Preface

New applications such as image processing, graphics, geographic data processing, robotics, office automation, information systems, language translation, and expert systems have developed various data organizations and algorithms specific to the application requirements. The growing importance of these applications has created a need for general studies on data organization and algorithms as well as for specific studies on new database management systems and on filing services. The main goal of this conference was to examine advances in techniques of permanent and temporary data organization in different fields of computer science by sharing experience and knowledge. Four well-known experts A. Colmerauer, L. Davis, R. Piloty and M. Rabin were invited to address the key issues in their fields.

The Program Committee received 89 submissions from Europe, America, Asia and Australia. Each submission was reviewed by four PC members and sometimes by external referees. After laborious deliberations, 27 articles were selected for full presentation and we asked 8 authors for short communications. In addition to the four invited talks, the conference program included the panel on data organizations for logic programming, chaired by M. Freeston (ECRC, FRG). The conference was opened by A. Bensoussan, the President of INRIA. Two advanced and extensive tutorials preceded the conference: on spatial data bases, by H. Samet from the University of Maryland (USA) and on neural information processing, by H. Tirri from the University of Helsinki (Finland).

The Program Committee of Fodo-89 was co-chaired by W. Litwin (INRIA France) and H.J. Schek (ETH, Switzerland). The members were:

D.J. Abel (Australia)	G. Levy (France)
S. Abiteboul (France)	P.C. Lockeman (FRG)
M. Atkinson (UK)	F. Luccio (Italy)
D.S. Batory (USA)	A. Machinouchi (Japan)
C. Beeri (Israel)	Y. Masunaga (Japan)
P. Buneman (USA)	T. Merrett (Canada)
C. Costilla (Spain)	J. Nievergelt (USA/Swizerland)
S. Crespi-Reghizzi (Italy)	Th. Ottman (FRG)
U. Dayal (USA)	Sh. Peleg (Israel)
J.L. Encarnação (FRG)	R. Piloty (FRG)
H.D. Ehrich (FRG)	C. Puech (France)
Ph. Flajolet (France)	N. Roussopoulos (USA)
M. Freeston (FRG/UK)	R. Sacks-Davis (Australia)
A. Gagalowicz (France)	Y. Sagiv (Israel)
S. Ghosh (USA)	H. Samet (USA)
S. Gottlob (Austria)	P. Scheuermann (USA)
Th. Haerder (FRG)	M. Scholl (France)
T. Jaervi (Finland)	N. Spyratos (France)
L. Kalinichenko (USSR)	K. Subieta (Japan)
Y. Kambayashi (Japan)	K. Tanaka (Japan)
W. Kim (USA)	A.M. Tjoa (Austria)
E. Kuhn (Austria)	P. Valduriez (USA)
B. Lang (France)	K.Y. Whang (USA)
P.A. Larson (Canada)	B. Yao (USA)

We would like to give our thanks to all Program Committee members as well as to all the reviewers for their care in evaluating the submitted papers.

We are particularly pleased to thank C. Delobel, the Conference Chairman, for giving us the opportunity to design the FODO-89 program and for his aid whenever we need it.
We also acknowledge the great help of the International Organization Committee: S. Ghosh (IBM Research, San Jose, USA) Chairman, Y. Kambayashi (University of Kyushu, Japan) Asian coordinator, V. Lum (Naval Postgraduate School, USA) American coordinator. The same gratitude concerns the Local Organization Committee at INRIA: Th. Bricheteau, S. Abiteboul and M. Scholl. Furthermore, we would like to thank our Conference Secretariat: M. Chazal, S. Gosset, as well as all other members of the Department of External Relations at INRIA who helped us to set up the Conference. Finally, we thank our sponsors.

Previous FODO conferences were held in 1981 in Warsaw, and in 1985 in Kyoto. FODO-89 is being held in Paris, in the Ministry of Research and Technology building. This building is at the medieval site of Montagne Ste Geneviève in the middle of the Latin Quarter. It is the former historical site of the well-known French Ecole Polytechnique, founded in 1794. Many top French scientists originate from these walls. It is also worth noting that the place is located at Descartes street. We thank the French Ministry of Research and Technology for the unique opportunity to enjoy the stimulating and relaxing atmosphere of this exceptional setting.

Paris, June 1989

Witold LITWIN   Hans-Jörg SCHEK

Program Committee co-Chairmen

Lecture Notes in Computer Science

Edited by G. Goos and J. Hartmanis

3

W

F
D
a

3r
P
Proc

Springer-Verlag

Berlin Heidelberg New York London Paris Tokyo Hong Kong

Volume Editors

Witold Litwin
Institut National de Recherche en Informatique
et en Automatique (INRIA), Domaine de Voluceau – Rocquencourt
B.P. 105, F-78153 Le Chesnay Cedex, France

Hans-Jörg Schek
Institut für Informationssysteme, ETH Zürich
ETH Zentrum, CH-8092 Zürich, Switzerland

CR Subject Classification (1987): H.2–4, I.1–4

ISBN 3-540-51295-0 Springer-Verlag Berlin Heidelberg New York
ISBN 0-387-51295-0 Springer-Verlag New York Berlin Heidelberg

Printing and binding: Druckhaus Beltz, Hemsbach/Bergstr.
2145/3140-543210 – Printed on acid-free paper

TABLE OF CONTENTS

NEW TECHNOLOGIES

BASIC DATA STRUCTURES

SHORT PRESENTATIONS

DATA ORGANIZATIONS FOR LOGIC PROGRAMMING

MULTIDIMENSIONAL DATA

ENGINEERING THE OBJECT ORIENTED DBMSs

INTERFACES AND FORMAL MODELS

NEW APPLICATIONS

DATA SHARING

OPERATING SYSTEMS AND DATA ORGANIZATION

ITOSS: An Integrated Toolkit For Operating System Security.[1]

(Extended Abstract)

Michael Rabin
Aiken Computation Laboratory
Harvard University
Cambridge, MA 02138

J. D. Tygar
School of Computer Science
Carnegie Mellon University
Pittsburgh, PA 15213

Public and private organizations maintain large systems of files to be accessed by many users. Clearly, access to information in these files must be regulated so that specific items are made available to specific users, in accordance with rules and limitations deemed appropriate by management. The totality of these rules and limitations constitute the (information) *security policy* of the organization.

Nowadays such systems of files reside within computer systems, usually on secondary memory devices such as magnetic or optical disks or magnetic tapes. The files are accessed through computers, on terminals or printers, in a time-shared mode on a single computer, or in a distributed system of computers and file servers linked together. Computer systems are governed by operating systems which, among other tasks, implement and regulate the total user interaction with the system, including user access to the file system. Any hostile impingement on the integrity of the operating system poses grave dangers to the security of the file system, as well as to the proper intended behavior of the computer. Thus security requirements include the protection of operating systems from unauthorized incursion and subversion.

We feel that a method or *model* for implementing secure operating systems should posses the following attributes:

1. It should include mechanisms allowing the transaltion of any desired well specified security policy into the behavior of the given operating system.

[1]This research was supported in part under NSF research grant DCR-81-21431 at Harvard University. The second author received additional support from graduate fellowships from IBM and NSF.

2. It should provide software support and tools for facilitating the above process of translation.

3. It should ensure the proper intended behavior of the system even under malicious attacks.

4. Finally, despite its vital importance, computer security must be achieved at just a modest cost of system performance degradation.

Our approach to the problems of computer security, while bringing to bear some sophisticated algorithms, is at the same time pragmatic. We do not axiomatize the notions and mechanisms of security. Neither do we propose to conclusively demonstrate that a large software system possess certain security properties by carrying out formal verification. In fact, there are solid scientific reasons to believe that such global verification is not possible, and in practice formally verified secure system kernels have been found to have serious weaknesses [Benzel 84], [DeMillo-Lipton-Perlis 79], [Jelen 85], [McLean 85], [McLean 86], [Thompson 84].

What we rather do is to prepare a list of desired and essential properties that a computer system should possess so that a security policy can be reliably and conveniently implemented by users. The issue of security is viewed as that of controlling the access of users to files and of protecting the integrity of the operating system. This is effected through a series of new concepts, mechanisms, calculi, and software support constructs. Taken together these tools (the word is used in the colloquial sense rather than as in "software tools") comprise the *ITOSS (Integrated Toolkit for Operating System Security) model* for computer security. This model is general in scope and applicability and was also implemented in detail for the UNIX BSD 4.2 operating system.

Users act in the system through computing processes which make system calls requesting access to files. In our system, processes $\mathcal{P}$ have privileges V, and files $\mathcal{F}$ have protections T. We develop a formal calculus for representing privileges and protections by *security expressions*, and a semantics for the interpretation of such expressions as having values which are certain set constructs. We define the relation of a *privilege V satisfying a protection T* ($V \Rightarrow T$). By stipulation, a process $\mathcal{P}$ with privileges V will be allowed to access a file $\mathcal{F}$ with protection T if $V \Rightarrow T$. An efficient algorithm is developed for determining, for given expressions V and T, whether $V \Rightarrow T$.

Our treatment of privileges and protections includes *non-monotone* privileges, a construct of *indelible* protections; and a mechanism for enforcing *confinement* (see [DOD 85], [Lampson 73]).

The next tool of ITOSS is that of *incarnations*. From an organizational point of view, the significant entity is not the individual user as a person but the *role*, such as department head or bank teller, in which he interacts with the computer system. We therefore enable the organization to dynamically specify a set of entities $I_1, I_2, \ldots$ called *incarnations*, where each I_i is endowed with the privilege V_i deemed appropriate for the organizational role that I_i represents. The privilege V_i is passed to the processes created on behalf of I_i. A particular user (person) $\mathcal{U}$ will have specific incarnations $I, I', \ldots$, associated with him. When $\mathcal{U}$ logs in he chooses the incarnation representing the role in which he intends to interact with the file system. By use of windows, he can simultaneously interact in several roles, without danger of security tresspasses.

The incarnations mechanism has several benefits. It allows precise tailoring of access privileges to needs of the work to be done by a user in a computer session. Access privileges can be specified according to work roles and can be effortlessly shifted around by system managers simply by removing or adding incarnations to a user.

Up to now we have described passive protection mechanisms. A *sentinel S* is a pointer to an executable file (program), call it F_S. The sentinel S may be incorporated as part of the protection header of a file $\mathcal{F}$. The code in F_S, and the decision whether to protect a particular file F by S, are made by system managers. The operating system includes code which, upon a system call to open a file $\mathcal{F}$, scans the header of $\mathcal{F}$ and creates sentinel processes $S_1, S_2, \ldots$, where S_i runs the code F_{S_i}, corresponding to the sentinels $S_1, S_2, \ldots$, listed in the header. Actually, the sentinels appear in the header in sentinel *clauses* of the form $C \rightarrow S$, where C is a *triggering condition*. The operating system tests C and invokes S as a process if and only if C is true.

Sentinels have many security and system applications. For example, we may write an audit program $F_{S_{\text{audit}}}$ which will record details of accesses to file $\mathcal{F}$ in a file $\bar{\mathcal{F}}$. For a sensitive file $\mathcal{F}$, one may include the sentinel S_{audit} in the protection. When such a file $\mathcal{F}$ is opened, the sentinel S_{audit} is invoked. The system passes to S_{audit} certain parameters which may include the file name of $\mathcal{F}$, an identifier of the process $\mathcal{P}$ which made the call to open $\mathcal{F}$, the name of the file $\bar{\mathcal{F}}$ into which the access to $\mathcal{F}$ by $\mathcal{P}$ will be recorded, etc.

It is important to emphasize that, as a rule, the decision to have any particular sentinel S, the code of F_S, the list parameters to be passed to S, and the decision as to which file $\mathcal{F}$ will be protected by a clause $C \rightarrow S$ (and with which C), are all made by the system management. ITOSS provides the general sentinel *mechanism* as a *tool* which may then be employed by management for any purposes deemed useful.

In every computer installation there is a group of users, the system programmers, each of whom necessarily possesses extensive access privileges. Thus for UNIX, system programmers have "root", i.e. total, privileges. This poses very serious security threats. In ITOSS we have the *secure committee* tool. This mechanism allows management, if they so desire, to subject an incarnation I_{comm} to a committee of n users $\mathcal{U}_1, \ldots, \mathcal{U}_n$ (more accurately, n incarnations $I_1, \ldots, I_n$ of these users), a quorum of q of whom are required to invoke and later control I_{comm}.

Secure committees with any specified privileges are created by system management according to need, and the system can support any number of such committees. We shall explain later how to initiate this process so as to ensure security from the start. Secure committees have additional security applications beyond "watching the guards".

Additional security tools of ITOSS are *fences*. These include a method of "fingerprinting" system calls and files, and comparing fingerprints at appropriate points during the progress of the computation. A discrepancy between a pair of fingerprints which ought to be the same is an indication that some inadvertent or maliciously induced departure from the intended course of the computation has occurred. Fences are incorporated as modules into the kernel and run as part of the kernel code. They serve as a second line of defense against possible security weaknesses. Since it is possible to incorporate flexible variants of fences into operating system kernels *after* their completion, there is a good chance that consequences of any security error in a given kernel will be blocked at runtime by the fence.

In our implementation of ITOSS in conjunction with UNIX 4.2, we introduced finger-printing at the top level of system calls, and again at the device driver level. This fence uncovered a hitherto unknown security breach arising from a possible race between `link()` and `chmod()` calls referring to a file. Even if the original code were left uncorrected, the un-intended change of protection would be consistently blocked by the fence, and the attempted, unauthorized change of protetction of a file would be brought to our attention whenever arising during run time.

A centrally important feature of ITOSS is that when incorporated into an operating system it provides for more than just one option of a security policy. The tools of ITOSS allow the specification and implementation of a wide variety of organizational security policies.

Current proposals for high-security operating systems entail a serious degradation of system performance as a price for enhanced security. An important focus of our work is this issue of efficiency. The overall approach adopted by us, coupled with carefully chosen data structures and very fast algorithms for the frequently repeated security functions, results in a highly efficient system. In tests comparing our system with pure UNIX 4.2, we found no more than a 10% degradation of performance resulting from incorporating ITOSS.

Altogether, we feel that the tools developed in this work lead to the following security advantages:

1. ITOSS provides user-privilege and file-protection structures rich and fine-grained enough to faithfully express and implement any desired security policy. Furthermore, our formalism allows convenient and succinct expression of privileges and protections.

2. The coarseness of privilege/protection structures in existing security systems forces system designers, in certain instances, to confer excessive privileges of access on user and computing processes. These excessive privileges may then be employed by users and processes to subvert file and system security. The rich structure of privileges and protections of ITOSS, coupled with the tool of incarnations, allows tailoring of user and process privileges to the exact access requirements of the tasks to be performed. This circumvents many possible security pitfalls and dangers.

3. Sentinels provide convenient and reliable mechanisms for guarding against inadvertent or malicious failures of a user to follow security procedures, and for monitoring, auditing, and controlling access to sensitive files.

4. We provide system defenses against so-called "Trojan Horses" in application programs. These "Trojan Horses" are programs submitted by an unscrupulous party for general use within the system, and containing code which when run by an unsuspecting user will illegally read, modify, or destroy his files. These defenses may be effected through the use of incarnations, fences, sentinels, non-monotonic protections, indelible protections and other ITOSS mechanisms.

5. Fences provide a "second line of defense", i.e. measures for detecting unauthorized changes of files and attempts to perform illegal accesses to files, reporting on the former and preventing the latter.

6. In existing computer systems there are always individual users, such as system programmers, with total access privileges. No system safeguards are provided against such pivotal individuals, should they wish to subvert the system's security. The mechanism of secure committees solves this problem.

7. The overhead cost in performance degradation resulting from running ITOSS is small (less than 10% slowdown over pure UNIX 4.2 operation.)

8. By implementing suitable changes, ITOSS can be incorporated into any existing operating system with a relatively modest programming effort, and will confer on that system the security protections of ITOSS.

Finally, a word on how ITOSS will be used. This system is intended for installations and organizations, such as banks, hospitals, corporations, and government departments, where security of information is an important issue. We envision that in such organizations, management will formulate a security policy, i.e. define organizational roles as well as classes of files (depending on security considerations) and specify, based on work needs, for every role, the set of files that can be accessed by users acting in that role.

The computer installation will have "security engineers" who are system analysts and programmers familiar with the tools and provisions of ITOSS, and also with the organization served by the system. These security experts will assist management in formulating the organization's security policy.

Actually we expect that with time and experience, security policies typical to various industries such as banking, retailing, and government, will emerge. Management of a particular organization will adopt and adapt a standard policy to its needs, without having to start from scratch.

The security engineers will implement the organization's security policy. This will include the creation of classes of privilege and protection expressions; the creation of incarnations;

the assignment of privileges to incarnations and of protections to files. After proper system initialization, the assignment of protections to newly created files will as a rule be automated. Security engineers will decide which sentinel programs to choose from a standard library, and what new sentinels to create. They will create and install secure committees for performing extra sensitive tasks.

The day to day maintenance of security will also be in the hands of the security engineers (acting as a secure committee, if so prescribed by policy). They will initially introduce users into the system and assign incarnations to those users according to instructions from management. The security engineers, together with other system programmers (also acting as a secure committee), will be responsible for ongoing changes in the operating system, the file system modifications, and the updating of security features.

The features and mechanisms of ITOSS will be mostly transparent to the ordinary user. The user will be presented, after he logs in using his personal password, with a menu of the incarnations available to him. These will be stated in everyday terms such as: "Manager of Loans", "Member of Committee on Salaries", "Personal Matters." Once the user makes a selection of an incarnation, his access privileges and the protections for the files that he creates are automatically determined. He is oblivious to the details of privileges and protections, and to the existence of sentinels which may guard files that he accesses. The flexibility of ITOSS allows management to depart from the transparent-to-user mode, if so desired. For example, security policy may permit a user to set and modify protections, including sentinels, to his private files which he accesses in the Personal Matters role (incarnation) that may be available to him. All such details are questions of policy, and any kind of policy is implementable in ITOSS.

We feel that this division of labor and responsibilities for security between management, expert security engineers, and users, coupled with the tools and flexibly employable protections of ITOSS, will provide usable, reliable, and appropriate protection for information systems.

Privileges and Protections

From management's point of view the issue of the security of information can be expressed as follows: We have a group of users and a dynamically changing body of information, which for the purposes of this work will be thought of as being organized in units called files. Management wants to define and enforce a regime specifying, for every user $\mathcal{U}$ and every file $\mathcal{F}$, whether $\mathcal{U}$ is allowed to access $\mathcal{F}$.

We view the security problem in the context of an operating system. In this environment the files reside in some kind of storage. Users have computing processes acting on their behalf.

Thus the security problem is reduced to being able to *specify* for every process $\mathcal{P}$ present in the system and every file $\mathcal{F}$ whether $\mathcal{P}$ will be allowed to access $\mathcal{F}$ and being able to *enforce* the specified regime. On the most general level, such a regime can be specified and enforced in one of the following three equivalent ways: We can create and maintain an *access matrix M* in which $M[i,j] = 1$ if and only if process $\mathcal{P}_i$ is allowed access to file $\mathcal{F}_j$. [Lampson

74] Alternatively, each process $\mathcal{P}_i$ may be provided with a *capability list* $L_i = (j_1, j_2, \ldots)$ so that $\mathcal{P}_i$ may access $\mathcal{F}_j$ if and only if j appears in L_i. The dual to this approach provides each file $\mathcal{F}_j$ with an *access control list* $L'_j = (i_1, i_2, \ldots)$ so that $\mathcal{P}_i$ may access $\mathcal{F}_j$ if and only if i appears in L'_j. When a process attempts access to a file, the operating system checks the access matrix, the capabilities list, or the access control list to see if this access should be permitted. The dynamically changing nature of the ensembles of processes and files and the large number of objects involved render such a regime difficult to specify and to update. Also, large capability lists for processes or long access control lists for files give rise to storage and runtime inefficiencies.

Our approach is to approximate these most general schemes by associating with every process $\mathcal{P}$, a list of *privileges* V called the *combined privileges* and with every file $\mathcal{F}$ a list of *protections* T called the *combined protections*. Access of $\mathcal{P}$ to $\mathcal{F}$ is allowed if V *satisfies* (is sufficient for overcoming) T. We shall do this so as to satisfy the following criteria:

1. The privilege/protection structure must be sufficiently rich and fine grained to allow modelling of any access-control requirements arising in actual organizations and communities of users.

2. A formalism must be available so that users can rapidly and conveniently specify appropriate privileges for processes and protections for files.

3. There must be a rapid test whether a combined privilege V satisfies a combined protection T.

When thinking about access of a process $\mathcal{P}$ to a file $\mathcal{F}$, we actually consider a number of access modes. For the purpose of this work we concentrate on the following modes:

1. Read

2. Write

3. Execute (i.e. run as a program)

4. Detect (i.e. detect its existence in a directory containing it)

5. Change Protection

This list of modes of accesses can be readily modified or extended to include other modes, according to need. Of these modes, Read, Execute, and Detect are henceforth designated as *non-modifying*, while Write and Change Protection are henceforth designated as *modifying*.

Both the combined privileges and the combined protection each consist of five privileges or protections, respectively, one for each of the access modes. Thus a process $\mathcal{P}$ has five privileges $(V_{rd}, V_{wr}, V_{ex}, V_{dt}, V_{cp})$ associated with it, where V_{rd} is the read privilege, V_{wr} is the write privilege, etc. Similarly, a file $\mathcal{F}$ has five corresponding protections $(T_{rd}, T_{wr}, T_{ex}, T_{dt}, T_{cp})$

associated with it. When process P makes a system call to read F, the system will check whether V_{rd} satisfies T_{rd} before allowing the access. The other access modes are handled similarly. The detailed implementation is somewhat more complicated, and an check of a privilege may involve looking at several components of the protection. The reason for this complication is to provide for confinement.

From now on we shall treat just a single privilege/protection pair $\langle V, T \rangle$, which can stand for any of the pairs $\langle V_{rd}, T_{rd} \rangle$, etc. In fact, $\langle V, T \rangle$ can stand for $\langle V_X, T_X \rangle$, where X is any additional access mode that an operating system designer may wish to single out.

As will be seen later, each privilege and protection have a finer detailed structure. Thus a privilege V_X, where X is a mode of access, will have several components.

Sentinels: An Overview

The mechanisms described above form a passive, *pure access scheme;* they describe when a process P can access a file F but the mechanisms perform no other action. While the pure access scheme gives us much power, there are basic security functions that it can not support. Thus, if we wanted to audit accesses to F, that is record the names of all users who accessed a file F, we would have to either modify the operating system kernel or modify all application code that might access F. Since modifying and testing new code would be a laborious and dangerous process, this solution could only be rarely used and then with great difficulty. We extend the pure access scheme with *sentinels*. Sentinels allow us to conveniently add functions such as auditing. These functions can be customized to reflect any special needs an organization may have.

Here is how a sentinel for a file F works: Roughly speaking, a sentinel S is a name, listed in a F's protection header, of an executable file F_S. When any process P opens F, the operating system schedules F_S for execution as a process S. The process S is passed some parameters that allow it to perform various operations. The sentinel programs can be written to perform any desired action.

For example, if the security engineers wish to have an audit fucntion, they create a sentinel named, say, S_{audit} and write an appropriate program $F_{S_{audit}}$. The program $F_{S_{audit}}$ will accept as parameters the identity of the process P accessing a file F, the name for F and for the file $\bar{F}$ *into* which the access to F is recorded, and any other specified paremters. The code of $F_{S_{audit}}$ will realize the desired manner in which the access to F will be recorded in $\bar{F}$.

Suppose we only wished to record access when a member of a certain class of users accessed F. We could attach a sentinel S which checked whether the user accessing F belonged to the class. If he did, S would record the fact; if he did not, S would abort. While this is an adequate solution, it would be even better if we could keep overhead costs down by keeping process creation to a minimum. To allow this, we further extend the form in which a sentinel appears in a protection header to include a *trigger* condition R. Then sentinel S is only scheduled for execution by the operating system kernel when F is accessed *and* the process meets the trigger condition R.

Enhanced functionality is achieved by separating sentinels into different classes. Auditing simply requires that S make the necessary records in the audit file when P reads F. A more sophisticated form of sentinels will take action only when certain records are read. For example, certain records in F might have a keyword `secret` attached to them. We may wish to have a sentinel S guarding F which will allow most accesses, but restrict access to `secret` records. The first example requires only an asynchronously running process, but the second example requires that S be able to continually monitor and approve individual I/O operations between P and F. To achieve such mode of operation, we introduce two types of sentinel mechanisms: *asynchronous* sentinels which run independently of P and *synchronous sentinels* (also called *funnels*) which "lie between" P and F. By "lie between", we mean that S is able to inspect and approve all I/O operations from P to F. (In our implementation, funnels utilize UNIX *named pipes*. [Ritchie-Thompson 74], [Kernighan-Plauger 76], [Leffler-Fabry-Joy 83])

A very sophisticated attack might try to read a file F protected by an asynchronous sentinel S and then crash the operating system before S can perform its function. To prevent this, we further specialize sentinels to allow *Lazarus* processes which will, if interrupted by a system crash, be rerun when the operating system is rebooted.

When a sentinel S runs as a process, it must, as all processes, have some privileges. One choice an implementor could pick would be to have all sentinels run as the system user. This would not conform to the philosophy of this work which always calls for tailoring privileges to be the minimal ones necessary to perform the task at hand. In addition this would mean that we could not allow individual users to attach sentinels for their own purposes. To allow sentinels to be used in the widest possible context, we give each sentinel file F_S an assigned privilege V_S. When the sentinels is scheduled by the operating system, it will run with privilege V_S. A sentinel file is a special case of an exectuable file.

It should be emphasized that we introduce sentinels as an operating system supported mechanism or tool. A particular version of ITOSS may come with a repertory of some standard sentinels which security engineers may use. But the sentinel tool allows security engineers to write any additonal sentinel files to perform useful security functions, and to routinely and effortlessly deploy sentinels as protections for files.

A *sentinel* S is an ordered tuple $\langle F_S, t \rangle$ where F_S is the name of a file, and t is the type, 1, 2, or 3 indicating that the sentinel S is

1. *Asynchronous,*

2. *Synchronous,*

3. *Lazarus.*

Suppose a process P attempts to access a file F. Suppose further that P's privilege for that access mode is V_P and F's protections for that access type are T including a sentinel S. First, the operating system tests whether $V_P \Rightarrow T$. This determines whether P can access F. But regardless of the result, S can be executed as a sentinel. The operating system checks to make sure that F_S exists and is executable. If it is, S is created by the operating system with privileges V_S and executes according to type t.

To reduce unnecessary executions of F_S from being activated, we would like to express a trigger condition R specifying when S should be run by the operating system. There are several possibilities for expressing conditions R. We chose to use our privilege/protection scheme for this purpose, but it is easy to imagine other good choices for expressing trigger conditions.

Incarnations and Secure Committees: Overview

A centrally important issue in secure operating and file systems is the correct and prudent management of privileges and protections, i.e., of access rights to files. There are several problems and dangers arising from the way access rights are assigned to *users* in existing systems.

A person often has a number of roles in which he is active within an organization, and which give rise to his interaction with the file system. In existing systems a user is usually presented to the operating system by a single entity through his login name, and this entity determines his access rights without regard to the purpose of his current computer session.

Assume that a user wishes to play a computer game. The program that he runs may have been inadequately tested and may contain Trojan Horse code. But the user's process running the program has access to *all* the files available to that user, so that the Trojan Horse code can cause serious damage.

Another difficulty arises when we have to add or revoke access rights. Assume that person $\mathcal{A}$ is in charge of a certain department and is chairman of a certain committee. These roles require access rights to two, possibly overlapping, sets of files. When person $\mathcal{A}$ is replaced by person $\mathcal{B}$ as chairman, the revocation of his access rights to the relevant files, and the assignment of these rights to $\mathcal{B}$ is a cumbersome and error prone process in existing systems.

In ITOSS the basic entities on whose behalf computing processes run are abstracted as *incarnations*. Each incarnation has combined privileges which will be attached to the processes created by it, and a scheme for attaching combined protections to the files created by these processes.

The set of incarnations is specified and dynamically updated by management, and generally reflects the organizational work roles. Each user has a number of associated incarnations with his login. When he logs in, he selects an appropriate incarnation from a menu of the incarnations available to him.

Consider the user $\mathcal{A}$ mentioned before. The security engineers create incarnations $\mathcal{I}_{headX}$, $\mathcal{I}_{chmnY}$ to represent the roles of head of Department X and chairman of Committee Y, and an incarnation $\mathcal{I}_{min}$ with minimal privileges. If user $\mathcal{A}$ wishes to run the game program, he invokes the incarnation $\mathcal{I}_{min}$ which has no access rights to any significant files. If $\mathcal{A}$ is replaced by $\mathcal{B}$ as chairman of Committee Y, the security engineers remove $\mathcal{I}_{chmnY}$ from the incarnations available to $\mathcal{A}$ and associate it with $\mathcal{B}$.

A concern equally important to the aforementioned control of privileges of processes is the correct assignment of protections to files. ITOSS proves means for *automatic assignment* of headers, including combined extended protecteions, to files. This stands in contrast to most previous schemes which placed the brunt of responsibility for protection files on the individual user who created the file. In practice, the prevailing approach worked poorly: non-expert users who did not fully understand the working of the operating system would give incorrect security specifications. ITOSS, with its far richer ensemble of security mechanisms, would be an even greater challenge to non-expert users. Moreover, even well-informed users acting in an uncoordinated fashion could not properly manager the assignment of the global resource or individual securons.

Our innovation allws us to shift this responsibility to the security engineers. The protection assignment is performed by an operating system mechanism which takes into account the context in which a given file was created, insuring that filew will always be created with appropriate protections.

A prevalant difficulty with system security features is that they are generally unused by users of the computing system. The automated nature of ITOSS solves this problem.

In existing systems there are always some users, such as the system programmers, who have access to all of the system's resources and files. This arrangment poses obvious security dangers. In ITOSS, every role is represented by an incarnation. Usually an incarnation is assigned to a user who may in addition control several other incarnations, i.e., one user controls several incarnations. Dually, the *secure committee* tool allows management to subject control of any incarnation $\mathcal{I}$ to a *committee* of n users, so that a *quorum* of q committee members is required to invoke the incarnation $\mathcal{I}$ and execute commands through it.

Assume that the security engineers decide to create a secure committee SCOMM with certain access privileges, and wish to have SCOMM governed by a quorum of at least q of the users $\mathcal{U}_1, \ldots, \mathcal{U}_n$. They create a *committee incarnation* $\mathcal{I}_{\text{comm}}$ and *committee-member* incarnations $\mathcal{I}_1, \ldots, \mathcal{I}_n$ where $\mathcal{I}_j$ is assigned to user $\mathcal{U}_j$. If $k \geq q$ users $\mathcal{U}_{i_1}, \ldots, \mathcal{U}_{i_k}$ need to invoke $\mathcal{I}_{\text{comm}}$, then each $\mathcal{U}_{i_j}$ selects his committee-member incarnation $\mathcal{I}_{i_j}$. Every $\mathcal{U}_{i_j}$, $1 \leq j \leq k$ then makes through $\mathcal{I}_{i_j}$ a system call to invoke $\mathcal{I}_{rmcomm}$. These calls by $\mathcal{I}_{i_1}, \ldots, \mathcal{I}_{i_k}$ may involve, for greater security, "pieces" of a secret password in a manner explained in Section 4.3. The system creates $\mathcal{I}_{\text{comm}}$ only after having such $k \geq q$ calls from SCOMM members.

The operating system records the identifiers of the incarnations $\mathcal{I}_{i_1}, \ldots, \mathcal{I}_{i_k}$ (here $q \leq k$) representing the users participating in the session. After the incarnation $\mathcal{I}_{\text{comm}}$ is invoked, every command by a joint shell owned by $\mathcal{I}_{\text{comm}}$ must be approved by all committee members participating in the session. Each participating member acts from his terminal and gets every system command for his inspection and approval.

The creation of secure committees, like all other security functions in ITOSS, is entrusted to the security engineers. As mentioned in the introduction, the security engineers and system programmers may also be organized into various secure committees, with possibly different quorums depending on the tasks and access privileges of the committee in question.

Validation

Once an implementor has specified a language for expressing security constraints and provided a mechanism for enforcing them, the task he faces is to *validate* the resulting system so to show that it is free of errors. Validation is an important issue not just for security but for software engineering in general, and a large number of methods, such as formal verification, testing, structured walkthroughs, have been proposed for dealing with this problem. In practice, none of these methods guarantee software without errors; they merely increase the confidence a user has in the system.

Validation for security is special because in many cases we are trying to prohibit some event from occurring. We propose a general method, *fences*, for providing a "second test" of security conditions.

The term "fence" was first applied to the IBM 7090 computer to describe a memory protection mechanism. [Bashe *et al* 86] In this context, a fence was a pointer into memory which separated user and system memory. Memory beyond the fence was accessible only in system mode, and this was enforced by independent hardware.

In our usage, a fence is any low-overhead hardware or software feature which enforces security conditions by testing values independently of the main stream of execution, allowing operations to be performed only if they do not violate security conditions.

Fingerprints

In the course of his research on string matching, the first author proposed a special hash function, called a *fingerprint*. [Rabin 81] His fingerprint function $F_K(x)$ hashes a n-bit value x into a m-bit value ($n > m$) randomly, based on a secret key K. The interesting point is that given a y, if K is unknown, then no one can find an x such that $F_K(x) = y$ with probability better than 2^{-m}.

(Briefly, Rabin's algorithm picks an irreducible polynomial p of degree m over the integers modulo 2. The coefficients of p, taken as a vector, form the key K. The bits in the input x are taken as the coefficients of a $n-1$ degree polynomial q. Let r be the residue of q divided by p in $Z_2[x]$. r is a $m-1$ degree polynomial, and its coefficients, taken as a vector, form $F_K(x)$. A software implementation of this algorithm merely consists of a sequence of very fast XOR operations. [Rabin 81] gives this algorithm in greater detail. [Fisher-Kung 84] describes a very fast systolic hardware implementation of this algorithm.)

With the fingerprinting algorithm, we can install powerful fences. Suppose we wish to guarantee that a file $\mathcal{F}$ has not been tampered with. One way we could protect against this is by installing a synchronous sentinel to guard $\mathcal{F}$. However, $\mathcal{F}$ would still be vulnerable to attacks on the physical disk. As a second-tier protection, we could have the synchronous sentinel guarding $\mathcal{F}$ keep an independent fingerprint of $\mathcal{F}$ elsewhere in the operating system. If $\mathcal{F}$ was changed illicitly, the sentinel would instantly detect it unless the fingerprint was also changed. Since the fingerprint is provable impossible to forge with accuracy greater than 2^{-m}

unless the key *K* is known, it is impossible for the opponent to change $\mathcal{F}$ without eventually coming to the attention of the sentinel.

Bibliography

[Bashe 86] Bashe, C. J., L. R. Johnson, J. H. Palmer, and E. W. Pugh. *IBM's Early Computers* MIT Press, Cambridge, Massachusetts, 1986.

[Benzel 84] "Analysis of a Kernel Verification." *Proceedings of the 1984 Symposium on Security and Privacy*, Oakland, California, May 1984, pp. 125–131.

[Daley-Dennis 68] Daley, R. C., and Dennis, J. B. "Virtual Memory, Processes, and Sharing in MULTICS." *Communications of the ACM,* **11**:5, pp. 306–312 (May 1968).

[DeMillo-Lipton-Perlis 79] DeMillo, R. A., R. J. Lipton, and A. J. Perlis. "Social Processes and Proofs of Theorems and Programs." *Communications of the ACM,* **22**:5, (May 1979).

[Dijkstra 68] Dijkstra, E. W. "The Structure of the 'THE' Multiprogramming System." *Communications of the ACM,* **11**:5, pp. 341–346 (May 1968).

[DOD 85] *Trusted Computer System Evaluation Criteria.* Computer Security Center, Department of Defense, Fort Meade, Maryland. (CSC-STD-001-83) March 1985.

[Grampp-Morris 84] Grampp, F. T., and R. H. Morris. "UNIX Operating System Security." *AT&T Bell Laboratories Technical Journal,* **63**:8b, pp. 1649–1672 (October 1984).

[Jelen 85] Jelen, G. F. *Information Security: An Elusive Goal.* Program on Information Resources Policy, Harvard University, Cambridge, Massachusetts. June 1985.

[Lampson 73] Lampson, B. W. "A Note on the Confinement Problem." *Communications of the ACM,* **16**:10, pp. 613–615 (October 1973).

[Lampson 74] Lampson, B. W. "Protection." *ACM Operating Systems Review*, **19**:5, pp. 13–24 (December 1985).]

[McLean 85] McLean, J. "A Comment on the 'Basic Security Theorem' of Bell and LaPadula." *Information Processing Letters,* **20**:3, pp. 67–70 (1985).

[McLean 86] McLean, J. "Reasoning About Security Models." Personal Communication, 1986.

[Organick 72] Organick, E. I. *The Multics System.* MIT Press, Cambridge, Massachusetts, 1972.

[Rabin 81] Rabin, M. O. "Fingerprinting by Random Polynomials." TR-15-81. Center for Research in Computing Technology, Harvard University, Cambridge, Massachusetts. 1981.

[Ritchie-Thompson 74] Ritchie, D. M. and Thompson, K. "The UNIX Time-Sharing System." *Communications of the ACM,* **17**:7, pp. 365–375 (July 1974).

[Schroeder-Saltzer 72] Schroeder, M. D., and J. H. Saltzer. "A Hardware Architecture for Implementing Protection Rings." *Communications of the ACM,* **15**:3, pp. 157–170 (March 1972).

[Shamir 79] Shamir, A. "How to Share a Secret." *Communications of the ACM,* **22**:11, pp. 612–613 (November 1979).

[Thompson 84] Thompson, K. "Reflections on Trusting Trust." *Communications of the ACM,* **27**:8, pp. 761–763 (August 1984).

[Wulf-Levin-Harbison 81] Wulf, W. A., R. Levin, S. P. Harbison. *HYDRA/C.mmp.* McGraw-Hill, New York, NY, 1981.

HEURISTIC REORGANIZATION OF CLUSTERED FILES

Peter Scheuermann and Young Chul Park
Department of Electrical Engineering
  and Computer Science
Northwestern University
Evanston, Illinois 60201   U.S.A.

Edward Omiecinski
School of Information
  and Computer Science
Georgia Institute of Technology
Atlanta, Georgia 30332   U.S.A.

Abstract

The problem of file reorganization which we consider involves altering the placement of records on pages of a secondary storage device. In addition, we want this reorganization to be done in-place, i.e., using the file's original storage space for the newly reorganized file. The motivation for such a physical change is to improve the database system's performance. For example, by placing frequently and jointly accessed records on the same page or pages, we can try to minimize the number of page accesses made in answering a set of queries. The optimal assignment (or reassignment) of records to clusters is exactly what record clustering algorithms [1,2,4,9] attempt to do. However, record clustering algorithms usually do not solve the entire problem, i.e., they do not specify how to efficiently reorganize the file to reflect the clustering assignment which they determine. Our algorithm is a companion to general record clustering algorithms since it actually transforms the file. The problem of optimal file reorganization is NP-hard [3]. Consequently, our reorganization algorithm is based on heuristics for which we prove three important observations.

1. Introduction

One of the ways in which the performance of a database system can be improved is through reorganization based on record clustering [6]. In this paper, we deal with a single file, containing multi-attribute records which are grouped into pages (i.e, blocks) in secondary storage. The target records of a multi-attribute query will usually be distributed over the entire file space and the number of pages accessed in the file can be as many as the number of target records for the query [7]. Thus, the objective of record clustering and reorganization is to reduce the expected number of page accesses. The result of a query Q_i is the set of records, in the file, which satisfy the conditions specified in the query. By using some directory (or directories), it is possible to access only those pages containing one or more records in the answer of the query. A common measure of the efficiency of answering a query is the number of page accesses required to retrieve the desired records [7]. If each page retrieved, in response to a query, contains only one record, then many pages will be accessed. On the other hand, if each retrieved page contains many records, then few pages will be accessed.

Record clustering algorithms [1,4,9] assign frequently and jointly accessed records to the same page(s) in such a way that the total number of pages accessed in response to a set of queries, with some probability of occurrence, can be minimized. Record clustering algorithms usually focus on finding an optimal clustering but stop short of specifying an optimal procedure for rearranging the records, in the file, to match the clustering [8,9]. We consider this rearrangement of records to be our file reorganization problem. The reorganization process involves bringing pages from the file into a main memory buffer area, constructing new pages by rearranging records on the pages in the buffer and writing new pages back to the file. The cost of reorganization equals the number of pages that must be transferred from (to) secondary storage to (from) main memory. The problem of optimal file reorganization has been shown to be NP-hard [3]. Therefore, our approach will be to develop a heuristic algorithm.

2. Previous Research on File Reorganization

In [1], a clustering algorithm, which is tightly coupled to the reorganization, is presented. Their clustering approach is to sort the records of the file in ascending order of the concatenated key. The concatenated key $A_1, A_2, ..., A_k$ is selected such that the attributes appear in nonincreasing order of their probability of appearence in a query. Since sorting is expensive, i.e., producing a total ordering of all records, they propose a partial-sort method that restricts the sorting to those records that can fit into the buffer. So the reorganization is efficient but is limited to their clustering method. In addition, experimental evidence [4,9] has shown that the partial-sort clustering method performs very poorly.

In [9], an adaptive record clustering scheme is introduced. They present an elegant as well as conceptually simple clustering algorithm. Their algorithm does not classify queries into types nor does it collect individual query statistics. Preliminary experiments has shown very good results [9]. Once the clusters have been determined, they assign reocrds in each cluster, i.e., from the first cluster to the last cluster, to pages. They have a few cases which they consider when deciding whether a new page or an existing page can be used. We consider this a logical assignment of records. We do not consider this an effective approach for reorganization for the following reasons.

1) Reorganization is constrained by the size of the main memory buffer area.
2) The actual numbering of the clusters is somewhat arbitrary and as such, the set of pages which currently store records from $cluster_{i-1}$ and $cluster_i$ may be disjoint. Thus, the pages which are brought into the buffer when constructing $cluster_{i-1}$ will be of no use when constructing $cluster_i$. This could cause an excessive number of page faults.

Another approach for file reorganization based on record clustering is the dynamic_cost_reorganization algorithm [3]. However, as we will show, there exist some problems and limitations with this method. Since we want to later compare our algorithm with the dynamic_cost_reorganization algorithm, we will briefly review it here. The algorithm assumes that input and output to the secondary storage device is accomplished by using a main memory buffer area of fixed size. Two mappings are required as input, one is PG which corresponds to the old (file) state and the other is NPG which corresponds to the new (file) state. These mappings satisfy the following:

$$PG : R \rightarrow P$$
$$NPG : P' \rightarrow 2^{R'}$$

where R = set of record identifiers,
P = set of physical page numbers,
P'_R = set of logical page numbers and
$2^{R'}$ = set of subsets of R of size ≤ pagesize.

To implement the mapping PG, there is a Page_table which associates with every record identifier, the physical page number on which it resides. This introduces another level of indirection between any directory (index) and the data file, but has the advantage that moving records within the data file does not affect the directory. Normally, in a tree structured directory [5,7], the leaves contain pointers to records. In this case, the leaves contain record identifiers. As previously mentioned, the output of a record clustering algorithm is assumed to be a set of logical pages: 1,2,...,M where each logical page contains at least one record and at most pagesize records. The records for each logical page are mutually exclusive such that NPG(i) ∩ NPG(j) = ∅ for 1 ≤ i,j ≤ M and i ≠ j. Logical page 0 is a special case and is the set of records in R which are not related to any logical page i, where 1 ≤ i ≤ M. Given the above two mappings, PG and NPG, the mapping D : P' → P is defined as follows: D_k = {PG(r) | r ∈ NPG(k)} where k ∈ P'. Thus D_k gives the set of physical pages which contain record(s) of logical page k. Buffer is the set of physical pages currently residing in the buffer. D'_k is the set of pages containing record(s) of logical page k and currently residing in secondary storage, i.e., $D'_k = D_k$ - Buffer. The dynamic_cost_reorganization algorithm of [3] is shown below.

Algorithm: dynamic_cost_reorganization
    Begin
        While all the logical pages are not constructed do
        Begin
            1: Determine the current logical page, clp, based on the cost function
                function cost(k) = $|D'_k| / |D_k|$;
            2: Determine physical pages to be swapped from the buffer using the
                fewest_records buffer paging policy;
            3: Bring in D'_{clp} physical pages;
            4: Rearrange the records in the buffer such that all the records which
                make up clp are contained on a single physical page;
            5: Write the physical page which contains clp to secondary storage;
            6: Rearrange records in the buffer such that records which belong to the

same logical page are grouped together as follows:
  a) for each logical page, k, which has records in the buffer, set
     $S_k = \{r \mid r \in NPG(k) \text{ and } PG(r) \in Buffer\}$;
  b) Order the above sets, excluding S_0, by nonincreasing size to obtain
     $S_1', S_2', ..., S_n'$;
  c) Allocate the sets in order: $S_1', ..., S_n'$, and s_0 to buffer
     pages in order $1, 2, ..., |Buffer|$;

End;
End;

The fewest_records buffer replacement policy (step 1.2) is to select the pages in reverse order of consolidation, i.e., page[|Buffer|],...,page[1], where page[x] represents the page in position x in the buffer. However, the dynamic_cost_reorganization algorithm suffers from the following problems and/or limitations.

1. The buffer capacity in pages must not be less than the page size in records, otherwise, the algorithm does not work in some cases.

2. If there is not enough buffer space to bring in D'_{clp} physical pages, several physical pages in the buffer are written to disk to make enough free buffer space. It may be inefficient to write out those physical pages at once before trying to construct clp, the current logical page, with the given buffer status.

3. If the number of records of clp is less than the pagesize, then other records are put on the page, e.g. page p, which is written to disk. If some of the records of another logical page k are contained on physical page p, then for the construction of logical page k, page p has to be brought into the buffer again. The construction of logical page clp may be destroyed.

4. Some logical pages do not need to be processed. For example, if there is only one physical page which contains records for logical page k, then logical page k does not need to be processed.

In the next section, we present our cluster_reorganization algorithm which works for any size of main memory buffer (i.e., ≥ 2 pages) and solves the previously mentioned problems. We assume a paged buffer system as well as the existance of a Page_table. The same mapping definitions and same notations will be used to enhance the ease of cross-referencing with the dynamic_cost_reorganization algorithm [3].

3. Efficient File Reorganization

This section deals with the problem of efficiently reorganizing the file, for a given record clustering. We assume that the dominating cost for reorganization is that incurred by page accesses to/from secondary storage [7]. Input and output to the secondary storage device is accomplished by using a main memory buffer area of fixed size. Thus, our goal is not only to reorganize the file but to minimize the number of pages swapped in and out of the buffer during the reorganization process. As mentioned, the mappings PG and NPG are used. Buffer, D_k, D'_k and clp are defined exactly as in the previous section. We need to define one more mapping, LPN : R $\rightarrow$ P' which is defined as LPN(r) = k, where r $\in$ NPG(k) such that LPN gives the logical page number for the corresponding record. Before we explain our cluster_reorganization algorithm, we need to present the following definitions.

1) A **void_record** r is a record which is not related to any logical page, i.e., LPN(r) = 0.

2) A **nonvoid_record** r is a record which is related to any one of the logical pages, i.e., LPN(r) = k where $1 \leq k \leq M$.

3) A **void_physical** page p is a physical page that consists only of void_records, i.e., for each record r $\in$ p, LPN(r) = 0.

4) A **perfect_physical** page p is a physical page where for each record r $\in$ p, LPN(r) = k and k $\neq$ 0. Hence D_k = {p}.

5) A **composite_physical** page p is a physical page which contains records from multiple logical pages and there is a record r $\in$ p such that LPN(r) = k, k $\neq$ 0 and D_k - {p} $\neq$ $\varnothing$.

6) A logical page is in the **ready_state** if all the records related to that logical page reside in the buffer.

7) A logical page is in the **perfect_state** if all the records related to that logical page reside in a perfect physical page.

The following notations are also used:

X = current available buffer space, i.e., Buffer_capacity - |Buffer|,

N_p = number of nonvoid_records in physical page p,

TVR = total number of void_records in the buffer,

RS = set of logical pages which are in the ready_state,

PS = set of logical pages which are in the post_ready_state,

MAX = subset of RS whose combined number of records for each constituent logical page $\leq$ pagesize and maximum among other subsets,

|MAX| = the number of constituent logical pages for set MAX and

SIZE = the combined number of records for each constituent logical page for set MAX.

To bring clp into the ready_state, it is necessary to bring in D'_{clp} physical pages from secondary storage into the buffer. If there is space in the buffer (i.e., X $\neq$ 0), there is no problem in bringing in a physical page from secondary storage. However, if X = 0 and D'_{clp} $\neq$ $\varnothing$, i.e., X = 0 while there are some physical pages which have to be brought into the buffer, then to bring in the next physical page in D'_k, a page frame needs to be made available in the buffer. In this situation, to free a page frame, the following steps are used:

step 1: Try to construct a perfect_physical page
step 2: If step 1 is not possible then try to construct a void_physical page
step 3: If steps 1 & 2 are not possible then build a composite_physical page
step 4: Write the above constructed physical page to secondary storage

When step 3 is satisfied, we call it overflow. However, if $X = 0$ and $D'_k = \emptyset$, i.e., if $X = 0$ after bringing in all the physical pages in D'_k into the buffer, then to continue the reorganization process, we also need to follow the above steps. In this case, if step 3 is satisfied, it is called underflow.

Once clp is brought into the ready_state and SIZE plus TVR is greater than or equal to the pagesize, then it is possible to make a perfect_physical page. However, to reduce the possibility of overflow or underflow when the next logical page is constructed, the following two steps are used.

step A: While $|MAX| = 1$ & SIZE = pagesize do
        construct a perfect physical page using records of logical page in MAX
step B: If $X = 0$ then follow the above 4 steps for freeing a page frame.

Overflow and underflow are not desirable situations since they propagate additional page accesses. So the reorganization algorithm must try to minimize the possibility of those situations. The possibility of overflow/underflow is directly related to the order of logical page construction and by the access sequence of those physical pages related to each logical page. The sequence of bringing in those physical pages which are related to each logical page will be discussed first. Afterwards, the dynamic order of logical page construction, as directed by our cost function, will be shown. To bring logical page k into the ready_state, we must bring in D'_k physical pages from secondary storage into the buffer. Let the result of sorting those physical pages in D'_k in nondecreasing order of nonvoid_records in each physical page be denoted as the bring_in_sequence, BIS. There are three observations concerned with overflow and underflow conditions which are related to BIS. These observations are proved in the appendix and provide some measure of the "goodness" of our algorithm. For these observations and for the cost function which will be explained next, the following notations are used.

$$Y_k = \max(N_1, N_2, ..., N_m) \text{ where } \{1, 2, ..., m\} = D'_k$$
$$Z_k = \sum_{i=1}^{m} N_i - Y_k$$

Observation 1: If BIS of D'_k causes overflow when bringing logical page k into the ready_state, then any other sequence also causes overflow.

Observation 2: If $(X - 1) * \text{pagesize} + \text{TVR} \geq Z_k$ then logical page k does not cause overflow by using BIS.

Observation 3: If $X \geq 2$ and $(X - 2) * \text{pagesize} + \text{TVR} \geq Z_k$ then logical page k does not cause overflow or underflow by using BIS.

Because of overflow and underflow, in some cases it is possible to be faced with the situation where some physical pages are brought into the buffer and written out repeatedly without making any progress. This condition, which causes an infinite looping, is referred to as thrashing. Bringing clp into the ready_state might cause thrashing. Checking whether this will happen is very difficult. So, instead of checking thrashing, it is much easier to check whether clp and the current buffer contents contain the possibility of causing thrashing. Thus, the thrashing_possibility (TP) is defined as true if clp causes overflow or underflow in the presence of at least one ready_state logical page. Therefore, once clp is decided according to the dynamic cost function which will be explained later, TP of clp is always checked before trying to bring clp into the ready_state.

If TP of clp is true, then instead of bringing clp into the ready_state, we try to construct a perfect_physical page with logical pages in the ready_state and void_records in the buffer. If there is not a sufficient number of void_records in the buffer, then one physical page which has the maximum number of void_records in secondary storage, needs to be brought into the buffer.

All the composite_pages on disk should be brought into the buffer at least once to finish the reorganization process. Our objective is to minimize the total number of pages swapped in and out of the buffer. Based on the above three observations for the given buffer contents, the logical page which has the minimum possibility of causing overflow or underflow is the one which has minimum Z_k. Moreover, after bringing a logical page into the ready_state or perfect_state, we want to increase the probability of having sufficient buffer space. To accomplish this, we select a logical page which has minimum cost among logical pages which are not in either the perfect_state nor ready_state. Our cost function is defined as follows:

$$\text{COST}(k) = \text{cost to bring logical page } k \text{ into the ready\_state} = (Z_k, Y_k),$$
$$\text{COST}(i) < \text{COST}(j) \text{ if } Z_i < Z_j \text{ or } Z_i = Z_j \text{ and } Y_i < Y_j.$$

The above cost function takes into account the entire contents of the buffer. According to this cost function, our heuristic rule for the selection of clp is the following. Find a logical page which has minimum Z_k value, i.e., a logical page that has the minimum possibility of causing overflow or underflow. If there is more than one logical page which has the same Z_k value, then select the one which has the minimum Y_k value, i.e., one with the largest number of void_records on a single physical page. The purpose of our cost function, COST(k), is to provide a means for ranking those logical pages which are not in the perfect_state. This allows us to determine a sequence of constructing logical pages which will hopefully minimize the total number of disk accesses for reorganization. A high level version of our algorithm follows.

Algorithm **cluster_reorganization**;
Begin
step 0: /* Initialization */
    Find COST for each logical page & sort COST table in nonincreasing order;
    Find logical pages, already in the perfect_state & delete them from the COST table;
step 1: /* Reorganization */
    While the COST table is not empty do
    Begin
    1.1: Find clp of minimum cost among logical pages in the COST table & $\neg$ in ready_state;
        If all the logical pages in the COST table are in the ready_state then set clp to 0;
    1.2: If clp $\neq$ 0 and clp contains thrashing possibility (TS) then set clp to 0;
    1.3: if clp = 0 then
        Begin
            $D'_{clp} := \emptyset$;
            If not possible to make a perfect_physical page then
                Begin
                    Find a physical page p on disk which has a minimum number
                        of nonvoid_records;
                    If p is not a perfect_physical page and # of nonvoid records < pagesize
                    or p is a perfect_physical page and # of nonvoid records < SIZE
                    Then $D'_{clp} := \{p\}$
                    Else
                        Since there is an insufficient # of void records in the buffer to
                        continue reorganization, create additional void records by
                        changing records from some logical page into void records;
                End;
        End;
    1.4: While clp is not in the ready_state do
        Begin
            While buffer is not full and clp is not in the ready_state do
             Fetch a physical page for clp with a minimum number of nonvoid_records;
            If the clp is in the ready_state
            Then
                 To reduce the possibility of overflow/underflow when the next logical page
                    is constructed, write out perfect physical pages whose size = pagesize;
            If no clp, or a clp & no free buffer space & there are pages in the ready_state
            Then
              Make this page into a perfect_physical page, if possible;
            If no available buffer space and total # of void records $\geq$ pagesize
            Then
                 construct and write out void_physical page p;
            If no available buffer space
            Then
                 Construct and write out composite_physical page p;
        End;
    1.5: For each logical page k whose cost has been changed & whose
        status is not the perfect_state do
        Find COST(k) and insert k into the proper position in the COST table;
    End;
step 2: /* Buffer clearance */
    For each physical page p in the Buffer do
        write out physical page p to secondary storage;
End;

4. A File Reorganization Example

    To illustrate our cluster_reorganization algorithm, we provide the following simple example.

Example: Assume that the pagesize is 4 records, the buffer_capacity is 3 pages, and NPG and PG are given as follows:

NPG

A: A_1 A_2 A_3
B: B_1 B_2 B_3 B_4
C: C_1 C_2 C_3 C_4
D: D_1 D_2 D_3 D_4

PG

A_1 1 A_2 2 A_3 3 B_1 1
B_2 3 B_3 4 B_4 5 C_1 1
C_2 2 C_3 4 C_4 5 D_1 1
D_2 3 D_3 3 D_4 5 b_1 2
b_2 2 b_3 3 b_4 4 b_5 5

For the above two mappings, A through D represent logical pages and A_1 through D_4 represent their corresponding record identifiers. The integer which follows each record identifier, in PG, indicates the physical page where the corresponding record resides. Each b_1 represents a void_record. The cost for each logical page is calculated using the cost function, $COST(k) = (Z_k, Y_k)$. Those costs are sorted and are stored in the COST table as follows.

$$COST(k) : (5,4)\ (8,4)\ (9,4)\ (9,4)$$
$$k :\quad A\quad\ C\quad\ B\quad\ D$$

Logical page A becomes clp and to bring logical page A into the ready_state, physical pages 1, 2 and 3 are brought into the buffer (Fig. 1a). Records for logical page A are collected on physical page 2 (Fig.1b) and are written to disk (Fig. 1c).

BUFFER

1 A_1 B_1 C_1 D_1
2 A_2 b_1 b_2 C_2
3 A_3 B_2 D_2 b_3
TVR= 3
RS= {A}
(a)

BUFFER

1 b_1 B_1 C_1 D_1
2 A_2 A_1 b_2 A_3
3 C_2 B_2 D_2 b_3
TVR= 3
RS= {A}
(b)

BUFFER

1 b_1 B_1 C_1 D_1

3 C_2 B_2 D_2 b_3
TVR= 2
RS= ∅
(c)

Figure 1: Buffer Contents

The updated costs for logical pages are as follows:

$$COST(k) : (3,3)\ (3,3)\ (3,3)$$
$$k :\quad B\quad\ C\quad\ D$$

According to the COST table, logical page B becomes clp. Alternatively, logical page C or D could have been selected. $D'_B = \{4,5\}$, and the bring_in_sequence is 4 and 5 (or 5 and 4 since both pages have the same number of nonvoid records). Physical page 4 can be brought into the buffer but, there is no room in the buffer to accomodate page 5, and overflow is encountered (Fig. 2a). At this point, the only alternative is to construct a composite_physical page, since neither a perfect_physical page nor a void_physical page can be made (Fig. 2b). After the composite_physical page is written to secondary storage, physical page 5 is brought into the buffer (Fig. 2c).

BUFFER

1 b_1 B_1 C_1 D_1
3 C_2 B_2 D_2 b_3
4 B_3 C_3 D_3 b_4
TVR= 3
RS= ∅

(a)

BUFFER

1 b_1 B_1 C_1 B_3
3 C_2 B_2 b_4 b_3
4 D_1 D_2 D_3 C_3
TVR= 3
RS= ∅

(b)

BUFFER

1 b_1 B_1 C_1 B_3
3 C_2 B_2 b_4 b_3
5 B_4 C_5 D_4 b_5
TVR= 4
RS= {B}

(c)

Figure 2: Buffer Contents

Now, logical page B is in the ready_state. The records of logical page B are collected on physical page 1 (Fig. 3a) and written out to disk. The updated COST table becomes the following.

$$COST(k) : (0,4) \ (0,4)$$
$$k : \quad C \quad \ D$$

At this point, logical page C becomes clp. To bring logical page C into the ready state, the physical page in $D'_C = \{4\}$ has to be brought into the buffer. Physical page 4 is brought into the buffer (Fig. 3b), the records of logical page C are collected on physical page 5 (Fig. 3c). Physical page 5 is written out to disk. The updated COST table is shown below and logical page D becomes clp with $D'_D = ∅$.

$$COST(k) : (0,0)$$
$$k : \quad D$$

The records of logical page D are collected on physical page 4 (Fig. 3c) and written out to disk. The remaining page in the buffer, which contains void_records is also written out to disk.

BUFFER

1 B_2 B_1 B_4 B_3
3 C_2 b_1 b_4 b_3
5 C_1 C_5 D_4 b_5
TVR= 4
RS= {B}

(a)

BUFFER

4 D_1 D_2 D_3 C_3
3 C_2 b_1 b_4 b_3
5 C_1 C_5 D_4 b_5
TVR= 4
RS= {C,D}

(b)

BUFFER

4 D_1 D_2 D_3 D_4
3 b_5 b_1 b_4 b_3
5 C_1 C_5 C_3 C_2
TVR= 4
RS= {C,D}

(c)

Figure 3: Buffer Contents

Now, the buffer is empty so the reorganization process is finished. The total number of disk accesses is 12 and all logical pages are in the perfect_state.

5. Experimental Results for File Reorganization

In this section, we present the results of a number of file reorganization experiments. For each experiment, we compare our cluster_reorganization algorithm with the dynamic_cost_reorganization algorithm [3]. In [3], it was shown, for certain assumptions (which we are not restricted to), that the dynamic_cost_reorganization algorithm makes approximately 40% fewer page accesses than a reorganization strategy that uses a linear ordering. Linear ordering means that logical pages are converted into perfect_physical pages in order of their logical page names (or numbers). In our experiments, we randomly generate records for 25 logical pages where the pagesize is 10 records. The record identifiers for the file are in the range from 1 to 1000. Tables I and II represent the experimental results for a buffer capacity of 10 and 20 pages respectively. For each fixed size buffer capacity, the size of a logical page is determined as a percentage of the size of the physical page. It varies from 1% to 100% in some cases, 50% to 100% in others and is set to 100% in the remaining cases. Another parameter in our experiments is the hit ratio, i.e., the percentage of physical pages containing relevant logical pages. In our experiments, the hit ratio varies from 30% to 100%. In the third and fourth columns in each table, the number of disk accesses necessary for the reorganization is shown for cluster_reorganization and dynamic_cost_reorganization algorithms, respectively. In the last column, we show the difference of disk accesses by (DYN - CLU) / DYN, where CLU and DYN represent the number of disk accesses made by cluster_reorganization and dynamic_cost_reorganization algorithms, respectively. We also compared the correctness of each reorganization algorithm by checking the number of logical pages which were not constructed correctly. Those numbers are represented in the fifth and sixth columns in each table for cluster_reorganization and dynamic_cost_reorganization, respectively.

From our experiments, we find that cluster_reorganization generates a correct result for any value of buffer capacity, hit ratio and logical page size. Moreover, the number of disk accesses required for cluster_reorganization is much less than that of dynamic_cost_reorganization and when the buffer capacity is greater than or equal to the pagesize, the number of disk accesses is mostly optimal. Due to the assumptions made by the dynamic_cost_reorganization algorithm, in general it will not work correctly (or possibly not terminate) when the buffer capacity is less than the pagesize or when the logical page size does not equal the physical page size. If it does terminate in either of those cases, as evidenced in our experiments, around 30% of the logical pages are not correctly constructed. Considering those results, we find that our cluster_reorganization algorithm is superior to the dynamic_cost_reorganization algorithm since our algorithm is more general and makes fewer page accesses.

6. Conclusion

In this work, we have developed an efficient heuristic algorithm for the problem of file reorganization which involves changing the placement of records on pages of secondary storage. Our algorithm utilizes heuristic functions to decide the reorganization sequence of logical pages and to decide the bring-in sequence of physical pages.

We have also considered the problem of overflow, underflow and thrashing which could occur during the reorganization period. With regard to the above situations, we proved three important observations about our algorithm. First, we proved that if our bring-in sequence of physical pages causes overflow when constructing a given logical page, then any other access sequence of those physical pages also causes overflow. The other two observations, which we proved, give us conditions, that if satisfied, show that underflow and overflow will not happen for our bring-in sequence.

In addition, we did a comparison with another approach [3] which showed that our algorithm is more general and caused fewer page faults during the reorganization. In addition, it generated the correct result for the given record clustering input.

Table I. Buffer capacity = 10 pages

logical pagesize in %	hit ratio	page accesses		logical pages not made by		difference in %
		CLU	DYN	CLU	DYN	
1_100	30	60	94	0	8	36.2
1_100	40	80	118	0	6	32.2
1_100	50	100	132	0	7	24.2
1_100	66	132	164	0	6	19.5
1_100	73	142	170	0	4	16.5
1_100	84	166	190	0	6	12.6
50_100	30	60	92	0	10	34.8
50_100	40	80	108	0	8	25.9
50_100	47	94	118	0	8	20.3
50_100	64	128	152	0	6	15.5
50_100	84	168	186	0	6	9.7
50_100	90	180	204	0	7	11.8
100	30	68	74	0	0	8.1
100	40	86	96	0	0	10.4
100	50	104	110	0	0	5.5
100	60	122	130	0	0	6.2
100	78	156	162	0	0	3.7
100	85	170	178	0	0	4.5
100	96	192	198	0	0	3.0

Table II. Buffer capacity = 20 pages

logical pagesize in %	hit ratio	page accesses		logical pages not made by		difference in %
		CLU	DYN	CLU	DYN	
1_100	30	60	92	0	7	34.8
1_100	38	76	116	0	6	34.5
1_100	48	96	124	0	9	22.6
1_100	52	102	136	0	8	25.0
1_100	62	124	156	0	8	20.5
1_100	78	156	180	0	8	13.3
50_100	30	60	88	0	8	31.8
50_100	40	80	108	0	8	25.9
50_100	50	100	116	0	5	13.8
50_100	60	120	152	0	9	21.1
50_100	72	144	168	0	8	14.3
50_100	86	172	198	0	10	13.1
100	30	60	60	0	0	0.0
100	40	80	80	0	0	0.0
100	50	100	100	0	0	0.0
100	60	120	120	0	0	0.0
100	69	138	138	0	0	0.0
100	80	170	170	0	0	0.0
100	96	192	192	0	0	0.0

References

[1] M. Jakobsson, "Reducing Block Accesses in Inverted Files by Partial Clustering," Information Systems , Vol. 5, 1980, pp. 1-5.

[2] J. Liou and S. B. Yao, "Multidimensional Clustering for Database Organizations," Information Systems , Vol. 2, No. 4, 1977, pp. 187-198.

[3] E. Omiecinski, "Incremental File Reorganization Schemes," VLDB Conference Proceedings , Stockholm, Sweden, 1985, pp. 346-357.

[4] E. Omiecinski and P. Scheuermann, "A Global Approach to Record Clustering and File Reorganization," in Research and Development in Information Retrieval ,ed. C. J. van Rijsbergen, Cambridge Press, 1984, pp. 201-219.

[5] P. Scheuermann and M. Ouksel, "Multidimensional B-trees for Associative searching in Database Systems," Information Systems , Vol. 7, No. 2, 1982, pp. 123-137.

[6] G. Sockut and R. Goldberg, "Database Reorganization - Principles and Practice," ACM Computing Surveys , Vol. 11, No. 4, 1979, pp. 371-395.

[7] T. J. Teory and J. P. Fry, Design of Database Structures , Prentice-Hall, Englewood Cliffs, NJ, 1982.

[8] C. Yu and C. Chen, "Information System Design: One Query at a Time," ACM SIGMOD Conference Proceedings , Austin, Texas, 1985, pp. 280-290.

[9] C. Yu, K. Lam, M. Siu and C. Suen, "Adaptive Record Clustering," ACM TODS , Vol. 10, No. 2, 1985, pp. 180-204.

Appendix

Observation 1: If BIS of D'_k causes overflow when bringing logical page k into the ready_state, then any other sequence also causes overflow.

Proof: Let the result of sorting $D'_k = \{1,2,...,m\}$ in nondecreasing order of nonvoid_reocrds in each physical page in D'_k be 1,2,...,m. Let the number of nonvoid_records be $e_1, e_2,...,e_m$ in each physical page 1,2,...,m; respectively. If $m \leq X$, then no sequence causes overflow, so in the following two cases, only consider the situation where $M > X$.

Case I: RS = $\varnothing$

Because there is no logical page, in the ready_state, which is contained in the buffer, a perfect_physical page cannot be constructed until all the physical pages in D'_k are brought into the buffer. So, an overflow could occur only when $X = 0$, the total number of void_records in the buffer is less than the pagesize, and one or more physical pages in D'_k are not in the buffer. Assume that n, ($n \leq X$ and $n < m$), physical pages are brought into the buffer. Because $(e_i + e_{i+1} + ... + e_{i+n-1})$ is greater than or equal to $(e_j + e_{j+1} + ... + e_{j+n-1})$, where $i < j$, we know that if $(TVR + e_i + ... + e_{i+n-1})$ is less than the pagesize then $(TVR + e_j + ... + e_{j+n-1})$ is also less than the pagesize. This means that if BIS causes overflow then any other sequence also does.

Case II: RS $\neq \varnothing$

To make room in the buffer, if some number of logical pages are in the ready_state, there are enough void_records to construct a perfect_physical page and $X = 0$; then this perfect physical_page will be written to disk. If $(TVR + SIZE + e_i + ... + e_{i+n-1})$ is less than the pagesize then $(TVR + SIZE + e_j + ... + e_{j+n-1})$ is also less than the pagesize. Therefore, if BIS causes overflow then any other sequence also does. $\square$

Observation 2: If $(X-1) * pagesize + TVR \geq Z_k$, then logical page k does not cause overflow by using BIS.

Proof: Let the result of sorting $D'_k = \{1,2,...,m\}$ in nondecreasing order of nonvoid_records in each physical page be $1,2,...,m$. If $X \geq m$ then it does not cause overflow. Therefore, assume that $X < m$ and that the first X-1 physical pages were brought into the buffer according to the bring_in_sequence. After bringing in X-1 physical pages, the number of void_records in the buffer will be $TVR + e_1 + ... + e_{X-1}$. Because $Z_k = N_1 + ... + N_{X-1} + N_X + ... + N_m$, it is obvious from the given condition that $TVR + e_1 + ... + e_{X-1} \geq N_X + N_{X+1} + ... + N_{m-1}$. Because only X-1 physical pages were brought into the buffer, there is room for one more physical page. Now, physical page X can be brought into the buffer and because $TVR + e_1 + ... + e_{X-1} \geq N_X + N_{X+1} + ... + N_{m-1}$, N_X nonvoid_records from physical page X can be replaced by N_X void_records. Physical page X becomes a void_physical page and can be written to disk. This leaves $TVR + e_1 + ... + e_{X-1} - N_X$ void_records and room for one page in the buffer. Now physical page X+1 can be brought into the buffer and because $TVR + e_1 + ... + e_{X-1} - N_X \geq N_{X+1} + ... + N_{m-1}$, N_{X+1} nonvoid_records from physical page X+1 can be replaced by N_{X+1} void_records and physical page X+1 becomes a void_Physical page and can be written to disk. This leaves $TVR + e_1 + ... + e_{X-1} - N_X - N_{X+1}$ void_records and room for one page in the buffer. With the same approach for X+2,...,m-1 physical pages; m-X void void_physical pages can be made and room for one page can be made in the buffer at each step. Now, the last physical page can be brought into the buffer without causing any overflow. Therefore, if BIS is used and $(X-1) * pagesize + TVR \geq Z'_k$, then there will be no overflow when bringing logical page k into the ready_state. $\square$

Observation 3: If $X \geq 2$ and $(X-2) * pagesize + TVR \geq Z_k$, then logical page k does not cause overflow or underflow by using BIS.

Proof: Because $(X-2) * pagesize$ is less than $(X-1) * pagesize$, it is trivial to prove that if $(X-2) * pagesize + TVR \geq Z_k$, then by using the bring_in_sequence, logical page k does not cause overflow. Now, we want to prove the second part of this observation. From the first part of this observation, after bringing in m-1 physical pages from disk, at least two buffer frames will be free. Hence, the last physical page can be placed in either of the two buffer frames and overflow will not occur. $\square$

Cluster Mechanisms Supporting the Dynamic Construction of Complex Objects

H. Schöning   **A. Sikeler**

University Kaiserslautern, Department of Computer Science, D-6750 Kaiserslautern, West Germany

Abstract

Non-standard database applications require adequate modeling facilities for their application objects which in general have an internal structure to be maintained by the database system. For this purpose, the database system has to provide fast access to such an object as a whole as well as to its components. In systems which support complex objects with a statically established structure, clustering of the objects' components along this structure is a widespread means to enhance efficiency. Systems which support the dynamic definition of complex objects' structures, however, cannot predict the characteristics of accesses to the database, and therefore have more problems in finding a storage structure that is useful for at least the majority of the accesses. In this paper, we propose a cluster mechanism that supports the flexibility and dynamism of the molecule-atom data model at the efficiency of static structure clustering. We discuss different alternatives for its design, taking into account the query processing strategies of the underlying database system. We address some problems concerning optimization that emerge from the dynamic structure definition and show some possible solutions.

1. Introduction

Non-standard database applications such as 3D-modeling for workpieces or VLSI chip design [DD86] require for various reasons adequate modeling facilities for their application objects. The notion of complex objects [BB84] is used to indicate that such objects have an internal structure maintained by the database system and that access is provided to the object as a whole as well as to its components. Obviously, interactive applications such as CAD require reasonable response times, and therefore demand efficient access to the complex objects provided by the database system. In systems which support complex objects with a statically established structure (e.g. NF^2 [SS86]), clustering of the objects' components along this structure is a widespread means of enhancing efficiency [Da86, DPS86]. Systems which support the dynamic definition of complex objects' structures, however, cannot predict the characteristics of accesses to the database, and therefore have more problems in finding a storage structure that is useful for at least the majority of the accesses. In this paper, we study a cluster mechanism (the so-called atom-cluster type) that is designed to support a lot of different database requests rather than to materialize a single object structure or query result. It may be compared to a materialized view, a database snapshot or a cached procedural field.

The conventional way to process queries on a relational view is to use query modification which translates the corresponding queries into ones on the base relations [St75]. An alternative approach, however, is to materialize a view, which means that the resulting relation is actually stored [BLT86, Ha87, SI84]. As a consequence of updating to the base relations, the materialized views may also require changes. These changes may be either executed at the end of each transaction, i.e. the materialized view is always up-to-date, or deferred by updating a materialized view just before data is retrieved from it [Ha87].

Database snapshots [AL80, LHMPW86], which are a related mechanism, are periodically refreshed, read-only replicas of a selected portion of the database which is defined by a query on one or more base relations. Snapshots are especially interesting in database applications which require the freezing of the database state e.g. for analysis, planning or reporting or in a distributed database serving as cost effective substitute for replicated data. Snapshots are not guaranteed to reflect the actual state of the database.

Another direction in materializing query results investigates the support of database procedures [SAH87]. Queries are stored in so-called procedural fields, i.e. attributes, in the same way data is stored in a relation. Accessing such a procedural field implies the execution of the queries stored in this field. However, performing such an access will be generally slow. Hence, the result of these queries may be cached, i.e. computed once and stored within a specifically assigned area on secondary storage, the cache [Se87].

Similar to these approaches, we investigate the physically clustered materialization of a complex object type. In the next chapters we introduce our data model and the architecture of our data base system. The dynamic construction of molecules during query processing is described in chapter 4. Based on this, we discuss restrictions on the complexity of molecules materialized as atom clusters in chapter 5. Finally we consider the use of atom-cluster types in the process of molecule construction (chapter 6).

2. The Molecule-Atom Data Model

The molecule-atom data model (MAD model [Mi88a]) has been introduced to support the use of dynamically defined complex objects. Complex object types (molecule types) are defined in terms of their components, which may be either complex object types or basic object types (atom types). An atom type consists of some attribute types, and therefore may be compared to a relation in the relational model. The corresponding objects, called atoms, are similar to tuples. We allow a richer selection of data types than most conventional database systems do. Particularly, the two special data types IDENTIFIER and REFERENCE are used to explicitly express relationships between atoms. The *IDENTIFIER* attribute, which is present in each atom exactly once, contains a system-defined primary key (surrogate) to uniquely identify the atom. *REFERENCE* attributes contain one or more IDENTIFIER values, all pointing to atoms of the same atom type (typed references). There must be a corresponding "back reference" for each REFERENCE attribute, i.e., if atom type A has a REFERENCE attribute pointing to atom type B (for short, "REFERENCE attribute to B"), then atom type B must contain a corresponding REFERENCE attribute to A. Also, if the REFERENCE attribute of atom a contains the IDENTIFIER of atom b, the corresponding REFERENCE attribute of atom b has to contain the IDENTIFIER of a. This structural integrity (which is based on referential integrity) is enforced by the operations of the MAD model. Thus, there is a means to reflect 1:1, 1:n, and n:m relationships among atoms in a direct and symmetric way. The relationships between atoms, which are manifested by the values of the REFERENCE attributes, lead to the so-called atom network. So far, the MAD model is similar to the entity-relationship model [Ch76].

The relationships installed by REFERENCE attributes can be used for the definition of molecule types. The notation A.ab-B.bc-C means, for example, that for each atom a of type A all atoms of type B ("B atoms") that are referenced by a's REFERENCE attribute ab and all C atoms referenced by attribute bc of these B atoms are grouped to a molecule. This definition assigns a direction to the relationships between A and B, and B and C respectively. Hence, a molecule can be seen as a directed subgraph of the atom network having one root, the so-called *root atom* (in contrast to the *component atoms*). If A has only one REFERENCE attribute to B, A-B may be written instead of A.ab-B. Fig. 2.1 illustrates some molecule types and corresponding molecules for a sample database.

Besides hierarchical structures as introduced above, the MAD model also allows network-like and recursive molecule type definitions. When an atom type has more than one predecessor in the molecule type graph, an atom of this type only belongs to a corresponding molecule, if it has references to at least one atom of each of the predecessor types which also has to belong to a corresponding molecule (network-like semantic). Recursive molecule types repeat a component molecule type in several recursion levels. Recursion level 0 of a recursive molecule consists of a molecule of the component molecule type. All molecules of the component molecule type which are referenced by the recursion-defining REFERENCE

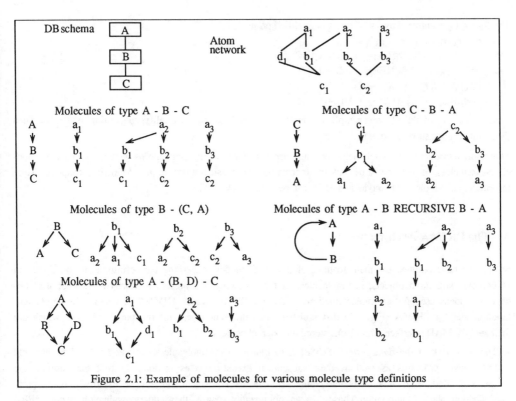

Figure 2.1: Example of molecules for various molecule type definitions

attribute of a component molecule on level i form the level i+1 of recursion. If a component molecule appears in more than one recursion level, it only belongs to the lowest one. Thus, cycles in the recursive molecule are avoided, and the termination of this operator computing the transitive closure is guaranteed.

Sets of molecules can be inserted, deleted, updated or retrieved (selected) using the SQL-like molecule query language (MQL). We concentrate on the SELECT-statement, which is the most complex statement. It is used to extract a set of molecules of a certain type from the database. Its general form is

```
SELECT     <projection_clause>
FROM       <molecule type definition clause>
WHERE      <restriction clause>
```

The **molecule type definition clause** determines the environment (molecule type) to work on. If more than one molecule type is present in this clause, this defines a cartesian product of the molecule types.

The **restriction clause** contains a condition ranging over the environment molecule type. It may be of arbitrary complexity, and may contain quantifiers and SELECT-statements (nested sub-queries). Only those molecules which fulfil this condition (molecules that *qualify*) are members of the result set. If no restrictions are to be imposed, "WHERE <restriction clause>" may be omitted.

The **projection clause** specifies, which parts of the molecules are to belong to the result. According to this clause, atoms or attributes are removed from the qualifying molecules. A value-dependent projection is possible ("qualified projection") and can be specified using a SELECT-statement with the special molecule type definition clause "RESULT".

The resulting molecules are molecules of the type specified in the molecule type definition clause, which qualify under the conditions of the restriction clause and have undergone the projection specified in the projection clause.

The following example shows the effects of qualified projection:

```
SELECT    C,(  SELECT    B
               FROM      RESULT
               WHERE     B.Att₁=7)
FROM      C - B - A
WHERE     FOR ALL A: A.Att₁>0
```

Assume that b_2 of the above example fulfils $B.Att_1=7$ and a_2 and a_3 qualify concerning $A.Att_1>0$. Then the result set consists of the molecule c_2-b_2.

This short introduction to MQL neglects many aspects of our query language as well as of our data model. Nevertheless, it will be sufficient to understand the considerations in the following chapters. More information about the MAD model and MQL can be found in [Mi88b].

3. The PRIMA Architecture

So far, we have outlined the main features of the MAD model concerning the definition and manipulation of complex structured objects, i.e. molecules. In the following, we present a short overview of the concepts and ideas used for its implementation within the PRIMA system [HMMS87, Hä88]. Our implementation model for PRIMA (Fig. 3.1) distinguishes three different layers for mapping molecules which are visible at the MAD interface onto blocks stored on external devices:

- The main task of the *data system* [Sch88] is to transform the molecule-set-oriented MQL interface into lower level programs as well as their subsequent execution. This is done by first transforming the user-submitted MQL statements into valid, semantically equivalent, but not necessarily optimal query evaluation plans (compilation phase). In an optimization phase, these query evaluation plans (QEPs) are rearranged according to different heuristics in order to speed up their processing. Subsequently, these QEPs are evaluated yielding the desired result (execution phase). A detailed description of a QEP as well as of its evaluation during the execution phase follows in chapter 4.

- The *access system* [Si88a] provides an atom-oriented interface similar to the tuple-oriented interface of the Research Storage System (RSS) of System R [As81]. However, the access system is more powerful than RSS as outlined in the following. It allows for direct access and manipulation of a single atom as well as navigational atom-by-atom access to either homogeneous or heterogeneous atom sets. Manipulation operations (insert, modify, and delete) and direct access (retrieve) operate on single atoms identified by their logical address (or surrogate) which is used to implement the IDENTIFIER attribute as well as the REFERENCE attributes. In performing manipulation operations, the access system is responsible for the automatic maintenance of the referential integrity defined by the REFERENCE attributes by adjusting the appropriate back references.

  Different kinds of scan operations are introduced as a concept to manage a dynamically defined set of atoms, to hold a current position in such a set, and to successively deliver single atoms. Some scan operations, however, are added in order to optimize retrieval access. Therefore, they may depend on the existence of a certain redundant storage structure. The *atom-type scan* delivers all atoms in a system-defined order based on the basic storage structure which always exists for each atom type. Similarly, the *sort scan* processes all atoms according to a specified sort criterion thereby utilizing the basic storage structure. However, since sorting an entire atom type is expensive and time consuming, a sort scan may be supported by an additional storage structure called sort order. Thus, a sort order consists of a homogeneous atom set materializing a sort operator. The *access-path scan* provides an appropriate means for fast value-dependent access based on different access path structures such as B-trees, grid files, and R-trees. The *atom-cluster type scan* as well as the *atom cluster scan* speed up the construc-

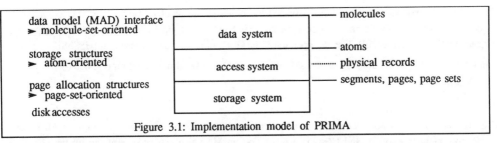

Figure 3.1: Implementation model of PRIMA

tion of frequently used molecules by allocating all atoms of a corresponding molecule in physical contiguity using a tailored storage structure called atom-cluster type. These atom clusters are the main subject of the rest of the paper.

The underlying concept is to make storage redundancy available outside the access system by offering appropriate retrieval operations (i.e. the choice of several different scans for a particular access decision by the optimizer of the data system), whereas in the case of update operations storage redundancy has to be concealed by the access system. As a consequence, physical records are introduced as byte strings of variable length which are stored consecutively in the containers offered by the storage system. Depending on the underlying storage structure, a physical record corresponds to either an entire atom (basic storage structure, sort order) or to a set of heterogeneous atoms (atom-cluster type). This establishes an n:m relationship among atoms and physical records which has to be maintained by a sophisticated address structure assigning each IDENTIFIER value a set of physical addresses and vice versa.

- The *storage system* [Si88b] as the lowest layer of PRIMA pursues two major tasks: It manages the database buffer and organizes the external storage devices, thus being responsible for the data exchange between main storage and disk storage. For this purpose, the database is divided into various segments consisting of a set of logically ordered pages. All pages of a segment are of equal size, and can be chosen for each segment independently to be 1/2, 1, 2, 4, or 8 kbytes, being kept fixed during the lifetime of a segment. Thus, the page size may be adapted to the specific access pattern of the segment in order to diminish either the conflict rate or the number of IO operations. The five page sizes, however, are not sufficient when considering the mapping process performed by the access system. Therefore, *page sequences* are introduced as predefined page sets supported by physical clustering. A page sequence is a set of logical consecutive pages of a segment which contain (from the viewpoint of the access system) one single object spanning these pages [DPS86]. Additionally, the storage system provides the means to handle not only such predefined page sets but also arbitrary page sets.

This overview may serve as a basis for the detailed discussion of the dynamic construction of molecules supported by an appropriate storage structure, i.e. the atom-cluster type, throughout the rest of the paper.

4. Query Processing in the Data System

When an MQL statement is given to the data system, it is compiled into an equivalent QEP forming a directed tree. The vertices of this tree are labeled with operators, while its arcs correspond to the data flow among the operators. The leaves of the QEP represent the operator "construction of simple molecules" (CSM), which builds up hierarchical, non-recursive molecules fulfilling some qualifications by using access system calls. The other vertices stand for operators like *recursion*, *aggregation*, etc.

The QEP may be subject to transformations by the optimizer, which is expected to generate a more efficient QEP by choosing appropriate access paths, selecting specific methods for each operator, and so on. Some of the possible choices for the CSM operator are discussed later.

When a QEP is executed, the operations indicated by its leaves are involved first, i.e., CSM operations are started. Whenever a molecule has been constructed, it is handed in a pipelined way to the next operator as indicated by the arcs in the QEP. The root operator of the QEP produces the final result set [HSS88].

Here we concentrate on the description of CSM, which constructs a set of molecules represented by

        SELECT   P
        FROM   M
        WHERE   Q(M).

M is the definition of a non-recursive hierarchical molecule type, P is a coherent subgraph of M, containing the root atom type of M, and Q(M) is a restriction on M, which can be determined by the consideration of a single molecule. As a consequence, Q(M) is not allowed to contain any queries.

Conceptually, CSM scans the root atom type of M. For each atom of this type CSM fetches the successor atoms according to M, then their successor atoms, and so on. When the whole molecule is fetched, it is checked against Q(M). If it qualifies, the molecule is added to the result set, otherwise all atoms belonging to the molecule are erased.

Considering this conceptual method reveals two points of inefficiency:

- All atoms of the molecule are fetched before Q(M) is tested, even those, which are not needed to check the molecule's qualification. If the molecule is discarded, the accesses to these atoms were senseless.
- Atoms shared by multiple molecules are fetched many times.

To avoid the first problem, the computation of the corresponding result set is done in two phases. The first one checks for molecule qualification accessing only atoms needed to decide Q(M). As soon as Q(M) cannot be fulfilled any longer, the next molecule is considered. If all qualifying molecules have been found, their remaining atoms are fetched in the second phase. In order to avoid multiple accesses to one atom, atoms that are likely to be needed by another molecule are stored in a main memory atom buffer.

The two phases may be interleaved, i.e., when the first qualifying molecule has been determined, the second phase may be started for this molecule immediately. While the second phase can be implemented straightforwardly (following the values of the corresponding REFERENCE attributes), the first phase offers a great choice of possible strategies. Depending on the restriction Q(M), the optimizer chooses an atom type to be fetched first and an appropriate access path, if available. Further atoms are accessed in a sequence which is likely to show disqualification as soon as possible (e.g., try to evaluate very selective parts of Q(M) first). This procedure is illustrated by the following example:

        SELECT   ALL
        FROM   A - B - C
        WHERE   EXISTS B: $A.Att_1=7$ AND $B.Att_1=A.Att_1$

First, A atoms fulfilling $A.Att_1=7$ are fetched (if possible, via an existing access path). For all these atoms, the corresponding B atoms have to be fetched using the REFERENCE attribute values of the A atoms, and tested for the condition $B.Att_1=A.Att_1$. If one of them fulfils this condition, the corresponding A atom is the root of a qualifying molecule, and the second phase may be started for this molecule.

In some cases there are more efficient ways to compute the result, than to navigate along REFERENCE attribute values. By comparing estimated selectivity and access costs the optimizer chooses one specific access sequence and determines which atoms will be stored in the atom buffer.

5. Materializing Atom Sets

Constructing molecules out of single atoms will generally be very slow. Since all atoms are distributed amongst different segments and pages, in the worst case one page request (i.e. an IO operation), has to be initialized for each atom. In order to avoid this extreme overhead a special storage structure is required which allows for the physical clustering of an atom set within a page sequence. Thus, all atoms belonging to such an atom set may be read into the database buffer by a single storage system call which in turn utilizes chained IO in order to minimize disk access time. In this chapter we discuss some alternatives in designing such a storage structure called atom-cluster type and its mapping onto the "containers" offered by the storage system. In particular, we would like to concentrate on the following problems:

- Which atom sets are to be materialized and how long?
- In which way is a materialized atom set to be updated due to a modification of the database?
- How are atom clusters utilized in constructing molecules?

In this chapter, we discuss the first two problems, whereas the third problem is treated in chapter 6.

5.1 Different Kinds of Atom-Cluster Types

The choice as to when to materialize molecules and when to dynamically construct them time after time is highly application-dependent (frequency of accesses, frequency of updates, etc. [Ha87]). Therefore, we delegate this choice to an experienced database administrator who may define and release an atom-cluster type representing a materialized molecule type by a corresponding statement, although we currently investigate, how this choice may be supported or even automated by the system. Nevertheless, we have to define how an atom-cluster type may look like compared to the resulting molecule set of an MQL query, especially when considering that an atom-cluster type has to be maintained by the access system due to modifications of the database. Therefore, we want to investigate each of the three clauses of a general SELECT statement with respect to the effects of a modification operation on a single atom on molecules which are materialized in the appropriate form.

Projection Clause

Concerning the projection clause, the most interesting part is the qualified projection, which allows for a value-dependent selection of atoms within a single resulting molecule. For this purpose, a qualification criterion is specified which is evaluated for each environment molecule defined by the molecule type definition clause (and selected by the restriction clause). Modifying an atom belonging to such an environment molecule may have the following effects on the corresponding result molecule:

- Due to the modification the qualification criterion of the qualified projection may become invalid for certain atoms. Thus, atoms that till now belonged to the result molecule have to be removed.
- On the other hand, the qualification criterion may become valid for certain other atoms. So, atoms that till now did not belong to the result molecule have to be included.

The complexity of the different possibilities may be demonstrated by a quite simple example. Suppose, we have a DB schema of three atom types A, B and C and a query defining a hierarchical molecule type A-B-C with a qualified projection selecting those submolecules B-C which exactly contain two atoms of type C (Fig. 5.1). For the given database this query results in a single molecule as indicated by the dashed circle. Inserting a new root atom generates a new molecule in either case (since no restriction clause is specified). The structure of the resulting molecule, however, depends on the qualified projection as is shown by inserting a2 with a reference to b1 and a3 with a reference to b2 (Fig. 5.1a). Inserting a new component atom, on the other hand, only causes an already existing molecule to grow, e.g. inserting c4 with a reference to b2 (Fig. 5.1b), or to shrink, e.g. inserting c4 with a reference to b1 (Fig. 5.1c). The latter holds for modifying an atom, e.g. removing the reference to b1 in a2, and for deleting a component atom, e.g. deleting c2, whereas deleting a root atom always results in the deletion of the whole molecule.

Therefore, the following actions are generally necessary in order to determine the effects of a modification operation on the appropriate molecules (without a restriction clause being specified):

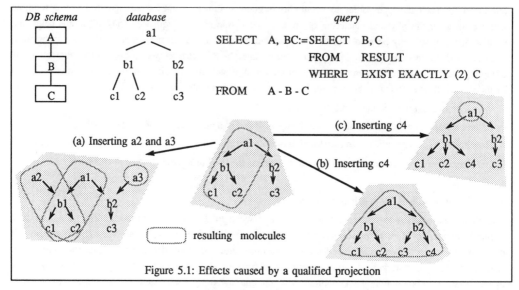

Figure 5.1: Effects caused by a qualified projection

- Inserting a root atom, generates a new molecule, which has to be constructed according to the molecule type definition clause. The participating atoms have to be selected based on the qualified projection.

- If a component atom is inserted or either atom is modified, all environment molecules containing the inserted or modified atom have to be constructed and the qualified projection has to be applied again to these molecules. The corresponding resulting molecules replace the original resulting molecules identified by the appropriate root atoms.

- When a component atom is deleted, a similar process has to be performed. Initially, the environment molecules containing the atom to be deleted have to be determined. These molecules have to be reconstructed without the deleted atom, the qualified projection has to be applied and again the original resulting molecules have to be replaced by the new ones.

- Deleting a root atom, however, results in deleting the associated molecule.

Thus, molecules have to be constructed and possibly complex qualification criteria have to be evaluated in order to determine the effects of a simple modification operation concerning the appropriate molecules. This, however, is the task of the data system. As a consequence, the projection clause allowed in an atom-cluster type definition is restricted to the key word ALL:

```
SELECT    ALL
FROM      <molecule type definition clause>
WHERE     <restriction clause>
```

Restriction Clause

The effects of a restriction clause may be compared to those of a qualified projection. The sole difference is that the corresponding qualification criterion determines whether or not an environment molecule really belongs to the result set. Therefore, the following situations may be distinguished (Fig. 5.2):

- The modification operation on a single atom violates the qualification criterion for certain molecules (Fig. 5.2b, 5.2c and 5.2d). As a result, these molecules have to be removed.

- Due to the modification operation the qualification criterion becomes valid for certain molecules (Fig. 5.2a and 5.2c) which now have to be materialized.

- In spite of the modification operation the qualification criterion remains valid for some molecules (Fig. 5.2a). Thus, these molecules have to be updated in the appropriate way.

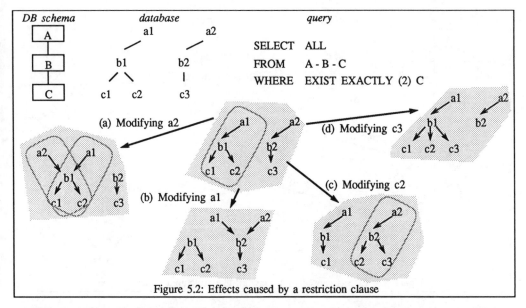

Figure 5.2: Effects caused by a restriction clause

Therefore, the following actions have to be performed when initializing a modification operation on a single atom:

- When inserting an atom, first of all the environment molecules containing the inserted atom have to be constructed and the qualification criterion has to be evaluated for each of them in order to determine those resulting molecules which either have to be materialized from scratch or which replace the original resulting molecules. Furthermore, for each environment molecule which does not qualify it has to be checked whether or not a corresponding result molecule exists which then has to be removed.

- If an atom is modified, two steps are necessary. In a first step, the existing resulting molecules containing the atom to be modified have to be removed. In the second step, the same procedure as for an insertion is mandatory. The environment molecules containing the modified atom are constructed, the qualification criterion is evaluated, and molecules are either materialized anew, replaced or removed.

- When deleting an atom, again the environment molecules containing the atom to be deleted have to be constructed. Within these molecules the atom has to be removed and the molecules have to be reconstructed in the appropriate way. Evaluating the qualification criterion delivers those resulting molecules which have to be materialized, replaced, or removed, respectively.

And again, the majority of these actions are in the responsibility of the data system. Therefore, the atom-cluster type definition is further restricted to a query of the following form:

```
SELECT    ALL
FROM      <molecule type definition clause>
```

Molecule Type Definition Clause

With respect to the molecule type definition clause we have to distinguish between hierarchical, network-like and recursive molecule type structures:

- With a network-like molecule type structure similar problems occur as in the case of a qualified projection. This is due to the semantics of a net structure (cf. chapter 2): Inserting an atom may establish a net structure, i.e. some molecules have to be expanded, deleting an atom may violate the net structure, i.e. atoms have to be removed from some molecules, and modifying an atom may cause both cases to arise (Fig. 5.3). Thus, similar actions as in the case of a qualified projection are necessary, most of

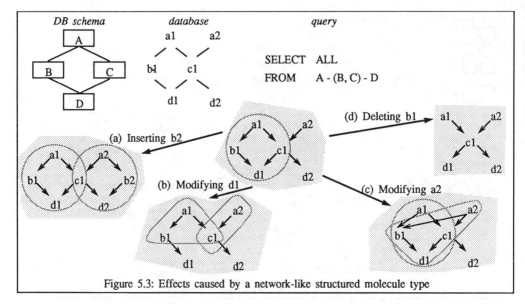

Figure 5.3: Effects caused by a network-like structured molecule type

which are a task for the data system, and, as a consequence, network-like molecule type structures are not allowed within an atom-cluster type definition.

- In the case of a recursive molecule type structure the construction of the corresponding molecules is based on a breadth-first strategy, in order to guarantee that each component molecule referenced in more than one recursion level only belongs to the lowest one. However, when inserting a new atom or modifying or deleting an existing atom, the breadth-first strategy may cause different results in relating atoms to a certain recursion level. Therefore, the corresponding molecules have to be reconstructed by either of the modification operations being once again the task of the data system.

- With a hierarchical molecule type structure, however, a simple evaluation of the "down" and "up" references is sufficient in order to determine the molecules affected by a modification operation as we will demonstrate later on. This evaluation may be performed by the access system, since, in any case, the access system has to check the REFERENCE attributes with respect to the referential integrity.

As a consequence, only molecule types with a hierarchical structure may be materialized. Thus, an atom-cluster type definition looks like the following:

      DEFINE ATOM_CLUSTER_TYPE <name> AS
          SELECT   ALL
          FROM   <one hierarchical structured molecule type)

5.2 Maintaining an Atom-Cluster Type

In the case of a hierarchical structured molecule type the access system is able to decide on its own which materialized molecules, i.e. atom clusters, are affected by an update operation to the database.

Inserting an atom

If the atom to be inserted corresponds to a root atom, a new atom cluster has to be generated. For this purpose, the corresponding "down" REFERENCE attributes specified in the atom-cluster type definition have to be evaluated and the referenced atoms have to be collected. For these atoms, in turn, the "down" REFERENCE attributes have to be evaluated until the leaf atoms are reached. The inserted root atom as well as the collected atoms are gathered up in a new atom cluster.

If the atom to be inserted corresponds to a component atom, the "up" REFERENCE attribute pointing to the predecessor of the appropriate atom type has to be evaluated in order to determine the corresponding predecessor atoms of the inserted atom. For each of these predecessor atoms the physical address of the appertaining atom clusters can be extracted from their address structure. These atom clusters have to be expanded by the inserted atom as well as by its successor atoms which are collected in the same way as above by evaluating the appropriate "down" REFERENCE attributes.

Modifying an atom

If the modification does not affect a REFERENCE attribute that defines the structure of an atom cluster, all atom clusters to which the modified atom belongs have to be determined by utilizing the address structure of this atom and within these atom clusters the corresponding atom has to be modified in the appropriate way. Thus, the usual management of replicas has to be performed.

If an "up" REFERENCE attribute pointing to the predecessors of the corresponding atom is modified, the old attribute value has to be compared to the new attribute value in order to determine those predecessors which are removed and those which are added. For each new predecessor the same procedure as for inserting an component atom may be applied. If predecessors are removed, the modified atom as well as its successors have to be removed from the corresponding atom clusters.

If a "down" REFERENCE attribute referring to successors of the atom is modified, the old attribute value and the new attribute value must be again compared in order to determine those successors which are removed or added, respectively. Each new successor as well as its successors have to be included into the atom clusters determined by the modified atom. Each removed successor as well as its successors, however, have to be deleted from the corresponding atom clusters.

Deleting an atom

If a root atom is deleted, the whole atom cluster determined by this atom has to be removed. If a component atom is deleted, this atom as well as all its dependent atoms, i.e. successors, have to be removed from the atom clusters determined by the deleted atom. This may be done in the same way as deleting a successor which has to be removed when an atom is modified.

In either case, if an atom is added to or removed from an atom cluster, the address structure of the corresponding atom has to be modified in order to indicate all existing replicas of an atom.

However, one special case has to be considered in more detail. A single atom may be multiply included in an atom cluster if the relationship between two atom types is multi-valued. In this case, a corresponding atom may have more than one predecessor within an atom cluster. As a consequence, if atoms are stored without duplicates within an atom cluster, appropriate information has to be kept in order to decide quickly whether or not an atom really has to be added to or removed from an atom cluster. This information, however, is part of the storage structure of an atom cluster which we will describe in the following.

5.3 The Storage Structure of an Atom-Cluster Type

The concept of atom clusters has been introduced in order to speed up construction of frequently used molecules by allocating all atoms of a corresponding molecule in physical contiguity. For this purpose different steps in mapping an atom cluster onto a page or page sequence are introduced:

From a logical point of view an atom cluster corresponds either to a heterogeneous or to a homogeneous atom set described by a so-called *characteristic atom*. This characteristic atom simply contains references to all atoms, grouped by atom types, belonging to the atom cluster (Fig. 5.4a). Moreover, the characteristic atom contains for each reference to such an atom an appropriate reference. Thus, the characteristic atom

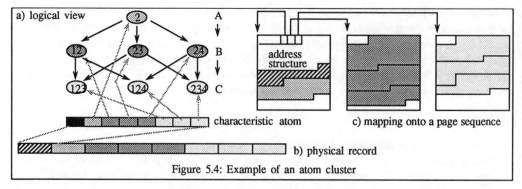

Figure 5.4: Example of an atom cluster

has to be evaluated in order to determine whether or not an atom really has to be added to or removed from an atom cluster or whether only the characteristic atom has to be adapted.

Each atom cluster is mapped onto a so-called physical record, i.e. a byte string of variable length containing the characteristic atom as well as all atoms referenced by the corresponding characteristic atom (Fig. 5.4b). All atoms are included only once although there may exist multiple references to one atom.

The physical record, in turn, is mapped onto a page or a page sequence depending on its current length. If the record goes beyond the page size assigned to the segment of the corresponding atom-cluster type, this record is mapped onto a page sequence. Otherwise, the record is mapped onto a single page. Within a page multiple records may be stored subsequently without intermediate space, whereas a page sequence always contains a single physical record. The mapping of a physical record onto a page sequence is performed as follows (Fig. 5.4c): All atoms of a single atom type are placed into a subrecord. All subrecords are subsequently mapped onto pages. If a subrecord exceeds the free space available within a page, a new page is allocated. If a subrecord requires multiple pages, these pages are exclusively used by the subrecord. However, in order to quickly locate an atom within an atom cluster, i.e. within a page sequence, an additional address structure is required which also depends on the current length of the physical record. If a record fits into a single page, no additional address structure is necessary, since a sequential search is always performed within a page. If the record is spread over a page sequence, the address structure initially consists of a simple table indicating the (first) page to which the appropriate subrecord is mapped for each atom type. In addition, each subrecord which requires multiple pages contains a further table indicating the page in which it is stored for each atom in order to avoid an exhaustive sequential scan over these pages.

This mapping mechanism described so far goes beyond other approaches concerning clustering of heterogeneous record sets, e.g. the physical representation of an NF^2 tuple [SS86] implemented in AIM-P [Da86] or DASDBS [DPS86] and the proposal of [KCB88], because we deal with replicated data and guarantee the automatic maintenance of consistency among these replicas.

5.4 Retrieval on Atom-Cluster Types

Concerning the retrieval operations on atom-cluster types and atom clusters one has to consider that the access system provides an atom-oriented interface, i.e. it is not possible to pass an atom cluster as a whole across the interface between the access system and the data system. Therefore, when accessing an atom cluster the appropriate characteristic atom is delivered, whereas the remaining atoms have to be requested by additional operations. As a consequence, the access system offers two different scan operations supporting a simple and efficient processing of atom clusters:

The *atom-cluster type scan* allows for the sequential processing of all atom clusters, i.e. characteristic atoms, of a certain atom-cluster type. In order to restrict the result set of such a scan an unqualified projection clause as well as a qualification criterion may be specified. Using a projection clause those atom types, i.e. the references to the corresponding atoms, are defined which are needed for further processing. The qualification criterion selects those atom clusters satisfying the corresponding condition, which has to fulfil the so-called single-scan property [DPS86], i.e. it has to be decidable during a single scan through an atom cluster. If this condition refers to the IDENTIFIER values of certain atoms which have to be contained in the desired atom clusters, the access system may utilize the corresponding address structure in order to speed up processing by determining the associated atom clusters without access to the data.

Since the atom-cluster type scan only delivers the characteristic atoms of the qualified atom cluster, the remaining atoms may be selected by either utilizing the corresponding IDENTIFIER values for direct access or by utilizing an atom cluster scan.

The *atom cluster scan* supports the sequential processing of all atoms of a certain atom type within a single atom cluster. Again, a projection clause as well as a selection criterion (decidable on a single atom) may be specified in order to restrict the result set to the attributes of these atoms which are required.

6. Using Atom Clusters for Efficient Molecule Construction

The usefulness of clustering atoms of heterogeneous types is obvious in systems that support static hierarchical objects, e.g., NF^2-tuples [SS86]. All records belonging to a structured tuple form a cluster, yielding minimal costs when accessing the whole tuple. Restrictions referring to the internal structure of the tuple can be evaluated very cheaply, since the structure is reflected by the cluster, and all data needed are in main memory after the cluster has been read. Furthermore, when access to subrecords is allowed only by reference to the whole tuple, there is no need for other, redundant data representations.

The MAD model, however, allows the dynamic definition of complex objects (molecules), as described in chapter 2. Therefore, it is more difficult to determine, which atoms should be clustered following a molecule type structure. On the other hand, when the optimizer chooses an access sequence for *construction of simple molecules*, it has to decide, whether or not existing atom clusters should be used. To give some hints, when the use of atom clusters may enhance efficiency, we consider the two phases of query evaluation introduced in chapter 4. We illustrate the different cases by examples, which suppose the existence of an atom-cluster type A-B-C, and of a fast access path on $A.Att_1$.

The first phase decides whether a molecule fulfils Q(M). If Q(M) contains conditions which reference the molecule structure, i.e., require parts of the molecule to be built up before the condition can be tested, an atom-cluster type scan, possibly enhanced by an appropriate selection criterion, may be useful, because it allows cheap access to all atoms involved. In the following example, the condition cannot be evaluated before the whole molecule is built up. The most efficient way to do so is to use the atom-cluster type.

```
SELECT    ALL
FROM      A - B - C
WHERE     EXIST EXACTLY (4) C: C.Att₁=A.Att₂
```

An atom-cluster type scan delivers the characteristic molecule of an atom cluster. The atoms of this cluster are then available in main memory, and thus can be cheaply accessed either by direct access using their IDENTIFIER value or by an atom cluster scan (cf. chapter 5).

An important criterion for the use of atom clusters in the first phase is the coincidence of the direction of the molecule type structure with that of the atom-cluster type. In the following example the atom-cluster type is of no use:

```
SELECT    ALL
FROM      C - B - A
WHERE     EXIST EXACTLY (4) A: C.Att₁=A.Att₂
```

Since access to an atom cluster is very fast when the IDENTIFIER value of one of its atoms is known (cf. chapter 5), it may be combined with an access path scan, as in the following example:

```
SELECT    ALL
FROM      A - B - C
WHERE     A.Att₁=7 AND FOR ALL C: C.Att₁>A.Att₃
```

In this case, all A atoms with $Att_1=7$ are determined via the access path scan. Then, the corresponding atom clusters are read to evaluate the rest of the condition. A more complex case occurs, if there is no access path on $A.Att_1$. One could use an atom type scan instead of the access path scan, accessing the rest of the molecule as above, or could alternatively employ an atom-cluster type scan with the selection criterion $A.Att_1=7$. The condition FOR ALL C: $C.Att_1>A.Att_3$, however, cannot be evaluated within the access system, as described in chapter 5. Which of these two alternatives is better depends on the selectivity of $A.Att_1=7$. If it is high, the first one is preferable, because checking the condition is cheaper. If it is low, the first alternative again causes many fetches of A atoms by the atom cluster access which are already in memory due to the atom type scan and already known to the data system.

While the second phase of query evaluation normally has no impact on the decisions concerning the first phase, this does not hold, when atom-cluster types are available. If, for example, molecule type and atom-cluster type have an identical structure, the second phase becomes very cheap, if the atom-cluster type is used to evaluate the restriction in the first phase. Therefore, costs of both phases have to be taken into consideration for optimization purposes. The following case illustrates that the considerations made during the first phase (last example) can be utilized for the second phase, too:

```
SELECT    ALL
FROM      A - B - C
WHERE     A.Att₁=5
```

Here again, the question is whether to use an atom type scan and access the atom cluster by its IDENTIFIER value, or to use an atom-cluster type scan with an appropriate selection criterion.

Even if the direction of the molecule type structure and that of the atom-cluster type structure do not match, atom-cluster types can be useful to traverse the molecule (in opposite direction). In the following example, it is a promising approach to look for the qualifying A atoms first, possibly supported by an access path. The corresponding C atoms can be found cheaply by reading the atom clusters of type A-B-C containing these A atoms. Afterwards the remaining atoms of types B and A have to be fetched by direct access using the appropriate REFERENCE attribute values:

```
SELECT    ALL
FROM      C - B - A
WHERE     EXISTS A.Att₁ = 7,
```

Atom-cluster types may accelerate the second phase, even if they are only subgraphs of the molecule types, as shown below:

```
SELECT    ALL
FROM      D - A - B - C
```

Since access to atom clusters via its root's IDENTIFIER is fast, A-B-C submolecules referenced by D atoms may be fetched in this way.

The discussion above shows the difficulty of optimizer decisions when atom-cluster types have to be taken into account. Access strategies become much more complex, and cost models have to be developed which cope with the critical parameters introduced above.

7. Conclusions

Dynamism in complex object definitions, as supported by the MAD model, requires new concepts for clustering. In the PRIMA system, heterogeneous sets of atoms can be clustered according to a specific molecule structure. This storage structure is kept redundantly, and therefore serves only for efficiency enhancement. It is managed by the access system, which guarantees transparency of this redundant data for all update operations but, in turn, offers operations to retrieve atoms via atom clusters. To keep the division of labor between access system and data system, the complexity of atom cluster definitions has to be restricted to correspond to a single hierarchical molecule type without any projection or restriction. Since the access to an atom cluster causes all appertaining atoms be loaded into main memory, the construction of a corresponding molecule can be done very efficiently. Thus, the dynamism of molecule type definition provided by the MAD model can be achieved in many cases at the efficiency of cluster mechanisms for static structures.

In spite of this quite simple structure it is difficult to decide whether the construction of molecules by the data system should be done with or without the use of existing atom clusters. For these reason, we see the following major fields for further research:

- Finding a good access strategy is more complicated than in the conventional case, if atom-cluster types are defined. Therefore, the optimizer must be extended by new rules and new cost models, which have to be developed.

- The usefulness of each atom-cluster type definition has to be checked, in order to destroy the definition when the update overhead goes beyond the efficiency gain for retrieval. For this purpose, appropriate statistics have to be kept. On the other hand, one needs hints, as to which atom-cluster type definitions could be useful to enhance efficiency. It still has to be investigated which kinds of statistics are required for these task. Furthermore, if there is any good heuristic to support either of both decisions, the system should initialize the corresponding actions by itself rather than by order of the database administrator.

- The structure of an atom-cluster type must be chosen very carefully. It is to support as many queries as possible, and as good as possible. Thus, one has to find a good compromise between "completeness" (i.e., all atoms of the molecule type definition clause of a query are contained in the atom-cluster type with the appropriate structure) and "generality" (i.e., the optimizer chooses the structure for the evaluation of many database requests, which in general means, for many different queries). If atom clusters of one type overlap (i.e., do not represent a strongly-hierarchical structure), an atom-cluster type scan causes several atoms be read multiply from disk. This should obviously be avoided. When the atom clusters are accessed using the value of their root atom's IDENTIFIER attribute, however, they may serve well to enhance the speed of a query evaluation. Thus, the usefulness of atom-cluster type definitions depends even on optimizer strategies. For this reason, we claim for a system controlled atom-cluster type definition, as already mentioned above.

Acknowledgement

We would like to thank T. Härder and B. Mitschang for their helpful comments on a earlier version of this paper which helped to improve the presentation of the important issues. Thanks are also due to H. Neu and I. Littler for preparing the manuscript. Furthermore, we would like to thank the anonymous referees for their fruitful comments and the inspiration of new ideas.

References

AL80   Adiba, M.E., Lindsay, B.G.: Database Snapshots, in: Proc. 6th VLDB, Montreal, 1980, pp. 86-91.

As81   Astrahan, M.M., et al.: A History and Evaluation of System R, in: CACM 24:10, 1981, pp. 632-646.

BB84   Batory, D.S., Buchman, A.P.: Molecular Objects, Abstract Data Types and Data Models: A Framework, in: Proc. 10th VLDB, Singapore, 1984, pp. 172-184.

BLT86   Blakeley, J.A., Larson, P.-A., Tompa, F.W.: Efficiently Updating Materialized Views, in: Proc. SIGMOD Conf., Washington, 1986, pp. 61-71.

Ch76   Chen, P.P.: The Entity-Relationship-Model - Toward a Unified View of Data, in: ACM TODS 1:1, 1976, pp. 9-36.

Da86   Dadam, P., et al.: A DBMS Prototype to Support Extended NF2-Relations: An Integrated View on Flat Tables and Hierarchies, in: Proc. SIGMOD Conf., Washington, 1986, pp. 356-367.

DD86   Dittrich, K.R., Dayal, U. (eds): Proc. Int. Workshop on Object-Oriented Database Systems, Pacific Grove, 1986.

DPS86   Deppisch, U., Paul, H.-B., Schek, H.-J.: A Storage System for Complex Objects, in: [DD86], pp. 183-195.

Ha87   Hanson, E.N.: A Performance Analysis of View Materialization Strategies, in: Proc. SIGMOD Conf., San Francisco, 1987, pp. 440-453.

Hä88   Härder, T. (ed.): The PRIMA Project - Design and Implementation of a Non-Standard Database System, SFB 124 Research Report No. 26/88, University Kaiserslautern, 1988.

HMMS87 Härder, T., Meyer-Wegener, K., Mitschang, B., Sikeler, A.: PRIMA - A DBMS Prototype Supporting Engineering Applications, in: Proc. 13th VLDB, Brighton, 1987, pp. 433-442.

HSS88   Härder, T., Schöning, H., Sikeler, A.: Parallelism in Processing Queries on Complex Objects, appears in: Proc. Int. Symp. on Databases in Parallel and Distributed Systems, Austin, Texas, 1988, pp. 131-143.

KCB88   Kim, W., Chou, H.-T., Banerjee, J.: Operations and Implementation of Complex Objects, in: IEEE Transactions on Software Engineering 14:7, 1988, pp. 985-996.

LHMPW86 Lindsay, B., Haas, L., Mohan, C., Pirahesh, H., Wilms, P.: A Snapshot Differential Refresh Algorithm, in: Proc. SIGMOD Conf., Washington, 1986, pp. 53-60.

Mi88a   Mitschang, B.: Towards a Unified View of Design Data and Knowledge Representation, in: Proc. 2nd Int. Conf. on Expert Database Systems, Tysons Corner, Virginia, 1988, pp. 33-49.

Mi88b   Mitschang, B.: Ein Molekül-Atom-Datenmodell für Non-Standard-Anwendungen - Anwendungsanalyse, Datenmodellentwurf und Implementierungsaspekte, Ph.D. Thesis, University Kaiserslautern, 1988.

SAH87   Stonebraker, M., Anton, J., Hanson, E.: Extending a Database System with Procedures, in: ACM TODS 12:3, 1987, pp. 350-376.

Sch88   Schöning, H.: The PRIMA Data System: Query Processing of Molecules, in: [Hä88], pp. 101-115.

Se87   Sellis, T.K.: Efficiently Supporting Procedures in Relational Database Systems, in: Proc. SIGMOD Conf., San Francisco, 1987, pp. 278-291.

SI84   Shmueli, O., Itai, A.: Maintenance of Views, in: Proc. SIGMOD Conf., Boston, 1984, pp. 240-255.

Si88a   Sikeler, A.: Buffer Management in a Non-Standard Database System, in: [Hä88] pp. 37-67.

Si88b   Sikeler, A.: Supporting Object-Oriented Processing by Redundant Storage Structures, in: Proc. Int. Conf. on Computing and Information (ICCI '89), Toronto, 1989.

SS86   Schek, H.-J., Scholl, M.H.: The Relational Model with Relation-Valued Attributes, in: Information Systems 2:2, 1986, pp. 137-147.

St75   Stonebraker, M.: Implementation of Integrity Constraints and Views by Query Modification, in: Proc. SIGMOD Conf., San Jose, 1975, pp. 65-78.

DATA ORGANIZATIONS FOR EXTENDED DBMSs

Query Optimization in an Extended DBMS

Beng Chin Ooi
Computer Science Department
Monash University
Victoria Australia 3168

Ron Sacks-Davis
Computer Science Department
Royal Melbourne Institute of Technology
Victoria Australia 3000

ABSTRACT
Conventional Data Base Management Systems (DBMSs) are not generally effective for applications such as geographic data processing where data have spatial characteristics and queries involve on spatial relationships. These DBMSs can however be extended by supplementing them with special processing subsystems and new indexing structures and by augmenting the query interface language. DBMSs supporting an SQL interface are now widely used. The GEOgraphic Query Language (GEOQL) [18] is an extension of SQL proposed for geographic applications and supports both spatial and aspatial operations. In this paper, we propose a global optimization strategy for the hybrid queries so that a general query involving both spatial and aspatial selection can be executed efficiently. We show that the method is feasible.

1. INTRODUCTION

The query optimizer is an important part of a relational database management system. The main task is to select an efficient query evaluation plan for a given query. However, most optimizers in existing systems have been designed for conventional data models, which are not capable of supporting applications like CAD/CAM or geographic data analysis. The design of extensible DBMSs [2, 6, 8, 15] has been the current focus, attempting to construct a generalized DBMS that can support unconventional applications easily. Another approach that has been widely advocated [1, 17] is to extend an existing DBMS for new applications. With the latter approach, an existing DBMS is supplemented by new indexing structures and evaluation subsystems in order to process spatial queries. An objective of the approach is to take advantage of existing mature techniques for aspatial query evaluation while providing, at low costs, efficient implementation of spatial indexing techniques for general queries. This paper describes an optimization strategy based on this approach.

To extend a DBMS for geographic applications, it is necessary to augment the external language and to provide a special processing subsystem to evaluate predicates that cannot be efficiently processed by a conventional DBMS. It is also necessary to construct an extended optimizer to execute the hybrid queries efficiently and to support new indexing/file structures [14] Ideally, a GIS must provide a storage and information processing architecture that integrates both the aspatial (attributes) and spatial components of the database. In such an integrated system, a user would be presented with a single query language, capable of expressing selection criteria that include both spatial and aspatial qualifications. One such query language is GEOQL which augments SQL with spatial operators to provide an interface that supports both spatial and aspatial query predicates. In this paper, an extended optimization is proposed with the GEOQL as the intended query language.

Consider the following query which locates all 'Wellington' roads that intersect railways.

```
SELECT    railway.name
FROM      road, railway
WHERE     road.name = 'Wellington' and
          road intersects railway.
```

The response to such queries depends on the ability of the optimizer to find an efficient query evaluation plan. Without considering how selections and projections may be performed, there are several global strategies to execute the above query. After retrieving all roads with the name 'Wellington' using conventional selection techniques, two techniques exist for finding intersecting railways. A spatial index can be used to reduce the number of railway entities that must be processed, or else each railway must be examined in turn. If the *road* relation is very large and no index exists in the attribute *name*, it may be more efficient to perform the intersection test first using a spatial index. Ultimately, an optimizer must be able to make a choice among these schemes and select the low level operations.

The proposal of a general method for extending an existing DBMS such that spatial queries can be optimized as a whole is the main aim of this paper. In the next section, a general overview of the method is presented. In Section 3, necessary logical transformation is discussed. A decomposition strategy that breaks a GEOQL query into a set of spatial and aspatial queries is presented in Section 4. In Section 5, query rewriting rules ensuring the query correctness and the query formulation strategy which generates all plausible query evaluation plans are presented. In Section 6, we discuss our implementation and the limitations of our approach. The conclusions are given in Section 7.

2. EXTENDING TECHNIQUES

2.1. Overview of An Extended System Architecture

New applications such as geographic applications require extra auxiliary indexing structures to facilitate the query retrieval based on the new (e.g. spatial relationships in a GIS) relationships. These new indexing structures cannot be supported in a conventional DBMS as they require different search and evaluating strategies. In order to evaluate the new predicates, a special subsystem is required. In an extented SQL-based DBMS, this subsystem interfaces with the SQL backend through which it accesses the database, and performs necessary spatial operations. On top of these two processors, the SQL backend and the special processor, is an extended optimizer responsible for determining an efficient query evaluation plan. The architecture of the extended system is illustrated in Figure 1. The *graphical display* unit which accesses graphical data provides the display of retrieved data in the form of maps.

2.2. Extended Optimization

Making use of an existing SQL backend is our primary intention. To this end, a GEOQL query is broken into subqueries that are either totally spatial or aspatial such that totally aspatial subqueries can be executed by an existing SQL backend, and the spatial subqueries can be executed by the newly installed spatial processor. Once the subqueries are formed, they are executed in an order that minimizes the overall query cost. The strategy consists of the following four major steps:

(1) *Logical Transformation*: As part of the optimization, the query tree produced by parsing the initial query is rearranged such that the new representation is more amenable to efficient evaluation. As well as including conventional logical transformations (e.g. redundancy removal), a GEOQL query tree must be restructured so that the spatial indexing

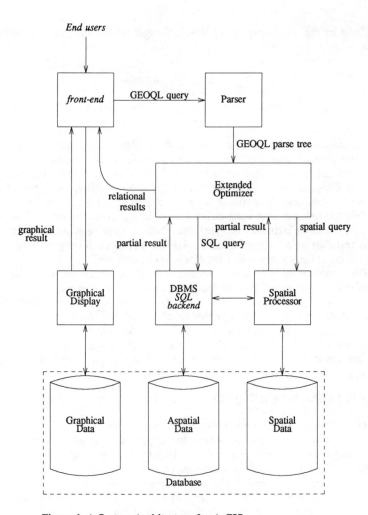

Figure 1. A System Architecture for A GIS.

can be used whenever possible.

(2) *Decomposition*: The parse tree produced by stage 1 is partitioned into subtrees which are either totally spatial or aspatial. Each subtree represents a subquery which must be executed by the query processor. The aspatial subqueries will be executed by the existing SQL backend and spatial subqueries which cannot be processed by the SQL backend will be executed by the spatial processor.

(3) *Plans Formulation and Selection*: From the set of subqueries obtained in the previous step, different orders (known as Subquery Plans (SQPs)) are formed. The best or cheapest is chosen among all subquery sequences.

(4) *Plan Execution*: From the chosen subquery sequence, SQL subqueries are passed to the SQL backend and spatial subqueries are passed to the spatial processor.

Figure 2 shows the extended optimization model.

The full syntax of GEOQL is presented in [18] In summary, it extends SQL to include predicates of the form

geo_term geo_op geo_term

where *geo_op* is one of the spatial operators (*intersects, adjacent, join, ends_at, contains, situated_at, within, closest* and *furthest*) and *geo_term* is one of the following:

(1) a geographic entity class (i.e. a *geo_obj* as defined by a table or variable name).
(2) a virtual geographic entity of the form
      (a) *line joining geo_obj and geo_obj*, or
      (b) *geo_obj bounded by geo_obj and geo_obj*.
(3) a window definition (x_1, x_2, y_1, y_2) where (x_1, y_1) and (x_2, y_2) are the top-right and bottom-left corners of the window, or a WINDOW keyword that assumes the current window in which a skeleton map is displayed as the coordinates.

For the definition of virtual objects, in case 2(a), the two *geo_obj*s must be points, and in case 2(b), the first object must be a line or a region and the latter two *geo_obj*s must define points or lines that intersect the first *geo_obj* (or its boundary if it is a region).

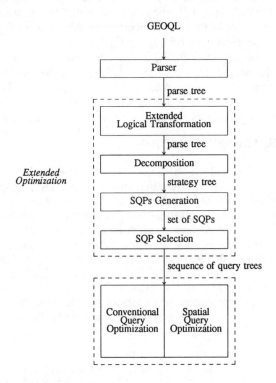

Figure 2. An Extended Optimization Strategy

Since SQL supports nested formulations of queries, algorithms which transform a nested query to an equivalent unnested query are an important component of a SQL query processor. As GEOQL spatial predicates do not allow subqueries as operands, the GEOQL language introduces no new nesting complexity as compared to SQL, and so the existing SQL unnesting algorithms [7,11] can be applied with only minor modifications to transform a GEOQL nested query into a set of partially ordered unnested queries. The result of this unnesting is a sequence of unnested GEOQL queries. Unnesting is considered a preprocessing stage, and the optimization strategies that follow consider each unnested query in isolation; consequently the only scope for optimization between the nested components occurs in the unnesting phase.

GEOQL is an extension of SQL, hence an existing SQL parser can be easily extended for GEOQL queries. For subsequent query transformation, it is highly desirable that the structure used to represent a parsed GEOQL query allows a great degree of freedom for restructuring. The parse tree used is a *multiway* tree, in which an internal node may have more than two children.

For the discussions below, we consider the predicate tree only when the other parts of the parse tree are immaterial to the context of discussion. Further we consider a predicate tree as consisting of internal nodes representing logical operators (and/or) and external nodes representing atomic predicates.

In what follows, we use $P_k(S_j)$ to denote kth predicate defined over a set (jth set) of relations. In order to distinguish a spatial predicate from an aspatial predicate, we put a superscript s on a predicate (e.g. P_k^s) when the predicate is spatial and a when it is aspatial (e.g. P_k^a). When the type of predicate is not important to the context of discussion, we simply use P_k. For a logical expression we write $log\_op(P_1(S_1), P_2(S_2), ..., P_n(S_n))$ to denote the disjunction or conjunction of the predicates $P_1(S_1)$, $P_2(S_2)$, ... , and $P_n(S_n)$, where log_op is *or* or *and* respectively. A conjunction of SQL predicates defined over the same number of relation(s) and same relation(s) is treated as a single predicate whenever possible. For example, $(P_1(S)$ and $P_2(S))$, is treated as $P_3(S)$, where P_3 is a symbolic name given to the compound predicate. $Q_m(S_n)$ is used to denote the mth query defined over the nth set of relations.

3. LOGICAL TRANSFORMATION

As in SQL, several GEOQL queries with different syntactic forms but with the same semantics may be formed. These alternative syntactic forms may exhibit different potential for execution optimization, and greatly increase the complexity of the optimization procedures. One of the preprocesses involved in query analysis is to convert all queries into some canonical form [9], with the objective of reducing the syntactic variants amongst semantically equivalent queries and yielding syntactic forms that are most amenable to the optimization heuristics. Assuming that a syntactically correct query is translated into a parse tree, the predicate subtrees corresponding to the WHERE clause are initially simplified as in [10].

As shown in [13], it is important to make use of spatial indexes whenever possible. Therefore, the representation of predicates in the predicate tree must not cause an early Cartesian product to be formed when this product may inhibit the use of spatial indexes.

Consider the following predicate.

```
road is adjacent to lake and
(lake.usage = "recreational" or
road.name = "Princess Highway").
```

If the *or* predicate is executed first, the cross product formed precludes the use of spatial indexes for the spatial predicate. However the expression in the following equivalent form would not inhibit the use of spatial indexes on both spatial predicates.

```
(road is adjacent to lake and
road.name = "Princess Highway") or
(road is adjacent to lake and
lake.usage = "recreational").
```

Note also in this example that the restrictions may be used to reduce the cost of evaluating the spatial expressions and no cross product is involved.

Another objective of logical transformation is to reduce the number of terms in an expression by identifying identical terms. This objective can conflict with the logical transformation stated above. Allowing the use of spatial indexes is given higher priority than reducing the number of terms. Thus the transformation required on top of the existing conventional logical transformations can be stated as follows:

$$\text{and}(P_1^s(S_1), \text{or}(P_2(S_2), P_3(S_3))) \Rightarrow \text{or}(\text{and}(P_1^s(S_1), P_2(S_2)), \text{and}(P_1^s(S_1), P_3(S_3)))$$
$$\text{if } (S_1 \cap S_2 \text{ or } S_1 \cap S_3) = \text{true}$$

The above transformation is necessary, irrespective of the predicate types of P_2 and P_3. Note that the above transformation has no effect on the following expression:

```
lake.usage = "recreational" and
road.name = "Princess Highway" and
(lake is adjacent to road or
lake is adjacent to railway)
```

For this expression, the spatial predicates are not impeded from using spatial indexes and can be more efficiently evaluated by using the partial results of the restrictions. No transformation is necessary.

All aspatial predicates are grouped according the relations they references. For example, the predicate $P_1^a(\{R_1\})$ and $P_2^a(\{R_1, R_2\})$ and $P_3^a(\{R_1\})$ are grouped as follows: $(P_1^a(\{R_1\})$ and $P_3^a(\{R_1\}))$, $P_2^a(\{R_1, R_2\})$.

4. DECOMPOSITION

A well known technique used in query optimization is to decompose a query into simpler components to reduce the complexity of optimization. In general, the simpler subqueries are designed to reference fewer relations than the original query [20, 21] In our context, an unnested GEOQL query is decomposed into simpler subqueries that are either purely spatial or purely aspatial to enable global ordering of subqueries such that an overall evaluation cost is minimized.

Consider the example in Figure 3. The temporary relation created by $P_2^a(S_2)$ may affect the strategy employed in evaluating $P_5^s(S_5)$ if both predicates reference some common relations. On the other hand, the partial result of an earlier execution of P_3^a or P_4^a will not affect the execution of P_5^s irrespective of the relations in S_3 and S_4. Hence, P_5^s, P_6^a and $\text{or}(P_3, P_4)$ should be detached as subqueries. P_1^a and P_2^a should form another two subqueries if S_1 or S_2 intersected S_5; otherwise the conjunction of the two predicates would form just one subquery. A more complicated decomposition policy would form P_1^a and P_2^a as two subqueries if S_1 or S_2 intersected any of S_3, S_4, S_5 and S_6. However, this more complicated strategy could lead to severe increase in the cost of determining the optimal subquery sequence. The strategy we have adopted is to form subqueries
(1) for each spatial predicate.

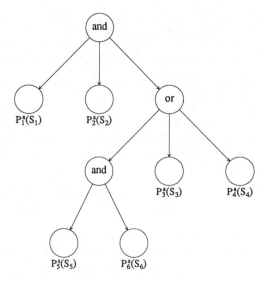

Figure 3. Grouping of Predicates.

(2) for each SQL predicate (which may be compound) that is related to a spatial predicate by a conjunction and references the relation (relations) involved in the spatial predicate.

(3) for the remaining SQL predicates in a logical expression, which do not satisfy condition (2).

The decomposition scheme maps a GEOQL expression $\log\_op(P_1, P_2, ..., P_k)$ into a query expression $\log\_op(E_1, E_2, ..., E_n)$, where E_i is either a query expression or a query $Q_k(S_k)$. More precisely, it is a mapping of a predicate tree into a tree whose internal nodes are logical operators, and external nodes are queries (pointers to corresponding query trees). We call the data structure formed by the decomposition algorithm the *strategy tree*. Figure 4 illustrates such a mapping. With such representation, the dependency of the subqueries is captured without any ordering.

A join, $R_1.A = R_2.A$, where one of the relations does not participate in any other predicates and the target list (answer) is implicitly a restriction. Hence, we regard such a join as a restriction in our decomposition algorithm.

As an example of the decomposition strategy, the following contrived query (disregard its semantics) is provided to illustrate the power of the decomposition strategy:

```
SELECT    road.name, railway.name
FROM      road, region, railway
WHERE     road.name ≠ region.name and
          road is adjacent to region and
          railway.name ≠ 'R10' and
          (region.name = 'Monash University' or
           region.name = 'RMIT').
```

Four subqueries formed by the decomposition strategy are given in Figure 5.

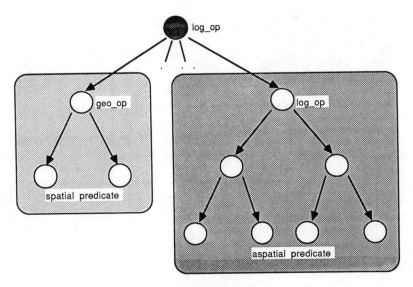

(a). A Predicate Tree.

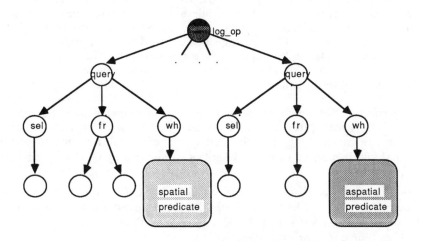

(b). A Corresponding Strategy Tree.

Figure 4. Mapping of a Predicate Tree to a Strategy Tree.

Q_1:	SELECT	*
	FROM	region, road
	WHERE	road is adjacent to region.
Q_2:	SELECT	*
	FROM	region
	WHERE	region.name = 'Monash University' or
		region.name = 'RMIT'.
Q_3:	SELECT	*

```
           FROM    road, region
           WHERE   road.name ≠ region.name.
   Q₄:     SELECT  *
           FROM    railway
           WHERE   railway.name ≠ 'R10'.
```

Figure 5. Subqueries Formed by the Decomposition.

The strategy tree for the above query is an internal node with an *and* logical operator pointing to four offspring subqueries. Note that Q_1, Q_2 and Q_3, and Q_4 are formed under conditions 1, 2 and 3 respectively.

It should be noted that the decomposition algorithm only decomposes a query into multiple subqueries, it does **not** specify any execution order for the subqueries, and the strategy tree allows us to arrange the subqueries in any order we prefer so long as the final answer is correct. Hence the SELECT clause of subqueries cannot be defined until the full ordering is known.

5. SUBQUERY SEQUENCING

5.1. Results Formation

Since a strategy tree is semantically equivalent to the predicate tree from which it originates, the subqueries in the strategy tree and their corresponding predicates in the original query tree exhibit the same dependencies. While ordering the subqueries, the dependencies captured by the strategy tree structure can be well expressed by the *introduction of extra SQL queries* and/or *terms rewriting*. The extra queries are used to merge multiple partial results (temporary relations), while the technique of terms rewriting propagates the partial result of a query to another query. Three result rewriting rules are introduced in this section to ensure the correctness of the final result. These conditions for which these rules are applied are *mutually exclusive*.

If two subqueries that are connected by a conjunction, reference some common relations and executed independently, then the partial results must be merged by a natural join. However, if a subquery (subquery Q_a) uses the partial result of the other subquery (subquery Q_b), then no natural join is required since the result that is produced by Q_a also satisfies the selections in Q_b.

Result Rewriting Rule 1. Given an expression and$(Q_1(S_1), Q_2(S_2))$ and the precondition $S_1 \cap S_2 \neq \emptyset$. Let $I = S_1 \cap S_2$ and let $C \subseteq I$. Suppose Q_1 is evaluated before Q_2, resulting the partial result T_1. Then for each $R \in C$ if $C \neq \emptyset$, replace R by T_1 in Q_2, and

(1) if $C = I$, no further rewriting is necessary.

(2) if $C \subset I$ (C may be $\emptyset$) and suppose T_2 is the temporary relation produced by Q_2 and A_1, ..., A_n are the common unqualified attributes in I, then the following SQL query (an equijoin) is introduced to merge the partial results:

```
           SELECT†  *
           FROM     T₁, T₂
           WHERE    T₁.A₁ = T₂.A₁ and
                    T₁.A₂ = T₂.A₂ and

                    ...

                    T₁.Aₙ = T₂.Aₙ.
```

Using a restricted instance of a base relation or a base relation with indexes is determined by the optimizer to minimize the processing cost.

Consider the following example. For simplicity, all attributes are selected in this example. Suppose that the attributes of R_i consist of $\{A_1, A_2\}$.

Q_1:	SELECT	*
	FROM	R_i, R_j
	WHERE	$P_1(R_i, R_j)$ and $P_2(R_i)$.
Q_2:	SELECT	*
	FROM	T_2, R_j
	WHERE	$P_1(T_2, R_j)$.
$T_2=$	SELECT	*
	FROM	R_i
	WHERE	$P_2(R_i)$.
Q_3:	SELECT	*
	FROM	T_{3a}, T_{3b}
	WHERE	$T_{3a}.A_1=T_{3b}.A_1$ and $T_{3a}.A_2=T_{3b}.A_2$.
$T_{3a}=$	SELECT	*
	FROM	R_i
	WHERE	$P_2(R_i)$.
$T_{3b}=$	SELECT	*
	FROM	R_i, R_j
	WHERE	$P_1(R_i,R_j)$.

Q_1 can be thought of as first fetching a tuple of R_i. If P_2 is true, fetch all the tuples of R_j such that P_1 is true. Then the result is projected as the final answer. This is operationally the same as Q_2, except Q_2 will have the partial result of R_i for which P_2 is true stored as the temporary relation T_2. Then for each tuple of T_2 and for all tuples of R_j, the result is formed if P_1 is true. Another way which is similar to Q_2, is firstly evaluating P_1 and then, based on the partial results, P_2 is evaluated. Alternatively, P_1 and P_2 are evaluated independently, and a join of two temporary relations on the common attributes is performed. This is expressed as Q_3. Hence the three queries produce the same answer.

The evaluation of a query can be visualized as firstly forming the Cartesian product of all the relations that are referenced, and then evaluating the predicates.

When two conjuncted subqueries reference different relations, the order of their evaluation is not important to cost saving. However, the partial result must be propagated to become part of the final answer. Subquery Q_4 in Figure 5 is a case in point. The partial result of Q_4 must participate in the final answer.

Result Rewriting Rule 2. We are given an expression and$(Q_1(S_1), Q_2(S_2))$, and a condition S_1 ⋔ S_2. Suppose that Q_1 is evaluated before Q_2, then put the temporary relation T_1 produced by Q_1 in the FROM clause of Q_2.

---

† since this is meant to be a natural join, only one of the joining attributes would be selected.

Consider the following example.

Q_4:	SELECT	*
	FROM	R_i, R_j, R_k
	WHERE	$P_1(R_i, R_j)$ and $P_2(R_k)$.
Q_5:	SELECT	*
	FROM	R_i, R_j, T_5
	WHERE	$P_1(R_i, R_j)$.
$T_5=$	SELECT	*
	FROM	R_k
	WHERE	$P_2(R_k)$.

Both predicates P_1 and P_2 can be evaluated independently, and the answer is the cross product of the partial results of P_1 and P_2. This is the same as forming the cross product of R_i, R_j and R_k, and then retaining the tuples for which P_1 and P_2 evaluate to true at the same time. For Q_5, P_2 is evaluated first and the result is stored as T_5. Then for each tuple of R_i, and for each tuple of R_j, the two tuples are merged if P_1 is satisfied and the resultant relation is then crossed with T_5. As P_1 and P_2 can be evaluated independently, the sequence of evaluation is immaterial.

Two disjuncted subqueries that reference different sets of relations must be made union compatible and hence, each partial result must be "crossed" with the relations that are not referenced by the subquery.

Result Rewriting Rule 3. Given an expression or($Q_1(S_1)$, $Q_2(S_2)$, ..., $Q_k(S_k)$), we let $S = S_1 \cup S_2 \cup ... \cup S_k$. The FROM clause of Q_i ($i = 1 .. k$) is rewritten with the set S as the referenced relations. Suppose T_i is the temporary relation produced by Q_i, then the result is formed by:

Consider the following example.

Q_7:	SELECT	*
	FROM	R_i, R_j, R_k
	WHERE	$P_1(R_i, R_j)$ or
		$P_2(R_j, R_k)$.
Q_8:	T_{8a} UNION T_{8b}.	
$T_{8a}=$	SELECT	*
	FROM	R_i, R_j, R_k
	WHERE	$P_1(R_i, R_j)$.
$T_{8b}=$	SELECT	*
	FROM	R_i, R_j, R_k
	WHERE	$P_2(R_j, R_k)$

Q_7 can be thought of as firstly forming the Cartesian product of all the relations and duplicating them as two temporary relations. Then evaluate P_1 on one of the temporary relation and P_2 on the other. The results obtained by both evaluations are then unioned to form the final answer. This is equivalent to Q_8.

Notice that the first rewriting rule does not handle a general case like $log\_op(E_1, ... , E_n)$, where E_i may be a subquery or an expression. Consider the example: and($Q_1(R_1)$, or($Q_2(R_1$, $R_2)$, $Q_3(R_1)$)) and suppose Q_1 is the first to be evaluated. Suppose we choose to to use the partial result of Q_1 in evaluating Q_2 but not Q_3 for some reason (like using indexes). Then a natural join between the results of the *or* expression and the results of Q_1 is required. However, if both Q_2 and Q_3 use the partial result of Q_1, then the partial result can be considered as being propagated to the *or* expression and hence no extra natural join is required.

The partial result relation of one subquery may be used as a substitute for a base relation of another subquery if the first common ancestor of both subqueries is an *and* node. In Figure 6, any of the partial results of Q_1^a, Q_2^a, Q_3^a and Q_4^s may be used by Q_5^s and Q_6^a. A child of an *and* node may use its brothers' results. Suppose insteads of Q_6, we have an *and* node with two child subqueries. These two subqueries may then use partial result of each other and the partial results of Q_i ($1 \leq i \leq 4$) but not of Q_5^s.

6. SQP FORMULATION

For n subqueries, n! distinct sequences of subqueries - subquery plans (SQPs) can be formulated by the brute force method. Without pruning techniques, the optimizer would be unacceptably slow. Hence a rule-based and heuristic strategy is required to reduce the number of SQPs considered. Following the conventional DBMSs, a rule-based optimizer should employ certain "*rules*" or "*musts*", to avoid the generation of sequences that are obviously ineffective, and heuristics to further prune the search space.

The set of subqueries formed by the decomposition strategy is generally small. However, it is important not to consider any alternatives that are obviously ineffective. Heuristic techniques are used to generate SQPs that are efficient. A relaxed heuristic uses less rules and hence produces more alternatives than those produced by a stricter heuristic which has more rules. A disadvantage of a stricter heuristic is that the likelihood of a good alternative being rejected is higher.

The following rules are proposed to reduce the subquery sequences being generated and thereby reducing the search space for finding the best sequence.

Heuristic Rule 1. For an expression $and(Q_1(S_1), ..., Q_i(S_i), ..., Q_n(S_n))$, if $S_i \pitchfork (S_1 \cup ... \cup S_{i-1} \cup S_{i+1} \cup ... S_n)$ then $Q_i(S_i)$ is executed just before the result is required.

The execution of Q_i does not affect any intermediate results of Q_j for $1 \leq j \leq n$ ($i \neq j$), therefore the sequencing of its execution is not important. To avoid rereading the partial result of

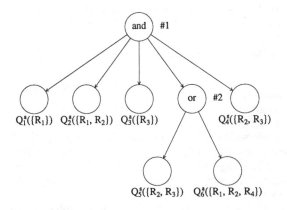

Figure 6. Use of Partial Results.

Q_i which is not required till the formation of the final answer, the merging of the partial result can be postponed until n-2 sibling subqueries have been evaluated. One of n-1 queries, Q_j (j ≠ i), is not executed before Q_i so that the partial result of Q_i may be propagated to the final answer through that query (as in Result Rewriting 2).

The above rule is applicable for a general case in which there is more than one independent subquery. However, for each *and* node of the strategy tree, the decomposition strategy will produce at most one query for which the referenced relations do not exist in the other conjuncted queries.

Heuristic Rule 2. For an expression $or(Q_1(S_1), ..., Q_n(S_n))$, the order of execution of subqueries is immaterial to cost saving. Hence the queries may be executed in any specific order.

Since the subqueries are independent, that is, one does not depend on the evaluation of another, it is immaterial which subquery is executed first. The above rule states that the sum of the cost in executing subqueries is invariant to the order of the subqueries. However, if the *or* expression is part of a conjuncted expression, say $and(Q_{p1}, ..., Q_{pm}, or(Q_1, ...,Q_n))$, then the queries in the disjunction may use the partial result of the conjuncted ancestor queries ($Q_{p1}, ..., Q_{pm}$). The order of execution of the *or* query expression is important with respect to queries $Q_{p1}, ...,$ and Q_{pm}, so the whole disjunction is treated as a single entity. The following illustrates some of the subquery sequences of the example shown in Figure 6:

$$[Q_1^a, Q_2^a, Q_3^a, Q_4^s, (Q_5^s, Q_6^a)]$$
$$[Q_1^a, Q_2^a, Q_3^a, (Q_5^s, Q_6^a), Q_4^s]$$
$$[Q_1^a, Q_2^a, (Q_5^s, Q_6^a), Q_3^a, Q_4^s]$$
$$[Q_1^a, Q_2^a, (Q_5^s, Q_6^a), Q_4^s, Q_3^a]$$
$$...$$
$$[(Q_5^s, Q_6^a), Q_2^a, Q_3^a, Q_4^s, Q_1^a].$$

While subqueries in [...] are conjuncted, subqueries in (...) are disjuncted.

For each *or* node of the strategy tree, the decomposition strategy will produce at most one child node which is an aspatial query although there may be a number of child nodes representing spatial queries.

Heuristic Rule 3. For an expression $and(Q_1(S_1), ...,Q_i^a(S_i), ..., Q_j^a(S_j), ..., Q_k^s(S_k), Q_n(S_n))$, suppose $|S_i| = 1$, and $|S_j| = 1$, and $S_i, S_j \subset S_k$, then at least one of Q_i^a or Q_j^a must be executed before Q_k^s. □

The argument follows from the fact that outer relation should be as small as possible to reduce the search.

6.1. Generating SQP

During the generation of different SQPs, it is necessary to minimize the number of SQPs for which cost estimation is performed. A method for generating SQPs has been proposed by [5]. This method generates different plans lexicographically [3,5,19] in such a way that all arrangements with common initial subsequences are generated consecutively. In this way, the rejection of next few sequences with the same initial subsequence can be made without having to examine them. The method advocated by Er [5] is outlined in Appendix B and is used in our query formulations.

Following the hueristic rule 2, the maximum number of sequences that may be generated is

$$\left\{ \prod_{\text{all } and \text{ node}} \text{number of children!} \right\}.$$

To specify the order of execution, the strategy tree may be

rearranged such that the depth first left to right traversal produces the desired order. Alternatively, an array that describes the ordering can be used. For the example in Figure 6, one of the sequences may be represented as follows:

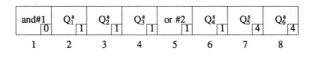

SQP: $[Q_1^a, Q_2^a, Q_3^a, (Q_5^s, Q_6^s), Q_4^a]$.

Figure 7. SQP Array.

An entry consists of a query or a logical operator and the parent index (the inner box). The first entry is always a logical operator and is followed by the children. The SQP can be obtained by recursively scanning the array from left to right. Start from the first entry, its child entries are searched from left to right. When a child entry is a logical operator, the process is repeated from that point. For the array in Figure 7, on reaching entry 4, the search for entries 6 and 7 starts. Searching for the remaining children of the 1st entry resumes when the searching of the children of 4th entry is completed.

While constructing an SQP, the attributes in the SELECT clause of subqueries are selected if they are required for further evaluation or the answer.

6.2. Cost Estimation

The query decomposition strategy discussed so far, in general, provides a means for separating spatial and aspatial predicates such that an existing SQL backend can be used to evaluate aspatial predicates. In order to choose a near optimal subqueries sequence, cost estimation is required. A complicated cost model is expensive to run. Indeed, the cost of running the optimizer may sometimes overshadow the benefits obtained. A trade off between the optimization effort and execution cost must be taken to minimize the total evaluation cost (execution cost + optimization cost).

The cost of processing query Q in the form of its equivalent subquery sequence is sum of the cost processing each individual subquery. To minimize the cost of the query, it is necessary to choose the subquery sequence which incurs least cost. Let the minimum cost of processing Q(S) be C(Q(S)). Then

$$C(Q(S)) \equiv \min_{\text{all k sequences}} \left\{ \sum_{i=1}^{N_k} C(Q_i(S_i)) \right\}$$

where N_k is the number of subqueries in kth subquery sequence, and $C(Q_i(S_i))$ is the cost of processing ith subquery in kth sequence.

The proposed extended optimization model can utilize the cost model of the SQL backend to estimate SQL query costs. Making use of the SQL backend cost model however undesirably makes the extended optimizer dependent on a particular backend. In addition, there will be an increase in the overall evaluation cost due to the fact that the execution strategy of each SQL query is practically examined twice. Instead of using the cost model employed by the SQL backend, an empirical parametric cost model would be sufficient to provide a reasonable cost estimation. Such a cost model would use a set of queries, which are deemed to be a representative set, to estimate the execution for different classes of queries, and the cost estimation should involve only a small number of parameters. The cost of the subquery $C(Q_i(S_i))$ is dependent on the type of Q_i (e.g. queries with pure selections) and the cardinality of S_i and the availability of indexes for S_i. This gives a fairly crude estimation. Should a more accurate cost estimation be necessary, the cost function may be tuned as more queries are processed. However, since we are trying to optimize the cost globally, it may be sufficient to use a simple cost estimation model which could be substituted with a finer estimation model if so required. Finding an estimation model itself is a hard problem [4, 16] therefore, it is not within the scope of this thesis to give any precise new estimation model. Rather, we assume the use of an existing estimation model, which may be simplistic but relatively useful as in [20].

7. DISCUSSION

To check the correctness of the algorithm and to justify the feasibility in terms of implementation, an experimental system was built on top of a DBMS called Relational Test Bed (RTB) [12] which was designed to allow fast implementation of small research databases.

The implementation confirmed that the rewriting rules are correct and that for each GEOQL query, all sequences produced by the decomposition algorithm and SQP formulation algorithm gave the same answer. Simple queries that involve three result rewriting rules were used for the tests [14]. The results obtained by different SQPs were exactly the same.

The major limitation with the extended optimization model is that we must be able to access the existing DBMS at more than the user's level. The unnested aspatial subqueries formed by the decomposition strategy are syntactically and semantically correct. It would be very inefficient to submit each query individually and then make use of the temporary results as part of the execution strategy. We need to able to control the buffer management and to access temporary storage without having to submit the decomposed unnested aspatial queries at the user's level. Using SQL queries with INTO clauses introduces more problems than just creating temporary tables, expensive rereading operations are also required.

8. CONCLUSIONS

An optimization model for GEOQL-like augmented SQL has been proposed. Many of the techniques employed by the proposed extended optimizer are based on existing methods used in current optimizers. Although, the strategy is proposed for a particular extension of SQL, we believe the same method can be used for other languages that are based on SQL.

The major contribution of this paper is a global optimization strategy for extensions of SQL which require additional indexing structures to materialize the additional relationships. The proposed strategy does not require *extensive modifications* of existing DBMSs. The optimization strategy consists of the following modules: extended logical transformation, decomposition, the generation of subquery sequences, and the selection of the best subquery sequence. Queries are transformed into logically equivalent queries that are more efficient to evaluate. As the SQL backend is not capable of evaluating the spatial components of the extended language, the decomposition breaks a query into several subqueries so that the SQL backend can be used for SQL (UA) subqueries, and a spatial processor, a subsystem for evaluating spatial selection criteria, processes spatial subqueries. With an unordered set of subqueries, all plausible different arrangements of subqueries are considered. This involves the generation of plans and the heuristic pruning of the search space so that only plausible plans are examined.

While such optimizer may not produce the best strategy, it can however produce a reasonable strategy. The approach is simple. It will not involve a substantial increase in the costs. The extension to the DBMS is minor: the SQL parser is modified to parse a larger set of predicates and the extended optimizer is built on top of the existing optimizer.

REFERENCES

1. D. J. Abel and J. L. Smith, "A Kernell-Shell Approach to an Extended Relational Spatial Database Management System", *Unpublished paper, CSIRO Canberra*, 1987.
2. D. S. Batory and M. Mannino, "Panel on Extensible Database Systems", *Proc. ACM SIGMOD Int. Conf. on Management of Data*, Washington D.C., May 1986, 187-190.
3. F. W. Burton, V. J. Kollias and J. G. Kollias, "Permutation Backtracking in Lexicographic Order", *The Computer Journal 27*, 4 (1984), 373-376.
4. S. Christodoulakis, "Implications of certain assumptions in database performance evaluation", *ACM Transactions on Database Systems 9*, 2 (June 1984), 163-186.
5. M. C. Er, "An efficient implementation of permutation backtracking in lexicographic order", *The Computer Journal 30*, 3 (1987).
6. J. C. Freytag, "A rule-based view of query optimization", *Proceedings of SIGMOD '87*, San Francisco, California, May 1987, 173-180.
7. R. A. Ganski and H. K. T. Wong, "Optimization of nested SQL queries revisited", *Proceedings of SIGMOD '87*, San Francisco, California, May 1987, 23-33.
8. G. Graefe and D. J. DeWitt, "The EXODUS optimizer generator", *Proceedings of SIGMOD '87*, San Francisco, California, May 1987, 160-172.
9. P. A. V. Hall, "Optimization of single expressions in a relational data base system", *IBM Journal of Research and Development 20*, 3 (May 1976), 244-257.
10. M. Jarke and J. Koch, "Query optimization in database systems", *ACM Computing Surveys 16*, 2 (June 1984), 111-152.
11. W. Kim, "On optimizing an SQL-like nested query", *ACM Transactions on Database Systems 7*, 3 (September 1982), 443-469.
12. K. J. McDonell, "An overview of the relational test bed (RTB)", *Technical Report 81, Dept. Comp. Sci., Monash University, Vic., Australia*, 1986.
13. B. C. Ooi, K. J. McDonell and R. Sacks-Davis, "Spatial kd-tree: an indexing mechanism for spatial database", *Proceedings of the Eleventh IEEE Computer Software and Applications Conference*, Tokyo, Japan, October 1987, 433-438.
14. B. C. Ooi, "Efficient Query Processing for Geographic Information Systems", *PhD Thesis, Monash University*, 1988.
15. J. A. Orenstein and F. A. Manola, "PROBE spatial data modelling and query processing in an image database application", *IEEE Trans. on Softw. Eng. 14*, 5 (1988), 611-629.
16. P. Richard, "Evaluation of the size of a query expressed in relational algebra", *Proc. ACM SIGMOD Int. Conf. on Management of Data*, New York, April 1981, 155-163.
17. N. Roussopoulos, C. Faloutsos and T. K. Sellis, "An efficient pictorial database system for PSQL", *IEEE Trans. on Softw. Eng. 14*, 5 (1988), 639-650.
18. R. Sacks-Davis, K. J. McDonell and B. C. Ooi, *GEOQL - a query language for geographic information systems*, Royal Melbourne Institute of Technology, Melbourne, Australia, July 1987.
19. R. Sedgewick, "Permutation generation methods", *ACM Computing Surveys 9*, 2 (June 1977), 137-164.
20. E. Wong and K. Youssefi, "Decomposition - a strategy for query processing", *ACM Transactions on Database Systems 1* (1976), 223-241.
21. S. B. Yao, "Optimization of query evaluation algorithms", *ACM Transactions on Database Systems 4*, 2 (June 1979), 133-155.

An Algorithm for Insertion into a Lattice: Application to Type Classification

M. Missikoff

IASI-CNR, Viale Manzoni 30, Roma, Italy

M. Scholl

INRIA, 78153 Le Chesnay, France*

Abstract

The focus of this paper is on updates of a type hierarchy structured as a lattice. We propose below algorithms for inserting a new type into a specific lattice of types used in the knowledge base system MOSAICO [Mi87]. Such a structure is closely related to the concept of *complete objects* as defined in [Di88] and to the *Concept Lattices* studied in [Wi82].

1   Introduction

Typing is a concept of programming languages: data is usually structured as a cartesian product (record type) or disjoint sum. The structuration of data is also fundamental in Database systems. The relational model [Co70] allows to structure data as sets of record types and has been advocated to be an effective way of processing sets. However relational data types have rapidly been perceived as relatively poor for various applications. This limitation gave rise to various models and systems having richer data typing.

Most of these new approaches allow any combination of the set and cartesian product constructors to build up data types. Among these approaches, the most important ones are semantic data models [HK87], nested relations models [Oz88], complex object models [Ba86, AB88] and, last but not least, object oriented systems [Ba88].

The same requirements and trends hold for knowledge base systems [KBS85] in the field of Artificial Intelligence. Among the numerous features of object oriented systems, we retain type inheritance.

---

*This research was partially supported by a grant of the french PRC BD3 and was initiated while the author was on leave at IASI-CNR

1.1 Type inheritance

The "taxonomic" organization of data as a hierarchy of types is systematically used in object oriented programming as well as in object oriented database systems or in some knowledge base systems.

At any level of the hierarchy, data types inherit all of the attributes of data types higher up in the hierarchy. The usual semantics associated to this types hierarchy is a set inclusion semantics: the set of objects of a given type is included in the set of objects of higher types. If t is higher than u, u is often said to *specialize t*, or t to *generalize u*.

1.2 The classification problem

If it is clear that typing and inheritance bring a richer semantics to systems for data intensive applications, there is nothing such as a standard for a typing system: the systems vary on the constructors used for defining a type (record, set, list,...) as well as on the definition of the type hierarchy (trees, directed acyclic graphs, various kinds of lattice structures, ...). Furthermore, the typing mechanisms vary from one application to the other: as an example, typechecking has not the same meaning for programming languages, object oriented database systems or classification applications [To86].

We are interested in the design of a type hierarchy where the correct placement of any type inserted into the hierarchy is fundamental and always enforced. As an example of these applications, we take MOSAICO, a knowledge base system, a prototype of which is currently developed at CNR-IASI, Rome [Mi87]. MOKA is a tool of MOSAICO which helps the user to correctly construct the schema. In particular, it displays any portion of the hierarchy and inserts new types into the hierarchy, enforcing the resulting structure to be consistent.

In the Omega [At86] and KL-ONE [BS85] systems, a classification algorithm properly connects a new description to other descriptions related by inheritance. Taxonomic reasoning as a deduction process exploiting the organization of objects in hierarchies of classes is also central to clustering analysis in the fields of statistics and pattern recognition [MS83, Di88]. CAD databases are another example of application in which there exist development tools, that enforce consistency after updates of object classes such as inserts or movings in the type hierarchy.

1.3 Algorithms for type insertion into a lattice

The focus of this paper is on updates of a type hierarchy structured as a lattice. We propose below algorithms for inserting a new type into a specific lattice of types used in MOSAICO. A similar structure is used in the Entity-relation model with inheritance, MORSE [Bo84]. Such structures are closely related to the concept of *complete objects* as defined in [Di88] and to the *Concept Lattices* studied in [Wi82].

As mentioned above, type constructors as well as type hierarchies vary from one system to the other. To illustrate the mechanism, we use a simple type system borrowed from [Ca84]. Informally, an object type is a record of atomic types, an atomic type being an attribute name associated to a subset of a given domain, called range. A type can be specialized by adding new atomic types and/or by choosing a smaller range in the domain of an atomic type. Multiple inheritance is allowed.

The key feature of the proposed lattice stucture is the concept of common *generator*. To simplify, whenever two different types share a common subset of atomic types, we assume that there exists a third type in the hierarchy, generalization of the two types, which is a record built up on the common atomic types. To illustrate the insertion mechanism, we give in Figure 1.1, 5 instances of lattices before and after insertion of a new type. For the sake of clarity each type is only represented by its set of attributes (we omit the ranges supposed to be the same at any level of the hierarchy). In examples 2 to 5, we use integers for attibute names: 134 represents the record type with attribute names 1,3 and 4. Observe that the insertion of a new type induces the insertion of other *hidden* types (underlined in Figure 1.1).

This approach has resulted particularly effective in the design of knowledge bases for complex applications. In such applications, it is difficult to proceed linearly top-down, introducing first the most general types and then specializing them in a number of subtypes, sub-subtypes, and so forth.

On the contrary, during the design process, when the user introduces a concept (type), he has no global knowledge of which (super)type he or another user will require later on. Then it appears easier to introduce a number of types at an intermediate level and then proceed in both ways: downward specializing types and upward finding generalizations of types previously introduced.

In the proposed type hierarchy, the existence of a common generator, for types with common attributes, allows us to derive a number of generalizations from the types actually introduced by the user. Hidden types derived by the insertion algorithm that do not appear of any interest can be dropped at the end of the design process, while those of use are kept explicitly.

As mentioned above, the proposed lattice structure is closely related to Wille's *Concept Lattices* [Wi82]:

The set of explicit (user) types E (a *context*) together with the set of derived (hidden) types form a complete lattice L (*Concept lattice*) such that E is supremum-dense in L, i.e. $L = \{\vee X \mid X \subseteq E\}$, where $\vee$ is the join operator.

The algorithms we propose below for inserting a new type may then be viewed as incremental algorithms for deriving the *concept lattice* associated to a given *context*.

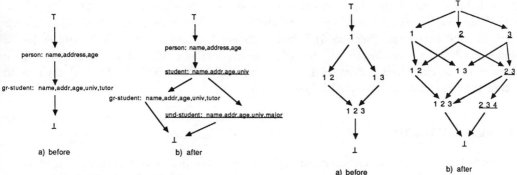

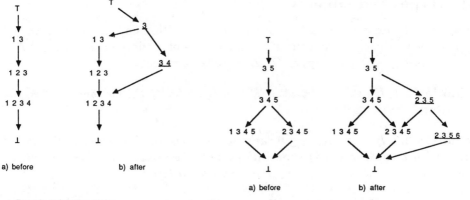

Figure 1.1 Examples of Lattices

After having defined the type system and the lattice structure (Section 2), we give two algorithms for inserting a new type into the lattice. If the first one (Section 3) sounds natural, the second one (Section 5) is more efficient but less intuitive and requires for its understanding and validation, the use of some properties of the lattice structure. These properties are exhibited in Section 4. Some remarks on the extension of the algorithms to richer type systems are given in the last section.

2 Definitions

We introduce in this section a simple type system. We first give the definition of types and objects, we then structure types into a lattice structure called M-lattice.

2.1 Types and Objects

We assume the existence of a finite set of domains with names $D_1, D_2, \ldots, D_n$. We also suppose the existence of two countably infinite sets of attribute names $\mathcal{A}$ and $\mathcal{B}$. Let Δ_i be any subset (possibly empty) of D_i. Δ_i is called a range.

Definition 2.1 *If $a \in \mathcal{A}$ is a name and Δ_i a range ($\Delta_i \subseteq D_i$, for some i), then $t = a : \Delta_i$ is an* **atomic type**.

Definition 2.2 *If $t_1, \ldots, t_k$, $k \geq 0$, are atomic types and b a name in $\mathcal{B}$, then $t = b : [t_1, \ldots, t_k]$ is a* **tuple(record) type** *with name b. Two record types cannot have the same name. For each r in $\Delta_1 \times \cdots \times \Delta_k$, r is an object of type t.*

Let T be the set of record types. We denote by A_t the set of attribute names of record type t. Let $a \in A_t$ be an attribute name in t . We denote by $\Delta_{a,t}$ the range of the atomic type corresponding to a in t:

$$A_t = \{\ldots, a : \Delta_{a,t}, \ldots\}$$

2.2 M-lattice

Let $\vee$ be the function $T^2 \to T$ defined as follows:

$$z = x \vee y$$

where $x, y \in T$ and z is such that:

$$A_z = A_x \cap A_y,$$

and for all $a \in A_z$

$$\Delta_{a,z} = \Delta_{a,x} \cup \Delta_{a,y}$$

Let $\geq$ be the following partial order on T:

$$x \geq y, \ x, y \in T, \ iff \ A_x \supseteq A_y \ and, \ for \ all \ a \in A_y, \ \Delta_{a,x} \subseteq \Delta_{a,y}$$

Let U be a subset of types: $U \subset T$. Assume $\{U, \geq\}$, is a meet-semilattice[1]. Assume also that U is closed under $\vee$. Clearly, U is a join-semilattice, where for any pair (x, y) in U $x \vee y$ is the unique greatest lower bound (GLB). Therefore, U is a lattice, called *M-lattice*.

Let S be a subset of types: $S \subset T$. Assume $\{S, \geq\}$ is a lattice in which we do not coerce the 'generator' of two types to be present, i.e. S is not necessarily closed under the above function $\vee$. It is similar to the lattice on record and variant types as defined in [Ca84] and restricted to structures ([Ca84] includes also subtyping on functions). Call it C-lattice. A M-lattice is a C-lattice. Indeed, if we denote by $\vee_c$ the join operation of C-lattices, then:

$$z = x \vee y \Rightarrow z = x \vee_c y$$

But, the converse is not true.

Then the results in [Ca84] on the semantics of types (lattices of objects where the ordering is set inclusion) hold for M-lattices.

The "Top" type ($\top$) is the empty record type: a type with no atomic type. A record type $t = b : [t']$ with only one atomic type $t' = a : D_i$ (with range the domain itself) has a unique supertype, $\top$. The record type whose set of properties is A itself and whose range for each property is the empty set is a subtype for all other types. It is called the "Bottom" type ($\perp$).

3   An Algorithm for Insertion into an M-lattice

We are given an M-lattice of types $\{U, \geq\}$. We want to insert a new type x into the M-lattice and coerce the resulting structure to be an M-lattice. The new set of types $U \cup \{x\}$ after insertion of x, is not necessarily an M-lattice, i.e. it is not necessarily closed under $\vee$. The insertion of x may require the insertion of additional types (hidden types).

In the first example of Figure 1, before insertion, the M-lattice includes four types: $\top$, *person*, *gr-student* and $\perp$. Upon insertion of *und-student*, another type, *student* with atomic types: name, address, age, university, has to be inserted.

Thus we are looking for the inductive closure of $U \cup \{x\}$ under $\vee$. In order to provide a fast navigation through the lattice, the latter is usually represented as a graph. A graph representation of the lattice includes an explicit information on the links between a type and its immediate supertypes and subtypes.

However, representing the lattice as a graph complicates the insertion mechanism. The algorithm below computes the inductive closure for an M-lattice $\{U, \geq\}$ represented by a

---

[1]Standard definitions and results on lattice theory can be found in [Bi79]

directed acyclic graph (dag) $D = [U, E]$ in which nodes are record types and there is an edge from node x to node y, iff $x < y$ and there is no z such that $x < z$ and $z < y$. In other words, there is an edge from x to y, if x is an immediate supertype of y. x is then called a *father* of y, and y is called a *son* of x.

Before getting into the algorithm, we need some notations. Let $SUP(x)$ be the set of supertypes of x: $SUP(x) = \{y \in U \mid y < x\}$. Let $FATHERS(x)$ be the set of fathers of x. $FATHERS(x)$ is the set of maximal elements of $SUP(x)$. Similarily, one defines the set of subtypes of x: $SUB(x)$, and the set of immediate subtypes, or *sons*: $SONS(x)$. Finally, we denote by $COMP(x)$ the set of types which have at least one atomic type in common with x, but which are not comparable: $COMP(x) = \{y \in U \mid x \vee y \notin \{x, y, \top\}\}$.

We give below a simple algorithm which, given the dag D representing M-lattice U, produces a dag D_+ representing an M-lattice after insertion of type x:

ALGORITHM A1

INSERT(x,U)

1. compute $FATHERS(x), SONS(x), COMP(x)$:

    (a) for all $y \in U$
    - if $y = x$ then $x \in U$, RETURN
    - if $x \vee y = y$ then $SUP(x) \leftarrow SUP(x) \cup \{y\}$,
    - if $x \vee y = x$ then $SUB(x) \leftarrow SUB(x) \cup \{y\}$,
    - if $x \vee y > \top$ then $COMP(x) \leftarrow COMP(x) \cup \{y\}$,

    (b) compute $FATHERS(x)$ and $SONS(x)$ respectively from $SUP(x)$ and $SUB(x)$

2. $U \leftarrow U \cup \{x\}$: *create-node x*

3. update the edges

    (a) for all $f \in FATHERS(x)$, *create-edge $f \rightarrow x$*
    (b) for all $s \in SONS(x)$, *create-edge $x \rightarrow s$*
    (c) for all edges $f \rightarrow s$, if any, where $f \in FATHERS(x)$ and $s \in SONS(x)$, *delete-edge $f \rightarrow s$*

4. generate virtual nodes (hidden types): *if $COMP(x) \neq \emptyset$, then for all $c \in COMP(x)$*

    (a) $v \leftarrow x \vee c$
    (b) INSERT(v,U) □

This algorithm inserts one (x) or several nodes (v) in the dag D representing the M-lattice $\{U, \geq\}$. It uses as primitives, (i) *create-node* which adds a node to the set of nodes U, (ii) *create-edge (delete-edge)* which adds (deletes) an edge to (from) the set of edges E.

The first step is a naive way of traversing the dag in order to get the set of immediate supertypes of x, the set of immediate subtypes of x and the set of types which are non comparable to x. There are of course more performant algorithms for doing the job, one of which, is implemented in OSAICO which uses this M-lattice structure, although on richer types [Mi87].

The second and third steps actually insert x into D.

The fourth step enforces the resulting dag D_+, to be an M-lattice by possibly inserting recursively some new hidden types, until the resulting dag represents an M-lattice.

Intuitively, at each step, a node is inserted in the right position, i.e. in between his immediate supertypes and subtypes and edges are possibly deleted (step 3.c) to insure that in the graph, there is no edge between x and $y > x$, if there is a node z such that $x < z < y$.

Note that, if the lattice were not to be represented by a graph and if we only require the inductive closure of U, the simple algorithm below would compute this inductive closure:

ALGORITHM A2

INSERT(x,U)

1. $U \leftarrow U \cup \{x\}$

2. Get $COMP(x)$: for all $y \in U$

    - if $y = x$ then $x \in U$, RETURN
    - if $x \vee y \notin \{\top, x, y\}$ then $COMP(x) \leftarrow COMP(x) \cup \{y\}$

3. if $COMP(x) \neq \emptyset$ then for all $c \in COMP(x)$

    - $v \leftarrow x \vee c$
    - INSERT(v,U)

□

Intuitively, the recursive call of the INSERT procedure until $COMP$ is empty is extremely expensive. In the following section, we exhibit some properties of M-lattices which allow the design of a faster algorithm to be shown later.

4   Some properties of M-lattices

We first show that, given a set of user types $U \subset T$ and a type $x \in T$, the computation of the inductive closure of $U \cup \{x\}$ under join ($\vee$), denoted by $(U \cup \{x\})^+$ takes a single pass (Section 4.1):

$$(U \cup \{x\})^+ = U \cup V$$

where $V = f(U)$ and f is defined as

$$f : U \to V$$

$$f(y) = y \vee x, \ y \in U$$

We then show that $\{V, \geq\}$ is an M-lattice and that $\{U \cup V, \geq\}$ is an M-lattice (Section 4.2).

4.1   Closure of $U \cup \{x\}$ under $\vee$

Lemma 4.1 $(U \cup \{x\})^+ = (U \cup \{x\})_+$, *under join.*
  where, if A is a set, $S \subset A$ and g a function of arity n, $A^n \to A$,

$$S_+ = \bigcup_{i \geq 0} S_i$$

$$S_0 = S$$

$$S_{i+1} = S_i \cup \{g(x_1, \ldots, x_n) \mid x_j \in S_i, \ j \in [1, n]\}$$

Proof:
see Lemma 2.3.1, p.19 in[Ga86], for example.

Theorem 4.1 *If U is closed under join, then $(U \cup \{x\})^+ = (U \cup \{x\})_1$, under join.*

Proof:
From Lemma 4.1, we must show that:

$(U \cup \{x\})_+ = (U \cup \{x\})_1$, under join.

Since U is closed under $\vee$, we have:

$$(U \cup \{x\})_1 = U \cup \{x\} \cup \{x \vee y \mid y \in U\}$$

In order to show that $(U \cup \{x\})_1$ is closed under $\vee$, three cases have to be considered:

  1. both t and $u \in U$: then U is closed under $\vee$, by assumption.

2. both t and $u \in V = \{v = x \vee y \mid y \in U\}$:

Then
$$t \vee u = (y_1 \vee x) \vee (y_2 \vee x)$$
where $y_1, y_2 \in U$. From the commutativity and associativity properties of $\vee$,
$$t \vee u = (x \vee x) \vee (y_1 \vee y_2)$$
Using idempotence of $\vee$ and since $y_1 \vee y_2 = y' \in U$, we have:
$$t \vee u = x \vee y'$$
By definition of V, $x \vee y' \in V$. Therefore $t \vee u \in V$ and V is closed under $\vee$.

3. $t \in V$ and $u \in U$:

There exists $y_1 \in U$ such that $t = y_1 \vee x$. Then:
$$t \vee u = (y_1 \vee x) \vee u$$
By associativity and commutativity,
$$t \vee u = x \vee (y_1 \vee u)$$
Since $y_1, u \in U$, so does $w = y_1 \vee u$. By definition of V, $x \vee w \in V$. Therefore $t \vee u$ is in V.

Thus $(U \cup \{x\})_1$ is closed under $\vee$. $\square$

Theorem 4.1 suggests that the computation of the inductive closure can be done in a single pass of insertions of new types, the elements of V which are not in U.

4.2 Lattice isomorphism

We have already defined the function f where $f(u) = u \vee x$, for all $u \in U$.

The kernel of f is the following equivalence relation:

$$given \ u, t \in U, \ then \ u \equiv t, \ iff \ u \vee x = t \vee x$$

Lemma 4.2 *Each class of the kernel of f has a unique minimal element.*

Proof
It is easy to show that for any $v = f(y)$, $f^{-1}(v)$ is closed under $\vee$. Assume $f^{-1}(v)$ has two minimal elements y_1 and y_2, then $y_1 \vee y_2$ has also v as an image by f. Since $y_1 \vee y_2$ is $\leq y_1, y_2$, y_1 and y_2 are not minimal elements, which is a contradiction. $\square$

Let U^* be the set of class representatives modulo $\equiv$, where we take the minimal type as canonical representative for each class. The restriction of f on U^* is a bijection:

- let $NC = \{u \in U \mid u \vee x = \top\}$ (NC stands for non comparable), The class representative of NC is $\top$: $f(NC) = f(\top) = \top$.

- $f(SUB(x)) = x$. The class representative of $SUB(x)$ is its minimal element s: $f(s) = x$.

- $SUP(x)$ is a set of fixpoints for f: $f(SUP(x)) = SUP(x)$. $\forall y \in SUP(x), f(y) = y$.

- $f(COMP^*(x)) = f(COMP(x))$. The set of class representatives is:
  $COMP^*(x) = \{y \in COMP(x) \mid if \ y' \in COMP(x) \ and \ y \vee x = y' \vee x, \ then \ y \leq y'\}$

  This suggests a simple optimization of algorithm A: it is enough to run step 4 for the types of $COMP^*(x)$.

$U^* = \{\top \cup SUP(x) \cup COMP^*(x) \cup s\}$

Lemma 4.3 *Each type $v \in V$ either is in U or has a single son in U which is the canonical representative of $f^{-1}(v)$.*

Proof
From Lemma 4.2, there is a single minimal class representative $u \in U^*$ such that $f(u) = v$. We have: $f(u) = u \vee x \leq u$. Assume u is not a son, i.e. there exists $t \in U$ such that $f(u) < t < u$.

(1) From Lemma 4.2, $t \not\equiv u$. Then, since $u > t$, $f(u) > f(t)$ (isotonicity of $\vee$)

(2) but $u \vee t \vee x = t \vee x$, since $t < u$. Then $u \vee t \vee x = f(t)$

(3) we have also $u \vee t \vee x = u \vee x \vee t = f(u) \vee t$. But since $f(u) < t$, $f(u) \vee t = f(u)$ and $u \vee t \vee x = f(u)$

(4) from (2) and (3), $f(u) = f(t)$, which is a contradiction since $t \not\equiv u$.

Thus, u is the smallest subtype of $f(u) \in U$. $\square$

Lemma 4.4 $\{V, \geq\}$ *is an M-lattice.*

Proof

- V is a join semi-lattice
  for all v_1, v_2 in V, $v = v_1 \vee v_2$ is the GLB, since from Theorem4.1, V is closed under $\vee$;

- V is a meet semi-lattice
  x is an upper bound for all $v_1, v_2 \in V$. Assume there exists v_1, v_2 in V which have two distinct least upper bounds (LUB) g_1 and g_2. Let u_1, u_2 be the canonical representatives of $f^{-1}(v_1)$ and $f^{-1}(v_2)$.

  (1) Since their unique LUB $u_1 \wedge u_2$ is greater or equal to u_1, u_2, by isotonicity $f(u_1 \wedge u_2) \geq v_1, v_2$ (it is a lower bound for v_1 and v_2). Then since g_1 and g_2 are LUB's, $g_1, g_2 \leq f(u_1 \wedge u_2)$

  (2) let l_1, l_2 be the canonical representatives of $f^{-1}(g_1)$ and $f^{-1}(g_2)$. From (1), by isotonicity, $l_1, l_2 \leq u_1 \wedge u_2$. But also by isotonicity, $l_1, l_2 \geq u_1, u_2$ since $g_1, g_2 \geq v_1, v_2$.

  (3) since g_1 and g_2 are distinct, $l_1 \not\equiv l_2$. Therefore $l_1 \neq l_2$

  (4) From (2) and (3) l_1 and l_2 are two distinct LUB's. This is a contradiction, since U is a lattice and for any pair $u_1, u_2 \in U$ there is a unique LUB $u_1 \wedge u_2$

  Therefore there cannot exist $v_1, v_2 \in V$ with two LUB. All $v_1, v_2 \in V$ have a unique LUB. Then V is a meet semi-lattice.

Since V is a join semi-lattice and a meet semi-lattice, then it is a lattice. Since V is closed under $\vee$, it is an M-lattice.$\square$

Corollary f is a lattice isomorphism inducing a lattice structure on U^*.
$\forall u_1, u_2 \in U^*$:
$$f(u_1 \vee u_2) = f(u_1) \vee f(u_2)$$
$$f(u_1 \wedge u_2) = f(u_1) \wedge f(u_2)$$

Proof
The restriction f on U^* is a bijection.$\square$

Theorem 4.2 $\{U \cup V, \geq\}$ *is an M-lattice.*

Proof
From Theorem4.1, $U \cup V$ is closed under the $\vee$ operation. From the definition of M-lattice, it remains to show that, all $z_1, z_2 \in U \cup V$ have a unique LUB, $z \in U \cup V$.
If both $z_1, z_2 \in V$, then from Lemma4.4, they have a unique LUB $z \in V$. If they both are in U, since $\{U, \geq\}$ is a lattice, they have a unique LUB $z \in U$.

It remains to prove that any couple $u \in U - V$, $v \in V - U$ has a unique LUB. Note that neither u nor v are in $SUP(x)$. We now show that this unique LUB exists and is

$$u \wedge v = u \wedge s$$

where $s \in U^*$, $s = f^{-1}(v)$.

Indeed, if a unique LUB $w = u \wedge v$ exists,

- $w \in U$, since if w was in V, then $u \leq w \leq x$ that is $u \in SUP(x)$ which is a contradiction;

- **(1)** $u \wedge v \leq u \wedge s$, by isotonicity, since $v = f(s) < s$, by definition of f,

  (2) since $u \wedge v > v$, and $u \wedge v \in U$, there exists $v' \in V$ and $\sigma \in U^*$ unique son of v' (lemma 4.3) such that

    - $v \leq v' < \sigma \leq u \wedge v$.
    - Then, $u \wedge v = u \wedge v' = u \wedge \sigma$

  (3) Since $v \leq v'$ and since the restriction of f in U^* is a bijection, $s \leq \sigma$

  (4) Then $u \wedge s \leq u \wedge \sigma$ by isotonicity, and since $u \wedge v = u \wedge \sigma$, we have $u \wedge v \geq u \wedge s$

  (5) From (1) and (4), $u \wedge v = u \wedge s$.

Thus, $w = u \wedge v = u \wedge s$ is the unique LUB. $\square$

5 More efficient algorithms

The following algorithms are based on the above properties of M-lattices. According to the system and the queries to be run against lattice U, the latter may be represented by various data structures. A graph representation allows fast scanning of subtypes and supertypes of a given type. The price to be paid for this is slower update operations and more complicate insertion algorithms, as it will be seen below. However the following algorithms are more efficient than the algorithms of Section 3. We successively consider the cases where the lattice is represented as a set and the case where it is represented as a graph.

5.1 Set representation of the lattice

We assume lattice U is sorted according to the partial order $\geq$.

ALGORITHM B1

INSERT(x,U)

1. (get V): for all u in U, $v = f(u)$

2. (get $U \cup V$): merge of U and V $\square$

The resulting lattice is sorted. The first step has a $O(n)$ complexity, where n is the number of nodes of U. V is a sorted sequence with duplicates. The merge of the second step has a $O(n)$ complexity since both sequences to be merged are ordered.

Note that the complexity of the recursive algorithm A2 of Section 3 is $O(n^2)$ in the worst case (n hidden types have to be inserted).

5.2   Graph representation of the lattice

Let $D = [U, E]$ be the graph representing the lattice, where U is the set of nodes and E is the set of edges: there is an edge $u \to v$ if v is a son of u (u is a father of v), i.e. if $u < v$ and there is no t such that $u < t$ and $t < v$.

Without loss of generality, assume the graph is represented by a table with n sorted lines (one for each node) and with two columns: the first one represents the node (u) and the second one the set of fathers of u: $fathers(u)$. The lines are sorted according to $\geq$.

Let $\Delta = [V, \mathcal{E}]$ be the graph with set of nodes V and with set of edges $\mathcal{E}$: there is an edge $v_1 \to v_2$ if v_2 is a son of v_1. Graph Δ represents M-lattice V. From the corollary of Lemma 4.4, Δ is isomorphic to graph $D^* = [U^*, E^*]$ representing U^*.

Let $\Delta' = [U^* \cup V, E']$ be the graph such that:

$$E' = \{v \to u \mid u \in U^*, \; v \in V - U, \; v = f(u)\}$$

To each node u of U^* corresponds a node $v = f(u) \in V - U$ and an edge $v \to u$: this edge materializes the fact that u is the unique son of $f(u)$ in U (Lemma 4.3).

Then $D_+ = D \cup \Delta \cup \Delta'$ represents M-lattice $\{U \cup V, \geq\}$.

The algorithm below constructs graph D_+ in three steps:

1. it first constructs D^* representing U^* by scanning D in a depth-first order; the output is a sorted set of pairs $< u, fathers^*(u) >$ where $fathers^*(u)$ is the set of fathers of u in U^*.

2. it then constructs at the same time Δ and Δ', by scanning in a depth-first order D^*: to each node u of U^*, it associates a node $v = f(u)$ in Δ, an edge $v \to u$ in Δ' and edges in Δ from the father(s) of v to v. From the corollary of Lemma 4.4, $fathers(v) = f(fathers^*(u))$. The outputs of this step are two sequences $< u, fathers(u) >$ and $< v, fathers(v) >$ representing respectively $D \cup \Delta'$ and Δ which are sorted on u and v according to $\geq$.

3. the final step consists in merging these two sequences.

A simple optimization would consist in running steps 1 and 2 at the same time: this has not been done, for the sake of clarity.

We first give the overall algorithm without detailing step 1 (U^* computation). We then give the algorithm for step 1.

Algorithm B2

INSERT(x,U)

1. compute U^*

2. for all $u \in U^*$ do
   if $v = f(u) \neq u$, then

   - $V \leftarrow V \cup \{v\}$
   - $fathers(v) \leftarrow f(fathers^*(u))$ (*create edges in* Δ)
   - $fathers(u) \leftarrow fathers(u) \cup \{v\}$ (*create edge in* Δ')
   - if $fathers(v) \cap fathers(u) \neq \{\emptyset\}$ then
     - $fathers(u) \leftarrow fathers(u) - fathers(v)$ (delete some edges $fathers(v) \rightarrow u$)

3. $U \leftarrow U \cup V$ (*the two sorted sequences are merged*)

□

compute U^*

for all $u \in U$, do

1. $fathers^*(u) \leftarrow fathers(u)$

2. if $(\forall y \in fathers(u), f(y) \neq f(u))$,then $U^* \leftarrow U^* \cup \{u\}$ (*mark* u)

3. for all $y \in fathers(u)$, do:

   if y not-marked, then

   - $fathers^*(u) \leftarrow fathers^*(u) - \{y\}$
   - for all $z \in fathers^*(y)$, do
     - if $fathers^*(u) = \{\emptyset\}$, then $fathers^*(u) \leftarrow fathers^*(u) \cup \{z\}$
     - else, if $(\forall w \in fathers^*(u), z \not\leq w)$, then
       $fathers^*(u) \leftarrow fathers^*(u) \cup \{z\}$ □

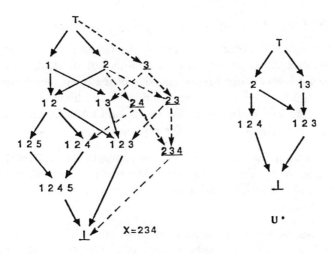

X=234

U•

u	fathers(u)	mark	fathers*(u)
T	Ø	•	Ø
1	T		T
2	T	•	T
12	1,2		2
13	1	•	T
125	12		2
124	12	•	2
123	12,13	•	2,13
1245	125,124		124
⊥	1245,123	•	124,123

Fig. 5.1 Algorithm B$_2$ on an example

u	fathers(u)	mark	fathers*(u)
T	Ø	•	Ø
35	T	•	T
345	35		35
1345	345		35
2345	345	•	35
⊥	1345,2345	•	2345

x = 2356

T
↓
35
↓
2345
↓
⊥

U•

Fig. 5.2 - Computation of U" on Example 4 of Fig. 1.1

Several remarks are in order:

1. the algorithm above constructs subgraph D^* by deleting some nodes from D : graph D is scanned breadth-first; each time a node is not marked, i.e is not kept in U^* because it is not the canonical representative of the equivalence class $(f(y) = f(u))$, then it is deleted (as well as all edges coming to and leaving this node). Its fathers are directly connected to its sons. Figures 5.1 and 5.2 illustrate on two examples, the computation of the sorted sequence representing D^*.

2. An upper bound on the complexity of this computation is $O(m^2)$, where m is the number of edges of U. The complexity of the two last steps of Algorithm B2 (computation of graphs Δ and Δ' and merge of the sorted sequences) is $O(n)$, where n is the number of nodes.

3. Figure 5.1 gives also the final graph D_+ after the insertion of type $x = 234$ (the dashed edges represent the graphs Δ and Δ'). Observe that nodes $\top$ and 2 are common to U and V.

4. By convention, in Algorithm B2, $f(\{\emptyset\}) = \{\emptyset\}$

5. Some edges may have to be deleted: if we have $v' \to v \in \Delta$ and if $v' \to u$ is in D, i.e. $v' \in U \cap V$, the insertion of $v \to u$ implies $v' < v < u$. Then $v' \to u$ has to be deleted (u is not anymore a son of v'). For instance, in example 3 of Figure 1.1, after having inserted edges $3 \to 13$ and edge $\top \to 3$, $\top \to 13$ is deleted.

6 Extensions

In this paper, we introduced algorithms for automatic type classification, for a simple type system.

We showed that the process of classification is not trivial, because of the natural but strong restriction imposed on the correctness of the type system, namely that if two types belong to the set of types, then their common *generator* type should also belong to the set of types.

For the sake of simplicity, we lost in generality in the choice of the typing system. Indeed, the only way of structuring data , was to use the record constructor borrowed from the programming language community.

The simple inheritance mechanism by refinement and specification together with the record structure on atomic types is probably enough to model many simple applications. However, most of the complex object models or the object-oriented type systems use both the set and tuple constructors, leading to richer type structures.

The extension of the type system to take into account the set constructor should not change the algorithm for classification. An alternate solution, which does not change the algorithm, is often used by the artificial intelligence community. Sets are represented by attaching to each atomic type of a record type, a repeating factor i.e., a maximal number of occurrences of objects of such an atomic type. The subtype partial order is extended accordingly: a type is refined by reducing the repeating factor of one of its atomic types. This strategy was chosen in the type system of MOSAICO.

Adding the set constructor allows the representation of complex structures (nested relations or complex objects). More important is the ability to represent types as tuples (or sets) of atomic types **as well as** already constructed non atomic types. This type sharing feature (composition of objects) is implemented in MOSAICO (where it is called *Entity Reference*) as well as in various knowledge base systems and object oriented systems (see for example O_2 [LRV88]). Composition of objects has for a consequence, the capability of sharing objects.

Since the algorithms proposed in this paper are independent of the partial order defining subtyping (inheritance), they apply to type systems including set construction and type sharing (as long as a partial order is defined on such types).

Acknowledgements: This paper benefits from the early contribution of F. Pirri who implemented the first version of MOSAICO's classification algorithm. Thanks also go to Y. Hanatani for the discussions we had on this paper.

7 References

[AB88] S. Abiteboul, C. Beeri, "*On the power of languages for the manipulation of complex objects*," INRIA research report, No 846, May 1988.

[At86] G. Attardi et Al., "*Taxonomic reasoning*," Proc. of ECAI Conference, Brighton, July 1986.

[Ba86] F. Bancilhon, "*A Calculus for Complex Objects*," Proc. of ACM PODS, Boston, March 1986.

[Ba88] F. Bancilhon, "*Object Oriented Database Systems*," Proc. of ACM PODS, Austin, Texas, March 1988.

[Bi79] G. Birkhoff, "*Lattice Theory*," Colloquium Publications, Volume 25, American Mathematical Society, Providence, RI, 1940, Third (revised) edition, 1979.

[Bo84] M. Bouzeghoub, "*MORSE: a functional query language and its semantic data model*," Proc. of 84 Trends and Applications of Databases Conference, IEEE-NBS, Gaithersburg, USA, 1984.

[BS85] Brachman R. J., Schmolze J.G., *"An overview of the KL-ONE Knowledge Representation System,"* Cognitive Science 9, 1985.

[Ca84] L. Cardelli, *"A Semantics of Multiple Inheritance,"* in Lecture Notes in Comp. Science, No 173, Springer Verlag, 1984.

[Co70] Codd, E.F., *"A relational model for large shared data banks,"* Comm. ACM 13:6, pp377-387, 1970.

[Di88] E. Diday, *"The symbolic approach in clustering and related methods of data analysis"*, H.H. Bock (editor, Elsevier Science Publishers B.V. (north-Holland), 1988, pp. 673-683.

[Ga86] J. Gallier, *"Logic for Computer Science,"* Harper and Row, Publishers, New York, 1986.

[HK87] Hull R., R. King, *"Semantic Database Modeling: Survey, Applications, and Research Issues,"* ACM Computing Survey, Vol. 19, No. 3, Sept. 1987.

[KBS85] *"Special Issue on Architectures for Knowledge Based Systems"*, Comm. of ACM, Vol. 28 n. 9, Sept. 1985.

[LRV88] C. Lecluse, P. Richard, F. Velez, *"O_2, an object oriented data model,"* Proc. of SIGMOD conference, Chicago, 1988.

[Mi87] M. Missikoff, *"MOKA: An User-friendly Front-End for Knowledge Acquisition,"* Int'l Workshop on Database Machines and Artificial Intelligence, Minowbrook (N.Y.), July 1987.

[MS83] R. Michalsky, R.E. Stepp, *"Automated construction of classifications: conceptual clustering versus numerical taxonomy,"* IEEE trans. on Pattern analysis and Machine Intelligence, Vol. 5, No. 4, 1983.

[Oz88] Special issue on *"Nested relations,"* Data engineering, (Z.M. Ozsoyoglu editor) Vol. 11, No. 3, Sept. 1988.

[To86] D.S. Touretzky, *"The Mathematics of Inheritance Systems,"* Morgan Kaufmann Publ., 1986.

[Wi82] R. Wille, *"Restructuring lattice theory: an approach based on hierarchies of concepts,"* Proc. of the symposium on ordered sets (I. Rival editor), Reidel, Dordrecht-Boston, 1982, pp. 445-470.

Duplicate Detection and Deletion in the Extended NF^2 Data Model

K. Küspert, G. Saake*, L. Wegner§
IBM Heidelberg Scientific Center, D-6900 Heidelberg, West Germany
*on leave from TU Braunschweig, FB Informatik, D-3300 Braunschweig, West Germany
§Gh Kassel - Universität, FB Mathematik, D-3500 Kassel, West Germany

Abstract. A current research topic in the area of relational databases is the design of systems based on the Non First Normal Form (NF^2) data model. One particular development, the so-called extended NF^2 data model, even permits structured values like lists and tuples to be included as attributes in relations. It is thus well suited to represent complex objects for non-standard database applications. A DBMS which uses this model, called the Advanced Information Management Prototype, is currently being implemented at the IBM Heidelberg Scientific Center. In this paper we examine the problem of detecting and deleting duplicates within this data model. Several alternative approaches are evaluated and a new method, based on sorting complex objects, is proposed, which is both time- and space-efficient.

1. Introduction

Within the last decade, the *relational data model* [Co70] has been widely accepted as a basis for commercial database management systems (DBMS's). In the relational model, all data are organized as homogenous collections of tuples within database tables (*relations*). The *tuples* consist of a non-homogenous collection of *attributes*. According to the so-called first normal form (short 1NF) postulate, all attributes must be 'atomic', for instance of type BOOLEAN, INTEGER, REAL, or CHARACTER. The major and well-known benefits of relational database systems are the structural simplicity of the data model combined with a powerful, descriptive query and data manipulation language (DML), e.g. QUEL [St76] or SQL [Ch81].

In the last few years, however, it became increasingly clear that the pure relational (1NF) data model is not very well suited to the management of *complex data objects* in a DBMS. These complex objects occur in many so-called 'advanced' or 'non-standard' application areas, e.g. in engineering (design objects for construction purposes, ...), office automation (structured documents with figures and images, ...), and science (molecule structures in chemistry, ...). If the user wants to retrieve a complex data object as a whole, for instance to display a large engineering design object on the screen or to provide it as input for a construction simulation, a large number of *join* operations are required to (re-)assemble the data object from the corresponding 'flat' tuples and 'flat' tables of a 1NF DBMS. These non-trivial join operations on large amounts of data are very unhandy from the user's point of view, rather error-prone in coding, as well as extremely resource (CPU time and I/O) consuming during execution.

The *NF^2 data model* [AB84, JS82, Ro85, SS86] is one approach to overcome these limitations of missing 'object orientation' in the 'pure' relational model. This data model (NF^2 = NFNF = Non First Normal Form) combines the 'pure' relational data model and the hierarchical data model, as known, for instance, from IMS [Da81, SJ77]. Attributes in tuples may again be (sub-)relations, i.e. the 1NF postulate is given up deliberately. These concepts of 'nested relations' or 'relations with relation valued attributes' in the NF^2 data model enable the user to map complex objects to *one* NF^2 relation instead of dispersing the data over *several* 'flat' relations.

Finally, the *extended NF^2 data model* [Da86, Pi87] is a further development of the NF^2 data model to capture some additional - for certain applications very important - structural concepts like ordered relations (usually called *lists*), *multisets* (i.e. sets which may have duplicates [Kn73]), nested tuples and nested (multi)sets, etc. (see Sec. 2 for a more detailed description).

In the last five years, a DBMS prototype, the Advanced Information Management Prototype (AIM-P), based on the extended NF^2 data model, has been developed in a research project at the IBM Heidelberg Scientific Center. At its current stage, AIM-P supports most constructs of the extended NF^2 data model and offers a powerful, high level, SQL like query and data manipulation language, called HDBL (Heidelberg Database Language), for complex object manipulation [PT85, PA86, PT86, ALPS88]. One of the more recent research interests in this project is the provision of suitable mechanisms to *detect and delete duplicates* in the extended NF^2 data model.

In any relational DBMS - be it 1NF, NF^2 or extended NF^2 - the need to detect and delete duplicates arises under two different circumstances:

1. **Uniqueness on stored database tables:** The user declares a database table as being 'free of duplicates'[1] either for a single attribute or for a collection of attributes. This integrity constraint may be enforced via a primary or secondary key declaration formulated in the system's data definition language (DDL). In the *extended* NF^2 data model, the situation is somewhat more complicated since multisets, nested (multi)sets, etc. may occur where a key declaration in the straightforward sense cannot be done.

2. **Uniqueness on query results:** The user wishes to obtain a unique *query result*, even if the database tables are not necessarily free of duplicates. This may be the case if e.g. all *different* salaries shall be extracted from a personnel table. In most relational DBMS implementations, the user may add a clause like UNIQUE to the query statement (e.g. in SQL) to trigger 'on the fly' duplicate elimination when the query result is built up. The reader should note that according to relational database theory [Co70], a query result must always be a *set* in the mathematical sense, i.e. be free of duplicates. Duplicate elimination, however, is not cheap and most systems therefore trade set theory for performance and do duplicate elimination for query results only on user request (SELECT UNIQUE ...).

In most (1NF) relational DBMS products uniqueness on database tables (1) is usually checked and enforced via proper *indexes* (e.g. multiway trees, hash tables); uniqueness on query results (2) is usually achieved via *sorting* accompanied by duplicate elimination. In the case of the NF^2 and *extended NF^2 data model*, however, several new problems arise which have not yet been thoroughly investigated in database research and development:

- What does a term like 'unique' exactly mean for complex objects or parts of complex objects? Do we have to distinguish between different *kinds* of uniqueness, e.g. between 'partial uniqueness', which applies only to the outermost (top) level of a complex object and 'total uniqueness', which implies uniqueness on all levels (cf. [KF88] which recently introduced the terms *shallow* and *deep duplicate free*)?

- Which kind of indexes can be used to enforce uniqueness on (extended) NF^2 database tables?

- Is sorting still the most appropriate method for duplicate elimination 'on the fly' and if yes, how can complex objects, like VLSI circuit layouts, be sorted?

In this paper we primarily concentrate on the topic of duplicate detection and deletion when creating *query results*. We present some basic concepts and algorithms, and discuss a set of design alternatives. In an accompanying paper [SLPW89], DML constructs for requesting uniqueness from the user's point of view are presented in more detail.

---

1   Throughout this paper the terms 'unique' and 'free of duplicates' are used as synonyms.

2. Data Model and Problem Definition

The extended NF^2 (AIM-P) data model removes many of the unpleasant restrictions on building database structures. Similar to type constructions in programming languages, set-, list- and tuple-constructors can be orthogonally combined to form almost arbitrary object structures. In particular, lists - not supported in the pure NF^2 model - are a commonly used data structure in many applications. Figure 2.1 illustrates the three data models discussed above. Key words in upper case show legal starting points for database object structures.

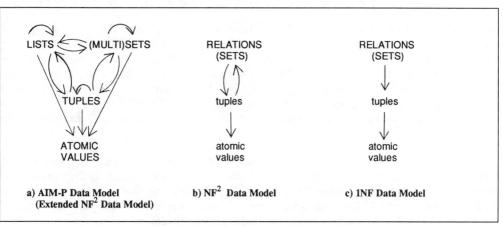

Figure 2.1: Comparison of three relational data models

Figure 2.2 shows an example for a relation in the extended NF^2 data model. The table gives the available seatings for various types of aircrafts. These types are grouped into three categories (represented as tuples in the database scheme) according to the routes flown. The table itself forms a set as indicated by

{SEATINGS}					
ROUTES	{AIRCRAFT}				
	TYPE	<SEATING_VERSIONS>			
		CODE	[SEATS_IN_CLASS]		
			F	B	T
National	B737	73C1 73C2	8 8	90 102	0 0
	B727	727E	8	131	0
	A310	AB31	18	181	0
Europe & Gulf Region	B727	727E	8	131	0
	A310	AB31	18	181	0
	A300	AB30 AB36	16 18	78 63	72 126
Intercontinental	DC10	DC10	22	76	136
	B747	74M1 74M2 747E	21 21 33	84 56 108	131 177 204

Fig. 2.2: Example for a table in the extended NF2 data model

the set brackets '{' and '}' around SEATINGS. SEATINGS has two attributes, an atomic attribute ROUTES and a non-atomic attribute AIRCRAFT which is again a set, i.e. unordered. For some aircrafts, the same type comes in different versions. The versions are grouped into lists, indicated by '<' and '>' around the attribute SEATING_VERSIONS. The versions are thus ordered, say in ascending sequence according to the lexical ordering of CODE which is the first attribute in SEATING_VERSIONS. The second attribute is SEATS_IN_CLASS, which is of type tuple (indicated by '[' and ']'). Each tuple SEATS_IN_CLASS has three components: F, B, and T for First, Business, and Tourist Class. Here, all three components are of the same type which, in general, does not need to be the case.

The example above contains no multisets. Indeed, if the table had been obtained by projection from the carrier's table of aircrafts in service, a result with possibly a dozen identical entries for each *type* of aircraft would be useless. In other circumstances, however, multisets play a useful role. One example would be a table (set) of medical records which is also made available for statistical research. To protect the individual, all attributes which serve to identify a patient, are hidden by the system for this class of users. Rather than adding an otherwise useless attribute 'NO_OF_MATCHING_INDIVIDUALS' to catch created duplicates by this implicit projection, it would save space and simplify queries to operate with multisets.

A situation where most data models are based on the concept of a set in the mathematical sense, yet implementations of these models usually handle multisets, is rather unsatisfactory. In the extended NF^2 model, the concepts of set and multiset are well separated. The data manipulation and retrieval language HDBL of the extended NF^2 data model contains explicit type conversions between the different relation types as well as implicit conventions for the type of query results [PT86].

As an example for duplicate detection we take the (flat) table in Figure 2.3 which relates employees to the files which they may access. The cardinalities of the result tables following projection on FILE_ID should be 4 (i.e. there are 4 distinct files in the table), 3 following projection on NAME, but 4 following projection on (NAME, EMP_NO) because there are two employees with identical NAME (jim) but distinct EMP_NO fields (1024, 9999). Figure 2.4 shows the projection on NAME and EMP_NO, followed by a sort on (NAME, EMP_NO), but preceeding duplicate deletion. With the sorted table in Figure 2.4 it is then quite obvious which tuples are duplicates and must be deleted.

Consider now the (extended) NF^2 data model. The same data as in Figure 2.3 might be arranged in nested format as shown in Figure 2.5. Assume we like to know how many files are distinct in terms of accessing employees. The natural way to proceed is to make a projection on ACCESSEE. Figure 2.6 shows the result before deletion of duplicates. The final result table, however, should have cardinality 3

{ACCESS_RIGHTS}		
NAME	**EMP_NO**	**FILE_ID**
susan	3189	customers
jim	1024	trends
jim	9999	budget
susan	3189	budget
jim	1024	customers
susan	3189	trends
jim	1024	accum-sales
peter	2705	budget
jim	9999	trends
susan	3189	accum-sales

Fig. 2.3: A flat table before projection

{ACCESS_TEMP}	
NAME	EMP_NO
jim	1024
jim	1024
jim	1024
jim	9999
jim	9999
peter	2705
susan	3189
susan	3189
susan	3189
susan	3189

Fig. 2.4: ACCESS_RIGHTS projected on NAME and EMP_NO

because both customers and accum-sales are accessed by {[susan, 3189], [jim, 1024]}. Of course, the question is how the DBMS can detect the duplicates. If sorting is the solution, then how can we order complex objects, i.e. is the set {[susan, 3189], [jim, 9999], [jim, 1024]} 'less' than {[jim, 9999], [susan, 3189], [peter, 2705]}?

The problem becomes even more subtle if nested projections are considered. Assume we project in the table from Figure 2.5 on NAME in ACCESSEE. The resulting table, preceding duplicate deletion, is also shown in Figure 2.6. An algorithm which assumes that subobjects are unique might be tempted to use the cardinalities of subobjects as a first criterion to decide on equality. Thus, unless deletion of duplicates is performed from the inside to the outside, {susan, jim, jim} and {susan, jim} might pass as two different objects.

On the other hand, if the result from the projection on NAME is explicitly specified as a multiset, but the projection on the reduced attribute ACCESSEE is supposed to be a set, then the method must distinguish between {susan, jim, jim} and {susan, jim}, yet delete one of the two instances of {susan, jim}. Similarly, if the attribute ACCESSEE were a list, <susan, jim> and <jim, susan> would be two distinct objects.

Another interesting aspect is the detection and deletion of duplicates relative to a subset of the attributes or parts of a value. As an example, a user might consider two entries in a table of scientific abstracts as identical if they agree on 'author(s)' and 'title', disregarding other attributes like 'journal',

{ACCESS_RIGHTS}		
FILE_ID	{ACCESSEE}	
	NAME	EMP_NO
trends	susan jim jim	3189 9999 1024
customers	susan jim	3189 1024
budget	jim susan peter	9999 3189 2705
accum-sales	jim susan	1024 3189

Fig. 2.5: ACCESS_RIGHTS in grouped form

{ACCESS_TEMP}		{ACCESS_TEMP}	
{ACCESSEE}		{ACCESSEE}	
NAME	**EMP_NO**	**NAME**	
susan jim jim	3189 9999 1024	susan jim jim	
susan jim	3189 1024	susan jim	
jim susan peter	9999 3189 2705	jim susan peter	
jim susan	1024 3189	jim susan	

Fig. 2.6: ACCESS_RIGHTS projected on ACCESSEE and on NAME

'year_of_publication', 'text_of_abstract'. Furthermore, a DBMS might use a procedure for long text fields whereby two texts are considered equal if they have the same length and a common prefix of, say, 100 characters.

In this context, where two objects are treated as duplicates, but can still be distinguished, the question arises which of the multiple 'identical' objects should be kept: any, always the first in a yet unspecified order, always the last? Moreover, should the 'set' of deleted duplicates be made available to the user? These questions become even more pressing when elimination of duplicates is offered for lists, creating something like a 'unilist' (not offered in the extended NF^2 data model). Here, the user may even want both the list of unique objects as well as the list of duplicates to retain the relative order of the input sequence. Without an additional hidden attribute, this could not be achieved by sorting alone.

Duplicate detection could also be used as a shortcut for the 'group-by' operator in HDBL. Consider e.g. going from the atomic attribute FILE_ID in ACCESS_RIGHTS to a set valued attribute FILE_IDS. This would group customers and accum-sales into the same tuple because they have matching AC-CESSEE's. These questions, however, are outside the scope of this paper and are treated in a discussion of the language interface [SLPW89]. We hope that these examples from the extended NF^2 data model and the list of problems to solve in detecting and deleting duplicates are sufficient explanation and motivation to look at duplicates in an orderly fashion in the next section.

3. An Ordering Relation for Complex Objects

Any algorithm for duplicate detection and deletion must include two decisions: (1) decide which two objects to compare next and (2) decide whether the two objects are equal. Moreover, we must keep in mind that we are really comparing object *representations*. For objects like (multi)sets, which may have many valid representations with respect to order, one way to answer (2) is to sort the objects internally.

To sort a collection of objects, a linear order relation "<" must be defined on the set S of possible objects, s.t. for any three objects a, b, c in S, the following conditions are satisfied:

1. Exactly one of $a < b$, $a = b$, $b < a$ is true (law of trichotomy).
2. If $a < b$ and $b < c$, then $a < c$ (law of transitivity).

We may assume that < is defined for atomic objects of the same type (integer, Boolean, real, and character). For texts (which might also be treated as atomic objects), lists, and tuples of atomic objects, the usual lexicographic order can be used, i.e. $A = a_1 a_2 \ldots a_n < B = b_1 b_2 \ldots b_m$ iff

1. $n < m$ and $a_i = b_i$ for $i = 1, 2, ..., n$ or
2. $\exists\, i \leq m : a_j = b_j$ for $j = 1, 2, ..., i-1$ but $a_i < b_i$.

Note that for tuples $[a_1, a_2, ..., a_n]$ we assume a declared order of the columns which needs not necessarily be left to right but must be fixed. The open point is what the ordering is between sets, resp. multisets, e.g. between $\{1, 4\}$ and $\{2, 3\}$.

Let $|S|$ denote the cardinality of (multi)set S. We propose as Definition 1 a recursive, transfinite ordering based on cardinality of (multi)sets and lexicographical ordering, i.e. $\{4\} < \{1, 4\}$ because $|\{4\}| = 1 < 2 = |\{1, 4\}|$ and $\{1, 3\} < \{1, 4\}$ because $|\{1, 3\}| = |\{1, 4\}|$ but $3 < 4$. Applying the order relation recursively to complex objects yields the following definition.

Definition 1 (cardinality-min-ordering):

For objects A and B of the same type, let
    $A < B$ iff
(0) A and B are **atomic** and $A < B$;
(1) A and B are **(multi)sets** and either $|A| < |B|$ or $|A| = |B|$ and $MIN(A) < MIN(B)$ or
    $|A| = |B|$ and $MIN(A) = MIN(B)$ and $A\backslash MIN(A) < B\backslash MIN(B)$,
    where $MIN(\{e_1, e_2, ..., e_n\}) = e_i$ with $e_i \leq e_j$ for all $i \neq j$ $(1 \leq i, j \leq n)$
    and $\{e_1, ..., e_i, ..., e_n\}\backslash e_i = \{e_1, ..., e_{i-1}, e_{i+1}, ..., e_n\}$, i.e. $X\backslash Y$ denotes X
    with Y removed;
(2) A and B are **tuples**, resp. **lists**, and either $FIRST(A) < FIRST(B)$ or
    $FIRST(A) = FIRST(B)$ and $A\backslash FIRST(A) < B\backslash FIRST(B)$ or
    A empty and B not empty,
    where $FIRST([e_1, e_2, ..., e_n]) = e_1$, resp. $FIRST(<e_1, e_2, ..., e_n>) = e_1$. ∎

As an example, let us order the elements of the powerset of set $S = \{1, 2, 3\}$. Definition 1 above yields

$$\emptyset < \{1\} < \{2\} < \{3\} < \{1, 2\} < \{1, 3\} < \{2, 3\} < \{1, 2, 3\} .$$

Clearly, this is not the only possible choice for defining the order. For sets we could have used $A < B$ iff $MAX(A) < MAX(B)$ or not used the cardinality at all. For lists, on the other hand, we could have included the length as a criterion. Note that tuples of the same type must have the same degree (arity).

Consider what happens if we do not include the cardinality as a first criterion for sets. The resulting order is given in Definition 2.

Definition 2 (no-cardinality-min-ordering):

For objects A and B of the same type, let
    $A < B$ iff
(0) A and B are **atomic** and $A < B$;
(1) A and B are **(multi)sets** and either $MIN(A) < MIN(B)$ or
    $MIN(A) = MIN(B)$ and $A\backslash MIN(A) < B\backslash MIN(B)$ or
    A empty and B not empty,
    where $MIN(\{e_1, e_2, ..., e_n\}) = e_i$ with $e_i \leq e_j$ for all $i \neq j$ $(1 \leq i, j \leq n)$
    and $\{e_1, ..., e_i, ..., e_n\}\backslash e_i = \{e_1, ..., e_{i-1}, e_{i+1}, ..., e_n\}$, i.e. $X\backslash Y$ denotes X
    with Y removed;
(2) A and B are **tuples**, resp. **lists**, and either $FIRST(A) < FIRST(B)$ or
    $FIRST(A) = FIRST(B)$ and $A\backslash FIRST(A) < B\backslash FIRST(B)$ or

A empty and B not empty,
  where $\text{FIRST}([e_1, e_2, ..., e_n]) = e_1$, resp. $\text{FIRST}(<e_1, e_2, ..., e_n>) = e_1$. ■

As an example we take again the powerset of the set $S = \{1, 2, 3\}$. The resulting sequence is

$$\varnothing < \{1\} < \{1,2\} < \{1,2,3\} < \{1,3\} < \{2\} < \{2,3\} < \{3\}.$$

We note that the *subset relation* (which is not a total ordering) is violated quite frequently and that S itself is "unnaturally" placed in the middle.

If sets are taken from a small ordered universe U, a set S can be represented as a bit-vector V_S (as e.g. in Pascal) where the i'th bit is 1 in V_S iff the i'th element in U is an element of the set S. Written from left to right (smallest element in most significant bit postition) and interpreted as binary coded integers, the powerset example above yields

$$\varnothing < \{3\} < \{2\} < \{2,3\} < \{1\} < \{1,3\} < \{1,2\} < \{1,2,3\}$$
$$000 < 001 < 010 < 011 < 100 < 101 < 110 < 111$$

which never violates the subset relation, i.e. forms a topological sort for "$\subseteq$", but is not "natural" either because $\{3\} < \{1\}$. A fairly natural ordering results from recording the smallest element in the numerically least significant position:

$$\varnothing < \{1\} < \{2\} < \{1,2\} < \{3\} < \{1,3\} < \{2,3\} < \{1,2,3\}$$
$$000 < 001 < 010 < 011 < 100 < 101 < 110 < 111.$$

For sets from a potentially infinite universe, we could achieve this ordering using the MAX-function without cardinality, i.e. $\{2, 3\} < \{1, 4\}$ because $\text{MAX}(\{2, 3\}) = 3 < 4 = \text{MAX}(\{1, 4\})$ and $\{1,4\} < \{2, 4\}$ because $\text{MAX}(\{1, 4\}\backslash 4) = 1 < 2 = \text{MAX}(\{2, 4\}\backslash 4)$. This yields Definition 3.

Definition 3 (no-cardinality-max-ordering):

For objects A and B of the same type, let
  $A < B$ iff
(0) A and B are **atomic** and $A < B$;
(1) A and B are **(multi)sets** and either $\text{MAX}(A) < \text{MAX}(B)$ or
  $\text{MAX}(A) = \text{MAX}(B)$ and $A\backslash\text{MAX}(A) < B\backslash\text{MAX}(B)$ or
  A empty and B not empty,
  where $\text{MAX}(\{e_1, e_2, ..., e_n\}) = e_i$ with $e_i \geq e_j$ for all $i \neq j$ $(1 \leq i, j \leq n)$
  and $\{e_1, ..., e_i, ..., e_n\}\backslash e_i = \{e_1, ..., e_{i-1}, e_{i+1}, ..., e_n\}$, i.e. $X\backslash Y$ denotes X
  with Y removed;
(2) A and B are **tuples**, resp. **lists**, and either $\text{FIRST}(A) < \text{FIRST}(B)$ or
  $\text{FIRST}(A) = \text{FIRST}(B)$ and $A\backslash\text{FIRST}(A) < B\backslash\text{FIRST}(B)$ or
  A empty and B not empty,
  where $\text{FIRST}([e_1, e_2, ..., e_n]) = e_1$, resp. $\text{FIRST}(<e_1, e_2, ..., e_n>) = e_1$. ■

Which definition to choose is largely a matter of taste and convenience. Figure 3.1 shows a listing of book descriptions, where each description can be a subset from {algorithms, data structures, programming}. Definition 1 (the leftmost column using cardinality first, then lexicographical ordering on equal size sets) is quite natural, but so is Definition 2 (middle column, order on repeated minimum element only), because the sets can be read as lexicographically ordered lists. Definition 3 (rightmost column, using the repeated maximum only) seems odd, yet the subset relation is never violated.

cardinality-min	no-cardinality-min	no-cardinality-max
{}	{}	{}
algorithms	algorithms	algorithms
data structures	algorithms data structures	data structures
programming	algorithms data structures programming	algorithms data structures
algorithms data structures	algorithms programming	programming
algorithms programming	data structures	algorithms programming
data structures programming	data structures programming	data structures programming
algorithms data structures programming	programming	algorithms data structures programming

Fig. 3.1: Three orderings of a list of book descriptions

As a final example we show the data from Figure 2.6 (subtable on the left) with all (sub)objects brought into ascending order according to Definition 1. The result is depicted in Figure 3.2.

The most compelling argument for using either Definition 1 (which we shall use from now on) or Definition 3 (no-cardinality-max-ordering) is the fact that they never violate the subset ordering, i.e. a sorted set of complex objects is always topologically sorted according to the partial subset relation. This even holds for multisets, where multiset X is a subset of multiset Y iff every distinct element in X occurs at least the same number of times in Y as it occurs in X, i.e. $\{a, b\}$ would be a proper subset of $\{a, a, b\}$. For Definition 1 this is trivially seen, for Definition 3 the proof is slightly more complicated, but straightforward, and is omitted here.

{ACCESS_TEMP}	
{ACCESSEE}	
NAME	EMP_NO
jim susan	1024 3189
jim susan	1024 3189
jim jim susan	1024 9999 3189
jim peter susan	9999 2705 3189

Fig. 3.2: ACCESS_TEMP ordered according to Definition 1

4. Alternatives to Sorting

Figure 3.2 indicates that sorting might provide a handle on the duplicate detection and deletion problem for the extended NF^2 data model. In this section we investigate whether there are alternatives to sorting.

4.1 Index Solution

An *index* is a mapping from attribute values to data objects. Consider a single attribute index for atomic values first. In order to decide whether a table is free of duplicates we could use the fact that if the index mapping is a function, then the indexed table is free of duplicates. Obviously, the inverse (an indexed table is free of duplicates only if it has an index with no multiple references) is false as can be seen from the following trivial example in Figure 4.1.

Neither FILE_ID nor NAME yields a key index on its own, yet the table has no duplicates. Still, existing index tables could be used to intersect the reference chains of length greater one between two indexes thus filtering out the only possible candidates. If no index tables exist, we could create them, say starting with the leftmost non-indexed attribute and proceeding to the next attribute as the need arises.

In the flat table ACCESS_RIGHTS from Figure 2.3, we could start with an index on NAME. For the entry susan we would have four references to tuples, for peter one, and for jim five references. Thus the tuple with NAME = peter could be eliminated as a candidate for duplicates. The remaining tuples would be selected into a temporary table and we could continue with an index on EMP_NO, either one for the whole temporary table or one per NAME value. This would split the set of tuples with NAME = jim into two subsets. Still, all reference chains per EMP_NO entry have length greater one and we had to look at the FILE_ID values for the tuples 'pointed to' in each chain. This would finally determine that the table is free of duplicates. Of course, a multi attribute index could also be used for that purpose.

The catch is that any intelligent sort would proceed in exactly the same way, i.e. it would never need to compare the EMP_NO fields of a tuple with NAME = jim with the EMP_NO field of a tuple with NAME = susan. Secondly, what if the table is ACCESS_TEMP in Figure 2.6? Now we need a complex object index. This is basically no problem, the index could conceptually be just a special NF^2 table with a 'pointer' attribute, but we are led back to the problem of detecting duplicates within the index!

Closely related to the idea of using an index with key property (i.e. where each entry 'points' to exactly one tuple) as a sufficient but not necessary condition for uniqueness, is the use of an additional attribute which will prove with high probability that the table is free of duplicates. As an example, consider an additional attribute NO_OF_ACCESSEES in Figure 2.5. It would record how many employees have access to each file, i.e. the cardinality of the set values. Given a projection on ACCESSEE (Figure 2.6), it would tell us immediately that only the first with the third tuple and the second with the fourth can be candidates for duplicates.

{ACCESS_RIGHTS}	
FILE_ID	NAME
customers	susan
customers	jim
accum-sales	susan
accum-sales	jim

Fig. 4.1: Attributes without key property but no duplicates

However, because it is only a sufficient indication of uniqueness, it does not solve our problem either. Moreover, cardinality of sets would be a data value stored internally by any NF^2 DBMS anyway and Definition 1 makes already use of this criterion. Unless a stronger 'signature' of tuples is used (cf. [FC84] for the use of signatures in document retrieval and the discussion of Hashing below), the use of artificial attributes under system or user control is a possible shortcut but not a solution in its own.

4.2 Hash-Function Solution

The idea is to specify a function f from the set V of (complex) values to, say, a set $A \subset \mathbb{N}$. If $A = \{1, ..., m\}$, $f(v) = i$ can be used as index into a hash table of size m and f would act as a *hash function*. Only values v_1, v_2 which cause a collision, i.e. which map to the same address, would be candidates for duplicate detection. If the hash function were perfect (i.e. an injective function) [Sp77] all colliding values were guaranteed to be duplicates. If the hash function were both perfect and minimal [Ci80, Ja81, Chang84], m could be set to the cardinality of the NF^2 table. If the function f were not minimal and would even produce a very large (sparse) table A, we could still use f to map the (complex) values into a list A' of signatures and then sort A' to detect duplicates.

An essential requirement is that f be a function, i.e. two values which are identical in the NF^2 sense must map to one value in A. For sets the ordering of elements is immaterial, thus we need a function $f(a_1,...,a_n)$ which is invariant on the ordering of arguments $a_1,...,a_n$. Any commutative operator will do, and $f(a_1,...,a_n) = (a_1 + ... + a_n)$ mod c for some constant c would be a candidate. If the elements a_i of the sets are not integers, an equivalent commutative operator must be used. For complex objects, the recursively computed hash values may be used as suggested by [KF88].

For lists and tuples order is relevant, i.e. $f(<1, 2>)$ should not be identical to $f(<2, 1>)$, resp. $f([1,2]) \neq f([2,1])$. Knuth [Kn73, p. 512] mentions multiword and variable lenght keys and notes that addition resp. exclusive *or* for folding the words makes use of all words in contrast to e.g. the mid-square technique for long character strings. Cichelli [Ci80] suggests using $h(k)=length(k) + g(\text{first character of } k) + g(\text{last character of } k)$. For the example above, i.e. the pair $f(<1, 2>)$, $f(<2, 1>)$, this fails. In general, a non-commutative operator between the elements of the complex key should give better results. Candidates would be subtraction, division, exponentiation, remainder with a subsequent operation that leads back to the natural numbers. In [KF88], addition combined with shifting for each added key is proposed. The authors also suggest keeping the computed hash values as tags with the objects and examine marking and interferencing as methods for avoiding repeated tests on duplicates.

However, hashing is not without pitfalls, as can be seen from the following example. Let a, b and c be pair-wise distinct complex objects and consider the set of sets $\{\{a, b\}, \{a, c\}\}$. Assume the unlikely, yet possible, coincidence where the hash function f yields $f(a) = f(b) = f(c) = k$. Thus the duplication detection algorithm must look inside a and b to determine that $\{a, b\}$ is indeed free of duplicates. The same happens for $\{a, c\}$. Both sets are marked "free of duplicates". On the next higher level, f uses the tagged hash values k yielding $f(\{a,b\}) = f(\{a, c\}) = k'$. Going again down one level, neither the tags nor the marking "free of duplicates" yield any clue as to whether $\{a, b\}$ is distinct from $\{a, c\}$ and we are back at the original problem.

Given a fixed table we could, in general, search for a perfect function, even a minimal one. This follows from Jaeschke's result [Ja81] which states that there always exist constants C, D, E s.t. $h(w) = int(C/(Dw + E) \bmod n)$, $n = |W|$ is a minimal perfect hashing function for a given arbitrary set W of positive integers. But it requires e.g. that the set W be sorted (!), is infeasible in the presence of many insertions and deletions or for large tables [Ja81] and is in any case computationally more expensive than sorting (Jaeschke reports 1.82^n iterations for n values to compute the minimal constant C as an experimental result).

Indeed, it is not necessary to use a minimal perfect hashing function to delete duplicates in minimal space without sorting. In [TW89a], a method is shown for detecting duplicates within an array and for moving these duplicates in place to the tail end of the array. The method requires in most instances several passes, but is independent of the hash function and has, on the average, a linear running time, i.e. it is much faster than sorting.

Hashing could also be used to test equality between sets. In [BKM86], Knuth suggests that equality of sets of integers be determined by inserting them into an ordered hash table. The two ordered hash tables are equal if and only if the two sets are equal. Since we must, in general, test equality between $n > 2$ sets, this would imply sorting the set of ordered hash tables. This seems less attractive than first sorting each set and then sorting the set of sets in some, yet unspecified, way. In summary, we see hashing as a very interesting speed-up which, however, must be backed up by a sorting method for degenerate cases. Whether it is ultimately easier to maintain a sorting order or a set of tagged hash values within typical NF^2 applications, further research and practical experience must show.

The final question is whether there is some method other than sorting, say some clever pairwise testing for equality, which would beat sorting. The answer is negative. For set equality, i.e. the question whether $A = \{A_1, ..., A_n\}$ and $B = \{B_1, ..., B_n\}$ are identical, Knuth ([Kn73], Sec. 5.3.3, Ex.23, p.209) mentions that under a suitable oracle any algorithm which only asks "Is $A_i = B_j$?" for certain i and j, must make at least $1/2*n(n+1)$ comparisons in the worst case.

For duplicates in a set (or list), Aho, Hopcroft and Ullman [AHU83, p. 292] mention that to "purge duplicates from a list requires at least $\Omega(n \log n)$ time under the decision tree model of computation." A similar result for detecting the maximal repeated element in a list can be found in [MS76, p.5].

5. Considerations for a Sorting Solution

The previous section indicated that sorting seems to be the best choice for duplicate detection and deletion in the extended NF^2 data model. We know (cf. Section 2) that the process of deletion has to go from the inside to the outside. To describe which requirements an efficient algorithm should fullfill, we partially sort ACCESS_TEMP from Figure 2.6 according to the order relation from Definition 1. The output should be a permutation of the input with duplicates removed, i.e. a set ACCESS_TEMP whose elements are set valued tuples[1] ACCESSEE, where the set elements are tuples of degree 2.

5.1 Basic Principle and Example

We use a simple Selectionsort to keep our example free of unnecessary algorithmic detail. Thus, we proceed from the top of the table to the bottom, select the minimum and move it to the front (top). According to Def. 1, for tuples A and B, $A < B$ iff FIRST(A) < FIRST(B), where FIRST(X) for tuples X is defined s.t. the first attribute is most significant and the last (rightmost) attribute is least significant and where MIN(X) for (multi)sets considers cardinality first. Note that we do not order (sort) objects inside more than needed. Sorting on all levels is in ascending order. Let card(X) denote the cardinality of (multi)set X and define fod(X) as a predicate which yields true iff object X is free of duplicates throughout. Note that we use the short-hand notation #i to identify the i'th tuple in Figure 2.6 (left subtable) and that card(#i) denotes the cardinality of the set valued field of tuple #i.

1. Pass (1. Minimum):

#1 is considered min. Is there a smaller object among #2 - #4 ?

---

[1]   ACCESS_TEMP might actually be defined as a set of set of tuples, but a set of set valued tuples might be more intuitive for those readers who expect a relation to be a set of tuples.

1. Test (Level 1): #1 < #2? According to Def. 1 we should consider cardinality first. However, we can use card(#1), resp. card(#2), iff we know that fod(#1), resp. fod(#2), holds. Thus we must delete duplicates in #1 and #2, i.e. 'sort' recursively #1 and #2. Of course, we only do this once and then store the fact that the sets are fod.

Applying again Selectionsort, [susan, 3189] in #1 is considered minimum.

1. Test (Level 2): [susan, 3189] < [jim, 9999]? The answer is no because 'jim' < 'susan'. Thus [jim, 9999] is considered minimum.

2. Test (Level 2): [jim, 9999] < [jim, 1024]? The answer is no because FIRST([jim, 9999]\jim) = 9999 > 1024 = FIRST([jim, 1024]\jim). Thus [jim, 1024] is the smallest element in #1 and is moved to the front. For the next sub-pass within #1, [susan, 3189] is again considered minimum.

3. Test (Level 2): [susan, 3189] < [jim, 9999]? The answer is no and [jim, 9999] is moved to the front as 2nd minimum. This completes the ordering of #1 and because all tests between tuples either yielded 'strictly less' or 'strictly greater', we did not find duplicates and card(#1) = 3.

Similarly, #2 is 'sorted' with one test and yields card(#2) = 2. Now the test on the outer level can be answered, i.e. #1 > #2 because card(#1) > card(#2). Thus #2 is the new minimum.

2. Test (Level 1): #2 < #3? We know card(#2) = 2, but #3 is not proven fod. Thus #3 is 'sorted' first. In three tests we order #3, find no duplicates, and card(#3) = 3. Note that at this time only the EMP_NO values for [jim, 9999] and [jim, 1024] in #1 entered a test. All other EMP_NO values were never looked at! This changes with the next test when we discover the first duplicate.

3. Test (Level 1): #2 < #4? Again, to determine card(#4), we sort #4. As a result we obtain card(#4) = card(#2) = 2. This implies that we must now look at successive minima in #2 and #4. The important observation here is that we should have stored the progress of the sort within each subset from previous passes. This way we can pick the minima without searching for them. The difference to storing the fod property is subtle and not well seen in this example. In other situations, however, a multiset might be marked fod but might not be completely ordered.

1. Test (Level 2): MIN(#2) = [jim, 1024] < [jim, 1024] = MIN(#4)? Since we note equality, we compare the second minima in both sets.

{ACCESS_TEMP}	
{ACCESSEE}	
NAME	EMP_NO
jim	1024
susan	3189
jim	1024
jim	9999
susan	3189
jim	9999
peter	2705
susan	3189
jim	1024
susan	3189

#2 (rows: jim 1024, susan 3189)
#1 (rows: jim 1024, jim 9999, susan 3189)
#3 (rows: jim 9999, peter 2705, susan 3189)
#4 (duplicate) (rows: jim 1024, susan 3189)

Fig. 5.1: ACCESS_RIGHTS ordered with duplicate deleted

2. Test (Level 2): MIN(#2\[jim, 1024]) = [susan, 3189] < MIN(#4\[jim, 1024]) = [susan, 3189]? Again the test yields equality, both #2 and #4 become empty and #4 (or #2) is identified and deleted as a duplicate. Subset #2 comes out as the minimum in the first pass and is moved to the front. Duplicate # 4 we move to the back.

The preceding Figure 5.1 shows the progress so far. Values in italics have entered a test at least once.

2. Pass (2. Minimum):

#1 is considered minimum. Is there a smaller object in the remaining 'list'?

1. Test (Level 1): #1 < #3? The answer is yes because card(#1) = 3 = card(#3), but MIN(#1) = [jim, 1024] < [jim, 9999] = MIN(#3). Thus #1 stays in front and duplicate elimination is completed. The final result is as in Figure 5.1 except that [*jim*, **9999**] in #3 should now be [*jim, 9999*] because the EMP_NO value 9999 entered the test in this pass.

5.2 Discussion of the Example

The example above explained the task of deleting duplicates by sorting. On the other hand, it might not make the reader enough aware of the differences between

*   sorting,
*   sorting throughout,
*   deleting duplicates, and
*   deleting duplicates throughout.

In Figure 5.2 we give another, more contrived example. Applying the same algorithm as above (to find out whether two files are identical w.r.t. their sets of accessees), Figure 5.2 could act as input and Figure 5.3 (with values which entered the sort in italics) would be the output. We note that the result is sorted but not sorted throughout. It contains no duplicates on the top level but it is not free of duplicates throughout. The reason is that we never have to compare the attribute values for ACCESSEE, thus never compute their cardinalities and thus never delete their duplicates.

Whether the user expects duplicate deletion throughout in Figure 5.3 is a question of the application and the language interface. From the algorithmic point of view, a sorting solution should provide both alternatives: do a complete depth-first recursive sort or - usually less expensive - sort subobjects only to the level needed. The second alternative requires that the sort within subobjects can be halted, that the progress can be recorded without much extra space, and that the sort within subobjects can be continued from this point later on. A sort with this property is said 'to *freeze* well'.

{ACCESS_RIGHTS}	
	{ACCESSEE}
FILE_ID	**NAME**
trends	susan jim jim
budget	jim susan peter

Fig. 5.2: Input to sort

{ACCESS_RIGHTS}	
	{ACCESSEE}
FILE_ID	**NAME**
budget	jim susan peter
trends	susan jim jim

Fig. 5.3: Output of sort

Similarly, if objects are known to be free of duplicates but are not ordered (and need not be ordered more than what is required for duplicate detection on a higher level), then it would be an advantage to have the minimum of a set with N elements delivered in O(N) time. Since we may expect that objects differ already on the first MIN value, considerable savings would result for the sort on the outer level.

Another pleasant property would be elimination of duplicates 'on the fly'. As we enter a subobject to sort it, we might discover duplicates. If they can be eliminated right away, we save redundant comparisons and data fetches in later visits. Some sorting algorithms can be modified this way. In general, a sort tailored to multisets can achieve a speed up from O(N log N) to O(N log k) on inputs of size N with k distinct key values [MS76, We85].

The last criterion discussed here is 'stability'. According to Knuth [Kn73, p. 4], a sort is *stable* if equal keys retain their relative input order. We carry this term over to duplicate detection and deletion where it implies that we pick the first instance of several objects with equal keys from a given input sequence and that the list of duplicates retains the relative input order on equal keys. The second property allows repeated applications of the algorithm to detect 2nd, 3rd, ... instances of 'identical' objects in sequence.

Clearly, a stable sort can be used for stable duplicate detection and deletion. Conversely, we conjecture that any stable duplicate detection and deletion which uses sorting must employ a stable sorting algorithm. However, this seems hard to prove because one has to argue over the set of all conceivable sorting methods. Note that most unstable sorting methods, like Quicksort, can be made stable if extra space is provided. Even some hashing methods can yield stable duplicate deletion if extra space of order N is provided.

On the other hand, stable methods, like Mergesort and Selectionsort, can loose their stability if duplicates are swapped with non-duplicates at random. We therefore include a column 'in situ' in the following table to indicate whether an algorithm uses less or equal than $O((\log N)^2)$ bits of extra space. Table I reviews the better known sorting algorithms with respect to the criteria discussed so far. In the following, we point out the relative merits of each method and the necessary modifications.

5.3 Comparison of Suitable Sort Algorithms

Delivering the minimum in $O(N)$ steps and then the next N-1 minima in $O(\log N)$ steps each gives a total sorting time of $O(N \log N)$. The first three methods in Table I are well known quadratic sorts. However, for small 'lists' of very large complex objects, Selectionsort might be the method of choice because it requires only N data movements [Se83, p. 95]. The algorithm is easily modified to have a stable list of duplicates in the back and requires no extra space.

The Mergesort - workhorse of most database systems - suffers from the fact that the minimum is not available until the last runs are merged. Freezing the sort then is not worth the effort anymore: it only takes $O(N)$ steps more to complete the sort. Deleting duplicates on the fly and stable deletion are easy to incorporate and give a speed up [BD83]. The prize to be paid here is extra space, usually in the order of $N/2$.

Radixsort and Shellsort are not attractive at all. Quicksort can be modified to move duplicates to the back [TW89b]. However, it is not stable unless linked list versions are used. Also, it has large time gaps — up to N steps per gap — in delivering the next minimum even if the total sorting time is made $O(N \log N)$ in the worst case, say using a median-find algorithm. Moreover, it requires saving the recursion stack to freeze the sort; using a stackless variant [We87] would lead to a rather complicated and slow solution. All in all, if stability and/or some extra space are no issues, efficient external versions of Quicksort can be modelled after [SW84, TW89b] but we would not consider it first choice.

<table>

Method	MIN in O(N)	next in O(logN)	freezes well	on-the-fly del.	stable	in situ
Selectionsort	yes	no	yes	yes	yes	yes
Insertionsort	no	no	yes	yes	yes	yes
Bubblesort	no	no	yes	yes	yes	yes
Mergesort	no	n.a.	no[1]	yes	yes	(no)[9]
Radixsort	no	n.a.	yes	no	(no)[8]	yes
Shellsort	no	n.a.	(no)[2]	no[3]	no	yes
Quicksort	yes[4]	yes[4]	(yes)[5]	(yes)[6]	(no)[8]	yes
Heapsort	yes	yes	yes	yes[7]	no	yes

</table>

TABLE I

Legend:

n.a. = not applicable

(1) difficult to freeze because of extra space, no sublist until after O(NlogN) time

(2) easy to stop but sorted sublist hard to detect

(3) would have to handle variable increments

(4) only on the average

(5) requires storing the recursion stack unless stackless variants are used [We87]

(6) best in linked list [We85]

(7) efficiency yet unknown [TW89b]

(8) stable for list versions

(9) stable in situ methods are known but are considered impractical

Much to our surprise, Heapsort fullfills all criteria but one. Following the heap building phase, the minimum (maximum) is at the root. Using Floyd's bottom up building method [Fl64], this only takes linear time in the worst case. Thereafter, the next key in sort order is returned after each heapify (sink in) step which takes O(log N) comparisons in the worst case. To freeze the heapsort, we need only one pointer indicating the rightmost leaf, everything else is contained in the regular structure of the heap.

On-the-fly deletion requires some non-trivial modifications [TW89b]. Whenever the rightmost leaf is swapped with the root and sinks down the heap, we also test for equality. If an equal key is detected, the key is swapped on the spot with the rightmost leaf which may either continue to sink down or climb up. This causes hardly any overhead. On the other hand, duplicates are usually detected very late in the process of sorting, namely when they become adjacent at the root. Empirical tests with this version of Heapsort indicate that a speed up from O(N log N) to O((N-M) log (N-M)) is possible, where M is the replication factor, i.e. $N = M*k$. This is substantially slower than the speed up for Quicksort and Mergesort (O(N log N) to O(N log k)). Moreover, Heapsort can also be turned into an efficient external sort [TW88] by using a heap of pages and merge operations between pages rather than exchanges of nodes.

The only obvious drawback with Heapsort is the fact that it is not a stable sort. If we insist on picking the first of several 'identical' objects, then it seems that a hidden attribute is the best solution. This attribute would record the index of the object relative to the input order. When objects with equal keys are detected, the 'index attribute' is compared and the object with smaller index value is kept. If the list of duplicates must be stable, we would then insert the other object into the list of duplicates using again the hidden index. Since Heapsort detects most duplicates as the root of the heap is removed, the insertion path is short.

Another alternative is to store the list of removed unique objects separately. This gives rise to a 'heap with holes' as described in [TW88]. Using a different arrangement for the heap we are then able to modify the sort to become stable at the expense of extra space. The resulting method now resembles Tree selection sort [Kn73, p. 142].

In summary, *Mergesort* is a safe choice if tables are always sorted throughout and if extra space is no issue. If objects need not come into physical sequence, linked list versions could be used. The modifications required for stable deletion are easy to incorporate. *Quicksort* in a stable linked list version for sorting throughout would be hard to beat performancewise. Special precaution has to be taken for the worst case. The necessary modifications can be taken from the literature. If sorting throughout is not required, *Heapsort* is best suited for the given task within the extended NF^2 data model. If stability is required, an extra attribute must be added. The necessary modifications for in situ duplicate deletion are outlined above but are not trivial.

6. Conclusion

Detecting and deleting duplicates in the extended NF^2 data model is a complex task both in terms of what needs to be offered to the user and in terms of implementation. Having introduced the notion of 'uniqueness' for tables, sets and lists in the extended NF^2 model, we introduced three ordering relations for complex objects. The definition which uses cardinality of sets and repeated minima as ordering criterion was picked as basis for the following discussion. We then reviewed existing and newly created indexes as well as hashing as possible alternatives to sorting for the given task. However, while both approaches can be used as a short-cut in many situations, they offer no general solution. The main reason is that duplicate deletion must handle complex objects which may contain duplicates themselves.

The recursive nature of the task is then shown in a detailed example where we apply a simple Selectionsort to a table with a set-valued attribute. The example illustrates that objects need to be sorted only up to the point where inequality can be detected. This gives rise to the notion of 'freezing' a sort within subobjects. Furthermore, the availability of the minimum in linear time rather than at the end of the sort is identified as a useful property. Finally, stability of duplicate deletion is introduced and is related to stable sorting methods.

Given these requirements, the popular sorting methods are reviewed and a modified Heapsort is selected as method of choice. As shown, Heapsort fullfills all criteria but stability which must be handled by a hidden attribute. At present, a preliminary implementation of a recursive Heapsort for nested complex objects is being tested. Further experience must show whether this unusual choice is justified.

References

AB84 Abiteboul, S., Bidoit, N.: Non First Normal Form Relations: An Algebra Allowing Data Restructuring. Rapports de Recherche No. 347, Institut de Recherche en Informatique et en Automatique, Rocquencourt, France, Nov. 1984.

AHU83 Aho, A.V., Hopcroft; J.E., Ullman, J.D.: Data Structures and Algorithms, Addison-Wesley, Reading, Mass., 1983.

ALPS88 Andersen, F., Linnemann, V., Pistor, P., Südkamp, N.: Advanced Information Management Prototype: User Manual for the Online Interface of the Heidelberg Database Language (HDBL) Prototype Implementation, Release 2.0, Technical Note TN 86.01, IBM Heidelberg Scientific Center, Jan. 1988.

BD83 Bitton, D., DeWitt, D.J.: Duplicate record elimination in large data files, ACM Trans. Database Syst., June 1983, pp. 255-265.

BKM86 Bentley, J., Knuth, D.E., McIlroy, D.: Programming Pearls: A Literate Program, Comm. ACM, Vol. 29, No. 6, June 1986, pp. 471-483.

Ch81 Chamberlin, D.D., et al.: Support of Repetitive Transactions and Ad Hoc Queries in System R., ACM Transactions on Database Systems, Vol. 6, No. 1, March 1981, pp. 70-94.

Chang84 Chang, C.C.: A study of an ordered minimal perfect hashing scheme, Comm. ACM, Vol. 27, No. 4, April 1984, pp. 384-387

Ci80 Cichelli, R.J.: Minimal Perfect Hash Functions Made Simple, Comm. ACM, Vol. 23, No. 1, Jan 1980, pp. 17-19.

Co70 Codd, E.F.: A Relational Model of Data for Large Shared Data Banks, Comm. ACM, Vol. 13, No. 6, June 1970.

Da81 Date, C.J.: An Introduction to Database Systems (3rd ed.), Addison-Wesley, Reading, Mass., 1981.

Da86 Dadam, P., et al.: A DBMS Prototype to Support Extended NF^2 Relations: An Integrated View on Flat Tables and Hie archies, Proc. ACM SIGMOD Int. Conf. on Management of Data, Washington, D.C., May 1986, pp. 356-367.

DGK Dayal,U., Goodman,N., Katz,R.H.: An Extended Relational Algebra with Control Over Duplicate Elimination, Proc. ACM Symp. PoDS, Los Angeles, Cal., March 1982, pp. 117-123.

FC84 Faloutsos, C., Christodoulakis, S.: Signature Files: An Access Method for Documents and its Analytical Performance Evaluation, ACM TOOIS, Vol. 2, No. 4, Oct. 1984, pp. 267-288.

Fl64 Floyd,R.W.: Algorithm 245, Treesort 3, Comm. ACM, Vol. 7, No. 12, Dec. 1964, p. 701.

Ja81 Jaeschke, G.: Reciprocal Hashing: A Method for Generating Minimal Perfect Hashing Functions, Comm. ACM, Vol. 24, No. 12, Dec. 1981, pp. 829-833.

JS82 Jaeschke, G., Schek, H.-J.: Remarks on the Algebra of Non First Normal Form Relations, Proc. ACM SIGACT-SIGMOD Symposium on Principles of Database Systems, Los Angeles, Cal., March 1982, pp. 124-138.

KF88 Khoshafian, S., Frank, D.: Implementation Techniques for Object Oriented Databases; in: Advances in Object-Oriented Database Systems, K.R. Dittrich (Ed.), Springer LNCS 334, Sept. 1988, pp. 60-79.

Kn73 Knuth, D.E.: The Art of Computer Programming, Vol. 3: Sorting and Searching, Addison-Wesley, Reading, Mass., 1973.

MS76 Munro, I., Spira, P.M.: Sorting and Searching in Multisets, SIAM J. Comput., Vol. 5, No.1, March 1976, pp. 1-8.

PA86 Pistor, P., Andersen, F.: Designing a Generalized NF^2 Data Model with an SQL-Type Language Interface, Proc. 12th Int. Conf. on Very Large Data Bases, Kyoto, Japan, Aug. 1986, pp. 278-288

Pi87 Pistor, P.: The Advanced Information Management Prototype: Architecture and Language Interface Overview, Proc. Troisièmes Journées Bases de Données Avancées, Port Camarque, France, May 1987 (invited paper).

PT86 Pistor, P., Traunmüller, R.: A Database Language for Sets, Lists and Tables, Information Systems, Vol. 11, No.4, 1986 pp. 323-336.

Ro85 Roth, M.A.: SQL/NF: A Query Language for ¬NF Relational Databases, Technical Report TR-85-19, Univ. of Texas at Austin, Dept. of Computer Science, Sept. 1985.

Se83 Sedgewick, R.: Algorithms, Addison-Wesley, Reading, Mass., 1983.

SJ77 IBM Systems Journal, Special Issue on IMS, Vol. 16, No. 2, 1977.

SLPW89 Saake, G., Linnemann, V., Pistor, P., Wegner, L.: Sorting, Grouping, and Duplicate Elimination in the Advanced Information Management System, IBM Heidelberg Scientific Center (in preparation).

Sp77 Sprugnoli, R.: Perfect hashing functions: A single probe retrieving method for static sets, Comm, ACM, Vol. 20, No. 11, Nov. 1977, pp. 841-850.

SS86 Schek, H.-J., Scholl, M.: The Relational Model with Relation-Valued Attributes, Information Systems, Vol. 11, No. 2, 1986, pp. 137-147.

St76 Stonebraker, M., et al.: The Design and Implementation of Ingres, ACM Trans. on Database Systems, Vol. 1, No. 3, Sept. 1976, pp. 189-222.

SW84 Six, H.W., Wegner, L.: Sorting a Random Access File in Situ, Computer Journal, Vol. 27, No. 3, pp. 270-275, 1984.

TW88 Teuhola, J., Wegner, L.: The External Heapsort, IEEE Trans. Softw. Eng., 1988 (in print).

TW89a Teuhola, J., Wegner, L.: Linear Time, Minimal Space Duplicate Deletion, Math. Schriften Kassel, No. 2/89, January 1989.

TW89b Teuhola, J., Wegner, L.: A tale of sorts: duplicate deletion in Quicksort, Mergesort and Heapsort, 1989 (in prep.).

We85 Wegner, L.: Quicksort for Equal Keys, IEEE Trans. on Computers, Vol. C-34, No. 4 (April 1985), pp. 362-367.

We87 Wegner, L.: A Generalized, One-Way, Stackless Quicksort, BIT, Vol. 27, No. 1, pp. 44-48, 1987.

EFFICIENCY OF DATA ORGANIZATIONS

FAST EXCHANGE SORTS*

Nachum Dershowitz
Department of Computer Science
University of Illinois
Urbana, IL 61801, USA

Hon–Wai Leong
Department of Computer Science
National University of Singapore
Singapore 0511

ABSTRACT

We present three variations of the following new sorting theme: Throughout the sort, the array is maintained in piles of sorted elements. At each step, the piles are split into two parts, so that the elements of the left piles are smaller than (or equal to) the elements of the right piles. Then, the two parts are each sorted, recursively. The theme, then, is a combination of Hoare's Quicksort idea, and the Pick algorithm, by Blum, et al., for linear selection. The variations arise from the possible choices of splitting method.

Two variations attempt to minimize the average number of comparisons. The better of these has an average performance of $1.075 n \lg n$ comparisons. The third variation sacrifices the average case for a worst–case performance of $1.756 n \lg n$, which is better than Heapsort. They all require minimal extra space and about as many data moves as comparisons.

1. Introduction

The sorting problem is: Given an array $a_1, a_2, \ldots, a_n$ of elements, rearrange them so that $a_1 \leq a_2 \leq \cdots \leq a_n$, where $\leq$ is a given linear ordering of elements. An *exchange sort* [Knut73] is one that goes about this task by repeatedly looking for a pair of elements a_i and a_j $(1 \leq i < j \leq n)$ that are inverted $(a_i > a_j)$ and exchanging them. By combining ideas from Hoare's Quicksort algorithm [Hoar61, Hoar62] and Blum, Floyd, Pratt, Rivest, and Tarjan's Pick algorithm [BlFP73] for linear selection, we have come up with a new scheme for exchange sorts.

One the one hand, we were interested in the possibility of improving the average case of Quicksort, and, on the other hand, in improving the worst case of Heapsort. The model under consideration is a comparison–based model; the *cost* of a method is measured by the number of

*This research was supported in part by the National Science Foundation under Grant DCR 85–13417.

comparisons required for sorting n elements. It is well–known [Knut73] that under this comparison–based model, sorting has cost $\Omega(n\lg n)$. Furthermore, there are well–known methods that are optimal to within a multiplicative constant. Heapsort [Will64] has both average– and worst–case performances of $O(n\lg n)$; asymptotically, its worst case is $2n\lg n$. Quicksort [Hoar61] has average–case performance of $1.39n\lg n$ [Knut73]. This was improved by Singleton [Sing69] to $1.19n\lg n$ using the median–of–three method, and can be made arbitrarily close to $n\lg n$ by increasing the sample size. However, Quicksort suffers from quadratic worst–case performance. In both Heapsort and Quicksort, the number of data–moves is the same order of magnitude as the number of comparisons. Binary–Insertion Sort [Knut73] is also optimal for this model, since it has worst–case performance of $O(n\lg n)$ comparisons; however, it requires $O(n^2)$ data–moves.

Briefly, our scheme is as follows: The array is maintained in small piles of sorted elements throughout the sorting process. Thus, the first step is to preprocess the input array into piles of sorted elements. This step is done only once; from then on, the piled structure is preserved. At each subsequent step, a particular pivot element is chosen and the piles are split into two parts so that all the elements in the left piles are smaller than all the elements in the right piles. Then, the two parts are each sorted, recursively. The theme, then, which we will call **Pilesort**, combines splitting around a pivot, as in Quicksort, with piling to find a pivot, as in Pick.

The variations we consider arise from different possibilities for splitting. Two variations attempt to minimize the average number of comparisons (over all possible input array permutations); another sacrifices average–case performance for an $O(n\lg n)$ worst–case that out–performs Heapsort [Will64, Floy64]. They all require some extra space and about as many data moves as comparisons; their practical value is limited to cases where comparisons are relatively expensive.

In the next section, we elaborate on the general scheme. Section 3 analyzes its time complexity. Three variations of the scheme are considered in Sections 4 and 5; experimental results are given in Section 6. We conclude with a brief discussion.

2. The Theme

The first step is to preprocess the input array, creating piles of three elements, each pile sorted. The result is shown in Figure 1, assuming (for simplicity) that n is a multiple of 3. This step costs at most n comparisons; on the average, it costs $8n/9$. From this point on, the piled structure will be maintained by the algorithm.

To sort a piled array, a *pivot–pile* is first selected, and its middle is used as the *pivot element*. Then the piles themselves are rearranged so that the middle elements of the left–piles are less than (or equal to) the pivot element, while the middle elements of the right–piles are greater than or equal to the pivot element. This is similar to Hoare's Partition except that key comparisons are based on the pile middles and that entire piles are being moved around. Different ways of choosing the pivot lead to different algorithms, as will be described in subsequent sections. We shall refer to this rearrangement as *Pile_Partition*. After *Pile_Partition*, the situation is as depicted in Figure 2.

At this point, note that elements in $W \cup Z$ are on the proper side of the partition, while elements in $X \cup Y$ may be greater or smaller than the pivot element. To complete the partitioning process, two things need to be done:

(a) The elements in $X \cup Y$ must be compared with the pivot element to determine if they are in the proper partition. This step takes $n/3$ comparisons.

(b) Restoring the pile structure.

Figure 1. After INITIAL_PILING

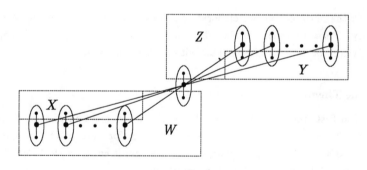

Figure 2. Configuration after PILE_PARTITION

In order to efficiently restore the pile structure, we note the following:

(i) A *loose* element can be merged with a pile of two *sorted* elements in 2 comparisons at most, and 5/3 comparisons on the average.

(ii) Three loose elements can be repiled in 3 comparisons at most, and 8/3 comparisons on the average.

(iii) Three piles of two elements can be merged into two piles of three elements by first comparing two maximal elements to form one pile of three, and then comparing the remaining loose element with the smaller, and, if necessary, the larger element of the remaining pile of two. This takes 3 comparisons at most, and 232/90 comparisons on the average (the average is over all possible arrangements of three piles of two elements).

The following procedures sketch the whole sorting scheme:

```
procedure Sort;
    begin
        Initial_Piling (1,N);
        Pilesort (1,N)
    end;

procedure Pilesort (L,R);
    begin
        if (R−L) ≤ Threshold
            then   Smallsort (L,R)
            else   begin
                        Pile_Partition (L,R,T);
                        Partition_Cleanup (L,R,T);
                        Pilesort (L,T−1);
                        Pilesort (T+1,R)
                   end
    end;
```

As in Quicksort [Knut73], a *Smallsort* routine is used whenever the array segment is so small that the overhead does not justify recursive calls. The *Partition_Cleanup* procedure does tasks (a) and (b) simultaneously. It is similar to the Partition phase of Quicksort and is applied to the X and Y elements. The elements in X are scanned until an element that is greater than the pivot (i.e. in the wrong partition) is found; then the Y-elements are scanned until one smaller than the pivot is encountered. These elements are broken off from their respective piles, interchanged, and inserted into the remaining piles of two. By (i) above, this takes at most 2 comparison per element moved and 5/3 comparisons on the average. This process is continued until all the elements of *either* X or Y are exhausted. Without loss of generality, assume that the elements in Y are exhausted. At this point, the remaining elements in X are scanned until three elements are found out of place. These form a pile that is moved to the right partition and the remaining remaining three piles of two are repiled into two piles of three. This will take, in the worst–case, 2 comparisons per element moved, and $(8/3 + 232/90)/3 = 472/270$ comparisons per element moved, on the average.

To summarize, *Partition_Cleanup* takes n comparisons in the worst case, $n/3$ to decide whether the element is in the proper partition and $2n/3$ for the actual moves. The average case, however, depends on how many elements get moved and on how they are moved.

Finally, once the piles are completely partitioned, the algorithm recursively sorts each of the two parts.

3. Analysis

Let cm be the cost to partition m piles in the *Pile_Partition* procedure. We assume that the pivot pile falls in the interval $[xm : (1-x)m]$ where $0 \leq x \leq 0.5$. Note that x is the split of the piles, not the elements themselves. Let α be the fraction of the elements in $X \cup Y$ that are interchanged in the *Partition_Cleanup* phase, and let A be the cost per element for such a move. Let β be the fraction of $X \cup Y$ that are moved from the larger partition to the smaller partition, and B, the cost per element for such a move. Thus, α is in the range $0 \leq \alpha \leq 2x$ and β is in the range $-(x-\alpha/2) \leq \beta \leq (1-x)-\alpha/2$ (β is negative if the elements are moved in the opposite direction). Then the cost for one pass is the sum of the following:

(i) $cn/3$ to select the pivot–pile and in the process, partition the *piles* themselves;

(ii) $n/3$ comparisons to compare the elements in $X \cup Y$ without repiling;

(iii) $A \alpha n/3$ for interchanging elements in X and Y; and

(iv) $B|\beta|n/3$ for moving the elements from one side to the other.

Since the resultant split of the elements (not just the piles) is $x + \beta/3$, the cost $T(n)$ for sorting n elements satisfies the following recurrence:

$$T(n) = \frac{(c+1)n}{3} + \frac{(A\alpha + B|\beta|)n}{3} + T\left(\frac{(3x+\beta)n}{3}\right) + T\left(\frac{(3-3x-\beta)n}{3}\right) \qquad (3.1)$$

A recurrence of the form $T(n) = kn + T(yn) + T((1-y)n)$ has a solution $T(n) = \gamma n \lg n$ where

$$\gamma = \frac{-k}{y \lg y + (1-y)\lg(1-y)}.$$

Therefore, the solution to recurrence (3.1) is given by

$$\gamma = \cfrac{-\cfrac{(c+1+A\alpha+B|\beta|)}{3}}{\left(\dfrac{3x+\beta}{3}\right)\lg\left(\dfrac{3x+\beta}{3}\right)+\left(\dfrac{3-3x-\beta}{3}\right)\lg\left(\dfrac{3-3x-\beta}{3}\right)} \tag{3.2}$$

It follows that the performance of the algorithm depends on two factors: the repiling cost $(A\alpha+B|\beta|)$ which depends on α and β, and the final split $(3x+\beta)/3$ which depends only on β. We note that the worst (maximum) repiling cost occurs when all the undetermined elements change sides in which case $\alpha=2x$, $\beta=1-2x$, but in this case the final split is $(x+1)/3$. On the other hand, the worst final split occurs when all the undetermined elements in the smaller part move to the larger part, namely $\alpha=0$, $\beta=-x$ and the split is $2x/3$. Thus, we have

$$T(n) = \begin{cases} \left[\dfrac{c+1+2Ax+B(1-2x)}{3}\right]n + T\left(\dfrac{(x+1)n}{3}\right) + T\left(\dfrac{(2-x)n}{3}\right) \\[2em] \left[\dfrac{c+1+Bx}{3}\right]n + T\left(\dfrac{2xn}{3}\right) + T\left(\dfrac{(3-2x)n}{3}\right) \end{cases} \tag{3.3}$$

More generally, with piles of height $2h+1$, the worst case recurrences are

$$T(n) = \begin{cases} \left[\dfrac{c+h+2hAx+Bh(1-2x)}{2h+1}\right]n + T\left(\dfrac{(x+h)n}{2h+1}\right) + T\left(\dfrac{(h+1-x)n}{2h+1}\right) \\[2em] \left[\dfrac{c+h+Bhx}{2h+1}\right]n + T\left(\dfrac{(h+1)xn}{2h+1}\right) + T\left(\dfrac{(2h+1-(h+1)x)n}{2h+1}\right) \end{cases} \tag{3.4}$$

But it turns out that $h = 1$ (giving piles of height 3) is usually optimal. Though taller piles reduce the cost of pivot selection, they cost more to build and maintain, and make $X\cup Y$ proportionally larger.

4. Linear Selection

In this section, we present the first variation of our basic sorting scheme. We describe an (unimplemented) algorithm with worst–case performance of $1.756n\lg n$ comparisons, which is better Heapsort.

We first note that if, in the *Pile_Partition* procedure, the median of the pile middles (i.e. $x=0.5$) can be found in linear time in the worst–case, then the procedure to divide the piles would take linear time in the worst–case. Furthermore, at least one third of the elements would be in each of the two parts. This guarantees that the resultant sorting algorithm is $O(n\lg n)$ in the worst–case. In fact, any linear time selection procedure that partitions the m piles so that the worst–case split is proportional to m will guarantee an $O(n \lg n)$ worst–case sorting method.

The fastest linear median selection algorithm is that of Schonhage, Paterson, and Pippenger [ScPP76] (improved in [Eber79]; see also [Knut73]). It has a $3k$ asymptotic upper bound on the number of comparisons to find the median of k elements. Thus, for worst–case performance, we have $x = 0.5$, $c = 3.0$, $A = B = 2$, and by (3.3) the worst case of this sorting algorithm is then given by $\gamma = \max(2, 1.815)$. In other words, $T(n) = 2n \lg n$ in the worst–case, as for Heapsort. The average case should be considerably lower.

To improve on the worst case, we need an approximation of the median that costs less to compute that still guarantees $O(n \lg n)$ worst–case running time. This may be accomplished by piling the middle elements themselves. First, the middle elements are grouped into piles of five elements (five turns out to be bettr than 3, as we will see below) and, then, the *median of their medians* is used as the pivot element. To be more precise, we expand *Pile_Partition* as follows:

P1: Pile the middle elements into piles of fives, so that the center element is their median.

P2: Use the median find algorithm to partition the piles of center elements.

P3: Move undetermined piles into the correct partition with respect to the median of medians. At the end of Step P2, we have the Hasse diagram shown in Figure 3 where each node in the diagram is a pile of three elements. Step P3, then moves the piles in $Q \cup R$ into the proper partition.

Step P1 costs $6(n/15) = 2n/5$, since it takes at most 6 comparisons to find the middle of five elements [Knut73]. Step P2 costs $3n/15 = n/5$, using the $3m$ worst–case median find algorithm. Lastly, Step P3 costs just $2n/15$ comparisons. Therefore, *Pile_Partition* costs $11n/15$ comparisons. Also, this method guarantees a worst–case split of the piles at $x = 3/10$ which occurs when all the undetermined piles in Q moves to the other side. Thus, the corresponding recurrence is given by

$$
T(n) = \begin{cases}
\dfrac{11n}{15} + \dfrac{n}{3} + \dfrac{2n}{3} + T\left(\dfrac{13n}{30}\right) + T\left(\dfrac{17n}{30}\right) \\[4mm]
\dfrac{11n}{15} + \dfrac{n}{3} + \dfrac{n}{5} + T\left(\dfrac{n}{5}\right) + T\left(\dfrac{4n}{5}\right)
\end{cases}
$$

giving $\gamma = \max(1.756, 1.755)$. Accordingly, the worst case is $1.756 n \lg n$, which is better than Heapsort's worst–case performance of $2n \lg n$.

If we replace the $3m$ median find algorithm of [ScPP76] by the slower $5.4305m$ Pick algorithm [BlFP73], the worst case of the sort will be $\max(1.920, 1.979) n \lg n = 1.979 n \lg n$ which is just under $2n \lg n$.

We can also consider grouping the *middle* elements into piles of three, instead of five. Then it costs $3n/9$ to pile the middles into groups of three, $3n/9$ to find median of middles, and $n/9$ to move undetermined piles, and the worst–case split of the piles is $x = 1/3$ and the recurrence is

$$T(n) = \begin{cases} \dfrac{7n}{9} + \dfrac{n}{3} + \dfrac{2n}{3} + T\left(\dfrac{4n}{9}\right) + T\left(\dfrac{5n}{9}\right) \\[2em] \dfrac{7n}{9} + \dfrac{n}{3} + \dfrac{2n}{9} + T\left(\dfrac{2n}{9}\right) + T\left(\dfrac{7n}{9}\right) \end{cases}$$

and $\gamma = \max(1.794, 1.745)$. Thus, the resultant sort has worst–case performance of $1.794 n \lg n$, which is still better than Heapsort.

5. Fast Selection

In order to improve the average case of Pilesort, we look for a median finding algorithm that has faster average–case performance. The best of these methods has an average case of $1.075 n \lg n$, which is better than $1.19 n \lg n$ of Singleton's median–of–three Quicksort.

The idea here is to always split the piles evenly into two parts using a fast median selection algorithm for *Pile_Partition*. We use the fastest known method, Select, by Floyd and Rivest [FlRi75a, FlRi75b] as modified by Brown [Brow76] which requires $1.5m$ comparisons on the average, to find the median of m elements. This variation of the sorting method is called Select–Pilesort.

The average case can be partially analyzed as follows: The worst–case split of the piles is $x = 0.5$. Substituting the average values for each of c, A and B, (viz. $c = 1.5$, $A = 5/3$, and $B = 472/270$) into (3.3), we get $\gamma = \max(1.389, 1.223)$. This analysis, however, assumes the worst distribution of undetermined elements. In order to get a better estimate, we have run extensive experiments to measure the empirical values of α and β. The results suggest that α is approximately 0.75 and β is small enough to be negligible. Substituting these into (3.2), we get the value $\gamma = 1.25$.

This variation of Pilesort can be significantly improved by eliminating the top–level recursive calls to Select from *Pile_Partition*. This is based on the observation that Select first uses the median of a *random sample* to partition the piles. If the sample median is indeed the exact median, Select terminates; otherwise, it calls itself recursively to find the exact median within the appropriate part. In most cases, however, there is already a fairly good partitioning of the piles and so there is little point in partitioning the piles further to get the exact median.

To further reduce the cost of *Pile_Partition*, we consider another variation, called *Random–Pilesort*. In our implementation, the middle pile is always chosen. To complete the procedure, the piles are partitioned about this pivot element. Thus, the cost of partitioning the piles is only $n/3$. However, we have no guarantee as to the worst–case split of the piles and so the analysis in Section 3 cannot be applied. Since the entire array is always partitioned around the median of three elements, it is natural to compare this sort with Singleton's variation of Quicksort, which requires an average cost of $1.19 n \lg n$ comparisons. Empirical results (see the next section) show that, on the average, γ is approximately 1.105 for Random–Pilesort.

To push this method further, one can use the median of three pile–middles as the pivot element. In our experiments, we uses the first, middle and last piles. This version of Random–Pilesort was found to perform slightly better.

6. Experimental Results

We implemented and tested the algorithms described in Section 5 in order to evaluate their average–case performances. Select–Pilesort uses the Select algorithm for choosing the pivot; Fast–Pilesort is the improved version using Select; Random–Pilesort uses Partition; Random–Pilesort-3 is the variation using three piles. For comparison, we also implemented Quicksort [Hoar61] and Singleton's median–of–three variation [Sing69], which we will call Quicksort-3. The implementations are all in Pascal and were tested on a CDC Cyber 175. A summary of the implemented algorithms is given in Figure 4.

Quicksort 1.338 ± 0.014	Hoare's Quicksort (partition about the middle element)
Quicksort-3 1.144 ± 0.008	Singleton's Quicksort (partition about median of first, middle, and last elements)
Select–Pilesort 1.415 ± 0.006	Fast median–finding variation of new scheme (uses Select to partition piles about median of pile middles)
Fast–Pilesort 1.093 ± 0.003	Improvement of Select–Pilesort (partition about the median of a sample)
Random–Pilesort 1.105 ± 0.006	Random partition variation of new sorting scheme (uses middle element of center pile as pivot)
Random–Pilesort-3 1.075 ± 0.003	Refinement of Random–Pilesort (uses median of middles of first, last, and center piles as pivot element)

Figure 4. Summary of the various sorts.

The data used to test the programs were randomly generated real numbers uniformly distributed over [10000.0 , 100000.0). This large range was chosen to minimize any chance of duplication of data values. For each sort, we ran the program on various data–sets of sizes $n = 1024, 2048, 4096, 8192$. For each size, we ran the program on sixteen different sets of random data. The mean values for γ obtained in these experiments are shown in the table below, along with their standard deviations. We use the formula $\overline{\gamma} \pm \dfrac{t_{s-1,0.025} \cdot \sigma}{\sqrt{s}}$ to obtain a *95%*

confidence interval for the values of γ where $\bar{\gamma}$ is the mean of γ, s is the sample size, σ is the standard deviation, and t is Student's distribution. These intervals are also given in Figure 4.

As is to be expected, the values of γ for Quicksort (1.338±0.014) and Quicksort–3 (1.144±0.008) are quite close to their theoretical values of 1.386 and 1.19, respectively. For Select–Pilesort, the overall average value of γ is 1.415±0.006. The discrepancy between this and the value 1.25, obtained in the previous section, is due to the fact that the actual cost of Select over the range of values $m \leq 8192/3$ was approximately $2m$, which is higher than the asymptotic average cost of $1.5m$ used in the previous section. With the more realistic value, the value of γ should be 1.417, in close agreement with the experimental results.

For Fast–Pilesort, where top–level recursive calls to Select are omitted, the value of γ drops dramatically to 1.093±0.003, which is better than the performance of Quicksort–3. The reason for the dramatic improvement is that after Select has partitioned the array about the median of a random sample, the split of the piles is reasonably close to 0.5. Insisting on finding the exact median, as in Select–Pilesort, requires an additional ck, where k is the size of the larger partition, which—with high probability— is about $n/2$. The effect of this variation is to choose as pivot element the median of a random sample of the elements, which explains why this algorithm performs better than Quicksort–3.

In Random–Pilesort the pivot element is just the middle of a random pile. Thus, Random–Pilesort effectively partitions the elements about the median of three elements. We found that Random–Pilesort has $\gamma=1.105\pm0.006$, which is slightly better than Quicksort–3.

	1024	2048	4096	8192	Overall
Quicksort	1.321	1.354	1.360	1.317	1.338
	.050	.058	.051	.048	.054
Quicksort–3	1.138	1.151	1.150	1.138	1.144
	.040	.030	.031	.020	.031
Select–Pilesort	1.406	1.416	1.417	1.422	1.415
	.031	.018	.020	.015	.022
Fast–Pilesort	1.087	1.092	1.098	1.096	1.093
	.017	.012	.007	.005	.012
Random–Pilesort	1.087	1.112	1.104	1.117	1.105
	.017	.032	.020	.014	.024
Random–Pilesort–3	1.067	1.074	1.080	1.080	1.075
	.015	.010	.009	.006	.011

Table 1. Means and standard deviations of γ.

In Random–Pilesort–3, the median of three pile middles is chosen as the pivot element, and so the pivot element is, in effect, the median of between 7 and 9 elements. As expected, the corresponding value of γ for Random–Pilesort–3 is 1.075 ± 0.003, better than that of all the other sorting methods we tried.

Note that Quicksort and Quicksort–3 have average cost $\gamma n \lg n$, while all the new algorithms require an additional $8n/9$ preprocessing cost, giving a total average cost of $8n/9 + \gamma n \lg n$. Finally, we note that the new sorting methods showed consistent performance: the value of γ did not change very much either for different data sets, nor for different values of n. The standard deviations for all the new methods were consistently less than 0.04 and are smaller than those for Quicksort and Quicksort–3. As is to be expected, the variances are smallest for Random–Pilesort and Select–Pilesort, which partition about the median of a small subset of the elements.

7. Conclusion

We have studied the performance of a new sorting scheme, called Pilesort, under the comparison–based model where the cost function is the number of comparisons needed to sort. The scheme combines ideas from Hoare's Partition algorithm and the linear time selection algorithm by Blum *et al.* It is robust in the sense that it can be implemented to obtain good worst–case or average–case performances.

Several variations of the scheme were studied. The first variation, using linear selection, was aimed at improving on the worst case of Heapsort, and is of theoretical interest. A simple implementation has a worst case of $2n \lg n$, the same as Heapsort. An improved version gave a worst–case performance of $1.756 n \lg n$ which is better than Heapsort.

The other variations sacrifice $O(n \lg n)$ worst case for a faster average case. A simple implementation, using a fast median–find algorithm, was found (empirically) to have $1.417 n \lg n$ average–case performance, which is comparable to that of Hoare's Quicksort. With a small change, this was improved to $1.093 n \lg n$. Using a random partition, the average case was found to be $1.105 n \lg n$, which is slightly better than that of Singleton's Quicksort. By selecting the median of three piles, rather than a pile at random, the performance improved to $1.075 n \lg n$.

The number of data–moves required by the new methods tends to be between two to three times that of Quicksort because of the need to moves piles of elements rather than one element at a time. Therefore, the new algorithms could be practical only in situations where key comparison is more expensive than data movement.

References

[BlFP73]   Blum, M., R. W. Floyd, V. Pratt, R. L. Rivest, and R. E. Tarjan, "Time Bounds for Selection," *Journal of Computer and System Sciences,* (1973), Vol. 7, pp. 448–461.

[Brow76]   Brown, T., "Remarks on Algorithm 489," *Trans. on Mathematical Software,* (1976), Vol. 3, No. 2, pp. 301–304.

[Floy64]   Floyd, R. W., "Algorithm 245 (Treesort3)," *Comm. of ACM,* (1964), Vol. 7, No. 12, p. 701.

[FlRi75a] Floyd, R. W., and R. L. Rivest, "Expected Time Bounds for Selection," *Comm. of ACM,* (1975), Vol. 18, No. 3, pp. 165–172.

[FlRi75b] Floyd, R. W., and R. L. Rivest, "Algorithm 489 (The Algorithm SELECT — for Finding the i–th Smallest of n Elements)," *Comm. of ACM,* (1975), Vol. 18, No. 3, p. 173.

[FrMc70]   Frazer, W. D. and A. C. McKellar, "Samplesort: A Sampling Approach to Minimal Tree Sorting," *Journal of ACM,* (1970), Vol. 17, No. 3, pp. 496–507.

[Hoar61]   Hoare, C. A. R., "Algorithm 63 (Partition); 64 (Quicksort); 65 (Find)," *Comm. of ACM,* (1961), Vol. 4, No. 7, pp. 321–322.

[Hoar62]   Hoare, C. A. R., "Quicksort," *Computer Journal,* (1962), Vol. 5, No. 1, pp. 10–15.

[Knut73]   Knuth, D. E., *The Art of Computer Programming, Vol. 3 (Sorting and Searching),* (1973), Addison–Wesley, Reading, MA.

[ScPP76]   Schonhage, A., M. S. Paterson, N. Pippenger, "Finding the Median," *Journal of Computer and System Sciences,* (1976), Vol. 13, pp. 184–199.

[Sing69]   Singleton, R. C., "Algorithm 347 (An Efficient Algorithm for Sorting with Minimal Storage)," *Comm. of ACM,* (1969), Vol. 12, No. 3, pp. 185–187.

[Will64]   Williams, J. W. J., "Algorithm 232 (Heapsort)," *Comm. of ACM,* (1964), Vol. 7, No. 6, pp. 347–348.

Efficient Organization of Semantic Databases

Naphtali Rishe

School of Computer Science
Florida International University —
The State University of Florida at Miami
University Park, Miami, FL 33199

This paper argues that semantic data models can have potentially more efficient implementations than the conventional data models. As a step towards realization of this potential, the paper proposes an efficient storage structure for semantic databases.

1. Introduction

Since [Abrial-74], many semantic data models have been studied in the Computer Science literature. Although somewhat different in their terminology and their selection of tools used to describe the semantics of the real world, they have several common principles:

- The entities of the real world are represented in the database in a manner transparent to the user. (Unlike that, in the relational model the entities are represented by the values of keys of some tables; in the network model the entities are represented by record occurrences.) Hereinafter, the user-transparent representations of real-world entities are referred to as "abstract objects". The "concrete objects", or "printable values", are numbers, character strings, *etc.* The concrete objects have conventional representations on paper and in the computer.

- The entities are classified into types, or categories, which need not be disjoint. Meta-

---

This research has been supported in part by a grant from Florida High Technology
and Industry Council

relations of inclusion are defined between the categories.

- Logically-explicit relationships are specified among abstract objects (*e.g.*, "person p1 is the mother of person p2") and between abstract objects and concrete objects (*e.g.*, "person p1 has first name 'Jack'"). There are no direct relationships among the concrete objects. In most semantic models, only binary relations are allowed, since higher order relations do not add any power of semantic expressiveness ([Bracchi-76], [Rishe-87-RM], [Rishe-88-DDF]), but do decrease the flexibility of the database and representability of partially-unknown information, and add complexity and potential for logical redundancy ([Rishe-88-DDF]).

The advantages of the semantic models versus the Relational and older models with respect to database design, database maintenance, data integrity, conciseness of languages, and ease of DML programming are known [Rishe-88-DDF]. This paper advocates the potential of semantic models to have efficient implementation.

Until now, several semantic data models have been implemented as interfaces to database managements systems in other data models, e.g., the relational or the network model [Tsur/Zaniolo-84]. (However, there are less typical, direct implementations, *e.g.* [Lien-81], [Chan-82], [Benneworth-81].) The efficiency of an interface implementation is limited to that of the conventional DBMS, and is normally much worse due to the interface overhead. The direct implementations are also commonly believed to have to be less time-efficient than the conventional systems, as a trade-off for the extra services that the semantic databases should provide. However, this author contends that the semantic models have potential for much more efficient implementation than the conventional data models. This is due to two reasons:

- All the physical aspects of representation of information by data are user-transparent in the semantic models. This creates greater potential for optimization: more things may be changed for efficiency considerations, without affecting the user programs. The Relational Model has more data independence than the older models. For example, the order of rows in the tables (relations) is transparent to the user. The semantic models have even more user-transparency. For example, the representation of real-world entities by printable values is transparent to the user. One may recall that not long ago the Relational Model was criticized as less efficient than the Network and Hierarchical models. However, it is clear now that optimizing relational database systems have potential of much higher efficiency than the network and hierarchical systems due to the data independence of the relational model.

• In the semantic models, the system knows more about the meaning of the user's data and about the meaningful connections between such data. This knowledge can be utilized to organize the data so that meaningful operations can be performed faster at the expense of less meaningful or meaningless operations.

In this paper, I use the Semantic Binary Model (SBM) [Rishe-88-DDF], a descendant of the model proposed in [Abrial-74]. This model does not have as rich an arsenal of tools for semantic description as can be found in some other semantic models, e.g. the IFO model [Abiteboul/Hull-84], SDM [Hammer/McLeod-81] (implementation [Jagannathan-88]), the Functional Model [Shipman-81] (implementation [Chan-82]), SEMBASE [King-84], NIAM ([Nijssen-81], [Nijssen/VanBekkum-82], [Leung/Nijssen-87]), GEM [Tsur/Zaniolo-84], TAXIS [Nixon-87], or the semi-semantic Entity-Relationship Model [Chen-76]. Nevertheless, the SBM has a small set of sufficient simple tools by which all the semantic descriptors of the other models can be constructed. This makes SBM easier to use for the novice, easier to implement, and usable for delineation of the common properties of the semantic models. The results of this paper are practically independent of the choice of a particular semantic model, and therefore they apply to almost all other semantic models.

The semantic binary model represents the information of an application's world as a collection of elementary facts of two types: unary facts categorizing objects of the real world and binary facts establishing relationships of various kinds between pairs of objects. The graphical database schema and the integrity constraints determine what sets of facts are meaningful, i.e. can comprise an instantaneous database (the database as may be seen at some instance of time.)

Formal semantics of the semantic binary model is defined in [Rishe-87-DS] using the methodology proposed in [Rishe-86-DN]. The syntax and informal semantics of the model and its languages (data definition languages, 4-th generation data manipulation languages, non-procedural languages for queries, updates, specification of constraints, userviews, *etc.*) are given in [Rishe-88-DDF]. A non-procedural semantic database language of maximal theoretically-possible expressive power is given in [Rishe-86-PS]. (In this language, one can specify every computable query, transaction, constraint, *etc.*)

The following section proposes an efficient storage structure for the Semantic Binary Model.

2. STORAGE STRUCTURE

2.1. Abstracted level

Every abstract object in the database is represented by a unique integer identifier. The categories and relations of the schema are also treated as abstract objects and hence have unique identifiers associated with them. Information in the database can then be represented using two kinds of facts, denoted xC and xRy, where x is the identifier associated with an abstract object, C and R are the identifiers associated with a category or a relation respectively, and y is either an identifier corresponding to an abstract object or a concrete object (a number or a text string). " xC " indicates that the object x belongs to the category C. "xRy" indicates that the object x is associated with the object y by the relation R. Logically, the instantaneous database is a set of such facts.

2.2. Goals

2.2.1. Efficiency of retrieval requests

At the intermediate level of processing queries and program retrieval requests, the queries are decomposed into *atomic retrieval operations* of the types listed below. The primary goal of the physical file structure is to allow a very efficient performance for each of the atomic requests. Namely, *each atomic retrieval request normally requires only 1 disk access*, provided the output information is small enough to fit into one block. When the output is large, the number of blocks retrieved is close to the minimal number of blocks needed to store the output information.

1. aC Verify the fact aC. (For a given abstract object a and category C, verify whether the object a is in the category C.)

2. aRy Verify the fact aRy.

3. $a?$ For a given abstract object a, find all the categories to which a belongs.

4. $?C$ For a given category, find its objects.

5. $aR?$ For a given abstract object a and relation R, retrieve all y such that aRy. (The objects y may be abstract or concrete.)

6. **?Ra** For a given abstract object a and relation R, retrieve all abstract objects x such that xRa.

7. **a?+a??+??a** Retrieve all the immediate information about an abstract object. (I.e., for a given abstract object a, retrieve all of its direct and inverse relationships, that is, the relations R and objects y such that aRy or yRa; and the categories to which a belongs.)

(Although this request can be decomposed into a series of requests of the previous types, we wish to be able to treat it separately in order to ensure that the whole request normally be performed in a single disk access. This will also allow a single-access performance of requests which require several, but not all, of the facts about an object, e.g. a query to find the first name, the last name, and the age of a given person.)

8. **?Rv** For a given relation (attribute) R and a given concrete object (value) v, find all abstract objects x such that xRv.

9. **?R[v1,v2]** For a given relation (attribute) R and a given range of concrete objects $[v_1, v_2]$, find all objects x and v such that xRv and $v_1 \leq v \leq v_2$. (The comparison "$\leq$" is appropriate to the type of v.)

2.2.2. Efficiency of update transactions

Efficient performance of update transactions is required, although more than one disk access per transaction is allowed.

A transaction is a set of interrelated update requests to be performed as one unit. Transactions are generated by programs and by interactive users. A transaction can be generated by a program fragment containing numerous update commands, interleaved with other computations. However, until the last command within a transaction is completed, the updates are not physically performed, but rather accumulated by the DBMS. Upon completion of the transaction the DBMS checks its integrity and then physically performs the update. The partial effects of the transaction may be inconsistent. Every program and user sees the database in a consistent state: until the transaction is committed, its effects are invisible.

A completed transaction is composed of a set of facts to be deleted from the database, a set of facts to be inserted into the database, and additional information needed to verify that there is no interference between transactions of concurrent programs. If the verification produces a positive result, then the new instantaneous database is: ((the-old-instantaneous-database) – (the-set-of-facts-to-be-deleted)) $\cup$ (the-set-of-facts-to-be-inserted).

2.3. Solution: a file structure achieving the goals

The following file structure supports the above requirements. The entire database is stored in a single file. This file contains all the facts of the database (xC and xRy) and also additional information described below and called inverted facts. The file is maintained as a B-tree. The variation of the B-tree used here allows both sequential access according to the lexicographic order of the items comprising the facts and the inverted facts, as well as random access by arbitrary prefixes of such facts and inverted facts.

The facts which are close to each other in the lexicographic order reside close in the file. (Notice, that although technically the B-tree-key is the entire fact, it is of varying length and on the average is only several bytes long, which is the average size of the encoded fact xRy. The total size of the data stored in the index-level blocks of the B-tree is less than 1% of the size of the database: e.g. each 10,000-byte data block may be represented in the index level by its first fact --5 bytes — and block address — 3 bytes — which would amount to 0.08% of the data block. Thus, all the index blocks will fit even into relatively small main memory.)

The file contains the original facts and additionally the following "inverted facts":

1. In addition to xC, we store its inverse $\bar{C}x$. ($\bar{C}$ is the system-chosen identifier to represent the inverse information about the category C. For example, it can be defined as $\bar{C} = 0\!-\!C$.) (If a category C_1 is a subcategory of category C_2, an object a belongs to C_1 and, thus, also to C_2, then we chose to store both inverted facts $\bar{C_1}a$ and $\bar{C_2}a$. When the user requests the deletion of the fact aC_2, it triggers automatic deletion of the facts aC_1, $\bar{C_1}a$, and $\bar{C_2}a$ in order to guarantee consistency.)

2. In addition to xRv, where v is a concrete object (a number, a string, or a value of another type), we store $\bar{R}vx$. Thus, the range query "?R[v1,v2]" is satisfied by all and only the inverted facts which are positioned in the file between $\bar{R}v_1$ and $\bar{R}v_2$HighSuffix. (HighSuffix is a suffix which is lexicographically greater than any other possible suffix.) Thus, the result will most probably appear in one physical block, if it can fit into one block.

3. In addition to *xRy*, where both x and y are abstract objects, we store $y\bar{R}x$. Thus, for any abstract object x, all its relationships xRy, xRv, zRx, and xC can be found in one place in the file: the regular and inverted facts which begin with the prefix x. (The infixes are: categories for xC, relations for xRy and xRv, and inverse relations $x\bar{R}z$ from which we find z such that zRx.)

Notice that facts xRa and xRv (x and a are abstract objects, v is a value) are inverted dissimilarly. This is because we have different types of atomic retrieval requests concerning abstract and concrete objects:

- There are range queries with concrete objects, e.g. "Find all persons salaried between $40,000 and $50,000". In such queries we know the identifier of the relation and partial information about the value. Therefore we need to use the inverted facts with $\bar{R}$ as the prefix. There are no range queries with abstract objects.

- On the other hand, we have multiple-fact retrievals about an abstract object, e.g. "Find all the immediate information about a given person p" (while such a request about a concrete object would be meaningless: "Find all the information about the number 5" makes no sense, as oposed to a meaningful query "Find information about item(s) whose price is $5".) Here we know the object, but do not know the identifiers of the inverted relations. We need to cluster together all the inverted relations of one object. Therefore, the inverted relation should appear in the infix.

The sorted file is maintained in a structure similar to a B-tree. The "records" of the B-tree are the regular and inverted facts. The records are of varying length. The B-tree-keys of the "records" are normally the entire B-tree-records, *i.e.* facts, regular and inverted. (An exception from this is when the record happens to be very long. The only potentially long records represent facts xRv where v is a very long character string. We employ a special handling algorithm for very long character strings.) Access to this B-tree does not require knowledge of the entire key: any prefix will do. All the index blocks of the B-tree can normally be held in cache.

At the most physical level, the data in the facts is compressed to minimal space. Also, since many consecutive facts share a prefix (e.g. an abstract object identifier) the prefix need not be repeated for each fact. In this way the facts are compressed further. The duplication in the number of facts due to the inverses is 100%, since there is only one inverse per each original fact (with a rare exception of the storage of redundant inverses of supercategories as described in (1)). The B-tree causes additional 30% overhead. (This overhead is because in a B-tree the data blocks are only 75% full on the average, though this can be improved by periodical reorganization. The overhead for the index blocks of the B-tree is no more than 1-2% since they contain only one short fact per every data block.) The total space used for the database is therefore only about 160% more than the amount of information in the database, i.e. the space minimally required to store the database in the most compressed form with no regard to the efficiency of data retrieval or update. Thus, the data structure described herein is more efficient in space and time than the conventional approach with separate secondary index files for numerous fields.

No separate index files are needed in the file structure proposed in this paper. The duplication of data (*i.e.* inverted relations) together with the primary sparse index which is a part of the B-tree effectively eliminate the need for secondary (dense) indices. Furthermore, it eliminates the horrendous I/O operations caused by sequentially retrieving along a secondary index, since the sequence of information represented by our primary sparse index is also stored in consecutive physical locations.

2.4. Secondary aspects of the file structure

Efficiency (time and storage) and flexibility of the file structure are enhanced by compression and encoding of the facts and the items therein, including: abstract objects; character strings of unlimited length; numbers with no global minimum, maximum or precision; identifiers for categories, relations, and their inverses.

A special technique [Rishe-88-CM] is employed to encode the numbers in the facts of the file so that:

1. Bitwise lexicographic comparison of the encodings coincides with the meaningful comparison of numbers. Thus, if n_1 is encoded by a byte string $b_1^1 b_2^1 b_3^1$ and n_2 is encoded by a byte string $b_1^1 b_2^2 b_3^2 b_4^2$, where $b_2^1 > b_2^2$, then $n_1 > n_2$. The standard representations of numbers do not allow bitwise comparison. (Consider, for example, the representation of floating point numbers by mantissa and exponent.)

2. There is no limit on arbitrarily large, arbitrarily small, or arbitrarily precise numbers. We wish to be able to compare and store in a uniform format integers, real numbers, numbers with very many significant digits, and numbers with just a few significant digits. We do not wish to set a limit on the range of the data at the time of the design or creation of the file. For example, the number π truncated after first 1000 digits is a very precise number (1000 significant digits). The number $10^{10^{10}}$ is large (10 billion decimal digits, but only one significant digit). We use the same format convention to represent both numbers. (The length of the representation is approximately

proportional to the number of significant digits: the representation of the second number is only a few bytes long, the representation of the first number is 425 bytes long.)

3. Every number bears its own precision, *i.e.* the precision is not uniform throughout the database. (This allows to treat integers, reals, values of different attributes with different precisions, in a uniform way in one file in the database.)

4. The encodings are of varying length and are about maximally space efficient with respect to their informational content. For example, the numbers 3,000,000 (with precision 500,000), integer 5 (precision 0.5), 0.000,000,000,000,000,7 (with precision 0.000,000,000,000,000,05) should require only a few bits each, while the number 12345678.90 should require many more bits. The number of bits in a number's representation is approximately equal to the amount of information in that number.

5. No additional byte(s) are required to store the length of the encoded representation or to delimit its end: the representation should contain enough information within itself so that the decoder would know where the representation of one number ends and of the next begins (within the same record in the file.) The absence of delimiters gives an additional saving in space, and also facilitates handling of records.

6. The representation of numbers is one-to-one. For example, there may not be several representation for 0, like 0.00, -0.0, 0E23, 0E0.

7. The encoding and decoding should be relatively efficient (linear in the length of the data string), but they need not be as efficient as comparisons. The database system can handle encoded numbers in all the internal operations, and translate them only on input/output from/to the external user.

3. Comparison to performance of implementations of the Relational Model

The system proposed herein is not less efficient, and normally more efficient, in both time and storage space than the relational model's implementations with multiple dense indices.

Let us consider a simple relational database composed of one relation T with attributes $A_1, A_2,..., A_n$. Let us assume that for each j there are queries of the type

$$\text{get } A_i \text{ where } A_j = c \tag{Q1}$$

and that each of those queries is required to be performed in a reasonable time.

The Relational model is technically a subset of the Semantic Binary Model. Specifically, the above relational schema is viewed in the Semantic Binary Model as a category T and relations A_i between the objects of T and values.

To assure reasonable time performance in the Relational model for each of the above queries, we need a dense index on each of the attributes A_i. There are n index files (or n indices combined in one file in some implementations.) The total size of the indices thus exceeds the size of the table T itself. Therefore the space overhead in the Relational model is greater than 100% and, thus, is greater than the space overhead in the proposed semantic implementation. Also, in the semantic implementation there is only one physical file, while there are many physical files in the relational implementations (and in some implementations there are as many files as $number\_of\_tables \times (1+number\_of\_attributes\_per\_table)$. The management of multiple files is not only a hassle but also contributes to additional space overhead due to allocation of growth areas for each file.

With respect to the time required to solve the simple queries of type Q1, it is the same in the best relational implementations and in the proposed semantic implementation. Namely, the time is

$$(1+number\_of\_values\_in\_the\_output) \times time\_to\_retrieve\_one\_block$$

(In the relational implementation, there will be one visit to the dense index on A_j, and for every $A_j = c$ found there, there will be one random access to the main table. In the semantic implementation, first the sub-query $?A_j c$ will be solved, and then for every match x found the sub-query $xA_i?$ will be evaluated.)

If in Q1 we desired to print many attributes A_i instead of just one, the same time results would be obtained in both implementations. Notice that in the semantic implementation proposed herein all the immediate information of an object, including all its attributes, is clustered together.

Now let us consider updates. Insertion of a row into the relational table takes replacement of one block in the main table and n blocks in the dense indices. In the semantic implementation there is insertion of the primary facts about the new object ob: $obA_1c_1, \ldots, obA_nc_n$ (all the primary facts will appear in contiguous storage in one block) and n inverse facts in possibly different n blocks. Thus, here, as well as in the other types of simple updates, the performance of the semantic implementation is not worse than that of the relational implementations supporting efficiency of queries.

The advantages in the semantic implementation's performance become even more significant for more complex queries and updates. Though the detailed analysis of these is beyond the space-limit of this paper, I would like to mention that, for example, queries requiring natural join in the relational implementations would be more efficient in the semantic implementation because there are direct explicit relationships between the categories instead of relationships represented implicitly by foreign key in the Relational Model. The gap in performance between the faster semantic implementation and the relational implementations increases even more when the relational keys are composed of more than one attribute and when the relationships between the tables are many-to-many, which requires an extra table to represent the many-to-many relationship in the relational implementations. The gap increases with the number of joins in the query. In general, the more complex the query is the greater is the advantage in the efficiency of the proposed semantic implementation versus the relational implementations.

Of course, there are also major efficiency advantages in the semantic implementation in support of semantic complexities of the real world, which are very awkwardly and inefficiently implemented in the relational implementations. These complexities include intersecting categories, sub-categories, categories with no keys, varying-length attributes, missing ("null") values, multiple values, etc.

4. CONCLUSION

We have implemented this data structure in a prototype DBMS at the University of California, Santa Barbara ([Vijaykumar-87], [Jain-87]). Our implementation allows single-processor multi-user parallel access to the database. Optimistic concurrence control is used.

Although the best results are obtained from our DBMS for the Semantic Binary Model, it can also be used efficiently with all other major semantic and conventional database models. This is due to the fact that the Relational, Network, and Hierarchical data models are technically subsets of the Semantic Binary Model (as shown in [Rishe-88-DDF]).

Currently, at Florida International University, we are working on a project, financed by the state government, to extend our semantic DBMS implementation into a massively-parallel very-high-throughput database machine [Rishe-88-AMPDM], to be composed of many (thousand[s]) processors, each equipped with a permanent storage device and a large cache memory. Our analysis has shown that the proposed file structure greatly increases the parallelism in the operations of the DBMS, which can be utilized by large-scale parallel machines.

Acknowledgment

The author gratefully acknowledges the advice of Narayanan Vijaykumar, Li Qiang, Nagarajan Prabhakaran, Doron Tal, and David Barton.

References

[Abiteboul/Hull-84] S. Abiteboul and R. Hull. "IFO: A Formal Semantic Database Model", Proceedings of ACM SIGACT-SIGMOD Symposium on Principles of Database Systems, 1984.

[Abrial-74] J.R. Abrial, "Data Semantics", in J.W. Klimbie and K.L. Koffeman (eds.), *Data Base Management*, North Holland, 1974.

[Benneworth-81] R.L. Benneworth, C.D. Bishop, C.J.M. Turnbull, W.D. Holman, F.M. Monette. "The Implementation of GERM, an Entity-relationship Data Base Management System". Proceedings of the Seventh International Conference on Very Large Data Bases. (Eds. C. Zaniolo & C. Delobel.) IEEE Computer Society Press, 1981. (pp 465-477)

[Bracchi-76] Bracchi,G., Paolini, P., Pelagatti, G. "Binary Logical Associations in Data Modelings". In G.M. Nijssen (ed.), *Modeling in Data Base Management Systems*. IFIP Working Conference on Modeling in DBMS's, 1976.

[Chan-82] Chan,A., Danberg,Sy, Fox,S., Lin,W-T.K., Nori,A., and Ries,D.R. "Storage and Access Structures to Support a Semantic Data Model" Proceedings of the Eighth International Conference on Very Large Data Bases. IEEE Computer Society Press, 1982.

[Chen-76] P. Chen. "The Entity-relationship Model: Toward a unified view of data." *ACM Trans. Databas Syst. 1*, 1, 9-36.

[Hammer/McLeod-81] M. Hammer and D. McLeod. "Database Description with SDM: A Semantic Database Model", *ACM Transactions on Database Systems*, Vol. 6, No. 3, pp. 351-386, 1981.

[Jagannathan-88] D. Jagannathan, R.L. Guck, B.L. Fritchman, J.P. Thompson, D.M. Tolbert. "SIM: A Database System Based on Semantic Model." *Proceedings of SIGMOD International Conference on Management of Data.* Chicago, June 1-3, 1988. ACM-Press, 1988.

[Jain-87] A. Jain. Design of a Binary Model Based DBMS and Conversion of Binary Model Based Schema to an Equivalent Schema in Other Major Database Models. M.S. Thesis, University of California, Santa Barbara, 1987.

[King-84] R.King. "SEMBASE: A Semantic DBMS." Proceedings of the First Workshop on Expert Database Systems. Univ. of South Carolina, 1984. (pp. 151-171)

[Leung/Nijssen-87] C.M.R. Leung and G.M. Nijssen. From a NIAM Conceptual Schema into the Optimal SQL Relational Database Schema, Aust. Comput. J., Vol. 19, No. 2.

[Lien-81] Y.E. Lien, J.E. Shopiro, S. Tsur "DSIS — A Database System with Interrelational Semantics". Proceedings of the Seventh International Conference on Very Large Data Bases. (Eds. C. Zaniolo & C. Delobel.) IEEE Computer Society Press, 1981. (pp 465-477)

[Nijssen-81] G.M. Nijssen "An architecture for knowledge base systems", Proc. SPOT-2 conf., Stockholm, 1981.

[Nijssen/VanBekkum-82] G.M.A. Nijssen and J. Van Bekkum. "NIAM - An Information Analysis Method", in Information Systems Design Methodologies: A Comparative Review, T.W. Olle, et al. (eds.), IFIP 1982, North-Holland.

[Nixon-87] B. Nixon, L. Chung, I. Lauzen, A. Borgida, and M. Stanley. Implementation of a compiler for a semantic data model: Experience with Taxis." In *Proceedings of ACM SIGMOD Conf.* (San Francisco), ACM, 1987.

[Rishe-86-DN] N. Rishe. "On Denotational Semantics of Data Bases." *Mathematical Foundations of Programming Semantics.* Proceedings of the International Conference on Mathematical Foundations of Programming Semantics, April 1985, Manhattan, Kansas (ed. A. Melton), Lecture Notes in Computer Science, vol. 239. Springer-Verlag, 1986. (pp 249-274.)

[Rishe-86-PS] N. Rishe. "Postconditional Semantics of Data Base Queries." *Lecture Notes in Computer Science, vol. 239 (Mathematical Foundations of Programming Semantics,* ed. A. Melton), pp 275-295. Springer-Verlag, 1986.

[Rishe-87-DS] N. Rishe, *Database Semantics.* Technical report TRCS87-002, Computer Science Department, University of California, Santa Barbara, 1987.

[Rishe-87-RM] N. Rishe. "On Representation of Medical Knowledge by a Binary Data Model." *Journal of Mathematical and Computer Modelling,* vol. 8, 1987. (pp. 623-626)

[Rishe-88-AMPDM] N. Rishe, D. Tal, and Q. Li. "Architecture for a Massively Parallel Database Machine" *Microprocessing and Microprogramming.* The Euromicro Journal. 1988, in press.

[Rishe-88-CM] N. Rishe. "A Compact Monotonic Universal Encoding of Numbers" Proceedings of the 26th Annual Conference of Southeast Region of the Association for Computing Machinery, 1988.

[Rishe-88-DDF] N. Rishe. *Database Design Fundamentals: A Structured Introduction to Databases and a Structured Database Design Methodology.* Prentice-Hall, Englewood Cliffs, NJ, 1988. 436 pages. ISBN 0-13-196791-6.

[Shipman-81] D.W. Shipman. "The Functional Data Model and the Data Language DAPLEX", *ACM Transactions on Database Systems,* v. 6, no. 1, 140-173, 1981.

[Tsur/Zaniolo-84] S. Tsur, C. Zaniolo. "An implementation of GEM — supporting a semantic data model on a relational backend." In *Proc. ACM SIGMOD Intl. Conf. on Management of Data, May 1984.*

[Vijaykumar-87] N. Vijaykumar. Toward the Implementation of a DBMS based on the Semantic Binary Model. M.S. Thesis, University of California, Santa Barbara, 1987.

The Path Length of Binary Trees

Rolf Klein
Institut für Informatik
Universität Freiburg
Freiburg
West Germany

Derick Wood
Department of Computer Science
University of Waterloo
Waterloo, Ontario
Canada

Abstract

More than twenty years ago Nievergelt and Wong obtained a number of new bounds on the path length of binary trees in both the weighted and unweighted cases.

For the unweighted case, the novelty of their approach was that the bounds were applicable to *all trees*, not just the extremal ones. To obtain these "adaptive" bounds they introduced what came to be known as the weight balance of a tree, subsequently used as the basis of weight-balanced trees.

We introduce the notion of the *thickness*, $\Delta(T)$, of a tree T; the difference in the lengths of the longest and shortest root-to-leaf paths in T. We then prove that an upper bound on the external path length of a binary tree is

$$N(\log_2 N + \Delta - \log_2 \Delta - 0.6623),$$

where N is the number of external nodes in the tree. We prove that this bound is tight up to an $O(N)$ term if $\Delta \leq \sqrt{N}$. Otherwise, we construct binary trees whose external path length is at least as large as $N(\log_2 N + \phi(N, \Delta) \Delta - \log_2 \Delta - 4)$, where $\phi(N, \Delta) = 1/(1 + 2\frac{\Delta}{N})$.

1 Introduction

The time taken by a search operation in a search tree depends on the length of the path from the root to the node that contains the desired information. More generally, the execution time an algorithm needs to reach a particular state from its initial state is related to the length of the corresponding path in the decision tree. Therefore, the path length of a tree is a cost measure of great importance for the analysis of algorithms.

It is customary to consider the *external path length* $EPL(T)$ of an extended binary tree T; that is, the total number of edges along all the paths from the root to the external nodes of T. If N denotes the number of external nodes (the *weight* of T), then $EPL(T)/N$ is just the average length of a path from the root of T to an external node.

It is more than twenty years since Nievergelt and Wong obtained bounds for the weighted and unweighted path lengths of a binary tree; see [10,11]. In [11], they proposed an upper bound for $EPL(T)$ in terms of N and the maximum weight balance of all of T's subtrees. Weight balance was subsequently used to define a class of balanced trees; see [9]. They together with Pradels obtained other bounds for the weighted case; see [8]. Our upper bound requires much less information about the tree. We start with the following observations. The external path length is a minimum if and only if all paths in T differ in length by at most one; that is,

$$EPL(T) = N(\log_2 N + 1 + \theta - 2^\theta)$$

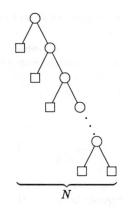

Figure 1: A snake.

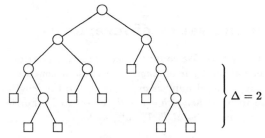

Figure 2: An example tree.

holds, where $\theta = \lceil \log_2 N \rceil - \log_2 N \in [0, 1)$; see Knuth [7], p. 194. This formula establishes a lower bound for the external path length. On the other hand, the path length takes its maximum value

$$\frac{N(N+1)}{2} - 1$$

if the tree is a "snake" as shown in Figure 1[1]. Here the shortest path is $N - 2$ levels shorter than the longest path.

We present an upper bound for the external path length in terms of the weight N and the maximal path length difference $\triangle$ (see Figure 2) by proving that

$$EPL(T) \leq N(\log_2 N + \triangle - \log_2 \triangle - \Psi(\triangle))$$

holds for all binary trees, where

$$\begin{aligned} \Psi(\triangle) &= \alpha - o(1) \geq 0.6622\ldots \\ \alpha &= \log_2 e - \log_2 \log_2 e = 0.9139\ldots \end{aligned}$$

and $o(1)$ tends to zero as $\triangle$ tends to infinity. For the tree in Figure 2, for example, we obtain the value 31.56 whereas its actual path length is equal to 30.

It is interesting to note that the ratio, rather than the difference, of the shortest and longest root-to-frontier paths has been used to define the α-balanced trees (see [12]), which become the red-black, half-balanced, or binary-B trees when $\alpha = 1/2$; see [1,3,13].

In Section 2, we first show, via the Kraft Inequality, that the external path length of a binary tree is related to the ratio of the geometric and the harmonic means of the integers 2^{l_i}, where l_i denotes the length of the i-th path. This is then used in Section 3 to obtain an upper bound for

---

[1]This and the following figures have been produced using TreeTEX; see [2].

the path length by applying a general theorem of Specht that imposes an upper bound on the ratio of means of arbitrary real numbers.

We continue in Section 4 by discussing the tightness of our upper bound. If $\triangle$ and N are integers of arbitrary, independent orders of magnitude, we can construct a tree whose path length is greater than

$$N(\log_2 N + \triangle - \log_2 \triangle - 4)$$

if $\triangle \leq \sqrt{N}$, and greater than

$$N\left(\log_2 N + \frac{1}{1 + \Theta(\frac{\triangle}{N})}\triangle - \log_2 \triangle - 4\right)$$

otherwise. Here $\Theta(\triangle/N)$ stands for a function whose order of magnitude is $\triangle/N$ up to constant factors, as usual. This shows that the upper bound for the external path length obtained here is tight if $\triangle \leq \sqrt{N}$ and quite sharp otherwise.

2 Path length and ratios of means

Let T be an extended binary tree. We count the *level* of nodes starting with level 0 at the root. The *access path* to a node at level j is of *length j*, because it consists of j edges. The *height h* of the tree T is the maximum level number or, equivalently, the length of a longest path in T. A node at level i is said to be at *height $h - i$ with respect to T*. Furthermore, $N = weight(T)$ denotes the number of external nodes of T. Finally, we let

$$EPL(T) = \sum_{i=1}^{N} l_i,$$

where l_i is the length of the path to the i-th external node.

First, we recall the definition of means. Let $a_1, \ldots, a_N$ and $q_1, \ldots, q_N$ be sequences of positive real numbers such that $q_1 + q_2 + \ldots + q_N = 1$. Then,

$$M_N^{[-1]}(a, q) = (\sum_{i=1}^{N} \frac{q_i}{a_i})^{-1}$$

is the *weighted harmonic mean* and

$$M_N^{[0]}(a, q) = \prod_{i=1}^{N} a_i^{q_i}$$

is the *weighted geometric mean* of the numbers $a_1, \ldots, a_N$ with weights $q_1, \ldots, q_N$.

Lemma 2.1 *Let T be a binary tree of weight N whose paths to the external nodes are of length $l_1, \ldots, l_N$. Let $a_i = 2^{l_i}$ and $q_i = \frac{1}{N}, 1 \leq i \leq N$. Then,*

$$\frac{M^{[0]}(a, q)}{M^{[-1]}(a, q)} = \frac{2^{\frac{EPL(T)}{N}}}{N}.$$

Proof: By Kraft's Theorem (usually referred to as the Kraft Inequality, see [4]) there exists a binary tree whose paths to the external nodes are of length $l_1, \ldots, l_N$ if and only if

$$\sum_{i=1}^{N} 2^{-l_i} = 1.$$

Hence,

$$M_N^{[-1]}(a,q) = \left(\sum_{i=1}^{N} \frac{2^{-l_i}}{N} \right)^{-1}$$
$$= N.$$

Furthermore,

$$M^{[0]}(a,q) = \left(\prod_{i=1}^{N} 2^{l_i} \right)^{\frac{1}{N}}$$
$$= 2^{\frac{1}{N} EPL(T)}.$$

$\square$

Inequalities involving means were first studied by the Pythagoreans and Euclid, and many interesting results have been obtained since; for example, it is well known that

$$M_N^{[-1]}(a,q) \leq M_N^{[0]}(a,q)$$

holds, for any sequences of numbers a_i and weights q_i. This yields immediately

$$EPL(T) \geq N \log_2 N.$$

In the next section we will use an upper bound for the ratios of these means discovered by Specht [14] in order to derive a new upper bound for the external path length of binary trees.

3   An upper bound for the external path length

Throughout this paper, $\triangle(T)$ denotes the difference between the length of a longest path from the root of T to an external node and the length of a shortest path from the root of T to an external node. We also refer to $\triangle$ as the *thickness of the fringe* of T.

Theorem 3.1 *Let T be a binary tree of weight N whose fringe is of thickness $\triangle$. Then*

$$EPL(T) \leq N(\log_2 N + \triangle - \log_2 \triangle - \Psi(\triangle)),$$

where

$$\Psi(\triangle) = \log_2 e - \log_2 \log_2 e - \frac{\triangle}{2^\triangle - 1} - \log_2 \left(1 - \frac{1}{2^\triangle} \right)$$
$$= \alpha - o(1) \geq \beta$$
$$\alpha = \log_2 e - \log_2 \log_2 e = 0.91392867\ldots$$
$$\beta = \alpha - \log_2 3 + \frac{4}{3} = 0.66229950\ldots$$

and e denotes the basis of the natural logarithm.

Proof: By Lemma 2.1,

$$\frac{2^{\frac{EPL(T)}{N}}}{N} = \frac{M_N^{[0]}(a,q)}{M_N^{[-1]}(a,q)},$$

where $a_i = 2^{l_i}$, l_i = length of the path to the i-th external node, and $q_i = \frac{1}{N}$, for $i = 1, \ldots, N$. By a theorem of Specht (Satz 1, (5.4) in [14]) we have

$$\frac{M_N^{[0]}(a,q)}{M_N^{[-1]}(a,q)} \leq \left(\frac{\frac{1}{B} - 1}{-\ln B} \right) e^{\left(-1 - \frac{\ln B}{\frac{1}{B} - 1} \right)}$$

if $B = \frac{M}{m}$ is such that $m \leq a_1, \ldots, a_N \leq M$. If $l = \min_i l_i$, then $B = \frac{2^h}{2^l} = 2^\Delta$ will do. The above exponential term equals

$$e^{-1} B^{1 + \frac{1}{B-1}},$$

whereas the left hand factor is equal to

$$\frac{1 - \frac{1}{B}}{(\log_2 e)^{-1} \Delta}$$

when we observe that $\ln x = (\log_2 e)^{-1} \log_2 x$ for the natural logarithm. Taking logarithms yields

$$\frac{EPL(T)}{N} - \log_2 N \leq \log_2 \left(1 - \frac{1}{2^\Delta}\right) + \log_2 \log_2 e - \log_2 \Delta$$
$$- \log_2 e + \left(1 + \frac{1}{2^\Delta - 1}\right) \Delta .$$

In order to complete the proof we note that the function $\log_2 \left(1 - \frac{1}{2^\Delta}\right) + \frac{\Delta}{2^\Delta - 1}$ takes its maximum value, over the positive integers, when $\Delta = 2$. □

We observe a certain similarity between the formula in Theorem 3.1 and the tight upper bound for the path length of AVL trees recently obtained by Klein and Wood [5], caused by the term $\log_2 \Delta$. Namely, for each AVL tree T we have

$$\Delta \leq \frac{1}{2} h(T) \leq \frac{1}{2} \gamma \log_2 N,$$

where $\gamma = 1/\log_2 \frac{1+\sqrt{5}}{2} = 1.4404\ldots$, which when substituted into the bound of Theorem 3.1 yields

$$EPL(T) \leq N(1.7202 \log_2 N - \log_2 \log_2 N) + O(N).$$

This bound is bigger than the tight upper bound

$$\gamma N(\log_2 N - \log_2 \log_2 N) + O(N)$$

in [5], but the presence of the term $\log_2 \log_2 N$ in the above equation is surprising!

4 High external path length trees

In order to investigate how close to reality the upper bound established in Theorem 3.1 is, we have to allow the parameters N and Δ to vary independently. If $\Delta = 1$, then $\Psi(\Delta) = \log_2 e - \log_2 \log_2 e = (1 + \ln \ln 2)/\ln 2$, and our upper bound takes the form

$$N(\log_2 N + 1 - (1 + \ln \ln 2)/\ln 2).$$

This is exactly the maximum value of the lower bound $N(\log_2 N + 1 + \theta - 2^\theta)$ for the external path length, for $\theta = -(\ln \ln 2)/\ln 2$; see Section 1 and Knuth [7], p. 194.

Next we consider the case $2^\Delta \leq N$.

Lemma 4.1 Let $\Delta = 2^a \geq 1$. Then, for each integer $s \geq 0$, there exists a binary tree T of weight $N = \Theta(2^{\Delta + s})$ whose fringe is of thickness Δ such that

$$EPL(T) \geq N(\log_2 N + \Delta - \log_2 \Delta - 2).$$

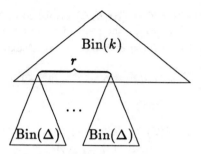

Figure 3: The tree $T_1(r, k, \triangle)$.

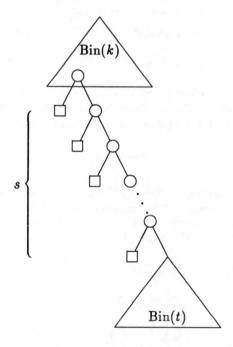

Figure 4: The tree $T_2(k, s, t)$.

Proof: (Sketch) Consider the tree $T = T_1(r, k, \triangle)$ displayed in Figure 3; a height k complete binary tree, r of whose external nodes are the roots of complete binary trees of height $\triangle$.

Since a complete binary tree $Bin(h)$ of height h has 2^h external nodes and external path length $h2^h$ we have

$$weight(T) = N = 2^k + (2^\triangle - 1)r$$

and

$$
\begin{aligned}
EPL(T) &= k(2^k - r) + r(k + \triangle)2^\triangle \\
&= kN + r\triangle\, 2^\triangle.
\end{aligned}
$$

Now let $k = \triangle - \log_2 \triangle + s = 2^a - a + s$ and $r = \triangle 2^{k-\triangle} = 2^s \geq 1$. Then, $EPL(T) = kN + \triangle^2 2^k$ and $N = \triangle 2^k(\triangle 2^\triangle + 2^\triangle - \triangle)/(\triangle 2^\triangle)$. We derive a lower bound of $k + \triangle - 1$ for $EPL(T)/N$ from these two equations and an upper bound of $k + \log_2 \triangle + 1$ for $\log_2 N$ from the second equation. Combining these two bounds we obtain the result. $\qquad\square$

In the above construction we were able to obtain a tree with its external nodes at two levels because $2^\triangle \leq N$. But if the fringe grows thicker (in relation to the weight) we have to place the external nodes at more than two levels in the tree. This tends to keep the maximal possible external path length smaller than the value of the upper bound. If $\triangle \leq \sqrt{N}$, however, then the difference from $EPL(T)/N$ is only a small additive constant, as the following lemma shows.

Lemma 4.2 *Let $\triangle = 2^a \geq 2$. Then, for each integer k in $[1, \triangle - a]$, there exists a binary tree T of weight $N = \Theta(\triangle 2^k)$ whose fringe is of thickness $\triangle$ such that*
A. $EPL(T) \geq N(\log_2 N + \triangle - \log_2 \triangle - 4)$ *holds if $\triangle \leq \sqrt{N}$ and*
B. $EPL(T) \geq N \left(\log_2 N + \frac{1}{1+\Theta(\frac{\triangle}{N})} \triangle - \log_2 \triangle - 4\right)$ *holds otherwise.*

Proof: This is omitted; see the full paper [6]. $\qquad\square$

Lemma 4.2 covers the case where $2^\triangle > N$ holds (by orders of magnitude). According to assertion A, the upper bound for EPL established in Theorem 3.1 is tight up to a small additive $O(N)$ term, if $\triangle \leq \sqrt{N}$. If $\triangle$ is increased beyond $\sqrt{N}$, then the coefficient

$$\rho = \frac{1}{1 + \Theta(\frac{\triangle}{N})}$$

of $\triangle$ in B begins to decrease. As long as $\triangle = O(N^\alpha)$ holds, however, for some real number $\alpha > 1$, the value of ρ still is arbitrarily close to 1 for large integers N. Only if $\triangle = \Theta(N)$ is the decrease of ρ substantial — but bounded, nevertheless. In fact, in the extreme case when the tree is a snake (see Figure 1), we have $\triangle = N - 2$ and

$$
\begin{aligned}
EPL(T) &= \frac{N(N+1)}{2} - 1 \\
&= N\frac{1}{2}\triangle + O(N) \\
&= N \left(\log_2 N + \frac{1}{2}\triangle - \log_2 \triangle\right) + O(N).
\end{aligned}
$$

This indicates that there is a difference between the world of reals where the upper bound of Theorem 3.1 is tight for all values of N and $\triangle$ and the real world of trees — but only a small one!

5 Concluding remarks

We have derived an upper bound for the path length in terms of the weight N and the thickness of the fringe, $\triangle$, namely

$$EPL(T) \leq N(\log_2 N + \triangle - \log_2 \triangle + O(1))$$

Then, we constructed binary trees with a high external path length to show that this bound is tight if $\triangle \leq \sqrt{N}$ and reasonably sharp otherwise.

Note that our bound is worse than the one of Nievergelt and Wong [11] for the specific example of Fibonacci trees. Since $\triangle(Fib(h)) = h/2$, we obtain the same bound as for AVL trees, namely $1.7202N(\log N - \log \log N) + O(N)$ which is worse than their $1.09N \log N + O(N)$ bound (If we state results modulo $O(N)$, we need not distinguish between internal and external path length.) But, our bound is much sharper for close-to-balanced trees! In this case their bound cannot be lower than $1.09N \log N + O(N)$, but our Theorem 3.1 yields upper bounds of the type $1.00N \log N+$ a precise $O(N)$ term, for each class of trees that has a $\triangle$ bounded by a constant! Also, we must emphasize that our bound needs much less information about the tree, so we cannot expect it to be uniformly better than [11].

The result obtained here raises a number of interesting problems for further research. For example, does our result extend to weighted binary trees? How much better a bound can be established if more information about the fringe is available?

Acknowledgements

This work was partially supported by a Natural Sciences and Engineering Research Council of Canada Grant No. A-5692 and by a grant from the Information Technology Research Centre. It was done during the first author's stay with the Data Structuring Group, the University of Waterloo, in 1986-1987.

References

[1] R. Bayer. Symmetric binary B-trees: Data structure and maintenance algorithms. *Acta Informatica*, 1:290–306, 1972.

[2] A. Brüggemann-Klein and D. Wood. Drawing trees nicely with TEX. *Electronic Publishing, Origination, Dissemination, and Design*, to appear, 1989.

[3] L.J. Guibas and R. Sedgewick. A dichromatic framework for balanced trees. In *Proceedings of the 19th Annual Symposium on Foundations of Computer Science*, pages 8–21, 1978.

[4] R.W. Hamming. *Coding and Information Theory*. Prentice-Hall, Inc., Englewood Cliffs, New Jersey, 1980.

[5] R. Klein and D. Wood. On the maximum path length of AVL trees. In M. Dauchet and M. Nivat, editors, *Proceedings of the 13th Colloquium on Trees in Algebra and Programming (CAAP '88), Springer-Verlag Lecture Notes in Computer Science 299*, pages 16–27, 1988.

[6] R. Klein and D. Wood. On the path length of binary trees. *Journal of the ACM*, 36, 1989.

[7] D.E. Knuth. *The Art of Computer Programming, Vol.3: Sorting and Searching*. Addison-Wesley Publishing Co., Reading, Mass., 1973.

[8] J. Nievergelt, J. Pradels, C.K. Wong, and P.C. Yue. Bounds on the weighted path length of binary trees. *Information Processing Letters*, 1:220–225, 1972.

[9] J. Nievergelt and E.M. Reingold. Binary search trees of bounded balance. *SIAM Journal on Computing*, 2:33–43, 1973.

[10] J. Nievergelt and C.K. Wong. On binary search trees. In C.V. Freiman, editor, *Information Processing 71*, pages 91–98, Amsterdam, 1971. North-Holland Publishing Co.

[11] J. Nievergelt and C.K. Wong. Upper bounds for the total path length of binary trees. *Journal of the ACM*, 20:1–6, 1973.

[12] H. J. Olivié. *A Study of Balanced Binary Trees and Balanced One-Two Trees*. PhD thesis, Departement Wiskunde, Universiteit Antwerpen, Antwerp, Belgium, 1980.

[13] H. J. Olivié. A new class of balanced search trees: Half-balanced search trees. *RAIRO Informatique théorique*, 16:51–71, 1982.

[14] W. Specht. Zur Theorie der Elementaren Mittel. *Mathematische Zeitschrift*, 74:91–98, 1960.

NEW TECHNOLOGIES

Efficient multiresolution image processing on hypercube connected SIMD machines

Larry S. Davis
P. J. Narayanan
Computer Vision Laboratory
Center for Automation Research
&
Institute for Advanced Computer Studies
University of Maryland
College Park, Maryland 20742

1. Introduction Image processing and computer vision applications have historically been important driving factors in the development of large-scale parallel computers. The principle reasons are the large amounts of data in an image (even a grey scale image from a standard television camera contains over one quarter of a million bytes of data) and the high number of processing steps involved in even the simplest image analysis algorithms. Cellular machines such as MPP[1], CLIP[2] and more recently, the Connection Machine[3] were designed to come as close as possible to the ideal goal of having one processor in the machine for each pixel in the image.

Yet our experience in processing images over the last decade or so indicates that many complex image analysis systems involve not only processing large images, but also small images derived from those large images. These small images might arise either because the original image is being processed using multiresolution algorithms or focus-of-attention algorithms.

Multiresolution image processing algorithms are a class of parallel techniques that operate on "pyramid" representations of images (Rosenfeld[4]). A pyramid is an exponentially tapered stack of square images, where the base of the pyramid is the original, full resolution image, and successive levels are constructed by a combination of averaging and sampling of the level below. The "classical" pyramid would be obtained by averaging nonoverlapping two by two neighborhoods at level i of the pyramid to determine the grey levels of pixels at level i+1.

An important advantage of pyramid image representations is that many features that are global in the original, full resolution image, become local at some level in the pyramid. So, for example, a large compact object in the original image eventually shrinks to a small spot at some level of the pyramid. Thus, one can apply relatively simple local operations to detect such features at high levels of the pyramid, and then delineate (i.e., outline) those features more accurately by selectively processing higher resolution versions of the image.

An additional computational advantage of the extra interprocessor connections provided by the pyramid is that such a machine is capable of measuring many image properties in a number of computational steps proportional to the logarithm of the diameter of the image. A comparable algorithm applied in a cellular machine would usually require a number of steps proportional to the diameter of the image. Consider as a very simple example the problem of deciding whether there exists a pixel in an image containing a particular value. In a cellular machine containing only horizontal and vertical connections, this is accomplished by having any processor containing the value transmit a message to a distinguished processor (e.g., the uppermost, leftmost processor). The entire operation is synchronized by having the processor furthest from the distinguished processor send an "end-of-computation" message. Since the distance that this special message must travel is the sum of the number of rows and columns in the image, the time taken to perform this operation is proportional to the diameter of the image.

On a pyramid machine, however, each processor containing the particular value would send a message to its parent; the root of the pyramid would act as the distinguished node. Since the distance from the root to any processor in the base is only the logarithm of the diameter of the image, the time taken to perform the operation on the pyramid machine is proportional only to the logarithm of the image diameter. For the pyramid machine, any processor at the base can be chosen to send the "end-of-computation" message. (Note that in neither case would one want the distinguished processor to count the number of cycles - which would allow it to conclude that the computation must have terminated unsuccessfully if no message arrived - because of the SIMD nature of computation; i.e., while the counting is being performed, no other processor can be performing useful work.)

Most models of pyramid machines assume a parallel computer with one processor for each pixel at each level of the pyramid (i.e., a pyramid of processors); see for example Tanimoto[5]. It is important to note, however, that many practical pyramid image analysis algorithms operate on only a single level of the pyramid at a time, perhaps computing a local representation of the image or transmitting information to an adjacent level. Thus, in a machine having one processor per pixel at each level, most of the machine is inactive at any step of the computation. We will describe how, for a hypercube connected machine, more of the available computational power can be brought to bear on processing even very high levels of the pyramid.

In focus-of-attention vision systems analysis is based on processing only subsets of the original high resolution image; these subsets correspond to predictions on the locations and appearance of image features based on either analysis of previous frames in a motion sequence or processing of other regions of the current image. So, for example, the system built in our laboratory for visual navigation of roads and road networks[6,7] was based on processing regions in the image predicted to contain the projections of important road features, such as road/shoulder boundaries and road markings. These predictions were derived from a three dimensional model of the road (developed on the basis of analyzing previous images in space and time) and an estimate of the location of the vehicle in that three dimensional model. There are two principle advantages to such focus-of-attention vision systems: first, of course, they require processing fewer pixels, which is critical on conventional, serial machines. But second, they allow us to utilize specialized image analysis algorithms which generally leads to robust performance. In our road navigation system, for example, we were able to predict the expected geometric (image orientation) and photometric (contrast) features of the road boundaries and markings and then used finely tuned feature detection algorithms to extract these highly constrained features within prediction windows. While such focus of attention vision algorithms can be implemented on a SIMD computer by selectively applying operations to the processors representing the pixels within a given window, such an approach is unnecessarily wasteful because the remaining processors are not performing any useful work.

So a common goal for both multiresolution processing and focus-of-attention processing is ideally, to utilize as many processors as possible at all stages of processing so that, ideally, the time required to perform any given operation on an image (or image window) would be proportional to the number of pixels in that image. If an image larger than the available machine is being processed, then this goal is relatively easy to obtain (for example, the image is broken into blocks, and the blocks are assigned to a processor - see Kushner and Rosenfeld[8] for a comprehensive treatment of methods for analyzing large images with relatively small cellular machines). However, when the available machine is substantially larger than the image to be processed, it is not so clear how such speedups might be achieved (even approximately).

In the remainder of this paper we will describe two different methods for processing small images effectively using large hypercube connected machines. The first of these methods, which is called a **fat pyramid (fat image)** is based on using many processors in the hypercube to represent single pixels at high levels of the pyramid (single pixels in a window of an original image). The second method, called a **replicated pyramid (image)**, is based on replicating the data associated with a given layer of the pyramid many times (replicating the window to be processed many times). We will briefly sketch how certain basic image analysis operations, such as histogramming, table lookup, and convolution can be performed on both of these representations. But first, we describe how **Gray codes** can be used to map arrays into hypercubes. The discussions in Sections 3 and 4 are taken from the paper by Bestul and Davis[9].

2. Gray codes and grids In [10] Chan and Saad describe how to embed a grid in a hypercube by the use of Gray Codes, which are number sequences in which the binary representation of two adjacent elements differ in exactly one bit position. The Gray Code used to construct both fat and replicated pyramids will be the **binary reflected Gray Code**, for which the i-bit sequence is obtained by appending a reversed copy of the i-1 bit sequence to itself, with each element prefixed by a 1.

So, for example, the 2-bit binary reflected Gray Code is {00,01,11,10} and the 3-bit code is {000,001,011,010,110,111,101,100}.

Consider a cell with grid coordinates (x,y), each of which have p bits, and let

$$g_x = g_{x,p-1}, g_{x,p-2} \cdots g_{x,0}$$

and

$$g_y = g_{y,p-1}, g_{y,p-2} \cdots g_{y,0}$$

be the x_{th} and y_{th} elements of the p-bit binary reflected Gray Codes, respectively. Then the hypercube address of this cell is taken as the concatenation:

$$g_{x,p-1}, g_{x,p-2} \cdots g_{x,0} \, g_{y,p-1}, g_{y,p-2} \cdots g_{y,0}$$

It is easy to see that the hypercube addresses of two cells adjacent in the grid will have addresses differing in exactly one bit position. Thus, any two such cells will be adjacent in the hypercube. This mapping is illustrated in Figure 1.

3. Fat pyramids and gray codes. In a fat pyramid, the size of a virtual processor associated with a node depends on the level of the node in the pyramid. Specifically, a processor at level $l+1$ will have four times as much storage, and possibly four times as much processing power, as a processor at level l. A fat pyramid allows for combining operations in which the amount of information per node increases with the level in the pyramid. In Section 1 it was pointed out that many pyramid image analysis algorithms have the property that only one level of the pyramid is active at any time during the execution of the algorithm. Our goal, then, is to multiplex the multiprocessor among all of the levels, with all of the processing cells being divided up among the nodes of a given level when that level is active.

Thus, if one cell were associated with each node at level 0, then there would be four cells cooperating to carry out computations at level 1, sixteen cells at level 2 and, in general, 4^l cells associated with each pyramid node at level l. Such an arrangement is called a fat pyramid.

In order for several cells to cooperate efficiently in performing some computation, it is desireable that there is a high degree of interconnectivity among them. This can be accomplished easily with a hypercube connected multiprocessor. At any level l of the pyramid, all of the cells of the hypercube are divided up among the nodes at that level, into block of 4^l cells per node. It is possible to do this so that blocks of cells implementing each node are themselves connected in a hypercube of dimension $2l$. Therefore, none of the 4^l cells in a block are more than $2l$ links apart. Also, if we define two processor blocks to be adjacent if any cell in one block is directly connected to some cell in the other block, then we can also arrange for all of the blocks at any given level to form a grid under this kind of adjacency.

Recall from Section 2 that we can embed a grid into a hypercube using Gray Code techniques. Again, let g_x and g_y be the p-bit Gray Codes for

7	4	12	28	20	52	60	44	36
6	5	13	28	21	53	61	45	37
5	7	15	31	23	55	63	47	39
4	6	14	30	22	54	62	46	38
3	2	10	26	18	50	58	42	34
2	3	11	27	19	51	59	43	35
1	1	9	25	17	49	57	41	33
0	0	8	24	16	48	56	40	32
	0	1	2	3	4	5	6	7

Figure 1

Hypercube To Grid Mapping

the components of the grid coordinates (x,y). If instead of concatenating g_x and g_y we instead interleave their bits to obtain:

$$g_{x,p-1} \; g_{y,p-1} \; g_{x,p-2} \; g_{y,p-2} \cdots g_{x,0} \; g_{y,0}$$

then we get not only a mapping from a hypercube to a grid which preserves adjacency, but we also get a natural hypercube-to-collapsed-fat-pyramid mapping in the following sense. This mapping allows the hypercube address of any cell in any block at any level l to be regarded as the concatenation of two binary numbers. The first is a 2(L-l) bit number (where L is the number of levels in the pyramid) determining the processor block the cell is in. The second is a $2l$ bit number giving the local address of the cell within the block. In other words, all of the cells comprising any block on any level l will have hypercube addresses which are in the range $k4^l$ to $(k+1)4^L$-1, for some k. This is illustrated in Figures 2 through 4.

This embedding of the fat pyramid into the hypercube was originally presented in Bestul and Davis[9]. That paper contained a description of an image histogramming algorithm based on the fat pyramid architecture. A report by Ziavras and Davis[11] describes in detail the implementation of an addition algorithm in the fat pyramid architecture. There, the bits of an operand to the addition operation are distributed across all of the cells used to represent a node in the fat pyramid. The hypercube connections are then used, effectively, to perform the carry look-aheads needed by a parallel addition algorithm. The addition algorithm is fundamental because it can be used to construct a multiplication algorithm, and finally a general convolution algorithm. Convolutions play a key role in many image processing algorithms (e.g., image enhancement, edge and local feature detection, etc.).

The fat pyramid addition algorithm was implemented on a 16K processor Connection Machine II (Ziavras and Davis[11]. The timing results were, unfortunately, very bad, making the fat pyramid addition algorithm efficient for only impractically large operands. This was due in large part to the amount of code needed to control the flow of information along the hypercube wires. Such inefficiencies have led us to explore less elegant, but more practical approaches, such as the replicated pyramid described in the following section.

4. Replicated pyramids. In a replicated pyramid, the cells in the hypercube are used to replicate, as many times as possible, the image stored at any given level of the pyramid. So, for example, if the image at the base (the 0'th level) of the pyramid has exactly as many nodes as there are cells in the hypercube, then only one copy of the image would be stored in the hypercube. At the first level there would be sufficient cells to store four copies of the reduced resolution image. In general, at the l'th level we would have 4^l copies of the reduced resolution image.

Again, it is straightforward to embed the replicated reduced resolution images into the hypercube using Gray Codes. Let (x,y) be the grid address of a node at the l'th level of the pyramid and let there be $2^L \times 2^L$

7	16	18	26	24	56	58	50	48
6	17	19	27	25	57	59	51	49
5	21	23	31	29	61	63	55	53
4	20	22	30	28	60	62	54	52
3	4	6	14	12	44	46	38	36
2	5	7	15	13	45	47	39	37
1	1	3	11	9	41	43	35	33
0	0	2	10	8	40	42	34	32
	0	1	2	3	4	5	6	7

Figure 2

Hypercube To Fat Pyramid Mapping

Division Of Cells Among Nodes At Pyramid Level 0

	0	1	2	3	
3	16 18	26 24	56 58	50 48
	17 19	27 25	57 59	51 49
2	21 23	31 29	61 63	55 53
	20 22	30 28	60 62	54 52
1	4 6	14 12	44 46	38 36
	5 7	15 13	45 47	39 37
0	1 3	11 9	41 43	35 33
	0 2	10 8	40 42	34 32

Figure 3

Hypercube To Fat Pyramid Mapping

Division Of Cells Among Nodes At Pyramid Level 1

16	18	26	24	56	58	50	48
17	19	27	25	57	59	51	49
21	23	31	29	61	63	55	53
20	22	30	28	60	62	54	52
4	6	14	12	44	46	38	36
5	7	15	13	45	47	39	37
1	3	11	9	41	43	35	33
0	2	10	8	40	42	34	32

Figure 4

Hypercube To Fat Pyramid Mapping

Division Of Cells Among Nodes At Pyramid Level 2

nodes in the image at the base of the pyramid. Then x and y can be represented using $L-l$ bit numbers. Let g_x and g_y be the $L-l$ bit binary reflected Gray Codes of x and y respectively. At the l'th level, we have 4^l images of size $2^{L-l} \times 2^{L-l}$ so that node (x,y) will be replicated 4^l times. If g_i is the $2l$ bit binary reflected Gray Code of i, then the hypercube address of the i'th copy of grid cell (x,y) at level l would be $g_i g_x g_y$.

We next briefly describe how the basic image processing operations of histogramming, convolution and table look-up can be efficiently computed at a given level of the reeplicated pyramid. We first consider constructing a one dimensional histogram of a data item (ordinarily grey levels, although other arbitrary local properties could have been previously computed) stored at level l of the replicated pyramid. Suppose that the grey levels occupy the range $[0, 2^r-1]$. Then during the first phase of the histogramming algorithm, each copy of the image at level l will compute the histogram for a subinterval of the range $[0, 2^r-1]$. If we let $s = 2^r/4^l$, then the 0'th copy would compute the histogram for grey levels $[0, s-1]$ and the i'th processor would compute the histogram for grey levels $[(i-1)s, is-1]$. At the second stage, the algorithm would in logarithmic time, exchange and combine histograms between pairs of image copies so that, finally, each copy of the image would have a complete instance of the histogram stored in a subset of its processors.

We now consider the first phase of the algorithm in more detail. At each step of the first phase, the algorithm computes the value of the final histogram for 4^l different values of the grey level. At the j'th step, image copy i will determine the histogram value for grey level $h_{i,j} = [(i-1)s + (j-1)]$ in the following way. First, all processors having grey levels of the form $[(i-1)s + (j-1)]$ **select themselves.** (Most SIMD machines, such as the Connection Machine, have a facility to apply a set of operations to only a subset of their processors. The subset is determined by having all of the currently selected processors apply a test to a value stored in local memory. If the test evaluates to true, then the processor becomes part of the selected set). This is straightforward to do. Before the first step of this phase, each processor determines to which histogram bin it will eventually contribute. This is done by simply subtracting $(i-1)s$ from its grey level. At the j'th step, any processor that computed a value of j initially will select itself. We can then count the number of processors in each image copy that have selected themselves. That count could be stored in the selected processor having highest hypercube address in each copy. Finally, those selected processors would transmit their counts to the appropriate processor in the local copy of the histogram. In the i'th copy this processor would be determined as follows. Let $g_{i,j}$ be the Grey Code of $h_{i,j}$. Then the selected processor in copy i would send its count to processor $g_i g_{i,j}$. In this way, consecutive grey levels will be stored in contiguous locations in the histogram. (Note: on the Connection Machine it as possible to count all grey levels in all copies simultaneously using the add-reduction operation. Here, all processors storing a given grey level send a message to the processor designated to count the number of occurrences of that grey level. The Connection Machine hardware can actually count the number of messages sent to any given processor during a single cycle of message routing, thus creating the histogram for the entire image in one send operation. Thus, on the Connection Machine, it is no faster to compute the histogram using a replicated algorithm than it would be to compute it using only a single copy of the input image.)

So, after the final step of phase 1, the entire histogram has been computed, although its values are distributed amongst the 4^l copies of the image. These copies are combined in $2l$ copy/merge steps. At step j, histograms are "swapped" between all copies i and $i+2^{j-1}$ mod 4^l. This is actually done by having the non-zero entries in each histogram copy their values into the corresponding locations of the paired histogram. The entire algorithm is illustrated for the simple case of $l=1$ in Figure 5.

In this figure, we show four replicated copies of a 4x4 image at the top. Each pixel contains a 3-bit grey level. Below these four copies, we show the histograms initialized to be all zeroes. At the end of the first iteration each copy has computed the histogram value for a single grey level. So, for example, copy 1 has counted the number of 0's in the input image (there is only one 0). After the second iteration, each histogram contains the count for two grey levels in the original image, and each grey level has been counted in exactly one of the copies.

The second phase is the merge/copy phase. During the first iteration, copies 1 and 2 and copies 3 and 4 exchange histograms. At the end of the first iteration both copies 1 and 2 contain histograms for the grey level [0,3] and copies 3 and 4 contain histograms for the grey levels [4,7]. During the second iteration, copies 1 and 3 and copies 2 and 4 exchange histograms. At the end of the second iteration, all copies have complete histograms of the original image. Subsequent processing of the histogram (which is a simple one dimensional image) can now proceed in parallel using similar techniques. In Bestul and Davis[9] we describe how Gray Codes can also be used for storing multidimensional histograms. The histogramming algorithm described above can also be extended directly to compute multidimensional histograms.

We next consider the operation of convolving a kxk convolution kernel at level l of the replicated pyramid. To simplify the discussion, we will assume that k^2 (the number of convolution weights) is less than 4^l. In this case, we will use only k^2 of the available copies to perform the convolution. Again, the algorithm proceeds in two stages. During the first stage, each copy of the image produces one of the summands for the final convolution. In the second stage, a logarithmic merge and copy algorithm is used to combine these partial results.

The first phase of the algorithm would procede as follows for a 3x3 convolution kernel. Here, each image copy is assigned one of the nine convolution weights. So, image copy 1 is assigned the convolution weight stored in the (-1,-1) location of the convolution kernal. Each processor in image copy 1 transfers its grey levels to the processor in relative grid location (1,1). All of the processors then multiply their local weights

Phase 1

Copy 1	Copy 2	Copy 3	Copy 4
2 1 3 7	2 1 3 7	2 1 3 7	2 1 3 7
2 6 0 7	2 6 0 7	2 6 0 7	2 6 0 7
5 4 5 3	5 4 5 3	5 4 5 3	5 4 5 3
2 4 1 3	2 4 1 3	2 4 1 3	2 4 1 3

i   01234567   i   01234567   i   01234567   i   01234567
H(i) 00000000   H(i) 00000000   H(i) 00000000   H(i) 00000000

Iteration 1

i   01234567   i   01234567   i   01234567   i   01234567
H(i) 10000000   H(i) 00300000   H(i) 00002000   H(i) 00000010

Iteration 2

i   01234567   i   01234567   i   01234567   i   01234567
H(i) 12000000   H(i) 00330000   H(i) 00002100   H(i) 00000012

Phase 2

Iteration 1

i   01234567   i   01234567   i   01234567   i   01234567
H(i) 12330000   H(i) 12330000   H(i) 00002112   H(i) 00002112

Iteration 2

i   01234567   i   01234567   i   01234567   i   01234567
H(i) 12332112   H(i) 12332112   H(i) 12332112   H(i) 12332112

Figure 5. Trace of the histogram algorithm.

(constant in any given image copy) by the transmitted grey levels. Generally, if copy i is assigned the convolution weight in kernel location (r,s), then all processors in copy i will transmit their grey levels to processors in relative grid locations (-r,-s).

During the second phase of the algorithm, a merge and copy algorithm similar in structure to the one used to combine histograms, is used to combine the partial convolutions. At the conclusion of the second phase, each image copy contains the complete convolution.

Finally, consider the table look-up operation, in which each pixel uses its grey level as an index into a table of length 2^r-1 to compute the value of an arbitrary function. Table look-up procedures are used to approximate complicated arithmetic operations (such as square roots and trigonometric functions used in gradient operations) and for display purposes. The table lookup algorithm is very similar to the histogramming algorithm. During the first phase, each image copy will compute the table look-up for a segment of the table. Recalling that $s = 2^r/4^l$, copy i will compute the table look-up for grey levels in the range [(i-1)s, is-1]. At the j'th step of phase 1 all processors having grey levels of the form [(i-1)s + j-1] will select themselves, and a segmented scan operation is used to copy the appropriate output value from the table to those selected processors. Finally, during phase 2 a copy/merge algorithm is used to combine the local results from each processor.

Notice that if sufficient local storage is available, then each processor can be given a complete copy of the table and in a single step each processor could read the appropriate entry from the table and compute its output value. We assume, however, that it is not generally practical to store copies of the table at each processor. Instead, one copy of the table is stored in a distributed fashion in each image copy, with the n'th entry of the table being stored in location $g_i g_n$, where g_n is the Gray Code of n. During each stage of phase 1, the appropriate processor in each copy activates itself to transmit the table output value to the selected processors.

5. Experimental results. We have implemented the histogramming, table look-up, and convolution algorithms for the replicated pyramid architecture. A single level of the replicated pyramid was implemented on the Connection Machine by configuring it as an **n X m X m** array of processors, where **n** is the number of copies of the **m X m** image. Communicationis efficient this way, since the Connection Machine automatically assigns subhypercubes to each copy of the image. Communication within each copy remains local and is independent of the communication within other copies. Also, the logarithmic merging step, typical of the second phase of all three algorithms, is very fast, because corresponding elements of different copies of the image are adjacent in the Connection Machine hypercube. A copy of the histogram of the image (in the case of the histogramming alogrithm) or the entire table (in the case of the table look-up algorithm) was stored in each copy of the image.

Histogramming and table look-up distribute the problem among the 4^l

copies available in such a way that each copy handles an equal number of grey-level values of the entire image. The implementation of these two algorithms are very similar so that we discuss below only the histogtramming algorithm.

The histogramming algorithms takes advantage of the Connection Machine II feature that if each processor sends a message to the processor that counts its grey-level value, then there will be as many collisions at each counting processor as the number of pixels with its specific grey-level value. Using the collision resolution strategy of counting all the colliding values, the histogram for the entire image can be computed in a single step. Thus, the histogramming algorithm implemented on a single level of a replicated pyramid cannot outperform a single copy histogram algorithm on the Connection Machine.

The convolution algorithm yields more interesting results on replicated pyramids. To compute a k X k convolution, k^2 copies of the image are required . (On the Connection Machine, the next power of 2 has to be chosen as the actual number of copies allocated , although only k^2 of them are used.) Each copy handles one of the kernel weights. In the first phase, each processor multiplies this kernel weight with its own grey level value and sends the product to the appropriate processor in the same copy. In the second phase, these products are summed to obtain the final result of the convolution at every processor of every copy.

Table 1 compares the time taken by the convolution algorithm implemented on the CM using a single copy against the replicated algorithm using k^2 copies. Each entry in the table contains two values. The first is the total time taken to perform the operation as measured on the host of the Connection Machine. This time includes the time taken to interpret the *LISP code on the host Lisp machine (which could have been absolutely speeded up if the *LISP compiler had been used). The second value is the time taken by the Connection Machine to perform the computation. Ideally, these two values should be very close (indicating high utilization of the more expensive Connection Machine), but practically there will always be some overhead for the host to interpret and transmit instructions to the Connection Machine.

The table indicates that the utilization of the Connection Machine is much higher for the replicated algorithm than for the single copy algorithm. This can be explained as follows. If there are a sufficient number of physical processors to store all k^2 image copies, then the replicated algorithm performs one multiplication step (in which all k^2 kernel multiplications are performed in parallel) and 2log k addition steps to compute the multi-copy convolution. In contrast , the single copy convolution algorithm has to perform k^2 steps of multiplications and additions, all under direction of the host computer. Thus, the host overhead is much higher for the single copy algorithm than for the replicated algorithm.

Kernel size	Single copy algorithm (total time, time on CM)	Multi-copy algorithm (total time, time on CM)
3 X 3	0.85, 0.07	0.36, 0.20
5 X 5	1.80, 0.21	0.54, 0.42
7 X 7	3.70, 0.45	0.98, 0.90
11 X 11	9.73, 1.28	2.06, 2.00

64 X 64 image using 8K processors on the CM.

Kernel size	Single copy algorithm (total time, time on CM)	Multi-copy algorithm (total time, time on CM)
3 X 3	0.92, 0.08	0.28, 0.09
5 X 5	1.94, 0.21	0.36, 0.22
7 X 7	3.66, 0.45	0.60, 0.52
9 X 9	6.11, 0.83	1.16, 1.12
11 X 11	10.64, 1.31	1.16, 1.12

64 X 64 image using 16K processors on the CM.

Table 1 - Results of convolution algorithms

6. Conclusion.   We have described two different methods for processing small images using large hypercube connected SIMD multiprocessors. The first method involves distributing the bits representing an individual operand across a set of processors, themselves connected in a hypercube and representing a single cell in an image.   The second method stores multiple copies of the image and attempts to decompose basic image analysis operations into pieces that can be performed in parallel on a SIMD machine.

There are many other basic image analysis algorithms to which the methods described in the paper can be applied in a straightforward way. For example, grey scale morphological operations (see, e.g., Haralick[12]) are implemented in much the same way as grey scale convolution; various types of image statistics useful for image texture analysis, such as coocurrence matrices or difference histograms, can be computed very quickly also.

Acknowledgements: We would like to thank Daniel Dementhon and Thor Bestul for comments and suggestions. The research was supported in part by funds from the Defense Advanced Research Projects Agency and the U. S. Army Engineer Topographic Laboratories under Contract DACA-76-88-C-0008.

References

1. K. E. Batcher, Design of a massively parallel processor, IEEE Transactions on Computers,31,377-384, 1982.

2. M. Duff, Parallel processors for digital image processing, in Advances in Digital Image Processing, (P. Stucki, ed.) Plenum Press, NY, 265-276, 1979.

3. D. Hillis, The Connection Machine, M.I.T. Press, Boston, 1983.

4. A. Rosenfeld, ed. Multiresolution Image Processing and Analysis, Springer, Berlin, 1984.

5.   Steve Tanimoto, Algorithms for median filtering of images on a pyramid machine, in Computing Structures for Image Processing, (edited by M. J. B. Duff), Academic Press, London, 1983, 123-142.

6. U. Sharma and L. Davis, Road boundary detection in range imagery for an autonomous robot, IEEE Trans. on Robotics and Automation, 4, 515-523, 1988.

7. A. Waxman, L. Davis, et al., A visual navigation system for autonomous land vehicles, IEEE Trans. On Robotics and Automation, 3, 124-141, 1987.

8. T. Kushner, A. Wu and A. Rosenfeld, Image processing on MPP, Pattern Recognition, 15, 121-130, 1982.

9. Thor Bestul and Larry Davis, On computing histograms of images in logn time using fat pyramids, University of Maryland Center for Automation Technical Report 271, February 1987 (a shortened version to appear in IEEE Trans. on Pattern Analysis and Machine Intelligence.)

10.T. G. Chan and Y. Saad, Multigrid algorithms on the hypercube multiprocessor, IEEE Trans. on Computers,35, 969-977, 1986.

11. Sotirios Ziavras and Larry Davis, Fast addition on the fat pyramid and its simulation on the Connection Machine, University of Maryland Center for Automation Technical Report 383, August 1988.

12. Robert Haralick, S. Sternberg, and X. Zhuang, Image ana;ysis using mathematical morphology, IEEE Transactions on Pattern Analysis and Machine Intelligence, 9, 1987, 532-550.

A HEURISTIC FOR CHANNEL ROUTING*

E. Lodi

Dipartimento di Informatica e Applicazioni, Università di Salerno

F.P.Preparata

Coordinated Science Laboratory, University of Illinois, Urbana

Abstract

In designing the layout of VLSI chips, channel routing plays a central role. A frequently used channel routing mode is known as Manhattan routing, where a two-layer channel is used to route a specified set of nets between two rows of terminals. If the net list contains long runs, the only way to reduce the number of channel tracks is by splitting horizontal segments of nets (jogging).

A new algorithm is proposed which uses a preprocessing to decide, before producing the routing, which nets must be split and where. Jogging a net effectively splits a run into two runs with approximately the same total length. The objective is achieved by finding a parameter m which represents the maximum desirable length for a run and minimizing the number of runs with length greater than m. This minimization is obtained by finding a minimum-cost matching in a weighted bipartite graph $G_m = (V, E)$. Node set V is partitioned in two sets: J and R, where J is a set of jogging requests associated to nets chosen as possible candidates for joggings while nodes in R are associated to channel columns. A heuristic is proposed to assign priorities to vertices of J and costs to vertices of R. The running time of the algorithm is $O(t \cdot n \cdot log n) + O(n\sqrt{n})$, where n is the number of nets and t is the number of tracks used. Quite satisfactory experimental results are also reported.

---

* This work has been supported in part by Ministero della Pubblica Istruzione of Italy and by the Semiconductor Research Corporation under Contract 87-DP109.

1.Introduction

Several different layout modes have been used in the study of channel routing. The traditional mode known as Manhattan routing assumes a two-layer grid, in which metal wires run on the top grid and poly wires on the bottom one. One layer is used only for vertical segments, the other for horizontal segments; a contact cut (via) is introduced for each layer change of a wire. Szymansky[1] showed that Manhattan routing is NP-hard.

Introduced in the early seventies [2], channel routing has been the subject of several heuristics in recent years [3,4,5,6,7,8,9,10,11,12,16]. In fact, channel routing is a key problem in the development of automated layout systems for integrated circuits. Moreover, the whole interconnecting phase can be viewed as a collection of channel routing problems. After dividing the entire layout region into nonoverlapping rectangular "channels", a global router determines which nets pass through each channel; subsequently a local channel router computes the detailed routing within each channel.

To address more precisely the problem, we can define a channel as follows. The *uniform grid* of the plane is the set of the lines $\{ x = i \mid i \in Z \}$ and $\{ y = j \mid j \in Z \}$. A t-track *channel* is a horizontal strip of the uniform grid delimited by the lines $y = 0$ and $y = t +1$ (*shores*), for integer t; lines $y = 1,2,...,t$ are the *tracks* of the channel. The number t is called the *capacity* of the channel. A grid point on either shore is called a *terminal*. The grid segment $x = c$, $0 \leq y \leq t +1$, is a *column* of the channel. A terminal in the lower shore is called a *lower* terminal,; similarly, for an *upper* terminal.

Definition 1. A (multiterminal) *net* is a pair of (not simultaneously empty) sequences of terminals on the shores $y = 0$ and $y = t +1$, respectively. For example, $N = ((p_1, \ldots , p_k)$, $(q_1, \ldots , q_h))$ with $p_1 < \ldots < p_k$, $q_1 < \ldots < q_h$. Such net is represented by a horizontal *spoked segment* from $\min(p_1 , q_1)$ to $\max(p_k , q_h)$, with a down-directed spoke for each p_i and an up-directed spoke for each q_j. (see Fig. 1 for an example).

A two-terminal net is denoted by a pair (p,q).

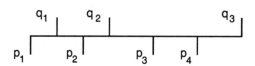

Fig. 1. Illustration of a multiterminal net as a spoked segment.

Definition 2. A channel routing problem (CRP) $\eta = \{N_1, \ldots , N_n\}$ is a collection of nets no two of which share a terminal (see Fig. 2 for un example).

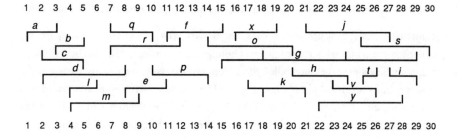

Fig. 2. A channel routing problem.

Definition 3. A *layout* of a CRP $\eta = \{N_1, \dots, N_n\}$ is a collection of connected subgraphs $\{w_1, \dots, w_n\}$ of the channel, such that w_i has a vertex at each terminal of net N_i.

Obviously only subgraphs in the form of trees need to be considered for the realization of $\{w_1, \dots, w_n\}$. A solution to a channel routing problem is an integer t, specifying the capacity of the channel and a set of subgraphs (wires) satisfying the restriction that two distinct wires can meet at a grid point only if it is a crossover point (see Fig. 3). The major objective of the problem is to minimize the number of tracks used to realize the routing. In addition to the capacity of the channel, a solution should also aim at minimizing other features, such as the number of additional columns, the maximum wire length, the number of vías, and the total wire length.

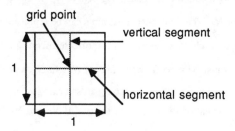

Fig. 3. A unit square with a crossover point

An important parameter of a channel routing problem is its *density d*, defined as the maximum, over all x, of the number of nets N_i crossing x, i. e. the nets for which at least one terminal is to the left of x and at least one terminal is to the right of x (in Fig. 2. d=6). Obviously the density is a lower bound on the minimum achievable capacity. It has been shown that a slightly different layout mode (the knock-knee mode, where two distinct wires can share a grid point where they both bend) allows one to solve a two-terminal net routing problem within a factor of two of channel density with two layers [13] and to achieve density with three layers [14]. Unfortunately, for the Manhattan mode, the density alone does not give, in general, a meaningful measure of the

routing requirements. In [15] it has been shown that at least $\sqrt{2n}$ tracks are necessary for any

problem which has n non trivial nets spanning $n+1$ contiguous columns. In [16] this behavior was

explained, introducing a new measure called *flux* . Roughly speaking, the density measures the

number of nets split by a vertical cut of the channel, while the flux measures the number of nets

split by a horizontal cut of the channel. More precisely, a routing problem has flux f if f is the

largest integer for which there exists a horizontal cut of the channel spanning $2f^2$ columns and

splitting at least $2f^2 -f$ nontrivial nets (in Fig. 2. $f = 3$). In [16] an algorithm is also given that

produces a Manhattan routing with $2d+O(f)$ tracks for every multiterminal net problem with

density d and flux f . The major feature of this algorithm consists of supplying a routing with

width at most a constant times the optimal value for all problems, although its behavior is not as

good as other heuristics for most practical problems.

2.Preliminaries

The adopted layout mode is such that the wires of any two nets N_i and N_j cannot overlap in

a column. If a column has an upper terminal of N_i and a lower terminal of N_j and if each net is

allowed just one horizontal segment, the horizontal segment of N_i must be necessarily placed in a

track above the one used for N_j. These vertical constraints can be represented by a directed graph

G_v , where each node corresponds to a net and an arc directed from N_i to N_j means that the

horizontal segment of N_i must be placed above that of N_j. In G_v a *root* is a node with no

incoming arcs, where a *leaf* is a node with no outgoing arcs; a *run* is a path from a root to a leaf

and the number of its nodes is called the *length* of the run. If N_i and N_j are two nets of a run,

$d(N_i , N_j)$ is called their *distance* and is equal to the number of arcs in the directed path between

N_i and N_j . For the problem of Fig. 2, the vertical constraint graph is shown in Fig. 4(a) where

there are six connected components corresponding to six runs r_1 (from a to k), r_2 (from a to r), r_3,

r_4, r_5 and r_6 whose lenths are 10, 12, 2, 1, 1 and 3 respectively.

We define *jogging* , or *doglegging* , the operation of splitting the horizontal segment of a net in

two or more subsegments and of connecting two consecutive subsegments by means of a vertical

segment. It is clear that without jogging some nets, the length of the longest run is a lower bound

to the capacity of the channel; in addition, jogging is necessary to handle cycles (see Fig. 5).

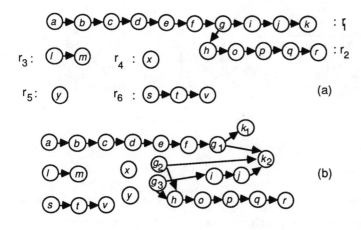

Fig. 4. Two vertical constraint graphs.

In Fig. 5 we show a jogging using an empty column; however, splitting of a horizontal segment adds a new node to G_v and changes the vertical constraints, resulting in a restructuring of G_v as we shall now discuss. A net $N = ((p_1, \dots, p_k), (q_1, \dots, q_h))$ is represented with $k+h$ -1 nodes (the number of its terminal minus one) as we split the horizontal segment of N at any of its terminals. We sort in increasing order the terminals of N and we associate one node in G_v to each horizontal segment of N contained between two consecutive terminals. Among these nodes there are no arcs. An arc from v_1 to v_2 still means that v_1 and v_2 share the same column, one for a lower terminal and the other for an upper terminal (see Fig. 6 for an illustration).

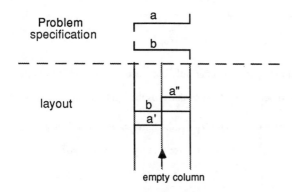

Fig. 5. A jogging used to solve a cycle

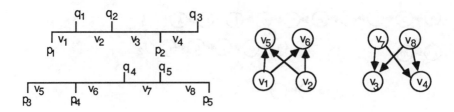

Fig. 6. An example of the vertical constraints for a general channel routing problem.

Fig. 7 shows the rearrangement of a run r_1 whose net N_i is split at an empty column; in Fig.7(a) we show the layout features and in Fig. 7(b) we show the modification of the portion of G_v pertaining to the run in question.

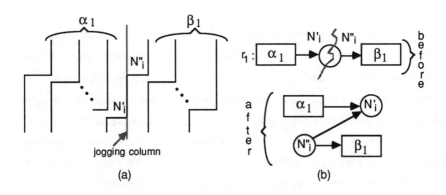

(a)   (b)

Fig. 7. Jogging at an empty column: run r_1 is effectively
split into two shorter runs $\alpha_1 N_i'$ and $N_i'' \beta_1$

Fig.8 shows the rearrangement of a run r_1 split at a partially occupied column, which has the upper terminal of a net e belonging to another run r_2. (Notice that e is the rightmost net of run r_2.) The net effect is that r_1 is split into two runs $\alpha_1 N_1'$ and $N_1'' \beta_1$, the latter of which is then spliced with r_2, of which it becomes the termination. We say in this case that r_1 and r_2 are *mated* at the jogging column.

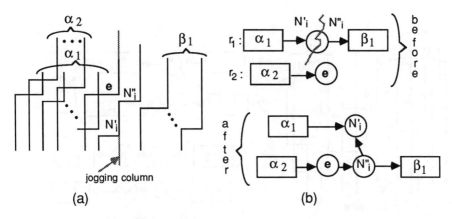

Fig. 8. Jogging at a partially occupied column (upper terminal) :
run r_1 is split into two runs, one of which is then spliced
(*mated*) with run r_2

The case in which the jogging column is also partially occupied, but has the lower terminal of a net h of a run r_2, is illustrated in Fig. 9 and deserves no additional comment.

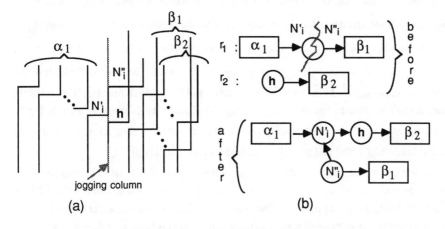

Fig. 9. Jogging at a partially occupied column (lower terminal): run r_1
is split into two runs, one of which is then spliced with run r_2

Finally we consider the most general case where net N_i of run r_1 is jogged at a fully occupied column; this column necessarily contains the upper and lower terminals, respectively, of two consecutive nets of a run r_2. The net result of the jogging is that the two runs are both split and cross-spliced (i.e. the initial segments of one with the final segments of the other, and viceversa). The situation is illustrated in Fig. 10.

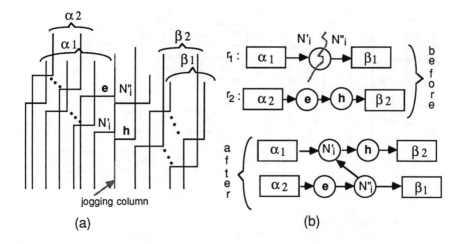

Fig. 10. Jogging at a fully occupied column. Both runs are space split,
and the resulting segments are cross-spliced.

As we mentioned earlier, to route a problem with a cycle r_1 , we must break it by choosing a net inside the cycle and a channel column h where it is convenient to make a jogging. Let $|r_1|$ be the length of r_1. If the jogging is done at an empty column, the resulting run will have length $|r_1|+1$ while in all the other cases (i.e. when column h is either partially or fully occupied by a run r_2), the resulting run length will be $|r_1|+|r_2|+1$. Therefore the choice must be done on the basis of the length of the resulting run. Moreover, since the splitting of a cycle is mandatory to route the problem, it must be done before executing the algorithm presented in the next section. Fig.11 illustrates the rearrangement of a cycle r_1 split at an empty column (Fig. 11(a)), at a partially occupied column (Fig. 11(b)) and at a fully occupied column (Fig. 11(c)).

As an additional example, Fig. 4(b) shows how the graph of Fig.4a must be changed if the nets $g = ((15)$, $(8,24,29))$ and $k = ((18,21)$, $(17))$ of Fig. 2 are split at columns 18 and 24 as previously outlined. Obviously nets of different runs can be put on the same track if they do not overlap horizontally. As mentioned earlier, to route a given net problem with density d and flux f the minimum channel width is at least $\max(d ,c \cdot f)$, for some constant c, but it is not entirely clear how these two measures interact. Clearly the density is an achievable bound on the number of tracks in problems consisting of runs of length one. On the other hand, consider the simple channel routing problem whose n nets represent each a shift to the right by one position. In this case, d is equal to one and f is equal to $\sqrt{n}$: the flux represents quite well the problem difficulty [15]. The algorithm proposed in [16] distributes empty columns uniformly across the channel, thereby dividing the channel columns into blocks of size f , each containing three empty columns. Therefore it makes use of a number of joggings proportional to f. Intuition suggests that this approach is successful when the flux can be related to the average length of runs, that is, the f empty columns will represent the columns of the roots and of the leaves of f runs each of which has length $2f-1$. Following this idea, a new heuristic is proposed that uses a parameter m to classify the runs into three sets I_r, S_r and L_r. The nets belonging to runs of I_r and S_r will not be split, while several nets belonging to runs of L_r will be split either at an empty column or at a column occupied by terminals of nets belonging to runs in S_r.

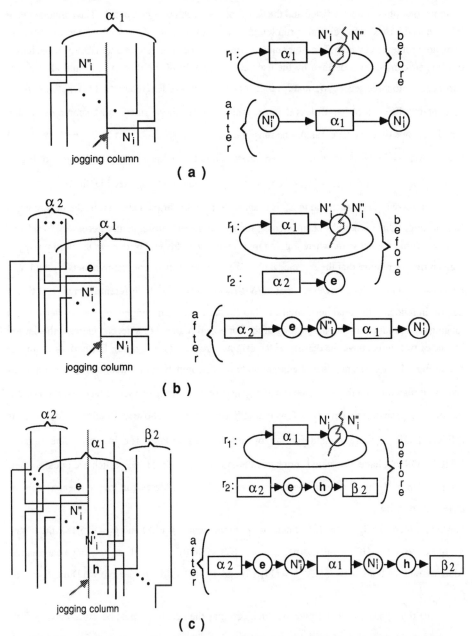

Fig. 11. Jogging of a cycle r_1 at an empty column (a), at a partially occupied column (b) and at a fully occupied column (c).

3. Description of the Algorithm

The algorithm consists of four phases; the first three phases are preparatory for the routing that takes place in the fourth phase.

In the first phase runs are listed and the flux f of the problem is computed . The parameter m is selected as the maximum desirable run length. Normally m is set equal to $2f$; however, because there are problems in which flux either understimates or overstimates the attainable average length of runs, m can be also defined by the user, independently of the flux. As a result, all runs are partitioned into three sets L_r, S_r and I_r. L_r contains the runs of length greater than m (long runs), S_r contains the runs of length less than or equal to $m/2$ (short runs) and I_r contains all the remaining runs (intermediate runs). The runs in L_r and in S_r are processed in the second and third phase respectively, while the runs in I_r are processed in the last phase. For the problem of Fig. 2, choosing $m = 4$, we have $L_r = \{r_1, r_2\}$, $S_r = \{r_3, r_4, r_5\}$ and $I_r = \{r_6\}$ (see Fig. 4(a)).

In the second phase each run in L_r is scanned to find the target nets, that is, the nets selected for splitting. (Once a net has been selected for splitting, it is subsequently necessary to select a column, within the net span, where jogging must take place; this will be done in the third phase.) In a given run we require that the distance $d\,(N_i\,,N_j\,)$ between two consecutive nets N_i and N_j be equal to $m{-}1$. Note, however, that $d\,(N_i,N_j)$ may be slightly different from $m{-}1$, if this is helpful in reducing the total horizontal overlap among target nets and the increase of density that joggings can produce. In fact the jogging of the horizontal segment of a net can increase the density by one or two units above the density of the original problem (see Fig. 12). Furthermore, suppose that in Fig. 12 N_1 corresponds to the target node in G ; comparing the situations illustrated in (a) and (b), it may turn out that the selection of N_2 as target net may be more advantageous. For this reason, for each target net N_i a few nets adjacent to N_i , whose collection is denoted as NEIGHBOR(N_i) are considered as of possible candidates for jogging. The nets in NEIGHBOR(N_i) have associated priorities (as indices of *desirability*) which are equal to their distance from N_i in G . Let T be the set of possible candidates for jogging, each with an associated priority.

For the problem of Fig. 2, the target nets of r_1 are the nets $d = (2,8)$ and $g_1 = (15,18)$; the target net of r_2 is $p = (14,10)$ (see Fig. 4(b)). All the NEIGHBOR() sets of these nets have cardinality equal to one and are $c = (5, 2)$, $f = (11, 15)$ and $o = (20, 14)$ respectively. Thus, $T = \{c, d, f, p, g_1, o\}$.

In the third phase, we determine at which columns the nets in T must be split; consequently runs in L_r are split and possibly mated (as illustrated in Figs.7-10) with runs in S_r . (Note that this heuristic mates long and short runs, thereby reducing the maximum length.)

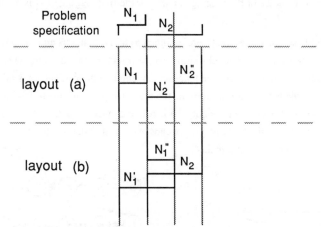

Fig. 12. Two different kinds of joggings.

We now show that this problem can be transformed into a min-cost matching problem in a suitably defined weighted bipartite graph $G_m = (V', E')$. The node set V' of G_m is partitioned into two sets: J and R. Node set J is a collection of jogging requests; that is the cardinality of J equals the number of target nets obtained in the previous phase of the techniques; specifically, each node in J is associated with a target net N_i and with the set of nets in NEIGHBOR(N_i) chosen as possible candidates for jogging. Node set R is a set of columns, which represent resources to be utilized to satisfy the jogging requests; specifically each node in R is associated either with an empty column or with the set of terminals of a run in S_r. The nodes in R are weighted: empty-column nodes have zero weight, while a node corresponding to a run in S_r has a weight equal to the run length. All edges in E' have a cost and a label; for $v_1 \in J$ and $v_2 \in R$, there is an edge $(v_1, v_2) \in E'$ if there is at least one net associated with v_1 which is intersected by at least one of the columns associated with v_2; if there is more than one net intersected, we select N as the one which minimizes the cost (i.e. N has minimum priority). In fact the cost of (v_1, v_2) is obtained by summing up the priority of N and the weight of v_2; the label is set to N.

It is clear that a matching of order j identifies j joggings. The min-cost criterion, and the selection of edge costs is the heuristic that matches joggings and columns.

After finding the minimum cost matching, runs in L_r and in S_r are properly rearranged as outlined in the previous section. Fig. 13(a) gives G_m for the example of Fig. 2. Bold edges indicate the solution found by the algorithm. Fig. 13(b) shows the resulting G_v ; where the initial part of r_1 is mated with r_3 at column 6, the final part of r_1 is mated with r_4 at column 16 and r_2 is split at the empty column 13. The choice of the jogging column for the first jogging of r_1 is made on the basis of the density.

In the fourth phase horizontal tracks are assigned to individual nets and the proper routing is determined for all the nets. The channel routing can be found by an algorithm where run nets are merged so as to minimize the length of the longest path length in the vertical constraint graph. This algorithm constructs the layout starting from the top track and performs the following actions: (i) it lists the runs in order of decreasing lenght; (ii) it fills the current track with the first net of the longest runs (in case of ties, the longest nets are chosen); (iii) it updates the runs and their lengths. This process continues until no net remains.

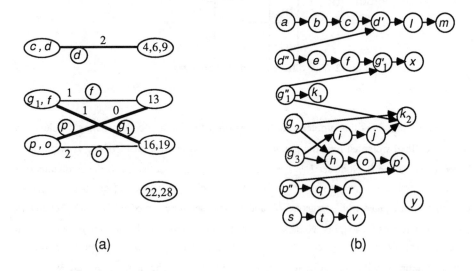

(a)   (b)

Fig.13 (a) The minimum cost matching found by the proposed algorithm for the problem of Fig. 2; (b) the resulting G_v .

4. Analysis of performance

To analize the performance of the algorithm, we shall evaluate the running time of each phase separately. Suppose that a channel has c columns, n nets and flux f. Furthermore, note that the size of T (the set of target nets) cannot be greater than $O(\sqrt{n})$.

In the first phase, the listing of the nets runs in time $O(c)$ and the computation of f runs in time $O(c \cdot f)$ [see 16]. In the second phase, selection of the target nets is accomplished in time $O(n)$;

similarly, the minimization of the horizontal overlap between target nets is done in time $O(n)$; because this task can be accomplished in time quadratic in the size of T (which is $O(\sqrt{n})$). In the third phase, finding the minimum cost matching is accomplished in time $O(n\sqrt{n})$ because the selected algorithm [17,18,19] has running time which is cubic in the size of T. Finally, rearrangement of runs is completed in time $O(n)$.

The running time of the fourth phase is $O(t \cdot n \cdot logn)$, since t tracks must be processed and steps (i), (ii) and (iii) outlined above collectively take $O(n \cdot logn)$ time.

Summing up, we conclude that the running time of the algorithm is $O(n \sqrt{n}) + O(t \cdot n \cdot logn)$.

We must point out, however, the following shortcomings of the current implementation of the algorithm:

- the only kind of jogging allowed is the one shown in Fig. 12 (a);

- set R consists only of columns inside the channel.

It is clear that the quality of the solution given by the algorithm depends on the choice of the parameter m and on how well resources in R can satisfy the jogging requests of target nets. Experimental results, reported in table 1, show routings with capacity t, $d \leq t \leq d+f$. Table 1 lists the caracteristics of eighteen examples and the resulting capacity obtained by the algorithm. Table 1 is subdivided in three sections. Let max denote the length of the longest run and let c be the number of channel columns. The first section has $max<d$, the second section has $max \sim d$ and the third section has $max>d$. Column 1 is the density, column 2 is the value of max, column 3 is the flux, column 4 is the ratio of the columns to the terminals and colum 5 is the capacity obtained by our algorithm. Fig.14 shows the channel routing obtained for the problem of Fig.2: it has optimal capacity and it makes three joggings.

d	max	f	c/n	t
24	5	4	1.2	26
26	6	4	2	27
13	8	2	2.1	15
10	4	2	2	11
18	13	4	1.5	20
28	6	5	1.2	30

First Section
max<d

d	max	f	c/n	t
8	8	2	1.4	8
7	8	2	2.4	8
8	10	2	2.4	10
8	11	2	1.8	9
6	8	2	2	7
6	7	2	1.7	7

Second Section
max~d

d	max	f	c/n	t
8	15	3	2.7	10
7	12	2	1.5	9
2	8	2	2.7	8
6	15	3	2	7
7	11	3	1.7	7
5	18	3	1.1	7

Third Section
max>d

Table 1. Features and resulting capacities of test examples.

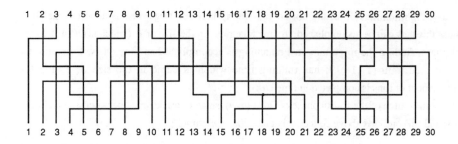

Fig.14. An optimal routing obtained by the proposed algorithm for the channel problem of Fig. 2.

References

[1]   Szymanski T.,"Dogleg Channel Routing is NP-complete", *IEEE Trans. on CAD,* CAD-4 (1985), 31-40.

[2]   Hashimoto, A. and J. Stevens, "Wire Routing by Optimizing Channel Assignment within Large Apertures", *Proc. 8-th Design Automation Workshop, IEEE* (1971), 214-224.

[3]   Kernighan, B., D. Schweikert, and G. Persky, "An Optimal Channel-Routing Algorithm for Polycell Layouts of Integrated Circuits", *Proc. 10-th Design Automation Workshop, IEEE* (1973), 50-59.

[4]   Hightower, D., "The Interconnection Problem: A Tutorial", *Computer* 7, 4 (April 1974), 18-32.

[5]   Asano, T., T. Kitchashi, and K. Tanaka, "On a Method of Realizing Minimum-Width Wiring", *Electronics and Communications in Japan,* J59-A, 2 (1976), 29-39.

[6]   Deutsch, D. N., "A 'Dogleg' Channel Router", *Proc. 19-th Design Automation Conference, IEEE* (1976), 425-433.

[7]   Persky, G., D. Deutsch, and D. Schweikert, "LTX - A Minicomputer-Based System for Automated LSI Layout", *Journal of Design Automation and Fault-Tolerant Computing* 1, 3 (May 1977), 217-255.

[8]   Kawamoto, T. and Y. Kajitani, "The Minimum Width Routing of a 2-Row 2-Layer Polycell-Layout", *Proc. 16-th Design Automation Conference, IEEE* (1979), 290-296.

[9]   Alford, S., "DYCHAR: A Channel Router which uses dynamic channel assignment", *MIT Bachelor's thesis* (May 1980).

[10] Yoshimura, T. and E. Kuh, "Efficient Algorithms for Channel Routing", *IEEE Trans. on CAD*, CAD-1, 1 (January 1982), 25-35.

[11] Rivest, R. L. and C. M. Fiduccia, "A 'Greedy' Channel Router", *Proc. 19-th IEEE Design Automation Conference,* (1982), 418-424.

[12] Burstein, M. and R. Pelavin, "Hierarchical Channel Router", *IEEE Trans. on CAD*, CAD-2, 4 (October 1983), 223-234.

[13] Rivest, R. L., A. E. Baratz and G. Miller, "Provably Good Channel Routing Algorithms", Proc. CMU Conference on VLSI Systems and Computations, (1981), 153-159.

[14] Preparata, F. P. and W. Lipski, "Optimal Three-Layer Channel Routing", *IEEE Trans. on CAD*, 33, 5 (May 1984), 427-437.

[15] Brown, D. and R. L. Rivest, "New Lower Bounds on Channel Width", *Proc. CMU Conference on VLSI Systems and Computations* (Computer Science Press 1981), 178-185.

[16] Baker, B. S., S. N. Bhatt and T. Leighton, "An Approximation Algorithm for Manhattan Routing", *Advances in Computing Research,* 2 (1984), 205-229.

[17] Carraresi,P. and C.Sodini, "An efficient algorithm for the bipartite matching problem", *EJOR,* 23 (1986),86-93.

[18] Edmonds, j. and R. Karp. "Theoretical Improvements in Algorithmic Efficiency for Network Flow Problems", *Journal of ACM,* 19 (1972), 248-264.

[19] Fredman, M. and R. Tarjan, "Fibonacci Heaps and their uses in Improved Network Optimization Algorithms", *Journal of ACM,* 34 (1987), 596-615.

BASIC DATA STRUCTURES

A LANGUAGE FOR THE P-ARY TREES.

application to the dynamic virtual hashing methods

Gerard LEVY

Université de Paris 9-Dauphine

Place du Maréchal de Lattre de Tassigny, 75775 Paris Cedex 16, France.

ABSTRACT

Dynamic (virtual) hashing methods (DVH) manage very large files by the means of an index which is, at least partially, stored in the core. Usually this index is a binary tree (b-t), and different implementations of DVH are based on the representations of the b-t using pointers or links to descendants or leaves. We show that it is also possible to represent a p-ary tree (p-t), and thus a b-t, with a word of a certain language, and to use this pointerless representation to perform all the operations needed by a DVH generalized to p-t's. We present this language, we study its operative properties, and we indicate how to perform the operations of search, insertion,...We compare our representation to the most usual ones, and we analyze the complexity of some algorithms in relation with this representation.

Key words : p-ary trees, representation of trees by words, languages, hashing methods, complexity of algorithms.

0. INTRODUCTION

Dynamic (virtual) hashing methods (DVH),first proposed by LARSON [1],LITWIN [2] , and FAGIN [3] , allow to manage very large files, through an index which is stored, at least partially, in the core of the computer. Usually this index is modelized by a binary tree (b-t), and the different representations of DVH are based on representations which use pointers or links to descendants or sons.

The caracteristics of DVH have been extensively studied, [4],[5],[6], and are presently well known. Essentially, for not too large files the index can be stored in the core, and one can reach any record by one disk access. For larger files, the index cannot be completely stored in the core. [3], and its extensions like MLTH

[7], [8], overcome this difficulty by splitting the index into pages which are stored in the external memory. With MLTH, for instance, one can reach any record with no more than two disk accesses, and range queries are allowed.

Recently, we have proposed, as an other extension of DVH, a method, called p-DVH, which uses for the indexes p-ary trees instead of binary trees [9]. The parameters and the performances of p-DVH have been analyzed and compared to those of DVH in [9]. As for DVH, the first implementations of p-DVH were based on the standard representations of trees by the means of links or pointers. On the other hand, during last years, many papers have been devoted to trees, essentially to their representations, their languages [10], their generating processes, [11] to [19], and the analysis of their parameters [6]. In some trends of this litterature trees are represented through words of different languages.

Following these trends, the main idea of our work is to show that it is possible to represent p-ary trees implied by p-DVH methods by the means of words of a certain language. We show that this representation is particularly efficient for our purpose, which is to perform all the operations involved in p-DVH methods. Our paper is organized as follows: - Section 1 defines our language for the p-ary trees; - Section 2 shows how to implement p-DVH methods with this language; - Section 3 gives results relative to p-DVH methods intrinsic performance; - Section 4 analyzes the complexity of some algorithms in relation with the words representation; - Section 5 compares our representation with the classical ones; - Section 6 concludes the paper.

1. A LANGUAGE FOR THE p-ARY TREES

Though there are many different ways to represent trees with words, a lot of them are not fitted to our purpose, since they have essentially been designed for generating and enumerating trees, [11] to [19], or managing algebraic expressions [10]. We shall propose here a representation of p-trees with words, which fits quite "naturally" our subject, and its related language which may be seen as a generalization of the well known language of "parentheses". We shall first give some definitions and properties of the p-ary trees, and then introduce our language.

1.1 The p-ary trees

Let p be a fixed integer, $p > 1$, and L a set with p elements. Without loss of generality, we take $L = \{0,1,...,p-1\} = [0..p-1]$. A *p-ary tree*, or *p-t*, $A = (S,G)$, is constituted of a non empty set S of nodes, and of a mapping $G : S \to S^p \cup \{\emptyset\}$, which associates to each internal node s the sequence $G(s) = (s_0,s_1,...,s_{p-1})$ of its *children*, and to each external node, or leaf, s, $G(s) = \emptyset$. Thus, a p-ary tree is a planar tree, since the children of each node cannot be exchanged.(Nevertheless, we will use here the same notation G(s) for the sequence of children and for their set {$s_0, s_1,...,s_{p-1}$}).We can give a graphical representation of such a tree. As at Fig 1.1 and 1.2, we draw a point for each node s, and connect s to its children by the means of lines to represent edges ; we do it in such manner that $s_0, s_1,...,s_{p-1}$ are under s and from left to right in this order .

For each node s , different from the root . there is an unique node s' such that s $\in$ G(s') ; we call s' the *father* of s, and we write s'= father(s)= $G^{-1}(s)$. The root r has no father ; we write father(r) = λ , assuming that $\lambda \notin S$.

More generally, we can define the different *links* of a p-ary tree as follows. We distinguish the links : father, son, brother, $f_0, f_1,..,f_{p-1}$.

(son(s) means "first son of s", and $f_i(s)$ is set for the i-th son of s, i$\in$L). Let us call $\underline{S} = S \cup \{\lambda\}$; each of the links is a mapping from S to $\underline{S}$ such that if G(s) = ($s_0,...,s_{p-1}$), we have

a) son(s) = s_0 ; b) brother(s_i) = s_{i+1}, for i<p-1, and brother(s_{p-1})= λ :

c) $f_i(s)$ = s_i, for i= 0,...,p-1; d) father(s_i) = s , for i= 0,...,p-1 , and father(root) = λ .

For each internal node s and each $s_i \in$ G(s) , the ordered pair (s,s_i) is an *edge* , and we attach to it the *label* g(s,s_i) = i $\in$ L. The *heigth* h(s) of a node s is equal to the number of edges of *path(s)* which is the unique path from the root to s .

We can give a *recursive definition* of the p-ary trees, which is equivalent to the first one, and which will be very useful . Let us call $\mathbb{T}$ *the set of all the p-ary trees, and* $\square$ *the tree which has only one node.* Then for any tree T of $\mathbb{T}$ we have:

a) either T =$\square$:

b) or T = <r,T_0,T_1,...,T_{p-1}> ,where r is the root ,and the different T_i belong to $\mathbb{T}$.

The equivalence results from the fact that if G(r) = ($r_0,...,r_{p-1}$), then each r_i is the root of the corresponding subtree T_i of T.

An obvious example of a p-ary tree is Q= <r,$\square$,$\square$,...,$\square$> .Q is the smallest p-t different from $\square$, and we call it the *basic p-ary tree*.

1.2 The language

Let L* be the free monoid generated by the alphabet L, completed by the sequence e of length 0 . The operation of concatenation associates to two words w, w' of L* the word w.w' of L* . For each w of L*, l(w) will denote its length, and for each element k of L, $n_k(w)$ will denote the number of occurences of k in w .

Now. let us *associate to each p-ary tree T its word* $\phi(T)$. by the means of the mapping ϕ: $\mathbb{T} \rightarrow$ L*, which is recursively defined by: a) if T = $\square$, then $\phi(\square)$ = e

b) else $T = \langle r, T_0, T_1, ..., T_{p-1} \rangle$ and $\phi(T) = 0.\phi(T_0).1.\phi(T_1)....(p-1).\phi(T_{p-1}) = \prod_{i \in L} i.\phi(T_i)$.

For instance, the word which corresponds to the basic tree Q is

$q = \phi(Q) = 0.e.1.e...(p-1).e = 0.1...(p-1)$. We call it the *basic word*.

As an other example, we associate to the tree of Figure 1.2 the word

$m = 0.(0.(e).1.(e).2.(e)).1.(e).2.(0.(e).1.(0.(e).1.(e).2.(e)).2.(e)) = 001212010122$.

We also associate to each node s of the p-ary tree $T = (S,G)$, a word $w(s)$ from L^*, called *the word of s* as follows: a) if s is the root , then $w(s) = e$; b) else $w(s) = w(G^{-1}(s)).g(G^{-1}(s),s)$.

Let us call $H = \phi(T)$. Our aim is to perform on the words of H all the operations that we usually do on the trees. To reach it, we need to study some properties of H, seen as a language. For a good understanding of these properties, we introduce several other languages named M, D, E, and we show how they are linked to H .

Definitions:

1) We call M the subset of L^* such that : a) $e \in M$; b) each m of M,different from e, can be written $m = \prod_{i \in L} i.m_i$,where all the m_i belong to M .

2) We call D the set of all the words m of L^* such that : a) for any two elements k,k' of L , we have $n_k(m) = n_{k'}(m)$; b) for any left factor m' of m , and any k,k' of L such that $k \le k'$, we have $n_k(m') \ge n_{k'}(m')$.

3) We call E the set of all the words $m = x_1...x_i.x_{i+1}....x_l$ of L^* such that for any subscript i, $1 \le i < l$, we have: a) if $x_{i+1} > x_i$, then $x_{i+1} = 1 + x_i$; b) if $0 < x_{i+1} \le x_i$, then $x_i = p-1$.

We can now establish the following results about the p-ary trees and the languages H, M, D, and E .

Property 1:*For each p-ary tree T, $\phi(T)$ is the word of the labels of its edges when it is visited in prefix order, and for each node s of T, $w(s)$ is the word of the labels of the edges of path(s).*

Property 2: a) *for any integer $p \ge 2$, we have $H \subset M \subset D \cap E$;*

b) *if $p = 2$, then we have $D \cap E = M = H$:*

c) *if $p > 2$, then H is a proper subset of $D \cap E$.*

Comments: part a) follows immediately from the definitions .

If $p = 2$, then we have $E = L^*$ and $D \cap E = D$. D is isomorphic to the "parentheses language", which is itself isomorphic to the language of the binary trees. But, if $p > 2$, M is a proper subset of D. For instance, in this case, if $n > 2$, $0^n.1^n...(p-1)^n$ is a word of D which does not belong to M . Moreover, there are words of $D \cap E$ which do not belong to M, such as, for example $m = 010012212$, for $p = 3$. Therefore, if $p > 2$, a word which belongs to D and E is not necessarily a word of M.

Property 3: *Each word which belongs to D, and therefore to M and to H, has respectively 'o' and 'p-1' for first and last digits, and a multiple of p for length.*

Property 4: *D is a left and right-cancellative monoid. (That is, for any three words m, m', and m" of L^*, if $m = m'.m"$ and if two of them belong to D, then the third belongs also to D.)*

Property 5: *M is a left and right-cancellative monoid.*

Property 6: *For each word m of M there is one unique sequence $(m_0, m_1,..,m_{p-1})$ $\in M^p$,such that $m = \prod_{i \in L} i.m_i$ .These m_i constitute "the decomposition" of m.*

Property 7 (of insertion): *For any two words m, m' of M, and for any two words s and t of L^* such that $m = s.t$, the word $s.m'.t$ belongs also to M.*

Property 8 (of deletion): *a) for any two words m, m' of M, if m' is a subword of m different from m or a left factor of m or a right factor of m, then m' is necessarily a subword of one word m_i from the decomposition of m;*

b) for any two words m, m' of M, if m' is a subword of m, then there exist two words s,t of L^* such that $m = s.m'.t$ and the word $m" = s.t$ belongs to M;

Property 9: *M can be generated with its subset (e,q) and the operation of insertion ,where e is the word of lenght 0, and q is the basic word.*

Theorem: *H and M are the same language.*

proofs:

Almost all the preceding properties can be easily proved by induction on the length of the words, if they are not obvious .(Full proofs may be found in [20]) .

Because of part a) of property 2, we just need to prove the reciprocal inclusion, and thus to etablish that for each word m of M one can find a p-ary tree T such that $\phi(T) = m$, to prove the theorem. Let us proceed, here again, by induction on $l(m)$. If $m = e$,then $T = \square$. Else, according to property 6, each word m_i of the decomposition of m is a word of M, and $l(m_i) < l(m)$. Therefore, by induction hypothesis, there exists a p-ary tree T_i such that $m_i = \phi(T_i)$. Let us call r_i the root of such a T_i , $i = 0,...,p-1$, let r be a node different from the r_i's , and $T = (S,G)$ the p-ary tree such that $G(r) = (r_0,...,r_{p-1})$, assuming that the T_i's are disjoint . Then we have $\phi(T) = 0.\phi(T_0).1.\phi(T_1)...(p-1).\phi(T_{p-1}) = 0.m_0.1.m_1...(p-1).m_{p-1} = m$. Q.E.D.

Comments: D, E, and M have been used here as "intermediate" languages to prove some properties of H. Moreover, D and E which are very similar to   the "parentheses language" will be used later on to obtain the decomposition of the words of H.

2.A DVH's IMPLEMENTATION BASED ON A REPRESENTATION BY WORDS

Till now, the implementations of the dynamic virtual hashing methods were based on a representation of the index by the means of pointers or links .Now we propose a pointerless representation based on the language H. To begin, we shall remind the definition of p-DVH's methods. After what, we shall study their implementation.

2.1 p-DVH's methods

In the context of dynamic (virtual) hashing, one has to manage dynamically a file R of records which are ordered pairs (key,data). Each key is a word of L^*, and each record is identified by its key. Thus, we shall consider from now, without loss of generality, that R is merely a subset of L^*. Usually R is too large to be entirely stored in the core, so it must be stored in the external memory, which is assumed to be constituted of a certain number of buckets of capacity b. To manage R we match it with an index $T(R)$, which is a p-ary tree, usually stored in the core, by associating to each leaf f of $T(R)$ one bucket noted $B(f)$, and by sending into $B(f)$ a subset $R(f)$ of R which will be defined precisely .

Definition: for each leaf f of the index $T(R)$, $R(f)$ is the set of all the keys c of R which have for left subword of length $h(f)$ the word $w(f)$. Thus, if for each word $c = c_1.c_2....c_k...c_l$ of L^*, we define $(c)_k$ to be $c_1...c_k$ for $k =1,...,l$, and $(c)_0 = e$, we have $R(f) = \{ c \in R \mid (c)_{h(f)} = w(f) \}$. Moreover, if we call F the set of all the leaves of $T(R)$, the following "*conditions of assignement*" must be satisfied :

a) $\forall f \in F : 0 \le |R(f)| \le b$; b) $\forall f, f' \in F: f \ne f' \Rightarrow R(f) \cap R(f') = \varnothing$; c) $\bigcup_{f \in F} R(f) = R$.

But , in what manner do we obtain $T(R)$ from R ? $T(R)$ is built dynamically in relation with the movements on R, as follows:

- Initially R is empty , $T(R)$ is $\square$, and an empty bucket is attached to the only node r, which can be seen both as the root and as a leaf of $T(R)$.

-Then, for each key c' of L^* that we consider, first we need to determine the unique leaf f of T. such that $B(f)$ contains or may contain c'. This leaf is entirely determined by $w(f) = (c')_{h(f)}$. Next, we have to see if c' belongs to $B(f)$:

- if c' does not belong to $B(f)$, and if this bucket is not full, we can insert c' in $B(f)$ without changing T;

- if c' does not belong to $B(f)$, and if this bucket is full, we must split $B(f)$ and send its contents into other buckets.This can be made by modifying   the index : the leaf f becomes an internal node such that $G(f) = (s_0,...,s_i,...,s_{p-1})$, where the s_i's are p new leaves to which we attach p new empty buckets $B(s_i)$. After that, we have the sets $R(s_i) = \{ c \in R(f) \cup \{c'\} \mid c_{h(f)+1} = i \}$, for $i = 0,...,p-1$.

They obviously satisfy the conditions of assignement b) and c), with $R(f)$ instead of R . For each i such thas $R(s_i)$ verifies also condition a) , we put the keys of this set into the bucket $B(s_i)$. Otherwise, we repeat the splitting procedure on the only s_i for which $R(s_i)$ contains $b + 1$ keys, and so on, untill the three conditions will be satisfied .

   - if c' belongs to $B(f)$, we may decide to delete it from this bucket.In this case, we may have to merge the contents of the buckets attached to the leaves "brothers " of f , in order to maintain the constraints of assignement, and thus to change the shape of the index .

This is the method that we shall implement. Although it is not the most general one, it works in the same manner, and it can be seen as a prototype of many different dynamic (virtual) hashing methods.

2.2 Implementation of the method

Since we want to use only words of L^* to implement our method,we have to solve the following problems:

1) given a word of L^*, how to recognize that it belongs to H ?

2) given a word of H, how to construct the corresponding p-ary tree, to know if a node is an internal or an external one, and to determine its links ?

3) given a key c of the file R, which is assumed to be a subset of L^* and to which is associated the p-ary index $T(R)$, how to find the unique leaf f such that c could belong to $B(f)$, and how to manage the possible splitting or merging operations in relation with the insertion or the deletion of c from R ?

2.2.1 Trees' words recognition Given a word $m = a_1.a_2...a_l$ of L^*, we must answer the question :does it belong to H ? Properties 2 and 3 are good criterions to provide quickly a negative answer to this question. However, even if m has the property 3 and if it is a word of $D \cap E$, this is not suffisant to insure us that it belongs to M, for $p > 2$. So, one way to answer our question is the next algorithm, which is a straightforward consequence of the property 9.

Algorithm 1 (recognition algorithm)

For each word m of L^* , let us build the following finite sequence ($m^{(k)}$) of words

a) $k := 0$; $m^{(k)} := m$;

b) while the basic word $q = 0.1...(p-1)$ is a subword of $m^{(k)}$, delete it from $m^{(k)}$. More accurately, we can say :while there exist words $m'^{(k)}$ and $m''^{(k)}$ of L^*,such that $m^{(k)} = m'^{(k)}.q.m''^{(k)}$, do $k := k +1$; $m^{(k)} := m'^{(k-1)}.m''^{(k-1)}$;

c) m belongs to H , if and only if $m^{(k)} = e$

(The complexity of Algorithm 1 will be analyzed later on).

2.2.2 <u>How to build a p-ary tree by the means of its word</u> Given the word m = $a_1.a_2...a_i...a_l$ of H, how to construct the corresponding tree T ?

From now, we shall suppose that T is a p-ary tree with l edges, and thus with l+1 nodes . Without loss of generality, we take S = { 0,1,...,l },and <u>S</u> = S ∪ {-1},where "-1" is a fictitious node that we use instead of "λ", formerly introduced. Moreover, we assume that the nodes of S are sorted in prefix order, starting with the root which is therefore the node with rank 0 . Depending on the context, we may have to build T entirely, or just to determine the links of some nodes .We shall study these two eventualities ,and provide methods to solve them.

2.2.2.1 <u>Sequential construction of the tree</u> Since, according to the property 1, m is the word of the labels of the edges of T, visited in prefix order, a_i is thus the label of the i-th edge in prefix order, and since the nodes of S are also in this order, this edge is necessarily of the form (j,i) , where j - father(i) , and we have to find j knowing i and a_i. To be more complete, we shall calculate for each node i of S , its links father(i), son(i) and brother(i) .

Keeping in mind the definitions of the links and property 2, we can see that only three mutually exclusive cases may occur :

a) if $a_i = 0$, then father(i) = i-1, and son(i-1) = i if i > 0 ;

b) if $a_i = 1 + a_{i-1}$, then brother(i-1) = i and father(i) = father(i-1) ;

c) if $a_i \neq 0$ and $a_{i-1} = p-1$, let us call j the greatest integer, smaller than i and such that aj ≠ p-1 ; then we have father(i)= father(j), brother(j)= i.

These three possibilities are shown on Figure 2, and solved as follows.

<u>Algorithm 2</u> (of sequential construction of T)

/*Given the word m = $a_1.a_2...a_l$ of H , this algorithm calculates the links father, son and brother in prefix order for all the nodes of T */.

```
Begin
   For i:=0 to l Do Begin father(i):=-1;brother(i):=-1;son(i):=-1; End;
   For i:=1 to l Do
       Begin
       If (a_i=0) Then Begin father(i):=i-1; son(i-1):= i ; End
               Else  If (a_i= 1+a_{i-1}) Then
                       Begin father(i):=father(i-1); brother(i-1):=i ; End
                       Else Begin
                               j:=i-1; While (a_j=p-1) Do j:=father(j) ;
                               father(i):=father(j); brother(j):= i ;
```

End;

End;

End.

2.2.2.2 Level by level construction of the tree

Given the word m of H, we want now to determine for each node i of S, its links $f_j(i)$, for $j= 0,...,p-1$.

Since H is a subset of D, we use the fact that m belongs to D to determine the words m_j which constitute the decomposition of m. After what, whe easily obtain the roots r_j of the different subtrees T_j of T , and we have $G(r) = (r_0,...,r_{p-1})$ and $f_j(r) = r_j$, for each j of L . This process of decomposition may then be applied to the word m_j , which also belongs to H , to obtain the links of r_j , and so on .

In what follows, we use the same conventions as before , and $f_j(i)=-1$ means that this link does not exist. Property 10,and algorithm 3 hereafter,are straight forward consequences of the fact that $m \in D \cap E$.

Property 10 *1) A node i of S is a leaf if and only if i = 1 ,or 1 ‹i ‹1 and $a_{i+1} \neq 0$;*

2) For each node i of S,1‹ i ‹1 . a) even $a_{i+1} \neq 0$: thus i is a leaf and we have $f_k(i)=-1$ for each k of L; b) or $a_{i+1} = 0$ and i is an internal node ; in this case , for each k of L $f_k(i)$ is the smallest integer $j \geq i+1$ such that $n_k(a_{i+1}...a_j)=n_0(a_{i+1}...a_j)$.

Algorithm 3

```
/* Given a word m= a₁...aₗ of H  and a node i of S, f₀(i),...,fₚ₋₁(i) are computed */
Begin
  Input i ∈ S ;
  For k:= 0 To p-1 Do  fₖ(i) := -1 ;
  If  Not ( i = 1 or  aᵢ₊₁ ≠ 0 ) Then
      Begin For k:= 0 To p-1  Do  n[k] := 0 ;  j := i+1 ;  k := 0 ;
              While ( k ≤ p-1 )  Do
                Begin  n[aⱼ] := n[aⱼ] + 1 ;
                        If ( n[k] = n[0] ) Then Begin  fₖ(i) := j;  k :=k+1 ; End ;
                        j := i + 1;
              End ;
      End;
  /* here  n[k]  means  nₖ(aᵢ₊₁...aⱼ) , that is the number of 'k' in  aᵢ₊₁...aⱼ  */
End .
```

2.2.3 Key retrieval

Given a word m= $a_1...a_l$ of H and a key c = $c_1...c_n$ of R, how to find the only leaf f of the index T such that c could be located in the bucket B(f) ? We call f *the leaf of c* and we write f= leaf(c). To answer this question we remember us that w(f) must be a left-factor of c . Following this idea, we are led to the next algorithm.

Algorithm 4

/* Given m = $a_1...a_l$ ∈ H and c = $c_1...c_n$ ∈ R, the algorithm determines leaf(c) */

Begin

s := root(T) ; /* thus s:= 0 ,here */ i := 1;

While (s is not a leaf of T , and j ≤ n) Do

   Begin k := c_i ; s := f_k(s) ; i := i + 1 ; End ;

If (s is a leaf) Then leaf(c) := s Else leaf(c) does not exist; /* c is too short */

End .

Remark: The link f_k(s) , which appears here, may be calculated with Algorithm 3 ; and " s is a leaf " is equivalent to (s=1 , or s < 1 and a_{s+1} ≠ 0), according to property 10 .

Once obtained leaf(f), we have to search c in the bucket B(f) , and eventually, to split this bucket in case of insertion, or to merge p buckets into one, in case of deletion. Let us for instance solve the insertion-splitting problem.

Algorithm 5 (splitting and insertion)

/* Given a word m = $a_1...a_l$ of H and a key c = $c_1...c_n$ of L* , we insert c into R . */

Procedure split(s:leaf) ;

Begin

Take p new nodes s_i , and p new empty buckets B(s_i) , i = 0,...,p-1 ;

change the index T = (S,G) into T' = (S',G') , where S' = S ∪ {s_0,...,s_{p-1}} ,and

G' - G on S-{s}, G'(s) - (s_0,...,s_{p-1}) , and G'(s_i) - ø for each i ;

for each i ,send into B(s_i) all the keys c of B(s) such that $c_{h(s)+1}$ = i;

return B(s) to the collection of empty buckets;

End;

Begin

s := leaf(c) ; j:= h(s); /* we assume that leaf(c) exists and that c ∉ B(s) */

While (|B(s)| = b) Do Begin split(s); j := j+ 1 ; k := c_j ; s:= f_k(s) ; End ;

put c into B(s) ;

End .

Remark :

The splitting operation is quite easy to realize on the word m = $a_1...a_i...a_l$;

indeed, if the leaf is the i-th node in prefix order, we just have to insert the basic word q into m after a_i, changing m into m' as follows

$m' = a_1...a_j.q...a_1 = a_1...a_j.\underline{0.1...(p-1)}...a_1$. From property 7 , we know that m' also belongs to H , and we have $m' = \phi(T')$. A similar algorithm may be designed to perform the operations of deletion and merging .

3. MAIN INTRINSIC PERFORMANCE FACTORS OF p-DVH METHODS

To do the paper as self-contained as possible, and to well situate p-DVH methods inside the family of managing methods for large files, we introduce here - from [9] - the main results about p-DVH . As it is well known, the main property of these methods is that any record can be found in exactly one disk access, once obtained leaf(c). The other performance is strongly dependent to the index. Because its size has evident repercussions on any implementation, its external path length gives an estimation of the retrivial time, its load factor indicates how are filled the buckets, and statistics on its leaves provide the numbers of full and empty buckets. As we are particularly interested by the very lage files, we shall assume that the file R *satisfies the statistical Poisso. hypothesis*. This means that its records are words, of possibly infinite length, of L, and that its size is a random Poisson variable, the mean value of which is ν This hypothesis, and a bucket's capacity of b, give the following asymptotic results , when ν becomes infinite :

(here the symbol ' $\simeq$ ' means " asymptotically equivalent to " .)

1) the mean number of internal nodes of the index is $N(\nu) \simeq \dfrac{\nu}{bLn(p)}$;

2) the load factor is $\tau \simeq \dfrac{Ln(p)}{p-1}$;

3) the mean number of buckets which contain q keys, $2 \le q \le b$, is

$$F_q(\nu) \simeq \frac{\nu}{q(q-1)Ln(p)}\left[1 - p^{(q-1)}\sum_{j=0}^{b-q}\binom{j+q-2}{j}(1-1/p)^j \right] \quad ;$$

the mean number of full buckets is $F_b(\nu) \simeq \dfrac{\nu}{b(b-1)}\left[1 - 1/p^{(b-1)} \right]$;

the mean number of empty buckets is

$$F_0(\nu) \simeq \frac{p\nu}{Ln(p)} U_p, \text{ with } V_p < U_p < p.V_p, \text{ and } V_b = \frac{1}{b(b-1)}(1-1/p)^{b+1};$$

4) the mean cost of insertion or deletion of one key is $I(\nu) \simeq \dfrac{\nu}{bLn(p)}$;

5) the mean value of the external path length of the index is $L(\nu) \simeq \nu \, Log_p(\nu)$. Several comments on to the comparizon between the classical case p=2 and the less one p > 2 are given in [9] .

4 . ANALYSIS OF THE IMPLEMENTATION BY THE MEANS OF WORDS

Beside the intrinsic performances of p-DVH methods, which are independant of the implementation, there are some other ones which depend on it, such as the amount of storage necessary to represent the index or the amount of time necessary to calculate the links when they are not explicitly given .We shall do first, some comparizons between our represention and the classical one ; and then compare it to the Luckaciewicz's one; and, to finish, give some results about the complexity of the algorithms previously described.

4.1 . Comparizon with classical representations of trees

For any index T, which is a p-ary tree with l edges ,and thus with l+1 nodes, if we use a representation by the means of pointers or links, we need about $p(l+1)$ links, since each node has p children . If we use our representation, we just need a word of length l of L^*. This represents an important save of storage. The counterpart lies in the time necessary to calculate the links f_k which appear when we have to determine a path through the index. Nevertheless this is a relatively small drawback, since the algorithm used to obtain these links has no back-track, and thus the time it needs is nearly proportional to the length of the key to search . Moreover, to reorganize the index in case of splitting or merging, we just have to insert or to delete one basic word into or from $\phi(T)$.

4.2 Comparizon with the Lukaciewicz's representation

Let us remind the Lukaciewicz's representation of trees [10] . This is a way to associate a word of some alphabet to any finite tree, and not only to a p-ary tree. But we shall just study here the case of p-ary trees, since we just need it. As for our representation, we shall proceed in a recursive manner. Thus ,let us call ρ : $\mathbb{T} \to \{0,1\}^*$ the mapping defined as follows:

a) if $T=\square$, then $\rho(\square)=0$; b) else $T =< r,T_0,T_1,...,T_{p-1} >$, and $\rho(T)=1.\rho(T_0).\rho(T_1)...\rho(T_{p-1})$
It is really easy to see that $\rho(T)$ may be obtained in the next but equivalent way: starting with the word w=e , we visit T in prefix order, beginning at the root. Each time we meet a node we append '1' to w if it is an internal node, and '0' if it is a leaf . For instance , for the tree of Figure 1.2 ,we have
$\rho(T) = 1.(1.0.0.0).0.(1.(0).1.(0.0.0).0) = 1100001010000$.

This kind of representation is very nice and more compact than our's, since for a tree with l edges it needs a word of $\{0,1\}^{l+1}$ instead of a word of $\{0,1,...,p-1\}^l$. Moreover, given a word m of $\{0,1\}^*$, there is a very quick criterion to see if m is the word of some p-ary tree . It is based on the homomorphism $\delta : <\{0,1\}^*, . > \to$ $<\mathbb{Z} , + >$, with initial values $\delta(0) = -1 , \delta(1) = p-1$, and such that $\delta(m.m') = \delta(m) + \delta(m')$ for any two words . Then the criterion states that a word m of $\{0,1\}^*$ is the word of a p-ary tree if and only if we have $\delta(m') \geq 0$ for any proper left factor m' of m , and $\delta(m) = -1$ .The time complexity of this algorithm is a $O(|S|)$, while the time complexity of Algorithm 1 is a $O(|S|^{1.5})$,as we shall see . But, on the other hand, this represention is less convenient than our's to calculate the links f_k which are extremely important in the implementation of p-DVH methods ; and the labels of the edges of the index, which are bearing all the information, are not appearent in the Lukaciewicz representation .

4.3 Time complexity of algorithm 1

If, to implement it. we choose for $m'^{(k)}$ the smallest left factor of $m^{(k)}$ such that $m^{(k)} = m'^{(k)}.q.m''^{(k)}$, and under an assumption of equiprobability, then we obtain in [21] the following result:

the mean cost of recognition, using algorithm 1, of the word of a p-ary tree with

n internal nodes, is asymptotically in n , $c_n \simeq \sqrt{\dfrac{\Pi p(p-1)}{8}} \, n\sqrt{n} \left(1 + o(\dfrac{1}{\sqrt{n}}) \right)$.

4.4 Time complexity of algoritm 2

Under the statistical hypothesis of equiprobability, we show, in [21] ,that :

asymptotically in n, the mean cost of construction of a p-ary tree with n internal nodes, using algorithm 2, is a O(n).

5. CONCLUSION

We have proposed a way to represent p-ary trees, in order to implement p-dynamic virtual hashing methods. From the points of view of storage amount and time complexity, our representation appears to be a compromise between the most usual ones and the Lukasiewicz's one. From the point of view of readability, our representation presents a major advantage on the other ones, since all the "semantics" of the index is immediatly accessible from its word.

To finish. let us indicate that some important aspects of access path structures . such as stability. reliability. fault tolerance and concurrency control need to be explored to achieve the present work.

Acknowledgment

The author is grateful to Dr. W. LITWIN at INRIA. for many valuable comments and suggestions during the preparation of the manuscript.

REFERENCES

[1] LARSON Per-Ake , "Dynamyc hashing", BIT 18 (1978), 184-201 .

[2] LITWIN Witold . "Virtual hashing. a dynamically changing hashing" ,
    4 th. Int .Conf on VLDB, Berlin(sept 1978) , 517-23 .

[3] FAGIN R., NIEVERGELT J., PIPPENGER N., STRONG H.R. , "Extensible hashing - a fast access method for dynamic files ", ACM-TODS ,4,3, (sept.1979) , 315-344 .

[4] KOUAKOU Jean. Thèse de Troisième Cycle. Université de Paris IX - 1986 .

[5] REGNIER Mireille, Thèse de Troisième Cycle,Université de Paris XI, 1983.

[6] FLAJOLET P. , REGNIER M. , SOTTEAU D. , "Algebraic methods for tries statistics ", Ann. Discrete Math. 25 (1985), 145-188 .

[7] LITWIN W., ZEGOUR D., LEVY G.,"Multilevel trie hashing", EDBT 88.,Venice .

[8] ZEGOUR Djamal Eddine, Thèse Université de Paris-Dauphine , 1988 .

[9] LEVY Gérard , " Analyse des performances du p-hachage dynamique virtuel ", Revue Modèles et Bases de Données (M.D.B.) ,N° 6 , 15-24 .

[10] Encyclopedia of Mathematics and its applications,Vol 17, Combinatorics and words , M. LOTHAIRE , Chap.11:"words and trees" , 1983, Addison-Wesley .

[11] KNOTT Gary D.,"A numbering system for binary trees", Comm. ACM,20 (1977), 113-115 .

[12] RUSKEY F. , HU T.C. , " generating binary trees lexicographically ", SIAM J. COMP.6 (1977), 745-758 .

[13] RUSKEY F., " Generating t-ary trees lexicographically ", SIAM J. COMP.7(1978), 706-712 .

[14] ROTEM DORON , VAROL Y.L. , " Generation of binary trees from ballot sequences",JACM25(1978),396-404 .

[15] ZACKS S. ,RICHARDS D. , " generating trees and other combinatorial objects lexicographically ", SIAM J. COMP.8(1979),73-81 .

[16] ZACKS S. , "Lexicographically generation of ordered trees ", Theoret. Comput.Sci.10(1980),63-82.

[17] PROSKUROWSKI A. , " On generation of binary trees ", JACM 27 (1980), 1-2 .

[18] SOLOMON M. , FINKEL R.A. , "A note on enumerating binary trees " , JACM 27 (1980) , 3-5 .

[19] LEVY G. , LITWIN W. , WANG Hong , " on generating binary and t-ary trees lexicographically ", Note interne INRIA (1988) .

[20] LEVY Gérard , " Arbres homogènes et mots associes ", Cahiers du centre de recherche IP9, Université de Paris-Dauphine (1985) .

[21] LEVY Gérard , " Etude de la complexité moyenne de deux algorithmes de reconnaissance des mots des arbres p-aires ", to appear .

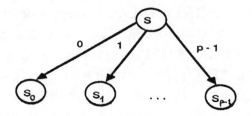

Figure 1.1

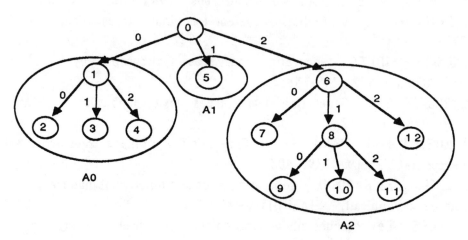

Figure 1.2: an example of ternary tree.

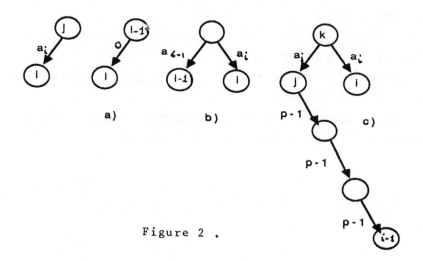

a)

b)

c)

Figure 2 .

Dynamic External Hashing with Guaranteed Single Access Retrieval

M.V. Ramakrishna
Walid R. Tout

Computer Science Department
Michigan State University
East Lansing, Michigan 48824 - 1027

ABSTRACT

The goal of the research on hashing as an access method is to arrive at a simple file organization scheme which guarantees single access retrieval from secondary storage, and is dynamic (can gracefully accommodate varying file sizes). There has been much progress in recent years in this regard. The Signature Hashing scheme for external files, proposed by Gonnet and Larson, guarantees single access retrieval [GL88]. But the scheme is static and implementation is complicated [LK84]. In this paper a simple external hashing scheme which guarantees single access retrieval is proposed and performance investigated. The scheme is dynamic, and its cost is better than that of Signature Hashing. An overview of the current state of the art and open problems are mentioned.

1. Introduction

Gonnet and Larson originally proposed a hashing scheme for external files which guarantees single access retrieval at the cost of storage space in internal memory, increased cost of insertions and additional internal memory probings [GL82]. Details of a practical implementation of the scheme was provided by Larson and Kajla in [LK84]. Gonnet and Larson provide additional details and an asymptotic analysis of the scheme in [GL88]. The basic motivation for the scheme is " ... accessing secondary storage is very slow, any technique that reduces the number of accesses, even at a fairly high cost of internal processing, is likely to reduce the total retrieval time" [GL88]. Tharp refers to the scheme as *Signature Hashing*, in his book on file processing [TH88]. We expect further research interest in this area and use the same terminology in this paper.

Signature Hashing is basically a modification of the double hashing scheme, in which the internal information stored enables to replace external accesses by internal probes. In this paper we take a new look at how and what information should be stored in internal memory to achieve single access retrieval. Implicit in this question is, how the overflows can be handled (stored and located) so that every record can be located in a single access to the external memory. The records hashed into non-full buckets can be retrieved in a single access. The records hashed into overflowed buckets have to be handled explicitly to guarantee single access retrieval. This is accomplished by using perfect hashing and separate storage area for overflow records. The corresponding details are stored in an internal dynamic table. If an entry is present for a primary bucket, it means that the bucket has overflowed and the entry has enough information to retrieve any of the keys in a single access. The absence of an entry for a primary bucket implies that it is a nonoverflowing bucket and hence accessing the bucket satisfies the retrieval command (whether it is a successful search or unsuccessful search). Since all the overflow records from an overflow bucket can be accessed, Linear Hashing can be readily adapted and hence the proposed basic scheme can be extended to be completely dynamic [LT80]. Before proceeding further, we summarize the state of the art of bounded access retrieval methods.

1. Signature hashing guarantees single access retrieval at the cost of internal memory space, internal probings for retrieval, increased cost and complexity of insertions. The scheme is completely static, i.e., the file size is fixed. Combining this scheme with linear hashing with linear probing, Larson recently extended this scheme to handle dynamic files [LS88].

2. Composite perfect hashing for external files proposed by Ramakrishna and Larson guarantees single access retrieval at the cost of internal memory space and increased cost of insertions (although, the scheme is simple). This scheme is based on external perfect hashing and is dynamic to some extent. A variant of the scheme is completely dynamic [RL88, RM86].

3. Bounded Disorder file organization proposed by Litwin and Lomet guarantees retrieval in two accesses (most retrievals require single access). This scheme is completely dynamic and enables efficient range searches [LL86].

4. Prompted by Signature Hashing and perfect hashing, Mairson has established that $\Omega(n)$ ''program size'' (in our case the internal memory space) is the lower bound for bounded access retrieval schemes [MR83, MR84] (details of these theoretical results are beyond the scope of the paper). All the schemes mentioned above including the one proposed in this paper are bounded by his theoretical limits.

5. If the directory is stored in internal memory, the Extendible Hashing scheme guarantees single access retrieval [FN79]. But the amount of internal storage required for such schemes, as Gonnet and Larson have already pointed out, is too large to be of practical value.

The Signature Hashing scheme

A brief explanation of the Signature Hashing scheme is provided here. There is an index table stored in the internal memory, with one entry per (external) bucket. Each entry consists of a separator of length d bits in which appropriate hash *signatures* are stored. A hash *signature* of length d for a key x is the first d bits produced by a secondary hashing function operating on the key x. For non-full buckets the value of the separator stored is the maximum possible signature, $2^d - 1$. For a full bucket, the minimum of the hash signatures of the keys overflowing from the bucket is the separator. Normal double hashing is used to store and retrieve the records. To retrieve a record corresponding to a key x, the primary hash address and the signature of x are computed. If the computed signature is less than the separator of the bucket, the required bucket has been found. Otherwise, proceed by calculating the next address and signature of the key until a bucket whose separator is greater than the signature of the key is found. Insertions are straight forward, if the bucket into which the key hashes is not full (and hence the separator of the bucket is 2^d-1). When an insertion causes a bucket to overflow, all the keys in the bucket (including the one being inserted) are sorted according to their signatures. A separator s is determined so that the number of keys having signatures less than or equal to s is as close to the bucket size b as possible: those keys are retained in the bucket. The value s is stored in the index table as the new separator, and all the records whose signatures are strictly greater than s are pushed out of the bucket and are inserted in their secondary addresses. This in turn may necessitate migration of keys stored in those buckets. Thus in essence, external probing has been replaced by internal probing and the index (separator) table stores enough information to terminate probing at the correct bucket address.

A critical look

In the Signature Hashing scheme described above, the separators stored for overflowing buckets are signatures, and for non-full buckets the information stored in the internal table is minimal. The analysis in [GL88] indicates that only a fraction of the total number of primary buckets overflow in general. The obvious question to ask is, what can be done to efficiently store information about overflowing buckets only? This reduces the internal memory space requirement, which is one of the costs of Signature Hashing. The other question is, are there other efficient methods of handling overflow records apart from the double hashing technique used in Signature Hashing? This line of thinking leads us to the hashing scheme proposed in this paper, which is simple in principle and implementation. Also, the preliminary analysis and simulations indicate that the proposed scheme performs better than the Signature Hashing.

Outline of the paper

The next section describes the proposed basic scheme. Section 3 provides a performance analysis of the scheme. Simulation results and a technique for improving storage utilization are presented in section 4. The extension of the basic scheme to make it dynamic are presented in section 5. The last section compares the proposed scheme with Signature Hashing and presents conclusions.

2. The proposed scheme

Basic idea

Starting from a simple hashing scheme, the basic problem is to place the overflow records appropriately and store suitable information in internal memory which enables to exactly determine the bucket address of any given key. Signature Hashing uses double hashing to handle overflows, and separators of the overflowing buckets enables exact determination of the bucket address of a given key. A fixed amount of internal space is reserved for all buckets in Signature Hashing, and the analysis in [GL88] indicates that only a small fraction of buckets overflow and hence inefficient use of internal table. The proposed scheme uses perfect hashing to handle the overflows, and overflows are stored in separate (from the prime area) overflow area. The details of the perfect hashing function, and pointer to overflow area are maintained in an internal table, which has an entry for each (and only) overflowing bucket. This information enables us to exactly determine the bucket address of a key hashing into overflowed buckets. For a key hashing into a non overflowing bucket, the absence of an entry for the bucket in the internal table indicates that the exact address has been found already. Since all the overflow records of any given primary bucket can be readily located, the proposed scheme can be extended to handle completely dynamic files by adapting Linear Hashing.

Further details

A given set of n records are to be stored in a hash file containing m primary buckets (on secondary storage), each having a capacity of b records. The number of records n is often expressed in terms of the load factor $\alpha = n/mb$. Let $H(\ )$ denote the hashing function which assigns each record an address in the range $0..m-1$. There is an auxiliary table stored in internal memory, with one entry for each of the overflowing primary buckets. This table is organized as a dynamic hash table, as proposed recently by Larson [LR88]. This table enables associative search, and its size depends on the number of entries stored in it (and does not have to be fixed at a high value a priori). We will refer to this internally stored table as IAT (internal auxiliary table).

Initially the IAT is empty (has no entries) and a corresponding entry is added each time a bucket of the hash file overflows. Let S_i denote the group of records which hash to address i by the hashing function $H(\ )$, i.e., $S_i = \{x \mid H(x) = i\}$. If the number of records in S_i is less than or equal to the bucket capacity b, group S_i is simply stored in bucket i and no entry is added to IAT. If the size of S_i is greater than b, perfect hashing is used to handle the overflow situation (more details of perfect hashing are given later). A perfect hashing function is determined to distribute the group of records S_i among m_i buckets, addressed as $0, 1, ..,m_i-1$. The overflowing primary bucket i forms the address '0' of the "overflow perfect hash table", the other (m_i-1) contiguous buckets are allocated from separate overflow area. An entry for bucket i is inserted into IAT containing a pointer p_i to the first of the overflow buckets, the number of buckets m_i, and parameter C_i of the perfect hashing function PHF_i. Thus, the exact bucket address for any given key x can be

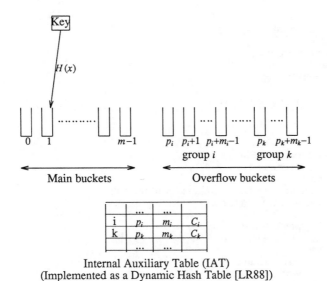

Internal Auxiliary Table (IAT)
(Implemented as a Dynamic Hash Table [LR88])

Figure 1. The proposed external hashing (basic) scheme.

determined by the function **address**(x) defined below.

```
address(x)
        compute i := H(x) ;
        search IAT for key i ;
        if there is no entry in IAT
                return(i) ;
        else
                retrieve information (p_i, m_i, C_i) from IAT ;
                if PHF_i = 0
                        return(i) ;
                else
                        return(p_i + PHF_i - 1) ;
        end;
```

The function first computes the primary hash address $i = H(x)$. A search is made for i in IAT. If there is no entry for i in IAT, it means the bucket i has not overflowed and hence the correct address has been found (i.e. address is i). If there is an entry, the perfect hashing function is evaluated with argument x, and the address evaluates to either bucket i or one of the overflow buckets. Detailed algorithms for retrieval, insertion and deletion are presented below. The details of perfect hashing follow.

```
retrieve(x)
      compute k = address(x) ;
      read bucket k ;
      search for record x ;
      if found
            return(record)
      else
            return("record not found") ;
end;


insert(x)
      compute primary address k = H(x) ;
      search IAT for key k ;
      if found
            compute exact bucket address i = address(x) ;
            read bucket i into buffer ;
            if bucket full
                  perfect-hash(group S_k) ;
                  update entry k in IAT ;
            else
                  insert x into buffer ;
                  write back bucket i ;
      else
            read bucket k ;
            if bucket full
            perfect-hash(group S_k) ;
                  create entry for k in IAT ;
            else
                  insert x into buffer ;
                  write back bucket k ;
end;
delete(x)
      compute k = address(x) ;
      search bucket k ;
      if found
            delete record and write back the buffer ;
            if the load factor of the group S_k becomes too small
                  perfect-hash(group S_k).
      else
            return("record not found") ;
end;
```

Finding Perfect Hashing Functions

A hashing function h is said to be perfect for a given set of records if it causes no overflows. If the records are stored using a perfect hashing function then any record can be retrieved in a single access. Sprugnoli was the first to define and investigate perfect hashing [SP77]. His methods of finding perfect hashing functions could handle only small static key sets of 10 to 20 elements. Ramakrishna and Larson investigated perfect hashing for external files. It is shown by analysis and simulations that perfect hashing functions can be found for large key sets (up to a few hundred elements), by simple trial and error method using $universal_2$ class of hashing functions [CW79]. With only 10 to 20 trials, each involving the evaluation of the hash addresses of the keys in the set, perfect hashing functions with good storage utilizations can be found. Analytical methods as well as more practical heuristics of external hashing are presented in [RL88, RM86]. We will not go into further details of the scheme here and the interested reader can refer to the cited literature. A brief outline of the function *perfect-hash*() is provided below.

```
perfect-hash(group Sᵢ) ;
    read all buckets of Sᵢ ;
    find perfect hashing function h (Cᵢ,.) for
      the records with mᵢ buckets (mᵢ to be determined) ;
    obtain mᵢ − 1 overflow buckets starting at bucket address pᵢ ;
    hash all the records into mᵢ buffers (using the perfect hashing function h (Cᵢ,.) ;
    write buffer '0' onto primary bucket i,
    and buffers 1,2,...,mᵢ−1 onto buckets starting at pᵢ ;
    return(pᵢ,mᵢ, Cᵢ ) ;
end ;
```

3. Performance Analysis

The proposed scheme is simple and guarantees optimal retrieval performance. Its practical significance depends on the following cost measures.

(a) Amount of internal storage required

(b) Cost of finding perfect hashing functions an the resulting storage utilization

In this section we present an analysis of the expected number of overflowing buckets (which corresponds to the number of entries in IAT). As for perfect hashing, a simple heuristic which was tailored for our purposes will be presented and the resulting storage utilization is analyzed.

Assume that keys are randomly hashed by the hashing function $H(\ )$, so that the probability of a key hashing to any particular bucket is $1/m$. (In view of the results presented in [RM88], this is not just an assumption convenient for analysis. It has been shown, using theory of pseudo-random number generators and $universal_2$ classes of hashing functions, that the theoretical performance measures of hashing can be achieved in practice by using hashing functions randomly chosen from the class H_1 of $universal_2$ hashing functions.) After hashing n keys, the probability of a bucket containing i records is given by the *Poisson* approximation,

$$P(\alpha,i) = \frac{e^{(-ab)} (\alpha b)^i}{i!}.$$

It follows that the probability of a bucket overflowing, $P_{ov}(\alpha)$, is given by,

$$P_{ov}(\alpha) = 1 - \sum_{i=0}^{b} \frac{e^{(-ab)} (\alpha b)^i}{i!}.$$

Figure 2 plots the probability of a bucket overflowing for different values of bucket size b and load factor α (which represents the expected number of buckets overflowing, as a fraction of the total number of buckets).

The size of the internal table IAT is directly dependent on the number of entries in it (since it is organized as a dynamic hash table). The expected number of entries in IAT is given by,

$$E(|IAT|) = mP_{ov}(\alpha)$$

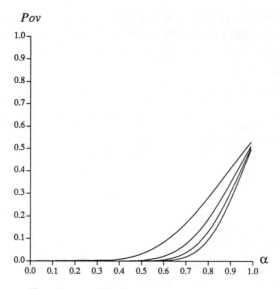

Figure 2. Probability of a bucket overflowing,
$b = 10, 20, 30, 40.$

The proposed scheme is aiming to exploit the small values of *pov* at practically acceptable load factors. We observe from the figure that, up to about 0.8 load factor, the expected number of entries in IAT is quite small (less than 10% of the buckets). Further discussion is postponed to section 4 and 6 (which also gives examples and comparison with Signature Hashing).

Storage utilization

We first compute the total expected number of buckets required to store n keys,

$$E(m) = \sum_{k=0}^{b} P(\alpha,k)m + \sum_{k=b+1}^{n} \{m\,P(\alpha,k)\}\,m_k$$

The first term above is essentially the expected number of non-full buckets. the second term is the total number of buckets, of all the groups of overflowing buckets. The above expression simplifies to,

$$E(m) = m + \sum_{k=b+1}^{n} \{mP(\alpha,k)\,(m_k-1)\}$$

The storage utilization for the file as a whole, λ, is given by,

$$\lambda = \frac{n}{E(m)b}.$$

Figure 3 plots the expected storage utilization λ as a function of load factor α, for various values of bucket size b. Most of the hashing schemes perform better as the bucket size b increases. We see from the figure that beyond a certain value of α, lower value of b yields better storage utilization. Also, the storage utilization is in the range of 60 to 75%

when the load factor α is less than 0.8 (this is the range we want to operate within. Higher values of α, although giving better storage utilization, are not practical because the size of the IAT increases drastically). These characteristics are because of fragmentation problems. Suppose b is 20 and a group S_i has 25 records, then 2 buckets have to be allocated resulting in a local storage utilization of only 62%. The problem is less pronounced with smaller bucket sizes, especially at higher load factors as evidenced by the plot for $b=10$. This suggests a simple way of increasing the storage utilization: reduce the overflow bucket size. Perfect hashing into two different bucket sizes has to be handled appropriately. These problems are dealt with in detail in the next section.

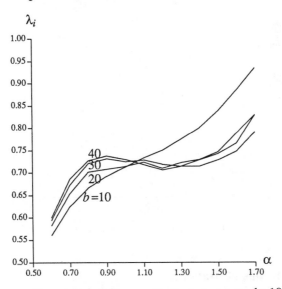

Figure 3. Computed storage utilization for bucket sizes $b=10$, 20, 30 and 40.

4. Simulation and improvements

To test the performance measures, we simulated several file loadings. A file consisting of over 10,000 userids from a large time sharing installation was used for simulation. Each key consists of up to eight alphanumeric characters. The keys were converted into integers and duplicates eliminated [LK84, RM86]. File loadings were simulated for different values of bucket sizes b. The experimental value of the storage utilization λ, after loading $n=\alpha mb$ records was computed as,

$$\lambda = \frac{n}{(number\ of\ buckets\ used)b}$$

Figure 4 compares the experimental storage utilization with that predicted by analysis in the last section. The main hashing function $H(\ )$ was chosen from a *universal*$_2$ class of hashing functions and the experimental results presented are the averages with 5 different hashing functions chosen at random (refer to [RM88] for details of how analytical results on hashing are related to practice). We observe that the two sets of results are in good agreement. There is a visible gap between the analytical and experimental results. This is due to the fact that the analysis does not exactly model the heuristic given for perfect hashing (the primary aim of the paper is to present the basic ideas and preliminary analysis).

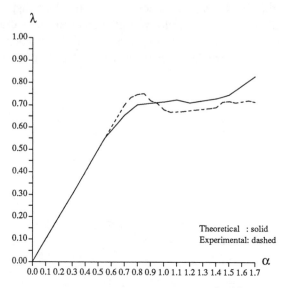

Figure 4. Storage Utilization for buckets size $b=20$.

Improving the storage utilization:

As already indicated, the storage utilization starts falling after a certain load factor due to the fragmentation problem. Initially, when very few buckets overflow, its effect is small. Beyond a certain point, a large number of records overflow and hence the allocated buckets are full. In between these two cases, the storage utilization reaches a peak. The bucket size has little effect on this peak value. The fragmentation problem can be overcome using smaller overflow buckets. We define the ratio R as,

$$R = \frac{primary\ bucket\ size}{overflow\ bucket\ size}.$$

The capacity of an overflow bucket is a fraction $1/R$ of the primary bucket size. The results presented so far correspond to the ratio $R=1$. Changing the size of primary buckets does not pose any problem for perfect hashing. The primary bucket is regarded as consisting of R buckets (each of size equal to the size of the overflow buckets) as shown in figure 5.

Obviously one would expect better storage utilization with increasing values of R. This is illustrated in Figure 6 which plots the storage utilization as a function of load factor (these are simulation results). The bucket size is fixed at 20, and there is one curve for each value of $R=1,2,4$ and 5. We see that very high storage utilization can be achieved with R greater than 4. Similar results were obtained with other bucket sizes.

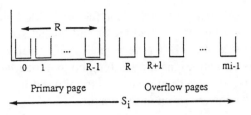

Figure 5. Overflow bucket size is a fraction
(1/R) of the primary bucket size.

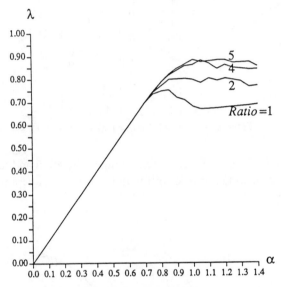

Figure 6. Storage Utilization for $b=20$ and
ratio $R=1, 2, 4$ and 5.

Cost of the scheme:

There are two costs associated with the scheme to be paid for its optimal retrieval performance:

(a) insertion cost

(b) internal memory space for IAT.

When an insertion is attempted, if the bucket to which the key hashes into is not already full, the cost is optimal (one read followed by a write). The probability of this event is quite large for perfect hashing tables as already shown in [RL88]. In our case, the probability is even higher in view of the non-full primary buckets. When the key does hash into a full bucket and a new perfect hashing function has to be found, there is computational and I/O cost involved for computing a new perfect hashing function and redistributing the records (this cost is lower than that of Signature Hashing). Some additional discussion may be found in section 6.

The size of the IAT depends on the load factor. Table 1 shows the number of entries in IAT for different values of the load factor and bucket sizes. When the load factor is below 0.8 or so, the size of the IAT is very small. This clearly indicates that the proposed scheme competes well with Signature Hashing up to a load factor of about 0.8 (note that in Signature Hashing, the insertion costs tend to infinity for higher load factors). Further details of the comparison are given in section 6.

α	20	30	40
0.1	0	0	0
0.2	0	0	0
0.3	0	0	0
0.4	0	0	0
0.5	0	0	0
0.6	1	0	0
0.7	4	3	1
0.8	10	10	6
0.9	24	22	22
1.0	42	42	42

Table 1: Size of IAT for $m=100$ and $b=20$, 30 and 40.

Figure 7 summarizes the results. The storage utilization and the size of IAT are plotted as a function of load factor α for different bucket sizes, keeping the ratio R constant at 5.

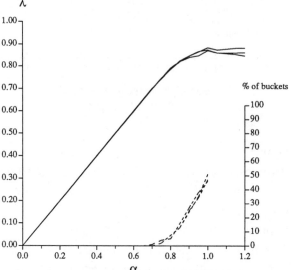

Figure 7. Solid line: Storage Utilization, dashed line: number of entries in IAT, for $b=20, 30$ and 40 and *ratio R*=5.

Worst case of hashing

One of the usual questions asked about hashing schemes is, what happens in the worst case? In our case, the *perfect–hash* ( ) has to be able to handle worst case key sets. Gonnet has shown that the fears of worst case are unfounded, and what is significant is the expected size of the worst case key set which has been shown to be $\Omega(\Gamma^{-1}(m))$ [GN81]. In view of the results in [RL88], there is no problem in handling these sizes for practically significant values of m.

5. Dynamic scheme

Since the overflowing records of any given bucket can be readily located, it follows that Litwin's Linear Hashing can be adapted to make the proposed scheme dynamic [LT80]. We assume the reader is familiar with Linear Hashing, and hence discuss the extension briefly.

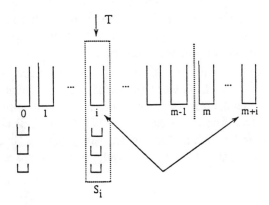

Figure 8. Dynamic scheme using *Linear Hashing*.

Figure 8 illustrates the dynamic version of the proposed scheme. There is a pointer T initially pointing to bucket 0, and two hashing functions h_0 and h_1. Whenever a decision is made to expand the file by one bucket, the group pointed to by T is split into two groups. Suppose T was pointing to group S_i, then it is split (accomplished by hashing function h_1) into two groups S_i and S_{m+i}. If there was an entry for S_i in IAT, it is replaced by 0/1/2 entries depending on the size of new S_i and S_{m+i}. Since this extension is straightforward we do not find it necessary to elaborate further in this regard.

6. Comparison with Signature Hashing and conclusions.

The proposed scheme is conceptually simple to implement as compared to Signature Hashing (an implementation some of the problems of signature hashing can be found in [LK84]). The proposed algorithms are straightforward and simple to implement, which in fact was the main motivation behind this work. Surprisingly, the cost involved with the proposed scheme also competes well with the Signature Hashing.

Considering the high probability of not having to recompute a perfect hashing function every time an insertion is made, the expected cost of an insertion is shown to be comparable to other hashing schemes including Signature Hashing [RL88]. Since a large fraction of primary buckets are not full, the overall expected cost of an insertion under the proposed scheme is even lower. However, we have not completely analyzed the insertion cost and is left as future work.

The size of IAT has been analyzed in terms of the number of entries (note that, as already mentioned, IAT can be organized as a dynamic hash table in internal memory as proposed in [LR88] and hence the number of entries determines the amount of storage used). Assuming 4 byte integer keys (longer alphanumeric keys can be converted to 4 byte integers using RADIX-conversion method [RM86]), each entry in IAT will be about 8-9 bytes long (4 bytes for C_i, 2 bytes for p_i and 2-3 bytes for m_i and i). This translates into about 4-6 bits per external bucket. This figure exactly agrees with the size of the internal separator table under Signature Hashing. Thus, below about 80% load factor, the internal memory space for the proposed scheme is lower than that for Signature Hashing. At higher load factors, the proposed scheme requires more internal space. But, at higher load factors, the insertion cost of Signature Hashing tends to infinity and hence those ranges of load factor are not of practical relevance.

Mairson has established that $\Omega(n)$ internal memory space is the lower bound to achieve single access retrieval. Given $\Omega(n)$ space, what information (and how) can be stored to minimize the complexity of the scheme (in terms of implementation, computation and I/O cost)? The proposed scheme and the results indicate that other kinds of information can be stored, which perform better than Signature Hashing and hence opens the problem, what is the best that can be achieved, given $\Omega(n)$ space?

References

[CW79]   Carter, L.J. and Wegman, M.L. *Universal classes of hash functions*. Journal of Computer and System Sciences, 18, 2(1979), 143 - 154.

[FN79]   Fagin,R., Nievergelt,J., Pippenger,N. and Strong,H.R. *Extendible hashing - a fast access method for dynamic files*. ACM Trans. on Database Systems, 4, 3(1979), 315 - 344.

[GL82]   Gonnet,G. H., and Larson, P. A. *External hashing with limited internal storage. In Proceedings of the ACM Symposium on Principles of Database Systems* (Los Angeles, CA.), ACM, New York, 1982, pp. 256-261.

[GL88]   Gonnet,G. H., and Larson P. A. *External hashing with limited internal storage*. Journal of the ACM, 35, 1(1988), pp. 161-184.

[GN81]   Gonnet,G.H. *Expected length of the longest probe sequence in hash code searching*. Journal of the ACM, 28, 2(1981), 289 - 304.

[LK84]   Larson, P.-A. and Kajla, A. *File organization - implementation of a method guaranteeing retrieval in one access*. Comm. of the ACM, 27,7 (1984), 670 - 677.

[LL86]   Litwin, W. and Lomet, D.B. *The bounded disorder access method,* Proc. 2nd Intn'l Conference on Data Engineering (Los Angeles, CA, 1988), 38-48.

[LR83]   Larson,P.-A. *Analysis of uniform hashing*. Journal of the ACM, 30, 4 (1983), 805 - 819.

[LR88]   Larson, P. A., *Dynamic Hash Tables* Comm. of the ACM, 31, 4 (1988), 446 - 457.

[LS88]   Larson, P. A., *Linear Hashing with Separators-A Dynamic Hashing Scheme Achieving One-Access Retrieval*. ACM Transactions on Database Systems, 13, 3 (1988), 366 - 388.

[LT80]   Litwin,W. *Linear hashing: A new tool for files and tables addressing*. Proc. 6th Intern'l Conf. on Very Large Databases, (Montreal, 1980), 212 - 223.

[MR83]   Mairson,H.G. *The program complexity of searching a table*. Proc. 24th Symposium on Foundations of Computer Science, IEEE Computer Society, 1983, 40 - 47.

[MR84]   Mairson,H.G. *The program complexity of searching a table*. Ph.D. Thesis, Department of Computer Science, Stanford University, 1984.

[RL88]   Ramakrishna, M.V. and Larson, P.A. *File organization using composite perfect hashing*. (to appear) ACM Trans. on Database Systems.
         Earlier version in Proc. ACM-SIGMOD Intern'l Conf. on Management of Data, (Austin, 1985), 190 - 200.

[RM86]   Ramakrishna,M.V. *Perfect hashing for external files*. Ph.D. Thesis, Department of Computer Science, University of Waterloo, Research Report CS-86-25, 1986.

[RM88]   Ramakrishna, M.V. *Hashing in practice, analysis of hashing and universal hashing*. Proc. ACM-SIGMOD Intern'l Conf. on Management of Data, (Chicago, 1988), 191 - 200.

[SP77]   Sprugnoli, R.J. *Perfect hashing functions: A single probe retrieving method for static sets*. Comm. of the ACM, 20, 11(1977), 841 - 850.

[TH88]   Tharp, A.L. *File Organization and Processing*. New York: John Wiley, 1988.

Partial-match Retrieval for Dynamic Files
using Linear Hashing with Partial Expansions

Kotagiri Ramamohanarao
John Shepherd

Ron Sacks-Davis

Department of Computer Science,
The University of Melbourne,
Parkville, Victoria 3052, Australia

Department of Computer Science,
Royal Melbourne Institute of Technology,
Melbourne, Victoria 3001, Australia

Abstract

The average number of disk accesses required to perform primary-key retrieval in systems using linear hashing can be reduced by employing the technique of partial expansions. This scheme maintains a more uniform distribution of records amongst the pages of the database file, thus reducing the average length of overflow chains and hence the average query cost. In this paper, we analyse the cost benefits of using linear hashing with partial expansions for partial-match retrieval and show that this type of indexing is effective for use with partial-match retrieval on highly dynamic files.

1. Introduction

Over the last decade, a number of hashing schemes have been developed for highly dynamic files. These methods maintain good retrieval performance and high storage utilisation independently of the size of the file. In this paper, we examine the method of *linear hashing* [3,7] so called because the file grows at a controlled rate by adding/removing one page at a time at the end of the file each time the number of records in the file increases/decreases by a fixed number L. Standard linear hashing has been improved by two independent techniques: *recursive linear hashing* [9] provides an effective method of handling overflow pages; *linear hashing with partial expansions* [2,7] improves the performance of the scheme by decreasing fluctuations in the storage utilisation. Linear hashing can be applied to both primary-key hashing and to multi-attribute hashing for partial-match retrieval. In this paper, we analyse the costs involved in answering partial-match queries using linear hashing with partial expansions.

We view a database as a collection of *files*, where each file contains *records* of a particular type. Each file is logically partitioned into a number of *pages*, where a page contains zero or more records up to a maximum B; all pages in the file are the same size. Each record consists of a number of *fields*, where each field is associated with a domain of possible values. The fields which may be specified in a query are called *attributes*; any other fields are not relevant to the considerations here. Let us assume that there are n attributes, $A_1, A_2, \cdots, A_n$. A *query type* is a subset of the attribute set $\{A_1, A_2, \cdots A_n\}$ which indicates the attributes that are *specified* in queries of that type. A *partial-match query* is a specification of the values of zero or more of these n attributes. The answer to a partial-match query is the set of records in the file which have the specified values for the specified attributes. *Primary key retrieval* may be regarded as a special case of partial-match retrieval where there is only one attribute, whose value must be specified in a query (that is, there is only one query type in primary key retrieval).

From a user's point of view, the most important aspect of database query performance is the average time taken to answer a query. The major time-cost involved in accessing current mass storage devices, such as disks, is the time taken to read or write a *page* of data. It is thus desirable to distribute the data in a file so as to minimise the number of pages which must be accessed in answering any query. However, in a partial-match retrieval system,

and it is not generally possible to arrange the data to minimise the page accesses for *every* query type. If we know the probability of asking a query of a particular type, then we can optimise the system to some extent by arranging (*clustering*) the data so that the most frequently asked queries are answered with lower cost than less frequently asked queries. In the context of partial-match retrieval, *multi-attribute hashing* schemes are a particularly interesting class of indexing schemes, as the indexing mechanism also provides a means of distributing the data over the pages of the file.

Linear hashing (*lh*) is a dynamic hashing technique that can be adapted to partial-match retrieval with multi-attribute hashing to enable it to handle dynamic files [5] without requiring periodic massive reorganisation of the index. However, because it allocates records to a new page by *splitting* a single existing page (distributing the records in a page between the original page and the newly added page), it suffers from considerable variation in storage utilisation as the file grows. This variation in storage utilisation results in variation in the average query cost, and, if one is unfortunate, the database might spend some time at a size where the average query cost is particularly high. A generalisation of linear hashing, linear hashing with partial expansions (*lhpe*) [2,7], performs splitting by re-distributing records from multiple pages and thus reduces the variation in the distribution of records. This, in turn, reduces both the average query cost and the cyclic fluctuation in query cost as the file changes size. However, in an *lhpe* scheme, the allocation of records to groups is controlled by a single attribute; in the context of partial-match retrieval, this may result in suboptimal organisation when the file is very small.

In section two, we review the technique of linear hashing with partial expansions for primary key retrieval as described in [7]. Section three introduces the partial-match retrieval problem. In section four, we analyse the differences between linear hashing with partial expansions for primary key retrieval and partial-match retrieval. Section five presents experimental results that show the expected performance for partial-match retrieval using linear hashing with partial expansions.

2. Linear Hashing with Partial Expansions

In linear hashing [3,7], a growing file undergoes a number of expansion stages. At the start of the dth expansion, the file contains $s = 2^d$ home pages. (There may also be overflow pages associated with each home page but we will delay further consideration of them until the analysis of the cost function.) The page in which a record is stored is computed by mapping the hash value of the key into the range of page numbers. As records are inserted into the file, new pages are added to the end of the file. The rate at which pages are added to and deleted from the file is determined by a system parameter called the *load control*, L: a new home page is appended to the file after the file size has increased by L records; a home page is removed from the end of the file after its size has decreased by L records; whenever a page is added or deleted, the load control counter is reset to zero. At the start of the dth expansion, a pointer called the *split pointer* (sp) will point to page 0 in the file. At a typical stage during the dth expansion (see figure 1), the file will contain $s + sp$ home pages, with the split pointer pointing at page sp.

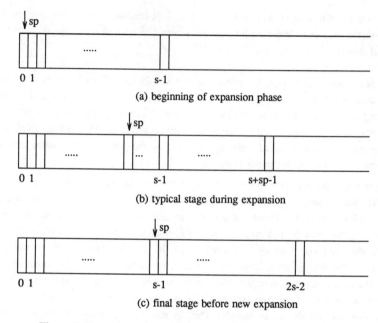

(a) beginning of expansion phase

(b) typical stage during expansion

(c) final stage before new expansion

Figure 1: Stages in expansion of a linear-hashed file

When a new page (page $s+sp$) is due to be appended to the file, page sp is *split*: the records that were in home page sp are distributed between pages sp and $s+sp$ by using an extra bit of hashing information (that is, by considering $d+1$ bits of the hash bit-string). The records for which the $d+1^{th}$ bit is 0 remain in page sp; the others are moved to page $s+sp$. The effect of this is that the pages which have already been split to the "left" of the split pointer (the *left pages*, numbered $0..sp-1$ and $s..s+sp-1$) are indexed as though the file were of depth $d+1$ (that is, contains 2^{d+1} pages), while pages which have not yet been split to the "right" of the split pointer (the *right pages $sp..s-1$*) are indexed as though the file were still depth d. After splitting, the split pointer is incremented by one. When the split pointer reaches s, the file size has doubled and the current expansion is completed. The file depth is then incremented to $d+1$ (doubling s) and sp is reset to the beginning of the file to start the next expansion.

While linear hashing provides a mechanism for dynamic hashing, there are some disadvantages to using a standard linear hashing scheme when trying to maintain a high load factor. Pages to the left of the split pointer and recently added pages (that is, the *left pages*) have approximately half as many records as the right pages. In order to maintain an overall high load factor, the right pages tend to carry a relatively high number of overflow pages compared to the left pages. This results in a higher average query cost when these overflow pages need to be searched in answering queries. Figure 2 indicates the average number of records per home page during a typical stage in the expansion of a linear hashed file.

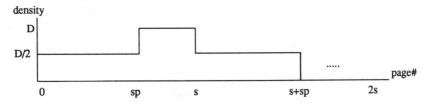

Figure 2: Record densities during expansion of a linear hashed file

The method of linear hashing with partial expansions (*lhpe*) [2,7,9] is a generalisation of linear hashing that maintains a more uniform distribution of records over the file as its size changes. This has several benefits: it gives better retrieval performance and the storage space in the home pages is better utilised, leading to shorter chains of overflow pages. The description of *lhpe* in this paper follows the description given in [7].

In an *lhpe* scheme, the file goes through a number of expansion phases as it doubles in size; this contrasts with linear hashing which has a single expansion phase each time the file size doubles. A new parameter known as the *group size* (G) is associated with the file; the file goes through G expansion phases as it doubles in size. Each of these expansion phases is known as a *partial expansion*. The file is initially partitioned into G groups, each of which contains 2^d pages. A split pointer, whose value ranges from 0 to 2^d-1, indicates the offset of the *split page* in each group. The split pointer is initially positioned so that the first page of each group is a split page. In a given partial expansion (see figure 3), there are g groups of size 2^d pages (where $G \leq g \leq 2G-1$), and a partial group of size sp. When the file size grows by one page, we add this new page to the partial group. The records in the split pages are then re-distributed amongst themselves and this new page, and the split pointer is advanced by one page. The partial expansion is complete when the size of the partial group reaches 2^d pages. When this happens, a new partial expansion is commenced; the value of g is incremented by one and the split pointers are reset to zero. When the value of g reaches $2G$, the file size has doubled and the file is then conceptually re-organised into G groups of 2^{d+1} pages, g is reset to G, and the next expansion phase begins. The partial expansion when $g = 2G-1$ is particularly important; since we do not wish to physically re-organise the records in the file when we change over to having G groups of size 2^{d+1}, we use an appropriate hashing function as shown in the algorithm below. Note that the standard linear hashing scheme is just an instance of linear hashing with partial expansions where $G=1$.

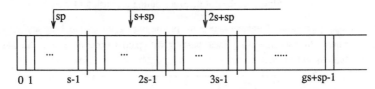

Figure 3: Typical stage during expansion of a linear hashed file with partial expansions

The page in which a record is stored is computed as two components: a group number and a page offset within the group. The offset for a record with key k when the groups are of depth d is given by a hashing function $h_{off}(k,d)$; this uses the depth of the group in the same manner as for standard linear hashing and maps the key into a value in the range $0..2^d-1$. The function h_{off} is required to have the property that

$$h(k,d+m) \bmod 2^d = h(k,d) \text{ when } d,m \geq 0$$

The group number for a record with key k when there are g groups in the file is given by a hashing function $h_{grp}(k,g)$; this maps the key into a value in the range $0..g-1$. The algorithm below describes the computation of the page address of a record in a file using linear hashing with partial expansions.

---

offset := h_{off} (key, d)
$d' := d$
if offset ≥ sp then

{ *maps to unsplit pages* }
group := h_{grp} (key, g)

else if g ≠ 2G-1 then

{ *this expansion not last partial expansion* }
group := h_{grp} (key, g+1)

else

{ *this expansion is last partial expansion* }
offset := h_{off} (key, d+1)
group := h_{grp} (key, G)
$d' := d + 1$

endif
page := $2^{d'}$ * group + offset

Algorithm: Computing multi-attribute hashing address with partial expansions

---

Figure 4 indicates the average number of records per home page during a typical stage in the expansion of an *lhpe* file. It shows that, rather than a single "peak" of high density, the file contains a number of smaller peaks; the greater the value of G, the closer the file is to a uniform distribution of records.

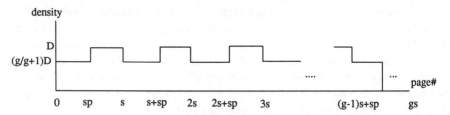

Figure 4: Record densities during expansion of a *lhpe* file

The average query cost of linear hashing for primary-key retrieval has been analysed in [7], and we follow their analysis here. In a scheme using linear hashing with partial expansions, each file has the five characteristic parameters given in table 1.

G:	group size
s_0:	initial segment size
B:	maximum number of records in each home page
b:	maximum number of records in each overflow page
L:	load control (number of record insertions after which a new home page is appended to the file)

Table 1: Characteristic parameters for *lhpe* files

Note that the standard linear hashing scheme is simply an instance of one of these schemes where $G = 1$. If N is the number of records inserted into the file, then we can define the properties of the file given in table 2.

$sp(N)$:	split pointer position
$lf(N)$:	load factor
$opl(N)$:	average overflow chain length for home pages left of sp
$opr(N)$:	average overflow chain length for home pages right of sp
$al(N)$:	average cost of retrieving records in home page plus overflow pages for home pages left of sp (in disk accesses)
$ar(N)$:	average cost of retrieving records in home page plus overflow pages for home pages right of sp (in disk accesses)
$ss(N)$:	average successful search cost (in disk accesses)
$us(N)$:	average unsuccessful search cost (in disk accesses)
$inl(N)$:	average cost of inserting record in home page left of sp
$inr(N)$:	average cost of inserting record in home page right of sp
$sc(N)$:	average cost of splitting
$in(N)$:	average insertion cost

Table 2: Properties of *lhpe* files

All costs are in terms of the number of disk accesses required to achieve the operation (including both reads and writes).

The value of sp is determined by a simple algorithm given in [7]. It is convenient to define a function W which indicates how many overflow pages are associated with a home page, given that there are k records in the home pages plus the associated overflow pages.

$$W(k) = 0, \ \text{ for } 0 \le k \le B$$

$$W(k) = j, \ \text{ for } B+(j-1)b+1 \le k \le B+jb$$

It is also convenient to use the following definitions for the probability of choosing a specific left or right page: $p_l = \dfrac{1}{(g+1).s}$ and $p_r = \dfrac{1}{g.s}$. In order to estimate the probability of k records hashing to a particular address when there are N records in the file and the probability of a given record hashing to that address is p, we use the binomial distribution given by:

$$b(k;N,p) = {}^nC_k(1-p)^{n-k}$$

The values of the other properties are then determined by the following formulae (also from [7]):

$$lf = \frac{N}{(g.s+sp).(B+b.op)} \tag{1a}$$

$$opl = \sum_{k=0}^{\infty} W(k)b(k;N,p_l) \tag{1b}$$

$$opr = \sum_{k=0}^{\infty} W(k)b(k;N,p_r) \tag{1c}$$

$$al = \sum_{k=0}^{\infty} (k+W(k)(k-(B+(W(k)-1)b/2))) \times b(k;N,p_l) \tag{1d}$$

$$ar = \sum_{k=0}^{\infty} (k+W(k)(k-(B+(W(k)-1)b/2))) \times b(k;N,p_r) \tag{1e}$$

$$ss = (g+1).\frac{sp}{N}.al + g\frac{(s-sp)}{N}.ar \tag{1f}$$

$$us = (1+opl).\frac{sp}{s} + (1+opr)\frac{(s-sp)}{s} \tag{1g}$$

$$inl = 2+\sum_{k=0}^{\infty} W(k+1)b(k;N,p_l) \tag{1h}$$

$$inr = 2+\sum_{k=0}^{\infty} W(k+1)b(k;N,p_r) \tag{1i}$$

$$sc = (g+1)(1+opl)+g(1+opr) \tag{1j}$$

$$in = \frac{(inl.sp+inr(s-sp))}{s} + \frac{sc}{L} \tag{1k}$$

Table 3 (from [7]) shows some typical values for these parameters when there are fifty records per page (that is, $B=50$).

lf	G	L	b	ss	us	in
0.849	1	51	14	1.202	1.968	3.112
0.845	2	45	8	1.064	1.486	2.703
0.850	4	44	7	1.029	1.272	2.577
0.855	8	44	7	1.021	1.213	2.716
0.949	1	69	7	1.985	5.016	6.274
0.946	2	56	4	1.425	3.610	5.041
0.950	4	54	4	1.239	2.795	4.369
0.955	8	54	4	1.206	2.655	4.592

Table 3: Typical values for *lhpe* file parameters

3. Partial-Match Retrieval with Linear Hashing

In the previous section, we described the notion of linear hashing for primary key retrieval. In this treatment, however, no mention was made of the actual method of obtaining a hash value to determine in which page a record would be located. For the primary key case, we can use any method of converting the key value into a bit-string which can be interpreted as a page number. In the case of partial-match retrieval, we use a multi-attribute hashing scheme to allocate records to pages; the concepts of linear hashing outlined above apply unchanged.

We again assume that the file contains 2^d pages, where $d>0$. Each record has n attributes and n associated hashing functions, h_i. Each h_i provides a mapping from the key space of attribute A_i to the set of all possible bit-strings of length d_i, where $d_i{\geq}0$ and $d_1+d_2+\cdots+d_n = d$. In a multi-attribute hashing scheme, the page in which a record is stored is computed as follows: for each attribute A_i, we hash its value to a string of length d_i bits using the hashing function h_i and interlace the bits of these strings (as indicated determined by a *choice vector*) to give the page number. The *choice vector* is indicates which attribute contributes each bit of the interlaced bit string and is determined using the bit-allocation algorithms described in [5]

We should, of course, choose the hash functions such that they distribute the records evenly among the pages. The clustering of the records depends on the choice of the values of the d_i. If, for example, $d_1=d$, then the clustering is determined solely by the value of attribute A_1. An *optimal clustering* is one which gives the minimum average cost for a query.

Let $Q \subseteq \{A_1, A_2, \cdots A_n\}$ be a query type, and p_Q be the probability that the user specifies a query of type Q. If an attribute A_i is specified in queries of type Q, then its value will contribute d_i bits of hashing information to the *query hash value*. For every attribute A_j that is not specified in queries of type Q, there will be d_j unknown bits in the query hash value. Since we need to investigate all possible values for the unknown bits, each unspecified attribute A_j requires us to examine 2^{d_j} times the number of pages. Thus, the average cost of a query is determined by:

$$C_{av} = \sum_Q p_Q \prod_{A_i \notin Q} 2^{d_i} \qquad (2)$$

where the summation is over all subsets $Q \subseteq \{A_1, A_2, \cdots A_n\}$. Note that the p_Q values for a particular system are determined by the use made of that system (although when the system is being designed we may have to estimate the expected usage of the various query types).

The problem of minimising the average cost is studied in [1,4,5]. The problem is: given p_Q values, find values for $d_1, d_2, \cdots, d_n$ that minimises the average query cost and satisfies the constraint that $d_1 + d_2 + \cdots + d_n = d$. Aho and Ullman [1] derived the optimal values of the d_i's in terms of the probability distribution in the *independent case*, that is, when the probability of specifying a particular attribute does not depend on the specification of any other attribute. However, this problem was shown to be NP-hard [6] for non-independent query probability distributions. In this case, there are heuristic algorithms that give good solutions [4].

The average query cost for linear hashing is determined in a manner similar to that above, except that there are two separate components because the file behaves as if it is split into two separate parts, one with size 2^{d+1} (the left pages) and the other with size 2^d (the right pages). For the left pages, the average query cost is computed as if the file were size 2^{d+1}:

$$CL_{av} = \sum_Q p_Q \prod_{A_i \notin Q} 2^{d'_i} \qquad (3)$$

where the d'_i are the number of bits allocated to the attribute A_i when the file size is 2^{d+1}. Note that each d'_i is equal to the corresponding d_i except for one, d'_j, which is equal to $d_j + 1$. For the right pages, the average query cost (CR_{av}) would be as given in equation (2). In order to determine the average query cost for the entire file, we must combine these two costs. We cannot simply sum them and divide by two, because there are generally different numbers of left and right pages in the file. If we assume that the references to pages which are caused by queries are spread uniformly over the file, then we can derive the following formula which takes into account the relative proportions of left and right pages:

$$CLR_{av} = (\frac{sp}{s}).CL_{av} + (\frac{s-sp}{s}).CR_{av} \qquad (4)$$

Using the definitions for the average overflow chain lengths for pages left and right of the split pointer (*opl* and *opr* in equations (1b) and (1c) respectively), we can account for the extra cost of overflows, to give the average query cost function for linear hashing schemes:

$$C(lh)_{av} = (1+opl).(\frac{sp}{s}).CL_{av} + (1+opr).(\frac{s-sp}{s}).CR_{av} \qquad (5)$$

4. Linear Hashing with Partial Expansions for Partial-match Retrieval

The predominant interest in primary key retrieval is to find the single record which satisfies the query with as few disk accesses as possible. The hashing scheme specifies a unique home page to examine and, in an effective hashing scheme, this will be the only page retrieved. Occasionally, the record is located in an overflow page associated with the primary page and so some overflow pages need to be read as well. Infrequently, the record will not exist in the database at all, and so the whole chain of overflow pages associated with the home page needs to be examined. Thus, the cost for a successful search is generally close to one page. The cost for an unsuccessful search is equal to the average length of overflow chains (plus one, to account for the primary page).

In partial-match retrieval, we are concerned only with the "unsuccessful" search cost, since we need to search all of the pages specified by the hashing to discover the complete set of matching records. A partial-match query will determine a number of home pages to be searched, and for each of these, we must also search the corresponding overflow pages. Thus, for partial-match retrieval, it is particularly important that overflow chains are kept as short as possible. *Linear hashing with partial expansions*, which minimises fluctuations in storage utilisation and thus reduces the average length of overflow chains, is thus an effective strategy for partial-match retrieval systems. One should also note that the insertion and deletion costs are the same whether we use a single-key hash value (for primary key retrieval) or a multi-attribute hash value (for partial-match retrieval).

There is, however, one disadvantage to this scheme in that one attribute (the *group attribute*) must be used to compute the group number for records. When this attribute is specified in a query, the group can be determined uniquely and so the query cost is the same as for partial-match retrieval in the standard linear hashing case. If this attribute is not specified, then the cost for that query type has to be multiplied by the number of groups in the file; since we cannot uniquely determine a group for the record, we must search at the determined offset(s) in every possible group.

In order to compute the average query cost for partial-match retrieval in an *lhpe* file, we need to formalise the above intuitive description. Let A_x denote the attribute which determines the group number of the record. As noted above in our analysis of the query cost for partial-match retrieval, for every attribute A_i which is not specified in a query, the average query cost is multiplied by 2^{d_i}. If the attribute A_x is not specified then the average query cost must also be multiplied by the number of groups g, to indicate that we need to examine all of the groups. We can now define the contribution to the query cost of a particular attribute, given the depth d (and a bit-allocation for that depth) and the number of groups in the file g:

$$attrcost(A_i, d, g) = \begin{cases} 2^{d_i} & \text{if } A_i \neq A_x \\ g \cdot 2^{d_i} & \text{otherwise} \end{cases} \quad \text{where } \sum_{i=1}^{n} d_i = d \tag{6}$$

The average query cost can now be defined for a given distribution of query types (at depth d and with g groups):

$$C(d, g) = \sum_{Q} p_Q \prod_{A_i \notin Q} attrcost(A_i, d, g) \tag{7}$$

where the Q ranges over all query types.

The above equation does not take into account overflow chain lengths and the difference between *left pages* and *right pages*. In addition, the case when there are $2G$ groups in the file has to be treated differently from the other values for g. Taking all of these factors into account yields the average cost of a query in an *lhpe* system:

$$C(lhpe)_{av} = (1+opl).(\frac{sp}{s}).C(d,g+1) + (1+opr).(\frac{s-sp}{s}).C(d,g) \quad \text{when } G \le g < 2G-1 \qquad (8a)$$

$$C(lhpe)_{av} = (1+opl).(\frac{sp}{s}).C(d+1,G) + (1+opr).(\frac{s-sp}{s}).C(d,g) \quad \text{when } g = 2G-1 \qquad (8b)$$

where *opl* and *opr* are as defined in equations (1b) and (1c).

The number of groups (G) affects the average query cost in two ways. First, having more groups reduces the average length of overflow chains (see the definitions for *opl* and *opr*), which in turn reduces the average query cost. Second, having more groups increases the query cost for query types which do not have the group attribute (A_x) specified, since we need to search all groups to answer these types of queries. Thus, in the case of partial-match retrieval, once we have increased the number of groups enough to minimise overflow chains (that is, to set $opl \approx 0$ and $opr \approx 0$), there is no benefit in increasing it further.

5. Performance of Linear Hashing with Partial Expansions

In order to test the effectiveness of linear hashing with partial expansions, we chose three sets of query probability distributions and evaluated the average query cost for various numbers of groups (G). The *minimal marginal increase* (*mmi*) algorithm described in [5] was used to determine optimal bit-allocations. In all cases, we are attempting to maintain a load factor of 0.95. We used the following parameters (derived from [7]) in all experiments:

G	s_0	B	b	L	lf
1	1	50	7	69	0.949
2	1	50	4	56	0.946
4	1	50	4	54	0.950
8	1	50	4	54	0.955

In the analyses below, we have ignored the cost of the query in which no fields are specified as it cannot be optimised by any method.

5.1. Aho & Ullman's Independent-attribute Distribution

The first probability distribution is taken from [1]. In this distribution the probability of an attribute occurring in a query is independent of the probability of other attributes occurring. The probabilities of the individual attributes are: $p_{A_1}=0.8$, $p_{A_2}=0.1$, $p_{A_3}=0.9$, $p_{A_4}=0.2$, and $p_{A_5}=0.5$. The full query probability distribution is given in the appendix, and we will denote it by PQ5 in the remainder of the paper. Table 4 shows the bit-allocations obtained for the PQ5 query distribution when $d=16$ for various values of G.

G	d_1	d_2	d_3	d_4	d_5	A_x
1	5	0	7	1	3	-
2	6	0	7	1	2	A_4
4	6	0	5	1	4	A_4
8	6	0	4	2	4	A_4

Table 4: Bit-allocations for PQ5 when $d=16$

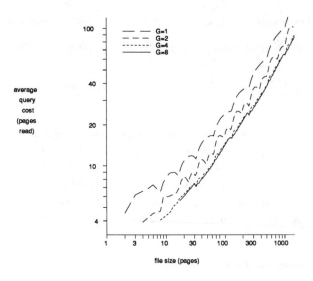

Graph 1: Average Query Cost vs. File Size for PQ5

It is clear from graph 1 that there is a significant improvement in the average query cost when linear hashing with partial expansions is used. For example, when there are 1000 pages in the file, the average cost falls from 101.54 when $G = 1$ to 64.37 when $G = 4$. It is also clear that when more groups are used, the fluctuations in performance are reduced. From the graph, it would not appear in this case that any significant benefit is gained by having more than four groups; the average query costs for four groups and eight groups are similar, and the update costs are greater when there are more groups.

5.2. Six-attribute Distribution

The next experiment used a random probability distribution for query types for a relation with six attributes taken from [8] (hereafter denoted PQ6). The query probability distribution for this case is given in the appendix. Table 5 and graph 2 give the results for the experiment using this probability distribution.

G	d_1	d_2	d_3	d_4	d_5	d_6	A_x
1	2	3	3	2	3	3	-
2	2	3	3	3	3	2	A_5
4	2	3	1	3	4	3	A_2
8	2	3	1	3	4	3	A_2

Table 5: Bit-allocations for PQ6 when $d=16$

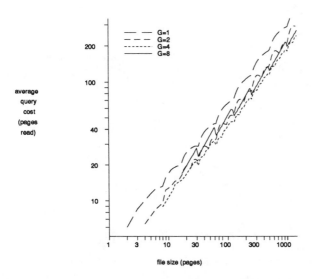

Graph 2: Average Query Cost vs. File Size for PQ6

Once again, we observe a similar performance improvement; in this case, however, having eight groups appears to impose a query performance penalty compared to the performance for four groups. This may indicate that four groups is sufficient to minimise the cost due to overflow chains, and that increasing G adds to the query cost by doubling the number of groups which need to be examined when the group attribute (A_2) is not specified (from the distribution in the appendix, the probability that A_2 is not specified is 0.5017).

5.3. Eight-attribute Distribution

The next experiment used a random probability distribution for query types for a relation with eight attributes (PQ8). Since there are 2^8 query types, space limitations prevent us from giving a description of the probability distribution. Table 6 and graph 3 give the results for the experiment using this probability distribution.

G	d_1	d_2	d_3	d_4	d_5	d_6	d_7	d_8	A_x
1	1	2	2	3	2	2	2	2	-
2	2	2	2	3	2	2	2	1	A_7
4	2	2	2	2	2	2	2	2	A_3
8	2	2	2	1	3	2	2	2	A_3

Table 6: Bit-allocations for PQ8 when $d=16$

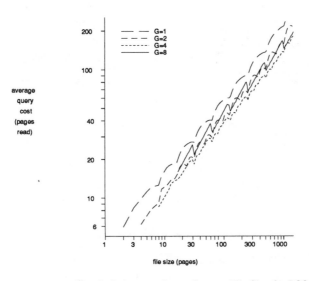

Graph 3: Average Query Cost vs. File Size for PQ8

5.4. Other Considerations

In the above analyses, we implicitly assumed that each attribute has an infinite domain (and thus can be allocated any number of bits). However, in practice attributes may have constraints on the size of their domains. For example, an attribute denoting *sex* can have at most two values; one should therefore allocate at most one bit to it. An attribute to denote *age* in years would range from zero to, say, 100, thus requiring a maximum of seven bits. Let 2^{dmax_i} denote the size of the domain of attribute A_i. Then the optimisation problem becomes to minimise the average query cost such that $d_1+d_2+ \cdots +d_n = d$ and $0 \le d_i \le dmax_i$ for $i=1,2, \cdots n$. Constraints on the d_i values generally have the effect of raising the average query cost once the constrained attributes have all of their allowed bits allocated to them. However, this occurs independently of any considerations with respect to the linear hashing scheme with partial expansions.

An additional method of improving the average query cost, which can be used in conjunction with linear hashing with partial expansions, is described in [10]. In this scheme, multiple copies of the data are stored, each of which uses a different bit-allocation to cluster the data. At query time, the database system uses the query type to determine which copy will result in the least number of pages being retrieved, and then uses that copy to answer the query. An experiment described in [10] using query distribution PQ5 indicated that using two copies of the data provided a performance improvement for the average query cost of ten times, while using four copies provided a performance improvement of nearly one thousand times.

6. Conclusion

We have examined the performance of query processing for partial-match retrieval using linear hashing with partial expansions. With a group size of four, we virtually eliminate the fluctuations in the load factor, and hence query cost, that occur in the standard linear hashing scheme. In addition, the reduction in overflow chain lengths from having four groups, reduces the average query cost by a considerable amount. Thus, linear hashing with partial expansions is an effective form of multi-attribute hashing for use with partial-match retrieval on highly dynamic files.

Acknowledgements

Thanks to Alan Kent for *graph+*, which made it so much easier to perform the analyses reported in this paper. Zoltan Somogyi was, as usual, an extremely thorough proof-reader and contributed to the clarity of the presentation by suggesting the density diagrams.

References

1.   A. V. Aho and J. D. Ullman, "Optimal partial-match retrieval when fields are independently specified", *ACM Transactions on Database Systems 4*, 2 (June 1979), 168-179.

2.   P. Larson, "Linear hashing with partial expansions", *Proceedings of the 6th International Conference on Very large Databases*, 1980, 212-233.

3.   W. Litwin, "Linear hashing: a new tool for file and table addressing", *Proceedings of the Sixth International Conference on Very Large Data Bases*, 1980, 212-223.

4.   J. W. Lloyd, "Optimal partial-match retrieval", *Bit 20* (1980), 406-413.

5.   J. W. Lloyd and K. Ramamohanarao, "Partial-match retrieval for dynamic files", *BIT 22* (1982), 150-168.

6.   S. Moran, "On the complexity of designing optimal partial-match retrieval systems", *ACM Transactions on Database Systems 8*, 4 (December 1983), 543-551.

7.   K. Ramamohanarao and J. W. Lloyd, "Dynamic hashing schemes", The Computer Journal, November 1982.

8.   K. Ramamohanarao, J. W. Lloyd and J. A. Thom, "Partial-match retrieval using hashing and descriptors", *ACM Transactions on Database Systems 8*, 4 (December 1983), 552-576.

9.   K. Ramamohanarao and R. Sacks-Davis, "Recursive linear hashing", *ACM Transactions on Database Systems 9*, 3 (September 1984), 369-391.

10.   K. Ramamohanarao, J. Shepherd and R. Sacks-Davis, "Partial-match retrieval using multi-key hashing with multiple file copies", *Proceedings of the International Symposium on Database Systems for Advanced Applications*, Seoul, Korea, April 1988.

Appendix - Query Probability Distributions

A.1 Aho & Ullman's Independent-attribute Distribution

Query type	P_Q	Query type	P_Q	Query type	P_Q
_,_,_,_,_	0.0072	A,B,_,D,_	0.0008	_,B,C,_,E	0.0072
A,_,_,_,_	0.0288	_,_,C,D,_	0.0162	A,B,C,_,E	0.0288
_,B,_,_,_	0.0008	A,_,C,D,_	0.0648	_,_,_,D,E	0.0018
A,B,_,_,_	0.0032	_,B,C,D,_	0.0018	A,_,_,D,E	0.0072
_,_,C,_,_	0.0648	A,B,C,D,_	0.0072	_,B,_,D,E	0.0002
A,_,C,_,_	0.2592	_,_,_,_,E	0.0072	A,B,_,D,E	0.0008
_,B,C,_,_	0.0072	A,_,_,_,E	0.0288	_,_,C,D,E	0.0162
A,B,C,_,_	0.0288	_,B,_,_,E	0.0008	A,_,C,D,E	0.0648
_,_,_,D,_	0.0018	A,B,_,_,E	0.0032	_,B,C,D,E	0.0018
A,_,_,D,_	0.0072	_,_,C,_,E	0.0648	A,B,C,D,E	0.0072
_,B,_,D,_	0.0002	A,_,C,_,E	0.2592		

Table A1: Five-attribute Independent Query Probability Distribution

A.2 Six-attribute Distribution

Query type	P_Q	Query type	P_Q	Query type	P_Q
_,_,_,_,_,_	0.0000	_,B,C,_,E,_	0.0196	_,_,C,D,_,F	0.0197
A,_,_,_,_,_	0.0027	A,B,C,_,E,_	0.0192	A,_,C,D,_,F	0.0179
_,B,_,_,_,_	0.0085	_,_,_,D,E,_	0.0128	_,B,C,D,_,F	0.0158
A,B,_,_,_,_	0.0197	A,_,_,D,E,_	0.0207	A,B,C,D,_,F	0.0280
_,_,C,_,_,_	0.0235	_,B,_,D,E,_	0.0068	_,_,_,_,E,F	0.0035
A,_,C,_,_,_	0.0226	A,B,_,D,E,_	0.0079	A,_,_,_,E,F	0.0186
_,B,C,_,_,_	0.0202	_,_,C,D,E,_	0.0242	_,B,_,_,E,F	0.0073
A,B,C,_,_,_	0.0023	A,_,C,D,E,_	0.0116	A,B,_,_,E,F	0.0009
_,_,_,D,_,_	0.0088	_,B,C,D,E,_	0.0312	_,_,C,_,E,F	0.0206
A,_,_,D,_,_	0.0035	A,B,C,D,E,_	0.0147	A,_,C,_,E,F	0.0252
_,B,_,D,_,_	0.0315	_,_,_,_,_,F	0.0194	_,B,C,_,E,F	0.0136
A,B,_,D,_,_	0.0239	A,_,_,_,_,F	0.0136	A,B,C,_,E,F	0.0232
_,_,C,D,_,_	0.0268	_,B,_,_,_,F	0.0199	_,_,_,D,E,F	0.0036
A,_,C,D,_,_	0.0106	A,B,_,_,_,F	0.0077	A,_,_,D,E,F	0.0310
_,B,C,D,_,_	0.0254	_,_,C,_,_,F	0.0176	_,B,_,D,E,F	0.0140
A,B,C,D,_,_	0.0051	A,_,C,_,_,F	0.0225	A,B,_,D,E,F	0.0127
_,_,_,_,E,_	0.0312	_,B,C,_,_,F	0.0044	_,_,C,D,E,F	0.0029
A,_,_,_,E,_	0.0216	A,B,C,_,_,F	0.0182	A,_,C,D,E,F	0.0190
_,B,_,_,E,_	0.0255	_,_,_,D,_,F	0.0248	_,B,C,D,E,F	0.0266
A,B,_,_,E,_	0.0029	A,_,_,D,_,F	0.0087	A,B,C,D,E,F	0.0011
_,_,C,_,E,_	0.0116	_,B,_,D,_,F	0.0220		
A,_,C,_,E,_	0.0009	A,B,_,D,_,F	0.0186		

Table A2: Six-attribute Random Query Probability Distribution

A.3 Eight-attribute Distribution

A complete definition of the eight-attribute random query probability distribution is rather voluminous and is omitted for the sake of brevity.

SHORT PRESENTATIONS

AN ANALYTICAL MODEL OF A DEFERRED AND INCREMENTAL UPDATE STRATEGY FOR SECONDARY INDEXES

Edward Omiecinski, Wei Liu and Ian Akyildiz
School of Information and Computer Science
Georgia Institute of Technology
Atlanta, GA 30332   U. S. A.

1. Introduction

The advantages of using an index for the retrieval of tuples from a relational database is well known. The benefit of having indexes is offset by the cost of maintaining the indexes in the face of updates. For some updates, the cost of maintaining the index may be greater than the cost of updating the desired set of tuples in the relation. In this paper, we describe a strategy for updating secondary indexes which can be classified as deferred and incremental. By deferred, we mean that the index is not updated when the user's update statement is executed. Rather, the appropriate changes are simply recorded for later update of the index. By incremental, we mean that only certain recorded changes will be applied to the index at a given time. We stress that only the index updates are deferred and that the tuple updates are performed by the user's update statement.

2. Previous Research

In [5], the use of a differential file is proposed. The differential file stores all updates, leaving the main file unchanged. Eventually, the differential file and main file are merged. In [5], they were interested in designing a Bloom filter which would indicate whether a given record could be found in the differential file.

In [3,6], the use of a differential file for updating a main file which is organized as a B+ tree is presented. In both [3] and [6], the approach is to perform an efficient batch update of the tree structured main file. In [3], they are concerned with determining the optimal time at which the batch update should take place. In [6], they use a tree structure for the differential file and assume that it can reside in main memory.

Instead of performing a batch update, others [1] have proposed to do incremental updating of the main file. Usually an update will be triggered by a query. In [1], the differential file does not contain the updated records but the update procedure.

In [2], an incremental and deferred update strategy is presented for the maintenance of text indexes. Their emphasis is on concurrency control methods and efficient data structures for the deferred update information.

3. Deferred and Incremental Index Update

Our deferred and incremental index update approach uses a differential file which grows as updates are executed and shrinks as queries are executed. A record in the differential file consists of the following attributes: a *TID*, the *old-key value* and the *new-key value*. For our purpose, we assume that the differential file is a simple sequential file with an update inplace capability. In addition, a record with a particular *TID* value occurs only once in the differential file.

The update procedure is simple and is shown below.

1. Access tuples to be modified (via a single index or file scan). If access is through the secondary index, then the query procedure (which follows) must be invoked.
2. Modify tuples.
3. For each indexed attribute, of the modified tuples, that has been modified:
   if the *TID* for this tuple does not appear in the differential file
       then write a new record to the differential file
   else update the *new-key value* for an existing record in the differential file

A naive query procedure, which uses the secondary index as the access method, is shown below.

1. Follow the appropriate path from the root to a leaf page of the index, (the leaf page contains key values and their associated *TID* lists).
2. Search the differential file for key values which match the requested key values contained on the leaf page.
   2.1 If the *old-key value*, from a record in the differential file, matches then delete the corresponding *TID* value from the *TID* list for the key and set the *old-key value* to null.
   2.2 If the *new-key value*, from a record in the differential file, matches then
       if the *old-key value* is null
           then
               insert the corresponding *TID* value in the *TID* list for the new key and set the *new-key value* to null
           else
               save the *TID* value in a temporary *TID* list.
   2.3 If both the *new-key value* and the *old-key value*, for a record in the differential file are null, then delete that record from the differential file.
3. If necessary, access the next leaf page and go to step 2.
4. Retrieve the tuples for the *TID* lists which have been found (including the temporary *TID* list). The *TID* lists contain any modifications as performed in step 2.

In [4], we prove that only one record in the differential file is needed per tuple, regardless of the number of key value changes that have taken place on any given tuple. We also prove in [4], that any *TID* will occur in the index at most one time and possibly be absent from the index during the deferred update.

4. Analytical Model of Differential File Size

Let us denote $P[size = s]$ as the probability that the differential file size is s, for

$s= 0,1,...,S_{max}$ and $P[i{\rightarrow}s]$ as the probability that the size of the differential file before the transaction is i, and after the transaction it is s. For a single update, a new record will be added to the differential file if and only if the *TID* of the record being updated is not contained in any of the existing differential file records. For a search transaction (single key or range of keys), if the *old-key value* for a differential file record is matched, then this value is set to $\emptyset$ and the indexed file is modified. A match on the *new-key value* will result in the record being deleted if and only if the *old-key value* in that record is $\emptyset$. Therefore, $P[i{\rightarrow}s]$ is determined by the number of records with the *old-key value* of $\emptyset$.

To characterize the above phenomenon, we use $P[empty\,|\,s]$ to denote the proportion of records with an empty *old-key value* when the differential file contains s records. It is obvious that for each record in the differential file of size s, the probability that its *old-key value* is empty is also $P[empty\,|\,s]$. The search transaction is treated as if it consisted of two steps. First, when the *old-key value* is matched, it is set to $\emptyset$. This results in $P[empty\,|\,s]$ being changed to a new value, $N(s,j)$, where $j= 1$ denotes a single key search and $j= 2,...,R_{max}$ denotes a range search consisting of 2 keys through R_{max} keys. The variable R_{max} denotes the maximum number of keys in a range query. The calculation of $N(s,j)$ will be given later. The second step is to match the *new-key value*. It should be noted that $P[empty\,|\,s]$ changes from transaction to transaction. Another consideration is, that if $P[size= s]= 0$ then $P[empty\,|\,s]$ is undefined. The above two considerations direct us in the calculation of $P^{(t)}[empty\,|\,s]$ where t denotes that t transactions have been processed. We use $P^{(t-1)}[empty\,|\,s']$ for all states s' that can reach s. That is, the differential file can change from a state having s' records to a state having s records. Also, $P^{(t-1)}[empty\,|\,s']$ is undefined if $P^{(t-1)}[size= s']= 0$.

Next, we develop an iteration model to calculate $P[size= s]$ based on $P[empty\,|\,s]$. Also, the maximum size of the differential file after t transactions have been processed can be easily predicted from the size distribution. We use the following notation in our model:

$Prob[up]$ = probability of update	K_{max} = number of unique key values
$Prob[ss]$ = probability of single key search	S_{max} = maximum size (in records)
$Prob[rs]$ = probability of range search	R_{max} = maximum number of keys in range search

Initially, we set $P^{(0)}[size= 0] = 1$ and $P^{(0)}[size= i] = 0$, for $i= 1,...,S_{max}$. All $P^{(0)}[empty\,|\,s]$ are undefined for $s= 1,..,S_{max}$. Iterate over equations (1 - 5), i.e., $t = 1,...,ceil$, until the difference between the average size of the differential file in two successive iterations is less than an epsilon $(\varepsilon= 10^{-4})$ value. The probability that after t transactions, the differential file size is s, is shown in equation 1.

$$P^{(t)}[size= s] = \sum_{i=0}^{S_{max}} P^{(t-1)}[size= i]\cdot P^{(t-1)}[i{\rightarrow}s] \tag{1}$$

where $P^{(t-1)}[i \to s]$ is computed by equation 4

$P^{(t)}[empty \mid s]$, in equation 2, is defined in a somewhat similar manner, except now, we have to take into account $Q^{(t-1)}[i \to s]$ for every i value that can lead us to a state with s records. $Q^t[i \to s]$, is defined in equation 5.

$$P^{(t)}[empty \mid s] = undefined, \qquad if \ P^{(t)}[size = s] = 0 \tag{2a}$$

$$P^{(t)}[empty \mid s] = \frac{\displaystyle\sum_{i=0}^{S_{max}} P^{(t-1)}[size = i] \cdot P^{(t-1)}[i \to s] \cdot Q^{(t-1)}[i \to s]}{\displaystyle\sum_{j=0}^{S_{max}} P^{(t-1)}[size = j] \cdot P^{(t-1)}[j \to s]} \tag{2b}$$

where $Q^{(t-1)}[i \to s]$ is defined in equation 5

The following equation yields the new proportion of records with an *old-key value* of $\varnothing$. This is relative to the differential file size and the number of keys which appear in a search request. This formula will be used in defining $Q^t[i \to s]$ as shown shortly.

$$N^{(t-1)}(s,j) = P^{(t-1)}[empty \mid s] + (1 - P^{(t-1)}[empty \mid s]) \cdot \frac{j}{K_{max}} \tag{3}$$

for $s = 1,..,S_{max}$ such that $P^{(t-1)}[size = s] > 0 \ \& \ j = 1,..,R_{max}$

Equations 4(a - d) depict the 4 possibilities for a transition in the differential file size.

$$P^{(t-1)}[s \to s+1] = Prob[up] \cdot (1 - \frac{s}{S_{max}}) \qquad (if \ P^{(t-1)}[size = s] > 0) \tag{4a}$$

$$P^{(t-1)}[s \to s] = Prob[up]\frac{s}{S_{max}} + Prob[ss]\left[1 - N^{(t-1)}(s,1) \cdot \frac{1}{K_{max}}\right]^s \tag{4b}$$

$$+ Prob[rs] \cdot \sum_{j=2}^{R_{max}} \frac{1}{R_{max}-1}\left[1 - N^{(t-1)}(s,j) \cdot \frac{j}{K_{max}}\right]^s \qquad (if \ P^{(t-1)}[size = s] > 0)$$

$$P^{(t-1)}[s \to s-\delta] = Prob[ss] \cdot \binom{s}{\delta}\left[N^{(t-1)}(s,1) \cdot \frac{1}{K_{max}}\right]^{\delta} \cdot \left[1 - N^{(t-1)}(s,1) \cdot \frac{1}{K_{max}}\right]^{s-\delta} \tag{4c}$$

$$+ Prob[rs] \cdot \sum_{j=2}^{R_{max}} \frac{1}{R_{max}-1}\binom{s}{\delta}\left[N^{(t-1)}(s,j) \cdot \frac{j}{K_{max}}\right]^{\delta} \cdot \left[1 - N^{(t-1)}(s,j) \cdot \frac{j}{K_{max}}\right]^{s-\delta}$$

$$(if \ P^{(t-1)}[size = s] > 0 \ \& \ for \ \delta = 1,..s)$$

$$P^{(t-1)}[i \to j] = 0 \quad for \ all \ other \ cases \tag{4d}$$

Again, we consider the possible state transitions for the differential file in equations 5(a - e). Except, that here we calculate the proportion of records in the differential file whose *old-key value* is ∅.

$$Q^{(t-1)}[0 \to 0] \text{ is not defined and is never used} \tag{5a}$$

$$Q^{(t-1)}[0 \to 1] = 0 \tag{5b}$$

$$Q^{(t-1)}[s \to s] = Prob[up] \cdot P^{(t-1)}[empty \mid s] + Prob[ss] \cdot N^{(t-1)}(s,1) \tag{5c}$$

$$+ Prob[rs] \cdot \sum_{j=2}^{R_{max}} \frac{1}{R_{max}-1} N^{(t-1)}(s,j) \qquad (if \ P^{(t-1)}[size=s] > 0)$$

$$Q^{(t-1)}[s \to s - \delta] = \frac{Prob[ss]}{Prob[ss] + Prob[rs]} \frac{s \cdot N^{(t-1)}(s,1) - \delta}{s - \delta} \tag{5d}$$

$$+ \frac{Prob[rs]}{Prob[ss] + Prob[rs]} \cdot \sum_{j=2}^{R_{max}} \frac{1}{R_{max}-1} \frac{s \cdot N^{(t-1)}(s,j) - \delta}{s - \delta} \qquad (if \ P^{(t-1)}[size=s] > 0)$$

$$Q^{(t-1)}[s \to s'] = 0 \qquad \text{for all other cases.} \tag{5e}$$

In [4], we compare our analytical model with a simulation model. We show that the expected maximum differential file size (in number of records) is only 16% of the number of records in the relation. In addition, we show in [4] that the model differs from the simulation by approximately 15% for the maximum differential file size.

References

1. Cammarata, S., "Deferring Updates in a Relational Database System," 1981 VLDB Conference Proceedings, 1981, 286-292.

2. Dadam, P., Lum, V., Praedel, U. and Schlageter, G., "Selective Deferred Index Maintenance & Concurrency Control in Integrated Information Systems," 1985 VLDB Conference Proceedings, 1985, 142-149.

3. Lang, S., Driscoll, J. and Jou, J., "Improving the Differential File Technique via Batch Operations for Tree Structured File Organizations," 1986 Data Engineering Conference Proceedings, IEEE, 1986, 524-532.

4. Omiecinski, E., Liu, W. and Akyildiz, I., "Analysis of a Deferred and Incremental Update Strategy for Secondary Indexes," Georgia Institute of Technology, Technical Report GIT-ICS-88-41, November 1988.

5. Severance, D. and Lohman, G., "Differential Files: Their Application to the Maintenance of Large Databases," ACM TODS, 1, 3, Sept. 1976, 256-267.

6. Srivastava, J. and Ramamoorthy, C., "Efficient Algorithms for Maintenance of Large Database Indexes," 1988 Data Engineering Conference Proceedings, IEEE, 1988, 402-408.

A Compact Multiway Merge Sorter using VLSI Linear-array Comparators

Tetsuji SATOH, Hideaki TAKEDA and Nobuo TSUDA
NTT Communications and Information Processing Laboratories
Kanagawa, Japan

1. INTRODUCTION

Sorting is one of the fundamental operations in relational database processing knowledge-base processing and image processing. A high-speed hardware sorter is necessary for sorting large amounts of data because too much CPU time is consumed for sorting even in a high-speed general-purpose computer. To overcome this CPU limitation, many kinds of hardware sorters have been proposed to increase sorting speed by using hardware parallelism and pipeline processing[1, 2]. However, ordinary hardware sorters are too large to be effectively used in database machines because their hardware configuration depends on the quantity of data to be sorted[3, 4]. For example, a pipelined two-way merge sorter[4] uses concatenated $\log_2 N$ two-way merge circuits, where N is the number of records.

The authors studied a basic principle of a high-speed multiway merge algorithm using a linear sorting array[5]. This algorithm is a potential basis for a compact and high-speed hardware sorter. This paper describes detailed algorithms and implementation techniques on a compact hardware sorter, whose architecture is independent of the number of records. The sorter embodies the multiway merge algorithm based on a data-driven string-selection technique and a pipelined parallel comparison technique. The number of merge ways, indicated by k, is expanded dramatically using these techniques, and the high-speed k-way merging is absolutely independent of k. By expanding the number of merge ways, the number of merging stages is decreased. A large number of records are usually able to be sorted with only two or three merge stages.

The compact sorter is mainly composed of a sorting array for record comparison and a working storage for record buffering. The sorting array is suitable for VLSI implementation because of its repeatability, and sorting speed is a function of array size. The working storage consists of large capacity dynamic-RAM chips and its size is determined by the number of records to be sorted. These devices are separately fabricated and can be combined in various sizes to suit the intended performance. Therefore, the sorter can satisfy the requirements for record capacity and sorting speed in a compact form.

2. SORT ALGORITHM

The multiway merge algorithm is one of the most popular sorting method known as external sorting in general-purpose computers[1]. The newly devised algorithm in the compact hardware sorter is essentially based on this algorithm.

2-1. HARDWARE CONFIGURATION

The sorter consists of a linear sorting array, a working storage and a merge controller, as shown in Fig. 1. The configuration of the array is cascade-connected sorting elements with one-dimensional linear array structure. Each element simply consists of two memories, a comparator and a few control circuits. The sorting array executes comparison-transferral actions synchronously in a pipelined parallel manner. In each sorting element, two records are compared, and the smaller or larger one is commonly selected and transferred to the neighboring element through a dedicated data path which is controlled by the previous comparative result. The sorting order, descending or ascending, determines whether the smaller or larger record is transferred.

Record flows in the sorting array for descending sorting order are shown in Fig. 2. In this figure, a record is represented by an arabic numeral. During the input operation, the

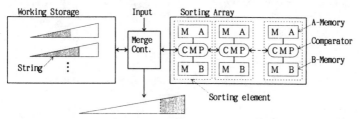

Fig.1 Block Diagram of Multiway Merge Sorter

smaller record in either MA or MB is selected and transferred to the rightward element synchronously in each sorting element. Conversely, during output operation, the larger record is selected and transferred leftward. Therefore the largest record in the array is always kept in the left-most sorting element at each input/output step. Sorting operation of k records is completed within the input and output of k records using ⌈k/2⌉ sorting elements, where ⌈k/2⌉ is the minimum integer greater than or equal to k/2.

The working storage can be realized in a small area circuit board using large-capacity dynamic-RAM chips. The multistage k-way merge operation, detailed in section 2-2 and 2-3, is executed by the merge controller.

2-2. MULTISTAGE MERGE ALGORITHM

Large number of records can be sorted in a series of sorting operations. This is called the multistage merge sort. In each k-way merge stage, k strings in the working storage are merged at one time and then re-stored there as a single string. The size of the string is the total number of records in all k strings. The multistage merge sort is executed by three types of stages as follows.

PRE-MERGE STAGE In this stage, the records are divided into k-record strings and all of them are sorted using the sorting array composed of ⌈k/2⌉ sorting elements. Sorted records are stored in the working storage as strings of size k. At the end of N record input, ⌈N/k⌉ strings are stored in the storage. The operation of this stage can be done during record input by the bi-directional sorting method described in section 3.

INTERMEDIATE MERGE STAGES In these stages, pure k-way merging described in section 2-3 is performed. In the first intermediate stage, strings generated in the pre-merge stage are successively merged. The maximum size of the generated strings is k^2 and the number of them is ⌈N/k²⌉. The number of strings in the working storage is decreased by one k-th in one stage. Merge operations are continued until the string number is below k.

OUTPUT MERGE STAGE Strings stored in the working storage can be merged and output in this stage because the number of strings is below k. The operations in this stage are similar to the intermediate merge stages except the handling the generated string. The generated string, which contains all the sorted records, is output to the host computer or any other device as needed.

Merge operations in all stages are accelerated by the sorting array. The stage number is ⌈log_k N⌉. For example, the 64-way merge sorter can handle 4k to 256k records in three merge stages; the pre-merge, one intermediate merge and the output merge stages.

The process of the multistage merging is shown in Fig. 3. In the pre-merge stage, input records are sequentially stored as strings of size k in the working storage starting from the bottom address. At the end of this stage, the auxiliary area is located above the area containing the strings. Intermediate merge operations are performed and keep a continuous single auxiliary area. The merge operation starts with the input of the last-stored string from the previous stage. The merged strings are stored continuously in opposite sequence. These operations are repeated in each stage. An auxiliary area is prepared for storing a merged string. Its capacity is equal to the maximum size of the strings stored in it. The auxiliary area capacity can be decreased to the value of (records capacity)/k when input strings in the output merge stage are equal.

2-3. MULTIWAY MERGE ALGORITHM

The multiway merge operation is achieved by using a newly devised data-driven string-selection technique. Records, read from the working storage, are identified with bank-tags. They are compared in the sorting array and output with their bank-tags. A continuous record flow using the bank-tag control is shown in Fig. 4. This figure shows an example of

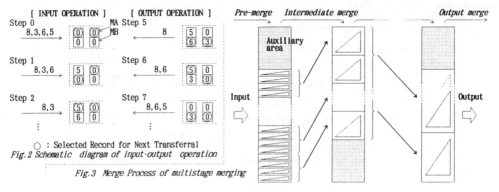

○ : Selected Record for Next Transferral
Fig. 2 Schematic diagram of input-output operation

Fig. 3 Merge Process of multistage merging

four-way merging in descending order.

M1-phase: In this phase, the sorting array is filled with the largest records in all merging strings. These largest records are located at the top of strings. The bank-tag indicating the string is attached to the record. A record with the bank-tag is input and compared in the sorting array. Four strings indicated by the bank numbers, #0 to #3, have been stored in the working storage. The top record, '8', in the #0 string is read out and input in the array with the bank-tag '0', as a '8-0'. The four records with bank-tags are compared with each other there. The largest record is kept in the left-most element at the end of the M1-phase.

M2-phase: In this phase, merge operations are performed successively. The largest record in the sorting array is immediately output with the bank-tag. This is the largest included in all merging strings. The second-largest candidate records are limited to any of the remaining ones in the array or the top one in the string indicated by the largest record's bank-tag. Therefore this top one is input to the array and is compared with the remaining candidate records. The successive multiway merging is achieved by this alternate record output-input operation. The M2-phase operation is continued until all merging strings are emptied. When any of the strings becomes empty, the record-input operation following the record-output operation whose bank-tag indicates a empty string is omitted. In this case, the output operation is continued.

The merging way number is only limited by the number of sorting elements in the array. The way number can be easily expanded by increasing the number of sorting elements.

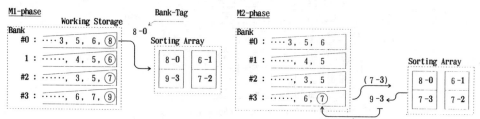

Fig. 4 Continuous Multiway Merging Diagram using Bank-tag

2-4. ADVANCED FEATURES OF THE NEW SORT ALGORITHM

The sort algorithm is achieved by the repetition of the multiway merge operation. Its advanced features are as follows.

- K, the number of merge ways, is increased dramatically by a data-driven string-selection technique and a parallel comparison technique.
- Perfect-successive k-way merging is achieved independent of k by these techniques.
- Very large amount of records can be sorted with a few k-way merge stages.
- It permits the construction a space efficient sorter that is both fast and flexible.

The hardware for k-way mergers consists of the sorting array, with ⌈k/2⌉ sorting elements, and the working storage which can store the whole record. By separating comparators and storage, the architecture of the hardware sorter is independent of the sorting speed and sorting record number. If sorting speed is paramount, then more comparators can be easily added in a cascaded manner. If the number of records is extremely large, then dynamic-RAM chips can be utilized to provide sufficient working storage capacity.

3. IMPLEMENTATION OF VLSI SORTING ARRAY

3.1 BASIC CONFIGURATION

The prototype sorting array chip is basically composed of cascade-connected 40 elements, as shown in Fig. 5. Each sorting element has a 1-byte wide comparator and two 16-byte memories. All neighboring elements are connected by a 1-byte wide data path.

The sorting operation is achieved by comparison-transferral actions in a successive pipelined manner. Fig. 5 shows an example of record sorting using 5 records, each of which consists of 4 bytes: v0-v3, w0-w3, x0-x3, y0-y3, and z0-z3. The records W, Y, and Z have already been input into the sorting array and have been quasi-sorted in descending order, that is Z is largest and W is smallest. The sorting sequence consists of transferral and comparison of single bytes. Record X is to be input and compared with record Z in four sequences. In the sequence stage indicated in this figure, x2 is input and compared with z2 which was read from memory MB1. Simultaneously, y2 is input to the second element, (Y was transferred resulting from the pervious record comparison in the first element,) and compared with w2 read from memory MA2. The comparisons and transfers continue until the last byte, x3, has been input. The comparison result is accumulated in the flag for comparison (FCMP) register within one record transfers. Based on the FCMP register value in the first element, the flag control circuit (FCTL) sets the switches, SWA, SWB, and SWC, to transfer the smaller record(of X or Z) to the second element and direct the byte-wide input of V to the comparator and then to the appropriate memory unit.

3.2 RECORD LENGTH EXPANSION

In the sorting array, records are kept and compared in each element. Therefore the record length is limited by the memory capacity on each element. The record-length expansion is achieved by cooperation between elements on the same sorting array chip or between chips. Records, whose lengths are over the memory capacity, can be handled by the element-connection method. Longer records are divided between the number of connected elements by handle the record length. Divided records are compared by the element in which they are stored. All the comparison results from the connected elements are accumulated for complete record comparison. The connected elements play the role of a single memory-expanded element. The record-length expansion is realized using only element combination circuits. These are mainly composed of bypass circuits for record transferring and circuits for accumulation of the comparison results.

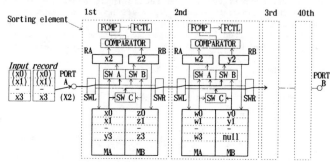

Fig. 5 Architecture of the prototype sorting array

3.3 BI-DIRECTIONAL SORTING METHOD

The sorting operation for k records is achieved within the successive k-record input and output time in the pre-merge stage. These input/output operations are alternately performed through the PORT-A as shown in Fig. 5. The input of new records through PORT-B is possible coincident with the output sorted records from PORT-A. To realize this function records input through PORT-A and PORT-B must be separated in the array.

The hardware configuration for bi-directional sorting is shown in Fig. 6. The flag, '0' or '1', is appended to the most significant bit (MSB) side of records. A couple of bit-reverse circuits are located on both sides of the sorting array to reverse all bits of input/output records. The record modification rule for bi-directional sorting is summarized in Table 1. In this case, both memories on all sorting elements are initially filled with the value '0' before record input.

By controlling both the flag value and bit-reverse circuits, any records input through PORT-A are always larger than any input through PORT-B. Thus, records input from PORT-A and PORT-B are separated automatically, moreover, the sorting order can be completely controlled independently each other. The sorting order is easily set up because the operation of sorting elements can be independent of the sorting order.

Table. 1 Record modification rules

Sort Order	Flag	Bit-reverse circuits	
		PORT-A	PORT-B
Ascending	'0'	Bit-reverse	through
Descending	'1'	through	Bit-reverse

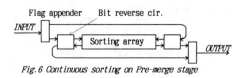

Fig. 6 Continuous sorting on Pre-merge stage

4. EVALUATION OF HIGH-PERFORMANCE SORTER

The VLSI sorting array chip used in the prototype hardware sorter contains 40 elements using 3-level hierarchical redundancy technology(7, 8). The chip can basically handle 80 16-byte records and several chips can be cascade-connected to increase the permissible record number. Records are continuously input and then output in a 1-byte wide data stream at a 3M-bytes/second throughput.

The 80-way merge sorter is composed in a small-sized single board. The main features of the sorter board are summarized in Table 2. Applied techniques to realize the compact and flexible sorter are also summarized in Table 3. Records of which length is less than 64 bytes can be sorted with the working storage. The single board sorter with an 8-MB working storage can sort 500k 15-byte records in 13.4 seconds.

The compact hardware sorter based on this architecture has been implemented in the Relational Database Processor (RINDA) (9,10). RINDA is connected to data-channels of general purpose computers, and performs on-the-fly search and pipeline sort operations. The hardware sorter in RINDA has the following characteristics.
- Merge operations in the pre-merge and output merge stage are performed within the record transfer time. Its merge speed is at least twice as fast as the prototype sorter for supporting the data transfer speed of a general purpose computer's channel.
- It must sort as long records as possible. Therefore, sorting record length is expanded to about 250 bytes by the element-connection technique.

Table 2 Features of the prototype sorter

Function	Multistage k-way merge sort
Record length	L < 64 bytes
Record number	N ; limited by the working storage capacity
Merge ways	k ; depends on the record length[*1]
	k = 80 (L<16B), 40 (L<32B), 20 (L<64B)
Merge speed	
Pre-merge stage	3.0 M-bytes/Second[*2]
Intermediate stage	1.5 M-bytes/Second
Output stage	1.5 M-bytes/Second
Configuration	
Merge controller	68020 micro-processor
Sorting array	A VLSI chip (including 40 sorting elements)
Working storage	8 M-bytes (1 M-bits dynamic-RAMs)
Board size	One square foot

*1 and *2 are achieved by techniques in Table 3.

Table 3 Applied techniques in the prototype sorter

Techniques	Effects
*1 : element-connection method	To increase the record length by a factor of four
*2 : Bi-directional sorting method	To simplify the sorting element's controller
	To accelerate the pre-merge speed by a factor of two

5. CONCLUSION

A multiway merge sorter using a newly devised merge algorithm has been proposed. It is composed of a sorting array for record comparison and a common working storage for record storing. The basic structure of the sorting array is linear, and its configuration is independent of the record length. The hardware can be realized in a small package because its components are very suitable for VLSI implementation. Separating the sorting array and working storage provides the flexibility to fulfill specific speed or capacity requirement, since the architecture is independent of those characteristics.

The k-way merge operation is performed independent of its way numbers using parallel comparison-transferral actions in the array. The number of merge ways is easily expanded by the data-driven string-selection technique using the bank-tag. The bank-tag is appended to the record in order to indicate the string which the record is stored in. The successive merge operation is performed using the string selection with the bank-tag. Also, Record length expansion is easily achieved by the element connection method. A single board prototype sorter using the VLSI sorting array chip can sort 500k 15-byte records in 13.4 seconds, including record input/output time.

REFERENCES
(1) D. E. Knuth, "The Art of Computer Programming, Vol. 3, Sorting and Searching", Addison-Wesley, 1973
(2) C. D. Thompson, "The VLSI Complexity of Sorting", IEEE Trans. on Computers, Vol. C-32, No. 12, pp. 1171-1184, Dec. 1983
(3) M. Kumar and D. S. Hirschberg, "An Efficient Implementation of Batcher's Odd-Even Merge Algorithm and Its Application in Parallel Sorting Schemes", IEEE Trans. on Computers, Vol. C-32, No. 3, Mar. 1983
(4) S. Todd, "Algorithm and Hardware for a Merge Sort Using Multiple Processors", IBM J. Res. Develop. Vol. 22, No. 5, pp. 509-517, Sept. 1978
(5) Satoh T. and Tsuda N., "A New Sorter Configuration using Linear Array Structure", 29th National Convention of IPS of Japan, pp. 769-770, Sept. 1984
(6) G. Miranker, L. Tang and C. K. Wong, "A Zero-Time VLSI Sorter", IBM J. Res. Develop. Vol. 27, No. 2, pp. 140-148, Mar. 1983
(7) Tsuda N., Satoh T., and Kawada T., "A Pipeline Sorting Chip", IEEE ISSCC Digest of Technical Papers, pp. 270-271, Feb. 1987
(8) Tsuda N. and Satoh T., "Hierarchical Redundancy for A Linear-array Sorting Chip", IFIP TC10/WG10.5 Workshop on Wafer Scale Integration, Sept. 1987
(9) Inoue U., Hayami H., Fukuoka H. and Suzuki K., "RINDA - A Relational Database Processor for Non-indexed Queries", International Symposium on Database Systems for Advanced Applications, Apr. 1989
(10)Takeda H. and Satoh T., "An accelerating Processor for Join Operations", Private report, Oct. 1988

USING LOGARITHMIC CODE-EXPANSION TO SPEEDUP INDEX ACCESS AND MAINTENANCE

Martin L. Kersten

Centre for Mathematics and Computer Science,
Kruislaan 413, 1098 SJ Amsterdam, The Netherlands

Keywords and Phrases : Data storage representations, access methods, main-memory DBMS.

1. Introduction

A growing awareness is that in the near future random access memory becomes a cost-effective storage medium for medium range databases [Garcia-Molina 83]. In 1984 an estimate of 250,000 dollar is given for a one Gigabyte main-memory system by the end of this decade [DeWitt 84]. Their guess has not been disproved since and several projects are underway to design and implement a main-memory DBMS [Bitton 86, Leland 87, Kersten 87].

One particular MMDB is being developed at the University of Wisconsin-Madison [Lehman 86a, Lehman 86b]. They discovered that the search algorithms for ordinary B-tree were too slow when compared with avl-trees and sorted heaps. Since the latter showed bad insertion performance, they invented a hybrid data structure, called the T-tree. A T-tree is a binary search tree in which each node contains a small, limited sized sorted heap. Moreover, each node represents a single, dynamically changing interval in the key space. The smallest and largest elements in the nodes are used to speed-up searching the T-tree node with the desired elements.

In this paper we too focus on the data structures for maintaining dynamic access paths to memory-resident relations. To obtain maximal benefit from the large main-memory we assume that the database as a whole fits in the available memory space, because previous analysis show that the performance quickly deteriorates when only a portion is mapped into a large buffer pool [DeWitt84]. However, we do not assume that memory is for free. Therefore, we are interested in data structures and algorithms with good time/space trade-offs. In particular, we focus on mapping a binary search tree to an array in an unconventional way, called a *virtual tree*. This way we obtain a simple, generic search procedure which uses implicit search information rather than explicit search pointers. Moreover, the mapping chosen results in reduced tree maintenance cost. In addition, we use *logarithmic code expansion* to factor-out boundary checks known at compile time.

Our experiments partly disproves the observations made by Lehman and Carey by presenting an array-based data structure and algorithms with excellent search performance and which incurs minimal space overhead. Moreover, the insert/delete algorithms can be balanced to obtain the best time/space trade-off for a given volatility rate.

The rest of this paper is mainly a summary of [Kersten 88]. In section 2 we describe virtual trees and describe a programming technique to improve their search performance. Section 3 discusses insertion cost of virtual trees.

2. Virtual trees

A good data structure for supporting range queries should support logarithmic search, does not incur too much overhead in search administration, takes into account the cost of the machine instructions, and works with reasonable large (constant sized) objects. The *virtual tree* is an attempt to fulfill all these requirements.

The structure of a virtual tree can best be introduced through an example. Therefore, consider a balanced binary-search tree with capacity 15. This tree is mapped to an array as shown in Figure 1. Moreover, any tree with less than 15 elements can be mapped into this array as well; provided you guarantee that each node remains accessible from the root. Looking at a binary search tree this way makes all pointers implicit and makes space overhead solely dependent on the size of the tree. In addition, searching in this data structure has become a bounded problem, at most 3 comparisons are needed to locate any element.

Definition A *virtual tree* of order k is a balanced-binary search tree of 2^k-1 nodes represented within a buffer of size 2^k-1.

Observe that a *virtual tree* is just one possible mapping from a binary search tree to an array. As such the technique is not new. Many storage representations for binary search trees can be found in [Knuth75]. In particular, the *virtual tree* resembles a *complete binary tree* mapped to an array. Conventionally, in the latter the childs of node i are found at location $2*i$ and $2*i+1$ rather than at positions $i-c$ and $i+c$ (c depends on the level). An advantage of the new mapping is that it greatly simplifies tree rebalancing, because it suffices to shift portions one element in either direction.

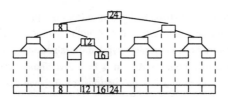

Figure 1 A virtual tree mapping

A potential problem of *virtual trees* is what we should do when 2^k elements are being stored. Two basic solutions exists. The general solution is to combine *virtual trees* into a forest, which by itself can be organised as a virtual tree. For example, the database can be represented with a T-tree in which the nodes themselves are organized as virtual trees. Another solution is to extend the array. This is possible when the underlying system includes a memory management unit that allocates physical memory pages upon demand. Here a virtual tree can be associated with a memory segment, whose size is determined by the number of dynamically allocated pages.

To use the virtual tree as a dynamic index we store references to tuples (or attributes) in the virtual tree. Under the assumption that tuples do not migrate we can use virtual memory addresses to the indexed fields directly. For the purpose of the remainder we assume that the tree has been partially filled with references. Empty slots are recognized by the NIL reference.

The general search algorithm for virtual trees, written in the language C, is shown Figure 2. This algorithm returns a reference to the tree element with the require value or NIL. The search parameters are, besides the value of interest, the root of the virtual tree and the initial stepsize. The latter tells how many elements we should move to the left or right after each comparison. It is divided in each phase to limit the search to tree elements. Testing a leaf node for the desired value is kept out of the loop.

```
long *BSAsearch(srchvalue, root, stepsize)
long srchvalue, **root, stepsize;
{
        while(stepsize>0){
                if( *root== NIL) return  NIL;
                if( srchvalue< ** root) root-= stepsize; else
                if( srchvalue> ** root)
                        root+= stepsize;
                else    return *root;
                stepsize= stepsize/2;
        }
        /* test leaf node */
        if( *root== NIL) return  NIL;
        if( srchvalue== **root) return *root;
        return NIL;
}
```

Figure 2 A search algorithm for virtual trees

```
#define Test(X)          if(*root == 0) return 0; \
                 if( srchvalue<**root) root -= X; else \
                 if( srchvalue>**root) root += X; else return *root;

long *BSAsrch15(srchvalue,root)
long srchvalue, **root;
{
        root +=7;
        Test(4); Test(2); Test(1);
        if( *root == 0) return 0;
        if( srchvalue == **root) return *root;
        return 0;
}
```

Figure 3 Search algorithm tree with code expansion

From a memory management point of view it is often advisable to use only a few different object sizes throughout a program. If we take this information into account during program development, we can develop a more efficient search algorithm for virtual trees as follows. The fixed object size means that in a *k*-order virtual tree only k steps are needed to locate an element. Moreover, the step-size at each point is a precisely known small constant. Thus, if we explicitly write out the code for each level in the tree we safe the boundary checks needed in the general solution given above. The effect is a *logarithmic code expansion* of the basic algorithms. The corresponding code, which uses the macro facility of C, is shown in Figure 3.

Such *logarithmic code expansion* is inspired by loop-unrolling optimization in optimizing compilers. However, no compiler will ever be able to apply this technique automatically to the algorithm shown in Figure 2, because it would require both a complete symbolic evaluation and knowledge about the possible initial values of *stepsize*. Note that, code-expansion is here *logarithmic* in the size of the tree only and since each additional level requires only a few instructions (ca. 12), we can ignore the code blow-up for most reasonably sized trees. (The code for searching an index over 1M tuples is about a 1K)

The prime point of interest is how the virtual trees behave compared with other algorithms used in Main-Memory Database Systems. Therefore, we have also implemented several candidate algorithms and obtained experimental performance figures through simulation. Figure 4 gives an overview of the search performance. The bottom of the picture denotes the order of the (virtual) trees being studied. We claim that the perceived behavior holds for larger trees as well.

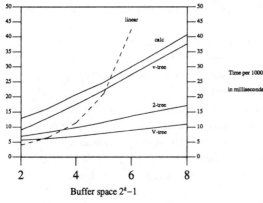

Figure 4 Search performance for search algorithm

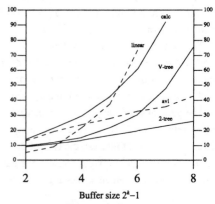

Figure 5 Performance of the insert operator

The line marked *linear* denotes the time when a sorted heap is searched in a linear fashion. The *calc* line reflects the performance of successive calculation of the sub-root. It is the method used in the study of Lehman and Carey to deal with array-based storage. The *2-tree* corresponds with a binary search tree implemented with pointers. It is the performance of a general algorithm which involves pointer chasing. (The results for the 2-tree also holds for the avl-tree) The performance of the virtual tree implementations are denoted by *v-tree* and *V-tree*, which correspond with the general solution (Fig. 2) and logarithmic code-expanded (Fig 3) solution, respectively. The performance figures shown reflect an implementation of the search algorithms in C under BSD 4.3 with optimized compilation on a 6 MIPS machine (Harris).

Comparing our results with those of Lehman & Carey we can observe the following. Their observation that calculated binary search in a sorted heap is expensive, is correct. However, the reasons are that expensive instructions are needed to locate the next comparison element and that the algorithm should continuously take into account the size of the heap. In other words, the boundary condition (the top of the heap) changes at run-time.

More importantly, our implementations of a virtual trees show that the search performance becomes better than the binary search tree when you freeze the maximum size of the problem at programming time and use (logarithmic) code expansion. It results in > 70% improvement over the sorted heap with calculated search and 35% over the binary search tree. It also shows that in our case the code-expanded solution is much faster than the general solution.

3. Insertion into a virtual tree

Insertion into virtual trees is only slightly more complicated than, for example, sorted heaps. For insertion the buffer is initialized with NIL references. Following the first element is placed in the middle. Subsequent inserts perform the search operation described above to find a duplicate or an empty slot in the tree. This process works for the first k insertions. Thereafter, it may happen that we bounce upon an already occupied array element. This means that part of the buffer should be shifted to make room for the new element.

Since we are forced to shift elements when the buffer becomes more and more filled, we can not expect a reduced complexity. Thus, insertion in virtual trees remains an $O(k^2)$ process. But, because we initially spread the gaps over all elements in the tree we get a significant improvement.

The critical remaining issue then is which way to shift. Several options can be considered. First we can look in either direction of the point of insertion for an empty slot. The closest one is used by shifting a portion into its direction. Observe that searching an empty slot only requires inspection of the leaf nodes, because a non-empty leaf implies a non-empty parent. By definition all non-leafs occupy even slots in our array.

Alternatively, under the assumption of a uniform key distribution we can take a lazy attitude and use an oracle to determine the shift direction. For example, when the most significant bit of the key value is set then we shift right, otherwise left. Unfortunately, this mechanism does not lead to an acceptable performance in practice. This can be seen as follows. In half of the cases the oracle provides the wrong decision, which means that after we have shifted a portion of the tree and encountered the buffer boundary, we should undo the effect by shifting the portion back into its original place and continue shifting in the proper direction. Since shifting becomes expensive in the end only, the errors made by the oracle are also noticable.

From the performance figures obtained from filling the index completely (Fig. 5), we may conclude that the layout of the tree elements over the buffer indeed reduces the shifting cost. But still the actual behaviour strongly depends on the insertion order. If the keys are submitted in-order then shifting won't occur and the virtual tree is equally fast as the binary search tree. The worst that can happen to a virtual tree is that during each insert all the nodes should be shifted. Fortunately, this can not occur, because the nodes are evenly spread as much as possible. This means that the worst-case performance, the line for calculated binary search (*calc*) won't be reached.

The performance of the insert routines can be further improved by taking a more liberal attitude towards space utilization, because the shift costs strongly depend on the filling of the buffer. If less then k elements are being inserted no shift occurs at all. Contrary, if the buffer is nearly full then on the average half of the available elements should be shifted. Therefore, it seems warranted to introduce a high-water mark which ensures that the buffer is not filled beyond a certain level. The time break-even point with binary search trees occurs at about 75%.

4. Summary

In this paper we have studied the performance of alternative representations of binary search-trees for indexing a relation kept in main-memory. It was shown that space/time performance of the common techniques, such as sorted heaps, and more complex data structures, such as avl-trees, can be improved considerably. In particular, when an upperbound is determined during program construction on the maximal size of the indices, an efficient mapping, called the *virtual tree*, from binary search tree to array exists. The resulting search structure ensures an upperbound on the number of comparisons for searching and maintenance will only start to deteriorate when the area set aside for holding the index is nearly full.

In addition, we showed that limiting the maximal size of the index structure permits judicious use of code-expansion, i.e. *logarithmic code expansion*, to further improve the performance of the algorithms.

For a search dominant environment our approach is better than the more space consumptive binary trees representations based on pointer chasing. In a volatile environment the space/time performance can be controlled precisely.

References

[Bitton86]
   Bitton, D. and Turbyfill, C., "Performance Evaluation of Main Memory Database Systems", Tech. Report TR 86-731, Jan. 1986.

[DeWitt84]
   DeWitt, D., R.Katz, Olken, F., Shapiro, L., Stonebraker, M., and Wood, D., "Implementation Techniques for Main Memory Database Systems," *Proc. ACM SIGMOD*, pp.1-8, June 1984.

[Garcia-Molina83]
   Garcia-Molina, H., Lipton, R.J., and Honeyman, P., "A Massive Memory Database Machine", Tech. report 314, September 1983.

[Kersten87]
   Kersten, M.L., Apers, P.M.G., Houtsma, M.A.W., Kuyk, E.J.A. van, and Weg, R.L.W. van de, "A Distributed Main-Memory Database Machine; Research Issues and a Preliminary Architecture," *Proc. 5th Int Workshop on Database Machines*, pp.496-511, Oct 1987.

[Kersten88]
   Kersten, M.L., "A Time and Space Efficient Implementation of a Dynamic Index in a Main-Memory DBS", CWI technical report CS-R8803, Jan 1988.

[Knuth75]
   Knuth, D., *The Art of Computer Programming Vol I and III*. Addison-Wesley, 1975.

[Lehman86a]
   Lehman, T.J. and Carey, M.J., "Query Processing in Main Memory Database Systems," *Proc. ACM SIGMOD Conference*, pp.239-250, May 1986.

[Lehman86b]
   Lehman, T.J. and Carey, M.J., "A Study of Index Structures for Main Memory Database Systems," *Proc. Conf. on Very Large Database*, pp.293-303, Sep 1986.

[Leland87]
   Leland, M.D.P. and Roome, W.D., "The Silicon Database Machine : Rationale, Design, and Results," *Proc. 5-th Int. Workshop on Database Machines*, pp.454-467, Oct 1987.

Concurrency In Multidimensional Linear Hashing

M. Ouksel
The University of Texas at Dallas
Computer Learning Research (CLEAR) Center
Richardson, TX 75083-0688

Jalal Abdul-Ghaffar
University of Petroleum and Minerals
Computer Science Department
Dhahran 31261

Abstract

Concurrency control schemes are developed to improve the throughput in a shared database by providing mechanisms which synchronize operations issued by concurrently executing processes. In this paper, we present efficient algorithms for concurrent operations in two structures; namely Multi-dimensional Linear Hashing and Interpolation-Based Index Maintenance. Both of these structures are extensions of Linear hashing to the multi-dimensional case. The concurrent scheme presented is an adaptation of the one proposed for linear hashing. The algorithms include searching for, inserting, and deleting data elements. These algorithms support a high degree of concurrency and are shown to be correct based on the restrictions imposed by the compatibility scheme.

1. Introduction

In recent years, researchers have devoted considerable attention to the design of file structures suitable for associative searching. To improve their throughput and the throughput of structures in general concurrency control schemes are also developed which provide mechanisms to synchronize operations issued by concurrently executing processes. Among the popular schemes are the ones designed for B-trees [1,4,5,10,12], Cartesian Product Files [7], grid files [11], and linear hashing [3]. Our objective is to design a scheme for two extensions of linear hashing [6] namely, multidimensional linear hashing [9] and interpolation-based index maintenance [2]. The concurrent scheme is an adaption of the one presented for linear hashing.

2. The data file

The storage space is divided into a contiguous logical address space of fixed size blocks called buckets or pages. Each bucket is capable of holding some number b of records. A bucket is the unit of transfer between secondary and primary memory. A data record is a d-dimensional tuple $K=(k_0, k_1, \ldots, k_{d-1})$ of values which correspond to attributes $A_0, A_1, \ldots, A_{d-1}$ respectively. Each component of the record is scaled and mapped to a rational number in the half open interval [0,1), a record is thus viewed as a point in the d-dimensional space $U^d=[0,1)$. Let $K=(k_0^0, k_1^0, \ldots, k_{d-1}^0)$ be the result of the mapping. As an example consider the two-dimensional case where $D_0=[0,50000)$ and $D_1=[0,80)$ a record K = (37500,10) will be mapped to $K^0=(37500/50000, 10/80)$ or (0.110,0.001) in binary.

The construction of the file is best illustrated by an example. To simplify the discussion only the two-dimensional case is presented. Thus, the data search space is viewed as a rectangle delimited by the cartesian product D_0 x D_1 of attributes A_0 and A_1 domains. The vector $K=(k_0^0, k_1^0)$ which is the mapping of the original record refers to the coordinates of this search space. The file initially consists of a single partition which embeds the whole search space. An insertion of a record to the database will be represented by exhibiting a dot in the graph. We shall assume that the data file bucket capacity $b_0=2$ and thus each partition may only contain at most 2 dots. When a partition overflows. Splitting the search space is necessary to maintain the data file bucket limit. For simplicity, we adopt a cyclic splitting in half policy along the various axes as illustrated in Figure 1.

An additional insertion to partition #1 will cause a split of the whole data space along axis #1. A partition can simply be represented by its coordinates (i,j). So in the example, see part(b) the possible pairs are (0,0),(0,1),(1,0),(1,1). A pair of coordinates represents the leading binary digits of the fraction part of k_0^0 and k_1^0 respectively. In other words, coordinates are simply prefixes of elements located in the subspace they determine. The length of these prefixes is exactly the interval partition level along the corresponding axis. For example, if we assumed the partition level along axis zero and axis one are 2 and 1 respectively, then the search space will look like Figure 2.

It is possible to deduce a simple one-to-one storage mapping, if partitions are split in a linear order. Let $C=(c_0^0, c_1^0, \ldots, c_{d-1}^0)$ denote the coordinates of the partition where K is contained. Each c_{ij}^0 indicates the j-th binary digit of c_i^0 starting from right, and assuming a cyclic splitting policy. Then the number of the partition in which a record $K=(k_0, k_1, \ldots, k_{d-1})$ may be contained is given by :

$$M(k,L)= \sum_{i=0}^{d-1} \sum_{j=0}^{L_i-1} 2^{d(L_i-1-j)} c_{ij}^0$$

where L_i, called **the interval partition level**, is the number of times a split along axis i occurred. Since the splitting policy is cyclic, the total number of splits is $\sum_{i=1}^{n} L_i$. It is called **the search space partition level**. The restructuring operation is inavoidable, but it is desirable to localize it to a minimum number of buckets in the file at a time and to minimize the number of times it is performed. The mapping discussed above allows us to localize the restructuring if linear order is assumed as in [9] in a dynamic environment since it satisfies the following property : M(k,L+1)= M(k,L) or M(k,L) + 2^L for $L = 0,1,...$ In other words, if a bucket is split, half will remain in the old bucket while the other half is assigned to a new bucket with a new logical number.

One possibility for restructuring is to maintain an approximately constant storage utilization. In this approach a split is performed only when the load factor exceeds some threshold. Unlike splitting, a merge is done only when the space utilization falls below some threshold. The load factor is defined as follows : LOAD FACTOR $=$ RECCOT $/$ (2^Lx'Bucket_size'), where RECCOT is the number of records in the file. It is referred to the above scheme as "controlled" restructuring. In controlled restructuring, it is possible that a data page may become full while the load factor is not affected. As a result, attempts to insert into a full primary bucket "collisions" are handled by creating a chain of overflow buckets associated with that particular bucket address.

Rather than restructuring the data space globally, the restructuring operation is now restricted to a single bucket chain at a time. The split operation is applied to each chain in linear order and cyclically. A split is performed on the bucket that is next in line to be split. A variable NEXT is used as a pointer to indicate the chain that should be split. The resulting modification in the data structure is movement of some records from the original bucket chain being split to a new primary bucket that is appended at the current end of the file. The new file structure is shown in Figure x. The variables NEXT and L are then updated as follows : **If** L = 0 **then begin** L := L + 1; NEXT := 0 **end else begin** Next := (NEXT + 1) mod 2**L; **If** NEXT = 0 **then** L := L + 1 **end;**

Unlike a split operation, a merge operation is performed on the bucket chain which is at the current end of the file and the bucket chain from which that particular bucket chain was generated due to a split. That is, undo the last split operation performed on the file. The variables NEXT and L are then updated as follows : **If** NEXT = 0 **and** L **not** = 0 **then begin** NEXT := (2**L - 1) - (2**(L - 1)); L := L - 1; **end else** NEXT := (NEXT - 1) mod 2**L;

Note that the structure presented above is the Interpolation-based Index Maintenance [2]. This structure subsumes the multi-dimensional linear hashing [9] since it is order-preserving; although this last property can also be satisfied since, as we have shown in [8], linear hashing can also be order-preserving.

3. Lock compatibility and convertibility

In order to regulate concurrent access we need a concurrency control which specifies the type of lock to be used by processes operating on some objects. A compatibility and convertibility graph CCG [1] specifies relations which must hold among the various types of locks on an object. The CCG of locks used in this scheme is shown in Figure 4. Processes can manipulate the various locks via three types of indivisible operations: Lock, Unlock and Convert.

For any two vertices α and β a solid edge directed from α to β means that a process with β-lock on an object would permit another process to put an α-lock on that object. A broken edge from α to β indicates that a process holding an α -lock on an object may convert it into β-lock. Two isolated vertices indicate that a process holding a lock of the first vertex type on an object would not permit another process to put a lock of the second vertex type on that object.

4. A concurrency scheme

The solution described below is an adaptation of the approach presented in [3] for concurrency in linear hashing files to the multi-dimensional case. In this solution, more than one reader may be reading a bucket simultaneously and no ordering is imposed on readers. Moreover, the FIND process can be performed concurrently with the processes INSERT and DELETE. The processes INSERT and DELETE may operate in parallel if they are accessing different bucket chains. The restructuring operations (SPLIT and MERGE) can be viewed as separate background processes in spite of the fact that they are called from the procedures INSERT and DELETE. That is, when the need for a SPLIT or a MERGE is determined by an INSERT or a DELETE process respectively, a separate asynchronous SPLIT or MERGE process is activated accordingly and associated with the calling process.

Clearly, concurrency is enhanced by allowing a process in its searching phase to operate in parallel with a SPLIT operation, but as in [3] there must be some means for it to reorient itself when the wrong chain is reached because of an out-of-date L value. The current value of L always reflects a smaller search space for new coming processes. Assume that a process in its searching phase is operating in parallel on the file structure shown in with a SPLIT operation. If the process decided, using the current value of L, that the record being searched for is located in bucket #1 which is also subject to a split operation as indicated by the variable NEXT, then that particular process may not find the designated record if the SPLIT process was able to split the bucket into two buckets before the process can gain access to it. In this scheme, each chain includes an additional field LOCALL that specifies the most recent split affecting this bucket. Storing LOCALL in the primary bucket ensures that the searching process can decide if it has the right chain without requiring the accuracy of the shared variable L. The modified file structure is shown in Figure 3.

Processes in their searching phase adopts the use of lock-coupling technique [4] on L, NEXT, and the bucket chains. The FIND process uses read-locks while the processes INSERT and DELETE use selective-locks. The SPLIT operation uses selective locks. The MERGE operation places exclusive locks on L, NEXT and both of the partner bucket chains being merged. After the values of the variables L and NEXT have been changed to reflect the smaller search space that will result from the merge, the locks on these variables are converted to selective locks, and processes entering their searching phase may then concurrently access the variables L and NEXT.

A process executing in its searching phase behaves as follows : the value of L is read and the value seen determines which bucket should be accessed initially. Let the private variable PRL record the value of L at the time it was read. Upon gaining access to a bucket, the process checks whether PRL matches that bucket's LOCALL, and if not, it increments its PRL value and recalculates the address M(K,PRL) until a match is found. The calculated address at each iteration will always be less than or equal to the address of the eventual destination. This can be concluded from the property discussed previously. Thus the bucket chain in which the desired record belongs should be reachable using this strategy as long as each address calculated is within the valid address space at the time of access. The two new chains resulting from a split appear atomically to other processes because of the order in which they are written to disk. Specifically, the chain at the new bucket address is written before the new version replaces the chain at the target bucket address. At this point, no information contained in the file points to the existence of this new bucket. Once the primary bucket at the head of the chain at the target address has been written, its LOCALL value indicates that the bucket has split and a new bucket has been incorporated into the file. After the reorganized chains are safely in place, the value of L and NEXT are changed to allow direct calculation of the address of the new chain. A process responsible for merging two buckets, holds exclusive-locks on both partners of the merge while it makes its changes. The read-lock held by the searching process prevents a MERGE from decreasing the size of the address space during the initial bucket access. Because of space limitations, only the pseudocode procedures for INSERT and SPLIT are presented (see Appendix). They show the locks on the additional variable RECCOT.

During the restructuring phase, the load factor is initially computed to determine if a split or a merge is still necessary. Indeed it may happen that another restructuring operation has just taken place or some processes have caused the load factor to be changed due to successive insertions or deletions and thereby preempting the need for another such phase.

5. Concurrency scheme correctness

During the searching phase of FIND, INSERT, and DELETE, locks are placed according to a well-defined ordering. Merges and Splits also respect the ordering in requesting their locks. Thus, deadlock can not occur. Searching for the record as part of a deletion, or for the place to insert as part of insertion, requires that the effect of previous updates (even those still active) be seen. Selective-locks are placed on the chains during the searching phase to serialize writers of the same individual buckets so that only up-to-date information is seen. This guarantees that there is no interference between concurrent executions of INSERT and DELETE.

At most, one restructuring operation can be executing at any time. Merges and Splits are completely serialized with respect to one another by incompatible locks on L and NEXT. All affected bucket chains are also locked by a restructuring process for the step. The SPLIT procedure allows, because of its selective-locks, only processes executing the FIND routine to concurrently access the chain being split. The exclusive-locks held during a merging process do not permit any concurrent use of the partner buckets of the merge. Processes executing FIND, INSERT, and DELETE are allowed to operate in parallel with a MERGE if they are working on a different bucket chain than the ones being merged. When the variables L and NEXT are updated to reflect smaller address space, the locks on them are converted to Selective-locks, and processes entering their searching phase may then access L and NEXT values.

6. Conclusion

In this paper, the design of a concurrency scheme for two extensions of linear hashing, namely multidimensional linear hashing and interpolation-based index maintenance was presented. These variations have the ability to handle growth in dynamic database environment and support range queries. A design of effective concurrent algorithms for search, insert, and delete were discussed. Each of the operations listed above required only constant amount of locking. This solution supported a high degree of concurrency. Almost all types of processes were allowed to proceed in parallel. As in other cases of concurrency in data structures, making modifications to the data structure has proved to be a useful technique for achieving higher degree of concurrency. As distributed configurations become widespread, lessening the problem of enhancing the degree of concurrency in data structures becomes very important in improving the performance of database systems.

7. References

[1] Bayer, R. and Schkolnick, M., "Concurrency of Operations on B-Trees," *Acta Informatica*, vol. 9, pp. 1-21, 1977.

[2] Burkhard, Walter A., "Interpolation-Based Index Maintenance," *Proc Second ACM-SIGACT-SIGMOD Symp on Principles of Database System*, pp. 76-85, 1983.

[3] Ellis, Carla S., "Concurrency in Linear Hashing," *ACM Transactions on Databases Systems*, vol. 12(2), pp. 195-217, June 1987.

[4] Kwong, Yat-Sang and Wood, Derick, "A new Method for Concurrency in B-Trees," *IEEE Transactions on Software Engineering*, vol. SE-8(3), pp. 211-222, May 1982.

[5] Lehman, Philip L. and Yao, S. Bing, "Efficient Locking for Concurrent Operations on B-Trees," *ACM Transactions on Database Systems*, vol. 6(4), pp. 650-670, December 1981.

[6] Litwin, Witold, "Linear Hashing : A New Tool for File and Table Addressing," *In Proceedings, 6th Conf on very Large Databases*, pp. 212-223, 1980.

[7] Onuegbe, E.O. and Du, H.C., "A Locking Scheme for Associative Retrieval," *Unpublished Paper,*

[8] Ouksel, M. and Scheuermann, P., "Multi-dimensional Storage Mappings," *Proc Second ACM-SIGACT-SIGMOD Symp. on Principles of Database Systems*, pp. 90-105, 1983.

[9]   Ouksel, M. and Scheuermann, P., "Implicit Data Structures for Linear Hashing Schemes," *Information Processing Letters*, vol. 29(4), pp. 183-189, 1988.

[10]   Sagiv, Yehashua, "Concurrent operations on B-trees with overtaking," *Proc of the 4th ACM-SIGACT-SIGMOD Symposium on Principles of Database Systems*, pp. 28-37, 1985.

[11]   Salzberg, Betty, "Concurrency in Grid Files," *Inform Systems Journal*, vol. 11(3), pp. 235-244, 1986.

[12]   Samadi, B.S., "B-Trees in A System With Multiple Users," *Inform Process Lett* , vol. 5(4), pp. 107-112, 1976 .

8. Appendix

Procedure INSERT(K); **Var** LL, Pntr, Bucket_chain, Lfactor, Reccount: Integer;

Begin LOCATE_BUCKET(K,Selective,Bucket_chain); /* Build a new chain and insert the new record if it does not exist */

If (inserted) **then** **begin** Lock(Read,L); Get_value(L,LL); Lock(Read,NEXT); Get_value(NEXT,Pntr); Lock(Selective,RECCOT); Get_value(RECCOT,Reccount); Reccount := Reccount + 1; Lfactor:= Reccount/((2**LL+Pntr)*Bucket_size); Put_value(Reccount,RECCOT); Unlock(Read,L); Unlock(Read,NEXT); Unlock(Selective,RECCOT); **end;** /* Replace the old chain by the new one */ Unlock(Selective,Bucket_chain);

if (Overflow) **then** SPLIT; **end;**

Procedure SPLIT; **Var** Target_bucket_chain : Integer; Lfactor, LL, Pntr : Integer; Reccount : Integer;

Begin Lock(Selective,L); Get_value(L,LL); Lock(Selective,NEXT); Get_value(NEXT,Pntr); Lock(Selective,RECCOT); Get_value(RECCOT,Reccount); Lfactor := Reccount/((2**L+Pntr)*bucket_size);

If (split is not necessary) **then** **begin** Unlock(Selective,L);Unlock(Selective,NEXT); Unlock(Selective,RECCOT); Terminate; **end**

else begin Unlock(Selective,RECCOT); Target_bucket_chain := Pntr; /* Allocate newchain and append it at the current end of the file. Move some of records in the target bucket chain pointed by NEXT to newchain. Write the primary bucket of the target chain with the new value of LOCALL */

if LL = 0 **then begin** LL:= LL + 1; Pntr := 0; **end**

else begin Pntr := (Pntr+1) mod 2**LL; **if** Pntr = 0 **then** LL := LL + 1; **end;**

Put_value(Pntr,NEXT); /* NEXT <— Pntr */ Put_value(LL,L); Unlock(Selective,L); Unlock(Selective,NEXT); Unlock(Selective,Target_bucket_chain); **end; end;**

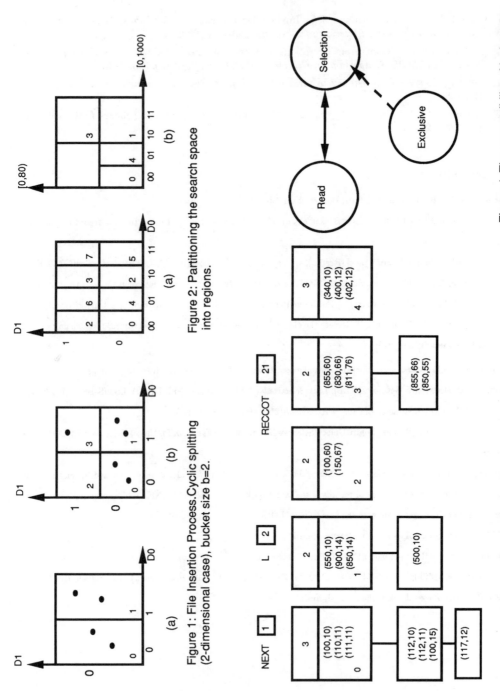

Figure 1: File Insertion Process.Cyclic splitting
(2-dimensional case), bucket size b=2.

Figure 2: Partitioning the search space
into regions.

Figure 3: The modified structure shown in linear order

Figure 4: The compatibility of lock types

Retrieving of parts with geometric similarity[*]

R. Schneider, H.-P. Kriegel, B. Seeger, S. Heep

Praktische Informatik, University of Bremen, D-2800 Bremen 33, FRG

Abstract

Todays CAD applications become less and less manageable if no database system is used. One of the most important queries in these applications is the retrieval of parts with geometric similarity. The information obtained from such similar parts will drastically reduce the overhead for production planning and construction.

In available retrieval and classification systems parts are described using attributes comparable to those in traditional database systems. In our paper, we suggest a system for retrieval of parts with geometric similarity which accesses to a database system storing the geometric data provided by the CAD system. By maintaining, storing and manipulating the complete geometric information of objects, our approach exhibits a flexibility and efficiency for similarity and other queries which is not known in available systems.

1. Introduction

In the following, we will consider a set of parts which were generated using a CAD-system. This set typically corresponds to the catalogue of parts of a company. With the demand for a new part, the retrieval of a similar part within the catalogue of parts may be useful for two reasons. On one hand, in the area of construction, reconstruction may be omitted partially or even completely when finding a similar or identical part. On the other hand, in the area of manufacturing similar parts require similar production processes yielding an even higher reduction of costs than in the area of construction.

The retrieval of similar parts will lead to the accessibility and reusability of present know-how. Furthermore the reuse of parts will result in a reduction of the multiplicity of parts and therefore will result in a reduction of administration overhead. Necessary conditions for the retrieval of similar parts is their storage in a database system. Before storing the parts we have to consider two possible ways of describing parts: • "explicit", i.e. the part is exactly specified (e.g. by a product drawing)
• "implicit", i.e. the part is described by attributes

---

*This work was supported by grant no. Kr 670/4-2 from the Deutsche Forschungsgemeinschaft (German Research Society)

The retrieval of similar parts determines, given the catalogue of parts of a company, the most similar part, as an optimum even the identical part. If the degree of similarity is either not specified or is not convenient in the particular application the result of the retrieval of similar parts may comprise a variety of similar parts.

In all commercially available systems (as e.g. the classification system of Opitz or the product design parameters (see DIN 4000) or the multivariate system for searching of similar parts) the object (part) will be described "implicitly" by attributes. The advantage of these systems is their simple embedding in a relational database system. On one hand, the resulting reduction of information may cause useless results, on the other hand the selection of attributes and the determination of their values is very cost-intensive. In our paper a new system for the retrieval of parts with geometric similarity will be presented which is based on an "explicit" representation of parts. The system was designed for a tool and die shop with the assistance of a major supplier in the German car manufacturing industry. Contrary to all current commercially available systems we do not use attributes, but the complete geometric description of the part, as it is available in the CAD-system. Thus a loss of information will be avoided. Additionally all the data to be stored in the database system supporting the similarity retrieval can be automatically derived from the data in the CAD-system. In our approach, it was necessary to restrict to a class of parts. For the given application the restriction to parts which are symmetric with respect to rotation proved to be convenient. As we will demonstrate later, such parts can be described uniquely by a 2-dimensional polyline (=contour) and by a rotation axis. For the similarity retrieval of parts which are "explicitly" described, a completely new query possibility was designed which guarantees a high standard of flexibility.

In this paper, we present a solution for the retrieval of parts with geometric similarity using a relational database system. The database system will be used for filtering a set of candidates from the catalogue of parts.

2. The normalized representation of rotation-symmetric parts in R^2

A part which is symmetric with respect to rotation, in the following called rotation-symmetric part, and which has no bores can be described in R^2 by specifying a simple closed contour (=K) and a rotation axis (=r), see fig. (1). Figure 2 will be referred to in section 3.

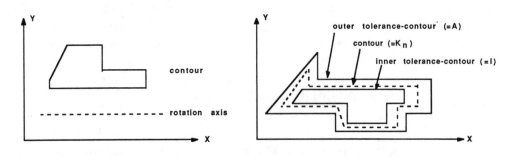

figure 1   figure 2

Remark:

Alt et al. have shown in their paper [AMWW 86] that the problem of congruence (= retrieval of identical parts) cannot be solved in an acceptable time. Consequently the retrieval of similar parts is only tractable if a normalized representation of the contours is given.

Normalization with respect to the y-axis: (Determine the grade (=m) of the rotation axis (=r))

case 1: $m = 0$, i.e. r is parallel to the x-axis. Determine the intersection point $s = (s_1, s_2)$ of r and the y-axis. Using the translation T (translation vector is $t = (0, - s_2)$), r is superimposed onto the x-axis. Additionally, we apply the translation T to K.

case 2: $m <> 0$.Determine the intersection point $S = (s_1, s_2)$ of r and the x-axis.The rotation R with the rotation point s and the rotation angle arctan (m) maps r onto the x-axis. R is also applied to K.

Normalization with respect to reflection at the x-axis:

Consider any vertex $E = (e_1, e_2)$ of K with $e_2 \neq 0$.

case 1: $e_2 < 0$, then perform a reflection of K with respect to the x-axis.

case 2: $e_2 > 0$, K is in the upper half-space $y \geq 0$.

Normalization with respect to reflection at the y-axis:

Determine the point $P = (p_1, p_2)$ (and $Q = (q_1, q_2)$) of the contour with maximum y-coordinate (with minimum x-coordinate). If there exists more than one, select the one with minimum x-coordinate (with minimum y-coordinate). Compute $p_1 - q_1 =: a$. Determine the reflection (=K_s) of the contour (=K) with respect to the y-axis. Now we can compute P_s, Q_s and a_s. Then the following three cases may arise:

case 1: $a_s < a$, then store K_s.

case 2: $a < a_s$, then store K.

case 2: $a = a_s$, then store K and K_s and note that K is identical to K_s.

3. The definition of contour-similarity

A rotation-symmetric part is uniquely identified by the normalized representation of its contour. The constructor or user can define the similarity of parts by specifying tolerances using an inner and an outer tolerance-contour. In a production environment, the specification of an inner tolerance contour rarely makes sense due to technological restrictions. Therefore, the inner tolerance contour (= I) is often identical to the contour (= K). As a result of a tolerance specification we are given two contours, where the outer contour (= A) completely contains the inner contour (= I). In particular, edges of I and A may partially or completely coincide (see fig. 2).

Definition 1 (contour-similarity) A newly constructed part is represented by a normalized contour (= K). Tolerances are specified by an inner tolerance-contour (= I) and an outer tolerance-contour (= A). Stored parts are represented by their normalized contours K_n. K is contour-similar to K_n iff K_n can be translated in x-direction such that A completely contains K_n and K_n completely contains I.

Due to space restrictions, it is not possible to present the complete algorithmic solution for the retrieval of contour-similarity in this paper. The interested reader is referred to [SKSH 89] for an exact description of this algorithm. We would like to emphasize that a prototype implementation of this algorithm is presently running and being investigated in the company mentioned in the introduction.

4. Embedding of the similarity retrieval in a relational database system

The contour-similarity retrieval is exclusively based on the geometry of the parts. We do not consider technological, functional or productional engineering properties. In a relational database system we can store in addition to the data of the contour also the product design attributes (machining methods,precision,material,....). Thus we can perform the contour-similarity retrieval as well as a retrieval by specification of product attributes (see fig. 3).

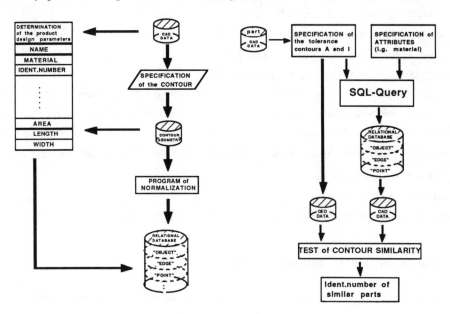

figure 3 : Storage of rotation-symmetric
parts in a relational database system

figure 4: schematic diagram of the
contour-similarity retrieval

Specification of the relations:

"object" : (oid,...,width)
•oid: object identifier
•idnr: identification number
•area: area of the object
•length:= $|max_x(oid)-min_x(oid)|$
•width := $|max_y(oid)-min_y(oid)|$

"edge" (oid,kid,pid_1,pid_2)
•kid: identifier of the edge
•pid_1: identifier of the startpoint
    of the edge
•pid_2: identifier of the endpoint
    of the edge

"point" (pid,x,y)
•x : x-coordinte of the point
•y : y-coordinate of the point

Specification of the SQL-Query:

SELECT object.oid,edge.kid,P1.x,P2.y
FROM   odject,edge,point P1,point P2
WHERE   object.oid = edge.oid AND (edge.pid$_1$=P1 AND edge.pid$_2$) AND
        (object.area $\geq$ area(I) AND object.area $\leq$ area(A) AND
        object.width $\geq$ width(I) AND object.length $\geq$ length(I) AND
        object.width $\leq$ width(A) AND object.length $\leq$ length(A) AND
        material = steel AND name = hub)
ORDER BY object.oid

5. Outlook

The essential contribution of this paper is the concept of using the geometric data of a CAD-system for the similarity retrieval of parts. These queries which are only to some extent supported by commercially available relational database systems, consist of complex geometric operations, such as the test of similarity (see[SKSH 89]).Therefore our new concept necessitates an additional algorithmic treatment. Presently, we investigate how these operations may be integrated and efficiently performed in an extensible database system. An approach similar to that proposed in the PROBE-project respectively DASDBS-project seems to be suitable (see [MO 86] respectively [PSSWD 87]. A first step towards an efficient processing of the queries is the integration of spatial access methods in a database system as proposed in [SK 88]. The practical importance of our method which is in a prototype-version operational in a tool and die shop results from the following facts. Our method avoids loss of information, automatically generates the data to be stored while keeping it consistent and offers a high degree of flexibility in the retrieval of parts with geometric similarity.

References :

[AMWW 86] Alt,H.,Mehlhorn,K., Wegener, H., Welzl, E.:´Congruence,Similarity and Symmetries of Geometric Objects`,in Proc. of the 3rd Ann. Symposium on Computational Geometry, Waterloo,June 1987,pp.308-319 (1987).

[MO 86] Manola, F., Orenstein, J.:´Towards a General spatial Data Model for an Object-Oriented DBMS´,in Proc. 12th Int. Conf. on Very Large Databases (1986).

[PSSWD 87] Paul,H.P.,Schek,H.J.,Scholl,M.H.,Weikum,G.,Deppisch,U.,´Architecture and Implementation of the Darmstadt Database Kernel System´,in Proc. ACM SIGMOD 1987 Annual Conference on Management of Data,pp.196-207 (1987).

[SK 88] Seeger, B., Kriegel, H.P.:´Techniques for Design and Implementation of Efficient Spatial Access Methods´,in Proc. 14th Int. Conf. on Very Large Databases,pp. 360-371 (1988).

[SKSH 89] Schneider, R., Kriegel, H.P., Seeger, B., Heep, S.,´A system for retrieval of parts with geometric similarity´, Technical Report 1/89, Informatik, Universitaet Bremen, FRG.

SEARCH FOR MULTI-COMPONENT OBJECTS IN LARGE SPATIAL DATABASES

Sudhakar Menon and Terence R. Smith
National Center for Geographic Information and Analysis,
The University of California, Santa Barbara, CA 93106

ABSTRACT

Many queries to spatial database systems concern spatial objects that may be conceptually modeled in terms of multiple components satisfying constraints on both attributes and spatial relationships. We investigate the performance of a new algorithm called Forward Constraint Propagation (FCP) that dynamically assembles the spatial locations of a multi-component object from a spatial database given a description of its components and their spatial relationships. The database stores the spatial locations of individual components in either object-based or location-based form. FCP embeds spatial constraint propagation within a heuristic tree search algorithm developed for the general constraint satisfaction problem. An experimental investigation based on a quadtree-structured database of "real-world" objects indicates that FCP outperforms eight alternative procedures in terms of time complexity.

1. The Multi-Component Spatial Search Problem

In a multi-component spatial search problem (MCSSP) for a spatial object O with n sub-objects $O_1, \ldots, O_n$, the sub-objects must satisfy specified unary constraints (such as size and shape) and binary constraints (such as distance and direction). Let $v_1, v_2, \ldots, v_n$ be variables characterizing respectively each of the n subobjects and taking values from a finite set of locations, D_i. The location of any sub-object is a point, a piecewise linear curve or a connected region in the plane whose boundary is a polygon.

Let the predicate P_i represent the conjunction of all k unary constraints on the location variable v_i ($P_i = P_{i_1} \bigwedge P_{i_2} \cdots \bigwedge P_{i_k}$) and let the predicate P_{ij} represent the conjunction of all binary constraints on the location variables v_i and v_j. A *location-set* for the object O is then a set of n locations $\{ x_1, x_2, \ldots, x_n \}$ with $x_i \epsilon D_i$ for $i = 1, \ldots, n$ such that :

$$P_1(x_1) \bigwedge \cdots \bigwedge P_n(x_n) \bigwedge P_{12}(x_1,x_2) \bigwedge \cdots \bigwedge P_{n-1,n}(x_{n-1},x_n) .$$

The MCSSP consists of determining all location-sets for the object O, given the domains of the n sub-objects. The MCSSP is a constraint satisfaction problem (CSP) in which the constraints between variables are *spatial* in nature and the values taken by variables are *locations* in space. It is easy to show that if no restrictions are placed on the spatial constraints, then the general MCSSP is NP-Complete.

2. An Algorithm for MCSSP

The performance of the basic tree search algorithm for the general CSP (i.e. Backtracking) may be improved by the use of consistency algorithms either as a preprocessing step (see Mackworth, 1977 and Mackworth and Freuder, 1985 who describe node, arc and path consistency algorithms) or during tree search, in which case Forward Checking (FC), Partial Looking Ahead (Haralick and Elliott,

1980) and Backmarking (Gaschnig, 1978) are three algorithms that dynamically enforce arc consistency conditions. In these algorithms for the general CSP, the domain of each variable is represented as an ordered set. During tree search, the values for any variable are examined sequentially and constraints are explicitly computed in order to check whether the value selected from the domain satisfies the constraints on the variable. These algorithms do not exploit the underlying structure of the variable domains.

Unlike these variants of the CSP algorithms, our new algorithm for solving the MCSSP, called the Forward Constraint Propagation algorithm (FCP), exploits the spatial nature of both the domain and constraints by using appropriate spatial data structures and retrieval algorithms. FCP embeds spatial constraint propagation within the FC heuristic tree search algorithm developed for the general CSP. A detailed algorithmic description of FCP, including its embedding in a spatial database using hierarchical quadtree data structures, may be found in Menon (1989). We note here that spatial constraint propagation is used to replace the explicit checking of constraints during backtracking by geometric search within constrained areas of the database. Depending on the geometric nature of object locations (points, lines, regions) and of the propagated constraints, the spatial window in the database in which search occurs may have an arbitrarily complex shape, which may be difficult to search efficiently. It may then be necessary to search within a larger area which is more efficiently accessed under the geometric data structure selected, and apply *filtering search* with explicit constraint checking being used to filter out retrieved examples that do not satisfy the required constraints.

The replacement of explicit constraint checking by constraint propagation is insufficient to prevent "thrashing" during backtracking when the number of sub-objects in a problem exceeds two. FCP therefore incorporates the "looking into the future" heuristic used by the FC algorithm of Haralick and Elliott (1980). The forward checks that enforce arc consistency between a current variable and future variables in the FC algorithm are replaced by forward constraint propagations that result in a search for future variables within constrained areas of the database in FCP. In order to apply spatial constraint propagation it is necessary to decide on a search order for the sub-objects. Order criteria include: domain size (smallest first); the structure of the underlying constraint graph (eg minimum width ordering Freuder, 1982); and object complexity (simplest first). Spatial Constraint Propagation requires the use of data structures that permit efficient retrieval of the subset of locations within a constrained window from the total set of locations in the database. The efficiency of this retrieval process depends on the specific data structures used for spatial indexing and storage of component locations within the spatial database.

3. An Experimental Evaluation of FCP and other Algorithms for MCSSP

A comparative experimental investigation of the performance of various procedures for the MCSSP, including FCP, was made. All evaluations were performed using procedures embedded in the spatial search module of KBGIS-II (see Smith, Peuquet, Menon and Agarwal, 1987), which is a GIS implemented at the University of California, Santa Barbara. The algorithms were tested on a database provided by the US Geological Survey. Nine algorithms were compared experimentally on a set of multi-component spatial search problems, namely: Backtracking, Unidirectional Arc-Consistency followed by Backtracking, Arc-Consistency followed by Backtracking, FC, Unidirectional Arc-Consistency followed by FC, Arc-Consistency followed by FC, Partial Looking Ahead, Backmarking and FCP. All algorithms *except FCP* employ explicit constraint checking. FCP and FC were compared to determine the utility of spatial constraint propagation. Each algorithm was investigated on the same set of multi-component spatial objects, consisting of region and linear sub-objects related by distance constraints. The following measures were made during each test run in order to investigate the time efficiency of the different procedures :

1. The total number of consistency checks used to verify spatial relationships between different sub-objects;

2. the total number of computations of constrained search windows;

3. the total number of database searches for single component sub-objects;

4. the total area of the spatial database searched;

5. the total CPU time taken by the system to answer the complete query.

The total number of consistency checks (1) and the total CPU time (5) were used to compare the different constraint checking algorithms. The total CPU time was included because the number of constraint checks alone is not an effective measure for the Backmarking algorithm (Haralick and Elliott, 1980). For a given multi-component object model, measures (2), (3) and (4) are identical for each of the 8 constraint checking algorithms and were included for comparison of the constraint checking algorithms with the FCP algorithm.

Two parameters were chosen to characterize the multi-component object models:

1. The Degree Of Constraint (DOC) in the model

2. The Constraint Graph Topology (CGT) for the model.

The DOC parameter was used as an index of the amount of pruning of the search space that was achievable by enforcing the spatial constraints imposed in a given multi-component object model, and may be defined as the average of the degrees of constraint for each of the edges of a constraint graph. Three values of this parameter were used (HIGH, MEDIUM, LOW). CGT was included as a parameter because the influence of different sub-object ordering and constraint inferring techniques was expected to vary with the graph topology, (CLIQUE and STAR topologies were investigated). Each of the spatial constraint satisfaction algorithms used an ordering for the nodes in each CLIQUE model that was based on domain size (smallest first) since all orderings are structurally equivalent.

Of the 8 constraint checking algorithms, FC used the smallest number of consistency checks for all test cases. FC was also the fastest algorithm, in terms of CPU time (confirming results obtained by Haralick, 1981, for the 8-Queens problem). Table 1 shows the performance of FCP and compares it with the performance of the FC algorithm for clique graphs with 3, 4 and 5 sub-objects respectively using all five measures. The net area of the database searched is expressed as a percentage of the total area of the database. The constraint checking operator used in this comparison was a fast centroid distance operator. Spatial constraint propagation was accomplished using rectangular constrained search windows on a quadtree based database. Each constraint propagation made by FCP results in a constrained window computation and a spatial database search (within the constrained window). The number of spatial database searches made by FCP is seen to be exactly one more than the number of constrained window computations because every search except the first is the result of a constraint propagation.

Table 1 : FC versus FCP
Operator : Centroid Distance between Polygons
GRAPH C3 (n=3)

DOC	ALGTHM	Checks	Props	Searches	Net Area	Area/Search	CPU
HIGH	FC	279	0	3	300	100.0	15.9
HIGH	FCP	30	14	15	166	11.1	38.3
MED	FC	431	0	3	300	100.0	18.7
MED	FCP	159	18	19	382	20.1	60.5
LOW	FC	564	0	3	300	100.0	22.1
LOW	FCP	305	20	21	675	32.1	87.8

GRAPH C4 (n=4)

HIGH	FC	645	0	4	400	100.0	26.2
HIGH	FCP	59	19	20	232	11.6	65.1
MED	FC	1185	0	4	400	100.0	44.4
MED	FCP	443	24	25	459	18.4	113.5
LOW	FC	3594	0	4	400	100.0	148.1
LOW	FCP	2652	29	30	914.1	30.4	295.8

GRAPH C5 (n=5)

HIGH	FC	661	0	5	500	100.0	49.0
HIGH	FCP	169	19	20	310.5	15.5	62.5
MED	FC	1340	0	5	500	100.0	61.7
MED	FCP	646	23	24	476	19.8	92.7
LOW	FC	3685	0	5	500	100.0	141.9
LOW	FCP	2725	28	29	706.0	24.3	212.8

Operator : Minimum Distance between Polygons
DOC : HIGH

GRAPH	ALGTHM	Checks	Props	Searches	Net Area	Area/Search	CPU
C3	FC	310	0	3	300	100.0	1024.5
C3	FCP	40	15	16	171	10.7	213.1
C4	FC	792	0	4	400	100.0	1207.5
C4	FCP	92	22	23	259	11.3	334.5
C5	FC	1127	0	5	500	100.0	3529.5
C5	FCP	385	23	24	3609	15.0	1431.2

The following observations may be made from these tables :

1   For all three sets of graphs the area per search for FCP increases as the DOC decreases, since the area of a constrained search window increases in size as the DOC decreases.

2   The number of searches made by FCP increases as the DOC decreases, since the number of total and partial solutions increases as the DOC decreases.

3.   At HIGH degrees of constraint the number of consistency checks made by FCP is a small fraction of the number of checks made by FC. For the HIGH degrees of constraint simulated in these queries the fraction ranged from 0.1 to 0.25. At LOW degrees of constraint, this fraction increases to between 0.6 and 0.8, since consistency checks performed by FCP are restricted to filtering the subsets of examples retrieved by constrained search. At LOW degrees of constraint, the number of examples found on each constrained search is large and the cost of filtering these found examples increases.

4.   At *all* degrees of constraint the number of constraint propagations made by FCP is a very small fraction of the number of consistency checks made by FC. While the number of constraint propagations made by FCP increases with a decrease in the degree of constraint (because of the increased number of partial solutions), this growth rate is far smaller then the growth rate in the number of constraint checks made by FC. This causes the ratio of the number of constraint propagations made by FCP to the number of checks made by FC to be actually smaller at LOW degrees of constraint. This ratio ranges from 0.01 at LOW degrees of constraint to approximately 0.04 at HIGH degrees of constraint.

5.   At HIGH degrees of constraint the net area of the database searched by FCP is less than the net area searched by FC, even though the number of searches made by FCP is more.

In the results reported in Table 1 the centroid distance operator used for distance constraint checking was extremely fast (although approximate when applied on polygon sub-objects). As a result FC was computationally faster in terms of CPU time. The last part of Table 1 shows the results, for HIGH degrees of constraint, when using a more expensive minimum distance between polygons operator. The average cost of the latter (more accurate) operator was approximately 150 times as high as that of the approximate centroid distance operator. The use of the minimum distance operator increases the net CPU costs of FC by a factor ranging from 50 to 150, if one includes the spatial database search costs. The increase in cost of FCP is by a much smaller factor (between 3 and 22). FCP is faster than FC by a factor ranging from 2.5 to 5 when using the minimum distance operator. The constraint values imposed in the models were not changed when switching to the more expensive operator. This accounts for the increased number of checks used by FC. The use of the minimum distance operator results in loosening the degree of constraint and increasing the number of solutions found, since the minimum distance between the boundaries of two regions may be less than the imposed value, d, even though the distance between their centroids is greater than d. The converse is not true. The comparative performance of the different algorithms when tested on STAR models is similar. For an evaluation of different graph oredering strategies see Menon (1989).

It is of interest to model explicitly the relationship between the number of constraint propagations made by FCP and the the number of checks made by FC as the number n of sub-objects increases. In the case of two sub-objects, the number of constraint checks made by FC is equal to the product of the domain sizes, whereas the number of propagations made by FCP is equal to the size of the domain of the first sub-object. Figure 1 shows a family of simple constraint graphs. Node i in such a graph is constrained only by node $i-1$. The graphs L1, L2 and L3 have 2, 3 and 4 nodes respectively. Such graphs are easy to analyze because :

1. there are no forward constraints leading from node i into any node other then node $i+1$. Hence the pruning achieved by both FC and FCP is identical to the pruning achieved by backtracking. ("looking into the future" has no value).

2. The only constraint leading into node i is rooted at node $i-1$. Thus each partial solution for nodes 1 through $i-1$ leads to a constraint propagation resulting in a search for node i.

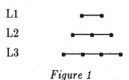

Figure 1

Suppose the size of the domains of all sub-objects is constant with each containing a locations. For any given location l for node i let f be the number of locations for node $i+1$ that satisfy the constraint between nodes i and $i+1$ when node i is assigned location l, where $1 \leq i < n$. Note that $1-f/a$ is the analog of the DOC. Assume that f is a constant over all nodes i, $i+1$ and locations l. The number of solutions found for L2 is then af. FC uses a^2 checks to find these solutions. FCP uses a propagations. Each solution for L2 represents a partial solution for the first two nodes in L3. The number of *additional* constraint checks made by FC on L3 is therefore $af \times a$ or $a^2 f$. The number of additional constraint propagations made by FCP on the L3 graph is af. The number of solutions found for L3 (by either algorithm) is af^2. Proceeding inductively in this manner it can be seen that the total number of checks made by FCP on such a graph with n nodes is $a^2 (f^{n-1}-1) / (f-1)$. The total number of constraint propagations made by FC is $a (f^{n-1}-1) / (f-1)$. Note that both the number of constraint checks and the number of constraint propagations increase *exponentially* with n even on such simple graphs when $f > 1$.

The *ratio* of the number of propagations made by FCP to the number of checks made by FC remains constant with n and is equal to $1/a$. Relative savings are therefore by a factor equal to the domain size of a sub-object. The *absolute* savings grow exponentially with n because of the exponential multiplicative factor.

4. Conclusions

Queries involving multi-component search on large spatial databases can be expected to possess high degrees of constraint. Of the 8 constraint checking algorithms investigated, Forward Checking (FC) was found to be the best overall algorithm for the task of spatial constraint satisfaction. The Forward Constraint Propagation (FCP) algorithm combines the "looking into the future" heuristic used by FC with spatial constraint propagation accomplished using spatial data structures that permit efficient access to the subset of locations within a constrained window. FCP is particularly appropriate for queries with a high degree of constraint, and for queries which involve costly constraint checking operators. The number of constraint propagations made by FCP is a small fraction, of the number of constraint checks made by FC. Analysis of a simple class of constraint graphs was used to show that this fraction grows smaller as domain sizes increase, but is independent of the number of sub-objects.

5. References

Freuder, E.C., 1982, A sufficient condition for backtrack free search, Journal of the ACM, vol. 29, pp. 24-32.

Gaschnig, J., 1977, A general backtrack algorithm that eliminates most redundant tests, Proc. of the International Joint Conference on Artificial Intelligence, Cambridge, MA, USA, p. 457.

Haralick, R.M. & Elliott, G.L., 1980, Increasing Tree Search Efficiency for Constraint Satisfaction Problems, Artificial Intelligence, vol. 14, pp. 263-313.

Mackworth, A.K., 1977, Consistency in Networks of Relations, Artificial Intelligence, vol. 8, pp. 99-118.

Mackworth, A.K. & Freuder, E.C., 1985, The Complexity of some Polynomial Network Consistency Algorithms for Constraint Satisfaction Problems, Artificial Intelligence, vol. 25, pp 65-74.

Menon, S, 1989, Spatial Search for Multi-Component Objects in a GIS using Symbolic Models and Hierarchical Data Structures, PhD Dissertation, University of California, Santa Barbara, CA, 93106.

Smith, T.R., Peuquet, D.J., Menon, S. & Agarwal, P., 1987, KBGIS-II A Knowledge Based Geographic Information System, Internation Journal of Geographical Information Systems, Vol I, no 2, pp 149-172.

OPTIMIZATION AT A HIGH LEVEL OF ABSTRACTION

Isabelle Richard and Elie Milgrom

Université Catholique de Louvain
UNITE D'INFORMATIQUE
Place Sainte-Barbe, 2
B-1348 Louvain-la-Neuve
Belgium

Abstract. This paper presents an optimization to an insertion algorithm for nearly complete binary search trees. The original algorithm was published recently by T.E. Gerasch in the *Communications of the ACM* ([Ger88]). Its insertion time is logarithmic in the best case, and linear in the worst case. With the optimization proposed here, some insertions that would require linear time with Gerasch's algorithm are handled in logarithmic time. The proposed optimization does not modify the worst case nor the best case behaviour of the algorithm.

1   Introduction

This paper presents an optimization to Gerasch's insertion algorithm for nearly complete binary search trees ([Ger88]). The original algorithm was expressed in Pascal, using a classical linked representation for binary trees. The optimization proposed here was discovered during an attempt to re-express Gerasch's algorithm in a very-high-level algorithmic pseudo-language, which we call Piola. One of the aims of the underlying work is to design means for algorithmic expression which allow to express algorithms and to analyze their complexity at a significantly higher level of abstraction than when using Pascal.

The algorithms presented in this paper are expressed in Piola. However, we concentrate here on the optimization of Gerasch's algorithm, not on the discussion of problems related with the expression of algorithms. Section 2 briefly presents those features of Piola which are necessary to *read* the algorithms of the next sections. Section 3 presents Gerasch's algorithm and the analysis of its complexity. Section 4 presents the proposed optimization and compares it with Gerasch's algorithm. This paper is a condensed version of [Ric88]; the full version presents a more detailed complexity analysis and contains more details about Piola.

2   Preliminary definitions and notations

Mathematical notations for binary trees.

Let T be a binary tree. $Nodes(T)$ denotes the set of nodes of T. The following function names will be used, with the obvious meaning: *root, l_child, r_child, parent, sibling.*

Direction names (*left, right*) are abbreviated: $Dir \triangleq \{l, r\}$. Boolean complementation is used to designate "the other direction": $\bar{r} = l$ and $\bar{l} = r$. In the above functions, direction names are considered as parameters. This allows to write c_child and $\bar{c}\_child$, where $c \in Dir$.

Keys from a set *Keys* are associated with each node of T by means of the function $key : Nodes(T) \longmapsto Keys$. The *depth* (or level) of a node in T is its distance to $root(T)$. $lev_i(T)$ denotes the sequence of nodes at depth i in T, from left to right.

If S is a sequence of nodes containing a and b, $S_{a \to b}$ denotes the sequence obtained by traversing S from a to b. If dir is a direction, $S_{a,dir}$ denotes the sequence obtained by traversing S from a, in direction dir, up to the corresponding endpoint of S.

Dummy nodes.

In Piola algorithms, *dummy nodes* will be defined to complete partial functions of the form $f : Nodes(T) \longmapsto Nodes(T)$. Intuitively, the dummy nodes of T give legal existence to expressions of the form $f(x)$, where $x \notin \text{dom}(f)$. Unless otherwise stated, all the dummy nodes are different from each other. Dummy nodes can be given a rigorous mathematical definition, but we shall not attempt to do so here.

$Dchildren(T)$ denotes the set of dummy children of T, i.e. the set of dummy nodes of the form $c\_child(n)$, where $c \in Dir$. Associating a key with a dummy child converts it into a true node and dissociating a key from a leaf converts it into a dummy child. If key k is not in the binary search tree T, the last element of the sequence $search\_path_T(k)$ is defined to be the dummy child where k could be inserted.

The "traverse" control structure.

"**traverse** S **reaching** $x \mid P(x)$" means that the sequence S must be traversed up to the first x verifying $P(x)$. If no condition $P(x)$ is indicated, the traversal terminates with the last element of S, which receives the name x. "**simultaneously_traverse** (S, S') **reaching** the first $x \mid P(x)$" means that sequences S and S' must be traversed, one element of each sequence at each step, and that the traversal terminates as soon as an x verifying $P(x)$ has been found, either in S or in S'. If a sequence terminates before an x is found, the search continues in the other one.

Additional keywords allow to express global actions that must be performed during the traversal, such as maintenance of an invariant or of explicit information (**maintaining**), detection of some particular element (**detecting** the first $y \mid Q(y)$), etc.

3 Brief presentation of Gerasch's algorithm

A binary tree T is *nearly complete to level l* if it is complete to level $l - 1$ and if $lev_l(T)$ is either empty or the last non-empty level of T. This is a balancing criterion for binary trees, because a nearly complete binary tree of n nodes has a depth of $O(\log_2 n)$. *NC_BST* denotes the set of all the *Nearly Complete Binary Search Trees* (to any level).

Let T be a binary search tree, nearly complete to level l and let k be a key to be inserted in T. Normal binary search tree insertion would insert k either in $lev_l(T)$ or in $lev_{l+1}(T)$, converting one of the dummy children p into a true node. Insertion at level $l + 1$ transgresses the balancing criterion; hence, T must be reorganized: room is made for k by displacing key values in T, from p, in infix order. The infix shift terminates when a shifted key can be inserted in a dummy node x at level l (see figure).

l is the *insertion depth* ($ins\_depth(T)$). Level l (resp. $l + 1$) is *the insertion level* (resp. *the transgression level*). $ins\_Dchildren(T)$ (resp. $trans\_Dchildren(T)$) is the set of dummy children at insertion (resp. transgression) level.

$infix(T)$ is defined as the sequence containing the true nodes, p and the insertion dummy children, in infix order. Hence, the infix shift of key values may be expressed as pushing_shift($infix(T)_{p \to x}$), where "pushing_shift" converts, by shifting, a sequence ending with a dummy (empty) node into a sequence beginning with a dummy node. (Note: "pulling_shift" is the inverse operation.)

A subtree S – and the node $root(S)$ – is *saturated* if it is impossible to insert a new key in S at the insertion level. The set of saturated nodes of T is noted $Sat(T)$.

If f is the first saturated node on $search\_path_T(k)$ (see figure), $sibling(f)$ is *not* saturated (because otherwise f would not be the *first* saturated node). Hence, a displaced key may be inserted in the corresponding subtree and the shift direction may thus be from f to $sibling(f)$. To identify the first saturated node easily, Gerasch associates additional information with each node. After effective insertion in a dummy node y at the insertion level, the saturation information must be updated for the nodes on the path from y to the root. This will be encapsulated in a procedure "update_sat$(y \in Nodes(T))$", whose time complexity is logarithmic in the worst case.

Gerasch's algorithm will require logarithmic time if no reorganization is needed (best case). The worst case occurs when the insertion position at the transgression level and the single free place left at the insertion level are located at the two infix endpoints of $infix(T)$. In that case, all the keys in T must be displaced and the time complexity is thus linear.

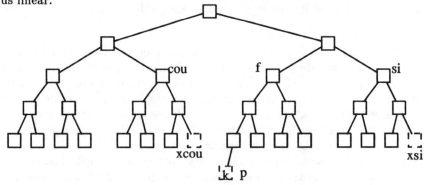

Gerasch's algorithm, expressed in Piola:
proc insert_G (**in** $k \in Keys$, **in/out** $T \in NC\_BST$) ;
    traverse $search\_path_T(k)$ **reaching** p
        detecting the first $f \mid f \in Sat(T)$
            let $c \in Dir \mid f = c\_child(parent(f))$
            (* f exists $\Leftrightarrow p \in trans\_Dchildren(T)$. Shift must be to the $\overline{c}$ of p *) ;
    if $key(p) = k$ $\longrightarrow$ **signal** (k already in T) ;
      $p \in ins\_Dchildren(T)$ $\longrightarrow$ $key(p) := k$; (* p has become non dummy *)
                                 update_sat(p) ;
      $p \in trans\_Dchildren(T)$ $\longrightarrow$ $key(p) := k$ (* PROVISIONAL *) ;
                                 (* restore balance: *)
                                 pushing_shift$(infix(T)_{p \to x})$
                                   where x is the first $x \in ins\_Dchildren(T)$,
                                      to the $\overline{c}$ of p ;
                               (* p is dummy again, x has become non dummy *)
                               update_sat(x)
    fi

4 Optimization of Gerasch's algorithm

As illustrated by the figure, Gerasch's strategy to determine the shift direction does not always choose the closest free node: in this example, Gerasch's algorithm will realize an infix shift towards xsi, thus causing $Nodes(T)/2$ key movements, while the infix shift towards $xcou$ would have required only two key displacements. Thus, the optimal shift length, d_{min}, may be constant when Gerasch's shift length, d_G, is linear. Choosing the optimal shift direction causes no savings in the best case (no reorganization is needed) nor in the worst case (only one free node left, at the other infix endpoint of T).

A first strategy to determine the optimal shift direction is to traverse $infix(T)$, from p, in both directions simultaneously, until a free node x is found. The overhead to find x is proportional to the infix distance $dist_{inf}(p, x) = d_{min}$, as the infix shift, thus causing no increase in complexity. With this strategy, it is not necessary to associate saturation information with the nodes.

Optimization: first strategy

proc insert_1 (**in** $k \in Keys$, **in/out** $T \in NC\_BST$) ;
    traverse $search\_path_T(k)$ reaching p ;
    if $key(p) = k$ $\longrightarrow$ **signal** (k already in T) ;
      $p \in ins\_Dchildren(T)$ $\longrightarrow$ $key(p) := k$; (* p has become non dummy *)
      $p \in trans\_Dchildren(T)$ $\longrightarrow$ $key(p) := k$ (* PROVISIONAL *) ;
                                  simultaneously_traverse$(infix(T)_{p,l}, infix(T)_{p,r})$
                                    reaching the first $x \in ins\_Dchildren(T)$;
                                    pulling_shift$(infix(T)_{x \to p})$
                                    (* p is dummy again, x has become non dummy *)
    fi

It is also possible to determine the optimal shift direction along $search\_path_T(k)$, considering three nodes of interest at each level: the node s on the search path and its closest unsaturated cousins to the left and right, l_u and r_u. (The *cousins* of a node are the other nodes at the same level. To avoid problems with missing unsaturated cousins, dummy cousins are defined – for more details see [Ric88].) At the insertion level, l_u and r_u are the free nodes closest to the left and right of p, respectively.

It can be proved that the infix distance of two nodes at the insertion level is twice their distance inside that level. The breadth-first numbering of the nodes (denoted nr) allows to compute distances inside a level by simple subtraction, and it is easy to maintain during the descent along the search path. This allows to determine whether l_u or r_u is closest to p in infix distance. This strategy uses the same saturation information as Gerasch's. The overhead to determine the optimal shift direction is logarithmic.

Optimization: second strategy

proc insert_2 (**in** $k \in Keys$, **in/out** $T \in NC\_BST$) ;
    traverse $search\_path_T(k)$ reaching p
          maintaining $\forall i \in \{0, ..., ins\_depth(T)\}$
               1) $l\_u, s, r\_u \in lev_i(T) \mid$
                    $\begin{cases} s \in search\_path_T(k) \\ \forall c \in Dir, c\_u \text{ is the closest unsaturated node to the } c \text{ of } s \end{cases}$
               2) $nr(x)$, for $x \in \{l\_u, s, r\_u\}$;

if $key(p) = k$ $\longrightarrow$ **signal** (k already in T) ;
   $p \in ins\_Dchildren(T)$ $\longrightarrow$ $key(p) := k$; (* p has become non dummy *)
                   update_sat(p) ;
   $p \in trans\_Dchildren(T)$ $\longrightarrow$ $key(p) := k$ (* PROVISIONAL *) ;
                   let $x \in \{l\_u, r\_u\}$, minimizing $dist_{inf}(p, x)$;
                   pulling_shift($infix(T)_{x \to p}$) ;
                   (* p is dummy again, x has become non dummy *)
                   update_sat(x)
fi

Comparison

Time requirements	insert_G	insert_1	insert_2
finding of p	l	l	l
determination of the shift direction:			
- determ. along $search\_path_T(k)$	l	—	l
- updating of saturation information	l	—	l
- search in $infix(T)$	—	0 or d_{min}	—
infix shift	0 or d_G	0 or d_{min}	0 or d_{min}
total	$l\,[+d_G]$	$l\,[+d_{min}]$	$l\,[+d_{min}]$

5 Conclusion

The paper proposes an optimization of Gerasch's insertion algorithm for nearly complete binary search trees: if an infix shift of key values must be realized, the shortest one will always be chosen. It has been shown that choosing the shortest shift never increases the complexity of the algorithm. In the most interesting cases, it decreases the time complexity from linear to logarithmic. The worst case remains linear.

Two implementation strategies have been proposed. One of those finds a free node during the descent along the search path. It uses the same additional information as Gerasch's algorithm. The other implementation strategy finds a free node by searching for it in both possible directions; it uses no additional information.

From the point of view of algorithm design, the more interesting point about the optimization of Gerasch's algorithm is not the optimization itself: in our opinion, it is the fact that it appeared during the re-expression of the algorithm – originally expressed in Pascal by Gerasch – in a very-high-level algorithmic pseudo-language.

Acknowledgments

We would like to thank Dr. T. Nguyen sincerely for his useful comments on an earlier version of this paper. Thanks are also due to the referees.

References

[Ger88] Thomas E. Gerasch. An insertion algorithm for a minimal internal path length binary search tree. *CACM*, 31(5):579–585, May 1988.

[Ric88] Isabelle Richard and Elie Milgrom. *Optimization at a high level of abstraction.* Research Report RR88-24, U.C.L., Unité d'Informatique, 1988.

A Spatial Database Shell for Relational Database Management Systems

D.J. Abel

CSIRO Division of Information Technology, Centre for Spatial Information Systems,
GPO Box 664, Canberra, ACT 2601, Australia

Abstract

SIRO-DBMS is a Spatial Information Systems database tool-kit implemented as a set of external attachments to a relational database management systems. It implements user data types through parameterised definitions of the user view of additional data types and of their internal representation. A spatial access method built on a 1-dimensional key and compatible with B-trees is also provided. Retrieval performance data with data sets of the sizes likely to be encountered in production systems are reported.

1. INTRODUCTION

The field of Spatial Information Systems (SIS) includes Geographical Information Systems, Land Information Systems and Automated Mapping/Facilities Management systems. SIS can be accurately placed within the broader field of technical database and shares many of the requirements of engineering (CAD/CAM) systems in such areas as support for complex objects, special access methods for relationships such as intersection and proximity and user-defined data types. Clearly the post-relational and extendible database management systems such as DASDBS (Schek and Waterfeld, 1986) and POSTGRES (Stonebraker and Rowe, 1986) will have a considerable influence in SIS. 'Lean and mean' solutions which are more directly aimed at particular classes of applications areas and which deliver some of the advanced concepts of research technical database management systems are also of potential interest to practitioners in implementing production systems.

This paper reports a 'lean and mean' system SIRO-DBMS (Spatial Information in a Relational Open-Architecture Database Management System) (Abel 1988a, 1988b), implemented both as a vehicle for continuing research and development and as a system able to be adopted for production use. While SIRO-DBMS adopts some of the concepts of the post-relational and extendible dbms, a design target has been to allow its adoption in large production systems. Unlike other SIS built around relational database management systems rdbms (e.g. Berman and Stonebraker, 1977), SIRO-DBMS avoids a single schema for geometric definitions and topological relationships. It is essentially a shell around off-the-shelf relational database management systems (rdbms) such as ORACLE, with the shell consisting of an extended relational data model, relational design forms for the internal representation of the geometry and topology of objects and procedural code to map user specifications of operations into those able to be performed directly by the kernel rdbms. As the rdbms is treated as a black box, SIRO-DBMS is implemented as a set of external attachments which communicate to the rdbms in SQL, an approach with benefits and pitfalls.

2. SHELL FACILITIES

The user data types enhance the relational data model by offering the user a high level view of the geometric description of spatial entities and of operations on them. SIRO-DBMS introduces a number of data types for the geometric description of objects by their location and extent. Five geometric data types are provided ('point', 'rectangle', 'line', 'polygon' and 'image') to cater for the usual coordinate representations of objects as well as the thematic representations of regions derived from satellite imagery.

SIRO-DBMS seeks to offer the database designer a range of options in internal representation of the non-trivial geometric data types, while making the choice of an internal representation transparent to the applications programmer. The philosophy has been that, as there are several relational design forms to represent a polygon (for example) with differing tradeoffs between storage required, ease of update and retrieval costs, it is more appropriate for the tradeoff to be selected case-by-case by the database designer than for SIRO-DBMS to impose a particular form in all cases.

There are three components to the implementation of the geometric data types. The first provides a parameterised mapping of the geometric data types into the atomic data types provided directly by the kernel rdbms. For example, the 'point' data type is mapped to two elemental spatial attributes, the x-coordinate of a point and the y-coordinate. The second element is the relational design, effectively the allocation of the set of elemental spatial attributes to one or more relations. These are also parameterised through a library of macro statements of retrieval operations to materialise geometric descriptions and pseudo-attributes from sets held under the various currently-defined relational forms. To execute an operation, the macro statement to be expanded and executed is chosen by SIRO-DBMS from statements of the attributes required and the presence of spatial or other qualifications (from the user specification of the operation) and from its knowledge of the relational design form (from an extended data dictionary). The third element of treatment of geometric data types is the recognition of the exact geometric descriptions of objects. SQL is a poor language to express tests such as the intersection of two polygons, so kernel rdbms facilities are used to deliver candidates which satisfy weakened forms of spatial qualifications, in terms of (for example) intersection of their minimum bounding rectangle with the bounding rectangle of a query window. A full test is then applied within the SIRO-DBMS shell, by code written in C. This requires that the generated SQL statement, where necessary, delivers the full geometric descriptions of objects to the shell.

The use of an rdbms as an implementation vehicle with SQL as the only communication between the shell and the kernel severely limits the choice of spatial access methods. The spatial access method of SIRO-DBMS is built on the approaches of Abel and Smith [1983, 1984] with an extended object referenced by an identifier of its smallest covering subquadrant

from a quadtree decomposition of the region. Orenstein's z-ordering [Orenstein, 1986] is based
on similar concepts.

The '1-key' approach is based on derivation of a single 1-dimensional key for an object from its
minimum bounding rectangle, allowing use of the key with ISAM data structures. Properties
of the key allow the simple expression of searches in SQL. Exepcted case performance is
estimated as O(N**0.5). The '4-key' approach generates up to four keys for an object by
fragmenting the object and indexing the object by the covering subquadrants of each of the
fragments. Search performance is estimated as O(logN) although, in an rdbms
implementation, a separate relation must be built as a 'spatial index'.

3. PERFORMANCE

The retrieval performance of SIRO-DBMS has been assessed empirically with two data sets
representative of applications in Land Information Systems and Geographical Information
Systems using a SUN 3/160 (10 Mhz) under SUNOS V3 and Version 5.1.17 of the ORACLE
rdbms. Solution costs are measured as elapsed times to initiate and complete a retrieval
operation (i.e. response times) with very light other load on the SUN from other users, a
simple but meaningful measure of performance. Abel (1989) presents more detailed
descriptions of the tests.

A first set of tests was measured reposnse times for retrieval of polygons intersecting a
rectnagular window from sets of 2529 to 306009 polygons with 4-key indexing. Large (55
polygons retrieved on average) and small (7 polygons) windows were used. Response times for
large windows ranged from 7.67 seconds (22761 polygons) to 4.98 (306009 polygons) and for
small windows from 2.25 seconds (22761 polygons) and 1.78 seconds (306009 polygons).
The second tests dealt with a point sets, of from 22949 points to 229290, again for retrieval of
objects within a rectangle. For small windows (7 points retrieved), the average response time

ranged from 0.51 seconds to 0.46 seconds and for large windows (57 points) from 1.36 to 1.51 seconds.

4. DISCUSSION

SIRO-DBMS has been implemented as a set of external attachments, treating the kernel relational database management system as a closed system. While such an approach has a number of disadvantages, SIRO-DBMS demonstrates that a useful and efficient 'lean and mean' spatial database tool-kit can be developed as a set of external attachments with a capacity for graceful extension. To the practitioner, the system offers advanced facilities compared to the Spatial Information Systems now available. These include an ability to integrate tightly commercial and spatial data processing systems, to establish genuine distributed databases and improved query performance. To the spatial database researcher, SIRO-DBMS is an opportunity to expose some of the capabilities of the next generation of database management systems to practitioners and to identify fresh problems.

References

Abel, D.J. (1988a), SIRO-DBMS User's Manual, TR-HA-88-1, CSIRO Division of
     Information Technology, Canberra, 168 pp.
Abel, D.J. (1988b), Relational database management facilities for spatial information
     systems, Proceedings of 3rd Intl Symp on Spatial Data Handling, Sydney, 9-18.
Abel, D.J. (1989), SIRO-DBMS: a database tool-kit for geographical information systems, Intl
     Jnl of Geographical Information Systems, to appear.
Abel, D.J. and Smith, J.L. (1983), "A data structure and algorithm based on a linear key for a
     rectangle retrieval problem", Computer Vision, Graphics and Image Processing, 24, 1-
     13.
Abel, D.J. and Smith, J.L. (1984), "A data structure and query algorithm for a database of
     areal entities", Aust Comput J, 16, 147-154.
Berman R. and Stonebraker, M. (1977), "GEO-QUEL: a system for the manipulation and
     Display of Geographic Data", Comp. Graphics 11, 186-191.
Schek, H.J. and Waterfeld, W. (1986), "A database kernel system for geoscientific
     applications", Proceedings. 2nd Intl Symp. on Spatial Data Handling, 273-288.
Stonebraker, M. and Rowe, L. (1986), "The design of POSTGRES", Proceedings ACM-
     SIGMOD, 340-355.

DATA ORGANIZATIONS FOR LOGIC PROGRAMMING

Une introduction à Prolog III

Alain Colmerauer
Professeur à l'Université Aix-Marseille II
Groupe Intelligence Artificielle
Unité de recherche Associée au CNRS 816
Faculté des Sciences de Luminy, Case 901
70 route Léon Lachamp,
13288 Marseille Cedex 9

Abstract. The Prolog III programming language extends Prolog by redefining the fundamental process at its heart; unification. Prolog III integrates into this mechanism, refined processing of trees and lists, number processing, and processing of complete propositional calculus. We present the specifications and the logico-mathematical model for this new langauge, in which we replace the notion of unification by the more appropriate concept of constraint resolution. The capabilities thus acquired by the language are illustrated by various examples.

Résumé. Le langage de programmation Prolog III est une extension de Prolog au niveau de ce qu'il a de plus fondamental, le mécanisme d'unification. Il intègre dans ce mécanisme un traitement fin des arbres et des listes, un traitement numérique et un traitement du calcul propositionnel complet. Nous présentons ici les spécifications et le modèle logico-mathématique de ce nouveau langage. A cette occasion nous remplaçons la notion même d'unification par celle plus appropriée de résolution de contraintes. Nous illustrons les possibilités accrues du langage à travers des exemples variés.

Table des matières

Introduction

Le langage de programmation Prolog a été initialement conçu pour le traitement des langues naturelles [2]. Son utilisation progressive pour résoudre des problèmes dans des domaines de plus en plus variés a mis en valeur ses qualités mais a aussi fait apparaître ses limites. Une partie de ces limites a pu être contournée par des implantations de plus en plus efficaces et des environnements de plus en plus riches. Il reste que le noyau même de Prolog, l'algorithme d'unification de Alan Robinson [7] est resté identique depuis quinze ans, et que ce noyau apparaît de plus en plus noyé dans un ensemble toujours croissant de procédures externes. Citons par exemple les procédures nécessaires à tous les traitements numériques. Ces procédures externes sont malheureusement d'un emploi difficile. Pour les appeler il faut être sûr que certains paramètres soient parfaitement connus, et ceci se heurte à la philosophie générale «prologienne» qui est de pouvoir parler n'importe où et n'importe quand d'un objet inconnu x.

Nous nous proposons donc de remanier profondément Prolog en intégrant au niveau de l'unification: (1) une manipulation plus fine des arbres, qui peuvent être infinis, avec un traitement spécifique pour les listes, (2) un traitement complet de l'algèbre de Boole, c'est-à-dire du calcul propositionnel, (3) un traitement numérique, comprenant l'addition, la soustraction, la multiplication par une constante et les relations $<$, $\leq$, $\geq$, $>$, (4) un traitement général de la relation $\neq$. Ainsi que nous l'avons fait pour décrire Prolog II [3], qui traitait déjà les arbres infinis et la relation $\neq$, ce remaniement passe par le remplacement du concept même d'unification par celui de résolutions de contraintes dans un domaine précis muni d'opérations et de relations précises.

L'objet de cet article est donc de décrire les fondements d'un nouveau langage baptisé Prolog III et d'illustrer ses possibilités à travers quelques exemples. Prolog III est bien entendu plus qu'une vue de l'esprit. Un prototype de son interpréteur fonctionne sur station SUN et a permis de tester les exemples proposés. Il s'exécutent tous dans des temps de l'ordre de quelques dixièmes de secondes sauf le remplissage d'un rectangle par neuf carrés qui prend quelques minutes. Le prototype a été réalisé conjointement par notre laboratoire (le GIA) et la société PrologIA. D'importantes aides financières ont été obtenues d'une part du Centre National d'Etudes des Télécommunications (marché 86 1B 027) et d'autre part des Communautés Européennes, dans le cadre d'un projet ESPRIT (P1219, 11O6) avec pour autres partenaires les sociétés Mercedes, Bosch et GIT.

Les valeurs possibles d'une variable

Dans les langages de programmation classiques une valeur est attachée à chaque variable. L'exécution d'un programme consiste alors à effectuer toutes sortes de modifications de ces valeurs, par le biais d'instructions d'affectation, et à obtenir des valeurs finales pour les différentes variables. En Prolog III une variable représente une valeur inconnue et le déroulement d'un programme ne vise pas à modifier cette valeur mais à la déterminer. Une variable se comporte donc exactement comme une inconnue mathématique dans une équation, comme par exemple x dans $x = (1/2)x + 1$. La différence principale est que x représentera quelque chose de plus complexe qu'un nombre: un *arbre*. Ces arbres seront composés de nœuds étiquetés par

(1) des identificateurs,
(2) des caractères,
(3) des valeurs booléennes,

(4) des nombres rationnels,
(5) le double signe <>.

En voici un

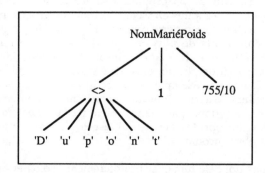

Les valeurs booléennes sont notées **1** et **0** et les nombres rationnels sont représentés par des fractions. L'ensemble des branches qui partent de chaque nœud d'un arbre est fini et ces branches sont ordonnées de gauche à droite. Une branche, par contre, peut être infinie. Un arbre réduit à un seul nœud est une *feuille* et nous ne ferons pas de différence entre une feuille et l'étiquette qu'elle porte. De ce fait les valeurs booléennes et les nombres rationnels seront considérés comme des cas particuliers d'arbres. Les arbres dont le nœud initial est le double signe <> sont des *listes* et servent à représenter des suites finies d'arbres, en l'occurrence la suite de leurs fils immédiats. De ce fait la feuille étiquetée <> représente la liste vide.

Les constantes connues

Pour représenter nos arbres nous disposerons de variables, que nous écrirons toujours en italique afin de les distinguer des identificateurs, de constantes pour nommer certains arbres particuliers et d'opérations pour construire des arbres à partir d'autres arbres. Un arbre sera donc représenté par une formule faisant intervenir ces trois ingrédients: les variables, les constantes et les opérations. Une telle formule, vue comme un objet syntaxique, sera appelée un *terme*. Voici les constantes connues:
(1) les identificateurs comme,

Pierre, RepasLéger, calcul12,

(2) les caractères comme,

'a', B', '4', '<',

(3) les valeurs booléennes,

0, 1,

(4) les entiers positifs ou nuls, comme,

0, 1,2 ,1987,

(5) la liste vide,

<>,

(6) les chaînes non vides comme la chaîne

"Et zut"

qui est l'arbre

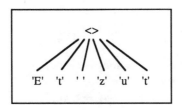

A part les chaînes, les constantes connues sont donc les étiquettes qui, comme nous l'avons déjà dit, sont assimilées à des feuilles. Il faut cependant noter que seuls les entiers positifs ou nuls sont prévus comme constantes numériques. Les autres nombres rationnels pourront être facilement représentés à l'aide des entiers positifs et des opérations de division et de changement de signe que nous introduirons plus loin. Il est aussi inutile de prévoir une constante particulière pour noter la chaîne vide, celle-ci étant identique à la liste vide <>.

Les opérations connues

Nous pouvons maintenant passer à l'énumération des opérations connues. Une opération sera tout simplement une application d'un ensemble de n-uplets d'arbres dans l'ensemble des arbres. On supposera que tous les n-uplets de cet ensemble sont de même longueur et cette longueur sera précisément l'*arité* de l'opération. Une opération d'arité n sera schématisée par une formule de la forme

$$a_1...a_n \rightarrow f(a_1...a_n),$$

où $f(a_1...a_n)$ désigne la notation utilisée pour représenter l'arbre résultant de l'application de cette opération sur le n-uplet $a_1...a_n$. Nous disposerons de trois types d'opérations: les opérations booléennes, les opérations arithmétiques et les opérations de construction d'arbres complexes.

Les opérations booléennes ne sont définies que si les opérandes sont des valeurs booléennes, c'est-à-dire des feuilles étiquetées par des booléens. Il y en a trois:
(1) l'opération *non*,

$$a_1 \rightarrow \neg a_1,$$

(2) l'opération *et*,

$$a_1 a_2 \rightarrow a_1 \wedge a_2,$$

(3) l'opération *ou* (non exclusif),

$$a_1 a_2 \rightarrow a_1 \vee a_2,$$

(4) l'opération qui produit **1** si les deux opérandes sont égaux et **0** s'il ne le sont pas,

$$a_1 a_2 \rightarrow a_1 \equiv a_2.$$

Les opérations arithmétiques ne sont définies que si les opérandes sont des nombres rationnels, c'est-à-dire des feuilles étiquetées par des fractions (ou des entiers) et, dans le cas de la division, uniquement si le deuxième opérande est différent de 0. Elles sont au nombre de six:
(1) l'opération neutre,

$$a_1 \rightarrow +a_1,$$

(2) le changement de signe,

$$a_1 \rightarrow -a_1,$$

(3) l'addition,

$$a_1a_2 \rightarrow a_1 + a_2,$$

(4) la soustraction,

$$a_1a_2 \rightarrow a_1 - a_2,$$

(5) la multiplication,

$$a_1a_2 \rightarrow a_1 \times a_2,$$

(6) la division,

$$a_1a_2 \rightarrow a_1/a_2.$$

Nous imposerons une importante restriction de *linéarité* sur les termes faisant intervenir ces opérations: dans une multiplication l'un des deux opérandes ne doit pas contenir de variables et, dans une division, le deuxième opérande ne doit pas contenir de variables. Enfin, afin d'alléger les écritures nous permettrons, quand cela ne prête pas à confusion, d'écrire a_1a_2 au lieu de $a_1 \times a_2$.

Les opérations de construction permettent de construire des arbres non forcément réduits à des feuilles. Il en existe quatre types:
(1) les constructions de listes, pour tous les n tels que $n \geq 1$,

$$a_1...a_n \rightarrow <a_1,...,a_n>,$$

(2) les constructions d'arbres, pour tous les n tels que $n \geq 2$,

$$a_1a_2...a_n \rightarrow a_1(a_2,...,a_n),$$

(3) la construction générale d'arbre,

$$a_1a_2 \rightarrow a_1[a_2],$$

(4) la concaténation de listes,

$$a_1a_2 \rightarrow a_1 \cdot a_2.$$

Les constructions de listes sont définies quels que soient les arbres a_i. Les constructions d'arbres ne sont définies que si l'arbre a_1 est une feuille. La construction générale d'arbre n'est définie que si l'arbre a_1 est une feuille et l'arbre a_2 une liste. La concaténation n'est définie que si les deux arbres a_1 et a_2 sont des listes. Ce que font exactement toutes ces opérations de construction se résume au schéma

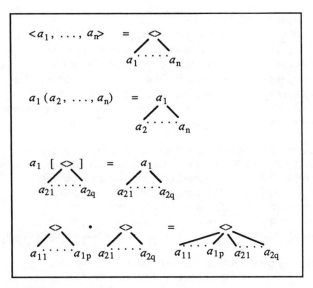

On remarquera les égalités

$$\langle a_1,\ldots,a_n \rangle = \langle\rangle(a_1,\ldots,a_n),$$
$$a_1(a_2,\ldots,a_n) = a_1[\langle a_2,\ldots,a_n\rangle]$$

et, lorsque a est une liste,

$$\langle\rangle[a] = a, \langle\rangle \bullet a = a \bullet \langle\rangle = a.$$

On remarquera aussi que pour noter une liste dont le premier élément est e et dont le reste de la liste est x on écrit

$$\langle e\rangle \bullet x$$

et que

$$e[x]$$

désigne un arbre absolument quelconque, l'étiquette de son nœud initial étant e et la liste éventuellement vide de ses fils étant x.

Comme on l'a fait pour la division et la multiplication on imposera une contrainte importante sur les opérations de concaténation figurant dans les termes: si l'opérande gauche est une variable x alors la longueur n de la liste qu'il représente doit être explicitement spécifiée par une contrainte de la forme $x:n$ dont nous allons parler. Il faut tenir compte dans cette restriction que la concaténation est une opération associative et qu'on ne fait aucune différence ici entre $(x\bullet y)\bullet z$ et $x\bullet(y\bullet z)$.

A l'aide des constantes et des opérations que nous avons introduites, nous pouvons représenter notre premier exemple d'arbre, indifféremment, par l'un des deux termes :
NomMariéPoids(<'D','u','p','o','n','t'>, **1**, 755/10),
NomMariéPoids("Dupont", **1**, 75+1/2).

Les relations connues

Un certain nombre de relations binaires et unaires sont connues. Les relations binaires permettent d'exprimer les contraintes suivantes sur les arbres:
$a_1 = a_2,$ les arbres a_1 et a_2 sont égaux,

$a_1 \neq a_2$, les arbres a_1 et a_2 sont différents,

$a_1 => a_2$, les arbres a_1 et a_2 sont des booléens et si a_1 vaut **1** alors a_2 vaut **1**,

$a_1 < a_2$, les arbres a_1 et a_2 sont des nombres et a_1 est inférieur à a_2,

$a_1 > a_2$, les arbres a_1 et a_2 sont des nombres et a_1 est supérieur à a_2,

$a_1 \leq a_2$, les arbres a_1 et a_2 sont des nombres et a_1 est inférieur ou égal à a_2,

$a_1 \geq a_2$, les arbres a_1 et a_2 sont des nombres et a_1 est supérieur ou égal à a_2.

Par «booléens» et «nombres» nous avons entendu ici des feuilles étiquetées par des valeurs booléennes et des feuilles étiquetées par des nombres rationnels.

Les relations unaires permettent d'exprimer les contraintes suivantes :

a : idt, le nœud initial de l'arbre a est étiqueté par un identificateur,

a : chart, le nœud initial de l'arbre a est étiqueté par un caractère,

a : boolt, le nœud initial de l'arbre a est étiqueté par un booléen,

a : numt, le nœud initial de l'arbre a est étiqueté par un nombre,

a : list, le nœud initial de l'arbre a est étiqueté par le signe <>,

a : n, du nœud initial de l'arbre a partent **n** branches, avec **n** connu.

Il est à noter que l'on peut simuler l'effet des quatre contraintes

$$t : \text{list}, \quad t : \text{boolt}, \quad t : \text{numt} \quad \text{et} \quad t : n$$

en introduisant de nouvelles variables x, y et y_i et en écrivant respectivement

$$t = <>[y], \quad t = (\neg x)[y], \quad t = (+x)[y] \quad \text{et} \quad t = x(y_1,...,y_n).$$

On utilise ici le fait que pour qu'une contrainte soit satisfaite la moindre des choses est que ses arguments soient des arbres bien définis. Il s'en suit que $\neg x$ et $+x$ désignent forcément des feuilles étiquetées par des booléens et des nombres.

Systèmes de contraintes

A partir des contraintes on peut construire des *systèmes* de contraintes qui sont des ensembles finis de contraintes, toutes à satisfaire en même temps. La première chose que Prolog III permet de faire est de résoudre de tels systèmes. Par exemple pour connaître le nombre x de pigeons et le nombre y de lapins qui ensemble totalisent 12 têtes et 34 pattes il suffira de poser la requête

$$\{x \geq 0, y \geq 0, x+y = 12, 2x+4y = 34\}?$$

et la machine répondra

$$\{x = 7, y = 5\}.$$

Pour connaître la liste z de 10 éléments qui produit la même liste si on lui concatène à gauche la liste <1,2,3> ou à droite la liste <2,3,1> il suffira de poser la requête

$$\{ z: 10, \ <1,2,3> \bullet z = z \bullet <2,3,1> \}?$$

pour obtenir

$$\{z = <1,2,3,1,2,3,1,2,3,1>\}.$$

On peut aussi résoudre les deux problèmes à la fois en posant la requête

$$\{x \geq 0, y \geq 0, z: 10,$$
$$\text{trio}(x+y, 2x+4y, <1,2,3> \bullet z) = \text{trio}(12, 34, z \bullet <2,3,1>)\}?$$

ou «trio» est un identificateur quelconque. Cette requête produit la réponse

$$\{x = 7, y = 5, z = <1,2,3,1,2,3,1,2,3,1>\}.$$

Le cœur d'un interpréteur Prolog III sera donc constitué d'un algorithme général de résolution de systèmes de contraintes. Cet algorithme permettra de décider si un système est soluble, c'est-à-dire s'il est possible d'attribuer aux variables des valeurs qui satisfont à toutes ses contraintes. Il permettra aussi, lorsque le système est soluble, de le simplifier afin de rendre apparentes ses solutions, c'est-à-dire les valeurs que doivent prendre les variables. Ces valeurs peuvent être uniques comme dans les exemples précédents, mais aussi multiples comme dans les trois systèmes simplifiés

$$\{0 \leq x, x \geq 3/4, x \neq 1/2\}, \{y => z\}, \{u = \text{père}(v)\}.$$

Si ces valeurs ne sont limitées d'aucune façon, le système simplifié sera le système vide {}. L'algorithme de résolution de contraintes remplace l'algorithme d'unification d'un Prolog classique. De ce fait il devra être efficace et d'une fiabilité telle qu'il puisse être considéré comme une boite noire par le programmeur. Ce sont ces deux raisons qui ont dicté le choix des opérations connues, des relations connues et des restrictions sur la multiplication la division et la concaténation.

A ce propos on notera que dans Prolog III une contrainte ne représente pas une valeur booléenne. Elle est, ou n'est pas, satisfaite pour certaines valeurs des variables. De ce fait il n'est pas possible d'écrire des choses comme $(x>2) \vee (x<1)$. D'ailleurs nos signes $\neg, \wedge, \vee, \equiv$ ne sont ni des connecteurs ni des relations, mais des opérations. Pour écrire $(x>2) \wedge (x<1)$ on écrira $\{x>2, x<1\}$ et pour affirmer $x \vee y$ on écrira $\{x \vee y=1\}$. Par contre on peut écrire $\{x=>y\}$ car => a été défini comme étant une relation. On notera aussi que dans Prolog III il n'existe pas de relation unaire permettant de contraindre un nombre rationnel à être un entier.

Signification d'un programme pour le programmeur

Nous pouvons maintenant expliquer dans toute sa généralité ce qu'est un programme en Prolog III. Il s'agit essentiellement d'une définition récursive d'un sous-ensemble d'arbres. Chaque élément de ce sous-ensemble, que nous appellerons un *fait*, représente une proposition considérée comme vraie par le programmeur. Une telle proposition pourrait être « Dupont est marié et pèse 75,5 kg » et être représentée par notre premier exemple d'arbre. L'ensemble des faits définis par un programme est généralement infini et constitue en quelque sorte une immense banque de données cachée. L'exécution du programme visera précisément à en dévoiler certaines parties.

Le programme proprement dit est un ensemble de *règles*: les règles auxquelles obéissent les *faits* que le programmeur a voulu définir. Chaque règle est de la forme

$$t_0 \rightarrow t_1 \ldots t_n , S$$

où n peut être nul, où les t_i sont des termes et où S est un système éventuellement absent de contraintes. Voici un tel ensemble de règles, c'est notre premier exemple de programme Prolog III. Il s'agit d'une amélioration d'un programme trop connu, mais toujours aussi pédagogique, le calcul de repas légers [3]:

RepasLéger(h, p, d) →
    HorsDœuvre(h, i) Plat(p, j) Dessert(d, k),
    $\{i \geq 0, j \geq 0, k \geq 0, i+j+k \leq 10\}$;

Plat(p, i) → Viande(p, i);
Plat(p, i) → Poisson(p, i);

HorsDœuvre(radis, 1) →;
HorsDœuvre(pâté, 6) →;
Viande(bœuf, 5) →;
Viande(porc, 7) →;

Poisson(sole, 2) →;
Poisson(thon, 4) →;

Dessert(fruit, 2) →;
Dessert(glace, 6) →.

Les variables qui figurent dans les règles sont bien entendu quantifiées universellement, c'est-à-dire que chaque règle $t_0 \rightarrow t_1 ... t_n, S$ n'est qu'une façon abrégée d'écrire toutes les règles *verrouillées* de la forme

$$a_0 \Rightarrow a_1 ... a_n$$

obtenues en donnant aux variables toutes les valeurs possibles qui satisfont le système éventuel S de contraintes et qui transforment les termes t_i en des arbres a_i bien définis. Voici quelques extraits de toutes les règles verrouillées du programme précédent:

....
RepasLéger(pâté,sole,fruit) ⇒
    HorsDœuvre(pâté,6) Plat(sole,2) Dessert(fruit,2) ;
....

....
Plat(sole, 2) ⇒ Poisson(sole,2) ;
....

....
HorsDœuvre(pâté,6) ⇒ ;
....

....
Poisson(sole,2) ⇒ ;
....

....
Dessert(fruit,2) ⇒ ;
....

Bien entendu, cette opération de *verrouiller* les règles est une opération purement mentale de la part du programmeur. La machine ne procédera pas ainsi, bien au contraire, elle essayera d'utiliser les règles en gardant leur maximum de généralité. Par contre les règles verrouillées ne font intervenir ni variables, ni contraintes, mais seulement des arbres. Leur signification est donc beaucoup plus claire.

Chaque règle verrouillée $a_0 \Rightarrow a_1...a_n$ peut s'interpréter de deux façons:
(1)   comme une *règle de réécriture* permettant de remplacer dans une suite d'arbres une occurrence de l'arbre a_0 par la suite d'arbres $a_1...a_n$ (lorsque $n = 0$ cela revient à effacer a_0 de la suite);
(2)   comme la *propriété logique* d'un sous-ensemble E d'arbres: « si tous les arbres $a_1,...,a_n$ appartiennent au sous-ensemble E alors l'arbre a_0 appartient aussi à E » (lorsque $n = 0$ cette propriété se résume à « l'arbre a_0 appartient à E »).

Comme nous l'avons vu, un programme représente l'ensemble cumulé des règles verrouillées provenant de toutes ses règles. Suivant que l'on considère l'une ou l'autre des deux interprétations précédentes, les *faits* définis par ce programme
(1)   sont les arbres effaçables par un nombre fini de réécritures;
(2)   forment le plus petit sous-ensemble d'arbres (au sens de l'inclusion) qui satisfait à toutes les propriétés logiques.

On montre que ces deux définitions sont équivalentes et on comprend pourquoi il y a hésitation sur la direction qu'il faut donner à la flèche d'une règle. Nous avons préféré le sens gauche droite qui correspond plus à ce que fait la machine. Les extraits de l'ensemble de règles verrouillées du programme précédent permettent d'effacer l'arbre

$$\text{RepasLéger(pâté,sole,fruit)}$$

par la suite de réécritures

$$\text{RepasLéger(pâté,sole,fruit)} \Rightarrow$$
$$\text{HorsDœuvre(pâté,6) Plat(sole,2) Dessert(fruit,2)} \Rightarrow$$
$$\text{Plat(sole,2) Dessert(fruit,2)} \Rightarrow$$
$$\text{Poisson(sole,2) Dessert(fruit,2)} \Rightarrow$$
$$\text{Dessert(fruit,2)} \Rightarrow.$$

Cet arbre est donc un fait défini par le programme. Si l'on considère maintenant ces extraits de règles verrouillées comme des propriétés logiques, on conclut successivement que les trois ensembles suivants sont constitués de faits définis par le programme

$$\{\text{HorsDœuvre(pâté,6), Poisson(sole,2), Dessert(fruit,2)}\},$$
$$\{\text{Plat(sole,2)}\},$$
$$\{\text{RepasLéger(pâté,sole,fruit)}\}.$$

Signification d'un programme pour la machine

Nous venons de montrer quelle est l'information implicite contenue dans un programme Prolog III, mais nous n'avons pas montré en quoi consiste l'exécution d'un tel programme. Cette exécution vise à résoudre le problème suivant: «étant donnés une suite $t_1.... t_n$ de termes et un système S de contraintes, trouver les valeurs des variables qui transforment tous ces termes t_i en des faits définies par le programme et ceci tout en satisfaisant à toutes les contraintes de S». Ce problème sera soumis à la machine en posant la *requête*

$$t_1.... t_n ,S ?$$

Deux cas particuliers retiendront notre attention. (1) Si la suite $t_1.... t_n$ est vide alors la requête se résume à demander de résoudre le système S. Nous avons déjà donné de tels exemples de requêtes. (2) Si le système S est vide (ou absent) et que la suite de termes est réduite à un seul terme alors la requête se résume à: «quelles sont les valeurs des variables qui transforment ce terme en un fait défini par le programme considéré». Ainsi si l'on se reporte à l'exemple précédent de programme, la requête

RepasLéger(h, p, d)?

permettra d'obtenir tous les triplets de valeurs pour h, p, d qui constituent un repas léger. Les réponses seront ici les systèmes simplifiés suivants:

$$\{h=\text{radis}, p=\text{bœuf}, d=\text{fruit}\},$$
$$\{h=\text{radis}, p=\text{porc}, d=\text{fruit}\},$$
$$\{h=\text{radis}, p=\text{sole}, d=\text{fruit}\},$$
$$\{h=\text{radis}, p=\text{sole}, d=\text{glace}\},$$
$$\{h=\text{radis}, p=\text{thon}, d=\text{fruit}\},$$
$$\{h=\text{pâté}, p=\text{sole}, d=\text{fruit}\}.$$

La façon de calculer ces réponses s'explique en introduisant une machine abstraite. Il s'agit d'une machine non-déterministe dont la seule instruction de base se décrit par les trois formules:

(1) $(W, t_0\, t_1...t_n\,, S)$,

(2) $s_0 \rightarrow s_1.... s_m\,, R$

(3) $(W,\, s_1...s_m\, t_1...t_n\,, S \cup R \cup \{s_0=t_0\})$.

La formule (1) représente l'état de la machine à un instant donné. W est un ensemble de variables à la valeur desquelles on s'intéresse, $t_0\, t_1...t_n$ est une suite de termes que l'on essaie d'effacer et S est un système de contraintes que l'on doit satisfaire. La formule (2) représente la règle du programme utilisée pour changer d'état. Au besoin on a renommé certaines de ses variables pour n'en avoir aucune de commune avec (1). La formule (3) est le nouvel état de la machine après application de la règle (2). Le passage dans ce nouvel état n'est possible que si le système de contraintes de (3) admet au moins une solution pour laquelle chacun des termes de la suite de termes de (3) représente un arbre bien défini.

Pour répondre à la requête $t_0...t_n, S$, la machine partira de l'état initial $(W, t_0...t_n, S)$, où W est l'ensemble des variables qui figure dans la requête, et passera dans tous les états qu'elle peut atteindre par itération de l'exécution de l'instruction de base, et ceci dans toutes les directions. Chaque fois qu'elle parviendra à un état dont la suite de termes est vide, elle simplifiera le système de contraintes qui lui est associé et le fournira comme réponse. Elle aura aussi la possibilité de simplifier au fur et à mesure tous les systèmes de contraintes qu'elle crée.

Reconsidérons notre premier exemple de programme et appliquons ce traitement à la requête

RepasLéger(h, p, d)?

L'état initial de la machine est

$(\{h, p, d\}$, RepasLéger(h, p, d), $\{\})$.

En appliquant la règle

> RepasLéger(h', p', d') $\rightarrow$ HorsDœuvre(h', i) Plat(p', j) Dessert(d', k),
> $\{i \geq 0, j \geq 0, k \geq 0, i+j+k \leq 10\}$

on passe à l'état

$(\{h, p, d\}$, HorsDœuvre(h', i) Plat(p', j) Dessert(d', k),

$\{i \geq 0, j \geq 0, k \geq 0, i+j+k \leq 10$, RepasLéger($h, p, d$)=RepasLéger($h', p', d'$)$))$

qui se simplifie en

$(\{h, p, d\}$, HorsDœuvre(h', i) Plat(p', j) Dessert(d', k),

$\{i \geq 0, j \geq 0, k \geq 0, i+j+k \leq 10$, $h=h'$, $p=p'$, $d=d'\}))$,

puis en

$(\{h, p, d\}$, HorsDœuvre(h, i) Plat(p, j) Dessert(d, k),

$\{i \geq 0,\ j \geq 0,\ k \geq 0,\ i+j+k \leq 10\}$).
En appliquant la règle

HorsDœuvre(pâté, 6) →

---

et en simplifiant on passe à l'état
$(\{h,p,d\},\ \text{Plat}(p,j)\ \text{Dessert}(d,k),\ \{h=\text{pâté},\ j \geq 0,\ k \geq 0,\ j+k \leq 4\})$.
En appliquant la règle

Plat(p', i) → Poisson(p', i)

---

et en simplifiant un peu on passe à l'état
$(\{h,p,d\},\ \text{Poisson}(p',i)\ \text{Dessert}(d,k),$
$\{h=\text{pâté},\ j \geq 0,\ k \geq 0,\ j+k \leq 4,\ p=p',\ j=i\})$.
qui se simplifie encore en
$(\{h,p,d\},\ \text{Poisson}(p,j)\ \text{Dessert}(d,k),\ \{h=\text{pâté},\ j \geq 0,\ k \geq 0,\ j+k \leq 4\})$.
En appliquant la règle

Poisson(sole, 2) →

---

on obtient
$(\{h,p,d\},\ \text{Dessert}(d,k),\ \{h=\text{pâté},\ p=\text{sole},\ k \geq 0,\ k \leq 2\})$.
Finalement en appliquant la règle

Dessert(fruit, 2) →

---

on obtient
$(\{h,p,d\},\quad,\ \{h=\text{pâté},\ p=\text{sole},\ d=\text{fruit}\})$.
On en conclut que le système
$\{h=\text{pâté},\ p=\text{sole},\ d=\text{fruit}\}$
constitue une des réponses à la requête posée.

Pour obtenir les autres réponses on procédera de la même façon mais en utilisant les autres règles. Il faut signaler qu'il existe mille façon de simplifier les contraintes et de vérifier si elles sont solubles. Il ne faut donc pas s'attendre à ce que la machine, qui utilisera des algorithmes très généraux, fasse les mêmes simplifications que celles que nous venons de présenter. Mais cela est absolument invisible pour le programmeur et n'a donc aucune importance.

Il ne reste plus qu'à illustrer les possibilités de Prolog III à travers d'autres exemples.

Calcul bancaire

Il s'agit de calculer la suite de versements successifs qu'il faut effectuer pour rembourser un capital emprunté à une banque. On suppose qu'entre deux versements s'écoule toujours le même temps et que pendant cette durée le taux d'intérêt réclamé par la banque est de 10%. L'ensemble des faits définis par le programme sera l'ensemble des arbres de la forme
VersementsCapital(x,c)
et où x est la liste des versements nécessaires pour rembourser le capital c avec un intérêt de 10% entre deux versements. Le programme lui-même se résume à deux règles:

VersementsCapital(<>, 0) →;
VersementsCapital($<v> \bullet x$, c) → VersementsCapital(x, $(1+10/100)c-v$);

La première règle exprime qu'il n'est pas nécessaire de faire de versements pour rembourser un capital nul. La deuxième règle exprime que la suite des $n+1$ versements pour rembourser un capital c consiste en un versement v et d'un suite s de n versements permettant de rembourser le capital c augmenté de 10% d'intérêts mais le tout diminué du versement v effectué.

Ce programme peut-être utilisé de différentes façons. Une des plus spectaculaires et de demander pour quelle valeur de v la suite de versements $<v,2v,3v>$ permet de rembourser 1000F. Il suffit de poser la requête

$$\text{VersementsCapital}(<v,2v,3v>,1000)?$$

pour obtenir la réponse

$$\{v = 207 + 413/641\}.$$

Voici une trace abrégée de ce calcul. On part de l'état initial
$(\{v\}, \text{VersementsCapital}(<v,2v,3v>,1000), \{\})$.
En appliquant la règle

VersementsCapital($<v'>\bullet x,c$) → VersementsCapital(x,(1+10/100)$c-v'$)

on passe à l'état
$(\{v\}, \text{VersementsCapital}(x,(1+10/100)c-v')$,
$\{\text{VersementsCapital}(<v,2v,3v>,1000)=\text{VersementsCapital } (<v'>\bullet x,c)\})$,
qui se simplifie en
$(\{v\}, \text{VersementsCapital}(x,(11/10)c-v'), \{v'=v, x=<2v,3v>, c=1000\})$,
puis en
$(\{v\}, \text{VersementsCapital}(<2v,3v>,1100-v), \{\})$.
Le lecteur vérifiera qu'en appliquant deux fois la même règle sur cet état on passe successivement dans les états simplifiés
$(\{v\}, \text{VersementsCapital}(<3v>,1210-(31/10)v), \{\})$,
$(\{v\}, \text{VersementsCapital}(<>,1331-(641/100)v), \{\})$.
En appliquant sur ce dernier état la règle

VersementsCapital $(<>,0)$ →

On obtient finalement
$(\{v\}, , \{1331-(641/100)v=0\}$
qui se simplifie en
$(\{v\}, , \{v=207+413/641 \})$.

Début de preuve de l'existence de Dieu

Le deuxième problème fait intervenir l'algèbre de Boole et a été proposé par George Boole [1] lui-même. Il s'agit de montrer que «quelque chose a toujours existé» à partir des 5 prémisses qui suivent.
(1) Quelque chose existe.
(2) Si quelque chose existe alors, soit quelque chose a toujours existé, soit les choses qui existent maintenant sont sorties du néant.
(3) Si quelque chose existe alors, soit ce quelque chose existe par la nécessité de sa propre nature, soit ce quelque chose existe par la volonté d'un autre être.
(4) Si ce quelque chose existe par la nécessité de sa propre nature alors quelque chose a toujours existé.
(5) Si ce quelque chose existe par la volonté d'un autre être alors l'hypothèse que les choses qui existent maintenant sont sorties du néant, est fausse.

L'ensemble des faits définis par le programme sera l'ensemble des arbres de la forme
$$\text{ValeurDeQuelqueChoseAToujoursExisté}(x)$$

où x désigne une valeur de vérité possible pour la proposition «quelque chose a toujours existé». On introduit 5 variables booléennes qui sont les valeurs de vérité possibles de 5 propositions:

    a : quelque chose existe,
    b: quelque chose a toujours existé,
    c : tout ce qui existe maintenant est sorti du néant,
    d : quelque chose existe par la nécessité de sa propre nature,
    e : quelque chose existe par la volonté d'un autre être.

Le programme consiste alors en l'unique règle

      ValeurDeQuelqueChoseAToujoursExisté(b) → ,
        $\{a = 1,$
        $a => (b \lor c) \land \neg (b \land c),$
        $a => (d \lor e) \land \neg (d \land e),$
        $d => b,$
        $e => \neg c\};$

Pour résoudre le problème on pose la requête
        ValeurDeQuelqueChoseAToujoursExisté(x)?
et l'on obtient bien l'unique réponse
$$\{x = 1\}.$$

Voici une trace abrégée du calcul de cette réponse. On part de l'état initial
    $(\{x\},$ ValeurDeQuelqueChoseAToujoursExisté(x), $\{\})$.
En appliquant l'unique règle on passe à l'état
    $(\{x\},$,
    $x=b,$
    $a = 1,$
    $a => (b \lor c) \land \neg (b \land c),$
    $a => (d \lor e) \land \neg (d \land e),$
    $d => b,$
    $e => \neg c\}.$
En éliminant les variables b et a ont obtient
    $(\{x\},$,
    $(x \lor c) \land \neg (x \land c) = 1,$
    $(d \lor e) \land \neg (d \land e) = 1,$
    $d => x,$
    $e => \neg c\},$
c'est-à-dire
    $(\{x\},$,$\{c = \neg x, e = \neg d, d => x, e => \neg c\})$.
En éliminant les variables c et e on obtient
    $(\{x\},$,$\{d => x, \neg d => x\})$
qui se simplifie en
    $(\{x\},$, $\{x = 1\}$.

Ici aussi il faut rappeler que la machine ne fera pas les mêmes simplifications que celles que nous avons présentées dans un but pédagogique. Elle en fera d'autres, sûrement plus compliquées, mais sûrement plus systématiques (voir la fin de l'article).

Problème de Lewis Caroll

Lewis Caroll nous a habitué à des problèmes plus difficiles que le problème précédent. Par exemple, étant donné les 18 phrases suivantes, (1) quel lien existe-t-il entre "avoir l'esprit clair", "être populaire"et "être apte à être député" et (2) quel lien existe-t-il entre "savoir garder un secret", "être apte à être député" et "valoir son pesant d'or" ?

1. Tout individu apte à être député et qui ne passe pas son temps à faire des discours, est un bienfaiteur du peuple.

2. Les gens à l'esprit clair, et qui s'expriment bien, ont reçu une éducation convenable.

3. Une femme qui est digne d'éloges est une femme qui sait garder un secret.

4. Les gens qui rendent des services au peuple, mais n'emploient pas leur influence à des fins méritoires, ne sont pas aptes à être députés.

5. Les gens qui valent leur pesant d'or et qui sont dignes d'éloges, sont toujours sans prétention.

6. Les bienfaiteurs du peuple qui emploient leur influence à des fins méritoires sont dignes d'éloges.

7. Les gens qui sont impopulaires et qui ne valent pas leur pesant d'or, ne savent pas garder un secret.

8. Les gens qui savent parler pendant des heures et des heures et qui sont aptes à être députés, sont dignes d'éloges.

9. Tout individu qui sait garder un secret et qui est sans prétention, est un bienfaiteur du peuple dont le souvenir restera impérissable.

10. Une femme qui rend des services au peuple est toujours populaire.

11. Les gens qui valent leur pesant d'or, qui ne cessent de discourir, et dont le souvenir demeure impérissable, sont précisément les gens dont on voit la photographie dans toutes les vitrines.

12. Une femme qui n'a pas l'esprit clair et n'a pas reçu une bonne éducation, est inapte à devenir député.

13. Tout individu qui sait garder un secret et qui sait ne pas discourir sans cesse, peut être certain d'être impopulaire.

14. Un individu à l'esprit clair, qui a de l'influence et l'emploie à des fins méritoires, est un bienfaiteur du peuple.

15. Un bienfaiteur du peuple sans prétention n'est pas le genre de personnes dont la photographie est affichée dans toutes les vitrines.

16. Les gens qui savent garder un secret et qui emploient leur influence à des fins méritoires, valent leur pesant d'or.

17. Une personne qui ne sait pas s'exprimer, et qui est incapable d'en influencer d'autres, n'est sûrement pas une femme.

18. Les gens populaires et dignes d'éloges sont, soit des bienfaiteurs du peuple, soit des gens sans prétention.

Chacune de ces 18 propositions est formée de propositions élémentaires reliées par des connecteurs logiques. A chaque proposition élémentaire on associe un nom, sous forme d'une chaîne de caractères, et une valeur logique représentée par une variable booléenne. L'information contenue dans les 18 propositions se résume alors en une seule règle formée d'un important terme de tête, d'une queue vide et d'une importante partie contraintes ;

Possibilité(<
<a,"avoir l'esprit clair">,
<b,"avoir reçu une bonne éducation">,
<c,"discourir sans cesse">,
<d,"employer son influence à des fins méritoires">,
<e,"être affiché dans les vitrines">,
<f,"être apte à être député">,
<g,"être un bienfaiteur du peuple">,
<h,"être digne d'éloges">,
<i,"être populaire">,
<j,"être sans prétention">,
<k,"être une femme">,
<l,"laisser un souvenir impérissable">,
<m,"posséder une influence">,
<n,"savoir garder un secret">,
<o,"s'exprimer bien">,
<p,"valoir son pesant d'or">>)   →,
{

$(f \wedge \neg c) => g$,

$(a \wedge o) => b$,

$(k \wedge h) => n$,

$(g \wedge \neg d) => \neg f$,

$(p \wedge h) => j$,

$(g \wedge d) => h$,

$(\neg i \wedge \neg p) => \neg n$,

$(c \wedge f) => h$,

$(n \wedge j) => (g \wedge l)$,

$(k \wedge g) => i$,

$(p \wedge c \wedge l) => e$,

$(k \wedge \neg a \wedge \neg b) => \neg f$,

$(n \wedge \neg c) => \neg i$,

$(a \wedge m \wedge d) => g$,

$(g \wedge j) => \neg e$,

$(n \wedge d) => p$,

$(\neg o \wedge \neg m) => \neg k$,

$(i \wedge h) => (g \vee j)$
};

Pour extraire une partie de l'information on introduit :

```
SousPossibilité(x) →
    Possibilité(y)
    SousEnsemble(x, y);

SousEnsemble(<>, y) →;
SousEnsemble(<e>•x, y) →
        ElémentDe(e, y)
        SousEnsemble(x, y);

ElémentDe(e, <e>•y) →;
ElémentDe(e, <e'>•y) → ElémentDe(e, y), {e ≠ e'};
```

Pour calculer les rapports éventuels qui existent entre "avoir l'esprit clair", "être populaire"et "être apte à être député" il suffit alors de poser la requête

SousPossibilité(<
        <p,"avoir l'esprit clair">,
        <q,"être populaire">,
        <r,"être apte à être député">>)?

La réponse est l'ensemble vide de contraintes

{},

ce qui veut dire qu'il n'y a aucun rapport entre "avoir l'esprit clair", "être populaire"et "être apte à être député".

Pour calculer les rapports éventuels qui existent entre "savoir garder un secret", "être apte à être député" et "valoir son pesant d'or" il suffit de poser la requête

SousPossibilité(<
        <p,"savoir garder un secret">,
        <q,"être apte à être député">,
        <r,"valoir son pesant d'or">>)?

La réponse est

$\{p \wedge q => r\}$,

ce qui veut dire que si on sait garder un secret et si on est apte à être député alors on vaut son pesant d'or.

Détection de pannes

Voici un problème de nature différente mais faisant toujours intervenir l'algèbre de

Boole et proposé en [6]. Il s'agit de détecter le ou les composants défectueux dans un additionneur qui calcule la somme binaire de trois bits x_1, x_2, x_3 sous forme d'un nombre binaire de deux bits y_1y_2. Comme on peut le voir ce circuit est formé de 5 composants numérotés de 1 à 5: deux portes *et* (marquées Et), une porte ou (marquée Ou) et deux portes *ou exclusif* (marquées OuX). On a aussi introduit trois variables u_1, u_2, u_3 pour représenter les sorties des portes 1, 2 et 4.

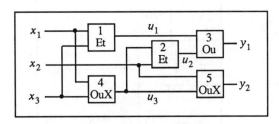

On introduit encore 5 variables booléennes p_i pour signifier que « la porte numéro i est en panne ». En faisant l'hypothèse qu'au plus un des cinq composants est en panne le programme qui lie les valeurs x_i, y_i et p_i est

Circuit(<x1,x2,x3>, <y1,y2>, <p1,p2,p3,p4,p5>) →
 AuPlusUnDeVrai(<p1,p2,p3,p4,p5>),
 {¬p1 => (u1 ≡ x1∧x3),
 ¬p2 => (u2 ≡ x2∧u3),
 ¬p3 => (y1 ≡ u1∨u2),
 ¬p4 => (u3 ≡ ¬(x1≡x3)),
 ¬p5 => (y2 ≡ ¬(x2≡u3))};

AuPlusUnDeVrai(P) → OuSurAuPlusUnDeVrai(P,p);

OuSurAuPlusUnDeVrai(<>, 0) →;
OuSurAuPlusUnDeVrai(<p>•P, p∨q) →
 OuSurAuPlusUnDeVrai(P, q),
 {p∧q = 0};

Si l'état du circuit nous amène à poser la requête
  Circuit(<1, 1, 0>, <0, 1>, <p1, p2, p3, p4, p5>)?
on diagnostique que le composant numéro 4 est en panne:
  { p1= 0, p2 = 0, p3 = 0, p4 = 1, p5 = 0 }.
Si l'état du circuit nous amène à poser la requête
  Circuit(<1, 0, 1>, <0, 0>, <p1, p2, p3, p4, p5>)?
on diagnostique que soit le composant numéro 1 soit le composant numéro 3 est en panne:
  { p1∨p3 = 1, p1∧p3 = 0, p2 = 0, p4 = 0, p5 = 0}.

Remplissage d'un rectangle par des carrés

Voici maintenant un problème qui met bien en valeur la partie numérique de Prolog III. Etant donné un entier n on s'intéresse à savoir s'il existe n carrés de dimensions distinctes qui peuvent être assemblés pour former un rectangle. Dans l'affirmative, on aimerait bien entendu connaître les dimensions de ces carrés, leurs positions et les dimensions du rectangle formé. Voici par exemple deux solutions à ce problème pour $n=9$.

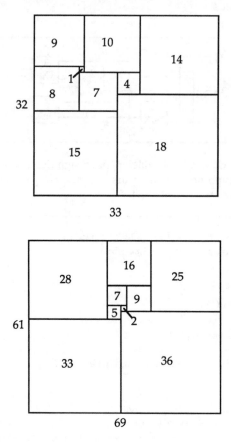

On désignera par a le rapport de la longueur du plus grand coté avec celle du plus petit coté du rectangle construit. On peut évidemment supposer que la longueur du plus petit coté est 1 et que la longueur du plus grand coté est a. Il faut donc remplir un rectangle de dimensions 1xa par n carrés tous distincts. En se référant au schéma qui suit, la base de l'algorithme de remplissage consistera
(1) à placer un carré dans le coin inférieur gauche du rectangle,
(2) à remplir de carrés la zone A,
(3) à remplir de carrés la zone B.
Le remplissage des zones A et B se fera récursivement de la même façon : placer un carré dans le coin inférieur gauche et remplir deux sous-zones.

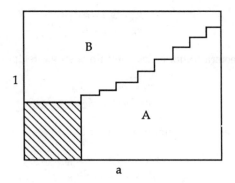

Précisons ce que nous entendons par remplir une zone ou une sous-zone. Une zone aura la forme suivante :

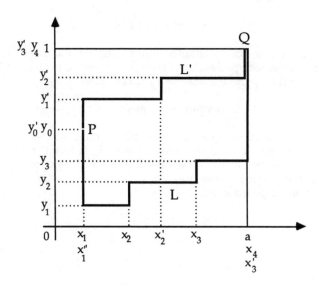

Elle est délimitée par une ligne brisée inférieure L allant d'un point P à un point Q et par une ligne brisée supérieur L' allant du même point P au même point Q. Le point P est placé n'importe où dans le rectangle à remplir alors que le point Q désigne le coin supérieur droit du rectangle. En introduisant deux axes de coordonnées dont l'origine est le coin inférieur gauche du rectangle à remplir, la ligne brisée inférieure sera représentée par la suite alternée

$$L = y_0, x_1, y_1, \dots, x_m, y_m,$$

et la ligne brisée supérieure par la suite alternée

$$L' = y'_0, x'_1, y'_1, \dots, x'_n, y'_n,$$

avec bien entendu

$$y_0 = y'_0,$$
$$x_1 = x'_1,$$

$$x_m = x'_n = a,$$
$$y_m = y'_n = 1.$$

Notre programme respectera toujours les conditions suivantes pour la ligne inférieur L :

$$x_1 < x_2 < ... < x_m$$
$$y_1 \leq y_2 \leq ... \leq y_n,$$

et les conditions suivantes pour la ligne supérieur L' :

$$x'_1 < x'_2 < ... < x'_n,$$
$$y'_0 \leq y'_1 \leq ... \leq y'_n.$$

On remarquera que la condition $y_0 \leq y_1$ ne figure pas pour la ligne inférieure L. Le cœur du programme sera la procédure

$$\text{Remplir}(L, C, L', C')$$

qui remplit de carrés une zone délimitée inférieurement par L et calcule sa limitation supérieure L'. Les carrées sont puisés dans le début de la liste C et C' est la liste des carrés qui restent. L'appel général au programme se fera par la requête

$$\text{RemplirRectangle}(n, a, C) ?$$

où n sera le nombre de carrés que l'on veut placer dans un rectangle. Le programme calculera la dimension possible 1xa du rectangle ($a \geq 1$) et la liste C de la dimension et de la position de chacun des n carrés. Chaque élément de C sera donc constitué de trois informations : la dimension du coté du carré et les deux coordonnées du coins inférieur gauche du carré. Voici le programme :

```
RemplirRectangle(n, a, C) →
    TousDistincts(n, C)
    Remplir(<1,0,0,a,1>, C, L, <>),
    {a ≥ 1};

TousDistincts(0, <>) →;
TousDistincts(n+1, <a(x,y)>•C) →
    TousDistincts(n, C)
    HorsDe(a, C),
    {n≥0};

HorsDe(a, <>) →;
HorsDe(a, <a'(x',y')>•C) -> HorsDe(a, C), {a ≠ a'};
Remplir(<y0,x1,y1>•L, C, <y0,x1,y1>•L, C) →,
    {y0 ≤ y1};
Remplir(<y0,x1,y1>•L, <a(x1,y1)>•C, L''', C''') →
    PlacerCarré(<x1,y1>•L, <x1+a>•L')
    Remplir(<y1+a,x1+a>• L', C, L'', C'')
    Remplir(<y0,x1>•L'', C'', L''', C'''),
    {y0 > y1, y1+a ≤ 1};

PlacerCarré(<x1,y1,x2,y2>•L, L') →
    PlacerCarré(<x2,y2>•L, L'),
    {y1 = y2};
PlacerCarré(<x1,y1>•L, L) →;
PlacerCarré(<x1,y1,x2>•L, <x1',y1,x2>•L) →,
    {x1 < x1' < x2};
```

Si on pose la requête

$$\text{RemplirRectangle}(9, a, C) \ ?$$

On obtient 8 réponses. Les deux premières que voici

{a = 33/32,
C = <(15/32)(0, 0), (9/16)(15/32, 0), (1/4)(0, 15/32),
(7/32)(1/4, 15/32), (1/8)(15/32, 9/16), (7/16)(19/32, 9/16),
(1/32)(1/4, 11/16), (5/16)(9/32, 11/16), (9/32)(0, 23/32)>},

{a = 69/61,
C = <(33/61)(0, 0), (36/61)(33/61, 0), (28/61)(0, 33/61),
(5/61)(28/61, 33/61), (2/61)(33/61, 36/61), (9/61)(35/61, 36/61), (25/61)(44/61, 36/61),
(7/61)(28/61, 38/61), (16/61)(28/61, 45/61)>}.

correspondent aux deux assemblages que nous avons dessinés. Les 6 autres réponses décrivent des assemblages symétriques de ceux-ci.

Manipulations d'arbres

Le dernier exemple illustre les possibilités de manipuler finement des arbres sans avoir recours à des fonctionnalités externes. Il s'agit de calculer la liste x des feuilles d'un arbre fini a. Voici le programme sans explications:

```
FeuillesDe(a, x) →
    FeuillesDarbre(a, x, <>);

FeuillesDarbre(e[<>], <e>•x, x) →;
FeuillesDarbre(e[u], x, x') →;
    FeuillesDeListe(u, x, x'),
    {u ≠ <>};

FeuillesDeListe(<>, x, x) →;
FeuillesDeListe(<a>•u, x, x'') →
    FeuillesDarbre(a, x, x')
    FeuillesDeListe(u, x', x'');
```

La requête
$$\text{FeuillesDe(mesure("Max",< } 180/100,\text{mètres}>,1), x)?$$
produira pour réponse
$$\{x = <\text{'M', 'a', 'x', } 1+4/5, \text{ mètres, } 1>\}.$$

Réalisation pratique

Terminons cet article par quelques informations sur notre tout premier prototype d'interpréteur Prolog III. Il est écrit en C, sauf certaines parties de l'environnement (de Pascal Bouvier) qui sont écrites en Prolog II. Par la suite, ces parties seront directement écrites en Prolog III. Le fait le plus marquant est la taille du programme de résolution de contraintes: 50 fois plus gros qu'un programme d'unification classique!

Le noyau de l'interpréteur Prolog III, conçu par Touraïvane, est essentiellement constitué d'une machine non déterministe à deux piles qui se remplissent et se vident conjointement. Dans la première on crée toutes les structures pour représenter la suite d'états à travers lesquels on est passé. Dans la deuxième on note par des couples adresse-valeur toutes les modifications que l'on fait sur la première pile et ceci afin de pouvoir faire les restaurations nécessaires lors d'un «backtrack». Un système général de récupération de mémoire permet de déceler les informations devenues inaccessibles et de récupérer la place qu'elles occupent en retassant les deux piles. Lors de ce retassement la topographie des piles est parfaitement préservée. Le noyau de l'interpréteur comprend aussi la partie principale de résolution d'équations et de contraintes de type ≠. Il s'agit essentiellement d'une extension des algorithmes utilisés dans Prolog II et décrits en [4]. Cette extension porte principalement sur le traitement des listes et sur le traitement des variables numériques qui ne sont pas astreintes à être positives.

Le noyau de l'interpréteur fait appel à deux sous-modules l'un pour le traitement de l'algèbre de Boole, l'autre pour tout ce qui est numérique. Le module algèbre de Boole a été conçu par Jean Marc Boï et Frédéric Benhamou. Les algorithmes utilisés sont ceux de Pierre Siegel [8]. Ils permettent d'une part de vérifier si un ensemble de contraintes booléennes est soluble et d'autre part de simplifier ces contraintes en un ensemble de contraintes ne faisant intervenir qu'un sous-ensemble donné de variables.

Le module arithmétique, écrit par Michel Henrion traite les variables astreintes à être non négatives (introduites pour éliminer les contraintes de type ≥). Il consiste essentiellement en la programmation de l'algorithme du Simplex de George Dantzig [5] avec un traitement subtil en cas de dégénérescence, c'est-à-dire lorsque des zéros apparaissent dans des endroits inopportuns. A cela il a fallu ajouter le traitement de certaines contraintes de type ≠. Le module comprend aussi les sous-programmes de base pour faire les opérations d'addition et de multiplication en précision infinie, c'est-à-dire sur des fractions dont le numérateur et le dénominateur sont codés par des suites de longueurs variables de mots.

Perspectives

Un produit commercial type interpréteur ou compilateur Prolog III ne devrait pas voir le jour avant deux ans. Ainsi que l'ont montré nos exemples ses applications seront très variées et l'expérience de Prolog nous enseigne que la plupart sont imprévisibles. Je vois cependant deux directions intéressantes. La présence des inégalités linéaires permet de résoudre certains problèmes traditionnellement abordés en recherche opérationnelle, minimisation de coûts, planification, etc, mais avec beaucoup plus de flexibilité. La présence de l'algèbre de Boole complète permet de mieux formuler les règles de raisonnement de systèmes experts: on n'est plus limité au raisonnement traditionnel du type « si ça et ça alors ça », on peut maintenant introduire des incertitudes logiques du genre « ceci ou cela est vrai » ou de vraies négations logique comme « ceci n'est pas vrai». D'ailleurs nous devrions en savoir rapidement davantage sur les applications de Prolog III. La prochaine étape de notre projet ESPRIT est d'utiliser notre prototype d'interpréteur pour programmer le système PROMOTEX de diagnostic de panne de moteur de voiture.

Remerciements

Je tiens à remercier le CEA et l'AMEDIA (Association Méditérannéenne pour le Développement de l'IA) pour leur aide financière. Je remercie aussi la compagnie DEC qui dans le cadre d'un «External Research Grant» nous a permis d'acquérir des matériels informatiques fort utiles à ce projet. Enfin je remercie les personnes du Ministère de la Recherche et de l'Enseignement Supérieur qui, à travers les deux Programmes de Recherches Concertés «Génie Logiciel» et «Intelligence Artificielle», ont soutenu des recherches sous-jacentes à ce projet.

Références

1. BOOLE GEORGE, *The Laws of Thought*, Dover Publication Inc., 1958.
2. COLMERAUER ALAIN, Henry Kanoui, Robert Pasero et Philippe Roussel, *Un système de communication homme-machine en français*, Rapport de recherche, Groupe Intelligence Artificielle, Université Aix-Marseille II, 1973.
3. COLMERAUER ALAIN, Prolog in 10 figures, *Communications of the ACM*, Volume 28, Numéro 12, Décembre 1985, 1296-1310.
4. COLMERAUER ALAIN, Equations and Inequations on Finite and Infinite Trees, Invited lecture, *Proceedings of the International Conference on Fifth Generation Computer*

Systems, Tokyo, Novembre 1984, 85-99.

5. DANTZIG GEORGE B., *Linear Programming and Extensions,* Princeton University Press, 1963.

6. GENESERETH MICHAEL R. ET MATTHEW L. GINSBERG, Logic Programming, *Communications of the ACM,* Volume 28, Numéro 9, Septembre 1985, 933-941.

7. ROBINSON ALAN, A machine-oriented logic based on the resolution principle, *Journal of the ACM,* 12 Decembre 1965.

8. SIEGEL PIERRE, *Représentation et utilisation de la connaissance en calcul propositionnel,* Thèse de Doctorat d'Etat, Faculté des Sciences de Luminy, Université Aix-Marseille II, Juillet 1987.

Prolog Programs
and Standard Data Bases

A. Caloini, S. Mainetti, P. Paolini

Politecnico di Milano - Dipartimento di Elettronica

This work has been partially supported by the INDOC project, of the ESPRIT program, financed by the Commission of the European Community.

Abstract

There is a growing interest in the development of advanced applications, i.e. applications making use of the paradigms and tools developed within the Artificial Intelligence community. On the other hand standard tools for Data Base management are needed to operative handle data for the traditional operative tasks. Therefore, in the near future, the advanced applications and the traditional ones will share the same Data Base.
For a number of reasons, explained in the paper, the authors believe that the Data Base will be handled by standard tools, while the advanced applications will be written with the proper Advanced Programming tools.
The paper examines some of the problems emerging from interfacing Advanced Programming tools with standard Data Base tools. A survey of existing approaches is presented; an original component (Conceptual Adapter) is proposed.
Although the issues are presented in general, the conclusions are supported by the experimental data obtained with a first implementation of the interface, implemented at the Politecnico of Milan. The current version implements an interface between Prolog and SQL Data Bases. The design and the implementation of other interfaces is planned.

1 INTRODUCTION

Our work stems from the belief, shared by a number of different authors ([Ull 85] [Fin 87] [Atk 87] [Boc 87b] [Iwa 88]), that the interfaces between Data Bases and tools for writing Artificial Intelligence applications, are of great practical and theoretical relevance.

Our belief, in particular, is that "intelligent applications" written with AI paradigms, but accessing large (or very large) amounts of data, will play a significant role for two key reasons:

AI paradigms open new powerful possibilities for the application writers;

most of the data currently handled by applications are handled by traditional Data Management tools (and a small percentage by Data Base tools).

Therefore, while we wait for the new generation tools (if they will ever come), we have to cope with the need of interfacing standard Data Base tools with AI programming tools.

The following are a few examples of intelligent applications:

- Triggers.
  These (usually small) applications are automatically invoked when exceptional conditions are detected (say, for example, overdrawing from a checking account, or alarm conditions in a plant).
  Their task is usually to "better understand" the situation and to invoke the proper (automatic or manual) recovery action.

- Constraint Checks.

Data manipulation operations must not violate constraints placed upon the Data Base. Constraints [Cer 88c] are evolving from simple functional dependencies to sophisticated formulas. AI languages are well suited in order to program these checks, which can be invoked whenever the application "feels" necessary.

- Data pre-analysis: to check data entry correctness.
  This is somewhat similar to the previous point, with a greater emphasis placed on size, and therefore on efficiency.

- Data post-analysis.
  It is likely that the first real merge between traditional applications and AI applications will happen in this direction.
  Think, for example, of a traditional accounting application. The data managed by such traditional application could also be used for financial forecasts or decision-support simulations. Traditional Programming Languages are not suited for this job, while AI Languages could be used to write applications which access the data generated by the traditional applications, and handle these innovative tasks.
  We are aware of several projects, in Italy, working along this line.

The above applications show the technical point which is the cornerstone of our approach: intelligent applications will share the data with more traditional applications.
If our assumption is assumed as valid, there are two possible consequences:

a A new generation of tools will handle, at the same time, Data and Knowledge, allowing the coexistence of traditional and Intelligent Applications.

b In the near future we need better interfaces between AI tools and Data Managers.
  The objective here is not of writing a persistent Prolog program; the problem is to allow the writing of AI (small) applications which need to access large amount of data, handled by standard Data Management tools.

We don't believe very much on the possibility "a" for a number of reasons. First of all, it didn't work for traditional applications. With the exception of the small percentage of applications implemented with special languages (such as fourth generation languages), almost all the applications are implemented interfacing traditional Programming Languages with Data Managers.

Moreover, there is a great investment on applications and Data Management already done. It is not likely that all these applications and Data Bases will be reimplemented just because new tools emerge.

Therefore we think that for a while there will be a great need for writing intelligent applications accessing Data handled by traditional tools.

For the purpose of this paper we will limit our observation to the interface of Prolog with Relational Data Bases. We do not believe at all that this is the proper combination (our doubts are more about Prolog than about Relational Data Bases, of course). Anyway we felt that it was a good starting point, in order to get quick results and to compare our work with what is being done by other researchers.

In Section 2 we define the requirements for our system. In section 3 we describe the architecture and the relevant features of our system. The features are described in general and also with references to the implementation carried on at the Politecnico of Milan. In section 4 further details about the current implementation, and the directions of our future work are provided. Section 5 contains the quoted references.

We will like to make clear that, although our current system is based upon a specific architecture (Prolog, of the Arity dialect, with SQL Data Bases, of the ORACLE and INFORMIX dialects), we have tried to work on general concepts and on their potentiality for effectiveness, rather than being carried away by the details of the specific tools we were working with.

2 OUR APPROACH: REQUIREMENTS

We have already pointed out in the introduction the reasons for interfacing existing environments: Data Base Management Systems already exist, and a large number of applications are developed using them. We have to cope with this situation.

Let us now list the most relevant requirements we have tried to deal with:

1) The Data Base is designed according to the need of traditional application environments. Therefore its logical structure is not necessarily directly suitable for the intelligent application.
   This requirement may derive from two practical situations:

   1a) The Data Base (and the traditional applicative environment) already exist, when the intelligent application is designed.

   1b) The Data Base is designed from scratch, but it is designed according with the needs of the traditional portion of the application (usually much heavier and operatively more important than the intelligent portion).

2) Even if point 1 is valid, the intelligent application should be written with a "view" of the Data Base suitable for its needs, that is making use of the proper conceptual structures which appear "the-most-natural" for the problem being attacked.

3) The writer of the intelligent application should not exploit the details of Data Base implementation, nor for conceptual or performance-related decision.
   The reason for this requirement is that the validity of the intelligent application should not be affected by changes of the Data Base implementation.

4) Intelligent applications should be developed with standard (or commonly used) languages and tools.
In the rest of the paper we will assume that intelligent applications are written in Prolog. We are planning to extend the principles of our approach to other tools (and frame-based tools and rule-driven tools are on top of our list).

5) The Data Base is implemented with standard Data Base tools.
In the rest of the paper we assume that the Data Base Manager is an SQL engine. We are planning to extend our approach to other relational dialects.

6) There must be some parameters which a Data Base Administrator (DBA) can use to optimize the performances of the accesses to the Data Base performed by the applications. This tuning of the parameters should not affect the validity (correctness) of the intelligent application, nor it should require a modification of the tools (for the Data Base or for the Intelligent Application).
Somehow the attempt of satisfying this requirement is driving most of our current research.

Just to make clearer our intention we could specify that we do not want

a) To design an "embedded-SQL" system.
Requirements <1,3>.

b) To modify the engine used for the intelligent application.
Requirements <2,4>.

c) To design a modified (or a new) Data Base Management System.
Requirements <1,5>.

d) To design a modified (or a new) AI tool.
Requirements <1,3,4>.

e) To force the intelligent application to deal with conceptually unsuitable data structures. Requirements <2>.

3 OUR SYSTEM: ARCHITECTURE AND RELEVANT FEATURES

Our system basically implements an interface allowing a Prolog program to access an SQL Data Bases. The need for such an interface originated in the course of an Office Automation project [Bar 87] [Pao 88], where a Prolog interpreter needed to access data, appearing in documents to be generated. These data were introduced in the application environment and handled via a DBMS (ORACLE at the beginning and INFORMIX later).

Designing this interface basically we kept in mind the requirements described in the previous section. We observed that interfacing the Prolog program and the Data Base we had a number of mismatches:

1) A conceptual mismatch

2) An operational mismatch

3) A buffering mismatch

Conceptual mismatch occurs because the (Prolog) application writer naturally use concepts (predicates) that do not have a direct counterpart in the relational Data Base. Nor could the Data Base be modified just to "please" the (Prolog) application programmer.

Our solution is the definition of a Conceptual Adapter, the job of which is of smoothing the conceptual differences between what is needed by the application and what is stored in the Data Base.

Needless to say that the Conceptual Adapter has a lot in common with standard relational views; but there are important differences. Apparently the performances are much in favor of the Conceptual Adapter solution (see experimental data below). Moreover, not all the DBMS support relational views.

Operational mismatches occur because the two systems which to be coupled necessarily handle different data structure with different "logics".

Think for example of the coupling between Prolog and an SQL Data Base Management System:

1) Prolog processes predicates one-at-a-time through the backtracking mechanism, while a relational DBMS returns the whole set of data satisfying a given query.

2) Prolog performs the 'next' statement implicitly through backtracking.

3) Prolog backtracking may cause implicit multiple accessing to the same set of data, for example during the evaluation of the clause

```
c2(Z,W):-
    p(X,Y),
    q(X,Z),
    r(Y,W).
```

backtracking to the next instance of q(X,Z) does not require accessing to a new set of data for r(Y,W).

We envision the use of Logical Buffers to overcome the operational mismatches. Each time the Data Base is accessed, retrieved tuples are buffered by the interface. The interface will transmit the tuples to the application (Prolog in our case) engine accordingly to its processing needs. We avoid unnecessary querying using a subsumption [Cer 86] based method: each buffer is properly Labelled to keep track of queries already satisfied.

Buffering in Data Bases is performed in several possible ways. One of the most effective ways of doing it is trying to figure out which data the application will need in the near future and keeping them in memory or bringing them to memory.

A very simple way of obtaining this result is to fetch from auxiliary memory more information than it is strictly needed. If a traditional application requires field A of a record, the whole record is brought into memory; other pieces of that record may become needed very soon. Same methods apply to full pages of data or more complex information structure.

Buffering mismatches occur since the way an intelligent (Prolog) application consumes information is unknown to the data manager. After partial information about a student is required, the next request could concerns the same information about another student, or additional information about the same student, or information about the classes the student has taken etc.

We observed that, in any case, the essence of any buffering scheme is of trying to bring and to keep into memory information which is not strictly needed. We also believe that only the application programmer can guess the "logic" which is being used to access data. Therefore we came to formulate the hypothesis that letting the application programmer, or better the DBA, to define clusters of concepts (Prolog predicates in our case), is the only way the interface could have a perception of how the application intends to proceed. The basic idea is very simple: whenever the application requires a piece of data belonging to a cluster, then the interface can guess that the rest of the cluster is a good candidate for buffering, since it is likely that the application will request it very soon. What can be done in practice, depends a lot on implementation details.

Summarizing what we have said so far, in order to improve the performances of our interface, we have devised three distinct mechanisms, the first two of which are used by almost everybody working on this topics. The third mechanism is somehow more original (at least in this context).
These mechanism are the following:

1) Logical Prefetching
   Data sets are retrieved, instead of single tuples;

2) Logical Buffering
   The tuples retrieved are logically labelled, in order to recognize if new requests are already satisfied, and if the data already in memory can be used to build up the answer.
   We should remark that we do not attempt the partial reuse of data (either the new request is exactly answered or we re-evaluate it from scratch). We believe, in fact, that the overhead of trying to figure out what to do with more sophisticated schemes greatly outweight the potential benefits.
   Moreover we should remark that our solution (as the solutions of everybody else) makes sense only if the Data Base is not concurrently shared among several users, that is to say that there are no updates, between one request and the next one.

3) Logical Clustering

Whenever data belonging to a cluster are requested, the full cluster is brought into memory. Guessing and experimental results seem to indicate that even this simple solution can dramatically improve performances.

In the following we will describe the system implemented (in a first rough version) at the Department of Electronics of the Politecnico of Milan, as a side-effect of the project INDOC [Bar 87] [IND 87] [Pao 88] [Gar 88].

In our system the application programmer has available a number of special predicates, that we call DBP's. These predicates are special only since the programmer must not define them. The ground facts corresponding to them are, in fact, computed by the interface when they are needed.

The Conceptual Adapter maps Prolog DBP's onto the corresponding Data Base tables through arbitrarily complex SQL statements. This simple technique allows a great deal of conceptual independence between the Prolog predicates used by the programmer and the actual Data Base structure.

The programmer can define and use its own predicates regardless of the Data Base structure and the DBA can maintain the Data Base without affecting Prolog applications.

A Conceptual Adapter is a collection of entities of the kind Functor(Arg1, Arg2, ...) ===> SQL query/operation; ex.

```
p($X,$Y) ===>
                SELECT  t1.x, t2.y
                FROM    t1, t2
                WHERE   t1.z = t2.z                (1)
                AND     t1.x = $X
                AND     t2.y = $Y
```

where the SELECT statement returned parameters orderly correspond to predicate arguments.

We used $-variables to indicate query parameters that may be
instantiated at runtime when the Prolog predicate is used by an
application.

Assume, for example, that a program invokes the Interface with the
request:

```
        ...
        p(X,Y),
        ...
```

where X is bound to the constant value x1. The interfaces access the
Data Base with the following query

```
                    SELECT t1.x, t2.y
                    FROM   t1, t2
                    WHERE  t1.z = t2.z
                    AND    t1.x = x1
```

The SQL statement above illustrated can be simplified to the
following

```
    p(X,Y) ===>
                    SELECT t1.x, t2.y
                    FROM   t1, t2
                    WHERE  t1.z = t2.z
```

The predicate "p" of the above example somehow represents a sort of
"Prolog view" of the Data Base.

As we have already said, buffering is necessary because an
Intelligent Application usually requests data in small chunks, while a
Data Base query retrieves sets of data. Therefore we need to
synchronize the data transfer from the Data Base to the application
language (Prolog in our case). This situation is exactly the same which
occur interfacing a relational Data Base with any other programming

language (say COBOL or C). The difference is that we didn't want the application programmer to deal with new constructs such as "Open Cursor", "Fetch" etc. as in embedded SQL.

Our system achieves synchronization using Buffers: when a DBP is encountered during a program execution our interface reads on the Data Base all the tuples matching the predicate. Retrieved tuples are stored in a Buffer and only the first one is returned to the program. Other tuples are returned if the program backtracks.

A Buffer may be scanned more than once by a single program line (see "3) - multiple access" by the beginning of this section) and also may be scanned contemporarily from different program execution points.

We will describe now how the notion of logical clustering is implemented in the current version of the system.

The following is the definition of a cluster

```
cluster(p1(X,Y,C),
        p2(X,Y,D)
        ).
```

We think of Clusters as entities: a student together with all his exams, for example.

Predicates in a Cluster are linked by some of their arguments in a join-like fashion: these links (Cluster Keys) are defined by means of common variables and are reflected in the query actually sent to the Data Base.

A Cluster has no entry point, this means it may be used by the interface regardless of which predicate required Data Base access (Triggering predicate).

In the current version we assume that the same predicate can not appear in more than one Cluster (therefore clusters can not overlap). Overlapping Clusters require that the interface is able to take difficult decisions: if the triggering predicate occurs in two different clusters, which one is the right one? How to deal with circular definitions?.

The definition of a Cluster is somewhat analogous to the creation of an index in a Data Base environment: it improves query efficiency without affecting semantics.

Obviously it may happen, sometimes, that using Clusters unnecessary data will be loaded in memory. Only a careful planning of the application environment may ensure that clusters significantly improve performances.

4 CURRENT IMPLEMENTATION AND FUTURE WORK

A first version of our system has been developed at the Politecnico di Milano. It implements all the features described in this paper (Buffering, Clustering, Subsumption, Memory Overflow Control, Paging, Garbage Collection). The preprocessor for the Source Prolog has also been implemented.

The prototype runs on MS-DOS and interfaces Arity Prolog to Informix or Oracle 4.1; communication modules are implemented in Microsoft C.

The main purpose of the implementation of this prototype is to test the performances of the different components of the interface, in order to locate possible bottlenecks, not easily identifiable by mere guessing.

The current version will be mainly used to test different solutions and software architecture. A new version will be attempted only when the different performance issues have been more clearly understood.

In the current version we emulate the Prolog inferential engine, keeping a partial track of program execution by means of internal variables. This computational overhead could be avoided if we could access the Prolog interpreter execution stack.

As far as the future is concerned, we are concurrently working on a number of directions:

- Improving the performances, trying different solutions.

- Extending the notion of Conceptual Adapter to different AI tools. Our first target will be frame-based or rule-based tools. Our main concern is the extension of the notion of Logical Buffering and of Clusters in a situation where the target structures are other the Prolog predicates.

- Trying to develop other concepts, similar to clusters, to improve the overall performances.

- Trying to get a better understanding of the requirements of real-life applications which make use of AI techniques and need to access standard Data Bases. For this purpose we will develop a number of applications, trying to analyse their inner working.

5 REFERENCES

[Atk 87] Atkinson M. P., Buneman O. P., "Types and Persistence in Database Programming Languages", ACM Computing Surveys Vol 19 No 2, June 1987.

[Bar 87] Barbic F., Celentano A., Garzotto F., Mainetti S., Paolini P., "Document Generation: Modeling and Techniques", INDOC Int. Rep., Sept. 1987.

[Boc 87b] Bocca J., Bailey P., "Logic Languages and Relational DBMSs: the Point of Convergence", Proc. Workshop on Persistent Object Stores.., Appin, UK, Aug 1987.

[Cer 86] Ceri S., Gottlob G., Wiederhold G., "Interfacing Relational Databases and Prolog Efficiently", Proc. First Int. Conf. on EDS, Charleston, 1986; Expert Database Systems, Kershberg L. (Editor), Benjamin/Cummings, 1986.

[Cer 88c] Ceri S., Garzotto F., "Specification and Management of Database Integrity Constraints through Logic Programming", Internal Report 88-025, Dipartimento di Elettronica, Politecnico di Milano, (Submitted to TODS 1988).

[Fin 87] Finkelstein R., "Lingua Franca for Databases", PC Magazine December 1987.

[Gar 88] Garzotto F., Paolini P., "The Role of Explanation in Office Automation: the Experience of the INDOC Project", Proc. 1st International Workshop on Explanation, AAAI Conf., Minneapolis (MN), Aug. 1988.

[IND 87] "Overall Approach Review: Application Definition and Functional Specification", Deliverable T1/D1-T2.1/D1, Esprit project 1542 "INDOC".

[Iwa 88] Iwashita Y., Sawamoto J., , 2nd International Expert Systems Conference, London, 1988.

[Pao 88] Paolini P., Garzotto F., Mainetti S., Barbic F., Celentano A., Liguori F., "Knowledge Based Document Generation", Proc. IFIP WG8.4 Workshop on Office Knowledge: Representation, Management and Utilization, Lamersdorff ed., North Holland, 1988 (to appear).
[Ull 85] Ullman J., "Implementation of Logical Query Languages for Databases", ACM TODS, Vol 10 No 3, Sept 1985, pp 289-321.

A Distributed Locking Algorithm for A Transactions System in Flat Concurrent Prolog

Ehud Reches, Ehud Gudes and Ehud Shapiro
Department of Computer Science
The Weizmann Institute of Science
Rehovot, Israel

Abstract

This paper reports on the design and the implementation of a distributed transactions-system for a *Universal File Server*. The system maintains consistency in a general purpose file-system by means of *concurrency control* and *crash recovery*. Both the distributivity of a transaction and the intra-transaction concurrency, are depicted by a single model which describes the transaction as a partially ordered set of operations. The main concurrency control algorithm described in this paper is a novel distributed locking management algorithm based on the two-phase-locking (2pl) protocol. The system is implemented in Flat Concurrent Prolog (FCP), a concurrent logic programming language. FCP lends itself to the development of new distributed algorithms which utilize the fine-grained concurrency and the powerful communication and synchronization mechanisms supplied by the language. The features of concurrent logic languages, which are useful for implementing file and database systems are demonstrated in this paper.

1 Introduction

This paper describes the design and the implementation of a *transactions-system*, written in *Flat Concurrent Prolog* (FCP). FCP is a concurrent logic programming language which enables elegant and simple implementations of distributed systems, and supplies powerful tools for inter-process synchronization and communication [9, 15, 16, 17]. The transactions-system maintains a consistent general purpose file-system of a distributed computer architecture [22]. It supports concurrent multi-client access by maintaining *concurrency-control*, and can handle system failures [1, 2, 3, 8].

In the design of the transactions-system we concentrated on the following topics:

- Generalization of the transaction concept.
  Traditionally a transaction has been described as a sequence of operations performed **serially**. A more general approach is to view a transaction as a partially ordered set of operations, some of which can be performed **concurrently**. we implement transactions according to this more general approach.

- Tree structured transactions.
  A transaction is structured as a tree in which the leaves are the basic file operations and some sub-trees can be executed concurrently. This structure improves

A prototype of the transactions-system was implemented on Logix — an FCP single user multi-tasking programming environment [7, 21].

There is a wide spectrum of configurations on top of which the file-system can be built. It can vary from a single machine with a single processor and a single disk server serving concurrent transactions, to a single multi-processor and multi-disk server, and to a network of nodes, each containing a single/multi processors and disk servers. Therefore, there may be several levels of distribution and parallelism in the system. Concurrency problems are handled similarly at each of these levels. The main effect of having a network and distributed transactions, is on recovery. In that case a commit protocol (e.g. two-phase-commit) should be employed to assure atomic transactions [2]. The implementation of such protocol in FCP is shown in [14]. Since in this paper we concentrate on concurrency control, we will assume in the implementation parts of this paper that the file server is implemented on a single node (which can be a tightly-coupled multi processor/ multi disk server) serving transactions which can issue operations to access multiple files, each of which may be served by a different processor.

There are three major contributions in this work:

1. The definition of a file and transaction system which can be mapped into systems with various levels of distribution and parallelism.

2. The implementation of the system in FCP. This implementation utilizes fully the inherent parallelism which exists in a transaction system. In particular, we show a novel implementation of a distributed lock manager in FCP, which is a central component in a transaction system.

3. We demonstrate the power, and the specific features, of FCP in particular, and concurrent logic languages in general, for implementing file and database systems.

The rest of the paper is structured as follows. Section 2 defines the file and transaction system model. In Section 3 the implementation in FCP of the overall system is sketched. In Section 4, the distributed lock manager is described in detail. Section 5 highlights the important features of FCP which are used for implementing file and database systems. Section 6 is the summary. For Sections 3 and 4, basic knowledge of FCP is assumed.

2 The File-system

A file is a sequence of atomic data items. It is not important for our discussion whether these items are bytes, ASCII characters or compound data objects; we name these atomic data items *records*. The file-system is a flat collection of files. At this level of the system there is no hierarchy (such as a directory system), and each file is independent in the sense that there is no replication of files and no division of a logical file into several physical files. These concepts can be implemented by higher levels of software.

The operations which manipulate files are: *append, truncate, modify* and *read*. A file is created by appending a sequence of records onto a new file name. Erasing a file is done by truncating it into a zero length file. The syntax of the basic operations is:

- read(P, N, D). P points to the first record to be read. N is the number of records to be read. The result is placed in buffer D.

- modify(P, N, D). P points to the first record to be modified. D is a buffer of N records which replaces the old (R[P] ... R[P+N−1]) records.

- append(N, D). D is a buffer of N records which are appended to the file.

- truncate(M). The file is truncated into M records.

Two operations *conflict* if the order of their execution influences the final state of the database. An example of a conflict between O_1 and O_2 which access the same file is when O_1 is modify(5,10,D1) and O_2 is read(3,5,D2). (A necessary condition for a conflict is that the respective ranges of the two operations overlap, the full conflict table is shown in [14].)

Transactions and Views

A transaction is a basic unit of database (file-system in our case) access. There are four requirements from a transactions-system: *serializability, atomicity, durability* and *isolation* [2]. A transaction in our model is a set of basic file operations. In most transaction systems, there is a total order of basic operations within a single transaction, especially for operations being executed in a single site of a distributed system. Such total order is not required in our model and a concurrent execution is the default for executing independent operations. Non-conflicting operations may execute concurrently, while conflicting operations must follow a locking protocol. (Our transactions model is basically a special case of the nested transactions model[10]).

We define a *view* as a set of operations accessing a range of records in a file. Using a view, a stream of operations may be executed, so long as the operation's subrange is within the view's range.

For example, a read view is defined as:
read_view(F, P, N, Stream_of_requests). F is the file name. P points to the first record of the range. N is the number of the range's records.
Stream_of_requests is a stream of atomic *read* operations.

Basically, a view reflects the non-concurrent part of a transaction, while views may be executed concurrently. Therefore, it is possible to use a single lock for the view's operations and thereby saving the overhead of many locks for each of the basic operations.

The conflict table for views is exactly the same as the conflict table of basic operations, the only difference being that each atomic operation there, is replaced by a sequence of more basic operations which share the same lock. Two non-conflicting views can be executed concurrently. A total order is imposed on the basic file operations within a view, and this property ensures that the final result of each view is deterministic.

We require from the client which produces a transaction to define an order between conflicting views of his. The system prevents the concurrent execution of two conflicting views from same transaction by adding the *lock state* property to a lock. A lock can be in one of two states: *hold* or *retain*. We use the lock states to distinguish between two periods in a lock's "life": From the moment at which the lock was set, to the end of the execution of its operations, the lock is in the *hold* state; from then on, until the lock is released, it is in the *retain* state. During the *hold* period of the lock, no other view of the transaction, with a conflicting lock, can be activated; an attempt to do so causes an error message to be sent to the client (the client may respond by aborting the transaction, or by trying to initiate the conflicting view later on). During the *retain* period of the lock, any view of the same transaction can be initiated without causing a conflict, since all the operations associated with the lock were already performed (obviously, the state of the lock is changed again to hold). During both periods, lock requests of *other* transactions which conflict with this lock, cannot be granted either. A similar solution for synchronizing sub-transactions is implemented in the Locus operating system [11].

The transaction is a tree structured construct. Two more levels are added above the view level — the *open_file* and the *open_transaction* levels. The *open_file* construct is a collection of views which manipulate the same file. The *open_transaction* is a collection of *open_file* constructs.

The *open_file* structure is: open_file(F, Parameters, Stream_of_views).

F is the file's name. *Parameters* might include operational details, such as buffer size, etc. *Stream_of_views* is a stream of views. The parameters of the open_file construct are inherited by the views belonging to this construct, this eliminates the need to include a file name in the view construct.

The *open_transaction* structure is: open_transaction(Stream_of_open_files).

Following is an example of a whole transaction (control operations will be described later):

```
open_transaction([
            open_file(f1, Param1,
                    [
                    read_view(0, 10, [
                                    read(0, 5, D1),
                                    read(5, 5, D4)]),
                        read_view(50, 10, [
                                    read(50, 1, D3),
                                    read(51, 1, D6)])]),
            open_file(f2, Param2,
                    [
                    modify_view(0, 15,[
                                    modify(0, 10, D2),
                                    modify(10, 5, D1?)])])])])
```

The transaction opens two files, two *read* views and two atomic requests for each view are performed on the first file. A *modify* view is opened for the second file and two modifications are performed. A set of concurrently running system processes read the tree and perform the required operations by modifying files or completing incomplete data structures (in the case of *read* operations). The system is allowed to execute the operations in any order it likes, as long as views' operations are performed serially and the rules of two-phase-locking are obeyed. Note that the data in *D1* is read from *f1* and is written on *f2*. The correct order between the read and the write operations is implicitly imposed by the semantics of FCP, using data-flow synchronization.

Recovery

Using the two-phase locking protocol, we can ensure that if all operations are performed and no failures take place during the execution, then the final result is correct. But the following problems might interfere with the execution: A deadlock situation might force the system to abort one of the transactions; a client might wish to abort a transaction as a result of a failure in the execution of one of the operations; and the system might fail in the middle of the execution. Two control operations are added to our model in order to deal with those problems — *commit* and *abort*. These operations are performed by *strict 2pl protocol* — locks of transaction T_i are released only after either commit or abort was performed [2]. This ensures complete isolation of transactions.

A transaction would look like: open_transaction([$Open\_file_1$ ... $Open\_file_n$, Control]), where *Control* is either *commit* or *abort*.

We said that, in principle, the system can process the transaction tree in an arbitrary order. This might contradict the requirement that an *abort* or a *commit* operation be the last to be performed. If the *commit* is executed too early, then some of the operations will not be committed. If operations are performed after an abortion, then undesirable effects of "non-existing" transactions will change the file-system. A solution, where the system is responsible for detecting a transaction termination, is described in [14].

3 The Implementation

In this section we sketch the implementation of the file-system model which was introduced. The lock-manager component is presented in detail in the next section.

We assume an underlying system that consists of a fail/stop FCP machine and a stable-storage. The FCP machine is a cluster of one or more processors which cooperate in executing FCP programs. The stable-storage supplies a low-level file-system. Fail/stop processors and stable-storage were suggested as the primitives of fault-tolerant systems [2, 1, 8]. There is an interface between the FCP machine and the low-level file-system via a *data-manager*. This data-manager presents to the FCP layer a flat set of files. Through the data-manager, it is possible to *read, modify, append* and *truncate* each file, and to ensure that all the modifications, up to a given instant, are "stable", by sending a *flush* request (flushing the data from the buffers into the stable-storage). Modifications prior to a *flush* operation are vulnerable to failures.

Implementation Principles

The main idea here is the distribution of control between several concurrently running processes. The system consists of several concurrently running cooperating servers who serve clients as well as each other. The system has a hierarchical structure, as any server might itself consist of several cooperating servers each of whom provides more basic services. In particular the following processes are defined:

Transaction:
A transaction consists of a tree of processes which is isomorphic to the client's tree-structured transaction. Each node in the structure has a process which consumes its stream of requests and executes its items. New processes are activated for compound requests; for instance, the root process of the transaction activates an open-file process for each client open-file structure. This method of process activation enables simple distribution of synchronization variables among the processes.

Recovery:
Each transaction is connected to a *recovery* process which manages a log-file and is responsible for performing a commit or an abort.

Coordinator:
Each file is accessed through a coordinator which receives all the file operations regarding that file. The scheduling protocol is distributed; transactions communicate with each other through common coordinators, not through a central manager. A detailed description of the coordinator can be found in Section 4.

The root process of each transaction is activated by the *transactions-server*. Two other servers are the *data-manager* and the *file-names-server*:

- **Transactions-server:** The *transactions-server* is responsible for activating new transactions and for giving them access to the *file-names-server* and to a *recovery-log* file.

- **Data-manager:** The *data-manager* serves as an interface between the underlying low-level file-system and the transactions-system by activating a data-manager process for each open file. It also performs the log-file operations on behalf of each transaction server.

- **File-names-server:** The *file-names-server* does the mapping from file names to file coordinators. A coordinator is a server which synchronizes the access into its file.

Figure 1 is a diagram of the transactions-system. As we said before, the structure of the system is hierarchical; this diagram presents the upper level.

OPEN-TRANSACTION REQUESTS

```
                    V
      ------------                                    ----------
     |TRANSACTIONS|                                  |  DATA/   |
     |            |                                  |  LOG     |
     |  SERVER    |        Log-files Service         |  MANAGER |
     |            |------->-------->-------->--------|          |
      ------------                                    ----------
           |                                               |
           | Mapping                                       |
           V Into                                          ^
           | Files                                         |
      -----------                                          ^
     |  FILE     |                                         |
     |  NAMES    |                                         |
     |  SERVER   |                                         |
     |           |------------>---------->----------->---------^
      -----------            Interface To The Data-Manager
```

Figure 1.

For space limitations, only the transactions-server is shown in more level of detail.

The Transactions-server

The *transactions-server* consumes a stream of *open_transaction* requests and spawns a transaction process for each request.

```
transactions_server(Init-phase,
                    N,
                    [open_transaction(Requests) | Open_tr_requests],
                    [merge(Opens_stream?) | To_names_server],
                    [open(N, To_log_file?, _Length) | To_data_manager]
) :-
        Init-phase? = done    |
        recovery(N,From_transaction?,From_views?,To_log_file),
        transaction(N,Requests?,From_transaction,
                    From_views1,Opens_stream),
```

```
merger(From_views1?,From_views),

N1 := N+1,

transactions_server(done,N1?,Open_tr_requests?,
                    To_names_server,To_data_manager).
transactions_server(_Done, _N, [], [], []).
```

The server starts to serve the clients when *Init-phase* is done, (the first argument). A log-file is opened by sending a request to the *data_manager*, and the *recovery* process receives access to it. The *open* request arguments are: The file name, the stream of requests and the file length, which is not used here. A *recovery* process is spawned for each transaction. It has two input streams: One from the transaction — for the *commit* and the *abort* requests — and one from the transaction's views which modify files. Requests from different views are merged into one stream by *merger*. After spawning a transaction, the unique Id is incremented.

4 The Lock Manager

In this section we describe the implementation of a central component of the file-system, the distributed lock manager.

We suggest a simple distributed locking protocol which is a natural solution in a system of concurrently running objects. It prevents the "bottleneck" effect of the central-table method, avoids the problems of table entries allocation and deallocation, and the need for table protection, and simplifies the linkage between a transaction's locks by employing a common logic variable. Setting or releasing of a lock takes only a few FCP reductions. An FCP process reduction, in turn, corresponds to several tens of conventional machine instructions.

There are two levels of concurrency in the implementation: Each file has its own locking manager. The locking managers of the different files run concurrently, and each locking manager runs a distributed locking algorithm described below.

Distributed Locking Algorithm

The basic concept in the design of the lock manager is that of a *lock process* which represents an active lock on some part of the file. Suppose we have a *parameters* domain and a *conflict* relation over it. If a pair {P1, P2} belongs to the conflict relation then we say that conflict(P1, P2) holds. At any instant, a group of *lock* processes are active. Each of them has a parameter *p* which belongs to *parameters*, and a communication channel *Terminate*. When a *terminate* message comes on *Terminate* the *lock* process should terminate. It is not allowed for any two *lock* processes, with P1 and P2 parameters and conflict(P1,P2) to be active at the same time. The *coordinator* process receives from its clients a stream of requests to activate new *lock* processes. A new process can be activated provided there is no conflict with existent processes.

The protocol is used in the following way: Each file in the system has a *coordinator*. Any view which accesses a file must have a *lock* process which was activated by the file's *coordinator*. This process serves as a lock of the view's subrange. Activation of a new *lock* has to be approved by the rest of the locks which refer to the same file, since some of them might have a conflict with it. Gaining a lock through a *coordinator* ensures the atomicity of a locking operation.

There are two basic approaches to solving the problem; to use a centralized algorithm or a distributed one. The first is easily implemented — the *coordinator* maintains a list of the current processes and their parameters, and is responsible for keeping this list updated. Whenever *coordinator* wants to activate a new process, it consults the list. The deficiency of the centralized algorithm is clear, the *coordinator* does all the computations and becomes a "bottleneck", while the *lock* processes are idle.
In the distributed algorithm, each process checks by itself whether or not it conflicts with the new process; the *coordinator* has to find a way to use these local computations in order to make a decision. The communication protocol is as follows:

1. The *coordinator* gets a request to activate a new *lock* process.

2. The *coordinator* broadcasts a message to all the active *lock* processes. The message consists of the new parameter and an address to which the processes can send an objection to the new process.

3. The *coordinator* waits for one of two events:
   a. An objection is received.
   b. All the *lock* processes have finished checking the new parameter, and no one sent an objection.
   If the first event takes place, then the request to activate the process is rejected. If the second event takes place, then the process is activated.

The *lock* processes are implemented by FCP processes, the *Terminate* communication channel by a shared logical variable, and the *coordinator* is a monitor, implemented by an FCP recurrent process [24].

Algorithm description: When the *coordinator* wants to activate a new *lock* process, it sends an incomplete message {p,*Reply*}, to all the *lock* processes, where p is the parameter of the new process and *Reply* is a logic variable (*Reply* is common to all the *lock* processes). Each *lock* process checks his parameter against p. If there is no conflict, then the *lock* process does nothing, otherwise, a message {conflict,Terminate} is written on *Reply*, where *Terminate* is the *lock*'s termination channel. The rejected client can use *Terminate* to detect the termination of his opponent and to initiate an activation request again whenever this happens (the process of releasing locks or changing their state is described in [14]). It can be done without busy-waiting if *Terminate* instantiation is used as the "waking" event. The *coordinator* therefore knows that if there is at least one objection to the new process then an appropriate message will eventually arrive on *Reply*.

Two major problems arise:

1. The *coordinator* must know whether all the *lock* processes have already checked the new parameter p.

2. Only one *lock* process should be able to write on *Reply*.

The first problem is addressed by using the short-circuit technique [16]. The *lock* processes are connected by a stream of Short-circuits, i.e., for each new activation request, a segment of a short-circuit is sent to all the *lock* processes. After each process has finished checking the {*p,Reply*} message, it "closes" its segment. When the circuit is closed, then the *coordinator* knows that the processes have finished.

One way of solving the second problem is to break the symmetry of the {*conflict,Terminate*} messages by giving a unique name to each *lock* process and changing the message to be: {*conflict,unique_name,Terminate*}. A more elegant way eliminates the need for the irrelevant *unique_name* information by using the test-and-set protocol. Test-and-set is implemented in FCP by instantiating *Reply* in two phases. In the first phase, *Reply* is bound to a read-only variable, thereby preventing other processes from executing their first phase. In the second phase, the read-only variable is bound to the message; it is still the case that no other process can perform the first phase. Hence, only the process which was the first to perform the first phase will succeed to write on *Reply*. Success in the first phase is equivalent to a positive result of the test, whereas a failure is a negative result. The implementation is shown in procedure *make_reply* in the next section.

The lock process

The following program describes the *lock* process. *From_coordinator* isthestream of *check_conflict* requests. *Left−Right* is the stream of short-circuits. While *Terminate* is still "unknown", i.e., the *lock* process is not terminated yet, a new request is checked, a reply process is activated, and finally the short-circuit is closed. As was mentioned before, *Reply* is not instantiated if a conflict wasn't detected. If an instantiation of *Terminate* is detected (second clause), then *lock* unifies the left and the right ends of the short-circuits stream, and terminates; by that unification, the *lock* actually "closes" all the short-circuit segments which will be sent by the *coordinator* in thefuture. At the third clause, the *lock* process is terminated immediately, before starting, b ecause a *not_ok* message is given to it by the *coordinator*, that is,a conflict was discovered, and therefore the lock process should not be activated at all (see also reply_client clause in the coordinator process; this is also the reason for the variabl OK).

```
lock(ok,
     [ check_conflict(Parameter1, Reply) | From_coordinator],
     [L | Left] - [R | Right],
     Parameter,
     Terminate
) :-
          unknown(Terminate) |
          check_conflict(Parameter1, Parameter, Result),
```

```
      make_reply(Result?, Reply, Terminate, Ok),
      send_ack(Ok?, L, R),
      lock(Ok?, From_coordinator?, Left-Right,
           Parameter, Terminate).
lock(ok,
     _From_sync,
     Left-Left,
     _Parameter,
     Terminate
) :-
      Terminate? = terminate | true.
lock(not_ok,
     _From_sync,
     Left-Left,
     _Parameter,
     Terminate
).
send_ack(ok, L, L).
```

Following is the *make_reply* process. If *no_conflict* was detected, then *Reply* is not instantiated (third clause). Otherwise, (first clause) a read_only variable is unified with *Reply* in the guard, which block any other trials to write on *Reply*. Then the message itself is written on *Reply* through a writable version of the intermediate variable. From this stage on no other *lock* can write on *Reply* since it isn't unifiable with a read_only variable. If *Reply* was already instantiated by another *lock* (second clause), then nothing has to be done. By this technique we achieve a nondeterministic atomic instantiation of a shared variable, and use it for mutual exclusion.

```
make_reply(conflict,
           Reply,
           Terminate,
           ok
):-
      Reply=Intermediate? | Intermediate={conflict, Terminate}.
make_reply(conflict,
           Reply,
```

```
            _Terminate,

            ok

    ):-         known(Reply)  | true.

    make_reply(no_conflict,

            _Reply,

            _Terminate,

            ok

    ).
```

The coordinator process

The following program describes the *coordinator*. An activation request — {parameter,Terminate} — comes on the *Requests* stream. It is a request to activate a *lock* process with a *Parameter* and a termination channel *Terminate*. A common incomplete *check_conflict* message is sent to all the active *lock* processes on *To_locks* stream. A *done* message is sent on the left side of the short-circuit. *reply_client* process sends a reply to the client, when the *done* message reaches the right end of the short-circuit. Note that it is impossible use *Reply1* as an answer to the client since a positive answer is given by not instantiating it, therefore *reply_client* is needed in order to make the positive answer explicit on *Reply*. Another product of *reply_client* is *Result*, which is used to decide whether a *lock* process should or shouldn't be activated. The new *lock* process receives a segment of the short-circuits stream and a capability to read the *To_locks* stream.

```
    coordinator([{{Parameter,Terminate},Reply} | Requests],

            [check_conflict(Parameter,Reply1) | To_locks],

            [done | Left]-[R | Right]

    ) :-

            reply_client(R?, Reply1, Reply, Result),

            lock(Result?, To_locks?, Right-Right1,

                    Parameter, Terminate),

            coordinator(Requests?, To_locks, Left-Right1).
```

Following is the *reply_client* process. At the first clause, following a *done* message from the short-circuit, an *ok* message is written on the common *Reply1* variable which was sent to the *locks*. A successful writing proves that no *lock* objects the new lo ck process, as no one has written on *Reply1*. An *ok* message is also sent on *Reply* and on *Result*. At the second clause, after *make_reply* failed to write *ok* on *Reply1*, a *not_ok* result is produced and the {conflict,Terminate} message is sent as a reply to the client.

```
    reply_client(done,ok,ok,ok).
```

```
reply_client(done,Conflict,Conflict,not_ok
):-

    Conflict \= ok | true.
```

Comments:

One may question whether this implementation of distributed-lock management is actually more efficient than a centralized table-based lock management. To answer this we emphasize two points. First, the lock manager is *pipelined*. Although one transaction cannot proceed until the short-circuit is complete, the lock manager can handle multiple transactions requests concurrently, which is impossible to do with a centralized manager. The coordinator itself cannot become a bottle-neck since it only passes requests to other processes. Second, in a multi-processor environment with an efficient implementation of FCP, checking for conflicts using process structures should not be less efficient than using data structures (such as a centralized hash-table). Furthermore, the list of relevant lock processes can be reduced by using hashing.

Another issue is the assumption throughout this paper that the underlying implementation of FCP is responsible for making the unification atomic. Even though this assumption requires algorithms such as 2pl protocol to be combined in the language implementation level, this is not a very strong assumption. The reason is, the ability to use FCP primitives for implementing much easily a wide range of systems without implementing special set of primitives for each of them. A similar assumption is often made in operating systems when one implement a synchronization primitive on top of a lower-level more basic one.

5 FCP Language Features for Implementing Transaction Systems

We suggest that using FCP (or another language with similar properties), we can easily implement *reactive parallel systems* [13]. Entities of those systems can be mapped into language entities very naturally. Needs of the system are met at the language level, without any special system primitives. The features of FCP which are used to implement the transaction-system (which is an example of a reactive parallel system) are briefly shown below. More details can be found in [14].

- The fine-grained parallelism with the cheap creation, suspension and termination of processes enables us to express several levels of concurrency (parallelism within a node as well as between nodes).

- Read-only variables are used for data-flow synchronization as well as for explicit synchronization.

- We use different abstractions of FCP programs. The operational point of view (the message passing model and the shared variables model); and the declarative point of view which enables us to hide implementation details.

- Flexible typing of data structures is essential for the implementation of the dynamically built tree-structured transaction.

- Powerful communication for dynamically changing set of processes can be implemented by sending communication channels (streams and channels) as part of a message (incomplete messages).

- The short-circuit technique is used in order to synchronize the transaction's tree of processes.

- The above features and techniques are used to implement a system of concurrently running modular objects (object oriented programming).

6 Summary

We described here a transactions-system for a distributed file-server, but most of the theory and implementation principles are applicable to other concurrent transactions systems. In particular, the distributed lock algorithm can be used by a distributed database manager, or by the kernel of a distributed operating system.

The system which was described here cannot yet serve a multi-user/multi-application operating-system. It is still necessary to design and build a Data-manager which will replace Unix as an underlying system and will be able to express the parallelism which was incorporated into the higher level. This Data-manager can employ *logic per track* devices in order to achieve low-level parallelism [6].

We believe, however, that the principles which were introduced for the abstract model, as well as for the refined model and the implementation can be the basis for highly distributed file-servers. This basis can be tailored in order to get the optimal solution when more specific targets have to be achieved.

References

1. Anderson, T., Lee, P.A. "Fault Tolerance Principles and Practice" Prentice-Hall, Englewood Cliffs, NJ, 1981

2. Bernstein P.A., V. Hadzilacos, N. Goodman, "Concurrency Control and Recovery in Database Systems", Addison-Wesley, 1987.

3. Bernstein, P.A., Goodman, N., Hadzilacos, V. "Recovery Algorithms for Database Systems" In Proc. IFIP 9th World Computer Congress, North-Holland, Amsterdam, 1983.

4. Date, C., "An Introduction to Databases Systems", Addison-Wesley, 1983.

5. Dijkstra E. W., "A Discipline of Programming", Prentice-Hall, 1976.

6. DeWitt D. J. "DIRECT - A Multiprocessor Organization for Supporting Relational Database Management Systems" IEEE Transactions on Computers, Vol. C-27, No 1, January 1979

7. Hirsch M. "The Logix System", M.sc. Thesis, The Weizmann Institute of Science, 1986

8. Lampson, B., Sturgis, H. "Crash Recovery in a Distributed Data Storage System" Technical Report, Computer Science Laboratory, Xerox, Palo Alto ResearchCenter, CA, 1976.

9. Mierowsky C., S. Taylor, E. Shapiro, J. Levy and M. Safra, "The Design and Implementation of Flat Concurrent Prolog", Technical Report CS85-09, The Weizmann Institute of Science, July 1985.

10. Moss E. B.," Nested Transactions: an Approach to Reliable Distributed Computing", MIT Press, 1985.

11. Mueller E. T., Moore J D., and G. Popek, "A Nested Transaction Mechanism for LOCUS", Proceedings of ACM-SIGOPS Conference, Bretton Woods, NH, October 1983.

12. Papadimitriou, C., "The Theory of Database Concurrency Control", Computer Science Press, 1986.

13. Pnueli A., "Specification and Development of Reactive Systems", in Information Processing 86, Editor Kugler H.J., Elsevier Science Publishers B.V. (North-Holland), IFIP 1986.

14. Reches E., E. Gudes, E. Shapiro, "Parallel Access to a Distributed Database and its Implementation in Flat Concurrent Prolog" Technical Report, CS88-11, The Weizmann Institute of Science, Rehovot, Israel, 1988

15. Shafrir A. and E. Shapiro, "Distributed Programming in Concurrent Prolog", Technical Report CS84-02, January 1984. Also chapter 11 in [20]

16. Shapiro E., "Concurrent Prolog: A Progress Report", IEEE Computer, August 1986.

17. Shapiro E., "A Subset of Concurrent Prolog and its Interpreter", ICOT Technical Report TR-003, February 1983. Also chapter 2 in [20].

18. Shapiro E., "Systems Programming in Concurrent Prolog", Proc. of 11th ACM Symp. on Principles of Programming Languages, Jan 1984, pp 95-105.

19. Shapiro E. and S. Safra, "Multiway Merge with Constant Delay in Concurrent Prolog", New Generation Computing, 4, 2 (1986), pp 211-216.

20. Shapiro E. (Editor), Concurrent Prolog: Collected Papers, Vols 1 and 2, MIT Press, 1987.

21. Silverman W., M. Hirsch, A. Houri and E. Shapiro, "The Logix system user manual", Technical Report CS86-21, The Weizmann Institute of Science, June 1986. Also Chapter 21 in [20].

22. Svobodova L., "File Servers for Network-Based Distributed Systems" ACM Computing Surveys, Vol. 16, 1984.

23. Tannenbaum A., "Computer Networks", Prentice-Hall, 1981.

24. Tribble E. D., Miller, M. S., E Shapiro, "Channels: A Generalizaton of Streams." Proc. 4th Int. Conf. on Logic Programming, MIT Press, 1987.

25. Ullman J., "Principles of Database Systems", Computer Science Press, 1982.

26. Verhofstad J. S. M., "Recovery Techniques For Database Systems", ACM Cmputing Surveys, Vol. 10, 1978.

27. Weinbaum D., E. Shapiro, "A Hardware Description Language Using Concurrent Prolog", proc. of CHDL, 1987. Also chapter 36 in [20].

MULTIDIMENSIONAL DATA

Advances in the design of the BANG file

M. W. Freeston

ECRC, Arabellastr. 17, D-8000 München 81, West Germany

ABSTRACT   A recent paper described a new kind of grid file - the BANG file - which, unlike previous grid file designs, has the important property that the directory never expands faster than the data, whatever the dimensionality of the file or the form of the data distribution. Experience with the first implementation of the BANG file has given new insights into its properties and behaviour, which have enabled significant improvements in performance to be obtained without compromising the conceptual simplicity of the original design:

- access to an individual tuple now always succeeds in a single pass down the directory tree, as with a B-tree;
- overflow or underflow of data or directory pages never leads to more page splits or merges than in a B-tree of the same directory depth;
- every direct representation of a sub-space of the data space is guaranteed to be a *minimal* representation - substantially improving the efficiency of range searches, partial match searches and joins.

The paper begins with a review of the original design in the light of its implementation. A detailed description is then given of the enhancements which have been found possible, with the theoretical foundations on which they depend. Finally, a selection of performance figures are given to demonstrate its characteristics.

1. Principles and definitions

Grid files [NIEV81 BURK83 HINR85 OZKA85 FREE87] adopt a direct geometric representation of the data: the tuples of an n-ary relation are represented as points in an n-dimensional hyperspace, the dimensions of which are the domains of the n attributes. The problem is how to allocate the tuples in this hyperspace to the set of disk blocks (or pages) in the file. In geometric terms the obvious thing to do is to divide up the data space into a set of hyperrectangles or block regions, each of which corresponds to a disk page. However, in order to maximise the storage efficiency of the file, the number of such regions, and the positions of their boundaries, have to be arranged so that each of the corresponding disk pages has a high data occupancy.

In the BANG file, data pages are accessed via a multi-level directory of block regions, stored in the same file as the data. When the insertion of a tuple into the file causes a disk block to overflow, then the disk page and the corresponding block region are split into two, and the directory is updated. The objective of the partitioning strategy is to obtain a 'best balance' i.e. nearest possible balance - between the occupancies of the two resulting regions. As with other grid file designs, the BANG file partitions the data space by a sequence of binary divisions in which the dimension selected for the next division is chosen according to a pre-defined order of cycling through all the dimensions. But it differs from previous designs (with the exception of [OHSA83]) in that, although the same partitioning sequence is applied throughout the data space, the partitioning *operation* is applied selectively to individual block regions. It is however more the way in which the block regions are represented and interpreted in the directory, rather than the method of partitioning itself, which gives the BANG file its characteristic properties.

A block region may be recursively partitioned many times before a new region is created: *any* size of region may be created within another, provided that the enclosed region is a member of the set of all block regions which could be created by the chosen partitioning sequence (figure 1a). The recursive partitioning is terminated when best balance is obtained between the two split regions, one of which always *encloses* the other (but see **minimality** below). It is important to emphasise that 'best-balance' does not mean *exact balance*. It is easy to show however that the division cannot be in a worse proportion than 2:1.

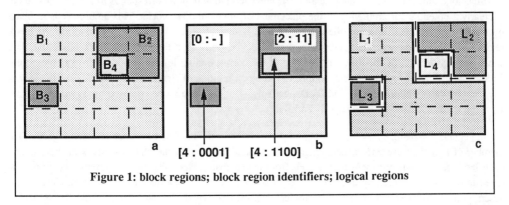

Figure 1: block regions; block region identifiers; logical regions

The number of partitions (i.e. the length of the partitioning sequence) required to create a particular block region is a measure of its *granularity*, and is termed the *level number* or simply *level* of the block region. (For example, if figure 1a represents the entire data space, then block region B_1 is at level 0, B_2 is at level 2, and B_3 and B_4 are at level 4). The level corresponding to the smallest block region so far created is called the *grid level*, and block regions of this size are termed *grid regions*. (In figure 1a, the grid level is 4, and regions B_3 and B_4 are grid regions).

A *block region identifier*, composed of a number pair *(level number, block region number)*, is assigned to every block region, and uniquely identifies it in the set of all possible block regions at every level. The block region number is generated as a binary string representing the partitioning sequence required to create the region. For example, suppose that in figure 1a the space is alternately partitioned about the vertical and horizontal dimensions, starting with the vertical. If the right and upper partitions are represented by **1** and the left and lower by **0**, then the block regions in figure 1a are represented by the identifiers shown in figure 1b. The level number thus indicates the length of the binary string, and since B_1 encloses the whole space, it is represented by its level number only: [0:-].

1.1. The mapping from tuple to enclosing block region

This mapping is well known [BURK83, OUKS83, OREN84]. The value of each of the **n** key attributes of the tuple is transformed - whatever the domain type - into a bit string, in such a way that the original ordering on the domain of the attribute is preserved, if the bit string is interpreted as an unsigned integer. (Character strings can generally be used directly, but the transformation of integers and reals is machine dependent). An n-dimensional binary key is then assembled from these bit strings by taking one bit from each cyclically, starting with the most significant bit. The order in which the **n** bit strings are visited defines the partitioning sequence of the corresponding n-dimensional tuple space. And as each bit is added to the key, the resulting bit string is the block region number of the next smaller block region which could enclose the tuple.

1.2. Logical regions

Since one block region can enclose another, and each block region corresponds to a disk block, there is clearly a potential for ambiguity in the placement of tuples in disk blocks. This ambiguity is resolved by introducing a further concept, the *logical region*. A logical region is a block region *minus* the block regions which it encloses. Thus, although every block region maps to a physical disk block, the data sub-space represented by the disk block is that of the corresponding logical region. For example, figure 1c shows the logical regions corresponding to the block regions of figure 1a. L_3 and L_4 are the spaces enclosed by the boundaries of B_3 and B_4 respectively. But L_2 is the space enclosed by B_1 *minus* B_2, and L_1 is the space enclosed by B_1 *minus* B_2 and B_3.

In general therefore, every logical region of the BANG file is defined by a *set* of block regions. One member of this set represents a rectangular space which encloses all the other members of the set. The enclosed block regions represent subtractions from the enclosing block region. This representation is achieved in practice by searching through the set of block regions in a particular order, as explained in the description of the directory below. The logical regions into which the data space of the BANG file is partitioned are therefore defined by block regions, but are not necessarily block regions themselves. In other words, *the logical regions do not have to be hyperrectangles*. They can contain concavities, and have internal as well as external boundaries. It is even possible for a logical region to be disjoint i.e. to be composed of subspaces which do not intersect and which have no common boundary. Most importantly, *a logical region always spans the space which it encloses*. This is not in general true for a block region. However, the logical regions and the sets representing them are - as the name implies - purely logical constructs. Only block regions are represented explicitly. But each data page holds the tuples mapping to a logical region, not to a block region. Likewise the partitioning algorithm attempts to balance the distribution of tuples between logical regions.

From this point on, *region* should be taken to mean *logical region* unless explicitly qualified as *block region*, or distinguished by the notation **L** or **B**. In some contexts however, the same reasoning holds equally for logical and block regions.

1.3. The directory of block regions

The BANG file has a tree structured directory with the self-balancing and update properties of a B-tree. The structure and storage order of the entries within the nodes (directory pages) of the tree is the key to the BANG file representation of the data space. Each level of the directory, from the leaves to the root, represents a recursive repartitioning of the data space into regions enclosing regions. Each node of the tree represents a logical region itself, and contains a set of entries which identify logical regions at the next lower level of the directory tree. The entries in the leaf nodes of the tree point to the data pages, each of which directly represents a logical region of the data space, and contains the set of (source) tuples located in that logical region. In the original version there was no defined ordering on the tuples within a data page. In the current version however, although the tuples themselves are not ordered, the page entry table of offsets to the start byte of each tuple is held in key order.

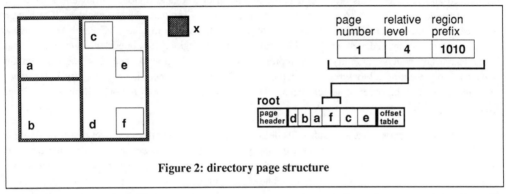

Figure 2: directory page structure

Each entry in the directory is a triplet representing a block region (figure 2). In principle, this triplet has the form:

[disk page number, level number, block region number]

However, it is not generally necessary to store the complete block region number in a directory entry, because the directory page itself corresponds to a block region, which encloses all the block regions represented within it. Therefore all entries within the same directory page must share the same partition sequence - and hence the same bit string in the block region number - down to the directory page level. Hence it is only necessary to store the *relative level number* i.e. the level relative to that of the enclosing directory page, and the *block region prefix*, which is the bit string for the relative entry level. A directory entry thus takes the form:

[disk page number, relative level number, block region number prefix]

In practice, a compromise is made between these two representations, for efficiency reasons. In order to be able to make comparisons by byte rather than by bit during directory search and update operations, remainder bits from the block region prefix at one directory level are carried down to the next. (Beware of confusing *directory level* with *partition level*. A directory page at one level of the directory tree may contain entries for block regions at many partition levels). Provided that the *absolute partition level* is accumulated during the descent of the directory tree, the position of the start bit of the next prefix can be easily computed. Note that directory entries are of variable length, depending on the length of the block region prefix. For this reason a page entry offset table is necessary in directory pages (figure 2).

1.4. Retrieval

The search for a tuple proceeds from root to leaf. At each directory level, the prefixes in the directory entries are compared with the corresponding prefix of the tuple search key i.e. with the same number of leading bits of the key. Every entry for which a match is found represents a block region which encloses the tuple either directly or indirectly. In principle, the search key is generated from the source tuple as described above, but in practice it is generated dynamically during traversal of the tree. When the search descends to a page at the next level, a comparison is made between the absolute level of the smallest block region in the page and the current length of the search key bit string. If the search key is shorter, it is extended.

The correct logical region is located within each directory page by the order in which the entries are maintained and searched. This order reflects the definition of a logical region. Entries are ordered lexically by block region prefix, so that every region precedes any regions which it encloses. The page is then searched in the reverse order, so that the first entry found which matches the search key is always that of the smallest, immediately enclosing logical (and block) region. It is important to emphasize that, if the search key matches an entry which represents some block region B, then it will also match any other entry representing a block region which encloses B. However, there is no ambiguity in locating a tuple in B, because the order of search means that the innermost enclosed region will always be found first.

For example, suppose that a search is made for a tuple which actually lies in region a of figure 2. (Region a may represent a data page, or a directory page at the next lower level). The first directory entry, searching in reverse lexical order (from right to left) is at level 4, so that the first 4 bits of the search key are generated from the tuple. The first and only entry found to match the key is $[p_3:2:01]$....where p_n is the number of the page pointed to by the nth entry in the directory page. Now suppose that the tuple lies in logical region c. In this case two directory entries match the generated key: $[p_1:1:1]$ and $[p_5:4:1101]$. But the latter is the first one found, so the search is correctly directed to page p_5. In practice, a modified binary search is used to find the matching key of highest level number.

1.5. Page splitting and merging

When a data page overflows and is recursively partitioned as previously described, an entry representing the newly created page is inserted in the directory page above. This in turn may cause overflow, and so on up the directory tree. Thus directory updates always propagate upwards from the leaves, and the tree remains balanced, as in a B-tree. Note that, when a directory page splits, the entry prefix defining the new page is inserted into the level above, and is stripped from the leading bits of every prefix within the new page. On merging, the inverse operation is required. But this *increases* the occupancy of the merged page, and so must be allowed for when deciding whether the merge can take place without immediately overflowing.

2. The spanning problem

The description of retrieval above assumes that the search will always terminate with a single pass down the tree. This requires that a logical region enclosing the position of the tuple will always be found at every directory level, wherever the tuple may be in the data space i.e. it requires that every logical region spans the space which it encloses. Although this might at first seem intuitively obvious, it is unfortunately not the case in the BANG file design as originally proposed. A data page directly represents a logical region of the data space. The tuples which it encloses are represented by points, which are indivisible i.e. however the space is partitioned on splitting, each point will lie on one side or the other of the partition. By contrast, directory pages represent the data space only indirectly - as regions of regions. But regions are not indivisible. When a directory page splits, it is possible that one of the logical regions which it contains will lie partly on one side of the partition, and partly on the other. An example is illustrated in figures 2 and 3.

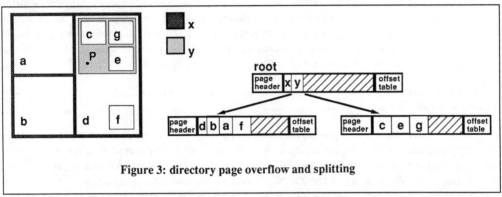

Figure 3: directory page overflow and splitting

In figure 2, the root directory page is shown to be full. (In practice a 1Kbyte page holds around 70 entries on average). Figure 3 shows the situation after insertions into region **d** cause it to overflow and split into regions **d** and **g**. The insertion of the entry for **g** into the root directory page forces it to split into pages **x** and **y**, and a new root page is created. But figure 3 shows that the new enclosed region **y** does not span the space which it encloses i.e. there is no entry in page **y**, or at any higher directory level, which represents the shaded area immediately surrounding point **P**. This area is still spanned by region **d**. A search for a tuple at point **P** will therefore proceed down the directory tree to the page representing region **y**, where the search will fail. All is not lost however. The search has to retreat to the directory level above, and to recommence descent of the tree at the entry representing the next larger (enclosing) region **x** which matches the key. Such a region will always exist when this condition occurs. In page **x** a match is found at the entry for data page **d**, which encloses point **P** as before, and the search succeeds.

Although in practice the average length of the search path has been found to be less than 3% longer than a direct traversal from root to leaf, the worst case requires a depth-first traversal of the entire directory. However improbable this event might be, it would clearly be better if the spanning problem could be avoided altogether. Fortunately it can be, so that a direct traversal from root to leaf is guaranteed. The sacrifice made for this in the current implementation of the BANG file is very small - an increase of less than 1% in the overall file size. Let us formalise the problem further:

Definition: a logical region **R** spans the space which it encloses if every point in that space maps to logical region **R**.

Note that this definition does *not* imply that, in a page **P** representing a region **R**, the union of all the logical regions represented by entries in **P** completely fills **R**. Spanning guarantees only that a tuple will always be inserted into the *logical* region to which it maps. But the search for a tuple could fail not only because the tuple is not present, but also because there exists no representation of the region enclosing the point to which it maps. However, according to the first of the axioms on which the design of the BANG file was originally based [FREE87]:

The union of all the sub-spaces [logical regions] into which the data space has been partitioned must span the data space.

i.e. there must be no *unrecorded* regions. We will see later that the enforcement of spanning allows us to relax this axiom. But let us for the moment accept the partitioning of the data space as so far described, for which the above axiom holds because page splits, merges or redistributions never result in unrecorded regions of the data space. Looking at figure 3 again, we see that the cause of the problem is of a very fundamental nature. A partition boundary (y) has been introduced which *intersects* the boundary of an existing logical region **d**. This situation has arisen because by definition the directory represents a hierarchy of enclosing regions i.e. the region which a directory page represents must enclose all the regions which it contains. So although region **y** is smaller than region **d**, **y** is nevertheless the enclosing region, by definition. This contradicts the self-evident axiom that a region must be larger than, or the same size as the region which it encloses. It also contradicts the second of the original BANG axioms:

If two sub-spaces into which the data space has been partitioned intersect, then one of these sub-spaces completely encloses the other.

Enclosure therefore allows *regions* to intersect, but not their *boundaries*. In figure 3, logical region **x** does not completely enclose logical region **d**. We see therefore that the requirement that every region must span the space which it encloses is equivalent to applying the second axiom rigorously at every level of the directory. We note that when the file is created the total data space must span, since it is represented by a single data page. We also note that, if two spanning regions merge, then the resulting merged region must also span, since no new partitions are introduced in the merging process. Therefore if spanning is maintained when a region is split then every region will always span. On the basis of these considerations we can now formulate an algorithm to split an overflowing page while maintaining spanning, and without triggering a chain of further overflowing pages.

2.1. Spanning algorithm

Let page **P** represent some region **L** which spans. Suppose now that **P** overflows and is split according to the best-balance algorithm. If the splitting boundary B_s coincides with that of one of the block region entries in **P**, then it cannot intersect any existing regions, and so the resulting split pages must both span. But if B_s does <u>not</u> coincide with any entry in **P**, then it may or may not intersect an existing boundary. Intersection will occur if and only if there exists an entry **B'** in **P** representing a block region which *encloses* B_s. If this is not the case, then the split pages must still both span. If however there is no entry coinciding with B_s but there exists some region **B'** enclosing B_s then a split of **P** on the boundary of **B'** will also span. But there is no guarantee that the partition about **B'** will divide the contents of **P** sufficiently evenly to resolve the overflow. To do so, each resulting split page must have an occupancy greater than or equal to the length of the insertion entry which caused the overflow. This is not an automatic consequence of an arbitrary page split when directory entries are of variable length.

We can nevertheless deduce a lower limit for the occupancy of region **B'**. The best-balance partition B_s is determined by a sequence of binary partitions of **P** until the occupancy of the enclosed region becomes less than or equal to that of the enclosing region. Therefore every region which encloses the best-balance partition must have an occupancy greater than half the occupancy of **P**. And the smallest (innermost) of these, B_s+, must have a lower occupancy than any other enclosing region. Conversely, any region which is *not* a member of the set of block regions into which **P** is partitioned to establish the best-balance boundary must have an occupancy *less* than half that of **P**. Suppose that B_s- is the region which has a higher occupancy than any other of these. Then whichever of B_s+ and B_s- more nearly approaches exact balance is the best balance which can be found for which spanning of the split pages can be guaranteed. This is a useful result, upon which a simple and efficient algorithm can be constructed:

- The exact balance point is computed from the occupancy of **P** and the length of the insertion entry.

- The best-balance partition B_s of **P** is found as previously described

- If there is an entry in **P** coinciding with B_s then **P** is partitioned on B_s

- Else if there is no entry in **P** enclosing partition B_s then **P** is partitioned on B_s

- Else B_s- is computed as follows:
  - the entries in **P** are scanned linearly to find the first region which is not a member of the partitioning set. Any entry whose prefix does not match the leading bits of B_s or whose prefix is longer than that of B_s is not a member of the partitioning set. Since the page entries are in prefix order, the region found will be followed immediately by a sequence of any other regions which it encloses, none of which can be members of the partitioning set.

  - the total length of all the entries in this sequence is accumulated, representing the occupancy of that part of **P** enclosed by the boundary of the first entry in the sequence.

  - when an entry is encountered which is not enclosed by the first in the sequence, then the scan algorithm is repeated. The accumulated total for each sequence found is compared with the previous largest found, and the larger of the two is retained, together with a pointer to the first entry in the sequence. At the end of the scan, the pointer indicates the location of B_s- in **P**, and the accumulated total is its occupancy.

  - the occupancy of B_s+ is now computed by notionally (though not yet physically) splitting **P** on this boundary.

  - the page is then physically split along whichever of the partitions B_s+ and B_s- has an occupancy closer to exact balance.

This algorithm will always succeed because, if no better spanning balance can be found, **P** will be split on the boundary of the insertion entry. This must be so because the size of the insertion entry represents a lower bound to the occupancy of B_s-. Note that other solutions may exist which give a better balance, but they must involve a partition boundary which does not coincide with any existing page entry. They cannot therefore guarantee spanning, without involving a much more time-consuming spanning-check algorithm.

3. Minimality

We have so far axiomatically assumed that there are no unrecorded regions of the data space (see **spanning problem** above). According to the partitioning algorithm so far given, a region on splitting divides into the *original* region, plus an *enclosed* region, so that the space spanned by a region is never reduced on splitting. However, as mentioned earlier, the enforcement of spanning allows us to relax this requirement. Recall that, in the original (non-spanning) version of the BANG file, a stored tuple might not be found in a direct pass from root to leaf of the directory. The search within a directory page could fail if the page did not span i.e. if there were no region in the page enclosing the point in the data space to which the tuple mapped. However, such failure cannot occur if spanning is guaranteed: if a tuple exists, then a region enclosing it exists also. But this guarantee does not require the representation of any part of the data space which contains *no* data points. We may therefore modify the original axiom on spanning to the following:

The union of all the logical regions into which the data space is partitioned at each directory level must span a sub-space of the data space which encloses all the recorded data.

Thus no region needs to be greater than the **minimal** size necessary to enclose all the regions or tuples which it contains. Although the maintenance of minimality increases update overheads, it is potentially well worth the extra effort. Any operations which involve searching some defined sub-space of the data space will benefit from being able to reduce that search space. In particular, the efficiency of such operations as relational joins, which depend on the intersection of two or more data spaces, may be substantially improved.

Suppose that directory page **P** representing region **L** contains a set of regions whose union is less than **L**. The search for a tuple **t** will fail in page **P** if there is no region enclosing **t**. This simply means that no stored tuple **t** exists, and so the search terminates. But note that this could now happen at any directory level. In general, therefore, the average path length of an unsuccessful search will be less than the depth of the directory tree. If a tuple insertion fails for the same reason, then an existing region in **P** must be extended to enclose **t** (see **Extensibility** below).

Note that the minimality of a region is not the same as the *minimal representation* of a region:

Definitions: *a logical region* **L** *is minimal if it is the smallest logical region which can enclose the contents of* **L**.

The minimal representation of a logical region **L** *is that representation for which the block region* **B** *immediately enclosing* **L** *is minimal.*

Block region **B** *is minimal if it is the smallest block region which can immediately enclose* **L**.

In the case of a data region enclosing a single data point (tuple), the region is minimal if its absolute level number is equal to the total length (in bits) of the tuple key.

Minimality is not an invariant property of a logical region, because certain update operations may change a region from minimal to non-minimal, and vice-versa: for example, a deletion in a minimal page, or insertion in a non-minimal page. On the other hand, insertions cannot cause minimal pages to become non-minimal. In order to maintain minimality, a check must be made during every such update, and minimality enforced. Unfortunately, as is explained below, enforcement is not always possible (or rather, practical). But it can be maintained to a very high degree, with little additional software and an acceptable average and worst-case processing overhead.

Algorithmically, the checking and maintenance of minimality is very easy, since directory page entries are stored in prefix order. Comparison of the prefixes of the first and last entries of page **P** representing region **L** shows how many leading bits of all the prefix entries in **P** are identical. If there are **b** such bits, then the minimal region to which **L** can be reduced is represented by appending the **b** bits to the directory page entry for **P**, and stripping them from the prefix of every entry in **P**. (This representation of the minimal page is also a minimal representation). A similar check can be made for data pages because, although the tuples are stored in random order, the page entry table is maintained in prefix order.

(There is, of course, no bit-stripping overhead for data pages.)

The extension of an entry prefix in the higher level directory page may of course cause overflow which, in the worst case, may propagate upwards to the root. But minimality introduces an additional problem. In the previous description of page splitting, it has always been assumed that the resulting regions consist of an enclosing region with the same boundary as before, plus a new enclosed region. The update passed to the directory level above therefore consists of a single insertion of the entry for the new page. It was pointed out above that, if this insertion causes the directory page to overflow, it is always possible to find a spanning partition, because at the worst the partition can be made on the boundary of the new entry i.e. a separate directory page is created for the new entry. The original directory page is unchanged, and must therefore still span, but no longer overflows.

However, although the splitting algorithm always automatically ensures that the enclosed split page is minimal, this is not necessarily so for the enclosing page. If minimality is **enforced**, it may be that the original enclosing page becomes reduced in size. In this case, the update passed to the directory level above becomes a deletion of the original entry, plus *two* new insertions - each with an entry prefix longer than the original. If such an update causes overflow, it is easy to find cases (although not easy to find a general existence proof) where no binary spanning partition exists. Clearly if either of the insertions alone can be made without causing overflow, then a spanning partition must exist if the second insertion causes overflow, by the same argument as for non-minimal splitting. But if neither insertion can be made without overflow, then either the spanning or the minimality requirement must be relaxed. Since the former choice would undermine the axiomatic foundation of the system, the simplest solution is to leave the original enclosing region non-minimal. This means that the update deletion and its replacement insertion are ignored, so that the full update is transformed into a single insertion.

The imposition of minimality on page splitting may cause leading bits to be stripped from the entries contained in the enclosing page as well as in the enclosed page. This may affect the position of the best-balance splitting partition, but since the minimality check needs so little effort, the effect can be calculated, for both pages, at each partition iteration. An additional refinement is to check for minimality *before* page splitting, to avoid the possibility of a series of preliminary partitions of empty space before any actual division of entries occurs.

The merging of pages is much simpler. It is not necessary to check minimality when two minimal data pages are merged, because the resulting page must also be minimal. A check must however always be made whenever directory pages are merged, because their minimality cannot be guaranteed. But since the size of a merged region cannot be less than that of the smaller of its component regions (even if they are not minimal) the subsequent update of page entries cannot cause overflow in the directory level above.

4. Extensibility

When the insertion of a tuple fails because no region can be found which encloses the point to which the tuple maps, then the representation of the data space must be *extended*. The objective is to increase the represented data space by the smallest amount necessary to enclose the inserted data point. A new region cannot be created to do this, because it would contravene the fundamental principle of a balanced tree structure: that all insertions are transmitted from a lower level of the directory tree. But an existing region can be extended. The 'smallest and nearest' existing region to the insertion point is the region which has the longest entry prefix matching the search key. There may be several regions which equally well meet this criterion, but some of them may be enclosed by others. Clearly, only unenclosed regions are candidates for extension.

The extension algorithm is quite simple, as it is a variation on the directory page search algorithm - indeed the two can be combined. A binary search locates a page entry which most closely matches the search key. This entry may be preceded by others which match the key equally well, representing regions which enclose the first one found. A linear search of these preceding entries is therefore made to find the outermost. The prefix of the selected entry is then truncated after the last bit which matches the search key, and the entry is updated in the page. Since the new entry prefix is shorter than the old, the update can always be made without causing page overflow. And since the region has been extended by only the minimum necessary to enclose the new data point, it must be minimal, even if it was not previously so.

At whichever directory level the insertion of a tuple may fail, it must also fail at all lower levels. So the extension algorithm may be repeated several times. However, even if the insertion fails at every directory level, the additional overhead is slight because of the simplicity of the extension algorithm, and because no additional pages are involved.

5. Performance Measurements

Figures A1-A4 (appendix) demonstrate the behaviour of a version of the BANG file in which the spanning algorithm has been implemented, but not minimality checking. Figure A1 measures the performance of a 2-dimensional file, in which both attributes are composed of a (different) randomly generated character string, 48 bytes long. The page size is 1 Kbyte. The first graph shows the average percentage occupancy of data pages as the file grows. The vertical lines indicate the points at which the directory expands to an additional level - in this example, to a maximum of three levels. The second graph shows the same information for directory pages, and the third shows the ratio of directory to total file occupancy. At first there is only one data page, and no directory. When ther data page overflows, it splits into two, so that the average data occupancy drops to something over 50%, and the first directory page (the root) is created. The irregular rise in the occupancy percentage of the first directory page, as compared with that of the first data page, is simply due to the fact that new entries are added to the directory page only when data pages (or directory pages) overflow. A direct correspondence can therefore be seen between the 'spikes' of the data-occupancy graph, and the 'steps' of the directory occupancy graph.

After the insertion of about 1000 tuples, the data occupancy shows little variation from about 67%. At this stage there are about 150 data pages, each containing 6 or 7 tuples on average, and the probability that a particular page will overflow at a particular overall file size is evidently about the same for all data pages - the graph of data occupancy becomes almost a horizontal line. The same is not true however for directory occupancy. The average length of a directory entry in this example is only about 10 bytes (including page offset table information) and a directory page of 1 Kbyte therefore contains about 100 entries when it overflows. This represents the addition of about 600 or 700 tuples which, if distributed uniformly throughout the data space, are almost equally likely to affect any leaf directory page, albeit indirectly via the overflow of data pages. Therefore directory pages at the same directory level tend to overflow at the same overall file size, which accounts for the steep oscillations in directory occupancy. As will be seen later, this effect is not observed for non-uniform data distributions. However, the average directory page occupancy for a uniform data distribution is again about 67%.

Although the first two graphs in figure A1 show that the same page occupancy level is achieved for both data and directory pages, this alone does not guarantee that the ratio of directory to data remains constant. This ratio is shown in the third graph. It will be seen that the ratio rapidly tends to a value of around 2%. The actual value of this ratio depends on the average number of entries per directory page i.e. the 'fan-out ratio', which depends on the average directory entry length and the page size.

Figures A2-A4 show the behaviour of the file, and the way in which the data space is partitioned, for a selection of non-uniform data distributions: data clusters, an inverse linear correlation, and a non-linear function (a sine curve). Integer attribute values were used in these examples. It will be seen that there is no significant variation in data or directory page occupancy, or data/directory ratio, whatever the data distribution. (The directory/total file size ratio is around 17% because a page size of only 200 bytes was used in order to test performance with a 4-level directory). Similar tests have been carried out for files of up to 8 dimensions, and no significant variation in occupancy levels has been observed.

6. Conclusion

The performance figures demonstrate the extreme insensitivity of the BANG file to variations in the data distribution. They also show that the introduction of spanning enforcement does not degrade data occupancy to any significant extent. A new version of the BANG file is currently being written to test the effectiveness of the second proposed spanning algorithm, and the effect of minimality checking and dataspace extension. There remains one important problem: the cyclic partitioning of the data space is carried out over the domains of the attributes, and not over their ranges. This can lead to a very uneven partitioning of the several dimensions. It is a weakness of all grid file designs so far, and ways of overcoming the problem are being actively sought.

There is a lot of work still to be done to investigate BANG file performance characteristics of partial match and range queries, and indeed all relational operations. So far, exact match, partial match and range queries have been implemented, as well as join operations. The performance of the BANG file in comparison with an equivalent one-dimensional fully-inverted file structure, (and variants) is also being investigated. In the view of the author, it is now feasible to replace the B-tree structure with a multi-dimensional structure in a database system. It therefore becomes important to know under what circumstances it would be advantageous to make use of such multi-dimensional capabilities, and when not. It is hoped to develop criteria which would help a database designer or administrator to decide. There is of course no reason why *all* the attributes in a relation should be included in the multi-dimensional index, and it is still possible to combine the values of a selected combination of attributes to form one or more concatenated keys. There are also circumstances in which it is clearly better to use only one dimension. Multi-dimensional file structures do not solve every access problem, but they do offer greater flexibility of data access, without the overheads of secondary indexing.

Acknowledgements

Thanks to all at ECRC, but especially the KB group, for their encouragement and enthusiasm. Particular thanks are due to Pierre Coste, who produced the pictures of the data distributions and has been of great assistance in testing and de-bugging the system. The author is also grateful for the support of Jean-Marie Nicolas throughout this research.

7. References

[ABEL83]   D.J. Abel, J.L. Smith
            A data structure and algorithm based on a linear key for a
            rectangle retrieval problem
            Computer Vision, Graphics and Image Processing 27,1,1983.

[BURK83]   W.A. Burkhard
            Interpolation-Based Index Maintenance
            Proc. ACM SIGMOD-SIGACT Symposium, 1983.

[FREE87]   M.W.Freeston
            The BANG file: a new kind of grid file
            Proc. ACM SIGMOD Conf., San Francisco, 1987.

[HINR85]   K.H. Hinrichs
            The grid file system: implementation and case studies of applications
            Doctoral Thesis Nr. 7734, ETH Zurich, 1985.

[NIEV81]   J. Nievergelt, H. Hintenberger, K.C. Sevcik
            The Grid File: an adaptable, symmetric multikey file structure
            Internal Report No. 46, Institut für Informatik,
             ETH Zürich, December 1981.

[OREN83]   J.A. Orenstein
            Algorithms and data structures for the implementation of a relational
            database
            Technical Report SOCS-82-17 (1982), School of Computer Science,
            McGill University.

[OUKS83]   M. Ouksel, P. Scheuermann
            Storage Mapping for Multidimensional Linear Dynamic Hashing
            Proc. of 2nd Symposium on Principles of Database Systems, Atlanta, 1983.

[OZKA85]   E.A. Ozkarahan, M. Ouksel
            Dynamic and Order Preserving Data Partitioning for Database Machines
            Proc. of 11th Int. Conf. on Very Large Data Bases, Stockholm, August 1985.

[OHSA83]   Y. Ohsawa, M. Sakauchi
            The BD-Tree: a new n-dimensional data structure with highly efficient
            dynamic characteristics
            IFIP 9th World Computer Congress, Paris, 1983.

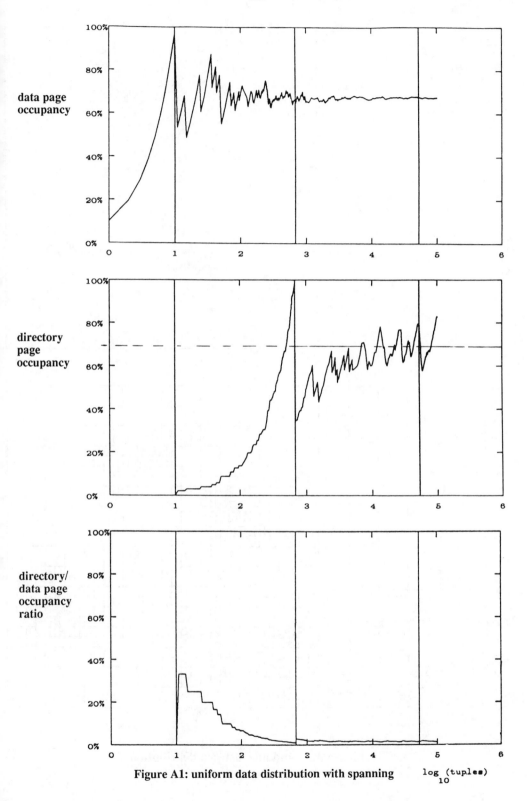

Figure A1: uniform data distribution with spanning $\log_{10}(\text{tuples})$

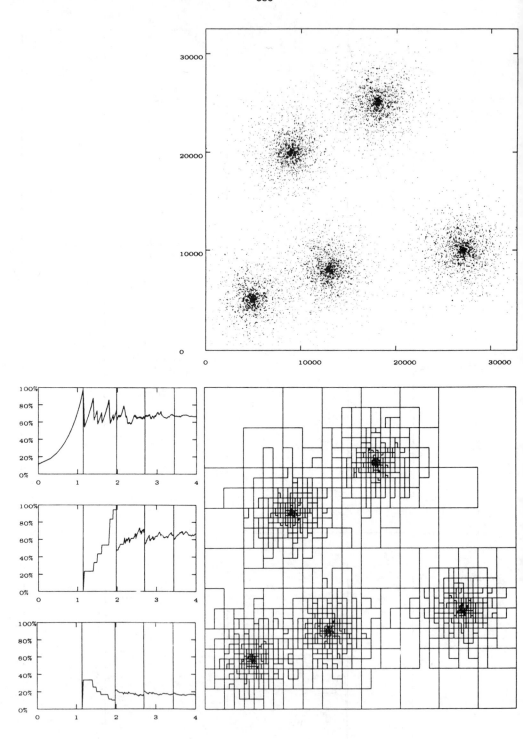

Figure A2: random clustered distribution

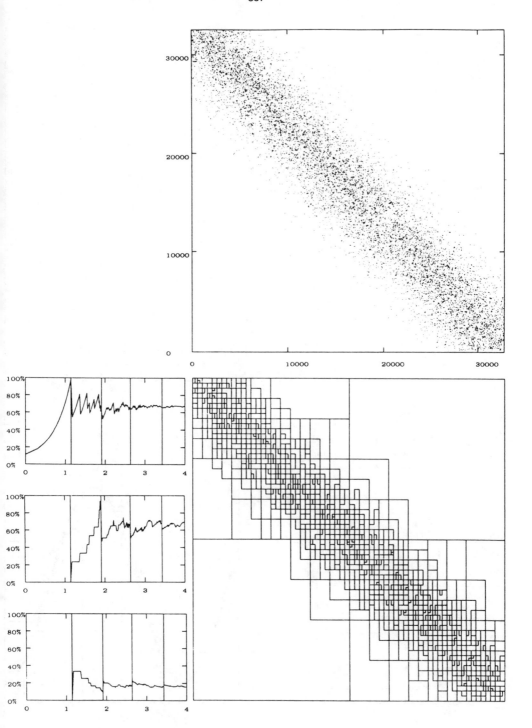

Figure A3: inverse linear correlation

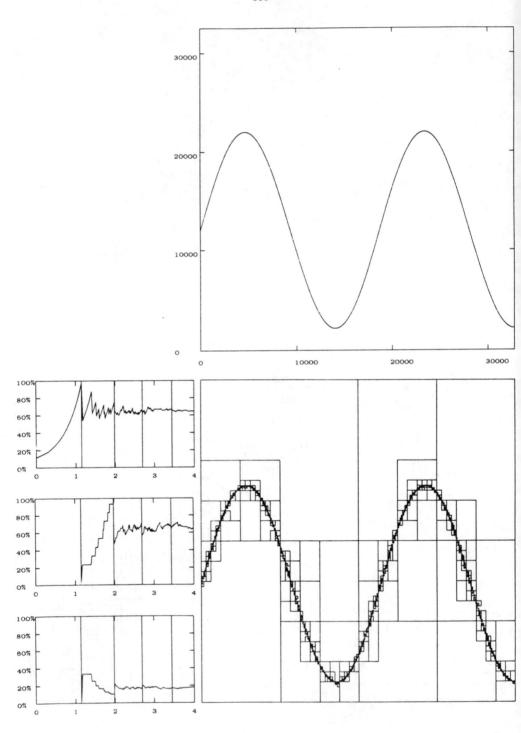

Figure A4: non-linear function (sine curve)

Manipulating Three-Dimensional Triangulations

Elisabetta Bruzzone
Leila De Floriani
Enrico Puppo

Istituto per la Matematica Applicata
Consiglio Nazionale delle Ricerche
Via L.B. Alberti, 4 - 16132 Genova (Italy)
Phone Number: 39-10-515510
Email Address: DEFLO@IGECUNIV.BITNET

Abstract

The three-dimensional symmetric data structure is a topological model of a three-dimensional triangulation. It is a generalization of the symmetric structure proposed by Woo [Woo85] for describing the boundary of a solid object. In the paper, we present the basic topological elements of a 3D triangulation and their mutual relations. We describe the 3D symmetric structure and present structure accessing algorithms for retrieving those relations which are not explicitly encoded in the structure. Finally, a minimal set of primitive operators for building and manipulating a 3D triangulation are discussed. Such operators are independent of the underlying data structure.

1. Introduction

Object representation plays an important role in a variety of applications, such as computer graphics, computer vision, robotics, computer aided design. Different object models are suitable for different applications. Object representation schemes can be classified into their major categories: boundary representations, constructive models and decomposition models [Man88]. Boundary representations describe an object in terms of the surfaces enclosing it, constructive models (like the CSG tree [Req81]) represent an object as a boolean combination of primitive volumetric component. Decomposition models can be further classified into space-based and object-based schemes. The former decompose the space into elementary volumes (usually, cubes) and describe the object in terms of the volume elements which belong to it. An example of a space-based model is the octree [Sam84]. Object-based scheme represent an object S as the combination of pair disjoint primitive 3D cells whose union cover S. Usually, tetrahedra are used as basic cells. Such a model object is called a three-dimensional triangulation. Three-dimensional tesselations are extensively used in the finite element method and in computer vision for the object reconstruction problem [DeF87]. Three-dimensional triangulations have several important properties like invariance through rigid transformations, ease of updating, computational efficiency, and suitability for both sparse and dense data [Boi88].

Usually a 3D triangulation is constructed from a set of points in the 3D space or from the boundary of an object and a set of internal points (which are either given or selected by the algorithm). This latter is usually the case when a finite element representation must be produced from a CAD model [Bow81].

Often, the use of a three-dimensional Delaunay triangulation [Boi84] is proposed to provide a global geometric structure encoding the neighborhood relations among the points of the given data set. Intuitively, a Delaunay triangulation T of a set S of points in the k-dimensional Euclidean space is a collection of simplexes tesselating the interior of the convex hull of S in such a way that the vertices of T are the points of S and the circumspheres of such simplices do not contain any point of S inside [DeF87]. Algorithms for computing the n-dimensional Delaunay tesselation of a set of points are discussed in [Bow81,Wat81]. The 3D Delaunay triangulation of the points defining the boundary of an object provides a volumetric representation of the convex hull of the object by a set of tetrahedra. If not all of the given points are on the convex hull, the object boundary can be sculptured by iteratively eliminating external tetrahedra, as described in [Boi84].

Several data structures for describing a triangulation of a set of points in the plane or any partition of the plane [DeF87,Pre85] or of the boundary of a solid object [Ans85,Bau72,Wei85,Woo85] have been proposed in the literature. Such structures store the basic entities defining the tesselation and their mutual relations. Also, basic operators for building and updating a boundary sheme, called the Euler operators, have been defined by several authors [Ans85,Man88,Wei86]. Less attention has been devoted to the problem of describing and manipulating a 3D tesselation. In [Dob87] Dobkin and Laszlo generalize the DCEL data structure used for describing arbitrary planar subdivisions [Pre85] to the case of volume decompositions.

In this paper, we define a data structure for encoding a 3D triangulation, and a set of structure accessing primitives operating on it. The data structure generalizes the symmetric structure [Woo85] to 3D triangular tesselations. Its space complexity is evaluated as well as the time complexity of the structure accessing algorithms which operate on the data structure. A minimally complete set of building and updating primitives, which generalize the Euler operators defined for classical boundary schemes, is defined. Such operators ensure that the topological validity of the object represented by the 3D tesselation is satisfied at each updating.

2. Primitive Topological Elements and Their Mutual Relations

In this section, we define the basic entities of a 3D triangulation and their mutual relations.

Let S denote a set of n distinct points in E3 (n>=4). Assume that the points of S are not coplanar. Let C denote the convex hull of S and D the closed volume bounded by C. A triangulation [Law77] of S is a tessellation of D composed of non-degenerate quasi-disjoint tetrahedra having the vertices at the points of S. The four basic topological elements defining a three-dimensional triangulation of a set of points are tetrahedra, triangles (also called facets), edges and vertices.

In some applications, the boundary B of the object described by the set S is explicitly specified as a collection of triangles, edges and vertices and is not necessarily convex [Boi84]. In this case, the concept of 3D triangulation of a set S generalizes to that of 3D triangulation of a set S constrained by a boundary B. B must define a compact orientable two-manifold surface [Wei86] and must be triangulated. B can be expressed as a tuple B=(FB,EB,VB), where FB, EB and VB denote the facets, edges and vertices forming B. Then, a 3D triangulation TD of set S constrained by B is a set of non-degenerate tetrahedra {ti} satisfying the following properties:

(i)   All vertices of each tetrahedron are elements of S
(ii)   The interiors of the tetrahedra are pairwise disjoint
(iii) Each facet is either in FB or is a common facet to two tetrahedra

¦(iv)   Each tetrahedron, facet or edge contains no other point of S other   than
        its vertices
(v)   The facets, edges and vertices of B belong to the triangulation
(vi)   The union of the {ti} is the volume in E3 enclosed by B

Note that, if B is the boundary of the triangulated convex hull of S, the above
definition reduces to that of 3D triangulation of a set S.

In the following, we will call three-dimensional triangulation a triangulation
of a set of points constrained by a boundary (which can possibly be the boundary
polygon of the convex hull of S). A three-dimensional triangulation, denoted
TD, can be expressed as a 4-tuple TD=(T,F,E,V) where T,F,E and V denote the
collection of the tetrahedra, facets, edges and vertices of TD, respectively.
The number of tetrahedra, facet and edges have been evaluated as a function of
the number n of the vertices of TD for the case when TD is a 3D Delaunay
tesselation.   It has been proven [Pre85] that a 3D Voronoi diagram of n points
has O(n^2) vertices and edges. Thus, a 3D Delaunay triangulation of n points,
which is dual with respect to the Voronoi diagram, contains O(n^2) tetrahedra,
O(n^2) facets and O(n) edges. Thus, any relational model of a 3D triangulation
will have an O(n^2) space complexity.

Sixteen pairwise ordered adjacency relations can be defined over the four
primitive topological elements, as shown in the adjacency schemata depicted in
figure 1. In this schemata, nodes describe topological elements, while each
arrows denotes an ordered relations between pairs of elements. Heavy arrows
denote constant relations. The sixteen ordered adjacency relations defined
between pairs of elements of a 3D triangulation can be calassified into four
categories according to the first element of each ordered pair.

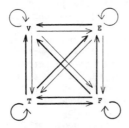

Figure 1

1. Tetrahedron-based relations

   1.1 **Tetrahedron-Vertex** (TV) (see figure 2a)
       $TV(t)=\{v1,v2,v3,v4\}$,   t in T
       {v1,v2,v3,v4}: set of vertices of TD belonging to t.
   1.2 **Tetrahedron-Edge** (TE) (see figure 2a)
       $TE(t)=\{e1,e2,e3,e4,e5,e6\}$,   t in T
       {e1,e2,e3,e4,e5,e6}: set of edges of TD belonging to t.
   1.3 **Tetrahedron-Facet** (TF) (see figure 2a)
       $TF(t)=\{f1,f2,f3,f4\}$,   t in T
       {f1,f2,f3,f4}: set of facets of TD belonging to t.
   1.4 **Tetrahedron-Tetrahedron** (TT) (see figure 2b)
       $TT(t)=\{t1,t2,t3,t4\}$,   t in T
       {t1,t2,t3,t4}: set of tetrahedra of TD sharing a facet with t.   A
       tetrahedron ti, i=1,...,4, is empty if t does not share facet fi with any
       tetrahedron of TD, i.e., fi is on the boundary.

Note: The four sequences defined above are consistent. For instance, vertices
      v1, v2, v3 belong to f1, v1, v2, v4 belong to f2, v2, v3, v4 belong to f3
      and v3, v1, v4 belong to f4 (see figure 2a).

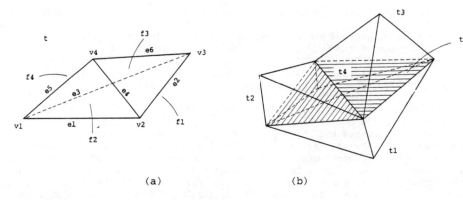

(a) (b)

Figure 2

2. Facet-based relations

2.1 Facet-Vertex (FV) (see figure 3a)
FV(f)=[v1,v2,v3], f in F
[v1,v2,v3]: sequence of vertices of TD bounding f (in counterclockwise order).

2.2 Facet-Edge (FE) (see figure 3a)
FE(f)=[e1,e2,e3], f in F
[e1,e2,e3]: sequence of edges of TD bounding f (in counterclockwise order).

2.3 Facet-Facet (FF) (see figure 3b)
FF(f)=[{f11,f21},{f12,f22},{f13,f23}], f in F
[{f11,f21},{f12,f22},{f13,f23}]: sequence of facet pairs sharing an edge with f.
{f1i,f2i}: unordered pair of facets of TD preceding and following f along edge ei and belonging to t1 and t2 respectively, where ei denotes the i-th edge bounding f and t1 and t2 the two tetrahedra sharing f (when t2 is empty, then FF(f)=[f11,f12,f13]). The facet pairs sequence is ordered according to the ccw order of the edges around f.

2.4 Facet-Tetrahedron (FT) (see figure 3b)
FT(f)={t1,t2}, f in F
{t1,t2}: unordered pair of tetrahedra of TD sharing f (t2 is empty if f belong only to one tetrahedron).

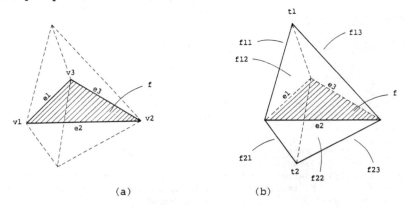

(a) (b)

Figure 3

3. Edge-based relations

3.1 Edge-Vertex (EV) (see figure 4a)
EV(e)={v1,v2}, e in E
{v1,v2}: unordered pair of vertices of TD which are extreme vertices of edge e.

3.2 Edge-Edge (EE) (see figure 4a)
EE(e)={[e1,e2,...,er],[e1',e2',...er']}, e in E
{[e1,e2,...,er],[e1',e2',...er']}: unordered pair of sets of edges of TD sharing a vertex with e.
[e1,e2,...,er]: sequence of edges of TD (ordered counterclockwise) sharing vertex v1 with e and bounding the facets sharing e.
[e1',e2',...er']: sequence of edges of TD (ordered counterclockwise) sharing v2 with e and bounding the facets sharing e.

3.3 Edge-Facet (EF) (see figure 4b)
EF(e)=[f1,f2,...,fr], e in E
[f1,f2,...,fr]: sequence of facets of TD sharing edge e (in counterclockwise order).

3.4 Edge-Tetrahedron (ET) (see figure 4b)
ET(e)=[t1,t2,...,ts], e in E
[t1,t2,...,ts]: sequence of tetrahedra of TD sharing edge e (in counterclockwise order).

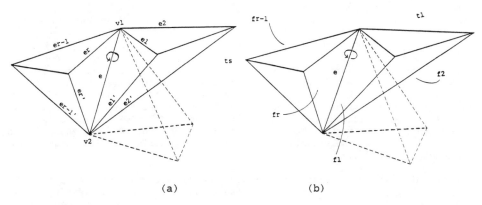

(a)   (b)

Figure 4

4. Vertex-based relations

4.1 Vertex-Vertex (VV) (see figure 5a)
VV(v)={v1,v2,...,vp}, v in V
{v1,v2,...,vp}: set of vertices of TD which are extreme vertices of the edges incident on v.

4.2 Vertex-Edge (VE) (see figure 5a)
VE(v)={e1,e2,...,ep}, v in V
{e1,e2,...,ep}: set of edges of TD incident on vertex v.

4.3 Vertex-Facet (VF) (see figure 5b)
VF(v)={f1,f2,...,fq}, v in V
{f1,f2,...,fq}: set of facets of TD sharing a vertex with v.

4.4 Vertex-Tetrahedron (VT) (see figure 5b)
VT(v)={t1,t2,...,th}, v in V
{t1,t2,...,th}: set of tetrahedra of TD sharing a vertex with v.

The previous sixteen relations can be classified into __constant__ and __variable__ relations depending on the number of elements involved in the second term of the relation. All tetrahedron- and facet-based relations are constant, while the edge- and vertex-based relations, with the exception of the EV one, are variable.

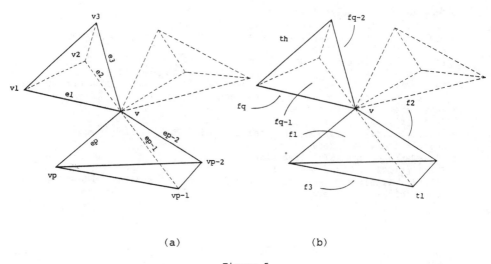

(a)   (b)

Figure 5

The topology of a three-dimensional triangulation is completely and unambiguously represented by the four primitive topological elements (T,F,E,V) together with a suitable subset R' of the set R of the sixteen adjacency relations. The relations in R' must be <u>sufficient</u> to describe TD unambiguously. In other words, it must be possible to retrieve from (T,F,E,V) and R' all relations in R-R' without any error or ambiguity. The VE is an example of a relation which is individually sufficient to describe a 3D tesselation unambiguously [Wei86].

Since encoding too many relations increases the storage cost of the resulting data structure (which will have in any case a quadratic space complexity), it is important to identify minimal subsets of relations which are capable of providing a sufficient topological description of the tesselation and ensuring the efficiency of the basic structure accessing algorithms.

3. The Three-Dimensional Symmetric Data Structure

In this section, we present a generalization to the 3D triangulation of the symmetric data structure which is used in geometric modeling to describe subdivisions of the boundary of a solid object into faces, edges and vertices [Woo85]. The complexity of the data structure is evaluated in terms of the cost of storing the adjacency relations encoded and of the time complexity of the basic structure accessing algorithms which retrieve those relations which are not explicitly encoded into the data structure.

The <u>three-dimensional symmetric data structure</u> encodes the <u>four</u> primitives elements and <u>six</u> relations, namely TF, FE, EV, VE, EF and FT, as described by the adjacency schemata in figure 6. The structure is called symmetric since each relation is stored together with its inverse one.

345

Figure 6

type

```
triangulation = record
                    tlist:^tetrahedron;
                    flist:^facet;
                    elist:^edge;
                    vlist:^vertex
                end

tetrahedron = record
                  nexttetrahedron: ^tetrahedron;
                  mark: boolean;
                  facets: array [0..3] of ^facet
                                             (*Tetrahedron-Facet relation*)
                  end;
facet = record
            nextfacet: ^facet;
            mark: boolean;
            tetrahedra: array [0..1] of ^tetrahedron;
                                             (*Facet-Tetrahedron relation*)
            edges: array [0..2] of ^edge;    (*Facet-Edge relation*)
            orientation: array [0..2] of boolean
        end;
edge = record
            nextedge: ^edge;
            vertices: array [0..1] of ^vertex; (*Edge-Vertex relation*)
            facets: ^facetlist                 (*Edge-facet relation*)
        end;
vertex = record
            nextvertex: ^vertex;
            x,y,z: real;
            edges: ^edgelist                   (*Vertex-Edge relation*)
        end;

facetlist = record
                nextfacet: ^facetlist;
                facet: ^facet
            end;
edgelist = record
               nextedge: ^edgelist;
               edge: ^edge
           end;
```

Figure 7

Figure 7 describes the 3D symmetric structure as a collection of Pascal record
type declarations. Primitive elements of the triangulation are stored in four
linked lists, corresponding to the four classes of elements. Head pointers of
these lists are contained in the fields of the record of type triangulation.
For each element in the triangulation, a record of the appropriate type exist in

the corresponding list. Such a record contains, besides a pointer to the next record in the list, some pointers storing the relations from that element to the other elements in the triangulation. Note that the <u>four</u> constant relations, TF, FT, FE, and EV (denoted by heavy arrows in figure 6), are encoded directly using arrays in the description of the records of type tetrahedron, facet and edge respectively. Encoding the two variable relations (EF and VE) requires two additional linked lists, implemented through records of type facelist and edgelist.

Some boolean fields are added to speed up the structure accessing algorithms described in the next section. The field <u>orientation</u> is used to retrieve the ccw order of the vertices along a facet f. An element of such an array, which corresponds to an edge e joining vertices v1 and v2, assumes the value <u>true</u> when the corresponding edge e appears on the facet f as (v1,v2), the value <u>false</u> when e appears as (v2,v1) on f. Mark fields are used by some structure accessing algorithms (see next section). By taking into account that (i) a facet belongs to the list of the facets associated with its <u>three</u> bounding edges and (ii) an edge belongs to the list of the edges of its <u>two</u> extreme vertices, the storage cost of the symmetric data structure is given by the following expression

$$5t+12f+8e+2n \qquad (3.1)$$

where t, f, e and n denote the number of tetrahedra, facets, edges and vertices of the 3D triangulation. Note that the storage space required for geometrical information or for the boolean fields has not been counted.

The remaining ten adjacency relations not explicitly stored into the structure can be expressed as combination of the six basic ones as described below. Such relations are classified according to their first term.

1. <u>Tetrahedron-based</u> relations
   TT=TF+FT
   TE=TF+FE
   TV=TF+FE+EV

2. <u>Face-based</u> relations
   FF=FT+TF+(FE)
   FV=FE+EV

3. <u>Edge-based</u> relations
   ET=EF+FT
   EE=EF+FE+(EV)

4. <u>Vertex-based</u> relations
   VT=VE+EF+FT
   VF=VE+EF
   VV=VE+EV

Note that tetrahedron- and facet-based relations are combination of constant relations, while the remaining ones are variable relations. Because of our definition of the Edge-Edge relation we need also EV relation to distinguish between the two lists forming EE(e). The same is true for the use of the FE relation in the FF one.

For instance, extracting the Tetrahedron-Edge relation, which means retrieving all the edges which bound a given tetrahedron t requires combining the Tetrahedron-Facet and the Facet-Edge relations, i.e., retrieving the facets bounding t and the bounding edges of each facet. Extracting, for example, the Edge-Tetrahedron relation can be done by concatenating the Edge-Facet and the Facet-Tetrahedron relations. In other words, the tetrahedra of TD sharing a given edge e are obtained by considering the facets of TD sharing e and the tetrahedra sharing each facet. The output size is thus the number of tetrahedra sharing e.

4. Structure Accessing Algorithms

In this section, we describe the algorithms which compute the relations which are not stored in the three-dimensional symmetric data structure classified as in the previous section. We will use the following primitive functions and procedures for manipulating a sorted list L [Aho83] (for some relations the order of the list is not meaningful):

- CREATE_EMPTY_LIST(L): creates an an empty list L.
- IS_AN_ELEMENT(L,x): returns the value _true_ if x is an element of list L; the value _false_ otherwise.
- IS_LAST_ELEMENT(L,x): returns the value _true_ if x is the last element of list L; the value _false_ otherwise.
- FIRST_ELEMENT(L): returns the first element of list L.
- NEXT(L,x): returns the element following x in L (it returns EOL(L), i.e., the end of list, if x is the last element of L).
- INSERT_LIST(L,x): inserts element x at the end of list L.

and the following boolean functions and procedures operating on the data structures storing the 3D triangulation:

- EQUAL(x,y): returns the value _true_ if element x is equal to element y; the value _false_ otherwise (x,y must be both elements of the same type, i.e., tetrahedra, facets, edges or vertices).
- MARK(x): marks element x as visited (it is used only for tetrahedra and facets).
- IS_MARKED(x): returns the value _true_ if element x has been visited, the value _false_ otherwise.
- RESETMARKS: reset marked elements of triangulation.
- IS_EMPTY(t): returns the value _true_ if tetrahedron t is empty; the value _false_ otherwise.

```
Procedure Tetrahedron_Vertex (t,Lv);
(* t:  tetrahedron of TD;
   Lv: list of the vertices belonging to t, i.e.  TV(t) *)
begin
     let TF(t)={f1,f2,f3,f4}; (*TF(t):  set of the facets of t*)
     Facet_Vertex(f1,Lv); (* returns in Lv of the vertices bounding f1*)
     Facet_Vertex(f2,Lv');
     let Lv'=[v1,v2,v3];
     for i:=1 to 3 do
             if not IS_AN_ELEMENT(Lv,vi) then INSERT_LIST(Lv,vi)
end.  (*Tetrahedron_Vertex*)

Procedure Tetrahedron_Edge (t,Le);
(* t:  tetrahedron of TD;
   Le: list of the edges of TD belonging to t, i.e.  TE(t) *)
begin
     CREATE_EMPTY_LIST(Le);
     let TF(t)={f1,f2,f3,f4}; (*TF(t):  set of the facets of t*)
     for i:=1 to 3 do begin
          let FE(fi)=[e1,e2,e3]; (*FE(fi):  sequence of the edges bounding fi*)
          for j:=1 to 3 do
               if not IS_AN_ELEMENT(Le,ej) then INSERT_LIST(Le,ej)
     end  (*for i*)
end.  (*Tetrahedron_Edge*)

Procedure Tetrahedron_Tetrahedron (t,Lt);
(* t:  tetrahedron of TD;
   Lt: list of the tetrahedra adjacent to t along  a  facet,  according  to  the
       order of the facets along the boundary of t, i.e.  TT(t) *)
begin
   CREATE_EMPTY_LIST(Lt);
   let TF(t)={f1,f2,f3,f4};  (*TF(t):  set of the facets of t*)
   for i:=1 to 4 do begin
        let FT(fi)={t1,t2}; (*FT(fi):  pair of tetrahedra sharing facet fi*)
        if EQUAL(t1,t)
```

```
                then INSERT_LIST(Lt,t2)
                else INSERT_LIST(Lt,t1)
        end  (*for*)
end.  (*Tehrahedron_Tetrahedron*)


Procedure Facet_Vertex (f,Lv);
(* f: facet of a tetrahedron of TD;
   Lv: sorted list FV(f) of the vertices bounding f *)
begin
    CREATE_EMPTY_LIST(Lv);
    let FE(f)=[e1,e2,e3];
    (*FE(f):  sequence of the edges bounding f in ccw order*)
    let EV(e1)={v1,v2};  (*EV(e1):  extreme vertices of e1*)
    if IS_CCW(v1,v2,f)
    (* IS_CCW(v1,v2,f) is a local boolean function that returns the value  true
    iff v2 follows v1 according to the ccw order of the edges bounding f *)
        then begin
            INSERT_LIST(Lv,v1);
            INSERT_LIST(Lv,v2)
        end  (*then*)
        else begin
            INSERT_LIST(Lv,v2);
            INSERT_LIST(Lv,v1)
        end;  (*else*)
    let EV(e2)={v3,v4};
    if EQUAL(v3,v1) or EQUAL(v3,v2)
        then INSERT_LIST(Lv,v4)
        else INSERT_LIST(Lv,v3)
end.  (*Facet_Vertex*)


Procedure Facet_Facet (f,Lf);
(* f:  facet of a tetradedron of TD;
   Lf: sorted list FF(f) of the facets pairs which are adjacent to f *)
begin
    CREATE_EMPTY_LIST(Lf);
    let FT(f)={t1,t2}; (*FT(f):  pair of tetrahedra sharing facet f*)
    let FE(f)=[e1,e2,e3]; (*FE(f):  sequence of the edges bounding f*)
    for i:=1 to 3 do begin
        f1i:=ADJACENT_FACET(t1,f,ei);
        (*ADJACENT_FACET(t1,f,ei) returns that facet of t1 (<>f)  which  shares
        edge ei with f.  This function uses relation TF*)
        if IS_EMPTY(t2)
            then INSERT_LIST(Lf,f1i)
            else begin
                f2i:=ADJACENT_FACET(t2,f,ei);
                INSERT_LIST(Lf,(f1i,f2i))
            end  (*else*)
    end  (*for*)
end.  (*Facet_Facet*)
```

The number of operations performed in each of the above procedures is constant.

```
Procedure Edge_Edge(e,Le);
(* e:  edge of a tetradedron of TD;
   Le: list EE(e) of the edges which are adjacent to e *)
begin
    CREATE_EMPTY_LIST(Le1);
    CREATE_EMPTY_LIST(Le2);
    Lf:=EF(e);  (*EF(e):  sequence of the facets sharing e*)
    let EV(e)={v1,v2};  (*EV(e):  extreme vertices of e*)
    f:=FIRST_ELEMENT(Lf);
    while f<>EOL(Lf) do begin
```

```
        Le':=FE(f); (*FE(f): sequence of the edges bounding facet f*)
        e1:=ADJACENT_EDGE(Le',e,v1);
        (*ADJACENT_EDGE(Le',e,v) returns that edge e' (<>e) in the list of
        the edge Le' bounding a given facet f which has v as an extreme
        vertex.  This function uses relation EV*)
        e2:=ADJACENT_EDGE(Le',e,v2);
        INSERT_LIST(Le1,e1);
        INSERT_LIST(Le2,e2);
        f:=NEXT(Lf,f)
    end;  (*while f<>EOF(Lf)*)
    Le:={Le1,Le2}
end.  (*Edge_Edge*)


Procedure Edge_Tetrahedron (e,Lt);
(* e: edge of a tetrahedron of TD;
   Lt: sorted list ET(e) of tetrahedra sharing e *)
begin
    CREATE_EMPTY_LIST(Lt);
    Lf:=EF(e);  (*EF(e): sequence of the facets sharing e*)
    f:=FIRST_ELEMENT(Lf);
    let FT(f)={t1,t2}; (*FT(f): pair of tetrahedra sharing facet f*)
    if IS_EMPTY(t2)
    (*we assume that, if f is on the boundary, t2 is always the empty
    tetrahedron*)
        then INSERT_LIST(Lt,t1)
        else if IS_CCW(t1,t2,e)
        (*IS_CCW(t1,t2,e) is a local boolean function that returns the value
        true, iff t2 follows t1 around e in ccw*)
            then begin
                INSERT_LIST(Lt,t1);
                INSERT_LIST(Lt,t2)
            end  (*then*)
            else begin
                INSERT_LIST(Lt,t2);
                INSERT_LIST(Lt,t1)
            end;  (*else*)
    f:=NEXT(Lf,f);
    while f<>EOL(Lf) do begin
            let FT(f)={t1,t2};
            if IS_LAST_ELEMENT(Lt,t1)
                then if not IS_EMPTY(t2) then INSERT_LIST(Lt,t2)
                else INSERT_LIST(Lt,t1);
            f:=NEXT(Lf,f)
    end  (*while*)
end.  (*Edge_Tetrahedron*)
```

The worst time complexity of procedures Edge_Edge and Edge_Tetrahedron is linear in the number of the facets sharing edge e.

```
Procedure Vertex_Vertex (v,Lv);
(* v:  vertex of a tetrahedron of TD;
   Lv: list VV(v) of other extreme vertices of the edges incident on v *)
begin
    CREATE_EMPTY_LIST(Lv);
    Le:=VE(v);  (*VE(v): set of the edges incident on v*)
    e:=FIRST_ELEMENT(Le);
    while e<>EOL(Le) do begin
            let EV(e)={v1,v2}; (*EV(e): extreme vertices of e*)
            if EQUAL(v1,v) then INSERT_LIST(Lv,v2) else INSERT_LIST(Lv,v1);
            e:=NEXT(Le,e)
    end  (*while*)
end.  (*Vertex_Vertex*)
```

The worst time complexity of procedure Vertex_Vertex is linear in the number of the edges incident on vertex v.

Procedure Vertex_Facet (v,Lf);
(* v: vertex of a tetrahedron of TD;
   Lf: list VF(v) of the facets sharing v *)
begin
    CREATE_EMPTY_LIST(Lf);
    Le:=VE(v); (*VE(v): set of the edges incident on v*)
    e:=FIRST_ELEMENT(Le);
    while e<>EOL(Le) do begin
            Lf':=EF(e); (*EF(e): sequence of the facets sharing e*)
            f:=FIRST_ELEMENT(Lf');
            while f<>EOL(Lf') do begin
                    if not IS_MARKED(f)
                    then begin
                            INSERT_LIST(Lf,f);
                            MARK(f)
                    end; (*then*)
                    f:=NEXT(Lf',f)
            end; (*while f<>EOL(Lf')*)
            e:=NEXT(Le,e)
    end; (*while e<>EOL(Le)*)
    RESET_MARKS;
end. (*Vertex_Facet*)

The worst time complexity of procedure Vertex_Facet is linear in the number of the facets incident on vertex v. Each of such facets is examined exactly two times since it appears in the EF list of its two bounding edges incident on v.

Procedure Vertex_Tetrahedron (v,Lt);
(* v: vertex of a tetrahedron of TD;
   Lt: list VT(v) of the tetrahedra sharing v *)
begin
    CREATE_EMPTY_LIST(Lt);
    Le:=VE(v); (*VE(v): set of the edges incident on v*)
    e:=FIRST_ELEMENT(Le);
    while e<>EOL(Le) do begin
            Edge_Tetrahedron(e,Lt); (* returns in Lt' of the tratrahedra sharing
            e *)
            t:=FIRST_ELEMENT(Lt');
            while t<>EOL(Lt') do begin
                    if not IS_MARKED(t)
                    then begin
                            INSERT_LIST(Lt,t);
                            MARK(t)
                    end; (*then*)
                    t:=NEXT(Lt',t)
            end; (*while t<>EOL(Lt')*)
            e:=NEXT(Le,e)
    end; (*while e<>EOL(Le)*)
    RESET_MARKS;
end. (*Vertex_Tetrahedron*)

By applying the same arguments as for procedure Vertex_Facet, we can prove that the worst time complexity of procedure Vertex_Tetrahedron is linear in the number of tetrahedra sharing vertex v.

Extracting the previous ten relations from the symmetric structure requires a constant number of operations for any constant relation or a number of operations which is linear in the size of the output for any variable relation.

Thus, no relation requires a number of operations which is linear in the total number of tetrahedra, facets, edges or vertices in TD. In this sense, the time complexity of the data structure can be considered optimal since no structure accessing algorithm requires searching the entire data structure. If we eliminate, for instance, the Edge-Vertex relation from the data structure, then retrieving the Edge-Vertex relation (as well as the TV, FV, VV and EV ones) would require examining all the vertices of TD and for each vertex scanning the list of the edges incident on it. The process of retrieving the EV relation would have a complexity which is linear in the total number of vertices and edges of TD.

5. A Minimal Set of Manipulation Primitives

In this section, we define a minimally complete set of primitive operators to build and modify a three-dimensional triangulation. Such operators, that we call Euler operators ensure that the topological validity condition expressed by Euler-Poincare formula in the form given below [Gre67] is always satisfied at each step of the triangulation updating process.

For convenience, we consider the case in which a 3D triangulation consists of several connected components. Each of such components, that we call a volume, is a maximal connected set of tetrahedra. If we denote by v the number of volumes in a 3D triangulation, Euler-Poincare formula becomes

$$n-e+f-t=v \qquad (5.1)$$

The topological validity of a 3D triangulation can be checked by applying formula (5.1). To avoid performing a validity check of a 3D triangulation after each updating, it is convenient to decompose each modification of the triangulation into a sequence of simple atomic steps provided by Euler operators. It can be proven that all valid 3D triangulations consisting of one or more volumes with no holes can be created with a finite sequence of Euler operators, and, conversely, given a 3D triangulation, there exists a finite sequence of operators that completely destroy the triangulation.

By analogy with the case of boundary models [Man88], every 4-tuple of mutually independent operators can be proven to be theoretically sufficient for describing all 3D tesselations satisfying formula (5.1). The set of the primitive operators selected is listed below with an informal description of their effect on the 3D triangulation. Only changes in topological entities are described regardless of any geometric information.

1. Constructive Operators

1. MAKE_VOLUME_VERTEX
   MVV($\overline{vm}$,v): creates a new volume vm by inserting a vertex v.
2. MAKE_EDGE_VERTEX
   MEV($\overline{vm}$,w,e,v): adds a new edge e having one end-point at an existing vertex w and the other one at a new vertex v to volume vm.
3. MAKE_EDGE_FACET
   MEF($\overline{vm}$,e1,e2,f,e): adds a new facet f bounded by the two existing edges e1 and e2 and by a new edge e to volume vm.
4. MAKE_FACET_TETRAHEDRON
   MFT($\overline{vm}$,f1,$\overline{f2}$,f3,t,f): adds a new tetrahedron t bounded by the three existing facets f1, f2, f3 and by the new facet f to volume vm.

2. Inverse Operators

1. KILL_VOLUME_VERTEX
   KVV($\overline{vm}$,v): eliminates a volume vm consisting of a single vertex v.

2. KILL_EDGE_VERTEX
   KEV($\overline{vm}$,e,$\overline{v}$): eliminates edge e and one of its extreme vertices v from volume vm.
3. KILL_EDGE_FACET
   KEF($\overline{vm}$,e,$\overline{f}$): eliminates an edge e and one of the facets f bounded by e from volume vm.
4. KILL_FACET_TETRAHEDRON
   KFT($\overline{vm}$,f,t) eliminates a facet f and one of the tetrahedron t bounded by f from volume vm.

Figure 8 shows an example illustrating the use of the above operators to construct a simple 3D triangulation.

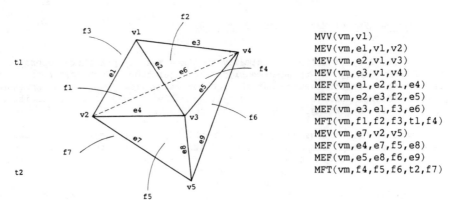

MVV(vm,v1)
MEV(vm,e1,v1,v2)
MEV(vm,e2,v1,v3)
MEV(vm,e3,v1,v4)
MEF(vm,e1,e2,f1,e4)
MEF(vm,e2,e3,f2,e5)
MEF(vm,e3,e1,f3,e6)
MFT(vm,f1,f2,f3,t1,f4)
MEV(vm,e7,v2,v5)
MEF(vm,e4,e7,f5,e8)
MEF(vm,e5,e8,f6,e9)
MFT(vm,f4,f5,f6,t2,f7)

Figure 8

6. Concluding Remarks

The problem of defining a data structure for storing a three-dimensional triangulation has been considered. The 3D symmetric data structure, which stores the form basic topology elements of a 3D tesselation and six ordered adjacency relations, has been defined. We have shown that extracting the ten relations which are not explicitly stored in the structure requires a constant number of operations for any constant relation (namely tetrahedron- and facet-based relations) or a number of operations which is linear in the output size for any variable relation.

A mutual set of primitive operators for building and manipulating a 3D tesselation has been defined. Such operators are independent of the data structure used to store the 3D tesselation and ensure the topological integrity of the tesselation. In other words, the use of such operators ensures that always 3D tesselations of objects bounded by compact oriented two-manifold surfaces and without holes are created at each step of the construction process. The minimality of such operators can be proven by considerations similar to those used by Mantyla [Man88] for proving the minimality of sets of Euler operators defined for boundary models.

Future work involves the investigation of generalizations of the DCEL data structure [Pre85] defined for planar sudivisions or of the modified winged-edge structure [DeF87] defined for two-dimensional triangulations, and comparisons with the 3D symmetric data structure proposed here.

Ackowledgement

The authors are grateful to Jean Daniel Boissonnat for suggesting the problem.

References

[Aho83] Aho, A.F., Hopcroft, J.E., Ullman, J.D., Data Structure and Algorithms, Addison Wesley Publ.,Reading, Ma., 1983.

[Ans85] Ansaldi S., De Floriani L., Falcidieno B., Geometric Modeling of Solid Object by Using a Face Adjacency Graph Representation, Computer Graphics, 19, 3, 1985, pp. 131-139.

[Bau72] Baumgardt, M.G., Winged-Edge Polyhedron Representation, Tech. Rep. CS-320, Stanford University, 1972.

[Boi84] Boissonnat, J.D., Geometric Structures for Three-Dimensional Shape Representation, ACM Trans. on Graphics, 3, 4, pp.266-286.

[Boi88] Boissonnat, J.D., Faugeras, O.D., Le Bras-Mehlman, E., Representing Stereo Data with Delaunay Triangulation, Proceeding IEEE Robotics and Automation, Philadelphia, April 1988.

[Bow81] Bowyer, A., Computing Dirichlet Tesselations, The Computer Journal, 27, 2, pp.165-171.

[DeF87] De Floriani, L., Surface Representations Based on Triangular Grids, The Visual Computer, 3, 1987, pp.27-50.

[Dob87] Dobkin, D.P., Laszlo, M.J., Primitives for the Manipulation of Three-Dimensional Subdivisions, Proc. ACM Conferenceon Computational Geometry, Waterloo, 1987, pp.86-99.

[Gre67] Greenberg, M.J., Lectures on Algebraic Topology, W.A. Benjamin, Inc., New York, 1967.

[Law77] Lawson, C.L., Software for Cl Surface Interpolation, Mathematical Software III edited by J.R. Rice, Academic Press Inc., 1977, pp. 161-164.

[Man88] Mantyla, M., An Introduction to Solid Modeling, Computer Science press, 1988.

[Pre85] Preparata, F.P., Shamos, M.I., Computational Geometry: an Introduction, Springer Verlag, 1985.

[Req81] Requicha, A.A.G., Representation of Rigid Solids: Theory, Methods ans Systems, Computing Surveys, 12, 4, 1981, pp. 437-464.

[Sam84] Samet, H., The Quadtree and Related Hierarchical Data Steructures, Computing Surveys, 16, 2, 1984, pp. 198-260.

[Wat81] Watson, D.F., Computing the n-dimensional Delaunay Tesselation with Applications to Voronoi Polytopes, The Computer Journal, 24, 1981, pp.167-171.

[Wei85] Weiler, K., Edge-based Data Structures for Solid Modeling in Curved-surface Environments, IEEE Computer Graphcs and Applications, 5, 1, 1985, pp.21-40.

[Wei86] Weiler, K., Topological Structures for Geometric Modeling, Ph.D. Thesis, Rensselaer Polytecnic Institute, Troy (NY), August 1986.

[Woo85] Woo, T.C., A Combinatorial Analysis of Boundary Data Structure Schemata, IEEE Computer Graphics and Applications, 5, 3, 1985, pp.19-27.

The Arc Tree: An Approximation Scheme
To Represent Arbitrary Curved Shapes

Oliver Günther
Department of Computer Science
University of California
Santa Barbara, CA 93106

Eugene Wong
Department of EECS
University of California
Berkeley, CA 94720

Abstract

This paper introduces the *arc tree*, a hierarchical data structure to represent arbitrary curved shapes. The arc tree is a balanced binary tree that represents a curve of length l such that any subtree whose root is on the k-th tree level is representing a subcurve of length $l/2^k$. Each tree level is associated with an approximation of the curve; lower levels correspond to approximations of higher resolution. Based on this hierarchy of detail, queries such as point search or intersection detection and computation can be solved in a hierarchical manner. We compare the arc tree to several related schemes and present the results of a practical performance analysis for various kinds of set and search operators. We also discuss several options to embed arc trees as complex objects in an extensible database management system and argue that the embedding as an abstract data type is most promising.

1. Introduction

The exact representation of curved geometric objects in finite machines is only possible if the objects can be described by finite mathematical expressions. Typical examples for such objects are paraboloids or ellipses, which can be described by functional equations such as $x^2/a^2+y^2/b^2=1$. Many applications, however, especially in computer vision and robotics, do not fit this pattern. The objects to be represented are rather arbitrary in shape, and some approximation scheme has to be employed to represent the data. Any finite machine can only store an approximate representation of the data with limited accuracy. In particular, the answer to any query is based on this approximate representation and may therefore be approximate as well.

Of course, the initial description of a curved object, coming from a camera, a tactile sensor, a mouse, or a digitizer may already be an *approximate* description of the real object. In most practical applications, this description will be a sequence of curve points or a spline, i.e. a piecewise polynomial function that is smooth and continuous. To support set, search, and recognition operators, however, it is more efficient to represent the data by a *hierarchy of detail* [Same84, Hopc87], i.e. a hierarchy of approximations, where higher levels in the hierarchy correspond to coarser approximations of the curve. Geometric operators can then be computed in a hierarchical manner: algorithms start out near the root of the hierarchy and try to answer the given query at a very coarse resolution. If that is not possible, the resolution is increased where necessary. In other words, algorithms "zoom in" on those parts of the curve that are relevant for the given query.

In this paper, we develop this theme of hierarchy of detail, focusing on the *arc tree*, a balanced binary tree that serves as an approximation scheme to represent arbitrary curved shapes. Section 2 gives a definition of the arc tree and shows how to obtain the arc tree representation of a given curve. Section 3 generalizes the concept of the arc tree to include other hierarchical curve representation schemes such as Ballard's strip trees [Ball81] and Bezier curves [Bezi74, Pavl82]. Sections 4 and 5 show how to perform point queries and set operations, such as union or intersection. Both sections also discuss the performance of our arc tree implementation. Section 6 outlines how to embed arc trees into an extensible database system such as POSTGRES [Ston86a], and section 7 contains a summary and our conclusions.

2. Definition

A *curve* is a one-dimensional continuous point set in d-dimensional Euclidean space E^d. For simplicity, this presentation is restricted to the case $d=2$. The generalization to arbitrary d (with the curve remaining one-dimensional) is straightforward. A curve is *open* if it has two distinct endpoints, otherwise it is called *closed*; see figure 1 for some examples. As mentioned in the introduction, in practical applications, curves are usually given as a polygonal path, i.e. a sequence of curve points, or as a spline, i.e. a piecewise polynomial function that is smooth and continuous.

Figure 1: A closed and two open curves.

The arc tree scheme parametrizes a given curve according to its arc length and approximates it by a sequence of polygonal paths. Let the curve C have length l and be defined by a function $C(t):[0,1]\rightarrow E^2$, such that the length of the curve from $C(0)$ to $C(t_0)$ is $t_0 \cdot l$. The *k-th approximation* C_k ($k=0,1,2...$) of C is a polygonal path consisting of 2^k line segments $e_{k,i}$ ($i=1..2^k$), such that $e_{k,i}$ connects the two points $C(\frac{i-1}{2^k})$ and $C(\frac{i}{2^k})$. See figure 2 for an example.

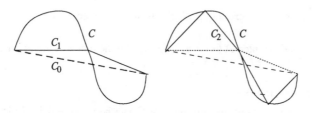

Figure 2: A 0th, 1st and 2nd approximation of a curve

Each edge $e_{k,i}$ can be associated with an arc $a_{k,i}$ of length $l/2^k$, which is a continuous subset of C. $C(\frac{i-1}{2^k})$ and $C(\frac{i}{2^k})$ are the common endpoints of $e_{k,i}$ and $a_{k,i}$. For $k\geq 1$, each k-th approximation is a refinement of the corresponding $(k-1)$-th approximation: the vertex set of the $(k-1)$-th approximation is a true subset of the vertex set of the k-th approximation.

More formally, the k-th approximation of C is defined by a piecewise linear function $C_k:[0,1]\rightarrow E^2$ as follows. Here, $\underline{t}$ and $\overline{t}$ denote $\frac{\lfloor t \cdot 2^k \rfloor}{2^k}$ and $\frac{\lceil t \cdot 2^k \rceil}{2^k}$, respectively.

$$C_k(t) = \begin{cases} C(t) & t \cdot 2^k = 0..2^k \\ \dfrac{\overline{t}-t}{\overline{t}-\underline{t}} \cdot C(\underline{t}) + \dfrac{\overline{t}-t}{\overline{t}-\underline{t}} \cdot C(\overline{t}) & \text{otherwise} \end{cases} \qquad t \in [0,1]$$

There are various criteria in common use that measure the error between a curve C and its k-th polygonal approximation C_k [Imai86]. In the case of the arc tree, one could use the maximum distance between a curve point and the corresponding point of the approximation:

$$\max_{0 \le t \le 1} d(C_k(t), C(t))$$

Here, d denotes Euclidean distance. This criterion will be referred to as (e1). Other possibilities include the maximum distance between a line segment $e_{k,i}$ and the curve points on the corresponding arc $a_{k,i}$ (criterion e2):

$$\max_{0 \le t \le 1} d(e_{k, \lceil t \cdot 2^k \rceil}, C(t))$$

or the maximum distance between the *line* containing $e_{k,i}$ (denoted by *line* $(e_{k,i})$) and the arc $a_{k,i}$ (criterion e3). For brevity reasons, the following theorem is presented without proof.

Theorem 1: According to any of the error criteria described above, the error between a curve C and its k-th approximation C_k is no more than $1/2^{k+1}$. $\square$

Lemma 2: Using any of the above error criteria, the sequence of approximation functions $(C_k(t))$ converges uniformly towards $C(t)$.

Proof: It follows from theorem 1 that the error converges towards zero for $k \to \infty$, which proves the lemma. $\square$

Moreover, for each approximation C_k there is a well-defined area that contains the curve. We have

Lemma 3: Let $E_{k,i}$ denote the ellipse whose major axis is $1/2^k$ and whose focal points are the two endpoints of the edge $e_{k,i}$, $C(\frac{i-1}{2^k})$ and $C(\frac{i}{2^k})$. Then the arc $a_{k,i}$ is internal to $E_{k,i}$.

Proof: (by contradiction) Let $X \in a_{k,i}$ denote a point external to $E_{k,i}$. Then

$$d(X, C(\frac{i-1}{2^k})) + d(X, C(\frac{i}{2^k})) > 1/2^k$$

Thus, the length of $a_{k,i}$ would be greater than $1/2^k$ which is a contradiction. $\square$

Corollary 4: The curve C is internal to the area formed by the union of the bounding ellipses, $\bigcup\limits_{i=0}^{2^k} E_{k,i}$

$(k=0, 1, ..)$. $\square$

See figure 3 for an example.

The family of approximations of a given curve C can be stored efficiently in a binary tree. The root of the tree contains the three points $C(0)$, $C(1/2)$ and $C(1)$ and is considered on level 0. If a tree node on level i contains point $C(\frac{x}{2^{i+1}})$ $(x=1 .. 2^{i+1}-1)$, then its left son contains point $C(\frac{2x-1}{2^{i+2}})$, and its right son contains point $C(\frac{2x+1}{2^{i+2}})$. We call this tree the *arc tree* of the curve C. The arc tree is an exact representation of C; each of its subtrees represents a continous subset of C. An inorder traversal of the first k $(k \ge 0)$ levels of the arc tree yields the vertices of the $(k+1)$-th approximation, sorted by increasing t. On the other hand, a breadth-first traversal of the first k levels yields these vertices in an order such that the first 2^i+1 vertices form the i-th approximation of C $(i=1,2 .. k+1)$. See figure 4 for an example.

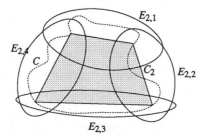

Figure 3: A curve C with its 2nd approximation C_2 and corresponding ellipses $E_{2,i}$.

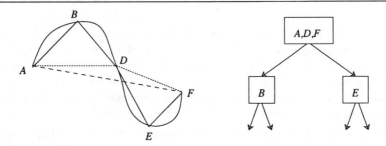

Figure 4: A curve with approximations and its arc tree. For a closed curve, it is $A = F$.

In practice, only a finite number of levels of the arc tree is stored. An arc tree with r levels is called an arc tree of *resolution* r. It is a balanced binary tree and it represents the 0th through $(r+1)$-th approximation of C.

An arc tree of resolution r can be constructed in two traversals of the given curve C. In the first round, one determines the length l of C. If C is a spline (or a polygonal path), l can be computed using the following formula for the arc length of an analytical curve. If the curve is given by $y = f(x)$, its length between the points $P_1(x_1, y_1)$ and $P_2(x_2, y_2)$ is

$$l = \int_{x_1}^{x_2} \sqrt{1 + f'^2(x)}\, dx$$

If it is given by $x = x(t)$, $y = y(t)$, its arc length is

$$l = \int_{t_1}^{t_2} \sqrt{x'^2(t) + y'^2(t)}\, dt$$

with $x_i = x(t_i)$ and $y_i = y(t_i)$. One may also attach a label to each knot of C indicating the length accumulated so far. This does not require any additional computation, but it will speed up the second round. In the second round, one picks up the curve points $C(\frac{i}{2^r})$ ($i \in \{0, 1..2^r\}$) and inserts them into the appropriate tree nodes while performing an inorder traversal of the tree.

Note that arc trees can be used to represent any given curve that can be parametrized with respect to arc length. This requirement poses no problem if the input curve is given as a polygonal path or a spline. Nevertheless, there remain problems with some curves such as fractals, for example [Mand77], or with curves that are distorted by high-frequency noise. In both cases the concept of arc length becomes somewhat meaningless and it is necessary to smooth the curve first before the parametrization can take place.

3. Generalization

The arc tree parametrizes the given curve by arc length and localizes it by means of bounding ellipses. At higher resolutions the number of ellipses increases, but their total area decreases, thus providing a better localization.

The arc tree can be viewed as just one instance of a large class of approximation schemes that implement a hierarchy of detail. Higher levels in the hierarchy correspond to coarser approximations of the curve. Associated with each approximation is a *bounding area* that contains the curve. Set and search operators are computed in a hierarchical manner: algorithms start out near the root of the hierarchy and try to solve the given problem at a very coarse resolution. If that is not possible, the resolution is increased where necessary.

In this section we will present several approximation schemes that are based on the same principle, but that use different parametrizations or bounding areas. For all of these schemes, it is fairly straightforward to obtain the representation of a given curve. Moreover, the algorithms for the computation of set and search operators are very similar to the corresponding arc tree algorithms, which are presented in sections 4 and 5. It is a subject of further research to conduct a detailed practical comparison of these schemes to find out which schemes are suited best for certain classes of curves.

The first modification of the arc tree concerns the choice of the ellipses $E_{k,i}$ as bounding areas. These ellipses provide the tightest possible bound but, on the other hand, ellipses are fairly complex objects, which has a negative impact on the performance of this scheme. For example, it is often necessary to test two bounding areas for intersection; if the bounding areas are ellipses, this operation is rather costly. Our implementation showed that it is in fact sometimes more efficient to replace the ellipses by their bounding circles; see section 5.1. The circles provide a poorer localization of the curve, but they are easier to handle computationally, which caused the total performance to improve. Other alternatives would be to use bounding boxes whose axes are parallel to the coordinate axes or to the axes of the ellipses. Both of these approaches, however, proved to be less effective than the bounding circles.

If the curves to be represented are polygonal paths with relatively few vertices, it is more efficient to break up the polygonal paths at their vertices rather than to introduce artificial vertices $C(\frac{i}{2^k})$ ($i = 1 .. 2^k - 1$). If a polygonal path has $n+1$ vertices $v_1 .. v_{n+1}$, it can be represented *exactly* by a *polygon arc tree* of depth $\lceil \log_2 n \rceil$ as follows. The root of the polygon arc tree contains the vertices v_1, $v_{\lceil n/2 \rceil + 1}$, and v_{n+1}. Its left son contains the vertex $v_{\lceil n/4 \rceil + 1}$, its right son the vertex $v_{\lceil 3/4 \cdot n \rceil + 1}$, and so on, until all vertices are stored. Clearly, the arc length corresponding to a node is no more implicit; it has to be stored explicitly with each node. In particular, at each node N it is necessary to know the lengths of the subcurves corresponding to N's left and right subtree. An example is given in figure 5.

It is easily seen that some of this length data is redundant. Indeed, with some care it is sufficient to store only one arc length datum per node. For this reason, the storage requirements for a polygon arc tree are only about 20% to 40% higher than for a regular arc tree of the same depth.

A data structure closely related to the polygon arc tree is the *Binary Searchable Polygonal Representation (BSPR)* proposed by Burton [Burt77].

There are other structures that also implement some hierarchy of detail. One of them is the *strip tree*, introduced by Ballard [Ball81]. As the arc tree, the strip tree represents a given curve C by a

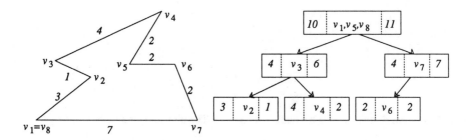

Figure 5: A polygon and corresponding polygon arc tree. The numbers in italics denote arc length.

binary tree such that each subtree T represents a continuous part C_T of C. C_T is approximated by the line segment connecting its endpoints (x_b,y_b) and (x_e,y_e). The root node of T stores these two end-points and two widths w_l and w_r, thus defining a bounding rectangle S_T (the *strip*) that tightly encloses the curve segment C_T. S_T has the same length as the line segment $((x_b,y_b),(x_e,y_e))$ and its sides are parallel or perpendicular to it. See figure 6 for an example of a curve and a corresponding strip tree. Clearly, this approach requires some extensions for closed curves and for curves that extend beyond their endpoints (fig. 7).

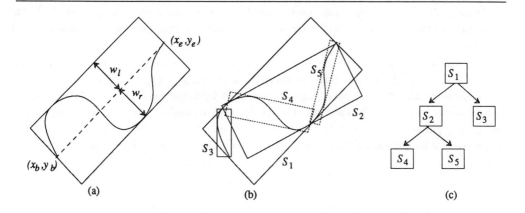

Figure 6: A curve with strip, a hierarchy of strips, and a corresponding strip tree.

When a strip tree is constructed for a given curve C, a curve segment C_T is subdivided further until the total strip width w_l+w_r is below a certain threshold. As it is a non-trivial operation to obtain the strip S_T for every curve segment C_T, the construction of a strip tree for a given curve may be quite costly. To subdivide C_T, one can choose any point of C_T that lies on the boundary of the corresponding strip S_T. Clearly, a strip tree is not necessarily balanced, which has a negative impact on its average-case performance. Note that arc trees are always balanced, which might give them an edge over strip trees in terms of average performance.

Also, a strip tree requires about twice as much space as an arc tree of same depth: each arc tree node stores a minimum of two real numbers and two pointers, whereas a strip tree node stores six real

Figure 7: A curve C that extends beyond its endpoints. There is no bounding box of length l that contains C.

numbers and two pointers. Note, however, that strip trees can be modified to require less storage. First, all subdivision points belong to more than one strip and are therefore stored in more than one node. The redundant data may be replaced by pointers or deleted; in the latter case, the strip tree algorithms given by Ballard would have to be somewhat modified. Second, rather than storing w_l and w_r, one may just store the maximum of these two widths. The corresponding strip is potentially wider and provides a poorer localization. In both cases, some loss in performance is likely, but it will probably be minor compared to the savings in storage space.

A generalization of the strip tree to higher dimensions is possible. The *prism tree* of Ponce and Faugeras, for example [Ponc87], approximates free-form solids in three dimensions by means of truncated pyramids. The arc tree, on the other hand, does not have an immediate equivalent in higher dimensions because the parametrization method (by arc length) is impractical to generalize to curved surfaces.

A very different approach to implement a hierarchy of detail is based on curve fitting techniques such as *Bezier curves* [Bezi74] or *B-splines* [Debo78]; see also [Pavl82] for a good survey of these and related techniques. A Bezier curve of degree m is an m-th degree polynomial function defined by $m+1$ *guiding points* $P_1 .. P_{m+1}$. The curve goes through the points P_1 and P_{m+1} and passes near the remaining guiding points $P_2 .. P_m$ in a well-defined manner. The points P_2 through P_m may be relocated interactively to bring the Bezier curve into the desired form. See figure 8 for two examples.

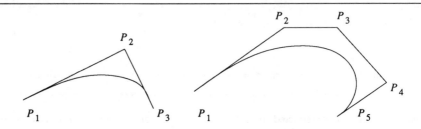

Figure 8: Examples of Bezier polynomials with three and five guiding points.

It can be shown that a Bezier curve lies within the corresponding *characteristic polygon*, i.e. the convex hull of its guiding points. Also, a Bezier curve B can be subdivided into two Bezier curves B_1 and B_2 of same degree. The characteristic polygons of B_1 and B_2 are disjoint and subsets of B's characteristic polygon. They therefore provide a better localization of B; see figure 9.

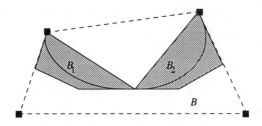

Figure 9: A Bezier curve B subdivided into two curves B_1 and B_2 with characteristic polygons.

Now we can derive a hierarchical representation of a given Bezier curve B as follows. The first approximation is the edge segment connecting B's endpoints; its bounding area is given by B's characteristic polygon. The second approximation is the polygonal path connecting the endpoints of B_1 and B_2; its bounding area is the union of the characteristic polygons of B_1 and B_2, and so on. There are various efficient subdivision algorithms to obtain B_1 and B_2 from a given B; see for example [Pavl82], pp. 221-230.

The main problem with this approach seems to be that not every curve can be approximated well by a low-order Bezier curve. A high-order Bezier curve, however, is harder to subdivide and has a more complex characteristic polygon, which has an adverse impact on the performance of this scheme. In practice, complex curves are often approximated by *several* third-order Bezier curves. This would mean that the bounding area of the first approximation is a union of convex polygons, which is already rather complex. Further approximations are then obtained by subdivisions of each one of these polygons. Nevertheless, this approach seems very promising and should be included in a practical comparison of the various approaches to implement a hierarchy of detail.

We expect arc or strip trees to be superior to Bezier curves if the curves to be represented are initially described by a long sequence of curve points and can only be described by high-order splines or a large number of simpler splines. This is often the case if curves are input from a digitizer pad or a mouse. On the other hand, if a curve is initially given by a few simple splines, it is probably more efficient to keep this representation and use spline subdivision algorithms as described above to implement a hierarchy of detail.

B-splines can be used in a way similar to Bezier curves to implement a hierarchy of detail. For appropriate subdivision algorithms, see [Bohm84].

Certainly, there are many more possibilities to implement a hierarchy of detail as a tree structure similar to the schemes presented above. Note that in all of these schemes it is possible to trade space with time as follows. Rather than storing all lower level approximations explicitly, one could keep the source description of the curve in main memory and compute finer approximations "on the fly" when needed. This approach can be viewed as a *procedural arc tree* as finer approximations are defined procedurally, i.e. by means of the appropriate subdivision algorithm that computes finer approximations from coarser ones. This approach seems particularly promising for the Bezier approach where highly efficient subdivision algorithms are available. In the case of arc and strip trees, the computations to obtain finer approximations are probably too complex to be repeated at every tree traversal.

As mentioned above, the algorithms for set and search operations for these various approximation schemes are all essentially the same. In the following two sections, we give the algorithms for the arc tree scheme. In most cases, the corresponding algorithms for the other schemes are simply obtained by replacing the ellipses $E_{k,i}$ by the corresponding bounding areas, viz., the characteristic polygons for the curve fitting approaches or the strips for the strip tree.

4. Hierarchical Point Inclusion Test

To demonstrate the power of the arc tree representation scheme, we first show how to answer point queries on the arc tree. Given a point $A \in E^2$ and a simple (i.e. non self-intersecting) closed curve C, a point query asks if A is internal to the point set enclosed by C, $P(C)$. For simplicity, we also describe this case by stating that A is internal to C, or that $A \in P(C)$.

The point inclusion test is performed by a hierarchical algorithm called $HPOINT$, which starts with some simple approximation C_{app} of C. For each edge $e_{k,i}$ of C_{app} ($i=1..2^k$), it checks if the replacement of $e_{k,i}$ by the arc $a_{k,i}$ may affect the internal/external classification of A. If there is no such edge $e_{k,i}$, then $A \in P(C_{app})$ is equivalent to $A \in P(C)$; $HPOINT$ uses a conventional algorithm for polygons to solve the point query $A \in P(C_{app})$? and terminates with that result. Otherwise, $HPOINT$ replaces each edge $e_{k,i}$, whose replacement by $a_{k,i}$ may affect A's classification, by the two edges $e_{k+1,2i-1}$ and $e_{k+1,2i}$. $HPOINT$ proceeds with the resulting polygon, which is a closer approximation of C.

If the maximum resolution has been reached without obtaining a result, then the problem cannot be decided at that resolution. In fact, there are boundary points (such as $C(\frac{1}{3})$) that cannot be decided at *any* finite resolution. There are three ways to resolve this situation: (i) the algorithm returns *unclear*, (ii) the algorithm considers the point a boundary point, or (iii) the arc tree is extended at its leaf nodes to include the source description of the curve; then, edges $e_{k,i}$ may eventually be replaced by arcs $a_{k,i}$ to allow an exact query evaluation. For $HPOINT$, we choose option (ii), thus considering the boundary as having a nonzero width. In our definition of the point inclusion test, where the given point set $P(C)$ is closed, $HPOINT$ returns $A \in P(C)$, accordingly.

We are left with the problem of how to find out quickly if the replacement of $e_{k,i}$ by $a_{k,i}$ may affect the internal/external classification of A. From lemma 3, we obtain

Lemma 5: Let $C_{k,i}$ denote the curve obtained from C by replacing the arc $a_{k,i}$ by the straight line $e_{k,i}$. If A is external to $E_{k,i}$ then $A \in P(C)$ is equivalent to $A \in P(C_{k,i})$.

Proof: Because A is external to $E_{k,i}$, A may not lie on or between $a_{k,i}$ and $e_{k,i}$. Therefore, the replacement of $a_{k,i}$ by $e_{k,i}$ may not affect the internal/external classification of A. $\qquad\square$

It is therefore sufficient to check if A is internal to $E_{k,i}$. If yes, the replacement of $e_{k,i}$ by $a_{k,i}$ may affect the classification of A, otherwise it may not. Letting the initial approximation be C_0, $HPOINT$ can be described more precisely as follows.

Algorithm HPOINT

Input: A point $A \in E^2$. The arc tree T_C of a simple closed curve C.

Output: $A \in P(C)$?

(1) Set the approximation polygon C_{app} to C_0, k to zero, and tag the edge $e_{0,1}$ of C_{app}.

(2) For each tagged edge $e_{k,i}$ ($i \in \{1..2^k\}$) of C_{app}, check if A is external to the ellipse $E_{k,i}$. If yes, untag $e_{k,i}$.

(3) If C_{app} has no tagged edges left, use a conventional point inclusion algorithm for polygons to determine if $A \in P(C_{app})$, return the result and stop.

(4) Otherwise, if k is less than the maximum resolution, $depth(T_C)$, replace each tagged edge $e_{k,i}$ by the two tagged edges $e_{k+1,2i-1}$ and $e_{k+1,2i}$, increase k by one and repeat from (2).

(5) Otherwise, A is a boundary point; return $true$ and stop.

Step (2) can easily be done by computing the distances from A to the two focal points of $E_{k,i}$. Step (4) can be performed by using C's arc tree in the following manner. Each edge $e_{k,i}$ is associated with the subtree whose root contains the point $C(\frac{2i-1}{2^{k+1}})$. Note that this is the curve point which corresponds to the center point of $e_{k,i}$ and which $e_{k+1,2i-1}$ and $e_{k+1,2i}$ have in common. If $e_{k,i}$ is to be replaced by $e_{k+1,2i-1}$ and $e_{k+1,2i}$, HPOINT obtains that point from the tree node and continues recursively on both subtrees of this node.

Steps (2) and (4) can now be performed during a top-down traversal of the arc tree. Each subtree can be processed independently of the others, which offers a natural way to parallelize the algorithm. If C_{app} has no more tagged edges, then the partial results are collected in a bottom-up traversal of the tree and put together to form the boundary of the final approximation polygon C_{app}. At this point, $A \in P(C)$ is equivalent to $A \in P(C_{app})$. Step (4) can be performed by Shamos' algorithm, where one constructs a horizontal line L through A and counts the intersections between L and the edges of C_{app} that lie to the left of A. If the number of intersections is odd, then A is internal, otherwise it is external. Shamos' algorithm requires some special maintenance for horizontal edges; see [Prep85] for details.

We implemented this algorithm on a VAX 8800 and ran several experiments to see how HPOINT's time complexity correlates with the complexity of the given curve C and with the location of A with respect to C. Our running times should not be considered in absolute terms as we did not make a great effort to optimize our code. However, the figures are appropriate for comparative measurements. Figures 10 and 11 show our results. Here, t is CPU time in ms, and r is the resolution at which the query was decided. The dotted polygons are the final approximations C_{app}, respectively.

Note that the use of alternative approximation schemes is unlikely to improve the performance of our algorithms. To test a given point for inclusion in a given ellipse has about the same complexity as the corresponding tests for a characteristic polygon (say, a convex quadrilateral) or a strip. On the other hand, the test is somewhat easier for circles or for boxes whose axes are parallel to the coordinate axes. In both cases, however, the localization of the curve that is provided by these areas is poorer than for the bounding areas above.

Our algorithm HPOINT is an application of the idea of *hierarchy of detail*, as described by Samet [Same84] or Hopcroft and Krafft [Hopc87]. It solves the point inclusion problem by starting with a very simple representation of C and introduces more complex representations only if they are required to solve the problem. The algorithm "zooms in" on those parts of C that are interesting in the sense that they may change the internal/external classification of the point A at a higher resolution. As our examples demonstrate, HPOINT terminates very quickly if A is not close to C. The closer A gets to C, the higher is the resolution required to answer the point query. Due to a quick localization of the interesting parts of C, the algorithm does not show the quadratic growth in the complexity of C that a worst-case analysis would predict.

5. Hierarchical Set Operations

In this section, we show how to detect and compute intersections between curves. Other set operations such as union or difference or set operations on areas can be computed in a similar manner [Gunt88]. Again, the idea is to inspect approximations of the input curves by increasing resolution and

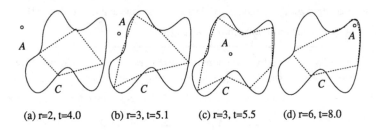

(a) r=2, t=4.0   (b) r=3, t=5.1   (c) r=3, t=5.5   (d) r=6, t=8.0

Figure 10: C is a spline with 12 knots.

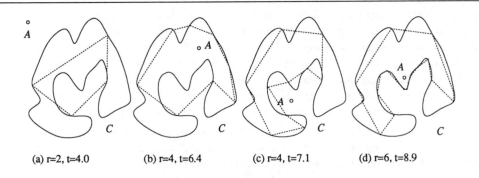

(a) r=2, t=4.0   (b) r=4, t=6.4   (c) r=4, t=7.1   (d) r=6, t=8.9

Figure 11: C is a spline with 36 knots.

to "zoom in" on those parts of the boundaries that may participate in an intersection.

5.1. Curve-Curve Intersection Detection

We first show how to test two given curves C and D for intersection. The hierarchical algorithm *HCURVES* starts with simple approximations C_{app} and D_{app} of C and D, respectively, and continues with approximations of higher resolutions where necessary. For brevity, the following lemma is presented without proof.

Lemma 6: The arcs $a_{k,i}$ and $b_{k,j}$ corresponding to the edges $e_{k,i}$ of C_{app} and $f_{k,j}$ of D_{app}, respectively, *must* intersect if the following three conditions are met:

(i) $e_{k,i}$ intersects $f_{k,j}$,

(ii) the two endpoints of $e_{k,i}$ are external to the ellipse $F_{k,j}$ corresponding to $f_{k,j}$,

(iii) the two endpoints of $f_{k,j}$ are external to the ellipse $E_{k,i}$ corresponding to $e_{k,i}$. $\square$

Now the algorithm *HCURVES* proceeds as follows. For each pair of edges, $e_{k,i}$ of C_{app} and $f_{k,j}$ of D_{app} $(i,j \in \{0,1..2^k\})$, *HCURVES* checks if their corresponding arcs *may* intersect. According to lemma 3, this can be done by testing if the corresponding ellipses $E_{k,i}$ and $F_{k,j}$ intersect. If yes, *HCURVES* puts tags on $e_{k,i}$ and $f_{k,j}$ and applies lemma 6 to see if the arcs *must* intersect. If yes, *HCURVES* reports an intersection and stops. After all pairs of edges have been processed, *HCURVES* checks if there are any tagged edges. If no, *HCURVES* reports no intersection and stops. Otherwise,

HCURVES replaces all tagged edges by the corresponding edges of the next higher approximation, increases k by one, and proceeds with the refined curves. If the maximum resolution has been reached and there are still tagged edges, *HCURVES* interprets the situation as an intersection of the boundaries and returns an intersection. More exactly, *HCURVES* can be described as follows.

Algorithm HCURVES

Input: The arc trees T_C and T_D of two curves C and D.

Output: $C \cap D \neq \phi$?

(1) Set the approximation polygons C_{app} to C_0, D_{app} to D_0, and k to zero.

(2) For each pair of edges $e_{k,i}$ of C_{app} and $f_{k,j}$ of D_{app} do

    (2a) Check if the two ellipses $E_{k,i}$ and $F_{k,j}$ intersect.

    (2b) If yes, tag $e_{k,i}$ and $f_{k,j}$; if conditions (i) through (iii) in lemma 6 are met or if $e_{k,i}$ and $f_{k,j}$ share one or two endpoints, return *true* and stop.

(3) If there are no tagged edges, return *false* and stop.

(4) If k is less than the maximum resolution, $\min(depth\,(T_C), depth\,(T_D))$, replace each tagged edge $e_{k,i}$ of C_{app} by the two edges $e_{k+1,2i-1}$ and $e_{k+1,2i}$. Similarly for each tagged edge $f_{k,j}$ of D_{app}. Increase k by one and repeat from (2).

(5) Otherwise, the maximum resolution has been reached; return *true* and stop.

We implemented this algorithm on a VAX 8800 with a few slight modifications to speed up execution. First, the test if the two ellipses $E_{k,i}$ and $F_{k,j}$ intersect is replaced by a test if the two circumscribing circles of $E_{k,i}$ and $F_{k,j}$ intersect. If those do not intersect then the ellipses do not intersect either. Otherwise, we assume that the ellipses may intersect and proceed accordingly. We made several experiments with more accurate tests, such as to test bounding boxes of the two ellipses for intersection, or to test the two ellipses themselves for intersection. In every case, the execution times went up between 25% and 60%. The more accurate tests required a significant amount of CPU time, but they only marginally reduced the number of tagged edges.

Second, rather than performing step (2) for each pair of edges $e_{k,i}$ of C_{app} and $f_{k,j}$ of D_{app}, we maintain a list to keep track which pairs of ellipses $(E_{k,i}, F_{k,j})$ pass the intersection test in step (2a). Then, step (2) is executed for a pair of edges $(e_{k,i}, f_{k,j})$ if and only if the ellipses $E_{k-1,\lceil i/2 \rceil}$ and $F_{k-1,\lceil j/2 \rceil}$, which correspond to their parent edges, intersect. Otherwise, it is known in advance that $E_{k,i}$ and $F_{k,j}$ do not intersect.

Figures 12 and 13 give several examples for the performance of the algorithm. Here, r denotes the resolution at which the algorithm is able to decide the query, and t denotes the CPU time in *ms*.

Again, it is not clear if the use of alternative approximation schemes might yield a better performance. The crucial operation in algorithm *HCURVES* is the test if two bounding areas intersect. In the case of circles, this is a trivial operation: two circles intersect if the distance between their centers is no more than the sum of their radii. The corresponding tests for boxes or characteristic polygons (say, convex quadrilaterals) are about two to three times as complex.

Note that the running times do not grow quadratically with the complexity of the input curves. The example in figure 13 (b) requires a large amount of CPU time due to the fact that the two curves are quite interwoven but do not intersect. It is therefore necessary to get down to fairly high resolutions in order to determine that there is no intersection. It seems that a case like this will require a lot of

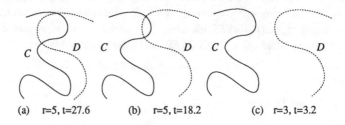

(a)   r=5, t=27.6   (b)   r=5, t=18.2   (c)   r=3, t=3.2

Figure 12: C is a spline with 13 knots, D a spline with 8 knots.

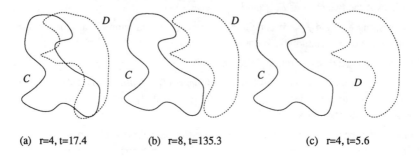

(a)   r=4, t=17.4   (b)   r=8, t=135.3   (c)   r=4, t=5.6

Figure 13: C is a spline with 24 knots, D a spline with 23 knots.

computation with any other intersection detection algorithm as well.

5.2. Curve-Curve Intersection Computation

The intersection is actually computed by the hierarchical algorithm $HCRVCRV$, which is a variation of algorithm $HCURVES$. $HCRVCRV$ does not test if two arcs *must* intersect, but continues the refinement until one of the following two conditions is met: (i) there are no more tagged edges, or (ii) the maximum resolution has been reached. In case (i), C and D do not intersect. In case (ii), each tagged edge of C_{app} is tested for intersection with each tagged edge of D_{app}. If two edges intersect, the intersection points are computed and returned.

We implemented this algorithm on a VAX 8800 with the same modifications as in the case of $HCURVES$. Figures 14 and 15 give two examples for the performance of the algorithm at various maximum resolutions r. P is an intersection point, d is the distance between P and its approximation, C_{app} and D_{app} are C's and D's final approximations, and t is CPU time required to compute all intersections.

Note that the running times do not increase quadratically with the number of edges, 2^r, or with the complexity of the input curves. In fact, the increase in CPU time is about cubical in r, i.e. polylogarithmic in the number of edges. The plot in figure 16 shows the increase in CPU time for both figures and for resolutions $r=2$ through $r=7$. The broken lines indicate the distance d between the actual intersection point P and the corresponding intersection point returned by the algorithm at maximum resolution r.

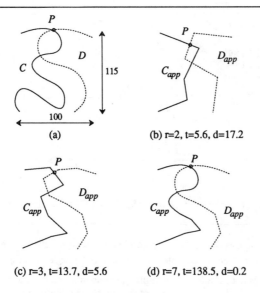

Figure 14: C is a spline with 13 knots, D a spline with 8 knots.

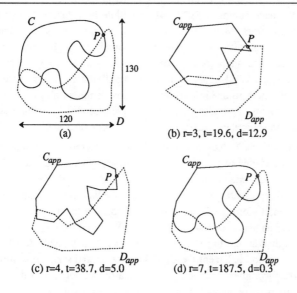

Figure 15: Both C and D are splines with 20 knots.

6. Implementation in a Database System

As the previous sections have shown, the arc tree is an efficient scheme to represent curves. In large-scale geometric applications such as geography or robotics, is is usually most efficient to have a separate data management component and to maintain a geometric database to store a large number of

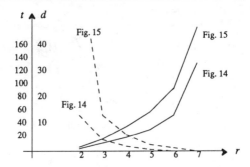

Figure 16: CPU time t and error d of algorithm *HCRVCRV* at various resolutions r.

geometric objects. In order to use the arc tree representation scheme efficiently in this context, it is therefore necessary to embed arc trees as complex objects in the database system.

There are three major ways to implement complex objects in an extensible relational database system such as POSTGRES [Ston86a], DASDBS [Paul87], or XRS [Meie87]. First, one may organize the data of a complex object in relational form and represent the object as a set of tuples, each marked with a unique object identifier. Then the algorithms may be either programmed in an external host language with embedded query language commands [RTI84], or within the database system by means of user-defined data types and operators [Wong85, Kemp87]. These approaches have been used in earlier attempts to extend relational database systems to applications in geography and robotics [Kung84, Gunt87]. Second, one supports a procedural data type to store expressions in the query language or any other programming language directly in the database. This approach is emphasized in the POSTGRES database system [Ston86b]. Third, one may define an abstract data type (ADT) with corresponding operators and abstract indices; see for example [Ston83]. The importance and suitability of ADT mechanisms for geometric data management has also been discussed by Schek [Sche86].

Although the arc tree is a useful representation scheme for the most important geometric operators, it should not necessarily be visible to the user. On the contrary, all set and search operators should be executed *without* revealing the internal representation scheme - the arc tree - to the user. The only operator where the internal representation may be visible to the user is the rendering of approximations of the curve. But even then, it seems preferable to offer an operator that maps an abstract object of type *curve* and a resolution into an approximation of the curve. Note that for none of the common operators the user needs to have explicit access to subtrees or to retrieve or manipulate details of the arc tree. On the other hand, it is important to implement the algorithms for set and search operations as efficiently as possible. The algorithms are complex, and their performance should not be impeded unnecessarily by an insufficient runtime environment or an inadequate implementation language.

Because of these considerations we believe that an embedding of the arc tree as an abstract data type (ADT) into an extensible database system is the superior solution to the problem. An ADT is an encapsulation of a data structure (so that its implementation details are not visible to an outside client procedure) along with a collection of related operators on this encapsulated structure. The canonical example of an ADT is a stack with related operators *new*, *push*, *pop* and *empty*. In our case, the user is given an ADT *curve*; each curve is represented internally as an arc tree, but this fact is completely transparent to the user. For a more detailed discussion of the arc tree embedding into a database system, see [Gunt88].

7. Summary

We presented the arc tree, a balanced binary tree that serves as an approximation scheme for curves. It is shown how the arc tree can be used to represent curves for efficient support of common set and search operators. The arc tree can be viewed as just one instance of a large class of approximation schemes that implement some hierarchy of detail. We gave an overview of several other approximation schemes that are based on the same idea, and indicated how to modify the arc tree algorithms to work with these schemes.

Several examples are given for the performance of our algorithms to compute set and search operators such as point inclusion or area-area intersection detection and computation. The results of the practical analysis are encouraging: in most cases, the computation of boolean operators such as point inclusion or intersection detection can be completed on the first four or five levels of the tree. Also, the computation of non-boolean operators such as intersection computation gives fairly good results even if one restricts the computation to the first few levels. Finally, it is described how to embed arc trees as complex objects in an extensible database system. It is argued that the embedding as an abstract data type is most efficient.

It is subject of future research to conduct a more comprehensive and systematic study of the arc tree algorithms and of the different possibilities to handle arc trees in an extensible database system. Also, we are planning to compare the arc tree to Ballard's strip tree and to Bezier curves, both theoretically and practically.

References

[Ball81]   Ballard, D. H., Strip trees: A hierarchical representation for curves, *Comm. of the ACM* **24**, 5 (May 1981), pages 310-321.

[Bezi74]   Bezier, P. E., Mathematical and practical possibilities of UNISURF, in *Computer Aided Geometric Design*, Academic Press, New York, NY, 1974, pages 127-152.

[Bohm84] Bohm, W., Efficient evaluation of splines, *Computing* **33** (1984), pages 171-177.

[Burt77]   Burton, W., Representation of many-sided polygons and polygonal lines for rapid processing, *Comm. of the ACM* **20**, 3 (March 1977), pages 166-171.

[Debo78] Deboor, C., *A practical guide to splines,* Springer, Heidelberg, 1978.

[Gunt87] Gunther, O., An expert database system for the overland search problem, in *Proc. BTW'87 - Database Systems for Office Automation, Engineering, and Scientific Applications*, Informatik-Fachberichte No. 136, Springer, Berlin, 1987.

[Gunt88] Gunther, O., *Efficient structures for geometric data management*, Lecture Notes in Computer Science No. 337, Springer-Verlag, Berlin, 1988.

[Hopc87] Hopcroft, J. E. and Krafft, D. B., The challenge of robotics for computer science, in *Algorithmic and geometric aspects of robotics*, Advances in robotics, Vol. 1, C. Yap and J. Schwartz (eds.), Lawrence Erlbaum Assoc., Hillsdale, NJ, 1987.

[Imai86] Imai, H. and Iri, M., Computational-geometric methods for polygonal approximations of a curve, *Comp. Vision Graph. Image Proc.* **36** (1986), pages 31-41.

[Kemp87] Kemper, A., Lockemann, P. C., and Wallrath, M., An object-oriented database system for engineering applications, in *Proc. of ACM SIGMOD Conference on Management of Data*, San Francisco, Ca., May 1987.

[Kung84] Kung, R., Hanson, E., Ioannidis, Y., Sellis, T., Shapiro, L., and Stonebraker, M., Heuristic search in data base systems, in *Proc. 1st International Workshop on Expert Database Systems*, Kiowah, S.C., Oct. 1984.

[Mand77] Mandelbrot, B. B., *Fractals: Form, Chance and Dimension*, W. H. Freeman & Co., San Francisco, Ca., 1977.

[Meie87] Meier, A., *Erweiterung relationaler Datenbanksysteme für technische Anwendungen*, Informatik-Fachberichte No. 135, Springer, Berlin, 1987.

[Paul87] Paul, H.-B., Schek, H.-J., Scholl, M. H., Weikum, G., and Deppisch, U., Architecture and implementation of the Darmstadt database kernel system (DASDBS), in *Proc. of ACM SIGMOD Conference on Management of Data*, San Francisco, Ca., May 1987.

[Pavl82] Pavlidis, T., *Algorithms for graphics and image processing*, Computer Science Press, Rockville, Md., 1982.

[Ponc87] Ponce, J. and Faugeras, O., An object centered hierarchical representation for 3D objects: the prism tree, *Comp. Vision Graph. Image Proc.* **38** (1987), pages 1-28.

[Prep85] Preparata, F. P. and Shamos, M. I., *Computational geometry*, Springer, New York, NY, 1985.

[RTI84] RTI, Relational Technology Inc., *INGRES/EQUEL/FORTRAN User's guide, version 3.0, VAX/VMS*, Oct. 1984.

[Same84] Samet, H., The quadtree and related hierarchical data structures, *Computing Surveys* **16**, 2 (June 1984), pages 187-260.

[Sche86] Schek, H.-J., Datenbanksysteme für die Verwaltung geometrischer Objekte, in *Proc. of the 16th GI Annual Meeting*, Informatik-Fachberichte No. 126, Springer, Berlin, Oct. 1986.

[Ston83] Stonebraker, M., Rubenstein, B., and Guttman, A., Application of abstract data types and abstract indices to CAD data, in *Proc. Engineering Applications Stream of ACM SIGMOD Conference*, San Jose, Ca., May 1983.

[Ston86a] Stonebraker, M. and Rowe, L., The design of POSTGRES, in *Proc. of ACM SIGMOD Conference on Management of Data*, Washington, DC, June 1986.

[Ston86b] Stonebraker, M., Object management in POSTGRES using procedures, in *Proc. 1986 International Workshop on Object-Oriented Database Systems*, Asilomar, Ca., Sept. 1986.

[Wong85] Wong, E., *Extended domain types and specification of user defined operators*, U.C. Berkeley, Memorandum No. UCB/ERL/M85/3, Feb. 1985.

ENGINEERING THE OBJECT ORIENTED DBMSs

Behavior Analysis of Object-Oriented Databases: Method Structure, Execution Trees, and Reachability (Extended Abstract)

Richard Hull[1]
Computer Science Department
University of Southern California
Los Angeles, CA 90089-0782
USA

Katsumi Tanaka
Department of Instrumentation Engineering
Faculty of Engineering
Kobe University
Rokkodai, Nada, Kobe 657
Japan

Masatoshi Yoshikawa
Institute of Computer Sciences
Kyoto Sangyo University
Kamigamo, Kita-ku, Kyoto 603
Japan

Abstract: A theoretical model for analyzing the behavior of method execution in object-oriented databases (OODBs) is introduced and used to study issues of reachability, nontermination, and well-typedness in the context of restricted classes of OODBs.

1 Introduction

Object-oriented databases (OODBs) have been receiving much attention in the last few years. These database systems combine features of semantic models [HK87] and of the object-oriented paradigm of programming languages [GR83]. Several research and even commercial OODB systems have already been developed [BCG+87, AH87, LRV88, PSM87, FBC+87]. However, there is currently a lack of a workable, flexible formalism for theoretical investigations of fundamental issues of OODBs. This paper proposes such a formalism, and uses it to study the basic issues of *nontermination*, *type-errors*, and *reachability*.

The primary features of OODB can be roughly divided into the structural (or static) and behavioral (or dynamic) ones as follows:

- structural aspects
  - direct representation of real-world objects
    * object identity
    * attributes (also called "instance variables")
  - explicit introduction of semantic constructs, e.g., generalization, aggregation etc.
  - integrity constraints, e.g., on the range of attributes
- (behavioral aspects)

---

[1]Research supported in part by NSF grant IST-8719875. Portions of this research performed while this author was visiting Kobe University, with partial support from the International Foundation for Information Science, Japan.

 — encapsulation of methods into types
 — flow of control based on message passing or method calls
 — object-dependent binding of method-names to method-implementations

The various structural features arising in OODBs have been studied for several years, for example, by using semantic models, and in more recent investigations such as [TY88], which proposes operations for abstraction of objects using different kinds of generalization hierarchies. However, these and other formal investigations do not take into account the behavioral aspects unique to OODB. The O_2 model [LRV88] presents a formal definition for a very rich object-oriented system, but no theoretical investigations have been performed with it to date. Also, the model for O_2 is primarily focused on signatures (types of receiver, parameters, and result); it is not as concerned with the contents or interaction of the method implementations.

As noted above, a fundamental component of the behavioral aspects of the object-oriented paradigm is the use of methods as the basic mechanism for contolling the flow of computation. This approach provides great expressive power; for example, it is easy to create recursive procedures in this paradigm. A second fundamental component of the object-oriented paradigm is *object-dependent binding* (sometimes called "late binding") of method-names to method implementations. Using this, a given method-name is interpreted in different ways depending on which class a target object belongs to. The use of object-dependent binding complicates the analysis of the ultimate behavior of a called method, and thus makes compilation and optimization of methods a complex task.

A fundamental contribution of the current paper is to introduce a formal model which can be used to analyze the behavior and interaction of methods in an object-oriented database. In particular, the model we introduce permits us to focus our study on the impact of object-dependent binding of method calls. Four contributions of this formalism can be identified: **(1)** It provides a formal but workable set of definitions describing the execution of methods in OODBs. **(2)** It has been used to obtain specific and useful theoretical results about OODBs **(3)** It naturally supports the definition of interesting families of OODBs, here based primarily on restricting the power of method implementations. **(4)** It can be extended in a graceful manner to incorporate features of OODBs not studied here. Notably, the formalism developed here was used as the starting point for a formal investigation of the expressive power of data access to object-oriented databases [HS89a].

The formalism presented includes a number of important, fundamental concepts which are relevant to the issues of compiling, type-checking, and optimizing OODB schemas. Foremost among these are the notions of *Method Execution Tree* (or *MET*), an abstract structure which describes the sequence of execution steps generated by a method call. Using this, a number of fundamental questions about OODBs are raised. For example, we ask whether invoking a given method leads to *unavoidable nontermination*, no matter what the underlying instance it is called on. It is clearly useful to be able to identify such methods, as they should be eliminated from any OODB schema. A second question concerns determining when one method is *reachable* from another, i.e., if there is some instance for which the execution of the first method invokes execution of the second. Reachability is a fundamental concept for describing the dynamic behavior of method execution. One particular application is to test whether all methods called by a given method have been defined for the classes on which they are called. Another question concerns whether a method has *bounded execution*, in that the total number of invoked methods is bounded. In that case, the method might be replaced by its "macro-expansion", in order to facilitate compilation. Finally, our approach allows us to analyze executions aborted due to *type-errors*.

The theoretical results of the paper focus primarily on two restricted classes of OODB schemas, here called *simple-retrieval* schemas and *update* schemas. Both of these are severely restricted versions of OODBs, but are nevertheless relevant because they can be viewed as models of fragments of practical OODB schemas. We show that most of the questions mentioned above are decidable for simple-retierval schemas, but are undecidable for update schemas. Taken together, these results provide a kind of lower and upper bound on how many object-oriented capabilities are needed to cause undecidability. We expect that continued research with our basic model will lead to additional insights in these and other directions.

In Section 2, we give motivating examples and explain the results of this paper intuitively. Section 3 gives formal defintions of the fundamental concepts introduced in this paper; in particular, several classes of method implementation and tools for the analysis of method execution are formally defined. Section 4 presents decidability results and algorithms for simple-retrieval schemas, and section 5 presents the undecidability results for update schemas. Some specific future research directions are mentioned in section 6.

This report is an extended abstract; some parts of this paper are quite abridged. In particular, some of the definitions are sketched, and proofs are omitted.

2 Motivating Examples

In this section, we give an intuitive explanation of the basic notions discussed in this paper together with illustrative examples. We use here an informal terminology which loosely parallels the formalism introduced in section 3. We assume the readers are familiar with the basic notions of object-oriented paradigm such as the inheritance of attributes and methods, computation based on method calls, etc.

Let us consider an OODB schema in Figure 1. In this figure, each rectangle represents a type with its type name and attribute-domain pairs inside; each arrow between rectangles represents an ISA relationship between corresponding types; and method implementations defined in each type is listed in the right-hand side or below the corresponding rectangle.

For example, type 'person' has two attributes 'age' and 'mentor' whose domains are 'integer' and 'person*', respectively. Here, 'person*' represents the union of the type 'person' and all (direct and indirect) subtypes of 'person' under a given ISA hierarchy; hence, each object which belongs to the type 'person' can have, as the attribute value of 'mentor', any object of which type is 'person', 'student', or 'professor'. Note that the domain of the attribute 'mentor' is defined as 'person*' in the types 'person' and 'student', whereas it is defined as 'professor*' in the type 'professor'.

Portions of an example for this schema which conforms to these domain constraints is given in Figure 2. In this figure, names such as Tom and Jim (informally) represent object identifiers. The arrows represent the value of the 'mentor' attribute for each object. For example, the mentor of Susan is Peter, and the mentor of Peter is Bill, and so on. (The 'age' and 'dept' attribute values are not shown). Note that the instance Figure 2 satisfies the domain constraints on the attribute 'mentor'.

Now we turn to the explanation of methods defined in each type. Figure 1 shows that 4 methods, **get-age**, **advisor**, **student-mentor** and **mentor-seniority** are defined in the type 'person'; 3 methods, **advisor**, **advisor-dept** and **student-mentor** are defined in the type 'student'; and 1 method **get-dept** is defined in the type 'professor'.

As for the syntax of sentences in method implementations, we will generally follow that of Smalltalk-80 with some minor differences which include: **(1)** For the representation of method invocations, "*method(receiver)*" syntax is adopted instead of "*receiver method*". For example, the sentence "get-dept(x)" in the method **advisor-dept** in Figure 1 is represented as "x get-dept" in Smalltalk-80. **(2)** "return" sentence instead of ↑, **(3)** each sentence except the last one ends with semicolon (;) instead of period (.). Also, we will follow the convention of dot-notation. For example, self.age in a method implementation represents an object stored in 'age' attribute of the receiver object of the method. (Formal definitions for the syntax and semantics of method implementations are given in section 3).

Note that among these methods, **advisor** and **student-mentor** are defined both in the types 'person' and 'student'. This is an example of *method overriding*, in which different implementations are defined with the same method-name in different types, which is one of the major characteristics of object-oriented paradigm. (In fact, method overriding is one reason which makes the analysis of method behavior difficult.) In order to uniquely identify a method-implementation we use pairs of the form (*method-name, type-name*)

The intuitive meaning of each method in Figure 1 is as follows:

- **get-age** returns the age of the receiver person object.

- **advisor** returns the advisor of the receiver's mentor when the receiver is a student. (It is recursively defined.) Otherwise, if the receiver is not a student, the advisor is the receiver himself/herself. Note that the returned object of the method implementation (advisor, student) can not be a student.

- **advisor-dept** returns the department to which the advisor of the receiver person object belongs.

- **student-mentor** returns *the closest* student mentor of the receiver person object. If the receiver is a student, the receiver himself/herself is returned. Otherwise, if the receiver is not a student, the "student-mentor" of the receiver's mentor is returned. Note the similarity between the two methods **student-mentor** and **advisor** in their recursive structures.

- **mentor-seniority** returns the difference of the ages of the receiver person object and his/her advisor.

- **get-dept** returns the department to which the receiver professor object belongs.

A method call is denoted by specifying a (method-name, type-name) pair, along with the object upon which the method is to be invoked, e.g., (advisor-dept, student)[Mark], If the type of the receiver object is known, the invoked method implementation is uniquely determined following the object-binding rule; in this case the type may be omitted, as in advisor-dept[Mark].

We now turn to the notion of method execution tree (MET), illustrated in Figures 3, 4 and 5 below. Informally, the MET of a method execution (m,t)[o] is a tree with (m,t)[o] as the root; and method executions invoked by (m,t)[o] as its ordered children; furthermore, each of these children could have their own children; etc. For example, the MET of (advisor-dept, student)[Mark] is given in Figure 3. Labels attached at the upper-right of nodes represent the return values of the corresponding method execution.

Figure 3 shows that (advisor-dept, student)[Mark] is successfully executed and its return value is C.S. (We assume that Peter belongs to C.S. department.)

There are cases, however, in which method executions do not complete successfully. These cases include: **(1)** nonterminating method execution (infinite MET), illustrated in Figure 4; **(2)** abortion of method execution caused by the invocation of an undefined methods, illustrated in Figure 5; and **(3)** abortion of method execution caused by an update violating a domain (or other) constraint. We also note that **(4)** (student-mentor, professor) has *unavoidable nontermination*, because for all instances, every execution will be nonterminating. Also, **(5)** (mentor-seniority,person) has *bounded execution*, because each MET for these has at most 3 nodes. **(6)** (advisor-dept,student) has *potential nontermination*, because at least one execution on some instance is nonterminating. **(7)** (advisor-dept,student) has *potential abortion*, because at least one execution on some instance is aborted (due to a type error) **(8)** (advisor,professor) is *reachable* from (advisor-dept,student) because there is some successful MET with root labeled (advisor,student) and some other node labeled (advisor, professor) (see Figure 3).

It is clear that identifying method-type pairs with unavoidable nontermination and/or abortion is highly desirable in the context of OODBs. Reachability and bounded execution are useful, because it could be used to "compile" the schema in such a way as to reduce the number of actual method calls. It is thus natural to ask whether any of these properties are decidable. If methods are allowed to have arbitrary computation power such decision problems are equivalent to the halting problem, and hence undecidable. However, there are restricted cases relevant in the context of databases in which these questions are decidable, or at least have a chance of being decidable; in the formal part of this paper we focus on such cases.

One class of OODB schemas defined here, called *retrieval schemas*, have implementations which permit method calls for retreivals, but do not permit updates. The schema of Figure 1 is a retrieval schema (although in that figure we use an abbreviated notation rather than the formal syntax described in section 3). A second class of OODB studied here, called *simple-retrieval*, includes further restrictions, which intuitively prevent returned values of method calls from affecting the overall flow of control of a method execution. (All method-implementation in Figure 1 except for advisor-dept are simple retrieval). Finally, *update* schemas are like retrieval schemas, but also permit updates to attribute values. Simple-retrieval and retrieval schemas are closely related to "derived attributes" of semantic models, because their computation is generally assumed to be free of side-effects.

As mentioned in the introduction, we show that many questions are decidable for simple-retrieval schemas, but are undecidable for update schemas. It remains open whether the questions are decidable for general retrieval schemas, and also, whether retrieval schemas can be simulated by simple-retrieval schemas.

3 Formal Definitions

This section presents a series of definitions which can serve as a formal framework for studying the kinds of questions raised in this paper. In these definitions we focus primarily on the restricted classes of database schemas which are formally studied in Sections 4 and 5 below; although it is clear how these definitions can be extended to permit the study of more general classes. In this extended abstract the discussion is rather terse, and in some cases, presents only sketches of the actual definitions.

Three topics are discussed in this section. First, we introduce notation for describing object-oriented database schemas and instances. Second we introduce three restricted classes of schemas, which are used in the formal study presented in Sections 4 and 5. Third, we present the notion of "Method Execution Tree" (MET), which records a body of relevant information about the execution of a single method call. We also note that the notion of MET can be used to formalize the various notions described in Section 2.

3.1 OODB schemas and instances

We begin with the notion of OODB schema, which consists primarily of types. Attribute (name)s and method (name)s are associated with types; ISA relationships are specified between types; and implementations are attached to some type-method pairs.

In the formal model, we assume the existence of 4 disjoint countably infinite sets: (1) $\mathcal{T}$ of (abstract) type (names); (2) $\mathcal{A}$ of attribute (names); (3) $\mathcal{M}$ of method (names); and (4) $\mathcal{I}$ of implementations. We also assume a fixed set (5) $BASIC$ of basic types, including, e.g., Integer, Real, Boolean, and Char. A basic object is an element of $\cup$ $BASIC$. In the current investigation, we assume that no subtype relationships hold between basic types.

Intuitively, attributes are analogous to the attributes of semantic data models, although in the current study all attributes are assumed to be single-valued. Implementations are fragments of executable code; these will be discussed in more detail below. Methods are abstract names which will be used (in the context of a given schema and given type) to refer to implementations.

Definition: A (database) schema is an ordered quintuple $S = (T, ISA, Att, Meth, Impl)$ where

1. T is a finite subset of $\mathcal{T}$.

2. (T, ISA) is a directed forest (with edges pointing from child to parent). If $(s, t) \in ISA$ we write s ISA t. Also, s is a subtype of t (t is a supertype of s), denoted $s \preceq t$ and $t \succeq s$, if there is a path from s to t in (T, ISA). (Note that each type is a subtype of itself.)

3. $Att : T \rightarrow \mathcal{P}^{fin}(\mathcal{A})$, such that: if s ISA t and $a \in Att(t)$, then $a \in Att(s)$.

4. $Meth : T \rightarrow \mathcal{P}^{fin}(\mathcal{M})$, such that: if s ISA t and $m \in Meth(t)$, then $m \in Meth(s)$.

5. $Impl$ is a partial function from $\{ (m, t) \mid m \in Meth(t) \} \rightarrow \mathcal{I}$, such that: if $m \in Meth(s)$ then there is some $t \succeq s$ such that $Impl(m, t)$ is defined. The function $Impl$ is also subject to other restrictions, which are described later.

We also define an induced function $Impl^*:\{ (m, t) \mid m \in Meth(t) \} \rightarrow \mathcal{I}$. In particular, $Impl^*(m, s) = Impl(m, t)$, where t is the least supertype of s for which $Impl(m, t)$ is defined. (The restriction of (5) above guarentees the existence of such a t.) Note that $Impl^*$ is a total function on $\{ (m, t) \mid m \in Meth(t) \}$.

We make the following remarks about this definition: (1) In the current investigation we do not permit "multiple inheritance". (2) Unlike some OODB models, we do not require that all types be subtypes of a given root type. (3) The restrictions of the functions Att and $Meth$ enforce a certain redundancy in schemas; namely the schema must explicitly mention the attributes and methods associated with a type, even if they are already associated with a supertype. This restriction simplifies some of the notation used below. (4) It is possible to have types s and t and a method m such that

$m \in Meth(s)$ and $m \in Meth(t)$, but there is no common supertype r of s and t such that $m \in Meth(r)$

We next define the notion of database instance of a schema. This will follow the general philosophy of, e.g., IFO. For this definition we assume the existence of a countably infinite set **(6)** $\mathcal{O}$ of *abstract objects*. Elements of $\mathcal{O}$ are viewed to be "uninterpreted" until they are included in a database instance.

Definition: Let $S = (T, ISA, Att, Meth, Impl)$ be a schema. A *(database) instance* of S is a pair $I = (O, A)$ where $O : T \to \mathcal{P}^{fin}(\mathcal{O})$, such that if $s \neq t$ then $O(s) \cap O(t) = \emptyset$. Using O, we define the function $O^* : T \to \mathcal{P}^{fin}(\mathcal{O})$ so that $O(t) = \cup\{O(s) \mid s$ is a subtype of $t\}$. Also, A is a total function from $\{(o, a) \mid a \in A(t)$ for that t such that $o \in O(t)\} \to \cup\{O(s) \mid s \in T\} \cup (\cup BASIC)$. We generally use $o.a$ to denote $A(o, a)$. For $t \in T$ we often write $I(t)$ $(I^*(t))$ to mean $O(t)$ $(O^*(t))$.

We note that the above definition prevents "dangling pointers", because the range of each attribute value is a basic object or an abstract object occuring in the instance. Also, no object can be in two incomparable types.

In the context of databases it is natural to associate constraints on the data which can arise in instances. In the current investigation we focus on a simple family of "domain constraints". These are used to restrict the values associated with object attributes.

Definition: Let $S = (T, ISA, Att, Meth, Impl)$ be a schema. A *domain constraint* on S is a formal expression '$(t, a) : p^*$' or '$(t, a) : B$' where $t \in T$, $a \in Att(t)$, and $p \in T$ or $B \in BASIC$. An instance I of S *satisfies* $(t, a) : p^*$ $[(t, a) : B]$ written $I \models (t, a) : p^*$ $[I \models (t, a) : B]$ if for each $o \in I(t)$: $p \in T$ implies $o.a \in I^*(p)$ $[o.a \in$ the domain of $B]$.

Thus, if p is an abstract type of a schema S, then the constraint $(t, a) : p^*$ requires that each a-value of objects in t must be taken from p *or its subtypes*; and the constraint $(t, a) : B$ requires that each attribute value be taken from the domain of B.

Definition: A *(constrained) schema* is a six-tuple $S = (T, ISA, Att, Meth, Impl, D)$, where $S' = (T, ISA, Att, Meth, Impl)$ is a schema, and D is a set of domain constraints for S' satisfying the following restrictions: **(1)** There is exactly one domain constraint for each type-attribute pair in S. **(2)** If $s \preceq t$ and $(t, a) : p^* \in D$, then there is some $q \preceq p$ such that $(s, a) : q^* \in D$. **(3)** If $s \preceq t$ and $(t, a) : B \in D$, then $(s, a) : B \in D$. An *instance* of S is an instance I of S' which satisfies each domain constraint in D.

3.2 Restricted families of implementations

We now turn to the family of implementations studied in this paper. In general, an object-oriented database model provides an imperative language for specifying implementations for methods. (This contrasts with "pure" object-oriented programming languages such as SMALLTALK, where even the most primitive operations are accomplished by method calls.) The imperative language may be an existing language (e.g., C), or might be developed specifically for the model. In any case, the language typically has special primitives for working with objects and their attributes. Also, the language may provide primitives for working with special data structures, such as set.

In the current discussion we study families of schemas in which the implementations use specific, restricted languages. We indicate here two such classes of implementations for which we have some theoretical results, and also indicate some other classes of implementations which are currently under investigation. The names we give to the classes of schemas are suggestive of their capabilities; however it is clear that because of the restrictions their overall expressive power is relatively weak.

We begin with the most restricted kind of implementation studied here:

Definition: An implementation is said to be *simple-retrieval* if it has the following form:

$$\textbf{var: } x_1, \ldots, x_n; y_1, \ldots, y_m;$$
$$s_1; \ldots; s_k; \textbf{return}(y_l)$$

where

1. $n \geq 0$, $m \geq 1$, $1 \leq l \leq m$; and
2. s_p has any of the following forms for $1 \leq p \leq k$:
   - (a) $x_i := \text{self}$
   - (b) $x_i := \text{self}.a$ (where $a \in \mathcal{A}$)
   - (c) $y_j := x_i$
   - (d) $y_j := m(x_i)$ (where $m \in \mathcal{M}$)
   - (e) $y_j := \theta(y_{k_1}, \ldots, y_{k_r})$, where θ is some arithmetic or other operation on *BASIC* types.

A *simple-retrieval schema* is a schema $S = (T, ISA, Att, Meth, Impl)$ such that $Impl(t, m)$ is a simple-retrieval implementation for each (t, m) on which $Impl$ is defined; and S satisfies the following **well-formed requirements:**

1. If $Impl(t, m) = i$ and 'self.a' occurs in i, then $a \in Att(t)$.
2. No variable is used before it is initialized.

The well-formed requirements will be used in the definitions of other classes of implementations. Intuitively, these focus on conditions which can be checked locally, i.e., with reference to only the implementation and its type.

We make the following observations about simple-retrieval schemas: **(1)** There are two kinds of variables (x_i and y_j); the x's are used to hold the 'self' object or its immediate attribute values, and the y's are used to hold the output of a method or a computation, or an x value. In simple-retrieval implementations, methods can only be applied to x variables, and only y values can be returned. In this way, the interaction of method calls is not affected by the values returned by the methods. **(2)** We do not provide a primitive for referring to an implementation in a supertype (such as 'super' in SMALLTALK or '$$' in VBASE). In general this feature can be simulated by explicitly including the contents of the supertype's implementation in the implementation of interest. **(3)** We do not provide primitives for manipulating sets (e.g., *add-element*) or other complex structures. **(4)** We do not include the ability to call methods with parameters. **(5)** Simple-retrieval implementations cannot update the data; in this sense they resemble the derived attributes of semantic data models.

The definition given above is quite specific as to the syntax permitted in simple-retrieval implementations. In the examples of Section 2 we used an *abbreviated* notation (e.g., permitting the statement $y := m(\text{self}.a)$). Modulo these abbreviations, all implementations of Figure 1 except that of (advisor-dept,student) are simple-retrieval.

The second class introduced relaxes the restriction that inputs to called methods must be self or self.a for some a.

Definition: An implementation is said to be *retrieval* if it has the same form as a simple-retrieval implementation, except: **(a)** there is no distinction between x and y variables; and **(b)** each statement has the form:

1. $x_i := \text{self}$

2. $x_i := \text{self}.a$ (where $a \in \mathcal{A}$)

3. $x_j := m(x_i)$ (where $m \in \mathcal{M}$)

4. $x_j := \theta(x_{k_1}, \ldots, x_{k_r})$, where θ is some arithmetic or other operation on *BASIC* type

A *retrieval schema* is a schema $S = (T, ISA, Att, Meth, Impl)$ such that $Impl(t, m)$ is a retrieval implementation for each (t, m) on which $Impl$ is defined; and S satisfies the well-formed requirements.

At present it remains open whether every retrieval schema can be "simulated" be a simple-retrieval schema.

The third class of schemas we present introduces the ability to perform side-effects. As will be seen in Section 5, this provides sufficient computational power to make many problems about schema behavior undecidable.

Definition: An implementation is said to be *update* if it has the form of a retrieval implementation, where each statement has one of the following forms:

1. $x_i := \text{self}$

2. $x_i := \text{self}.a$ (where $a \in \mathcal{A}$)

3. $\text{self}.a := x_i$ (where $a \in \mathcal{A}$)

4. $x_j := m(x_i)$ (where $m \in \mathcal{M}$)

5. $x_j := \theta(x_{k_1}, \ldots, x_{k_r})$, where θ is some arithmetic or other operation on *BASIC* type

An *update schema* is a schema $S = (T, ISA, Att, Meth, Impl)$ such that $Impl(t, m)$ is update implementation for each (t, m) on which $Impl$ is defined; and S satisfies the well-formed requirements.

The three classes introduced above are limited in many ways. Possible extensions include permitting one or more of the following in implementations: **(1)** statements of the form $x := \text{self}.a.b.c$ for attribute names $a, b,$ and c (This "nesting" of attributes does not appear to increase the expressive power of retrieval or update schemas, but may affect the power of simple-retrieval schemas.); **(2)** statements of the form: $y_1 := m(y_2; z_1, \ldots, z_k)$ (i.e., methods with parameters); **(3)** statements of the form: **if** ... **then** ... **else** ...; **(4)** statements of the form: **do** ... **while** ...; **(5)** statements of the form: **delete** o **from** t, and **insert** o **into** t; **(6)** primitives for set manipulation; and **(7)** primitives to create and delete objets in types.

3.3 Method execution trees

We now turn to an operational definition of the semantics of method calls. The definition used here is a faithful copy of the semantics given to method calls in actual object-oriented systems. The semantics is defined in terms of a labelled tree (where nodes have ordered children), called a "Method Execution Tree" (MET); the usual operational semantics is obtained from a MET by performing a depth-first traversal of it.

We first define METS for update schemas. It will be clear that this definition can be extended to incorporate essentially any class of implementations. It will also become apparent that METs for (simple-)retrieval schemas can be viewed as having simpler structure than update METs.

There are essentially three stages to the definition of MET. In the first stage, we focus on the kinds of label used for the nodes. In the second stage, we define "successful"

METs; and in the third stage we define "aborted" and "nonterminating" METS, which both correspond to unsuccessful computations.

For the first stage, we define the kinds of labels used for nodes:

Definition: Let $S = (T, ISA, Att, Meth, Impl, D)$ be a constrained schema. A *method call summary* (*mcs*) for S is a 3-tuple with one of the following forms:

> **completed:** $\langle (I_{in}, o_{in}), (m, t), (I_{out}, o_{out}) \rangle$;
> **aborted:** $\langle (I_{in}, o_{in}), (m, t), (-, -) \rangle$;
> **uncalled:** $\langle (-, -), (m, -), (-, -) \rangle$;

where **(1)** m is a method associated with type t. **(2)** I_{in} and I_{out} are instances of S. **(3)** $o_{in} \in I_{in}(t)$. **(4)** o_{out} is an object of I_{out} or a basic object.

Intuitively, an mcs holds a summary of a method call. (I_{in}, o_{in}) can be viewed as the pre-conditions of the call, and (I_{out}, o_{out}) the post-conditions. In particular, I_{in} is the database instance immediately prior to the call, and I_{out} is the database instance immediately after the call is completed (if it completes at all). o_{in} is the object on which m is called, and o_{out} (if defined) is the object returned by m on o_{in} in I_{in}. The type t is inferred from I_{in} and o. (We include t as an explicit part of the mcs, because it will facilitate the formation of various abstracts of METs.)

For the restricted schemas studied here there is no object creation or deletion, so the set of abstract objects in I_{in} will always equal the set of abstract objects in I_{out}, although attribute values may change. Furthermore, in the case of (simple-)retrieval schemas, method calls do not change the underlying database instance, so I_{in} and I_{out} will be identical; indeed, for these schemas I_{in} and I_{out} need not be explicitly mentioned in METs.

In the METs depicted in Figures 3, 4 and 5, each node is labeled by an mcs. However, we omitted reference to the input and output instance; and we presented each mcs $(o_{in}, (m, t), o_{out})$ by showing the expression $(m, t)[o_{in}]$ in the node, and the object o_{out} at the upper right corner of the node.

We now embark on the second stage of our definition, namely, of "successful" METs. To get started, we define a "weak-MET" to have the structure of METs, and ultimately define METs to be set of weak-METs which satisfy a number of conditions.

Definition: A *weak Method Execution Tree* (*weak-MET*) is a tree $M = (V, E, \lambda)$ where λ maps each node of M to an mcs.

To define successful METs we proceed in two steps: first focusing on method calls which do not themselves call any other methods, and second focusing on calls with arbitrarily large successful executions.

Definition: Let $S = (T, ISA, Att, Meth, Impl, D)$ be a constrained schema; $\mu = \langle (I_{in}, o_{in}), (m, t), (I_{out}, o_{out}) \rangle$ a completed mcs; and $M = (\{v\}, \emptyset, \lambda)$ where $\lambda(v) = \mu$. Suppose further that in S, $Impl^*(m, t)$ has variables X and hascommands $s_1; \ldots; s_n;$ **return**(x_l); and that no s_j involves a method call. Then M is a *successful Method Execution Tree* (*MET*), if **(1)** I_{out} is the result of applying the sequence $s_1; \ldots; s_n$ to I_{in}, where 'self' is interpreted as o_{in}; and **(2)** o_{out} is the object assigned to x_l after the execution of $s_1; \ldots; s_n$ on I_{in}, where 'self' is interpreted as o_{in}.

We now generalize to arbitrarily large finite trees:

Definition: Let $S = (T, ISA, Att, Meth, Impl, D)$ be a constrained schema; and $M = (V, E, \lambda)$ a weak-MET such that $\lambda(w)$ is a completed mcs for each node w of M. Then M is a *successful Method Execution Tree* (*successful MET*) if:

1. For each leaf w of M, the subtree of M with just w in it is a successful MET.
2. Suppose that w is a non-leaf node of M with children $w_1, \ldots, w_k$; that

$$\lambda(w) = \langle (I_{in}, o_{in}), (m, t), (I_{out}, o_{out}) \rangle; \text{ and that}$$
$$\lambda(w_j) = \langle (I_{in}^j, o_{in}^j), (m^j, t^j), (I_{out}^j, o_{out}^j) \rangle$$

for each $j, 1 \leq j \leq k$ (see Figure 3.3). Suppose further that in S, $Impl^*(m, t)$ has variables X and commands $s_1; \ldots; s_n$;**return**(x_l). Then there are *assignments* (i.e., partial functions from variables to objects) $\alpha_{in}^1, \alpha_{out}^1, \ldots, \alpha_{in}^k, \alpha_{out}^k$ where (for $1 \leq j \leq k$) α_{in}^j maps from X to objects in I_{in}^j and basic objects, and α_{out}^j maps from X to objects in I_{out}^j and basic objects, such that:

(a) There are exactly k commands in $s_1; \ldots; s_n$ involving method calls, which we denote by $s_{i_1}, \ldots, s_{i_k}$. Furthermore, s_{i_j} has the form $x_{q_j} := m^j(x_{p_j})$ (where x_{p_j} and x_{q_j} are in X) for $1 \leq j \leq k$.

(b) I_{in}^1 and α_{in}^1 are the result of applying $s_1, \ldots, s_{i_1 - 1}$ to I_{in} and the empty assignment, using o_{in} for 'self'.

(c) $o_{in}^j = \alpha_{in}^j(x_{p_j})$ for $1 \leq j \leq k$.

(d) α_{out}^j is identical to α_{in}^j, except that $\alpha_{out}^j(x_{q_j}) = o_{out}^j$, for $1 \leq j \leq k$.

(e) I_{in}^{j+1} and α_{in}^{j+1} are the result of applying $s_{i_j + 1}, \ldots, s_{i_{j+1} - 1}$ to I_{out}^j and α_{out}^j using o_{in} for 'self', for $1 \leq j < k$.

(f) I_{out} is the result of applying $s_{i_k + 1}, \ldots, s_n$ to I_{out}^k and α_{out}^k, using o_{in} for 'self'.

(g) o_{out} is the object assigned to x_l after applying $s_{i_k + 1}; \ldots; s_n$ to I_{out}^k and α_{out}^k, using o_{in} for 'self'.

For the third stage we define aborted and nonterminating METs. In this extended abstract we omit the formal definitions of these, and present only informal descriptions. An aborted MET models the situation where the execution of a method call is aborted in midstream. This might be caused by a *constraint violation*, because an attribute value assignment violates a domain constraint; or because of an *undefined method call*, in which a method m is called on an object o of type t, where $m \notin Meth(t)$. Both of these can be viewed as *runtime type errors*. An aborted MET M is a finite tree with a "critical" branch $B = v_1, \ldots, v_h$. Each node on B is labeled by an aborted mcs. Intuitively, M "looks like" a successful MET to the "left" of B; and to the right of B all of the nodes are labeled by uncalled mcs's. The MET of Figure 4 is aborted because of an undefined method call. A method call aborted due to constraint violation can arise only if updates are involved. A non-terminating MET is similar to a MET aborted due to an undefined method call, except that the critical branch is infinite.

Finally, we have

Notation: Let S be a constrained schema, I an instance of S, t a type of S, $o \in I(t)$, and $m \in Meth(t)$. Then $MET^I(m[o])$ or $MET^I(m, t[o])$ (the I may be omitted if understood from the context) denotes the MET for S and I whose root node has label of the form $\langle (I, o), (m, t), ? \rangle$, where $?$ is either (I', o') for some instance I' and object o', or $(-, -)$. In the former case the computation of $m[o]$ is called *successful*; otherwise it is called *unsuccessful*.

Using the above definitions, it should be clear how to formally define the various notions of reachability, unavoidable nontermination, etc., described at the end of Section 2. The formal definitions are omitted here. We do, however, include:

Definition: Let S be a schema, t a type of S, and $m \in Meth(t)$. Then (m, t) is *well-typed* if there is no aborted execution of (m, t).

As shown in the next section (Proposition 4.1), it is easy to identify the set of well-typed simple-retrieval schemas. On the other hand, this is undecidable for the class of update schemas.

4 Decidability in simple-retrieval schemas

In this and the next section we consider the issue of deciding various properties of restricted classes of OODB schemas. In the current section we focus on simple-retrieval schemas, and present algorithms (a) identifying well-typed schemas; (b) for identifying method-type pairs with necessarily nonterminating execution; and (c) for determining if one method-type pair is reachable from another one. We also discuss the issue of well-typed simple-retrieval schemas. The results and techniques used are of practical interest, because simple-retrieval schemas are closely related to some forms of derived attributes which arise in semantic database models. In Section 5 we show that these issues are not decidable for update schemas. Taken together, these results provide both a "lower bound" and an "upper bound" on the expressive power of OODB schemas with regards to decidability of certain fundamental properties.

We begin the discussion by identifying the set of (semantically) well-typed simple-retrieval schemas. To this end we introduce the notion of "syntactically well-typed" schemas:

Definition: Let $S = (T, ISA, Att, Meth, Impl, D)$ be a constrained simple-retrieval schema; (m, t) a pair in the domain of $Impl$; and that $Impl(m, t)$ has statements $s_1; \ldots; s_n; \mathbf{return}(x_l)$, where $s_{i_1}, \ldots, s_{i_k}$ are method calls. For each method call $s_{i_j} = y_j := m_j(x_j)$, let $c_j \in \{ \text{ self } \} \cup \{ \text{ self.}a \mid a \in Att(t) \}$ correspond to the "value" associated with x_j by $s_1, \ldots, s_{i_j - 1}$. Then $Impl(m, t)$ is *syntactially well-typed* if for each $j, 1 \leq j \leq k$, (1) if $c_j = $ self then $m_j \in Meth(t)$; and (2) if $c_j = $ self.a then the domain constraint for a in t has the form $(t, a) : p^*$ for some type $p \in T$, and $m_j \in Meth(p)$. Finally, the schema S is *syntactically well-typed* if $Impl(m, t)$ is syntactically well-typed for each pair (m, t) in the domain of $Impl$.

The following result is now straight-forward (proof omitted):

Proposition 4.1: Let S be a simple-retrieval schema. Then S is well-typed if and only if it is syntactically well-typed.

For the remainder of the section we restrict ourselves to the family of well-typed simple-retrieval schemas. We now turn to deciding nontermination and reachability. In this extended abstract we present an algorithm for deciding unavoidable nontermination (and for boundedness) for simple-retrieval schemas. Analogous algorithms for other questions have also been devised. Assume S is a fixed, well-typed, unrestricted simple-retrieval schema. To find the pairs (m, t) with unavoidable nontermination. This proceeds in two stages:

1. Elimination of calls of form $m'[\text{self}]$. (To do this, we first characterize of pairs (m, t) which have unavoidable nontermination because of a loop of calls $m_i[\text{self}]$. The implementations associated with these methods are replaced with $\bot$. In other method implementations, $m'[\text{self}]$ is replaced by a "macro-expansion" of m'.

2. In the context of simple-retrieval schemas which do not permit calls of form

$m'[\text{self}]$, characterization of pairs (m, t) which have unavoidable recursion.

We present an algorithm for the second step above.

Algorithm 4.2:

Input: well-typed, simple-retrieval schema $S = (T, ISA, Att, Meth, Impl, D)$ in which no implementations have a method call to 'self', and in which some implementations are designated as $\bot$.

Output: the set of all pairs (m, t) of S which have necessary nontermination, and the set of all pairs which have bounded termination.

Procedure:

1. Construct the annotated directed graph $G = (V, E, EG)$ where
   (a) $V = \{(M, t) \mid t \in T \text{ and } M \subseteq Meth(t)\}$.
   (b) $E = \{\langle (M, t), (N, s) \rangle \mid \text{for some attribute } a, s \prec p \text{ where } (t, a) : p^* \in D, \text{ and } N = \{n \mid \exists t, n(\text{self}.a) \text{ "occurs in" } Impl^*(m, t) \text{ for some } m \in M \}$.
   (c) EG is a function which maps each node $(M, t) \in V$ to a partition $EG(M, t)$ of the edges eminating from (M, t). Given (M, t), each element of the partition will have the form $\{(N, s) \mid s \prec p\}$, for some attribute $a \in Att(t)$, where $(t, a) : p^* \in D$ and where $N = \{n \mid n \text{ is "called on" } \text{self}.a \text{ by } Impl^*(m) \text{ for some } m \in M\}$.

2. "Mark" all nodes of G as "don't know".

3. If (M, t) is a node and some element m of M has implementation $\bot$ (from the removal of method calls of the form $n(\text{self})$), mark (M, t) as "nonterminating".

4. If (M, t) is a node with no out-edges and it is not marked "nonterminating", then mark (M, t) as "finite"

5. Recursively, until
   (a) If (M, t) is a node and $EG(M, t) = \{P_1, \ldots, P_n\}$ and for some i, *each* node in P_i marked nonterminating, then mark (M, t) as "nonterminating".
   (b) If (M, t) is a node and $EG(M, t) = \{P_1, \ldots, P_n\}$ and for each i, there is a node in P_i marked finite or OK, then mark (M, t) as "OK".
   (c) If (M, t) is a node and *all* out-edges of (M, t) point to a node marked finite, then mark (M, t) as "finite".

6. The set of pairs with necessary nontermination is $\{(m, t) \mid (\{m\}, t) \text{ is marked nonterminating or don't know}\}$; the set of pairs with bounded execution is $\{(m, t) \mid (\{m\}, t) \text{ is marked finite }\}$; and the set of pairs with possible successful execution is $\{(m, t) \mid (\{m\}, t) \text{ is marked finite or OK}\}$.

It is shown in the full paper that:

Lemma 4.3: Algorithm 4.2 is correct.

To summarize the section, we state:

Theorem 4.4: It is decidable, given a simple-retrieval schema $S = (T, ISA, Att, Meth, Impl, D)$ and two method-type pairs (m, t) and (m', t'), whether:

1. S is a well-typed schema.
2. (m, t) has necessarily nonterminating execution.
3. (m, t) has bounded execution.
4. (m', t') is reachable from (m, t).

5 Properties of update schemas are undecidable

In contrast with the results for simple-retrieval schemas, we have:

Theorem 5.1: Given an update schema $S = (T, ISA, Att, Meth, Impl, D)$ and two method-type pairs (m, t) and (m', t'), it is undecidable whether:

1. S is a well-typed schema.
2. (m, t) has necessarily nonterminating execution.
3. (m, t) has bounded execution.
4. (m', t') is reachable from (m, t).

These results are proved by reductions to the Post-Correspondence Problem (PCP). In each case, a schema is devised which takes as input encodings of problems P from PCP, and which has a given behavior depending on whether P has a solution or not.

6 Conclusions

In this paper we developed a workable formalism for studying the behavior of object-oriented database schemas, and used it to study fundamental questions concerning OODBs. It is our expectation that this model and its natural extensions can be used as the basis for a wide variety of theoretical investigations of the object-oriented paradigm in connection with its application to databases. We mention a few promising directions here.

A fundamental issue concerns the expressive power of various restrictions of OODBs, in connection with both queries and transactions. For example, it is known that Without restrictions, procedural query languages used with unrestricted OODBs have the power of all computable queries, and some calculus-style languages have power beyond the computable queries [HS89b]. It is thus interesting to consider the expressive power of different query languages on restricted classes of OODBs.

In the paper we focused on domain constraints. Another particularly important family of constraints on instances is to restrict object sets to be *acyclic* in various ways. This kind of restriction occurs frequently (e.g., in part-subpart hierarchies, in the ancestor relation, in supervisor hierarchies, etc.). The presence of these constraints might have significant impact on whether a given method-type pair has nonterminating execution or not.

Another family of questions raised in this paper concerns the structure of method executions. This uses the fundamental notion of *trace*, an abstraction of METs:

Definition: Let S be a schema, I an instance of S, t a type in S, m a method of t, and o an object in $I(t)$. Let $M = MET((m, t)[o]) = (V, E, \lambda)$. Then the *trace* of $m[o]$ (and $(m, t)[o]$) is the tree $trace_I((m, t)[c]) = (V, E, \lambda')$ where $\lambda'(v)$ is the middle coordinate of $\lambda(v)$ for each $v \in V$.

Natural families of traces are now defined by:

Definition: Let S be a schema, t a type of S, and $m \in Meth(t)$.

- $trace(m, t) = \{trace^I(m, t[o]) \mid I \text{ is an instance of } S \text{ and } o \in I(t)\}$.
- $trace(t) = \cup\{trace(m, t) \mid m \in Meth(t)\}$.
- $trace(t^*) = \cup\{trace(s) \mid s \text{ is a subtype of } t\}$
- $trace(S) = \cup\{trace(t) \mid t \text{ is a type in } S\}$.

These definitions provide the basis for a variety of questions concerning properties of families of traces, concerning issues such as closure properties and algebraic relationships.

References

[AH87]   T. Andrews and C. Harris. Combining language and database advances in an object-oriented development environment. In *Proc. Conf. on Object-oriented Programming Systems, Languages and Applications*, pages 430–440, 1987.

[BCG+87]   J. Banerjee, H.-T. Chou, J.F. Garza, W. Kim, D. Woelk, and N. Ballou. Data model issues for object-oriented applications. *ACM Trans. on Office Information Systems*, 5(1):3–26, January 1987.

[FBC+87]   D. H. Fishman, D. Beech, H. P. Cate, E.C. Chow, et al. Iris: An object-oriented database management system. *ACM Trans. on Office Information Systems*, 5(1):48–69, January 1987.

[GR83]   A. Goldberg and D. Robson. *Smalltalk-80: The Language and its Implementation*. Addison-Wesley, Reading, MA, 1983.

[HK87]   R. Hull and R. King. Semantic database modeling: Survey, applications, and research issues. *ACM Computing Surveys*, 19(3):201–260, September 1987.

[HS89a]   R. Hull and J. Su. On accessing object-oriented databases: Expressive power, complexity, and restrictions (extended abstract). In *Proc. ACM SIGMOD Symp. on the Management of Data*, June 1989. to appear.

[HS89b]   R. Hull and J. Su. Untyped sets, invention, and computable queries. In *Proc. ACM Symp. on Principles of Database Systems*, March 1989. to appear.

[LRV88]   C. Lecluse, P. Richard, and F. Velez. O^2: An object-oriented formal data model. In *Proc. ACM SIGMOD Symp. on the Management of Data*, Chicago, June 1988.

[PSM87]   Alan Purdy, Bruce Schuchardt, and David Maier. Integrating an object server with other worlds. *ACM Trans. on Office Information Systems*, 5(1):27–47, January 1987.

[TY88]   K. Tanaka and M. Yoshikawa. Towards abstracting complex database objects: Generalization, reduction and unification of set-type objects (extended abstract). In em Proc. 2nd Intl. Conf. on Database Theory; Lecture Notes in Computer Science, vol. 326, pages 252–266, 1988.

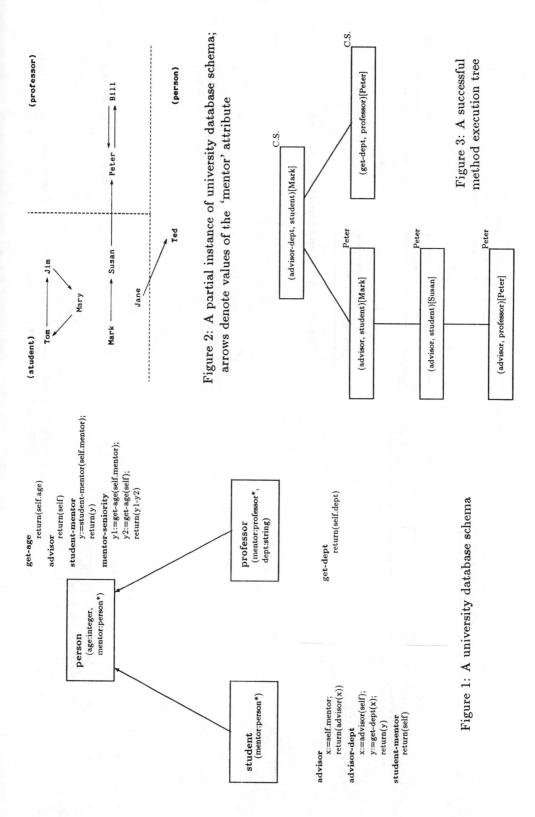

Figure 1: A university database schema

Figure 2: A partial instance of university database schema; arrows denote values of the 'mentor' attribute

Figure 3: A successful method execution tree

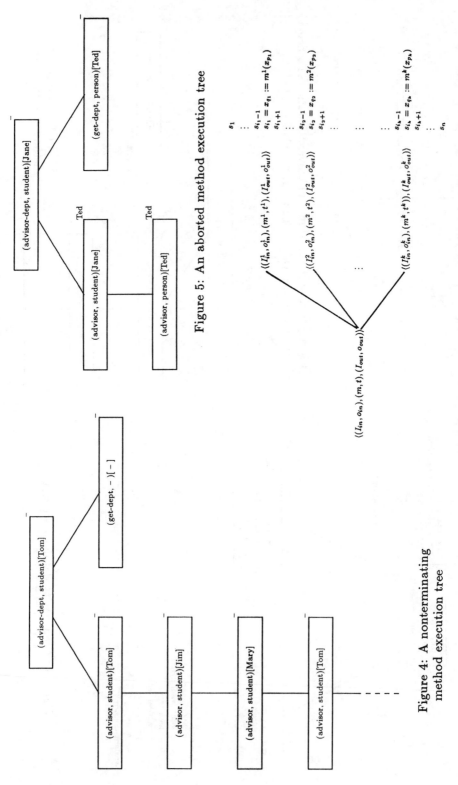

Figure 4: A nonterminating method execution tree

Figure 5: An aborted method execution tree

Figure 6: Illustration of part of definition of successful MET, showing a node and its children, with the tree branching horizontally.

Engineering the Object-Relation Database Model in O-Raid[1]

Prasun Dewan
Ashish Vikram
Bharat Bhargava
Department of Computer Science
Purdue University
W. Lafayette, IN 47907

ABSTRACT

Raid is a distributed database system based on the relational model. O-Raid is an extension of the Raid system and will support complex data objects. The design of O-Raid is evolutionary and retains all features of relational data base systems and those of a general purpose object-oriented programming language. O-Raid has several novel properties. Objects, classes, and inheritance are supported together with a predicate-based relational query language. O-Raid objects are compatible with C++ objects and may be read and manipulated by a C++ program without any "impedance mismatch". Relations and columns within relations may themselves be treated as objects with associated variables and methods. Relations may contain heterogeneous objects, that is, objects of more than one class in a certain column, which can individually evolve by being reclassified. Special facilities are provided to reduce the data search in a relation containing complex objects. The implementation of O-Raid extends the implementation of an existing distributed relational system called Raid.

1. INTRODUCTION

New emerging applications in manufacturing, robotics, image processing, and programming environments require managing databases that are more complex than those in applications such as banks and airline reservation systems. Current relational database management systems are limited in their support for these applications. These limitations are well documented in the database literature (recently in [6, 22, 24] and [25]). They include:

- *Complex Structures*: Complex data structures such as nested records, unions, and sequences need to be flattened into simpler values. This limitation results in both awkwardness of use and inefficiency, as several relations may have to be joined to retrieve

---

[1]This research is supported in part by NASA and AIRMICS under grant number NAG-1-676, and UNISYS.

the flattened representation of a complex entity.

- *Complex Operations*: Relational query languages restrict operations that can be invoked on stored data to selections, updates, joins, and projections. Complex data-specific operations need to be decomposed into these simpler operations, which is not always possible since a query language is not computationally complete.

- *Semantic Checks*: Relational databases cannot ensure that only semantically correct modifications are made to the database unless a separate subsystem to ensure integrity assertions is executed [17].

- *Semantic Actions*: Often a user may desire that an update to an entity trigger certain "side effects" or *semantic actions*. For instance, a user viewing an entity may wish to display its new value whenever the entity is updated. In the absence of support for such actions, each user has to ensure that the appropriate semantic action is triggered.

- *Generalization*: A user cannot create new entities as special cases of existing entities. As a result, information has to be duplicated in all specializations of a generic structure.

Recently, there has been interest in using the object model for managing databases. This model has been motivated by the research done in object-oriented programming languages such as Smalltalk [12] and C++ [27]. Object-oriented languages allow the encapsulation of data in *objects,* which respond to *messages* from other objects by executing *methods* that manipulate the state of the object stored in the *variables* of the object. Each object is an *instance* of a *class,* which describes the variables and methods of the object. A class can be a *subclass* of another class, in which case it inherits the variables and methods of its *superclass*.

Object-oriented languages solve limitations of the relational model as shown below:

- *Complex Data Structures*: Class declarations can be used to describe complex structures such as nested records, arrays, and unions (simulated by subclassing).

- *Complex Operations*: Objects can be associated with class-specific methods that are written in a computationally complete language and can be invoked by users to perform complex operations on the objects.

- *Semantic Checks and Actions*: Some object-oriented languages such as C++ allow an object to keep some of its variables private. These variables can be manipulated only by invoking methods on the object. The methods can ensure that only semantically correct changes are made to the object. Moreover, they can invoke methods on other objects to perform semantic actions.

- *Generalization*: Subclassing allows new classes to be created as specializations of existing classes.

While object-oriented programming languages overcome limitations of the relational databases, they do not provide many facilities available in database systems such as sharing, transactions, and efficient manipulation of large amounts of data. Recently, several object-oriented database systems such as GemStone [18], VBASE [1], and Orion [3] have tried to overcome limitations of object-oriented programming languages by extending them with database facilities. These systems provide data models that are fully integrated with general purpose programming languages, thereby eliminating the "impedance mismatch" problem in translating between language and database structures [2]. However object-oriented database systems take a "revolutionary" approach requiring that users abandon existing "time-tested" concepts and implementations and develop new ones. They offer relatively complicated (but computationally complete) programming languages which do not support relational operations such as joins and projections and force users to navigate through data. It is not obvious how ad-hoc queries can be supported in object-oriented database systems [7, 15].

The notion of a hybrid object-relation database model is attractive. Such a model can offer users the benefits of the object model without sacrificing any of the concepts (and possibly implementation) of existing relational database systems. Thus it represents an "evolutionary" approach towards overcoming limitations of current relational database systems.

Several systems have combined elements of the relational and object model to varying degrees using different approaches. For example, a system reported in [14] extends the relational model by including predefined geometric data types and operators. Iris [4, 11] provides both objects and an extension of the SQL query language for manipulating them. Postgres [22, 26], extends the relational model with procedure-valued attributes that can be used to model complex data. Exodus [8] provides sets of object values and references and a QUEL-like query language for manipulating elements of sets. DSM [23] supports binary and qualified relations in an object-oriented programming language.

We have engineered the object-relation model in the O-Raid system by extending an existing relational database system called Raid [5] (Robust and Adaptable Distributed Database System). Raid is a distributed database system that provides support for transaction processing, including transparency to concurrent access, crash recovery, distribution of data, and atomicity. O-Raid, supports the object-relation model by allowing relation attributes to be arbitrary objects. It offers C++ as a base language for defining objects in the database, and uses the facilities provided in the programming language for method invocation, inheritance, type checking, and overloading of function names and operators. It provides SQL++, an extensions of SQL, for interactively creating and manipulating relations and objects. Finally, it lets database objects be manipulated in C++ without "impedance mismatch".

Our work contributes in two main directions:

(1)   It proposes several new concepts including index variables and predicate functions, relations and columns as objects, static database variables, private pointers, reclassification of objects, and class relations.

(2)   It describes how a database system supporting the object-relation model may be engineered from an existing distributed relational database system and object-oriented programming language.

This paper is further organized as follows. Section 2, presents our design of O-Raid. Preliminary implementation notes are provided with the design. Section 3 gives an overview of the implementation. Section 4 discusses directions for further research. Finally, section 5 concludes the paper.

2. O-Raid

In the following subsections we describe the main components of O-Raid including relations, objects and classes, SQL++, and embedding of SQL++ in C++.

2.1. Relations

O-Raid relations are like Raid relations except that their attributes can be arbitrary C++ data structures including integers, strings, fixed and variable sized arrays, objects, and pointers to objects. A relation column containing objects is hierarchical, that is, it contains sub-columns storing the objects referred by the variables of the objects. Thus a postgres [26] like relation can be modeled by a relation containing one column.

Relations and their columns are themselves objects associated with variables and methods. The variables of columns and relations can be used to keep display, access, and other information common to members of the column such as display style (for instance, whether the elements of the column are to be displayed in a table, a pie chart, or a bar graph), colour, display width, and access list. The methods of columns and relations can be used to display or manipulate both their variables and their elements. For instance, in O-Raid a column/relation is associated with the default **print** method, which uses the information stored in the variables of the column/relation to print its elements.

2.2. Database Classes and Objects

A database class in O-Raid is composed of the declaration of a *base class* and (optional) declarations of its *readonly* variables, *own* and *private* pointers, *predicate functions*, and *column class*. We illustrate how database classes are defined in O-Raid through the example of the geometric classes *shape, rectangle*, and *triangle*.

Base Classes

A programmer creates a new database class by first defining a *base class* for it. The base class of a database class is a C++ class defining the public and private variables and functions (methods) of the database class. The concept of a base class defined in an existing object-oriented programming language allows us to use the implementation of method invocation and inheritance in the language. Moreover, it offers users of that language an evolutionary path towards the object-relation database model. We have chosen C++ as the base language because it is compatible with C and most of our current software is written in C.

The base class for *shape* is defined as follows:

```
class shape {
public:
        int x_coord, y_coord; /* coordinates of the centroid of the object */

        virtual int distance (shape other_shape)
        { --- }

        virtual bool operator<(shape other_shape);
        { --- }
}
```

The variables *x_coord*, and *y_coord* define the coordinates of the centroid of the object. The function *distance*, calculates the distance between the object and *other_shape*. The function ''<'' compares the object with another object.

The base class *rectangle*, is created as subclass of *shape*:

```
class rectangle : public shape {
        /* coordinates of end points of rectangles */
        int lower_left_x, lower_left_y, upper_right_x, upper_right_y;
public:
        rectangle(---) /* used for initialization */
        { --- }

        int area()
        { --- }

        void magnify(---)
        { --- }
}
```

In a similar manner the base class *triangle* is created to describe triangles. *triangle* and *rectangle* embellish the definition of *shape* by providing variables for storing the endpoints of shapes and functions for initializing shapes, calculating their area, and magnifying them.

NEWCLASS Declaration

Once a base class has been declared in C++, the corresponding database class may be registered with O-Raid by using the **NEWCLASS** declaration. For instance, the following **NEWCLASS** declarations may be used to create the database class *shape*:

```
NEWCLASS {
        class shape;
        file shape.c;
}
```

In this declaration, the programmer specifies the name of the new database class and the file containing the definition of the corresponding base class. The database classes *rectangle* and *triangle* may be similarly registered.

Public, Readonly, and Private Variables

C++ allows the programmer to divide the variables of an object into *public* and *private* variables. Public variables are accessible to clients of the object while private variables are accessible only to the functions of the object. O-Raid also provides the concepts of private and public variables of a database object. In addition, it allows the public variables of an object to be divided into *modifiable* and *readonly* variables.

Dividing the state of a database object into modifiable, readonly, and private variables serves the following purpose: It relieves the programmer from the overhead of defining trivial methods that simply read and write its state, while allowing him to support data abstraction, semantic checks, and semantic actions when necessary. Private variables can be used to keep implementation-dependent data of the object. Readonly variables can be used to keep public data associated with semantic checks and actions. Modifiable variables can be used to keep public data that does not need such protection.

Class *shape* and *rectangle* illustrate the use of public and private variables of an object. Class *rectangle* makes the representation of the rectangle private, thereby allowing the programmer to change the representation of the rectangle (for instance, to one storing two end points and a diagonal). Class *shape* makes the coordinates of the centroid of a shape public variables, which are modifiable by default, and can be explicitly declared to be readonly in a NEWCLASS declaration.

Column and Relation Classes

In O-Raid columns are also *objects* in that they are associated with instance variables and respond to messages. Each class is associated with a *column class*, which defines the class of columns containing instances of the class. The column class of a class is declared when the class is registered.

The following example illustrates the use of column classes. A class *shape_column* may be defined as follows:

```
class shape_column {
public:
        int max_x, min_x, max_y, min_y;
    ---
}
```

After this is registered with the system, it may be declared as the column class of *shape*, as shown below:

```
NEWCLASS {
        class      shape;
        file       shape.c;
        column class shape_column;
}
```

Now any column that contains objects of class *shape* will belong to class *shape_column*. In this example, the instance variables of *shape_column* define the limits of the x and y coordinates of the centroid of the elements of the column. Functions to initialize or change the position of these elements access these variables through embedded SQL++ to ensure that they are the correct range.

The notion of the column class of a class is analogous to the Smalltalk notion of the metaclass of a class. Like a metaclass, a column class can be used to define information common to several instances of a class. The main difference is that a metaclass of a class defines single class object that keeps information common to *all* instances of the class while a column class of a class defines several *column objects*, each one of which keeps information common to objects in that column. Note that column classes do not compete with the notion of Smalltalk metaclasses. Indeed, in O-Raid, the static variables of the class (discussed later) are similar to class variables in a metaclass and keep information shared by all objects of that class.

Like ordinary classes, column classes can be arranged in an inheritance hierarchy. A predefined class, *column*, provides default variables and functions of columns.

Similarly a relation is also an object belonging to some class, and keeps information common to all its tuples. The class of a relation is optionally specified using SQL++ at relation creation time. By default it is the predefined class *relation*.

Note that it is possible to allows users to specify classes of columns at relation creation time instead of the time the class of its elements is defined. The first alternative would allow different columns containing the same class of elements to be instances of different classes. We chose the second alternative because (a) it lets the programmer of a class assume that some of the properties of its instances are stored in the columns containing them, (b) it reduces the effort required by users to create relations, and (c) we did not see the need for the added flexibility of the first alternative.

Index Variables and Predicate Functions

O-Raid allows selected variables of an object to be used as keys of the relations containing them. The key of a relation can be declared at relation-creation time, as described in section 2.6, or at class registration time by using an **index** declaration. For instance, the user may include the declaration

    index upper_right_x, upper_left_y;

in the **NEWCLASS** declaration of *rectangle*. Any relation containing rectangles will then use *upper_right_x*, and *upper_left_y* as keys. The type/class of a key must be *comparable*, that is must define the '<' operator. This operator is system-defined for many predefined C++ types such as integers and reals, and can be explicitly defined for user-defined C++ classes.

Like Postgres, O-Raid allows a function without arguments that returns objects of a comparable class to be also declared as a key. The result of the function invocation is then recomputed and used for indexing the relation. For example the function *area()* in class *rectangle* could be made a key at class registration time by including the following declaration:

    index area();

O-Raid also supports the concept of *predicate functions* to provide efficient search of complex structures. We motivate this concept through an example. Assume that a boolean function, *overlap*, is defined in class rectangle:

```
bool overlap (rectangle rect)
{ return( (lower_left_x <= rect.upper_right_x) & ---)}
```

This function determines if the current object overlaps with its argument. Now assume that the function is used to select from a set of rectangles all those that overlap a particular rectangle. O-Raid has no choice but to invoke the compiled C++ function on *all* members of the relation and return those that satisfy the condition. The search could be made more, efficient however, if the variables *lower_left_x*, *lower_left_y*, etc that are used in the expression have been defined as keys in the relation containing these rectangles. The system could then use suitable physical representation of the relation such as a multi-index K-D-B tree [20] to reduce the search space at query resolution. However, the query processor would need to *interpret* this expression in order to perform the comparisons.

O-Raid supports interpretation of functions by allowing a function to be made a *predicate function*. Such a function contains a boolean expression that is interpreted by the query processor at run time. The query processor uses the expression to determine its search path through a B-Tree or K-D-B tree created to store the relation.

Own Values, Shared Pointers, Own Pointers, and Private Pointers

Like Exodus, O-Raid supports the notions of *own value*, *own pointers*, and *shared pointers*. In addition it supports the concept of *private pointers*. An own value is an object stored in a relation tuple or object variable, and is considered a part of the parent object or tuple. (A tuple itself may be considered as an object without functions whose public modifiable values are the components of the tuple.) It is copied and deleted with the parent object. An own pointer refers to another object, called its referent. It may be stored in variables of several objects in the database, but is owned by one of these objects, called its owner. It is copied and deleted with the owner. A shared pointer is like an own pointer except that its referent is equally shared by all objects that refer to it. A private pointer is like an own value in that its referent cannot be shared with other objects. We support both the notion of an own value and a private pointer because private pointers, unlike own values, can be used to define recursive types and can be reclassified, as discussed later.

The notion of a database pointer is different from the notion of a C++ pointer, in two respects: First, a database pointer is the OID (Object Identifier) of the referent while a C++ pointer is the virtual address of the referent. Second, C++ does not distinguish between own, shared, and private pointers. O-Raid considers C++ pointers declared in a base class to be shared database pointers, unless the programmer explicitly declares them to be **own** or **private** while registering the class.

The values and pointers stored in the variables of an object are kept with the object in the relation containing it. The indices stored in the referent of a private pointer of an object are also kept with the object to support efficient lookup of these values. Note that conceptually, it is possible to keep indices stored in referents of all pointers of an object with the object. However, this scheme requires back pointers from a referent to all objects that refer to it (to keep all copies of the indices consistent), which need to be updated whenever a reference to it is added or deleted.

Objects referred to by database pointers are stored in their *class relation*. For each class O-Raid creates a class relation which has the same name as the class. This relation stores objects of that class that are not own values.

Global and Static Database Variables

Objects in O-Raid may be accessed not only as parts of relations and other objects but also independently as *static* and *global* database variables. The former correspond to static variables declared in a C++ class and are used to keep information shared by all instances of the class. Static data of a class is kept in the variables of its class relation (which like other relations is also an object).

Global database variables are created and manipulated using SQL++ (discussed later). O-Raid defines the relation *global_variables* to map global variables to the OIDs they contain. This relation has three attributes, (1) *name*, which stores the name of the global variable, (2) *obj*, which stores the OID of the object referred by the variable and (3) *class*, which stores the type of the variable. Like other pointers, the pointers stored in global variables may be own, shared, or private. Global variables allow the database programmer to refer to database objects by name and allow the database designer the flexibility of designing the database as a collection of named objects.

Reclassification

Like C++ and other statically typed object-oriented languages, O-Raid allows variables declared as pointers to a class to refer to any subclass of that class. Only indices declared in that class can be used as keys of relations containing the pointers. Indices declared in a subclass of the class cannot be used as keys, since not all elements of relation columns containing these pointers may refer to objects of that particular subclass.

Objects often evolve and change their characteristics. For instance, a *person* object may become a *student* object, and later an *employee* object. Similarly, the shape of an object may change from a *triangle* object to a *rectangle* object. O-Raid supports such evolution by allowing the class of an object referred by a pointer variable to be changed to one of the valid classes for that variable. It replaces the object with an object of the new class that has the same values of variables common to the old and new class.

This technique of reclassifying *individual* objects complements the work done in Gemstone [19] and Orion [16] to allow evolution of *all* objects in a class by supporting changes to the class definition. We plan to support class evolution in O-Raid along the lines suggested by previous work.

3. SQL++

Like Postgres, Iris, and Exodus we extend an existing relational query language with constructs for supporting objects. We have chosen SQL as the base language and call the extended language SQL++. Our main extensions to SQL include constructs for supporting relations containing objects, global variables, column and relation objects, and copying of objects. We illustrate these extensions below using examples.

Relations Containing Objects

A user may create a new relation called *triangles*

    CREATE INDEX ON (obj) triangles (char name[20]; triangle *obj);

with attributes *name* and *obj* and key *obj*. The declarations of types of attributes follow C++ syntax. In the above example, *obj* is a shared pointer. Pointers may be declared to be own or private by prepending the keyword **own** or **private** to the name of the attribute.

A particular element can be added to the relation as follows:

    INSERT INTO triangles VALUES (name = "T1", obj = triangle(0,0));

In the above example, a C++ constructor function is used for initialization of the *obj* attribute.

The relation can be updated by either assigning new values to its objects or invoking functions, as illustrated below:

    UPDATE INTO triangles
        SET (obj.x_coord = 1, obj.y_coord = 1, obj.magnify(---))
        WHERE ((obj < triangle(1,1)) and (obj.area() <= 9))

Notice that the modifiable objects *x_coord,* and *y_coord* can be modified directly. Other objects may be modified only by invoking functions. The predicates involved in a WHERE clause can use results of function invocations, as illustrated by the above example. Standard C++ syntax is offered for invoking functions, and standard dot notation is provided for selecting variables of objects.

Public variables of objects stored in relations may be projected, as shown below:

    SELECT (obj.x_coord) INTO temp FROM triangles WHERE
    ((obj.x_coord > 0) & (obj.y_coord :

Moreover, relations containing objects may be joined. For example the following query

    SELECT(t1.name t2.name) FROM triangles t1, triangles t2
        WHERE ((t1.obj.x_coord = t2.obj.x_coord) and (t1.obj.y_coord = t2.obj.y_coord))

prints out the names of all pairs of triangles with a common centroid.

Global Variables, Relation and Column Objects

SQL++ provides constructs for creating and modifying objects referred by global variables, which parallel constructs for creating and modifying relations. For instance, a user creates a new global variable called *T* of type *triangle* by executing the following construct

    CREATE triangle *T SET (T = triangle(1,2));

where the SET part is optional and initializes the variable. The variables of the object denoted by *T* may later be updated as follows:

    UPDATE T SET (T.x_coord = 10, T.magnify(---));

Column and relation objects are created when the corresponding relation is created. The class of a relation can be optionally specified at relation creation time. For instance, the query

    CREATE shape_relation shapes(char name[20]; obj *shape);

creates a new relation *shapes* of class *shape_relation.* Relation objects are manipulated exactly as global variables. For instance, the query

UPDATE shapes SET(shapes.max_x = 10);

pdates the *max_x* variable of relation *shapes*.

The variables of column objects are updated and selected by queries that contain the eyword COLUMN to distinguish them from queries that update and select variables of bjects stored in the column.

opying Object Values and Pointers

SQL++ provides primitives for copying object values and pointers stored in the data-ase. It allows queries to be tied together by using an AND operator and allows values and ointers retrieved from the database to be assigned to variables, which may later be used to pdate other parts of the database. For instance the following query

SELECT (M = manager) FROM employee WHERE (name = "John")
AND INSERT INTO employee VALUES (name = "Joe", manager = M, ...);

etrieves the manager of the employee "John" in the variable *M* and assigns this value to the nanager field of the employee "Joe". In this example, *M* is a local variable whose scope is imited to the query. Object value and pointers may also be stored in and retrieved from glo-al variables, which are prefixed with a '%' to disambiguate them from local variables.

The following rules are used when an *rhs* is assigned to an *lhs*: If the *rhs* is a shared or wn pointer, or an own value, then the pointer or value, as appropriate, is directly assigned to he *lhs*. If the *rhs* is a private pointer, then a copy of the referent of the pointer is assigned to he *lhs*. Pointers are implicitly dereferenced when assigned to non-pointer variables and vice ersa. They may be explicitly dereferenced by using the "*" operator as in C++.

Thus in the above query if the *manager* field contains an object value then a copy of the alue is used in the update. Otherwise, the pointer is copied and changes to the referent ffects both employees.

.4. Embedding SQL++ in a C++ Program

Since SQL++ is not computationally complete, we allow it to be embedded in C++ pro-rams. It is conceptually possible to embed it in programs written in other programming anguages. However, it is easier to emebed it in C++ because there is a direct mapping etween C++ objects and database objects defined using C++ base classes.

A query executed from a C++ program may transfer data between C++ variables and the atabase. C++ variables used in a query are prefixed with a '$' to avoid confusing them with ocal query variables and global database variables. For instance, the following query may be nvoked from a C++ program:

SELECT ($s = name, $t = obj) FROM triangles WHERE (name = "T1");

where *s* should be a C++ string variable and *t* should be a C++ variable of class *triangle*.

The SELECT query may be associated with a C++ block statement, which is executed nce for every tuple selected. Thus the following query

```
SELECT ($s = name) FROM employees WHERE (salary > 50000) {
    printf("%s\n",s);
}
```

will print out the names of all employees with a salary greater than 50,000.

O-Raid automatically converts between the database and program representations of object values and pointers. When an object is read into memory, all it's components are also read and the OID's are replaced by valid memory pointers. Conversely, when a C++ object is written to the database, all its components are written to the database and the memory pointers replaced with OID's.

Our scheme is inefficient when only a few components of a large object are manipulated in the program. We do not currently allow reading and writing of components of an object or demand since it would require changes to the C++ compiler.

We ensure that if two objects with a shared component are read into memory the component is read once and remains shared in memory. Cycles in the database are also retained in memory. Conversely, we ensure that shared structures in memory remain shared in the database and cycles are retained.

To implement these features, O-Raid keeps in each program a table mapping OID's to memory pointers and vice-versa. This table is flushed at the end of each transaction.

3. Overview of the Implementation of O-Raid

We are implementing O-Raid by extending our current relational database implementation in Raid[5]. Raid is a message passing system, with server processes on each site. The servers manage concurrent processing, consistent replicated copies during site failures, and atomic distributed commitment. A high level, layered communication package provides a clean, location independent interface between the servers. The Raid servers are: User Interface(UI) - the front end invoked by the user to process queries, Action Driver(AD) - executes the transactions, Access Manager(AM) - provides write access to the database, Atomicity Controller(AC) - manages two commit phases of transaction processing to ensure global serializability, Replication Controller(RC) - maintains consistency of the replicated copies of the database and Concurrency Controller(CC) - ensures local serializability at a given site.

The initial implementation of O-Raid will change the UI, the AD and the AM. A new User Interface is being designed to parse and typecheck user SQL++ queries. It transforms valid queries into a sequence of instructions and passes these to the Action Driver. Queries are optimized using information about available indices and sizes of relations. It is also responsible for registering new classes.

The Action Driver is responsible for carrying out the inserts, updates and deletes. It loads and executes C++ functions as required. Both data and functions are cached. Certain system defined relations and certain functions (such as *print*) are preloaded. Changes to the database are maintained in a log file and are posted to the database at commit time.

The Access Manager is being changed to take care of all reads and writes to the database. The AD requests the AM for data whenever it needs to access it. The AM has been extended to provide more appropriate indexing methods such as K-D-B-Trees [20]

A pre-processor for C++ is being implemented to allow embedded SQL. A more detailed implementation will be the subject of another paper.

Future Work in O-RAID

We are extending the design of O-Raid in several ways. We are exploring class evolution, using ideas from Orion and GemStone. We are also exploring a "visual" alternative to the query interface for manipulating objects. The query interface requires the user to know the names and types of the variables of objects the messages that can be send to them. For instance, a user who enters the query

UPDATE INTO rel SET (obj.f1.f11 = 3, obj.f1.f12 = true, f2 = "foo", obj.f1.m1(3, true))
WHERE (obj.f3 == 3.0)

needs to know that $f1$ and $f2$ are modifiable variables of obj, $obj.f1$ refers to a structured object consisting of modifiable attributes $f11$ and $f12$, and the function $m1$, and so on.

We are designing a customizable structure-editing interface for manipulating objects. This will help the user both with the structure and protocol of objects. Structure-editing interfaces are extensions of the form interfaces provided by relational databases such as ADE [21] which let the user edit the contents of unstructured tuples. Structure-editing has been mainly explored in the context of programming languages. However it has also been used as a general paradigm for interaction [9]. We believe it is particularly suitable in a database supporting objects with complex structure and semantics. The nature of structure-editing interfaces and techniques for customizing them in a database environment are open research issues we are currently exploring.

Integration of objects and relations offers the opportunity to get the benefits of both models but raises the possibility of a complex non-uniform system. Implementation and evaluation is necessary to explore the usefulness of this approach. Our immediate goal is to complete the implementation of the current design. This will provide an estimate of the effort required to extend a relational model with object-oriented features. We plan to perform measurements that compare the costs of retrieving data encapsulated in relations and objects. We will use the system to store geometric objects, corporate army databases containing geographical, textual, and other complex data, and syntax tree, symbol tables, and other information about shared program modules.

Object-oriented systems have illustrated the usefulness of creating a programming environment based on the object model [10, 13]. A complimentary direction of research that builds a similar environment based on the object-relation model can be carried out. This model would replace or augment text files, hierarchical directories, command interpreters, and text editors of current environments with relations of objects, hierarchical relations, query interpreters, and graphical/structure-editors respectively.

5. Conclusions

An integrated object-relation model can offer the benefits of object model withou sacrificing the "time-tested" facilities of the current relational model. In this paper, we have described a system that supports this model. The paper makes two main contributions:

(1) It proposes several new concepts including index variables and predicate functions relations and columns as objects, private pointers, reclassification of objects, stati database variables, and class relations.

(2) It describes how a distributed database system supporting the object-relation mode may be engineered from an existing distributed relational database system and object oriented programming language.

We plan to use our implementation to support geometric, geographic, and program data bases, and to test algorithms that use semantics of objects to increase concurrency in a parti tioned database. Further research is needed to evaluate the usefulness of a hybrid-object rela tion model and build a programming environment based on this model.

Acknowledgement

We would like to thank Stephen Leung for his contributions to a preliminary version o this paper that resulted in the technical report(CSD-TR-781).

REFERENCES

[1] Timothy Andrews and Craig Harris, "Combining Language and Database Advances in an Object-Oriented Development Environment," OOPSLA '87 Proceedings, October 1987, pp 430-440.

[2] Malcolm P. Atkinson and O. Peter Buneman, "Types and Per- sistence in Database Pro gramming Languages," ACM Computer Surveys 19:2 (June 1987).

[3] Jay Banerjee, Won Kim, and Kyung-Chang Kim, "Queries in Object-Oriented Databases, Proceedings of the Fourth International Conference on Data Engineering, February 1988 pp. 31-38.

[4] David Beech, "A Foundation For Evolution From Relational To Object Databases," Advance in Database Technology - EDBT

[5] B. Bhargava and J. Riedl, "The RAID Distributed Database System" IEEE Transactions on Software Engineering, June 1989, Vol 15, No 6.

[6] Michael Blaha, William J. Premerlani, and James E. Rum- baugh, "Relational Database Design Using an Object-Oriented Methodology," Comm. ACM 31:4 (April 1988), pp. 414-427

[7] Toby Bloom and Stanley B. Zdonik, "Issues in the Design of Object-Oriented Database Pro gramming Languages," OOPSLA '87 Proceedings, October 1987, pp. 441-451.

[8] M. J. Carey, D. J. DeWitt, and S. L. Vandenberg, "A Data Model and Query Language for EXODUS," Proceedings of the SIGMOD International Conference on Management of Data June 1988, pp. 413-423.

[9] Prasun Dewan and Marvin Solomon, "Dost: An Environment to Support Automatic Genera tion of User Interfaces," Proceed- ings of the ACM SIGSOFT/SIGPLAN Software Engineering Sympo- sium on Practical Software Development Environments, SIG- PLAN Notices 22:1 (January 1987), pp. 150-159.

10] Prasun Dewan and Eric Vasilik, "Supporting Objects in a Conventional Operating System," San Diego Winter '89 Usenix Conference, February 1989, pp. 273-286.

11] D. H. Fishman, D. Beech, H. P. Cate, E. C. Chow, T. Con- nors, J. W. Davis, N. Derett, C. G. Hoch, W. Kent, P. Lyng- baek, B. Mahbod, M. A. Neimat, T. A. Ryan, and M. C. Shain, "Iris: An Object-Oriented Database Management System," ACM Transactions on Office Information Systems 5:1 (January 1987), pp. 48-69.

12] Adele Goldberg and David Robinson, Smalltalk-80: The Language and its Implementation, Addison-Wesley, Reading, Mass., 1983.

13] Adele Goldberg, Smalltalk-80: The Interactive Programming Environment, Addison-Wesley, Reading, Mass., 1984.

14] Ralf Hartmut Guting, "Geo-Relational Algebra: A Model and Query Language for Geometric Database Systems," Advances in Database Technology - EDBT '88, March 1988, pp. 506-526.

15] J.Ullman, "Database Theory - Past and Future," Proceedings of the PODS Conference, San Diego, CA., March 1987.

16] Won Kim, Jay Banerjee, Hong-Tai Chou, Jorge F. Garza, and Darrel Woelk, "Composite Object Support in an Object- Oriented Database System," OOPSLA '87 Proceedings, October 1987, pp. 118-125.

17] Angelika M. Kotz, Klaus R. Dittrich, and Jutta A. Mulle, "Supporting Semantic Rules by a Generalised Event/Trigger Mechanism," Advances in Database Technology - EDBT '88, , pp. 76-90.

18] Davis Maier, Jacob Stein, Allen Otis, and Alan Purdy, "Development of an Object-Oriented DBMS," OOPSLA '86 Proceedings, September 1986, pp. 472-483.

19] D. Jason Penney and Jacob Stein, "Class Modification in GemStone Object-Oriented DBMS," OOPSLA '87 Proceedings, October 1987, pp. 111-117.

20] R. Robinson, "The K-D-B-Tree: A Search Structure for Large Multi-Dimensional Indexes," Proceedings of 1981 ACM-SIGMOD Int. Conf. on the Mgt. of Data, April 1981, pp. 10-18.

21] Lawrence A. Rowe, "'Fill-in-the-Form' Programming," Proceedings of VLDB, 1985, pp. 394-404.

22] Lawrence A. Rowe and Michael Stonebraker, "The POSTGRES Data Model," Proc. 13th VLDB Conference, 1987 .

23] James Rumbaugh, "Relations as Semantic Constructs in an Object-Oriented Language," OOPSLA '87 Proceedings, October 1987, pp. 466-481.

24] G. Schlageter, R. Unland, W. Wilkes, R. Zieschang, G. Maul, M. Nagl, and R. Meyer, "OOPS - An Object Oriented Program- ming System with Integrated Data Management Facility," Proceedings of the Fourth International Conference on Data Engineering, February 1988, pp. 118-127.

25] Karen E. Smith and Stanley B. Zdonik, "Intermedia: A Case Study of the Differences Between Relational and Object- Oriented Database Systems," OOPSLA '87 Proceedings, October 1987, pp. 452-465 .

26] Michael Stonebraker and Lawrence A. Rowe, "The POSTGRES papers," Memorandom No. UCB/ERL M86/85, University of Cali- fornia, Berkeley, June 87.

27] Bjarne Stroustrup, The C++ Programming Language, Addison- Wesley, Reading, Mass., 1986.

ROOST:

A Relational Object Oriented System[†]

Nick Roussopoulos
Hyun Soon Kim

Department of Computer Science
College Park, Maryland 20742

Abstract

This paper presents ROOST, an object oriented data model for relational databases. ROOST defines objects as multi–level hierarchical aggregations of base relations, views, and/or other objects. It is a new, rather conservative approach, that is substantially different than those that follow the object oriented programming language approach. ROOST was designed to be easily portable to existing relational database systems. An object is structured as a hierarchical aggregation of subcomponents. Subcomponents are tables which are the media of relational databases, or other objects. The model includes languages for creating, manipulating, updating, and browsing objects. The proposed object model has been implemented on top of a relational database system.

1. Introduction

Object oriented systems are receiving wide attention these days in a varieties of areas such as office systems, database systems, programming languages, and artificial intelligence. An object oriented system can be loosely defined to be a system where data and its manipulations are encapsulated as one entity contrasting with their conventional counterparts where data and procedures are treated as two independent entities. Object oriented systems have the characteristics of abstraction of data, inheritance of properties, independence of data, and encapsulation of data and operations (modularity) [Derr86], [Keta86], [Kris81], [Lyng86], [Rowe87], [Wied86], [Wirt83], [Woel86], [Xero81]. These properties make object oriented systems capable of dealing with arbitrary data types in an environment that is constantly changing and developing. These properties also make object oriented systems suitable for encompassing complex multimedia data modes.

This paper proposes a new object oriented data model for relational databases. It extends some of the concepts of [Wied86]. In ROOST objects are collections of relational views which are the medium of relational databases. The concept of multi–level data schema is adapted by allowing objects to include other objects as their subcomponents. Inheritance is achieved through the construction and the support mechanism of relational views.

This is a rather conservative approach that provides no explicit message passing mechanism, but it offers a number of advantages. First of all, it relies on known relational database technology. Objects and abstractions are supported by well–defined and accepted query languages. Second, access methods and optimization techniques are well understood. Performance can be addressed at the logical level [Rous82a,b], [Sell88], which is an issue that has yet to be dealt in the more "pure" object oriented database systems. Third, since the basic building block is the relational view, supported by all relational systems, it is portable to all such systems and remains unaffected by changes in the lower level

[†] This research was sponsored partially by the National Science Foundation under Grant IRI–8719458 and the University of Maryland Institutes for Advanced Computer Studies.

implementation.

The proposed object model has been implemented on top of the Advanced Database Management System, ADMS, [Rous87b], which uses an *incremental access method* to provide high performance access to relational views [Rous87a].

Section 2 of this paper gives an overview of ROOST. Section 3 describes the Object Operation languages. Section 4 presents the capabilities of ROOST and the status of its implementation. Conclusions and further developments are in section 5.

2. The ROOST Object Oriented Data Model

This section describes the fundamental elements of ROOST. We define the concepts in terms of ADMS relational constructs. We will define the object definition and object manipulation languages in the following section.

2.1. Definition of an Object

An **object** for a relational database is defined to be a non–recursive hierarchical aggregation of sub-components. Subcomponents are either base relations, views, and/or other objects. Allowing an object to be a subcomponent of another object is a very important concept in achieving the hierarchical structure of ROOST. A base relation is a user defined table which has an independent existence, and a view is a table derived from one or more existing relations by an application of the relational algebra. Visually an object can be represented as n–ary tree where terminals are base relations or views, and nonterminals are other objects. Terminals and nonterminals do not have to be unique, allowing repetitive occurrence. Figure 2.1 illustrates an example of objects in a graphic representation.

There is no direct or indirect communication channel between one object to another object unlike those between objects in Smalltalk. Each object is highly independent but composite in structure like objects modeled in Engineering Information Systems [Rous86a], [Keta86]. Now let's look at the views in ADMS more closely since they are the basic building blocks of ROOST.

2.2. Views in ADMS

Views in relational database are defined as a query over the base relations or over other views. A view on a database permits a user in a database system to obtain access to a suitably limited amount of data. The view, as any relational query result, is also a relation.

A base relation in ADMS corresponds directly to a data file kept on secondary storage. A view, on the other hand, does not have independent existence and is maintained as an array of pointers called the *view index* [Rous82a]. The pointers in this index refer to tuples in the relations from which the view was derived and need be accessed in order to materialize the view. For the user, though, views appear like ordinary relations with the exception that they cannot be updated directly. View indexes are stored on disk to obtain persistency. In the sequel, we will assume that base relations are a special subset of views that are derived with an identity function. Unless it is specifically mentioned otherwise, whenever we refer to views, we imply that the same holds for base relations as well.

Updates to the underlying relations are reflected in the views by modifying the view index. A deferred and/or delayed update strategy is used to reduce and/or delay the overhead associated with the propagation of updates from the base relation updates to the view indexes. In the deferred case, only when a request to use the index is explicitly made, the propagation cost becomes the access cost of a view [Rous87b]. In the delayed case, views are updated periodically.

2.3. Properties of Object

The concept of object as presented in this paper will have the following desirable properties.

A. Inheritance

Two types of inheritance is supported by ROOST. The first is at the record instance level. Views automatically inherit changes made to the underlying base relations. This is done by the view support mechanism of the relational system that being Query modification [Ston75] or incremental access methods [Rous87a].

The second type of inheritance is structural. All properties and structure of an object is inherited by its encapsulating object. Since the construction of the objects follows the database paradigm that goes through a query language, meta–level management of the catalogs storing information about the objects is done at a high level. Therefore, inheritance of structural semantics can be done by defining objects that encapsulate all the structures pertinent to some aspect. Consistency is one such structural aspect that is discussed in a following section. We used this technique for capturing the semantics of consistency.

B. High and Multi Level Structure

Since objects are built using views on top of a relational database, this object model provides a high level structure. This frees users or application programmers from concerns of changes in the lower level relational database system. Changes that generate new views and the supporting mechanisms of relational views do not affect existing object structure.

Any predefined object can be a subcomponent of any other object other than its own ancestor. This characteristic makes an object a multi–level structure, and allows reuse of the object definition. Views cannot be removed from the system unless all objects that encapsulate it are removed.

C. Flexibility and Independence

Subcomponents can be freely attached and detached from an object. This removes the rigidity of a cluster [Jaco85] which is defined to be a relation having other relations built in as a substructure of it. In a cluster, once it is defined, the structure becomes permanent and can not be changed. A relation built in a cluster becomes a part of the cluster's structure and does not keep its independence. But a ROOST object's structure can be changed as desired by attaching, detaching, re–attaching, or replacing its subcomponents. This can be done because each subcomponent preserves its own independence.

D. Sharability

In the system view names are unique. But the same view can be shared by many objects. A view can be used more than once as a subcomponent of an object or of several different objects. This characteristic is particularly convenient for browsing objects that have many related views that need to be browsed simultaneously. The multiple occurrences of the same view in an object saves the user's unnecessary effort to search for the view back and forth within an object.

E. Random access of subcomponents

In accessing any terminal views or nonterminal objects, the path need not follow the hierarchical top down path. Views used as subcomponents are in existence independent of the existence of the encapsulating object and can be accessed individually through the ADMS relational language. Even though an object is used as a subcomponent of another object, the subcomponents of any object exist on their own right.

2.4. Object Catalog

There are three system catalogs, *relations, views, and objects* in ROOST. The catalog *relations* stores information about existing relations in the system. Catalog *views* stores information about how each view is derived. These are what all relational systems call *system's catalogs*. The catalog *objects*, which stores information about the structure of objects, is a meta schema file. It consists of two attributes, obj and subcomp. Obj is the object's identification, and subcomp is either the name of a base relation, a view, or an already defined object's id. When a new object is created, its obj and subcomp will enter the *objects* catalog. Since an object is defined in a multi–level way, the *objects* catalog is very important in tracing down each level of an object's subcomponent definition.

The *objects* catalog is the only place where all the information about objects are kept. Application programs access this catalog to find out about the structure of an object. This brings in a desirable level of independence equivalent to the one provided by the separation of schema and program in databases.

3. Object Operation Languages

In this section we will introduce the object operation languages with examples. In section 3.1 an object definition language is introduced to show how to define, duplicate, rename, remove, and flatten an object. In section 3.2 we show an object update language for changing an object's structure by attaching, detaching, or replacing subcomponents. In section 3.3 an object manipulation meta–language is introduced to operate collectively on all subcomponents of objects. In section 3.4 we look at an object browsing language for displaying objects, their attributes, their structure, and their catalog.

3.1. Object Definition Language

A) **create** <object> **with** <subcomp–list>

Creates an object with subcomponents. A subcomponent can be either a view or an already defined object other than any ancestor of the source object.

B) **duplicate** <source–object> **into** <target–object>

Creates a new target–object having the same subcomponents as the source–object. The source–object will still remain in the *objects* catalog.

C) **rename** <source–object> **into** <target–object>

Changes the name of a source–object into the target–object. All other objects, having the source–object as their subcomponent, receive the new name.

D) **kill** <source–object–list> [**global**]

Removes objects in the list from the *objects* catalog. If it is a global kill, all the descendent objects under the source object will be removed from the *objects* catalog also. A message will be issued telling which objects are removed.

E) **flatten** <source–object> **into** <target–object>

By traversing the source object n–ary tree from left to right the views under the source object will be collected and become one–level subcomponents of the target object.

Example: The database used for illustration is a University database. The base relations are:

College(name, location, head)
Department(dept, location, tel, head, college)
Faculty(ss#, name, dept, rank, degree)
Administrator(ss#, name, dept, position)
Student(ss#, name, dept, major, admission_date, u/g)
Course(dept, no, title, credit, time, location, instructor)

There are also views created using a SQL–like language:

f_{cs} :– **select** * **from** Faculty **where** dept = 'cs'
a_{cs} :– **select** * **from** Administrator **where** dept = 'cs'
s_{cs} :– **select** * **from** Student **where** dept = 'cs'
c_{cs} :– **select** * **from** Course **where** dept = 'cs'
f_{eng} :– **select** name,rank **from** Faculty F,Department D
　　　　where F.dept = D.dept **and** D.college = 'engineering'

Objects are created as follows. First, all the subcomponents used to create the department objects are the derived views. Figure 3.1 shows the graphical structure of each object.

create cs_dept **with** f_{cs} a_{cs} s_{cs} c_{cs}
create math_dept **with** f_{math} a_{math} s_{math} c_{math}
create phy_dept **with** f_{phy} a_{phy} s_{phy} c_{phy}
create art_dept **with** f_{art} a_{art} s_{art} c_{art}
create psy_dept **with** f_{psy} a_{psy} s_{psy} c_{psy}

Now we create objects whose subcomponents consist of other objects.

create coll_of_sci **with** cs_dept math_dept phy_dept
create coll_of_art_hum **with** art_dept psy_dept
create acad_orga **with** coll_of_sci coll_of_art_hum

Figure 3.2 shows the hierarchical structure of the created objects and a part of the *objects* catalog storing this structure.

3.2. Object Update Language

The following commands modify the structure of an object. The syntax of commands uses the following conventions:

The words in **bold face** are key words.
" | " is the alternation symbol.
" * " represents all the objects existing in the system.
" [...] " indicates that things enclosed by square brackets can be omitted.
The curly braces as in "{ A | B }" imply "either A or B".

A) **attach** <subcomp–list> **to** <source–object>

Appends a list of the new subcomponents to the end of the source object. The attached subcomponents can not be any ancestor of the source object or the source object itself to prevent infinite attachment.

B) **detach** <subcomp–list> | * **from** <source–object>

Removes a list of the subcomponents from the source object. Even if all the subcomponents are removed from the source object, the object will still remain with the NULL subcomponent in the *objects* catalog. Having an object with the NULL subcomponent prevents a dangling point problem from occurring.

C) **replace** [**all**] <subcomponent> **of** <source–object> **with** <subcomp–list>

Replaces a subcomponent of the source object with a list of the new subcomponents. But if the replacing subcomponent list contains any objects, they can not be the ancestors of the source object.

Example 1: First we attach the newly created meteorology department (met_dept) to coll_of_sci (figure 3.3). Then we derive undergraduate (cs_und) and graduate (cs_grad) student views from computer science students, s_{cs}, to show replacing and flattening an object.

```
create met_dept with f_met a_met s_met c_met
attach met_dept to coll_of_sci

cs_und :- select * from s_cs where u/g = 'undergraduate'
cs_grad :- select * from s_cs where u/g = 'graduate'
create cs_std with cs_und cs_grad
replace s_cs of cs_dept with cs_std
flatten cs_dept into flat_cs_dept
```

Figure 3.4 shows the replaced and flattened object cs_dept.

3.3. Object Manipulation Meta–language

This language allows the user to manipulate subcomponents of objects collectively. The meta–language is a generalization of the data manipulation language. Whereas the latter manipulates data at the tuple level, the meta–language manipulates objects, that are structures, at the schema level. The advantage of this operation is by executing one command the same type of the operation can be done on a group of views. These meta–language commands resemble MSQL, an extension of SQL to allow access to multiple databases [Litw87]. Like any other meta–level language, it can have sweeping effects on the underlying database. Therefore, it should be used with extra care. Especially when it comes to database updates.

The system has to generate new identifiers many times for the views resulted from meta–level operations.

3.3.1. Retrieval Meta–language

A) **group** <attr–list> **from** <source–object–list> | * [**into** <target–object>]

This operation collects views or base relations which contain all the attributes specified in the attribute list. When the <source–object–list> is given, the newly created target object consists of the qualified views selected from the subcomponents in the source object list, and its structure is flat. When the <source–object–list> is '*', the target object consists of the qualified views selected from all the views in the ADMS system.

group can be used for system's consistency control. For example, assume that several views are derived from a base relation, and then the underneath base relation is updated. An object can be created having the base relation together with the derived views from it as its subcomponents. By browsing this object, the user can see the effects that an update to a base relation has on the views dependent on it.

Example 2: Let's assume that some student records were deleted from the current student base relation due to graduation. To check if all the related records were also deleted from the views which are derived from the student relation we can use **group**.

group u/g **from** * **into** o1

This command will group all the views in the system, which have u/g as one of their attributes. The qualified relations will become the one–level subcomponents of the object, o1. Figure 3.5 shows the derivation chart which exhibits all the derived views in the system from the student relation, and the structure of the new object, o1.

B) **metaselect from** <source–object–list> **where** attr op { value | attr }
  [{ **and** | **or** } attr op { value | attr }] [**into** <target–object>]

This function performs the select operation on the terminal views of the source object. From each relation the tuples which satisfy the where clause will be selected. If a target object is specified, the system will generate a new name for each view, and the resulting views will become the subcomponents of the target object. The original structure of the source objects is not inherited by the target object, but the generated relations become one–level subcomponents of the new object. If no target object is specified, the qualified tuples of each relation will be directly displayed on the screen.

Example 3: metaselect from cs_dept art_dept **where** admission_date > '810901' **into** o2

For each relation under the source objects, cs_dept and art_dept it will be checked that whether it contains attribute, admission_date. In this example three relations, cs_und cs_grad, and s_{art} have the attribute admission_date. A select operation will be performed satisfying the where clause, and the system will provide new names, v1* for cs_und, v2* for cs_grad, and v3* for s_{art}. When names are generated by the system, a special character '*' will be concatenated at the end of each name to distinguish itself from the user provided names. Figure 3.6 shows the source objects coll_of_sci and art_dept, the derived views, and the object o2 with three qualified subcomponents v1*, v2*, and v3*.

C) **metaproject** <attr–list> **from** <source–object–list> [**into** <target–object>]

Projects the attributes in the <attr–list> from the the qualified views of the source objects. The <attr–list> should satisfy the boolean "and" function, and if a view has only a part of the attributes in the list, the view will not be considered as a qualified relation. When there is no **into** part, the views will be displayed immediately one by one on the screen. When there is **into**, the system will provide a new name for each derived view. The resulting object does not inherit the original structure of the source objects, but it becomes an object of one–level subcomponents which are the views of the projected attributes.

Example 4: metaproject dept ss# name **from** cs_dept **into** o3

The terminal relations f_{cs}, a_{cs}, cs_und, and cs_grad under the object cs_dept contain the attributes, dept, ss#, and name. The project operation will be done on these relations. And for the resulting views the system will generate the view name v4* for f_{cs}, v5* for a_{cs}, v6* for cs_und, and v7* for cs_grad. Figure 3.7 shows the source object cs_dept, the projected views, and the object o3 with new subcomponents.

D) **metaunique** <source–object> **into** <target–object>

Performs duplicate elimination on each view of the source object. The system provides new names for the resulting views. The target object does not inherit structure from the source object, but the resulting views become one–level subcomponents of it.

E) **metasnapshot** <source–object> **into** <target–object>

Converts all views of the source–object into base relations and tie them as subcomponents under the target–object. The system provides new names for the resulting base relations. The target object does not inherit structure from the source object, but the resulting views become one–level subcomponents of it. If the source–object dose not include any view, no conversion to base relation is done and the target–object is not created either. the resulting views become one–level subcomponents of it.

F) **metaindex** <source–object–list> **on** attr

Creates a secondary index on the given attribute of each view of the source objects, if there is such an attribute exists in each view.

G) **metarmindex** <source–object–list> on attr

Removes a secondary index on the given attribute of each view of the source objects, if there exists such an attribute in each view.

H) **metacount** <source–object–list>

Counts number of the tuples in each view of the source objects individually.

A notable omission from the meta–language is a **metajoin** operator. This was purposely left out because of our deep conviction that, in most cases, only meaningless objects can be built with such an operator. Because of that, and the fact that relational systems cannot protect the innocent users who may see those meaningless derived structures, we decided that we could serve best the users by not providing **metajoin** or similar operators.

3.3.2. Update Meta–language

Update meta–language is also a generalization of data update language.

A) **metainsert into** <source–object–list>

Performs an insert from a terminal operation to each base relation of the source objects. The insertions are done in sequence following the order of the relations entered in the structure of the object list. If any of the subcomponents is a view, it will be skipped and no insertion will be done. The format and attributes of each relation will be displayed before receiving tuples from the user to insert.

B) **metadelete from** <source–object–list> **where** attr op { attr | val }
   [{ **and** | **or** } attr op { attr | val }]

Deletes tuples from each base relation in the object list, which has the attributes and satisfies the where clause. The user is notified about which relations were affected by deletions, and how many tuples were deleted from each relation.

C) **metamodify** attr1 **to** val [attr2 **to** val [...]] **in** <source–object–list>
   where attr op { attr | val } [{ **and** | **or** } attr op { attr | val }]

Modifies the values of the attributes to new values on all tuples of each base relation of the source objects having the attributes and satisfying the where clause. The user is notified which base relations were modified and how many of their tuples were changed.

3.4. Object Browsing Language

Browsing is a necessary facility in any object oriented system because the user needs to access and utilize the additional structure imposed by the objects. This section describes the browsing capabilities of ROOST.

A) **browse** <source–object–list>

First, a lisp like source object definition is displayed to show to the user the object structure and to help one to navigate in the object. Since objects can also be subcomponents, to distinguish the objects from the views, the special characters "()" are being concatenated at the end of each object name. Then, the leaf nodes (views) are displayed one view per screen in a pre–order traversal. Note that ROOST provides scrolling on all directions inside a view (up, down, left, right), and navigation inside an object (next, previous, random subcomponent).

Example 5: Let's see an example by browsing the object, acad_orga:

browse acad_orga

Then the following will be displayed on the screen.

DEF : acad_orga(coll_of_sci(), coll_of_sci_hum())
    coll_of_sci(cs_dept(), math_dept(), phy_dept(), met_dept())
    cs_dept(f_{cs}, a_{cs}, cs_std(), c_{cs})
    cs_std(cs_und, cs_grad)
    math_dept(f_{math}, a_{math}, s_{math}, c_{math})
    phy_dept(f_{phy}, a_{phy}, s_{phy}, c_{phy})
    met_dept(f_{met}, a_{met}, s_{met}, c_{met})
    coll_of_art_hum(art_dept(), psy_dept())
    art_dept(f_{art}, a_{art}, s_{art}, c_{art})
    psy_dept(f_{psy}, a_{psy}, s_{psy}, c_{psy})

Then the views appear one after the other (one view per screen) traversing the objects in pre–order:

(f_{cs}, a_{cs}, cs_und, cs_grad, c_{cs}, f_{math}, a_{math}, s_{math}, c_{math}, ...).

The following commands provide information of the view schemas that constitute the objects.

B) **rad** <source–object–list> | *

The command **rad** is an acronym for "Relation, Attribute and Domain". If the option is '*', all the relations existing in the system and their attributes with their domain will be displayed. If <source–object–list> is given, all their descendent relations and their attributes with their domain will be displayed. If there is duplication of views among the collected views under the <source–object–list>, the view's information will be displayed only once.

Example 6: **rad** cs_dept

The following information will be displayed on the screen.

    f_{cs} : ss#(char11), name(char), dept(char), rank(char), degree(char)
    a_{cs} : ss#(char11), name(char), dept(char), position(char)
    cs_und : ss#(char11), name(char), dept(char), major(char),
        admission_date(char8), u/g(char1)
    cs_grad : ss#(char11), name(char), dept(char), major(char),
        admission_date(char8), u/g(char1)
    c_{cs} : dept(char), no(int), title(char), credit(int), time(char),
        room(char), instructor(char)

C) **adr** <source–object–list> | *

The command **adr** is an acronym for "Attribute, Domain and Relation". If the option is '*', all the attributes in the system with their domain will be displayed giving a list of the relation names having the attribute. Otherwise, attributes with its domain and its relations belonging to the source objects and their descendents will be displayed according to attributes.

D) **display** objects

Displaying the *objects* catalog is the same as displaying any other relation or view in ADMS. This command displays the *objects* catalog in its table form. Underneath each table there is a control panel of options to scroll in all directions and some other useful displaying commands.

E) **definition** <source–object–list> | *

Prints first the definition of the source object list (or of all objects in the system if * is specified) in a lisp like linear form. Then **rad** is applied to each terminal node.

Example 7: definition cs_dept

This will print on the screen a complete definition of the cs_dept object:

DEF : cs_dept(f_{cs}, a_{cs}, cs_std(), c_{cs})
    cs_std(cs_und, cs_grad)

    f_{cs} : ss#(char11), name(char), dept(char), rank(char), degree(char)
    a_{cs} : ss#(char11), name(char), dept(char), position(char)
    cs_und : ss#(char11), name(char), dept(char), major(char),
          admission_date(char8), u/g(char1)
    cs_grad : ss#(char11), name(char), dept(char), major(char),
          admission_date(char8), u/g(char1)
    c_{cs} : dept(char), no(int), title(char), credit(int), time(char),
          room(char), instructor(char)

4. Capabilities and Implementation Status of ROOST

The emphasis of ROOST is on the following capabilities: consistency checking, efficiency control, sharable access and reusability of definition, and ease of browsing.

Consistency Checking: Objects can be used for the system's consistency checking. As an example, assume that several views are derived from a base relation, and then the underlying base relation is updated. The operation **group** can create an object having the subcomponents of the base relation and all the views derived from that relation. Therefore, a user can be notified if a change on the base relation took place. Furthermore, a user can create objects using specific views and/or objects referencing the system's catalog for version updates and change propagation.

Performance Control: Execution of relational operators on objects has the effect of multiple query optimization [Sell88]. Executing a command on an object is the same as performing that operation repetitively on all the views belonging to that object. The qualified views under the source objects will be selected, optimized, and then executed. This allows the system to apply the same optimization techniques used in existing relational systems instead of implementing new techniques.

Sharable Access to Data and Reusability of Object Definition: In the *objects* catalog, names of relations are used to represent subcomponents. Therefore, a view can be used more than once as a subcomponent. It is sharing data by reference, not by copying data for each existence of a subcomponent. This permits the data, the terminal nodes of objects, to be effectively shared by different objects, and always the most updated views can be accessed at the same time. ROOST also supports reusability of object definition. Since the definition of each object is stored in the *objects* catalog, the same object can be reused in multiple places as the subcomponents.

Ease of Browsing: The object oriented model is associated with an interactive user friendly environment. The very definition of objects in this paper simplifies browsing through subcomponents. Since objects are a collection of subcomponents, by executing one command, all levels are accessed.

Implementation Status

ROOST has been implemented on our ADMS system that is running under Unix on Suns and Vaxes. The implementation is completely modularized and independent from the existing ADMS program. The ROOST languages are implemented using the ADMS programmatic interface language. This means, that the same can be easily translated on other relational systems.

5. Concluding Remarks and Future Research

ROOST, an object oriented data model for relational databases has been presented. ROOST defines objects as multi–level hierarchical aggregations of base relations, views, or other objects. ROOST was designed to be easily portable to any existing relational database system.

We are currently implementing versions on objects using the backlogs that are used for the deferred view update capability of ADMS. The additional capability of versions will allow the user to *freeze* versions of objects for a period that he desires. Historical queries on past versions will be allowed by extending the language of ROOST. We will report progress on ROOST versions in a forthcoming paper.

Future work on ROOST includes concurrency protocols for versions and long transactions. Research is also required on the languages of ROOST to obtain a "complete" set of operators on objects. Further research on optimization of access methods for historical queries on older versions is one of the most intriguing issues. Without performance, the object oriented approach will have no impact on the current or future databases.

6. References

[Derr86] Derrett, N., Fishman, D., Kent, W., Lyngbaek, P., Ryan, T., "An Object–Oriented Approach to Data Management," 1986 IEEE, pp. 330–335.

[Jaco85] Jacobs, B., "Applied Database Logic," Vol. 1, Prentice–Hall, Inc., 1985.

[Keta86] Ketabchi, M., Berzins, V., "Modeling and Managing CAD Databases," IEEE Computer Magazine, Jan. 1986.

[Kris81] Kristensen, B., Madsen, O., Moeller–Pedersen, B., Nygaard, K., "A Survey of BETA Programming Language," Norwegian Computing Center, Oslo, Norway, 1981.

[Litw87] Litwin, W. et al. "MSQL: A Multidatabase Language," INRIA Res. Rep. 695, (June 1987).

[Lyng86] Lyngbaek, P., "Atomic vs. Molecular Objects in Iris," Hewlett–Packard Laboratories, Palo Alto, California, STL–86–08, May 1986.

[Ston75] Stonebraker, M., "Implementation of Integrity Constraints and Views by Query Modification," Proc. ACM–SIGMOD, June 1975, pp. 65–78.

[Rous82a] Roussopoulos, N., "View Indexing in Relational Databases," ACM Transactions on Database Systems, Vol. 7, No. 2, pp. 258–290, June 1982.

[Rous82b] Roussopoulos, N., "The Logical Access Path Schema of a Database," IEEE Transactions on Software Engineering, Vol. SE–8, No. 6, pp. 563–573, November 1982.

[Rous86a] Roussopoulos, N., "Engineering Information Systems," Proc. of ACM SIGMOD, Washington, May 1986.

[Rous86b] Roussopoulos, N., "Principles and Techniques in the Design of ADMS±," IEEE, Computer Magazine, Vol.19, No. 12, December 1986, pp. 19–25.

[Rous87a] Roussopoulos, N., "The Incremental Access Method of View Cache: Concept and Cost Analysis," Dept. of Computer Science, Univ. of Maryland, March 1987.

[Rous87b] Roussopoulos, N., "Overview of ADMS: A High Performance Database Management System," Invited Paper, Fall Joint Computer Conference, Dallas, Texas, October 25–29, 1987.

[Rowe87] Rowe, L.A., "A Shared Object Hierarchy," in *The POSTGRES Papers*, M. Stonebraker and L. Rowe (Eds.), Memorandum UCB/ERL M86/85, Electronics Research Laboratory, University of California, Berkeley, June 1987.

[Sell88] Sellis, T. "Multiple Query Optimization," " ACM Trans. on Database Syst. Vol. 13, No 1, March 1988, pp. 23–52.

[Wied86] Wiederhold, G., " Views, Objects, and Databases," IEEE Computer, Vol. 19:12, December 1986, pp. 37–44.

[Wirt83] Wirth, N., "Programming in Modula–2," Springer–Verlag, Berlin, 1983.

[Woel86] Woelk, D., Kim, W., Luther, W., "An Object–Oriented Approach to Multimedia Databases," Proceedings of SIGMOD 86, May 1986, pp. 311–325.

[Xero81] The Xerox Learning Research Group, "The Smalltalk–80 System," BYTE, Aug. 1981, pp. 36–48.

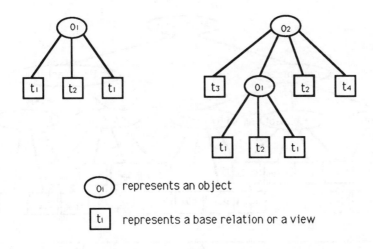

represents an object

represents a base relation or a view

Figure 2.1 objects in a graphic representation

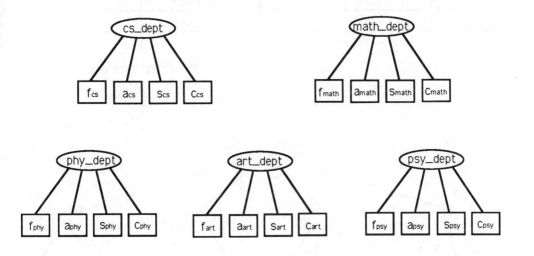

Figure 3.1 object structures

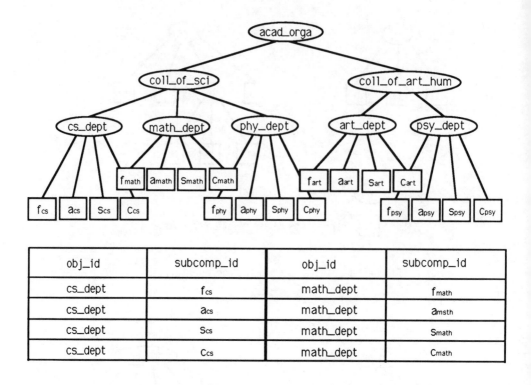

obj_id	subcomp_id	obj_id	subcomp_id
cs_dept	f_{cs}	math_dept	f_{math}
cs_dept	a_{cs}	math_dept	a_{msth}
cs_dept	S_{cs}	math_dept	S_{math}
cs_dept	C_{cs}	math_dept	C_{math}

Figure 3.2 object arca_orge and a part of the **objects** catalog

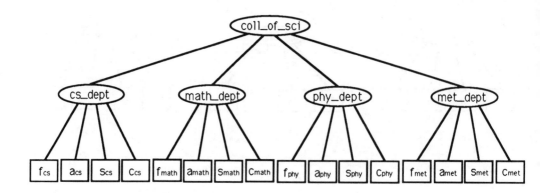

Figure 3.3 object coll_of_sci

creating cs_std   replacing S_cs with cs_std   flattened cs_dept

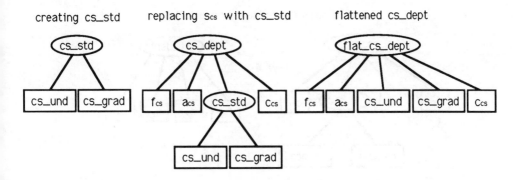

Figure 3.4

all the views derived from the base relation, student

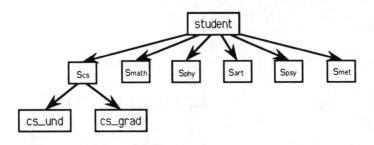

object o_1 created by the **group** operation

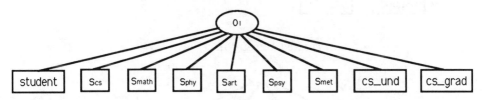

Figure 3.5

420

source objects, cs_dept and art_dept

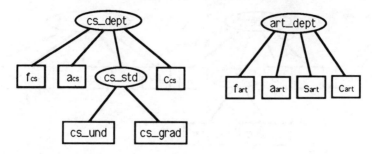

deriving views

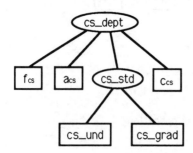

created target object, o2

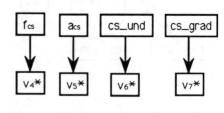

Figure 3.6

source objects, cs_dept

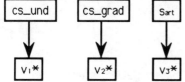

generating views

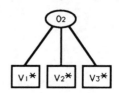

created target object, o3

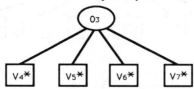

Figure 3.7

INTERFACES AND FORMAL MODELS

Complex-Statistical-Table Structure and Operators for Macro Statistical Databases

Lotfi Lakhal[1,3], Rosine Cicchetti[2,3]

and

Serge Miranda[3]

1- University of Tunis, ENSI, 2049, Ariana, TUNISIE.
2- CERAM, Sophia Antipolis BP 120, 06561 Valbonne cedex, FRANCE.
3- BAOU Project, University of Nice-CNRS, LISAN, Bat 3, Rue A. Einstein, 06560 Sophia-Antipolis, Valbonne, FRANCE.

Abstract

They are two kinds of Statistical DataBases (SDBs), micro and macro-SDBs. Micro-SDBs describe individual entities or events, they are mainly used for statistical analysis. Macro-SDBs contain only summary-data achieved by statistical-mathematical operations on micro-SDBs. In this paper, we propose a data-structure called Complex Statistical Table (CST) which offer a formal and homogeneous framework to develop macro-SDBs. In order to manipulate CST structure, we define two classes of operators : CST transposition operators making data-organisation dynamic and CST retrieval operators that work on CST instances. We also propose a discussion pointing out our approach contrasted with other contributions of this field.

Key-Words
Statistical databases ; Summary data ; Macro-data ; Micro-data ; Statistical Tables ;   Relational Statistical Table ; Complex Statistical Table ; Summary Table.

0 Introduction

Statistics consists in collecting, processing and analyzing data in order to learn from them and check their accuracy. Collected data or raw data are precise measures (variables), describing groups (populations) of persons, objects, facts,... (individuals) [SHOS82], [SHOS85]. Raw-data sets are generally called micro Statistical DataBases (micro-SDBs) [WONG84], [RAFA86] and are mainly used for statistical analysis [ANDE83]. Their fundamental feature is the great mass of managed data, incomparably more important than those of classical management applications (up to some giga-bytes) [BRY86]. In such micro-SDBs, where tape storage and batch processing are typically used, statistical investigation on the whole population is very long and expensive. So, statisticians have developed technics and tools (statistical packages for example : P-STAT [PSTA81], SPSS [NIE75],...) that summarize information, i.e. derive from directly-unworkable mass of raw-data, synthetic-data sets, called "summary-data sets", gathered in macro Statistical DataBases (macro-SDBs) or summary databases [JOHN81], [WONG84], [GHOS84], [OZSO85a] [RAFF86], [HEBR87],... The basic issue, therefore, consists in being able to represent and handle these summary-data, which express general tendencies on the studied population, in order to avoid processing statistical units that are micro-data.

In this paper, we describe a contribution to modelization and manipulation of summary-data. We first present the semantic of summary-data set and examine two signifiant approaches of such data representation. Then we detail the Complex Statistical Table (CST) data structure and present its manipulation operators, which are divided in two classes : transposition operators, that we describe and define in a complete way and retrieval operators, formalized in [CICC89a]. In decision support applications (involving statistical applications), it is difficult to anticipate definitely data structure and know the logical form in which data will be examined by users. Thus, it is necessary to change data organization or to work with a different data-aggregation level ; these later operations are very used, for example to make summary-data sets comparable [SHOS85], [OLKE86], [LATO86]. Since macro-data management is not an exception to this "rule", CST operators provide for such needs. Actually, transposition operators allow to modify CST organization, making this data-structure dynamic. With retrieval operators, users can refine attribute domains or aggregate macro-data.

This work is supported, in part, by French Departement of Education and Science - Direction de l' Evaluation et de la Prospective.

1 Semantic of summary-data set

Summary-data sets are aggregated-data sets according to a particular combination of criteria [JOHN81], [CHAN81]. They are characterized by two kinds of attributes : **summary attributes** or arithmetical variables, whose feature is to be quantitative and **category attributes** that permit to classify values of summary attributes. Category attributes frequently have an alphanumerical basic type and have generally (but not mandatory) small domain size [TURN79]. Summary attributes can only be of numerical type since their values are achieved by applying aggregative functions (SUM, AVG, COUNT, MIN, ...) on quantitative measures of a studied micro-data sub-set [KLUG81], [KLUG82], [OZSO85a].

For instance, in a macro-SDB concerning "student population", the summary-data set S1 permits to count the Nice students by sex, study year and discipline. S1 contains the category attributes SEX defined in the value set {W, M}, DISCIPLINE defined by {Computer science, Mathematics, Physics}, STUDY_YEAR defined by {1, 2}, and the summary attribute NB (number of students) defined by the integer set.

We can note several levels of complexity in the semantical contents of summary-data sets. Some, as S1 in the previous example, have a single semantic, others can represent several semantics, through different summary attributes, classified according to values of the same or different category attributes.

For instance, the summary-data set S2 permits to count the Nice students in graduate studies, by sex, discipline and study year (first semantic) and gives mean of student scholarship by sex and study year (second semantic).

It is very important to have a suitable data-structure in order to represent summary-data sets with a complex semantics. We summarize, in the following section, two significant contributions, providing for this need, and introduce, in an intuitive way, our proposal.

2 Statistical-Table related work and proposal

Statistical tables have been used for a long time by statisticians, to present achieved results (output form), as in statistical packages (P-STAT with the command TABLES or SPSS with BREAKDOWN and CROSSTABS). They are easy to comprehend (since they facilitate interpretation of macro-data) and deal with ergonomically (because of data rational organization). Recently, such tables have inspired some research contributions with summary-data modelization. The statistical table representation is seen as a logical structure with operators [GOSH84], [OZSO85a,b], but often limited (to simple tables) as in Rafanelli's approach [RAFA86]. Some of the most significant contributions, in this field, have been proposed by Ghosh [GHOS84] and Ozsoyoglu [OZSO84, 85a,b], [DATT86], which we shall in turn examine. These two approaches inspire us with a structure for summary-data, called Complex Statistical Table (CST), and suitable operators.

2.1 Ghosh's approach : Statistical Relational Table

Ghosh's summary-data model is based upon a data structure called **Statistical Relational Table** (SRT). SRT may be seen as a sub-set of the cross-product of summary-attribute and category-attribute value-sets. SRT presents values of one or several summary attributes, according to the same classification of category-attribute values, in the form of a crossed array. Category-attribute values appear in the row and column headings of the array and that of summary attributes correspond to the cells. For instance, let's consider a SRT allowing to count Nice students in graduate studies, according to sex, discipline and study year and gives mean of their scholarship, for the same classification. We try to represent in the following figure the two summary-attribute, called NB (number of students) and MS (mean of their scholarship), of this SRT.

SRT		STUDY_YEAR		
		1	2	MS
SEX	DISCIPLINE	NB		
	Computer science	45	42	1020
W	Mathematics	40	38	1100
	Physics	37	37	1000
	Computer science	58	55	1150
M	Mathematics	40	40	1400
	Physics	35	30	1550

Figure 0 : SRT Structure

SRT may present macro-data sets in a familiar way for statisticians. They can be manipulated through a set of operators (PROJECT, AGGREGATE, STATISTICS, SELECTION-PROCEDURES). Therefore, Ghosh's approach has some drawbacks. First of all, SRT involves several summary attributes, in an ambiguous way for the user, because SRT cells may correspond to several summary attributes, i.e. several semantics. Futhermore, SRT can represent summary data with a simple organization. Ghosh defines both SRT structure and manipulation operators in term of values, i.e. in an extensive way (using the relational data-model terminology [DATE81], [DELO82]). According to us, the intensive aspect may be included in the data structure definition, as well as in the manipulation facilities, in order to capture more semantics, to formalize SRT structure and to provide operators manipulating this structure and making data-organisation dynamic.

2.2 Ozsoyoglu and Ozsoyoglu's approach : SuMmary Table

To modelize summary data, Ozsoyoglu and Ozsoyoglu's approach introduces the **SuMmary Table** (SMT) structure. Compared with Ghosh's SRT, SMT permits to represent statistical macro-data sets with a complex organization. Furthermore, Ozsoyoglu and Ozsoyoglu's data model involves SMT scheme (intension) and values (extension). The SMT scheme is presented as an array, in which category-attribute names appear in the row and column headings, and summary-attribute names appear in the cells. The latter are structured, according to rows and columns, in a completely or partially different way (a single common dimension -row or column- or nothing in common). SMT rows (or columns) are actually organized according to category-attribute trees, grouped into row (or column) category-attribute forests. Thus it is possible to represent various semantics within the same SMT ; each one can be described by a Primitive SMT (PSMT). A PSMT is defined as a SMT with a unique summary attribute. This PSMT concept is very interesting, since every SMT can be broken down into a finite set of PSMTs. PSMT category attributes are ordered according to a "linear" tree, i.e. a tree having only one branch. For instance, in the statistical macro-SDB "student population", let's consider the SMT T1, that permits to count the Nice students in graduate studies, on one hand by sex, socio-professional class and study year; and on the other hand, by sex, discipline and study year. T1, whose scheme is given in figure 1, has two summary attributes : NB11 and NB12. T1 row- and column-structuration forests are reduced to one tree. For the columns, this tree is cut down into the unique root attribute : STUDY_YEAR. T1 may be broken down into two PSMTs P11 and P12 having respectively the summary attribute NB11 and NB12. The PSMT intensions are shown in figure 2.

T1		STUDY_YEAR
SEX	**CLASS**	**NB11**
	DISCIPLINE	**NB12**

Figure 1 : T1 scheme

P11		STUDY_YEAR
SEX	**CLASS**	**NB11**

P12		STUDY_YEAR
SEX	**DISCIPLINE**	**NB12**

figure 2 : P11 and P12 schemes

SMT extension is a summary-attribute-value table, structured according to row and column category-attribute-value forests. For example, T1 extension, whose scheme is shown in figure 1, is given in figure 3. The attribute CLASS in T1 has just four values : {Farmer, Worker, Manager, Others}. The other category attributes preserve their domains (see section 1).

SMT fits into the same research direction as Ghosh's SRT but with richer modelization facilities. Therefore, some aspects of Ozsoyoglu and Ozsoyoglu's approach require futher investigation, because of the luck of formalism in SMT and PSMT definition. This luck has consequential effects on SMT-manipulation operator definition (reduced to a simple syntactical description of operators, according to us).

T1				STUDY_YEAR	
				1	2
SEX	W	CLASS	Farmer	20	16
			Worker	30	25
			Manager	45	42
			Others	28	28
		DISCIPLINE	Computer sciences	45	42
			Mathematics	40	38
			Physics	37	37
	M	CLASS	Farmer	30	26
			Worker	32	30
			Manager	45	43
			Others	50	47
		DISCIPLINE	Computer sciences	58	55
			Mathematics	40	40
			Physics	35	30

Figure 3 : T1 extension

Ozsoyoglu and Ozsoyoglu define a language to manipulate SMT, called STL, in [OZSO85b], that includes relational algebra and specific operators as CONC, EX, SPLIT, MERGE, AGT... (not formaly defined). Therefore STL doesn't involve every operator defined by Ghosh (PROJECT for example) and doesn't offer operators working on SMT structure. In order to handle SMT values, the user must resort to relational algebra and operators conversing PSMT structure into the relational one and conversely. This twofold structure and the various manipulations to retrieve data are embarrasing for statisticians. They infer first of all SMT break-down into PSMTs (that are convertible into relation [IKED81], [KAMB82]) and then, after relational operator using, the PSMT composition, to make up the SMT result. Unfortunately, the SMT break-down is not unique and reversible, as illustrated by the following example.

Example : the SMT T'1, whose scheme is given in figure 4, has the same PSMTs as T1, and is equivalent to T1, in an informative way, but with a different row organization. This example shows that the "composition" of an ordered set of PSMTs, to make up a SMT, according to a common dimension -row or column- may produce different SMTs, semantically equivalent, but with a different organization. However, the category-attribute linear tree grouping, to achieve one forest, can be obtained in different ways.

T'1		STUDY_YEAR
SEX	CLASS	NB11
SEX	DISCIPLINE	NB12

Figure 4 : T'1 intension

2.3 Proposal : Complex Statistical Table

We introduce the CST structure, to avoid the non-reversibility of SMT break-down into PSMTs and to facilitate the formal expression of manipulation operators, while offering the user real abilities to define and handle arbitrarily-complex tables.

A CST is seen as a SMT, resulting from the composition, according to rows or columns, of N PSMT (N ≥ 1), which just makes a concatenation of their row or column category-attribute scheme (ordred set of category attributes). The definition of the CST rows (and columns) is a category-attribute multi-scheme (ordered set of schemes), providing each Statistical Table (ST) (equivalent to PSMT in an informative way) matches with a row and a column of the CST scheme. For example, the CST S1, with its ST identifiers, whose scheme is shown in figure 5, is achieved by composition according to the columns of the STs P11 and P12. S1 is equivalent to T1 and T'1 in an informative way. Its row category-attribute multi-scheme is the concatenation of the ST row category-attribute schemes. The extension of the CST S1 is schematized in figure 5. Its column category-attribute multi-scheme extension is reduced to the values 1, 2.

S1 / P11		STUDY_YEAR
P12		
SEX	CLASS	NB11
SEX	DISCIPLINE	NB12

S1 / P11 / P12				STUDY_YEAR 1	STUDY_YEAR 2
SEX	W	CLASS	Farmer	20	16
	W		Worker	30	25
	W		Manager	45	42
	W		Others	28	28
	M	CLASS	Farmer	30	26
	M		Worker	32	30
	M		Manager	45	43
	M		Others	50	47
SEX	W	DISCIPLINE	Computer sciences	45	42
	W		Mathematics	40	38
	W		Physics	37	37
	M	DISCIPLINE	Computer sciences	58	55
	M		Mathematics	40	40
	M		Physics	35	30

Figure 5 : S1 scheme and extension

The vision of a CST scheme, as a ST ordered set, inspires us with an easy-to-comprehend presentation, as shown in the previous figures, in the form of an array divided into four areas :

- the title area displays the CST name and its ST identifiers ;
- the row heading area represents the CST row category-attribute multi-scheme. Each row describes, from left to right, the ith scheme of the multi-scheme ;
- the column heading area presents, in the same way, the column category-attribute multi-scheme ;
- the cell area groups the summary-attribute names.

In the choosen presentation for the ST and CST extensions, the four areas of a ST or CST scheme are preserved. Every row (or column) of the row (or column) heading area describes, from left to right, an instance of the row (or column) category-attribute multi-scheme and summary-values appear in the cells. The advantage of such a presentation is to offer the user in the form of a single table, all the structural elements of a CST scheme. The user has always a double vision of the CST scheme, in terms of attributes and in terms of STs, so that manipulations are easier.

According to our CST intension, a same category attribute may "appear several times" in a CST scheme. Actually, this attribute may belong to several STs. Futhermore, this attribute extension may differ from a ST to another. This original possibility allowes to refine attribute domains (very used by statisticians), without ambiguity (and without using nul values), through ST identifier matrix. The hierarchical representation of category attribute in the SMT of Ozsoyoglu can't take into consideration, this case. In the following example (figure 6), the category attribute SEX has not the same extension in the STs P11 and P'12 (P11.SEX = {W, M}, P'12.SEX = {W}).

S'1 / P11 / P'12				STUDY_YEAR 1	STUDY_YEAR 2
SEX	W	CLASS	Farmer	20	16
	W		Worker	30	25
	W		Manager	45	42
	W		Others	28	28
	M	CLASS	Farmer	30	26
	M		Worker	32	30
	M		Manager	45	43
	M		Others	50	47
SEX	W	DISCIPLINE	Computer sciences	45	42
	W		Mathematics	40	38
	W		Physics	37	37

Figure 6 : S'1 intension

3 Complex-Statistical-Table Structure

We now define the ST and CST schemes and extensions and formalize the previous concepts, presented in an intuitive manner. It is important to note that STs represent **semantic units** for the user while CSTs offer them, within a unique structure, abilities to modelize several semantics. We show, at sub-section 4.1.3, that the CST break-down into a finite set of STs, is a unique and reversible loss-less decomposition, which avoids CST organization loss.

3.1 ST and CST scheme

ST scheme
Preliminary definition 1

> *Category-attribute scheme :*
> *We define a category-attribute scheme T as the ordered set of category attribute names, which structures the row or column dimension of a ST P. We use the following notation (involving the order existing within T), $Tr = [Ar_1,..., Ar_m]$ for the row scheme of P and $Tc = [Ac_1,..., Ac_n]$ for its column scheme.*

A ST intension or scheme, identified by its name P, is defined by the three-uplet P (Tr, Tc, SUMMARY) where Tr is the row category-attribute scheme of P, Tc is its column category-attribute scheme, that can be empty, i.e. without any attribute, providing Tr is not empty and conversely.

Futhermore, we have $Tr \cap Tc = \emptyset$ (else the ST semantical contents is unavaible). SUMMARY is the name of the single summary-attribute of P.

Example : the STs P11 and P12 (schemes in figure 2), permit to count the Nice students in graduate studies, by sex, discipline, study year and by sex, socio-professional class, study year.
These STs are intensively defined by :
  P11([SEX, DISCIPLINE], [STUDY_YEAR], NB11) ;
  P12([SEX, CLASS], [STUDY_YEAR], NB12).

CST scheme
A CST scheme, identified by its name S and having N summary attributes is achieved by grouping N STs : $P_{ij}(Tr_i, Tc_j, SUMMARY_{ij})$, according to row or column common structures, within a (m x n) matrix (with $n \geq 1$, $m \geq 1$ and $n \times m = N$), noted as MAT_ST(S). Each and every element P_{ij} ($\forall i \in$ [1...m], $\forall j \in$ [1...n]) of MAT_ST(S) is the ST identifier, constituting the ith row and j^{th} column of the CST scheme.
The MAT_ST(S) feature is defined by all the elements of a row (or column) whose index is k, i.e.
$\{P_{kj} / j \in [1...n]\}$ (or $\{P_{ik} / i \in [1...m]\}$) have the same row category-attribute scheme Tr_k (or column scheme Tc_k). We note :
fr : the application matching every row of MAT_ST(S) with the corresponding row category-attribute scheme : $\forall i \in [1...m]$, $\{P_{ik} / k \in [1...n] \}$ ----fr----> $\{Tr_i / i \in [1...m]\}$ and $fr(P_{ik}) = Tr_i$.
fc : the application matching every column of MAT_ST(S) with the corresponding column category-attribute scheme : $\forall j \in [1...n]$, $\{P_{jk} / k \in [1...m]\}$ ---fc----> $\{Tc_j / j \in [1...n]\}$ and $fc(P_{kj}) = Tc_j$.
fs : the application matching every element of MAT_ST(S) with its single summary attribute :
$\{P_{ij} / i \in [1...m], j \in [1...n]\}$ ----fs----> $\{SUMMARY_{ij} / i \in [1...m], j \in [1...n]\}$ and
$fs(P_{ij}) = SUMMARY_{ij}$.

Preliminary Definitions 2

> *Category-attribute multi-scheme :*
> *We call row (or column) category-attribute multi-scheme Fr (or Fc) of a CST S, the vector Fr (or Fc) whose m (or n) elements are achieved by applying fr (or fc) on MAT_ST(S).*
> $Fr = [Tr_1, Tr_2, ..., Tr_m]$ *(or $Fc = [Tc_1, Tc_2, ..., Tc_n]$).*

Remark : when all the schemes in a multi-scheme are empty, the multi-scheme itself is called empty. With this possibility, summary-data sets, that can be represented by Ghosh's Statistical Relational Table (i.e. having summary-attribute values classified according to the same category attributes) may be modelized by CST, in a non-ambigous way.

Summary-attribute matrix :

We call summary-attribute matrix of a CST S, noted as [SUMMARY$_{ij}$], i ∈ [1...m], j ∈ [1...n], the matrix achieved by applying fs on MAT_ST(S).

A CST scheme, identified by its name S, is defined by the three-uplet : S (Fr, Fc, [SUMMARY$_{ij}$]), i ∈ [1...m], j ∈ [1...n] where Fr and Fc are the row and column category-attribute multi-schemes of S and [SUMMARY$_{ij}$] is its summary-attribute matrix.

Remark : a CST may have an empty multi-scheme, but not both empty row and column multi-schemes (according to ST scheme definition).

Examples :
i) let's consider the CST S2 composed of four STs, whose schemes, illustrated in figure 7, are the following :
    P21([SEX, STUDY_YEAR], [DELAY], NB21) ;
    P22([SEX, STUDY_YEAR], [CLASS, SCHOLARSHIP], NB22) ;
    P23([SEX, DISCIPLINE], [DELAY], NB23) ;
    P24([SEX, DISCIPLINE], [CLASS, SCHOLARSHIP], NB24) ;
where DELAY represents for a student the number of years he's behind in his studies, and SCHOLARSHIP indicates whether a student has a scholarship or not.

P21		DELAY	P22		CLASS SCHOLARSHIP
SEX	STUDY_YEAR	NB21	SEX	STUDY_YEAR	NB22

P23		DELAY	P24		CLASS SCHOLARSHIP
SEX	DISCIPLINE	NB23	SEX	DISCIPLINE	NB24

Figure 7 : schemes of the ST components of S2

S2 (scheme in figure 8) is formaly and intensively defined as :
S2([[SEX, STUDY_YEAR], [SEX, DISCIPLINE]], [[DELAY], [CLASS, SCHOLARSHIP]], [[NB21, NB22], [NB23, NB24]]).

S2		DELAY	CLASS
P21	P22		
P23	P24		SCHOLARSHIP
SEX	STUDY_YEAR	NB21	NB22
SEX	DISCIPLINE	NB23	NB24

Figure 8 : S2 scheme

ii) let's consider the CST S3, composed of the STs P31 and P32, which respectively counts the Nice students in graduated studies, by sex, study year, and gives for the same classification, the mean scholarship (MNT32). The ST schemes, whose column scheme is empty, are as following :
    P31([SEX, STUDY_YEAR], [Ø], NB31) ;
    P32([SEX, STUDY_YEAR], [Ø], MNT32).
In the S3 intension, illustrated in figure 9, the column multi-scheme is empty, i.e. composed of two empty category-attribute schemes.

S3		Ø	Ø
P31	P32		
SEX	STUDY_YEAR	NB31	MNT32

Figure 9 : S3 scheme

3.2 ST and CST extension

ST extension
Preliminary definitions 3

Category-attribute cardinality and extension :
We call cardinality of a category attribute A in a ST P, noted as Card(A, P), the number of distinct values of A in P. The extension of A in P is defined as the ordered set of Card(A, P) values of A in P. It is noted as : $VAL(A, P) = [a_k \mid k \in [1...Card(A, P)]]$.

For instance, Card(SEX, P12) = 2 and VAL(SEX, P12) = [W, M].

Category-attribute-scheme cardinality and extension :
We define the cardinality of a row (or column) category-attribute scheme $Tr = [Ar_1, ..., Ar_m]$ in a ST P, as the number of possible combinations (tuples) of its category-attribute values in P. It is noted as Card(Tr, P). If $T = \emptyset$, Card(Tr, P) = 1, else it's defined as the mathematical product of A_i cardinalities :

$$Card(Tr, P) = \prod_{i=1}^{m} Card(Ar_i, P).$$

We define the extension of a row (or column) category-attribute scheme Tr in a ST P, as the ordered set of tuples, achieved as following :

$$VAL(Tr, P) = \bigotimes_{i=1}^{m} VAL(Ar_i, P) \text{ where } \otimes \text{ is the symbol of the ordered-set cross-product.}$$

If $Tr = \emptyset$, VAL(Tr, P) = { NUL}, where NUL stands for nul value.

For instance, Card([SEX, DISCIPLINE], P12) = 6 and VAL([SEX, DISCIPLINE], P12) = [(W, Computer sciences), (W, Mathematics), (W, Physics), (M, Computer sciences), (M, Mathematics), (M, Physics)].

Summary-attribute extension :
The summary-attribute extension in a ST : P(Tr, Tc, SUMMARY) is a two dimensional (Card(Tr, P) x Card(Tc, P)) matrix, noted as $VAL(SUMMARY, P) = [s_{tv} \mid t \in [1...Card(Tr, P)], v \in [1...Card(Tc, P)]]$, where every element s_{tv} is the SUMMARY value, structured according to row and column scheme values respectively matching with the tth tuple of VAL(Tr, P) and v^{th} tuple of VAL(Tc, P).

For instance, Card(NB12, P12) = 12 and VAL(NB12, P12) = [[45, 42], [40, 38], [37, 37], [58, 55], [40, 40], [35, 30]].

The extension of a ST P(Tr, Tc, SUMMARY) is defined by the three-uplet :
$VAL_{(P)}$(VAL(Tr, P), VAL(Tc, P), VAL(SUMMARY, P)) where VAL(Tr, P) and VAL(Tc, P) are respectively the row and column category-attribute scheme extension in P, and VAL(SUMMARY, P) is the extension of the summary attribute.

Example : the ST P12, whose scheme is given in figure 2, is extensively defined (figure 10) as :
$VAL_{(P12)}$ = ([(W, Computer sciences), (W, Mathematics), (W, Physics), (M, Computer sciences), (M, Mathematics), (M, Physics)], [(1), (2)], [[45, 42], [40, 38], [37, 37], [58, 55], [40, 40], [35, 30]]).

P12				STUDY_YEAR	
				1	2
SEX	W	DISCIPLINE	Computer sciences	45	42
	W		Mathematics	40	38
	W		Physics	37	37
	M		Computer sciences	58	55
	M	DISCIPLINE	Mathematics	40	40
	M		Physics	35	30

Figure 10 : P12 extension

CST extension
Preliminary definition 4

Category-attribute multi-scheme cardinality and extension :
Let's consider a row (or column) category-attribute multi-scheme $Fr = [Tr_1, ...Tr_m]$ in the scheme of a CST S. We define the cardinality of Fr in S, noted as Card(Fr, S), as the number of tuples associated with the schemes $[Tr_i / i \in [1...m]]$ of Fr in S. If Fr is empty, Card(Fr, S) = m ;

else, each Tr_i strutures the row dimension of a ST P_{ij} component of S. So, $\forall j \in [1...n]$,

$$Card(Fr, S) = \sum_{i=1}^{m} Card(Tr_i, P_{ij}).$$

We define the extension of a row (or column) category-attribute multi-scheme Fr in a CST S, as the ordered set of the extensions of all the row (or column) category-attribute schemes Tr_i of P.

$\forall j \in [1...n]$,

$$VAL(Fr, S) = \bigcup_{i=1}^{m} VAL(Tr_i, P_{ij}), \text{ where U is the concatenation of ordered sets.}$$

For instance, Card([[SEX, STUDY_YEAR], [SEX, DISCIPLINE]], S1) = 14 and VAL([[SEX, STUDY_YEAR], [SEX, DISCIPLINE]], S1) = [[(F, Farmer), (F, Worker), (F, Manager), (F, Others), (M, Farmer), (M, Worker), (M, Manager), (M, Others)], (F, Computer sciences), (F, Mathematics), (F, Physics), (M, Computer sciences), (M, Mathematics), (M, Physics)]]

Summary-attribute matrix-extension :
We define the extension of a summary-attribute matrix $[SUMMARY_{ij}]$, $i \in [1...m]$ and $j \in [1...n]$ in a CST S, noted as $VAL([SUMMARY_{ij}], S)$, the summary value matrix, composed of the (n x m) matrix $VAL(SUMMARY_{ij}, P_{ij})$ concatenated according to rows and columns as following :

$$VAL([SUMMARY_{ij}], S) = \bigcup_{j=1}^{n}c \bigcup_{i=1}^{m}r \; VAL(SUMMARY_{ij}, P_{ij})$$

where Ur and Uc are the symbols of matrix concatenation according to rows and columns.
Since $VAL([SUMMARY_{ij}], S)$ is a summary value matrix, we also use (in particular to formalize manipulation operator definition) the following notation :
$VAL([SUMMARY_{ij}], S) = [s_{tv} / t \in [1...Card(Fr, S)], v \in [1...Card(Fc, S)]]$

For instance, Card([NB11, NB12], S1) = 28 and VAL([NB11, NB12], S1) = [[[20, 16], [30, 42], [45, 42], [28, 28], [30, 26], [32, 30], [45, 43], [50, 47]], [[45, 42], [40, 38], [37, 37], [58, 55], [40, 40], [35, 30]]].

The extension of a CST : S(Fr, Fc, $[SUMMARY_{ij}]$), $i \in [1...m]$, $j \in [1...n]$, is defined by the following three-uplet : $VAL_{(S)}(VAL(Fr, S), VAL(Fc, S), VAL([SUMMARY_{ij}], S))$, where VAL(Fr, S) and VAL(Fc, S) are the row and column category-attribute multi-scheme of S, and VAL($[SUMMARY_{ij}]$, S) is the extension of the summary-attribute matrix.

Example : the CST S1, whose scheme is given in figure 6, is extensively defined by :
$VAL_{(E1)}$([[(F, Farmer), (F, Worker), (F, Manager), (F, Others), (M, Farmer), (M, Worker), (M, Manager), (M, Others)], [(F, Computer sciences), (F, Mathematics), (F, Physics), (M, Computer sciences), (M, Mathematics), (M, Physics)]], [(1), (2)], [[[20, 16], [30, 42], [45, 42], [28, 28], [30, 26], [32, 30], [45, 43], [50, 47]], [[45, 42], [40, 38], [37, 37], [58, 55], [40, 40], [35, 30]]]).

Remark : a ST is a particular case of CST and verifies its formal intensive and extensive definition.

4 Complex-Statistical-Table Operators

We define a set of basic operators to manipulate CST. **Our objective is to present, in a formal way, the fundamental primitives and their semantics.** These primitives are grouped into the two following classes : CST transposition operators and CST retrieval operators.
In order to clarify our presentation, we give for each operator, a short description of its function, its syntax, an example and the formal (intensive and extensive) definition of the CST result, refering to the CST operand(s).
Remark : an important statistical macro-data feature is data stability [SHOS82], therefore no storage operator or integrity constraint is defined.

4.1 Transposition operators

We group, in this class, two operators : CONCATENATE and EXTRACT, allowing to make up new CSTs or extract component STs ; and three operators : PERMUTE, ROTATE, DISPLACE, that restructure CST. First of all, their objective is to improve a CST presentation (according to the logical form that the user wants) or to prepare it, in order to facilitate later manipulations. They operate on the row (or column) category-attribute multi-scheme and the summary-attribute matrix, by re-organizing them, with possible consequential effects on their extension, providing a dynamic aspect to CST structure.

4.1.1 Concatenation operator
This binary operator concatenates two CSTs : S1 and S2, having a common (intensive and extensive) dimension (i.e. row or column category-attribute multi-scheme). If Fr (or Fc) is the same in S1 and S2, we call the operation column-concatenation (or row-concatenation). CONCATENATE doesn't modify the CST operand extensions, in the resulting CST.
The syntax of the operator is : CONCATENATE(d, CST1-NAME, CST2-NAME), where d must be replaced by "r" or "c", to express a row- or column-concatenation.

Example : the CST S1, whose scheme and extension are presented in figure 5, is achieved by the row-concatenation of the STs P11 and P12 : CONCATENATE(r, P11, P12).

In order to formalize the result of CONCATENATE, we consider two CST defined by :

$S1(F1r, F1c, [SUMMARY1_{ij}])$, $i \in [1...m]$ and $j \in [1...n1]$;

$S2(F2r, F2c, [SUMMARY2_{ik}])$, $i \in [1...m]$ and $k \in [1...n2]$;

with $F1r = F2r$ and $VAL(F1r, S1) = VAL(F2r, S2)$.

CONCATENATE(c, S1, S2) = S(Fr, Fc, [SUMMARY$_{if}$]), $i \in [1... m]$, $f \in [1 ... (n1+n2)]$,

where :
- $Fr = F1r = F2r$ and $VAL(Fr, S) = VAL(F1r, S1) = VAL(F2r, S2)$;
- $Fc = F1c \cup F2c$ and $VAL(Fc, S) = VAL(F1c, S1) \cup VAL(F2c, S2)$, where $\cup$ stands for ordered-set concatenation ;
- $[SUMMARY_{if}] = [SUMMARY1_{ij}] \cup_C [SUMMARY2_{ik}]$, where $\cup_C$ is the symbol of matrix concatenation according to columns and if $f \leq n1$ then $f = j$, else $f = k + n1$. Futhermore, $VAL([SUMMARY_{if}], S) = VAL([SUMMARY1_{ij}], S1) \cup_C VAL([SUMMARY2_{ik}], S2)$.

4.1.2 Extract Operator
This unary operator extracts from a CST S, one of its ST components P_{ij}, without having repercussion on the extracted ST extension. The used syntax is : EXTRACT(CST-NAME, ST-NAME).

Example : let's consider the CST S1 (scheme in figure 5). EXTRACT(S1, P12) returns the ST P12 (figures 2, 10).

Formally, let's have a CST : $S(Fr, Fc, [SUMMARY_{ij}])$, $i \in [1...m]$ and $j \in [1...n]$.
with $Fr = [Tr_1, ..., Tr_m]$ and $Fc = [Tc_1, ..., Tc_n]$.
EXTRACT(S, P_{ij}) = P(Tr, Tc, SUMMARY) where :
- $Tr = Tr_i$ and $VAL(Tr, P) = VAL(Tr_i, S)$;
- $Tc = Tc_j$ and $VAL(Tc, P) = VAL(Tc_j, S)$;
- $SUMMARY = SUMMARY_{ij}$ and $VAL(SUMMARY, P) = VAL(SUMMARY_{ij}, S)$.

4.1.3 CST break-down into STs

We give now the basic ideas, used in [CICC89b] to show that the CST loss-less decomposition, into a finite and ordered set of STs, is unique and reversible.

Let's consider a CST : $S(Fr, Fc, [SUMMARY_{ij}])$, $i \in [1...m]$ and $j \in [1...n]$.

with $Fr = [Tr_1, ... Tr_m]$ and $Fc = [Tc_1, ..., Tc_n]$.

The (m x n) ST components extraction is made by successive EXTRACT operations :
$EXTRACT(S, P_{ij}) = P_{ij} (Tr_i, Tc_j, SUMMARY_{ij})$.

To make up S, from the extracted STs, we use the row-concatenation operator, applied on all the P_{ij}, $i \in [1...m]$, successively for j varying from 1 to n. However, we successively obtain each column j of the ST-identifiers matrix of the CST : MAT_ST(CST).

Each column j is the result from (m-1) concatenation operations, defined in a recurrent way by :
$CONCATENATE(r, P_{1j}, P_{2j}) = RESULT_{1j}$ and $CONCATENATE(r, RESULT_{1j}, P_{3j}) = RESULT_{2j}$

and, $\forall i \in [2...(m-1)]$, $CONCATENATE(r, RESULT_{(i-1)j}, P_{(i+1)j}) = RESULT_{ij}$.

The n results $RESULT_{(m-1)j}$, $\forall j \in [1...n]$, must be concatenated according to column (using the same recurrent processes), in order to achieve the initial CST.

4.1.4 Permutation operator

This unary operator permutes the CST two dimensions, i.e. reverses its row and column category-attribute multi-schemes : Fr and Fc.
The syntax of this operateur is : PERMUTE(CST-NAME)

Exemple : let's consider the CST S1 whose scheme and extension are presented in figure 5.
PERMUTE(S1) returns the CST S4, whose scheme and extension, are the following :

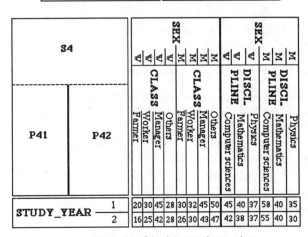

Figure 11 : S4 scheme and extension

Formally, let's consider a CST : $S(Fr, Fc, [SUMMARY_{ij}])$ $i \in [1...m]$ and $j \in [1...n]$.

PERMUTE(S) = S'(F'r, F'c, [SUMMARY'$_{ji}$]), where :

- F'r = Fc and VAL(F'r, S') = VAL(Fc, S) ;
- F'c = Fr and VAL(F'c, S') = VAL(Fr, S) ;
- [SUMMARY'$_{ji}$] = [SUMMARY$_{ij}$] and

  VAL([SUMMARY$_{ij}$], S) = [s_{tv}], $t \in [1... Card(Fr, S)]$, $v \in [1... Card(Fc, S)]$.

  PERMUTE transposes this summary-value matrix, so that :

  VAL([SUMMARY'$_{ij}$], S') = [s_{vt}], $v \in [1... Card(Fc, S)]$, $t \in [1... Card(Fr, S)]$.

4.1.5 Displacement operator

This unary operator changes the order of a category-attribute scheme T in a multi-scheme of a CST, by displacing a given attribute. DISPLACE operates both on the intension and extension of the scheme T, and on the extension of summary-attributes whose structuration involves T.

To displace the attribute A of T and insert it before the attribute B, the syntax is as follows :
DISPLACE(CST-NAME, ST-NAME.A, ST-NAME.B).

Example : the CST S5, illustrated in figure 12, is achieved from the CST S1 (figure 5) by the following operation : DISPLACE(S1, P21.DISCIPLINE, P21.SEX).

S5 P11 P51		STUDY_YEAR
SEX	CLASS	NB11
DISCIPLINE	SEX	NB51

S5 P11 P51				STUDY_YEAR 1	2
SEX	W	CLASS	Farmer	20	16
	W		Worker	30	25
	W		Manager	45	42
	W		Others	28	28
	M	CLASS	Farmer	30	26
	M		Worker	32	30
	M		Manager	45	43
	M		Others	50	47
DISCIPLINE	Computer sciences	SEX	W	45	42
	Computer sciences		M	58	55
	Mathematics	SEX	W	40	38
	Mathematics		M	40	40
	Physics	SEX	W	37	37
	Physics		M	35	30

Figure 12 : S5 sheme and extension

Formally, let's consider a CST : $S(Fr, Fc, [SUMMARY_{ij}])$, $i \in [1...m]$ and $j \in [1...n]$.

with $Fr = [Tr_1, Tr_2, ... Tr_m]$ a non empty multi-scheme.

Let's have the category-attribute scheme Tr_d of Fr : $Tr_d = [A_1,..., A_k, ..., A_p, ... A_u]$.

The user wants to displace the pth attribute of Tr_d and insert it before the kth one, with $1 \leq k < p \leq u$:

$\forall j \in [1...n]$,

DISPLACE(S, $P_{dj}.Ar_{dp}$, $P_{dj}.Ar_{dk}$) = S'(F'r, F'c, [SUMMARY'$_{ij}$]) $i \in [1...m]$ and $j \in [1...n]$; where :

- F'r = $[T'r_1, T'r_2, ... T'r_m]$ with :

  - $\forall i \in [1...m]$ and $i \neq d$ $T'r_i = T_i$ and $VAL(T'r_i, S') = VAL(Tr_i, S)$

  - $T'r_d = [A'r_{d1}, ..., A'r_{du}]$ with : $\forall y / y < k$ or $y > p$ $A'r_{dy} = Ar_{dy}$

    $\forall y / k \leq y < p$ $A'r_{dy} = Ar_{d(y-1)}$ and $A'r_{dp} = Ar_{dk}$.

    Every category attribute in S preserves its cardinality and extension in S'.

- F'c = Fc and VAL(F'c, S') = VAL(Fc, S) ;

- [SUMMARY'$_{ij}$] = [SUMMARY$_{ij}$]

  and if $i \neq d$, VAL([SUMMARY'$_{ij}$], S') = VAL([SUMMARY$_{ij}$], S)

  The quite long formal expression of VAL([SUMMARY'$_{ij}$], S'), according to VAL([SUMMARY$_{ij}$], S), in the case : i = d, is given in [CICC89b].

4.1.6 Rotating Operator

This unary operator allows to change the structuration dimension (row or column) of a category attribute, in a CST S, i.e. rotates this attribute, involved in a multi-scheme of S, into the other one. In order to return a semantically-consistent CST, the CST operand S must verify the following constraint : the attribute A, to be rotated, must belong to the row or column category-attribute scheme of all the STs of S. This condition (and the CST scheme definition) reduces the set of possible CST operands of ROTATE to the CSTs :

- having just a scheme structuring one of their dimension. The attribute A must be the last attribute of this scheme (case 1) ;
- having a category attribute multi-scheme, in which every scheme involves A as the last attribute. Futhermore A must have exactly the same extension in all the schemes (case 2).

ROTATE excludes A from its initial dimension ; A automatically becomes the last attribute of all the schemes in the other dimension.

The syntax of this operator is : ROTATE(d, CST-NAME, ATTRIBUTE-NAME), where d must be replaced by "c" if the attribute belongs to the column dimension, or "r" else.

Exemple : let's consider the CST SS'1, achieved from S1 as follows :
DISPLACE(S1, P11.CLASS, P11.SEX) = SS1 and DISPLACE(SS1, P12.DISCIPLINE, P12.SEX) = SS'1.
ROTATE(r, SS'1, SEX) returns the CST S6, illustrated below :

S6	STUDY_YEAR
P61	SEX
P62	
CLASS	NB61
DISCIPLINE	NB62

S6		STUDY_YEAR			
P61		1	1	2	2
		SEX		SEX	
P62		W	M	W	M
CLASS	Farmer	20	30	16	26
	Worker	30	32	25	30
	Manager	45	45	42	43
	Others	28	50	28	47
DISCIPLINE	Computer sciences	45	58	42	55
	Mathematics	40	40	38	40
	Physics	37	35	37	30

Figure 13 : S6 scheme and extension

We first consider the first case of CST operands and give the minor difference with the second case.

Formally, let's have a CST : $S(Fr, Fc, [SUMMARY_{ij}])$, $i \in [1...m]$ and $j \in [1...n]$, with :

- $Fr = [Tr_1, Tr_2, ...Tr_m]$;
- Fc reduced to a single non empty scheme, noted as $Tc = [Ac_1, Ac_2, ..., Ac_u]$, $u \geq 1$.

ROTATE(c, S, Ac_u) = S'(F'r, F'c, [SUMMARY'$_{ij}$]) where :

- $F'r = [T'r_1, T'r_2, ...T'r_n]$ and $\forall i \in [1... n]$, $T'r_i = Tr_i \cup Ac_u$;

  and $VAL(T'r_i, S') = VAL(Tr_i, S) \otimes VAL(Ac_u, S)$;

- F'c is reduced to a single scheme $T'c = [Ac_1, Ac_2, ... Ac_{u-1}]$ if $u > 1$; $T'c = \emptyset$ else ;

  $$VAL(T'c, S') = \overset{u-1}{\underset{y=1}{\otimes}} VAL(Ac_y, S) ;$$

- $[SUMMARY'_{ij}] = [SUMMARY_{ij}]$ and

  $VAL([SUMMARY_{ij}], S) = [s_{tv}]$ with $t \in [1...Card(Tr_i, S)]$; $v \in [1... Card(Tc, S)$].

  $VAL([SUMMARY'_{ij}], S') = [s'_{t'v'}]$ with $t' \in [1... Card(T'r_i, S')]$, $v' \in [1... Card(T'c, S')]$

let's set down : $I = INT(t' / Card(Ac_u, S))$ and $M = MOD(t' / Card(Ac_u, S))$,

$I' = INT(v'/ Card(Ac_u, S))$, where INT stands for integer part and MOD for modulo.

We have :

$$s'_{t'v'} = \begin{cases} {}^{S}(I)\ (I'+1)Card(Ac_u, S)\ ) & \text{if } M = 0, \\ {}^{S}(I+M)\ (I'Card(Ac_u, S) + M) & \text{else.} \end{cases}$$

In the second case of CST operands, the reasonning is analogous for all the scheme Tc_j in the multi-scheme of a CST S.

4.2 Retrieval operators

This class groups three operators that permit manipulations of CST operand(s) extension and produce new CST. These operators are the following : CUT, PASTE (that can be seen as CST-value extraction and CST-value concatenation) and AGGREGATE (to aggregate summary-data sets).

We give a complete description of the last operator and summarize the function of CUT and PASTE, formalized in [CICC89a].

4.2.1 CUT operator

This unary operator may be seen as the extension to CST of the relational operator SELECT. Actually, the user may only preserve the relevant values in a CST extension, by selecting category- or summary-values that verify a given condition or a boolean combination of conditions (linked by logical AND).

4.2.2 PASTE operator

This binary operator requires two CST operands S1 and S2, having the same scheme and makes up a new CST S, by "concatenating" a given category-attribute values in S1 and S2.

PASTE may be seen as the extension to CST of the relational operator UNION.

4.2.3 AGGREGATE operator

This unary operator is used to aggregate already-summarized data, according to a given category attribute. AGGREGATE operates both on the CST intension, by excluding the category attribute in the resulting CST scheme, and on the CST extension, by calculating new summary-values. These later are achieved by applying the aggregative function SUM.

The syntax of the operator is as follows :

AGGREGATE (CST-NAME, ST-NAME.CATEGORY-ATTRIBUTE-NAME).

Example :   Let's consider the CST S1 (figure 5). AGGREGATE(S1, P21.DISCIPLINE) gives the CST S7. Its scheme and extension are presented in the following figure :

S7		STUDY_YEAR
P11		
P72		
SEX	CLASS	NB11
SEX		NB72

S7				STUDY_YEAR	
P11				1	2
P72					
SEX	W	CLASS	Farmer	20	16
	W		Worker	30	25
	W		Manager	45	42
	W		Others	28	28
	M	CLASS	Farmer	30	26
	M		Worker	32	30
	M		Manager	45	43
	M		Others	50	47
SEX		W		122	117
		M		133	125

Figure 14 : S7 scheme and extension

Formally, let's consider a CST : $S(Fr, Fc, [SUMMARY_{ij}])$, $i \in [1...m]$, $j \in [1...n]$ with :
- $Fr = [Tr_1,..., Tr_m]$ and $Tr_k = [Ar_{k1},...Ar_{ku}]$, $u \geq 1$.
- $Fc = [Tc_1, Tc_2,...,Tc_n]$

AGGREGATE(S, $P_{kj}.Ar_{ku}$) = $S'(F'r, F'c, [SUMMARY'_{ij}])$, $i \in [1...m]$, $j \in [1...n]$,

where :
- $F'c = Fc$ and $VAL(F'c, S') = VAL(Fc, S)$;
- $F'r = [Tr_1, Tr_2,...,T'r_k, Tr_{k+1},...Tr_m]$, where

$T'r_k = [Ar_{k1}, Ar_{k2},..., Ar_{k(u-1)}]$ if $u > 1$, $T'r_k = \emptyset$, else.

$$VAL(T'r_k, S') = \overset{u-1}{\underset{y=1}{\otimes}} VAL(Ar_{ky}, S) ;$$

- $[SUMMARY'_{ij}] = [SUMMARY_{ij}]$, and

$VAL([SUMMARY_{ij}], S) = [s_{tv}]$ with $t \in [1... Card(Fr, S)]$, $v \in [1... Card(Fc, S)]$

$VAL([SUMMARY'_{ij}], S') = [s'_{t'v}]$ with $t' \in [1... Card(F'r, S')]$, $v \in [1... Card(F'c, S')]$

Then,

$$s'_{t'v} = \overset{Card(Ar_{ku}, S) \cdot t'}{\underset{t = 1+ (Card(Ar_{ku}, S) (t'-1))}{\Sigma}} s_{tv}$$

5 Conclusion

We now discuss about our CST contribution, both on the data structure aspect and operator aspect, and we contrast it with the summary-data representation approaches defined by Ghosh and Ozsoyoglu.
CST model encompasses representation facilities existing in Ozsoyoglu's Summary Table, but it seems simpler and richer.
The unique CST break-down into STs becomes then reversible (contrary to SuMmary Table (SMT)), and facilitates the manipulation-operator formal definition. Its second main advantage is to offer two equivalent visions : one in terms of attributes, one in terms of STs. From this twofold vision, an efficient and smart implantation may be achieved.

Futhermore, the CST model enriches SMT one by a formalization of the CST intension and extension. CST and SMT have equivalent abilities, that may be easily perceived, in an intuitive way, using the operator SPLIT of the STL language [OZSO85b] on a SMT, as many times as necessary to transform its definition forest into linear-tree ordered sets ; the result is a SMT, which is equivalent to the initial SMT (in an informative way) and verifies our formal definition of a CST.

CST also permits to represent summary-data sets, that can be modelized by Statistical Relational Table (SRT) of Ghosh.
A SRT may be seen as m STs ($m \geq 1$) having the same row and column category attribute scheme.
$P = ST_i(Tr, Tc, SUMMARY_i)$, $i \in [1...m]$ with :
$Tr = [Ar_1,..., Ar_v]$ and $Tc = [Ac_1, Ac_2, ..., Ac_u]$.
Every ST_i is equivalent to the result of u ROTATE operations, i.e. to ST'_i, defined as :

$ST'_i(T'r, T'c, SUMMARY'_i)$, $i \in [1...m]$

where $T'r = [Ar_1, ..., Ar_u, Ac_1, ..., Ac_v]$ and $T'c = \emptyset$

Thus, any Ghosh's SRT may be defined as a CST : $S(T'r, F'c, [SUMMARY'_j])$, $j \in [1...n]$; where :

$$F'c = \overset{m}{\underset{j=1}{U}} \emptyset ;$$ so, F'c encompasses m singletons whose unique element is $\emptyset$.

Remark : the ROTATE-operation sequence converts a SRT according to the form defined by Shu, Wong and Lum [SHU83].

The five transposition operators achieve all the CST possible re-organizations, by combining them. Except the ST extraction and the CST concatenation, directly inspired from the STL language (but completely formalized), other operators are original and do not seem to have been in other summary-data manipulation approaches.

Three operators permit the user to work on the CST or ST extension. Ghosh's operator PROJECT is interesting since it permits to select only relevant values in a CST extension. We define an operator called CUT, whose goal is the same as that of PROJECT, but its use is clearly defined and no ambigous. Futhermore, CUT is really efficient if the user may achieve a CST from its ST component values. This original possibility is offered by the operator PASTE.

To achieve aggregations on macro-data, we formally define the operator AGGREGATE.

The CST structure and its operators are a contribution to the statistical macro-data management study, whose advantage is a complete formalization. It may be used for a specific system or a built-on Relational -DBMS system. We have implemented it upon the DBMS ORACLE, in the context of a project between Nice University and the French departement of education and science.

Let's note that we also define some tools that work on CST presentation : one to display CST extension without value redundancy (in order to clarify it) and another to achieve all the additional required calculus for horizontal and vertical totals [CICC89b].

Acknowledgements :
We wish to thank Mr J.P. DISPAGNE (French Departement of Education and Science - Direction de l'Evaluation et de la Prospective) and N. LE THANH (University of Nice) for their valuable comments on the first draft of this paper.

References

[ANDE83]   Anderson G. D., Snider T., Robinson B., Toporek J. :
            "An integrated research support system for interpackage communication and handling
            analysis database operations". Proc. WSDBM Conf., (1983).
[BRY86]   Bry F., Thauront G. :
            "Gestion interne de données statistiques". Revue MBD, N° 4, (1986).
[CICC89a]   Cicchetti R., Lakhal L., N. Le Thanh, Miranda S. :
            "A logical Summary-Data Model for Statistical Databases".
            Proc. Int. Symp. on Database Systems for Advanced Applications, Seoul, (1989).
[CICC89b]   Cicchetti R. :
            "Gestion de données résumées statistiques".
            Thèse de Doctorat, Université de Nice, (1989).
[CHAN 81]   Chan P., Shoshani A. :
            "SUBJECT : A Directory Driven System for Organizing and Accessing Large
            Statistical Databases". Proc. VLDB Conf., (1981).
[DATT86]   Datta. A., Fournier B., Hou W.C., Ozsoyoglu G. :
            "The Design and Implementation of the SSDB". Proc. WSDBM Conf., (1986).
[DELO82]   Delobel C. :
            "Bases de données et systèmes relationnels". DUNOD Ed., (1982).
[DATE81]   DATE C. J. :
            "An Introduction to Database Systems". Addison-Wesley publishing Ed., (1981).
[GHOS84]   Ghosh S.P. :
            "Statistical Relational Tables for Statistical Database Management".
            IBM Res. Lab. San Jose, Ca, Tech. Rep. RJ 4394, (1984).
[GHOS85]   Ghosh S.P.
            "An Application of Statistical Databases in Manufacturing Testing".
            IEEE Transaction on Software Ingineering, Vol. SE-11, N° 7, (1985).
[HECK88]   Hecker G. A., Unger E. A. :
            "A user interface for database Creation, Use and Maintenance".
            Proc. ACM SIGSMALL/PC Conf., (1988).
[HEBR87]   Hebrail G. :
            "Définition de Résumés et Incertitude dans les Grandes Bases de Données".
            Thèse de Doctorat, Université de Paris-Sud, (1987).
[IKED81]   Ikeda H., Kambayashi Y. :
            "Additional Facilities of Conventional DBMS to Support Interactive Statistical
            Analysis". Proc. WSDBM Conf., (1981).
[JOHN81]   Johnson R.R. :
            "Modelling Summary Data". Proc. ACM SIGMOD Conf., (1981).
[KAMB82]   Kambayashi Y., Futagami K., Ikeda H. :
            "Implementation of a Statistical Database System HSDB".
            Proc. COMPSTAT Conf., (1982).

[KLUG81]   Klug A. :
              "ABE - A Query Language for Construction Aggregates-By Example".
              Proc. WSDBM Conf., (1981).
[KLUG82]   Klug A. :
              "Equivalence of Relational Algebra and Relational Calculus Query Languages Having
              Aggregate Functions". Journal ACM, Vol 29, N°3, (1982).
[KHOS85]   Khoshafian S. Bates D. M., DeWitt D. J. :
              "Efficient Support of Statistical Operators".
              IEEE Transaction on Software Ingineering, Vol. SE-11, N° 10, (1985).
[LAKH89]   Lakhal L., Cicchetti R. , Miranda S. :
              "A Relation and Table Language for Statistical Databases".
              Proc. MFDBS89. Lecture Notes in computer science, Springer Verglas, (1989).
[LATO86]   Latour P. :
              "La controverse entre SGBD classique et relationnel n'est-elle-pas un faux débat ?".
              Revue MBD, N° 2, (1986).
[LUO 81]   Luo D. Yao S.B. :
              "Form Operation By Example - a Language for Office Information Processing".
              Proc. ACM SIGMOD Conf., (1981).
[MALV88]   Malvestuto F. M. :
              "The Derivation Problem of Summary Data". Proc. ACM SIGMOD Conf., (1988).
[MCCA82]   McCarthy J. :
              "Meta-data Management for Large Statistical Database".
              Proc. VLDB Conf., (1982).
[NIE 75]   Nie H. W. :
              "SPSS-Statistical Package for the social sciences".
              McGraw-Hill Ed., (1975)
[NWOK84]   Nwokogba I., Rowan W. H. :
              "A Model for Integrated Statistical and Commercial Database".
              First Int. Conf. On Data Engineering, Los Angeles, (1984).
[OLKE86]   Olken F. :
              "Physical Database Support for Scientific and Statistical Database Management".
              Proc. WSDBM Conf., (1986).
[OZSO84]   Ozsoyoglu Z. M., Ozsoyoglu G. :
              "STBE - A Database Query Language for Manipulating Summary Data".
              First Int. Conf. On Data Engineering, Los Angeles, (1984).
[OZSO85a]   Ozsoyoglu Z.M, Ozsoyoglu G. :
              "A Language and a physical organization technique for summary-tables".
              Proc. ACM SIGMOD Conf., (1985).
[OZSO85b]   Ozsoyoglu G., Ozsoyoglu Z. M. :
              "Satistical Database Query Languages".
              IEEE Transaction on Software Ingineering, Vol. SE-11, N° 10, (1985).
[PSTA81]   P-STAT Users Manual, Princeton, New Jersey, (1981).
[RAFA86]   Rafanelli M., Fortunato E., Ricci F. L., Sebastio A. :
              "An Algebra for Statistical Data". Proc. WSDBM Conf., (1986).
[SATO81]   Sato H. :
              "Handling Summary Information in a Database : Derivability".
              Proc. ACM SIGMOD Conf., (1981).
[SHOS82]   Shoshani A. :
              "Statistical Databases : Characteristics, Problems and some Solutions".
              Proc. VLDB Conf., (1982).
[SHOS85]   Shoshani A., Wong H.K.T. :
              "Statistical and Scientific Database Issues".
              IEEE Transaction on Software Ingineering, Vol. SE-11, N° 10, (1985).
[SHU 83]   Shu N. C., Wong K. T. Lum V. Y. :
              "Forms Approach to Requirements Specification for Database Design".
              Proc. ACM SIGMOD Conf., (1983).
[SU 83]   Su S.Y.W. :
              "SAM* : A Semantic Association Model for Corporate and Scientific-Statistical
              Databases". Inform. Sci. Vol. 29, (1983).
[TURN79]   Turner M., Hammond R., Cotton F. :
              "A DBMS for Large Statistical Databases".
              Proc. VLDB, (1979).
[WONG84]   Wong H.K.T. :
              Micro and Macro Statistical/ Scientific Database Management".
              First Int. Conf. On Data Engineering, Los Angeles, (1984).

A DOMAIN THEORETIC APPROACH TO INCOMPLETE INFORMATION IN NESTED RELATIONAL DATABASES

M. Levene and G. Loizou
Department of Computer Science, Birkbeck College,
University of London, Malet Street, London
WC1E 7HX, U.K.

Abstract

Most previous approaches to incomplete information within the relational model depend on the specific semantics of the null types incorporated into this model. Herein we propose a model for incomplete information in nested relational databases which is independent of the semantics of the null types pertaining to incomplete information. Thus, the proposed model, called the *nested relation type* (NRT) model, allows user-defined null types, in addition to system-defined null types. The NRT model extends the nested relational model by incorporating a form of built-in inheritance. This allows us to define a partial order between nested-relations types and between the data values of these types. By utilizing these partial orders, we define an instance, over a NRT, to be incomplete when its information content may increase. In addition, we define an algebra for the NRT model, called the *NRT algebra*, which is shown to supercede known algebras for relations with nulls and for nested relations by showing *faithfulness* to these algebras. Finally, we investigate *monotonicity* of the operators of the NRT algebra, which allows us to predict how increasing or decreasing the information content of the instances in the database affects the user's view which is constructed from an algebraic expression over the instances in the database.

1. Introduction

Handling incomplete information in databases is very important since, in general, we do not expect to have a complete model of the real world. Most of the previous approaches to incomplete information in relational databases, such as those in [Bi, Co, GZ, IL, LerL, Ma, Za], and in nested relational databases, such as those in [AbB, LevL1, RKS], extend the relational model [Co] to accommodate null values associated with specific semantics. Thus the semantics of null values, for example, "value exists but is unknown at present" [Bi, Co, IL, Li, Ma], "value does not exist" [LerL] (cf. [AbB]), or "no information is available for a value" [Za] (cf. [LevL1, RKS]), govern the formalisms of the above models for incomplete information, and as a result different models have emerged. The lack of a unified model for incomplete information is accentuated by the fact that existing relational database management systems with an SQL interface [Ma, Ul] only support one type of null value, namely, "value unknown at present", which is, in general, too limiting.

The nested relational model [AbB, Gy, LevL2, OY, RKS, SS, TF, VF] was developed in order to extend the applicability of the relational model for non-business applications, such as computer aided design, image processing, office automation and text retrieval. With the said applications in mind it is hard to predict what types of null values are needed to model incomplete information, but the models for nulls in nested relations found in [AbB, LevL1, RKS] do not allow user-defined nulls, and do not even allow restricting the types of null values for any given domain. For example, if every PERSON must have a NAME, we should not allow nulls of type "does not exist" in the domain of NAME. In [RKS, Za] (cf. [BK]) an *information lattice* is defined on the underlying domains of the instances in the database; this allows us to measure the relative information content of these instances in the presence of null values. This notion is formalized by the partial order induced by the information lattice.

The model for incomplete information presented in this paper considers the relationship between the data types in the database, which we call nested-relations types, and the data values in the database, i.e., the instances of the data types. Hereafter we call the model presented in this paper the *NRT model*.

The algebra for the NRT model, called the NRT algebra, extends the algebra for nested relations of Gyssens [Gy], Thomas and Fischer [TF] and Van Gucht and Fischer [VF], for manipulating instances of nested-relations types. The NRT algebra can also be viewed as an extension of the algebra for relations with nulls [Za] to the NRT model. The main advantages of our algebra are its relative simplicity, since the operators of the NRT algebra (cf. [Co]) are well-known and well-understood [Ma, Ul], and its expressive power which supercedes that of all the above-mentioned algebras. Finally, we define and investigate two different properties of the NRT algebra. The first property we define is *faithfulness* (cf. [Ma, RKS]), which allows us to compare the NRT algebra with existing algebras for nested relations and for relations with nulls. Thus, we can formally show that the NRT algebra supercedes all the above-mentioned algebras. The second property we define is *monotonicity* of the operators of the NRT algebra (cf. [BDW] where monotonicity is defined in the context of a rule-based calculus for complex objects); this property allows us to predict how increasing or decreasing the information content of the instances in the database affects the information content of the user's view constructed from an algebraic expression over the instances in the database.

Nested-relations types and their instances (defined in Section 2) extend the nested relations and nested relation schemes found in [Gy, TF, VF] by including a form of built-in inheritance into the nested relational model. The concept of *inheritance* [Ba, BuA] allows us to recognize a common structure, between data types and their values, which may be shared. For example, an EMPLOYEE is a PERSON and thus the EMPLOYEE, say Bobby, may share the properties of himself considered as a PERSON. Providing inheritance is fundamental in *object-oriented database systems* [Ba, CM] as well as in some *database programming languages* (DBPLs) [AtB, BuA, BZ]. In the NRT model inheritance is defined by a partial order between nested-relations types (denoted as $\sqsubseteq^t$); thus, for example, PERSON $\sqsubseteq^t$ EMPLOYEE obtains. In order to define the notion of incomplete information, we define another partial order between instances of nested-relations types (denoted as $\sqsubseteq^v$), based on the information lattice of the underlying domains, provided the partial order, $\sqsubseteq^t$, obtains between the said nested-relations types. This leads us to defining an incomplete instance as an instance whose information content may increase with respect to (w.r.t.) the partial order on data values, i.e., $\sqsubseteq^v$. By using this definition of incomplete information, an instance of EMPLOYEE can be viewed as a more complete description of an instance of PERSON. Our approach is more fundamental than the previous approaches we have mentioned, since the NRT model does not depend on the given null types and it also holds for domains with no null values at all (in which case the bottom element, denoted as $\perp$, of the information lattice is known only to the DBMS).

The main contribution of this paper is that data types, incomplete information and inheritance are all dealt with, in a uniform manner, under one model, i.e., the NRT model, which extends the nested relational model. This gives rise to the primary application of the NRT model, i.e., in the area of the design of DBPLs [BZ] that provide *persistence* of data types and their data values (beyond the duration of a program) [AtB, Ba, BuA, Po]. The NRT model can provide an underlying data model for the design of a DBPL due to the following facts: in the NRT model data types and their data values are treated in a uniform fashion, inheritance is built into the model and the NRT algebra provides us with well-defined operators to manipulate persistent data.

The remaining sections of the paper are as follows. In Section 2, we introduce nested-relations types (NRTs) and their corresponding instances, and define a partial order on NRTs. In Section 3, we define incomplete information and a partial order on the data values in the database. In Section 4, we define the NRT algebra, which allows us to manipulate instances over NRTs, and in Section 5 we investigate two properties of the NRT algebra, i.e., faithfulness and monotonicity of its operators. Finally, in Section 6 we give our concluding remarks.

2. Nested-Relations Types and their Instances

In this section we define the data structures (and their data values), which are used in our NRT model for incomplete information. The motivation for defining NRTs and their instances rather than using one of the existing models for nested relations, found in [AbB, Gy, LevL2, OY, RKS, SS, TF, VF], is that these models lack the concept of *inheritance* found in object-oriented database systems [Ba, CM] and in some DBPLs [AtB, BuA, BZ]. NRTs and their instances supercede the nested relations and nested relations schemes of the above models, and allow rich data types with the modelling power of most existing database models [Ul].

Definition 2.1. A NRT is defined recursively as follows:

(1) $\emptyset$ is a NRT, denoted as the *empty-NRT*, with domain, $DOM(\emptyset) = \emptyset$.

(2) $N_1, N_2, ..., N_p$ are NRTs, denoted as *atomic-NRTs*, with corresponding non-empty domains, $DOM(N_1), DOM(N_2), ..., DOM(N_p)$.

(3) $N_1 \neq \varnothing$ is a *sub-NRT* of an atomic-NRT N_2, if $DOM(N_1) \subseteq DOM(N_2)$. A sub-NRT, N_1, is taken to be an atomic-NRT. (This allows us to add new atomic-NRTs to the predefined set of (2)).

(4) If $N_1, N_2, ..., N_m$ are NRTs, $m \geq 1$, then $N = (N_1, N_2, ..., N_m)$ is a NRT, denoted as a *molecular-NRT*, with domain $DOM(N) = P(DOM(N_1) \times DOM(N_2) \times ... \times DOM(N_m))$, where P(S) denotes the finite elements of the powerset of a set, S. (When it is convenient we consider $(N_1, N_2, ..., N_m)$ as a set of NRTs, i.e., $\{N_1, N_2, ..., N_m\}$, since the order of the N_i, $1 \leq i \leq m$, in the NRT, N, is immaterial).

A NRT, N, induces a graph, denoted as $G(N) = (V, E)$, where V is the set of vertices of G(N) and E is the set of its edges. We define G(N) recursively as follows:

(1) If N is the empty-NRT, then $V = \varnothing$ and $E = \varnothing$.

(2) If N is an atomic-NRT, then $V = \{v\}$, where the vertex, v, is labelled by N, and $E = \varnothing$.

(3) If $N = (N_1, N_2, ..., N_m)$ and $G(N_1) = (V_1, E_1)$, $G(N_2) = (V_2, E_2)$, ..., $G(N_m) = (V_m, E_m)$, then $V = \{v\} \cup V_1 \cup V_2 \cup ... \cup V_m$, where v is the initial vertex of G(N) and is labelled by N, and $E = \{(v,v_1), (v,v_2), ..., (v,v_m)\} \cup E_1 \cup E_2 \cup ... \cup E_m$, where $v_1, v_2, ..., v_m$, are the initial vertices of $G(N_1), G(N_2), ..., G(N_m)$, respectively.

We now restrict the definition of NRTs to *valid* NRTs, so as not to allow cyclic or ambiguous structures in the definition of a given NRT.

Definition 2.2. A NRT is *valid* if and only if (iff)

(1) the graph, G(N), is a rooted tree;

(2) the labels of the leaf nodes of G(N) are all atomic-NRTs; and

(3) if n, m are distinct nodes in G(N), then they are labelled by distinct NRTs.

Condition (1) of a valid NRT restricts our attention to hierarchical structures while condition (2) guarantees that a NRT, N, is well defined. On the other hand, condition (3) is similar to the *universal relation scheme assumption* [MUV], which guarantees that each component of a NRT, N, has a unique name. We note that condition (3) can always be enforced by creating new NRTs. From now on, we consider only valid NRTs, which we simply call NRTs.

Example 2.1. The tree, G(PERSON), for the NRT, PERSON, is shown in Figure 2.1 and the tree, G(EMPLOYEE), for the NRT, EMPLOYEE, is shown in Figure 2.2. The leaf nodes of G(PERSON), {FIRST, LAST, ADDRESS, CHILD}, denote the atomic-NRTs that define PERSON, while the leaf nodes of G(EMPLOYEE), {FIRST, LAST, CHILD, EADDRESS, JOB, SALARY, YEAR}, denote the atomic-NRTs that define EMPLOYEE. We also take EADDRESS to be a sub-NRT of ADDRESS.

Definition 2.3. An *instance*, I, of a NRT, N, is an element of DOM(N). In the boundary case, when $I = \varnothing$, we always take I to be an instance over the empty-NRT, $\varnothing$.

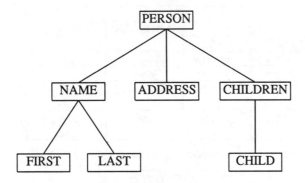

Fig. 2.1. The NRT, PERSON.

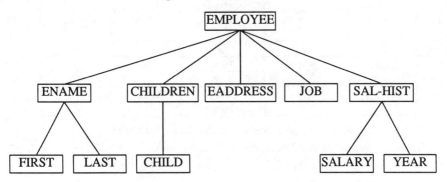

Fig. 2.2. The NRT, EMPLOYEE.

A *database type* is a collection, $\{N_1, N_2, ..., N_q\}$, of NRTs. A *database* is a collection of instances, $\{I_1, I_2, ..., I_q\}$, where each I_i is an instance over the NRT, N_i, $1 \leq i \leq q$.

Let I be an instance over a NRT, N = $(N_1, N_2, ..., N_m)$, t be a tuple of I, and $X \subseteq N$. Then t[X] is the restriction of t to X. If N is the empty-NRT and thus I = $\varnothing$, we assume that t[$\varnothing$] = $\varnothing$.

Example 2.2. An instance, I_1, of the NRT, PERSON, is shown in Figure 2.3 and an instance, I_2, of the NRT, EMPLOYEE, is shown in Figure 2.4. We note that these instances contain the null values {*unk, dne, ni*}, whose semantics we explain in Section 3. We also have that $\{I_1, I_2\}$ is a database over the database type, {PERSON, EMPLOYEE}.

We are now ready to define the partial order, $\sqsubseteq^t$, on NRTs, which describes the relative information content of NRTs.

Definition 2.4. The relative information content of two NRTs, N_1 and N_2, denoted as $N_1 \sqsubseteq^t N_2$, is defined to be true iff one of the following conditions holds:

(1) If N_1 is the empty-NRT, then $N_1 \sqsubseteq^t N_2$.

(2) If N_1 and N_2 are atomic-NRTs, then $N_1 \sqsubseteq^t N_2$, iff N_1 is a sub-NRT of N_2.

PERSON			
NAME		ADDRESS	CHILDREN
FIRST	LAST		CHILD
Gary	Kasparov	Moscow	*dne*
Bobby	Fischer	*dne*	*ni*
Tedd	Codd	San-Jose	Jack
			unk
Mia	Farrow	*unk*	Mary
			Jack

Fig. 2.3. An instance, I_1, of the NRT PERSON.

EMPLOYEE						
ENAME		EADDRESS	CHILDREN	JOB	SAL-HIST	
FIRST	LAST		CHILD		SALARY	YEAR
Gary	Kasparov	Moscow	*dne*	Chess	*ni*	80
					20	88
Bobby	Fischer	*dne*	*ni*	*ni*	*unk*	72
Tedd	Codd	San-Jose	Jack	Databases	*ni*	*unk*
			unk		30	88
Mia	Farrow	*unk*	Mary	Actress	*unk*	78
			Jack		40	88

Fig. 2.4. An instance, I_2, of the NRT EMPLOYEE.

(3) If N_1 and N_2 are molecular-NRTs, $N_1 = (N_1^1, N_2^1, ..., N_m^1)$, $N_2 = (N_1^2, N_2^2, ..., N_n^2)$, with $m \leq n$, then $N_1 \sqsubseteq^t N_2$, iff $N_1^1 \sqsubseteq^t N_1^2, N_2^1 \sqsubseteq^t N_2^2, ..., N_m^1 \sqsubseteq^t N_m^2$.

Let N_1, N_2 be NRTs, then N_1 and N_2 are *information-wise equivalent*, denoted as $N_1 \cong^t N_2$, iff $N_1 \sqsubseteq^t N_2$ and $N_2 \sqsubseteq^t N_1$.

Example 2.3. It can easily be verified that for the NRTs, PERSON and EMPLOYEE, from Example 2.1, PERSON $\sqsubseteq^t$ EMPLOYEE holds, and also that $\neg$(PERSON $\cong^t$ EMPLOYEE) holds.

3. Incomplete Information and a Partial Order on Data Values

In this section we formalize incomplete information in the context of the NRT model defined in Section 2. We show how the semantics of different null types can be incorporated into this model by defining an *information lattice* on the domains of atomic-NRTs [RKS, Za] (cf. [BK]). Our approach is more flexible than previous formalisms of incomplete information [AbB, Bi, Co, GZ, IL, LerL, LevL1, Ma, RKS, Za], as it is not dependent on the semantics of the given null types, and null types can be added or removed from the domain of an atomic-NRT, without affecting the formalism. We then proceed to define the relative information content of instances of NRTs, by a partial order, $\sqsubseteq^v$, on instances and tuples thereof referred to herein as *data values*. Our approach differs from those in [BK, RKS, Za] in the sense that $\sqsubseteq^v$ can obtain between any two data values in the database, only if $\sqsubseteq^t$ obtains between the corresponding NRTs of the given data values.

We first consider an atomic-NRT for null values, denoted as NULL, with domain, DOM(NULL). We assume that NULL is a sub-NRT of all the atomic-NRTs that have so far been defined. In the context of this paper, we let DOM(NULL) = {*unk, dne, ni, nr*}, whose meaning we now define.

(1) *unk* [Bi, Co, IL, Li, Ma] - "value exists but is unknown at the present time". For example, we may record that the ADDRESS of a given PERSON is unknown at the present time.

(2) *dne* [LerL] - "value does not exist" or "value is nonapplicable". For example, we may record that no CHILDREN exist for a given PERSON.

(3) *ni* [Za] - "no information is available for the value", i.e., it is either *unk* or *dne*. For example, we may record that a SALARY is either unknown or does not exist for an EMPLOYEE in a given YEAR.

(4) *nr* - "atomic-NRT is not relevant". For example, we may record that the NRT, JOB, is not relevant as a constituent component of PERSON.

We are now ready to define the *information lattice* [RKS, Za] (cf. [BK]) on DOM(N), for an atomic-NRT, N. The information lattice on DOM(N), denoted by *inf(N)*, induces the partial order, $\sqsubseteq^{inf(N)}$, among the elements of DOM(N), and is shown in Figure 3.1. We note that in [BO] such a domain is called a *tree-like* domain.

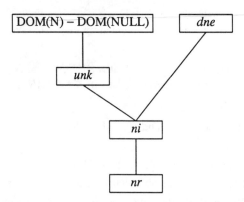

Fig. 3.1. The information lattice, inf(N), of DOM(N).

The partial order induced by inf(N) implies that $\forall$ v $\in$ (DOM(N) − DOM(NULL))

$$nr \sqsubseteq^{inf(N)} ni \sqsubseteq^{inf(N)} unk \sqsubseteq^{inf(N)} v, \text{ and that } nr \sqsubseteq^{inf(N)} ni \sqsubseteq^{inf(N)} dne.$$

Also, $\forall$ v $\in$ DOM(N) v $\sqsubseteq^{inf(N)}$ v is obviously implied.

We now make some remarks pertinent to the above.

(1) Users may define their own null values and add them to DOM(NULL) as long as their semantics are incorporated into inf(N), for an atomic-NRT, N.

(2) It is possible for users to define more than one atomic-NRT for nulls, i.e., *NULL*$_1$, *NULL*$_2$, ..., *NULL*$_n$, and assign to each one specific semantics. Thus *NULL*$_1$ $\sqsubseteq^t$ N_1,

$NULL_2 \sqsubseteq^t N_2$, ..., $NULL_n \sqsubseteq^t N_n$, where $N_1, N_2, ..., N_n$, are atomic-NRTs. For example, if an instance over the NRT, PERSON, cannot have either a non-existent or a non-relevant NAME, then we could have, $NULL_1 = \{unk\}$ with $NULL_1 \sqsubseteq^t$ FIRST and $NULL_1 \sqsubseteq^t$ LAST holding, and also $\neg$(NULL $\sqsubseteq^t$ FIRST) and $\neg$(NULL $\sqsubseteq^t$ LAST) holding.

(3) Herein it is immaterial whether for any v $\in$ DOM(NULL), the equality v = v holds or the inequality v $\neq$ v holds. We take the stand that v $\neq$ v is more natural, since when an instance with nulls is updated the two nulls may be replaced by two distinct non-null values.

(4) The user can disallow null values for a given domain, i.e., $\neg$(NULL $\sqsubseteq^t$ N) holds, for an atomic-NRT, N. In this situation the DBMS generates the bottom element, $\bot$, for inf(N), which can be interpreted as *nr*, but is not visible to the user (cf. [BK]).

We now define the relative information content of instances of NRTs by a partial order, $\sqsubseteq^v$, on instances and tuples thereof.

Definition 3.1. Let $t_1 \in I_1$ and $t_2 \in I_2$ be two tuples, where I_1 and I_2 are instances, respectively, of the NRTs, N_1 and N_2. (I_1, I_2, N_1, N_2 are not necessarily distinct.) Then, $t_1 \sqsubseteq^v t_2$, is defined to be true iff one of the following conditions holds:

(1) If N_1 is the empty-NRT, $\emptyset$, then $t_1 \sqsubseteq^v t_2$.

(2) If N_1 and N_2 are atomic-NRTs such that $N_1 \sqsubseteq^t N_2$, then $t_1 \sqsubseteq^v t_2$, iff $t_1 \sqsubseteq^{inf(N_2)} t_2$, where $\sqsubseteq^{inf(N_2)}$ is the partial order induced by inf(N_2). (We note that $t_1 = t_1[N_1]$, $t_2 = t_2[N_2]$).

(3) If N_1, N_2 are molecular-NRTs such that $N_1 \sqsubseteq^t N_2$ and $N_1 = (N_1^1, N_2^1, ..., N_m^1)$, $N_2 = (N_1^2, N_2^2, ..., N_n^2)$, with m $\leq$ n, then $t_1 \sqsubseteq^v t_2$ iff $\forall$ t $\in$ $t_1[N_i^1]$, $\exists$ t' $\in$ $t_2[N_i^2]$ such that t $\sqsubseteq^v$ t', $1 \leq i \leq m$.

We define the above tuples, t_1 and t_2, to be *information-wise equivalent*, denoted as $t_1 \cong^v t_2$, iff $t_1 \sqsubseteq^v t_2$ and $t_2 \sqsubseteq^v t_1$.

For the above instances, I_1 and I_2, we define the partial order, $I_1 \sqsubseteq^v I_2$, iff $\forall$ $t_1 \in I_1$, $\exists$ $t_2 \in I_2$, such that $t_1 \sqsubseteq^v t_2$. We note that $\sqsubseteq^v$, defined over instances, can be seen as an application of the *Hoare ordering* [BO, Gu] to the NRT model. Finally, we define the instances I_1 and I_2 to be *information-wise equivalent*, denoted as $I_1 \cong^v I_2$, iff $I_1 \sqsubseteq^v I_2$ and $I_2 \sqsubseteq^v I_1$.

We observe that if N_1 is a molecular-NRT, then the bottom element, $\bot$, w.r.t. $\sqsubseteq^v$ is $\emptyset$, otherwise if N_1 is an atomic-NRT, then $\bot$ is the null value *nr*.

Example 3.1. For the database, $\{I_1, I_2\}$, of Example 2.2, we have $I_1 \sqsubseteq^v I_2$, since PERSON $\sqsubseteq^t$ EMPLOYEE, and it can be verified that $\forall$ $t_1 \in I_1$, $\exists$ $t_2 \in I_2$ such that $t_1 \sqsubseteq^v t_2$. On the other hand, it can easily be verified that $\neg(I_2 \sqsubseteq^v I_1)$ holds. In order to demonstrate information-wise equivalence, we consider the instance $I_3 = I_1 \cup \{<\{$Gary, Kasparov$\}$, *unk*, $\{ni\}>\}$, over the NRT PERSON, where the union operator, $\cup$, is formally defined in Section

4. We have that $I_1 \cong^v I_3$, as required.

We can now formally define the notion of an instance with incomplete information from a domain theoretic point of view. We begin by defining the *completion* of an instance, I, over a NRT N; informally, it is the maximal information content that the instance, I, can contain.

Definition 3.2. The *completion* of an instance I, over N, is an instance J, over a NRT N_1, where $N \sqsubseteq^t N_1$ holds, and such that all the following conditions are true:

(1) $J \in \text{DOM}(N_1)$;

(2) $I \sqsubseteq^v J$;

(3) $\forall\, t \in J, \exists\, t' \in I$ such that $t' \sqsubseteq^v t$ (this condition ensures that there is a tuple-wise correspondence between I and J, and can be seen as an application of the *Smyth ordering* [BO, Gu] to the NRT model).

If I is equivalent to its completion, J, i.e., $I \cong^v J$, then we consider I to be *complete*. In the context of powerdomains, the definition of a completion J of I can be seen as an application of the *Egli-Milner ordering* (or as an application of the *Plotkin ordering*) [BO, Gu] between I and J, since condition (2) of Definition 3.2 induces an application of the *Hoare ordering* while condition (3) of Definition 3.2 induces an application of the *Smyth ordering*.

Definition 3.3. We define an instance I, over a NRT N, to be *incomplete*, iff the instance J is the completion of I, and I is not complete, i.e., $\neg(I \cong^v J)$.

This notion of incomplete information corresponds to our intuition that a database is an incomplete model of the real world iff there is a possibility of increasing the information content of the tuples in the database. Therefore, even a database with no null values is, in general, incomplete (in which case $\perp$ in inf(N), for a NRT, N, is known only to the DBMS). Definition 3.3 can be seen as an extension of Lipski's [Li] notion of incompleteness, in the sense that the completion of an instance I, over a NRT N, is usually not the maximal element in DOM(N) w.r.t. $\sqsubseteq^v$. Also, our definition of incompleteness can be viewed as specializing to the NRT model the approach to incomplete information taken in [BO], where powerdomains are used to provide semantics for the relational model and generalize many of the ideas in relational theory, including relations with nulls and nested relations. In our formalism of incomplete information one of the roles of integrity constraints [Ma, Ul] (a topic not dealt with in this paper) in the NRT model is to put limits on the minimum and maximum information content allowed in any given tuple. Thus, in the presence of integrity constraints, we constrain the completion of an instance I to satisfy a set of integrity constraints. In this framework I is defined to be *inconsistent* if no completion that satisfies the given set of integrity constraints exists. Buneman et al. [BDW] constrain the information content of an instance, I, to be "sandwiched" in between two instances, representing the *Smyth* and *Hoare* orderings. These two instances convey an over-approximation and an under-approximation of the information content of I, respectively, and give rise to the *sandwich ordering* [BDW]. In the NRT model the completion of an instance, I, over a NRT, N, provides the upper bound w.r.t. the information content of I, while the lower bound is the bottom element w.r.t. $\sqsubseteq^v$ in DOM(N), i.e., $\varnothing$

when N is a molecular-NRT. One way to set a more realistic lower bound than $\varnothing$ is to use the *mixed powerdomain ordering* suggested by Gunter [Gu], thus enforcing a minimal information content in tuples. Finally, we note a similarity between our approach to incomplete information and the representative instance approach [MUV] (and the nested representative instance approach [LevL1, LevL2]) in which the instances in the database are contained in a more complete, but unknown, representation of the real world.

4. The NRT Algebra

The NRT algebra presented in this section is an extension of the algebras for nested relations found in [Gy, TF, VF] for manipulating instances over NRTs. These algebras are minimal extensions of Codd's algebra for relations [Co], in the sense that the operators of Codd's algebra are extended in a natural way, i.e., tuples are considered as indivisible units. The other approach which considers the nested structure of tuples [AbB, LevL2, RKS, SS] is more flexible but adds complexity which is beyond the scope of this paper. In both approaches the NEST and UNNEST operators are added to the algebra to allow restructuring of the data. We note that, herein, we do not define a *transitive closure* [Ma] operator, which allows us to express a large class of recursive queries. If we view NRTs as persistent data types in a DBPL, then recursive queries can be programmed on demand.

Let N_1 and N_2 be NRTs such that $N_1 \sqsubseteq^t N_2$ and $N_1 = (N_1^1, N_2^1, ..., N_m^1)$, $N_2 = (N_1^2, N_2^2,$ ..., $N_n^1)$, with $m \le n$. We now define PAD(t, N_2) which pads a tuple, t, over $N_1 \ne \varnothing$, with null values of type, *nr*; the result is a tuple, t', over N_2. If $N_1 = \varnothing$ then PAD$(t, N_2) = \varnothing$.

For a tuple, t, over a NRT $N = (N_1, N_2, ..., N_m) \ne \varnothing$, the *assignment* of a null value v, v $\in$ DOM(NULL), to t[N] is denoted by t[N] $:\equiv$ v, and is defined thus: $\forall N_i \in N$, if N_i is an atomic-NRT, then $t[N_i] := v$, otherwise $t[N_i] :\equiv v$.

Definition 4.1. Let N_1, N_2 be NRTs as above. Then for a tuple, t, over $N_1 \ne \varnothing$, PAD(t, N_2) yields a tuple t', over N_2, such that:

(1) If N_i^1, $1 \le i \le m$, is an atomic-NRT, then $t'[N_i^2] := t[N_i^1]$ otherwise $t'[N_i^2] :=$ PAD$(t[N_i^1], N_i^2)$; and

(2) $\forall N_i^2$, $m+1 \le i \le n$, $t'[N_i^2] :\equiv nr$.

We next define the set operators union ($\cup$), difference ($-$) and intersection ($\cap$). Let N_1 and N_2 be NRTs as defined above and such that $N_1 \sqsubseteq^v N_2$, with corresponding instances I_1, I_2. Then

Union: $I_1 \cup I_2 = \{\texttt{PAD}(\texttt{t}, N_2) \mid \texttt{t} \in I_1 \text{ or } \texttt{t} \in I_2\}$ is an instance over the NRT, N_2.

Difference: $I_2 - I_1 = \{\texttt{t} \mid \texttt{t} \in I_2 \text{ and } (\forall \texttt{t}' \in I_1 \neg (\texttt{t} \sqsubseteq^v \texttt{PAD}(\texttt{t}', N_2)))\}$ is an instance over the NRT, N_2.

Intersection: $I_1 \cap I_2 = \{\texttt{t} \mid \texttt{t} \in I_2 \text{ and } \texttt{t}' \in I_1 \text{ and } (\texttt{t} \cong^v \texttt{PAD}(\texttt{t}', N_2))\}$ is an instance over the NRT, N_2.

We now define the projection operator (Π). Let $N = (N_1, N_2, ..., N_m)$ be a NRT and I be an instance over N, then, where $X \subseteq N$,

$$\Pi_X(I) = \{ t[X] \mid t \in I\} \text{ is an instance over the NRT, } N = (X).$$

The next operator we now define is the Cartesian product operator ($\times$). Let N_1, N_2 be NRTs with corresponding instances, I_1, I_2, and induced trees, $G(N_1) = (V_1, E_1)$, $G(N_2) = (V_2, E_2)$, respectively. Moreover, we constrain V_1 and V_2 to be pairwise disjoint; this constraint can always be enforced by generating new sub-NRTs and NRTs, which is equivalent to renaming [Ma].

$$I_1 \times I_2 = \{t \mid t[N_1] \in I_1 \text{ and } t[N_2] \in I_2\} \text{ is an instance over the NRT, } N = (N_1, N_2).$$

For the selection operator (σ), we define a *predicate*, pred, over a NRT $N = (N_1, N_2, ..., N_m)$,

$$\text{pred} ::= N_i \text{ comp-op } t_i \mid N_i \text{ comp-op } N_j,$$

where $N_i, N_j \in N$, t_i is an instance over a NRT, N_i, and comp-op $::= \sqsubseteq^\nu \mid \cong^\nu \mid =$.

Let I be an instance over N, then

$$\sigma_{pred}(I) = \{t \mid t \in I \text{ and } t \text{ satisfies pred}\} \text{ is an instance over } N, \text{ where } t \text{ satisfies pred if}$$

(1) pred $\leftarrow N_i$ comp-op t_i, then $t[N_i]$ comp-op t_i evaluates to *true*; or

(2) pred $\leftarrow N_i$ comp-op N_j, then $t[N_i]$ comp-op $t[N_j]$ evaluates to *true*.

Finally, we define the NEST and UNNEST operators for a NRT, $N = (N_1, N_2, ..., N_m)$, and an instance, I, over N. Let $N_i \in N$ with $N_i = (N_1^i, N_2^i, ..., N_n^i)$, $X \subseteq N$, $Y = N - X$ and $Z = N - N_i$. Then

$$NEST_{N'=(X)}(I) = \{t \mid \exists\ t' \in I \text{ such that } t'[Y] \cong^\nu t[Y] \text{ and } t[N'] \cong^\nu \{t''[X] \mid t'' \in I \text{ and } t''[Y] \cong^\nu t[Y]\}\} \text{ is an instance over the NRT, } N = (Y, N').$$

$$UNNEST_{N_i}(I) = \{t \mid \exists\ t' \in I \text{ such that } t[Z] \cong^\nu t'[Z] \text{ and } t[\{N_1^i, N_2^i, ..., N_n^i\}] \in t'[N_i]\} \text{ is an instance over the NRT, } N = (Z \cup \{N_1^i, N_2^i, ..., N_n^i\}).$$

We conclude this section by showing that in our approach to incomplete information nesting or unnesting of the empty set, $\emptyset$, which has generated so much controversy [AbB, Gy, GZ, LerL, LevL1, RKS, SS], causes no information loss or semantic ambiguity. Firstly, we note that $\emptyset$ conveys the minimal information content that an instance may assume. It can easily be verified that unnesting $\emptyset$ over $\emptyset$ is undefined, leading us to interpret $\emptyset$ over $\emptyset$ as an "undefined instance". On the other hand, nesting $\emptyset$ over $\emptyset$ results in $\emptyset$ over $\emptyset$, since by Definition 2.3, if an instance $I = \emptyset$, we consider the NRT of I to be $\emptyset$. For a non-empty NRT

N, we need to consider the case, where $N' \in N$ is an atomic-NRT. Now, the interpretation of the empty set depends on whether $\emptyset \in DOM(N')$ or not. If $\emptyset \in DOM(N')$ then the empty set is just another value in $DOM(N')$, as shown in the following example, and is treated as any other value in $DOM(N')$. On the other hand, if $\emptyset \notin DOM(N')$ then there is obviously no problem.

I:

N	
A	B
$\emptyset$	$\emptyset$
$\emptyset$	b

Fig. 4.1.

I':

N	
A	B'
	B
$\emptyset$	$\emptyset$
	b

Fig. 4.2.

Example 4.1. Let $N = (A, B)$ be a NRT, $\emptyset \in DOM(A)$, $\emptyset \in DOM(B)$, and I be an instance over N, as shown in Figure 4.1. Then the instance $I' = NEST_{B'=(B)}(I)$ is the instance over the NRT, $N = (A, B')$, shown in Figure 4.2, and correspondingly the instance $I = UNNEST_{B'}(I')$, over the NRT, $N = (A, B)$, is shown in Figure 4.1.

We interpret this semantics of $\emptyset$, as being "a value invisible to the user"; however, a different meaning, such as "does not exist" [AbB, LerL], "no information" [RKS] or even "unknown" [LevL1], can be given to $\emptyset$ by repositioning $\emptyset$ in the information lattice, inf(N'), of the NRT N'.

5. Properties of the NRT Algebra

In this section we define and investigate two properties of the NRT algebra. The first property to be defined is *faithfulness* (cf. [Ma, RKS]) of an algebra, which allows us to compare the NRT algebra with existing algebras for nested relations and with existing algebras for relations with null values. The second property to be defined is *monotonicity* of operators of the NRT algebra, which allows us to predict how increasing or decreasing the information content of the database affects the user's view constructed from an algebraic expression over instances in the database.

Definition 5.1. An algebra, $algebra_1$, for a data model, $model_1$, is *faithful* to another algebra, $algebra_2$, of a data model, $model_2$, if

(1) any allowable instance, I, of $model_2$ is also an allowable instance of $model_1$; and

(2) manipulating any set of allowable instances, $\{I_1, I_2, ..., I_n\}$, of $model_2$ with $algebra_1$ gives the same result as manipulating the same set of instances with $algebra_2$.

Proposition 5.1. The NRT algebra is faithful to the nested relational algebras defined in [Gy, TF, VF].

Proof. (Sketch) The result follows by the definition of the NRT algebra, since this algebra is equivalent to those in [Gy, TF, VF], whenever the instances manipulated by the NRT algebra contain no null values, i.e., $\forall$ N such that N is an atomic-NRT $\neg(NULL \sqsubseteq^t N)$ holds. $\square$

Proposition 5.2. The NRT algebra is faithful to the algebra for relations with nulls defined in [RKS] (cf. [Za]).

Proof. (Sketch) The result follows by restricting the instances manipulated by the NRT algebra to be over atomic-NRTs and letting DOM(NULL) = {*unk, dne, ni*}. ☐

Corollary 5.3. The expressive power of the NRT algebra supercedes those of the algebras for nested relations found in [AbB, Gy, LevL2, RKS, SS, TF, VF]. ☐

We now define *monotonicity* of the operators of the NRT algebra (cf. [BDW] wherein monotonicity is defined in the context of a rule-based calculus for complex objects).

Definition 5.2. Let *bin-op* be a binary operator and *un-op* be a unary operator of the NRT algebra. Then

(1) Let N_1, N_2, N_3 and N_4 be NRTs such that $N_1 \sqsubseteq^t N_3$ and $N_2 \sqsubseteq^t N_4$. Also, let $I_1, I_2,$ I_3 and I_4 be any corresponding instances of these NRTs such that $I_1 \sqsubseteq^v I_3$ and $I_2 \sqsubseteq^v I_4$. Then, if I_1 *bin-op* I_2 and I_3 *bin-op* I_4 are defined, *bin-op* is a *monotone operator* iff $(I_1 \text{ bin-op } I_2) \sqsubseteq^v (I_3 \text{ bin-op } I_4)$.

(2) Let N_1 and N_2 be NRTs such that $N_1 \sqsubseteq^t N_2$, and let I_1 and I_2 be any corresponding instances such that $I_1 \sqsubseteq^v I_2$. Then, if *un-op*(I_1) and *un-op*(I_2) are defined, *un-op* is a *monotone operator* iff *un-op*(I_1) $\sqsubseteq^v$ *un-op*(I_2).

The intuition behind the monotonicity of operators of the NRT algebra is as follows. The user's view of the database corresponds to the result of computing queries over instances in the database. If all the operators of the algebra are monotone, then increasing (decreasing) the information content of the incomplete database, increases (decreases) the content of the user's view. It turns out, however, that not all the operators of the NRT algebra are monotone. Thus, increasing (decreasing) the information content of the database may, in general, decrease (increase) the information content of the user's view. In our context of incomplete information, the monotonicity of an operator of the NRT algebra may be seen as a characteristic inherent in the operator rather than an undesirable property of the algebra. On the other hand, faithfulness is a desirable property, since it gives us a reference point as to the expressive power of the algebra and allows us to compare different algebras with each other.

The following theorems show, for each operator of the NRT algebra, whether it is monotone or not. We omit the proofs, because of their length, for the operators that are monotone; these proofs consist of tracing the definitions of the given operators in a step-by-step fashion.

Theorem 5.4. The union operator ($\cup$) is a monotone operator. ☐

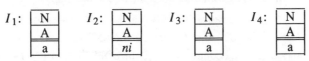

Fig. 5.1. The instances for the proof of Theorem 5.5.

Theorem 5.5. The difference operator ($-$) is not a monotone operator.

Proof. Let I_1, I_2, I_3 and I_4 be instances over the NRT, N = (A), shown in Figure 5.1. This is a counterexample, since N $\sqsubseteq^t$ N, $I_1 \sqsubseteq^v I_3$ and $I_2 \sqsubseteq^v I_4$ but $\neg((I_1 - I_2) \sqsubseteq^v (I_3 - I_4))$ holds; in fact, $I_1 - I_2 = \{a\}$, while $I_3 - I_4 = \varnothing$. $\square$

Theorem 5.6. The intersection operator ($\cap$) is not a monotone operator.

Proof. Let I_1 and I_2 be instances over the NRT, N = (A, B'), where B' = (B), shown in Figures 5.2 and 5.3, respectively. Also, let I_3 and I_4 be instances over the NRT, N = (A, B'), where B' = (B), shown in Figures 5.4 and 5.5, respectively. This is again a counterexample, since N $\sqsubseteq^t$ N, $I_1 \sqsubseteq^v I_3$ and $I_2 \sqsubseteq^v I_4$, but $\neg((I_1 \cap I_2) \sqsubseteq^v (I_3 \cap I_4))$ holds; in fact, $I_1 \cap I_2 = \{<a_1, b_1>\}$, while $I_3 \cap I_4 = \varnothing$. $\square$

I_1:

N	
A	B'
	B
a_1	b_1

Fig. 5.2.

I_2:

N	
A	B'
	B
a_1	b_1

Fig. 5.3.

I_3:

N	
A	B'
	B
a_1	b_1

Fig. 5.4.

I_4:

N	
A	B'
	B
a_1	b_1
	b_2

Fig. 5.5.

Theorem 5.7. The projection operator (Π) is a monotone operator. $\square$

Theorem 5.8. The Cartesian product operator ($\times$) is a monotone operator. $\square$

Theorem 5.9. The selection operator (σ) is not a monotone operator.

Proof. Let I_1, I_2 be instances over the NRT, N = (A, B), shown in Figures 5.6 and 5.7, respectively. This is a counterexample, since N $\sqsubseteq^t$ N and $I_1 \sqsubseteq^v I_2$, but $\neg(\sigma_{A \sqsubseteq^v B}(I_1) \sqsubseteq^v \sigma_{A \sqsubseteq^v B}(I_2))$ holds; in fact, $\sigma_{A \sqsubseteq^v B}(I_1) = \{<ni, ni>\}$, while $\sigma_{A \sqsubseteq^v B}(I_2) = \varnothing$. $\square$

I_1:

N	
A	B
ni	ni

Fig. 5.6.

I_2:

N	
A	B
a	b

Fig. 5.7.

Theorem 5.10. The NEST operator is not a monotone operator.

Proof. Let I_1, I_2 be instances over the NRT, N = (A, B), shown in Figures 5.8 and 5.9, respectively. Also, let $I_3 = NEST_{B'=(B)}(I_1)$ and $I_4 = NEST_{B'=(B)}(I_2)$ shown in Figures 5.10 and 5.11, respectively. This is a counterexample, since N $\sqsubseteq^t$ N, $I_1 \sqsubseteq^v I_2$ and $\neg(I_3 \sqsubseteq^v I_4)$ holds. $\square$

Theorem 5.11. The UNNEST operator is a monotone operator. $\square$

I_1:

N	
A	B
ni	b_1
ni	b_2

Fig. 5.8.

I_2:

N	
A	B
a_1	b_1
a_2	b_2

Fig. 5.9.

I_3:

N	
A	B'
	B
ni	b_1
	b_2

Fig. 5.10.

I_4:

N	
A	B'
	B
a_1	b_1
	b_2

Fig. 5.11.

The following theorem shows that although the NEST operator is not monotone, nesting does not affect the information content of the instance being nested in the following sense: A nest operation on an instance can always be reversed by an unnest operation without any loss of information.

Theorem 5.12. Let I_1, I_2 be instances over corresponding NRTs, $N_1 = (N_1^1, N_2^1,..., N_m^1)$, $N_2 = (N_1^2, N_2^2,..., N_n^2)$, with $m \leq n$, such that $N_1 \sqsubseteq^t N_2$ and $I_1 \sqsubseteq^v I_2$. Let $X_1 \subseteq N_1$ and $X_2 \subseteq N_2$, then the NEST and UNNEST operators satisfy the following property

$$UNNEST_{N'_1}(NEST_{N'_1 = (X_1)}(I_1)) \sqsubseteq^v UNNEST_{N'_2}(NEST_{N'_2 = (X_2)}(I_2)).$$

Proof. The result follows, since, by Theorem 1 in [TF] and Lemma 1 in [VF], we have that $UNNEST_{N'_1}(NEST_{N'_1 = (X_1)}(I_1)) = I_1$ and that $UNNEST_{N'_2}(NEST_{N'_2 = (X_2)}(I_2)) = I_2$. $\square$

6. Concluding Remarks

In this paper we have introduced a model for incomplete information, called the NRT model, from a domain theoretic point of view. The NRT model extends the nested relational model [Gy, TF, VF] by incorporating a form of inheritance built into the data structures of the model, i.e., NRTs and their instances. Our approach can be viewed as a specialization of the work in [BO], where powerdomains are used to provide a general framework for several relational concepts, including relations with nulls and nested relations. In order to formalize incomplete information we defined two partial orders, one on NRTs and the other on their instances. The partial order on NRTs, $\sqsubseteq^t$, describes the relative information content of NRTs, while the partial order on instances of NRTs, $\sqsubseteq^v$, describes the relative information content of instances of NRTs. This led us to define an incomplete instance as an instance for which the information content of tuples may be increased. In this setting, incomplete information does not depend on the specific semantics of the null values allowed in instances, as is the case with the previous approaches in [AbB, Bi, Co, GZ, IL, LerL, LevL1, Ma, RKS, Za]. The advantage of our approach to incomplete information is that users can define the null types appropriate for each domain of an atomic-NRT, within the NRT model. These null types may include, in addition to system-defined null types, user-defined null types. We then went on to define the NRT algebra which extends the algebras for nested relations [Gy, TF, VF] and the algebra for relations with nulls [Za]. We showed that the NRT algebra supercedes the algebras in [AbB, Gy, LevL2, RKS, SS, TF, VF] for nested relations, by proving faithfulness of the NRT algebra to the algebras in [Gy, TF, VF]. For each operator of the NRT algebra we established whether it is monotone or not. Monotonicity of the operators of the NRT algebra implies that increasing (decreasing) the information content of the instances in the database increases (decreases) the information content of the user's view, which is constructed from an algebraic expression over the instances in the database. It turns out that the operators: union, projection, Cartesian product and UNNEST are monotone, while the operators: difference, intersection, selection and NEST are not monotone. For the NEST operator we showed that the usual property that no information is lost when applying NEST to an instance [TF, VF] holds for the NRT algebra.

The primary application of the NRT model is in the area of designing DBPLs [BZ] that provide for persistence of data [AtB, Ba, BuA, Po], due to the the following reasons:

(1) The NRT model treats data types and their values in a uniform manner.

(2) NRTs provide rich data types for modelling business and non-business applications.

(3) The NRT model has built-in inheritance.

(4) The NRT algebra provides a well-defined theoretical basis for manipulating and updating persistent data.

(5) Incomplete information can be modelled in a very flexible manner in the NRT model.

Acknowledgement. One of us (M. L.) would like to express his thanks to the Wingate Foundation for supporting this work.

References

[AbB] ABITEBOUL S., AND BIDOIT N. 1986. Non first normal form relations: an algebra allowing data restructuring. *J. Comput. Syst. Sci. 33*, 3, pp. 361-393.

[AtB] ATKINSON M. P., AND BUNEMAN O. P. 1987. Types and persistence in database programming languages. *ACM Comput. Surv. 19*, 2, pp. 105-190.

[Ba] BANCILHON F. 1988. Object-oriented database systems. Invited talk in *Proceedings of ACM Symposium on Principles of Database Systems*, pp. 152-162, also as Technical Report Altair 16-88, INRIA, Rocquencourt, France.

[BDW] BUNEMAN P., DAVIDSON S., AND WALTERS A. 1988. A semantics for complex objects and approximate queries. In *Proceedings of ACM Symposium on Principles of Database Systems*, pp. 305-314.

[Bi] BISKUP J. 1981. A formal approach to null values in database relations. In *Advances in Database Theory Volume 1*, Gallaire H., Minker J., and Nicholas J. M. Eds. Plenum Press, New York, pp. 299-341.

[BK] BANCILHON F., AND KHOSHAFIAN S. 1986. A calculus for complex objects. In *Proceedings of ACM Symposium on Principles of Database Systems*, pp. 53-59.

[BO] BUNEMAN P., AND OHORI A. 1988. Using powerdomains to generalize relational databases. *Theor. Comput. Sci.*, to appear.

[BuA] BUNEMAN P., AND ATKINSON M. 1986. Inheritance and persistence in database programming languages. In *Proceedings of ACM SIGMOD International Conference on Management of Data*, pp. 4-15.

[BZ] BLOOM T., AND ZDONIK S. B. 1987. Issues in the design of object-oriented database programming languages. In *Proceedings of Conference on Object-Oriented Programming Systems, Languages, and Applications*, pp. 441-451.

[Co] CODD E. F. 1979. Extending the database relational model to capture more meaning. *ACM Trans. Database Syst. 4*, 4, pp. 397-434.

[CM] COPELAND G., AND MAIER D. 1984. Making smalltalk a database system. In *Proceedings of ACM SIGMOD International Conference on Management of Data*, pp. 316-325.

[Gu] GUNTER C. A. 1988. A logical interpretation of powerdomains. Research Report MS-CIS-88-31, Department of Computer and Information Science, University of Pennsylvania, Philadelphia, USA.

[Gy] GYSSENS M. 1987. The extended nested relational algebra. Technical Report 87-11, Department of Mathematics and Computer Science, University of Antwerp, Belgium.

[GZ] GOTTLOB G., AND ZICARI R. 1988. Closed world databases opened through null values. In *Proceedings of International Conference on Very Large Databases*, pp. 50-61.

[IL] IMIELINSKI T., AND LIPSKI JR. W. 1984. Incomplete information in relational databases. *J. ACM 31*, 4, pp. 761-791.

[LerL] LERAT N., AND LIPSKI JR. W. 1986. Nonapplicable nulls. *Theor. Comput. Sci. 46*, pp. 67-82.

[LevL1] LEVENE M., AND LOIZOU G. 1988. A universal relation model for nested relations. In *Proceedings of the International Conference on Extending Database Technology*, pp. 294-308.

[LevL2] LEVENE M., AND LOIZOU G. 1988. A universal relation interface for a nested database. Research Report LL-88-01, Department of Computer Science, Birkbeck College, University of London, UK.

[Li] LIPSKI JR. W. 1979. On semantic issues connected with incomplete information databases. *ACM Trans. Database Syst. 4*, 3, pp. 262-296.

[Ma] MAIER D. 1983. The Theory of Relational Databases. Computer Science Press, Rockville, Md.

[MUV] MAIER D., ULLMAN J. D. , AND VARDI M. Y. 1984. On the foundations of the universal relation model. *ACM Trans. Database Syst. 9*, 2, pp. 283-308.

[OY] OZSOYOGLU Z. M., AND YUAN L.-Y. 1987. A new normal form for nested relations. *ACM Trans. Database Syst. 12*, 1, pp. 111-136.

[Po] POULOVASSILIS A. 1988. FDL: An integration of the functional data model and the functional computational model. In *Proceeding of the 6th British National Conference on Databases*, pp. 215-236.

[RKS] ROTH M. A., KORTH H. F., AND SILBERSCHATZ A. 1985. Null values in ¬1NF relational databases. Research Report TR-85-32, Department of Computer Science, University of Texas at Austin, USA.

[SS] SCHEK H.-J., AND SCHOLL M. H. 1986. The relational model with relation-valued attributes. *Inf. Syst. 11*, 2, pp. 137-147.

[TF] THOMAS S. J., AND FISCHER P. C. 1986. Nested relational structures. In *Advances in Computing Research 3*, Kanellakis P. C., and Preparata F. Eds. JAI Press, Greenwich, pp. 269-307.

[Ul] ULLMAN J. D. 1982. Principles of Database Systems. Computer Science Press, Rockville, Md.

[VF] VAN GUCHT D., AND FISCHER P. C. 1988. Multilevel nested relational structures. *J. Comput. Syst. Sci. 36*, 1, pp. 77-105.

[Za] ZANIOLO C. 1984. Database relations with null values. *J. Comput. Syst. Sci. 28*, 1, pp. 142-166.

A Formal Definition of Binary Topological Relationships*

Max J. Egenhofer
National Center for Geographic Information and Analysis
and
Department of Surveying Engineering
University of Maine
Orono, ME 04469, USA
MAX@MECAN1.bitnet

Abstract

The exploration of spatial relationships is a multi-disciplinary effort involving researchers from linguistics, cognitive science, psychology, geography, cartography, semiology, computer science, surveying engineering, and mathematics. Terms like *close* and *far* or *North* and *South* are not as clearly understood as the standard relationships between integer numbers. The treatment of relationships among spatial objects is an essential task in geographic data processing and CAD/CAM. Spatial query languages, for example, must offer terms for spatial relationships; spatial database management systems need algorithms to determine relationships. Hence, a formal definition of spatial relationships is necessary to clarify the users' diverse understanding of spatial relationships and to actually deduce relationships among spatial objects. Based upon such formalisms, spatial reasoning and inference will be possible.

The topological relationships are a specific subset of the large variety of spatial relationships. They are characterized by the property to be preserved under topological transformations, such as translation, rotation, and scaling. A model of topological relations is presented which is based upon fundamental concepts of algebraic topology in combination with set theory. Binary topological relationships may be defined in terms of the boundaries and interiors of the two objects to be compared. A formalism is developed which identifies 16 potential relationships. Prototypes are shown for the eight relationships that may exist between two objects of the same dimension embedded in the corresponding space.

1 Introduction

Queries in spatial databases, such as Geographic Information Systems, image data bases, or CAD/CAM systems, are often based upon the relationships among spatial objects. For example, in geographic applications typical spatial queries are "Retrieve all cities which are within 5 miles of the interstate highway I 95" or "Find all highways in the states adjacent to Maine." Current commercial query languages do not sufficiently support such queries, because these languages provide only tools to compare equality or order of simple data types, such as integers or strings. The incorporation of spatial relationships over spatial domains into the syntax of a spatial query language is an essential extension beyond the power of traditional query languages [Egenhofer 1988].

Some spatial query languages support spatial queries with some spatial relationships; however, the diversity, semantics, completeness, and terminology of these relationships vary dramatically. While

---

*This research was partially funded by grants from NSF under No. IST 86-09123 (Principal Investigator: Andrew U. Frank) and Digital Equipment Corporation. The support from NSF for the NCGIA under No. SES 88-10917 is gratefully acknowledged.

some terms may be specific to particular applications, in general all spatial relationships are founded upon fundamental principles of geometry. A consistent and least redundant approach requires that the common concepts are identified at the geometry level in the form of a fundamental set of spatial relationships. These generic relationships can then be applied for the definition of application-specific relationships. In CAD/CAM, for instance, the expressions *left* and *right* are preferred, while geographic applications use the terms *East* and *West* describing possibly the same relationships. The terms in both applications rely upon the same geometric concept: (1) the two objects of interest are either disjoint or neighbors, and (2) a strict order relation ('<' or '>') defines the sequence of the objects along a one-dimensional carrier.

The development of a coherent, mathematical theory of spatial relations to overcome shortcomings in almost all geographic applications is one of the goals being investigated by the National Center for Geographic Information and Analysis [Abler 1987]. A formal definition is a prerequisite for the reasoning about the relationships among spatial objects. It is important to identify those crucial features which make humans distinguish one spatial situation from another, or which make them judge two situations as the same. A formal approach will be beneficial for several reasons: (1) The formalism serves as a tool to identify and derive relationships. Redundant and contradicting relations can be avoided such that a minimal set of fundamental relationships can be defined. (2) The formal methods can be applied to determine the relation between any two spatial objects. Algorithms to determine relationships can be specified exactly, and mathematically sound models will help to define formally the relationships. (3) The formalism is expected to help prove the completeness of the set of relationships. (4) The fundamental relations can be used to combine more complex relations.

Such a formal approach must be capable of dealing with spatial objects of various dimensions as well as objects in various spaces. Mapping two objects into a lower space should not affect their topological relationship, provided the object can exist in the lower space. Likewise, the projection into a higher space should not change the relationship between the two objects.

The scope of this paper is to provide a formal framework for reasoning about topological relationships, a particular subset of the wide range of spatial relationships. Topological notions include the concepts of continuity, closure, interior, and boundary, which are defined in terms of neighborhood relations. In this context, topological equivalence is considered a crucial criterion for comparing relationships among objects. Topological properties often conflict with metric ones. It is important to keep in mind that topological equivalence does not preserve distances; therefore, distance is excluded from all considerations in this paper to avoid any confusion between metric and topology. Instead, the subsequent investigations will be based upon continuity which is described in terms of incidence and neighborhood.

The spatial objects considered within the context of this paper are restricted to the following subset:

- All objects are represented as simplicial complexes, a model for spatial objects which will be discussed in section 4.

- All objects are cells, i.e., their boundary is not empty.

- All objects are not self-intersecting.

- All objects are connected.

- All objects are of genus 0, i.e., they have no holes.

Moreover, the underlying space must be topological and open. Space, such as the closed surface of a globe, will not be considered.

A systematic approach is necessary to identify similar relationships and to discriminate dissimilar ones. The dimensions of the objects to be compared and the underlying space are crucial for the occurence of certain relationships. The higher the dimension of the space, the greater is the variety of relationships between two of its objects. Likewise, objects of a higher dimension have the potential for more relationships than objects of lower dimensions. For example, the set of relationships between two polygons has more distinct relationships than the set between two points. The cardinality of the set is then the Cartesian product of the dimensions of the two objects and the underlying space.

The relationships for which the formalism will be verified are characterized as follows:

- All relationships are invariant under topological transformations.

- The relationships are of Boolean type and can hold for exactly two objects (binary relations).

Only relationships between two n-dimensional objects in the corresponding n-dimensional space will be investigated. This is to show the similarities of relationships between two objects of the same dimension and considered a first step toward an object-oriented view of spatial relationships.

The rest of this paper is organized as follows: Section 2 discusses various formalisms to describe spatial relationships. In section 3 the notion of *topological relationships* is introduced and a motivation is given for the use of topological means to specify these relationships. Section 4 and 5 present a spatial data model necessary for the definition of topological relationships and an algebraic interpretation of fundamental spatial operations, respectively. A set of topological relationships is defined in terms of bounding and interior faces in section 6.

2   Formalisms for Spatial Relationships

Three classes of spatial relationships are discriminated which are based upon different spatial concepts [Pullar 1988]. It appears natural for each class to develop an independent formalism describing the relationships.

- Topological relationships are invariant under topological transformations, such as translation, scaling, and rotation. Examples are terms like *neighbor* and *disjoint*.

- Spatial order and strict order relationships rely upon the definition of order and strict order, respectively. In general, each order relation has a converse relationship. For example, *behind* is a spatial order relation based upon the order of *preference* with the converse relationship *in_front_of*.

- Metric relationships exploit the existence of measurements, such as distances and directions. For instance, "within 5 miles from the interstate highway I 95" describes a corridor based upon a specific distance.

This classification is not complete since it does not consider *fuzzy* relationships, such as *close* and *next_to* [Robinson 1987], or relationships which are expressions about the motion of one or several objects, such as *through* and *into* [Talmy 1983]. These types of relationships can be considered as combinations of several independent concepts. Motion, for example, may be seen as a combination of spatial and temporal aspects.

So far, three different formal approaches for the definition of spatial relationships exist in the literature. The first one is based upon distance and direction in combination with the logical connectors AND, OR, and NOT [Peuquet 1986]. The relationship *disjoint (A, B)*, for example, is defined by the constraint that the distance from any point of object A to any point of B is greater than 0. This approach has two severe deficiencies: (1) It is not possible to model *inclusion* or *containment*, unless 'negative' distances are introduced. Peuquet defines the relationship *touching*, for example, by the distance which "equals to zero at a single location and is never less than zero" [Peuquet 1986]; however, by definition, distances are symmetric and a violation of this principle would lead to strange geometries. (2) The lack of appropriate computer numbering systems for geometric applications [Franklin 1984] impedes the immediate application of coordinate geometry and distance-based formalisms for spatial relationships. The assumption that every space has a metric is unnecessarily complex and promotes the confusion about two different concepts—metric and topology.

The formal definition of spatial relationships in the context of a geo-relational algebra is based upon the representation of spatial data in the form of point sets [Güting 1988]. Binary relationships are described by comparing the 'points' of two objects with conventional set operators, such as *equal* and *less than or equal*. For example, the relationship *inside (x, y)* is expressed by *points (x)* ⊆ *points (y)*. This point set approach is in favour of raster representations in which each object can be represented as a set of pixels, but it is not easily applicable to vector representation. A serious deficiency inherent to the point set approach is that only a subset of topological relationships is covered with this formalism. While *equality, inclusion*, and *intersection* can be described, the point set model does not provide the necessary power to define *neighborhood* relationships. A crucial characteristic of neighborhood is that the *boundaries* of two objects have common parts, while the *interiors* do not. These distinct object parts cannot be distinguished with the point set model; therefore, pure point set theory is not applicable for the description of those relationships which rely upon interior or bounding parts only.

A third approach was developed for the representation of relationships among 1-dimensional intervals in a 1-dimensional space [Egenhofer 1987b] [Pullar 1988]. It is based upon the intersection of the boundary and interior of the two objects to be compared and distinguishes only between "empty" and "non-empty" intersection. Table 1 shows the specifications of the minimal set of mutually excluding topological relationships among one-dimensional intervals.

(i1, i2)	$\partial \cap \partial$	$^{\circ} \cap ^{\circ}$	$\partial \cap ^{\circ}$	$^{\circ} \cap \partial$
disjoint	$\emptyset$	$\emptyset$	$\emptyset$	$\emptyset$
meet	$\neq \emptyset$	$\emptyset$	$\emptyset$	$\emptyset$
overlap	$\emptyset$	$\neq \emptyset$	$\neq \emptyset$	$\neq \emptyset$
inside	$\emptyset$	$\neq \emptyset$	$\neq \emptyset$	$\emptyset$
contains	$\emptyset$	$\neq \emptyset$	$\emptyset$	$\neq \emptyset$
covers	$\neq \emptyset$	$\neq \emptyset$	$\emptyset$	$\neq \emptyset$
coveredBy	$\neq \emptyset$	$\neq \emptyset$	$\neq \emptyset$	$\emptyset$
equal	$\neq \emptyset$	$\neq \emptyset$	$\emptyset$	$\emptyset$

Table 1: The minimal set of topological relationships among intervals in a one-dimensional space described by the intersection of boundaries ($\partial \cap \partial$), interiors ($^{\circ} \cap ^{\circ}$), boundary with interior ($\partial \cap ^{\circ}$), and interior with boundary ($^{\circ} \cap \partial$).

This method is superior to the other two formalisms because it describes topological relations by purely topological properties. In this paper it will be shown that it can be generalized for objects of higher dimensions than only one-dimensional intervals.

3 Topological Relationships

Figure 1 shows an introductory example upon which the phenomena of topological relationships will be explained. The two objects A and B are such that humans would use terms like *overlap* or *intersect* in order to describe their relationship.

461

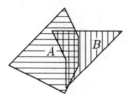

Figure 1: Two intersecting objects.

A particular characteristic by which the *overlap* relationship can be described is the relation among the object parts. For example, the boundaries coincide in two points, both boundaries run through the opposite interior, and both interiors are partially identical. Figure 2 visualizes this concept comparing both boundaries, both interiors, boundary of one with interior of the other, and, reversely, interior of one with boundary of the other.

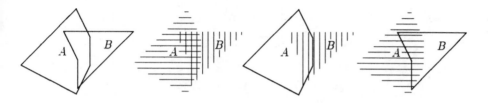

Figure 2: Comparing boundaries and interiors of two overlapping objects.

Another relationship between the same two objects is shown in Figure 3. Here, the common parts are only the coinciding boundary parts, while all other object parts do not have any commonality with the opposite parts.

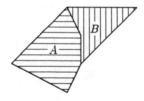

Figure 3: Two neighboring objects.

Compared to a similar situation shown in Figure 4, the only difference is that the common boundary has one edge less; however, this difference does not influence the judgement of the relationship between the two objects and humans will still use the same term describing the relationship.

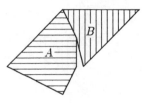

Figure 4: Two neighboring objects A and B sharing a common edge.

Finally, Figure 5 shows two objects that are not neighbors. Similar to the previous modification, only a slight change was made; however, this time the two objects are not *neighbors* but *disjoint* from each other.

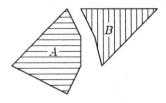

Figure 5: Two disjoint objects A and B.

These observations lead to two statements about the way to describe formally topological relationships:

Statement 1 *The topological relationship R between two spatial objects o1, o2 can be defined by comparing boundary and interior of o1 with the corresponding and opposite parts of o2.*

The second statement about the specification of spatial relationships can be derived from the pragmatic approach above:

Statement 2 *It is sufficient to consider "empty" and "non-empty" as values for the intersections of object parts.*

The two definitions guarantee complete coverage. Any further, more detailed relationship may be defined as a subset of one of them.

In order to define the crucial object parts *boundary* and *interior* for each object, a topological data model for spatial objects is needed.

4 A Model for the Representation of Spatial Data

In the mathematical theory of combinatorial topology, a sophisticated method has been developed to classify and formally describe point sets. This theory has been used for modeling spatial data [Corbett 1979] and their composition. Recently, combinatorial topology was applied to spatial data models in Geographic Information Systems (GIS) [Frank 1986] [Herring 1987], both for two-dimensional [Egenhofer 1987a] and three-dimensional [Carlson 1987] geometry. Their implementation demonstrated the simplicity of using a straight mathematical theory [Egenhofer 1989] [Jackson 1989]. Subsequently, a brief introduction will be given of the concepts of the simplicial model relevant for the definitions of the topological relationships. More details, especially about operations upon simplicial complexes, are described elsewhere [Egenhofer 1989].

4.1 Simplex

Spatial objects are classified according to their spatial dimensions. For each dimension, a minimal object exists, called *simplex*. Examples for minimal spatial objects are 0-simplices representing nodes, 1-simplices which stand for edges, 2-simplices for triangles, 3-simplices for tetrahedrons, etc.

Any n-simplex is composed of (n+1) geometrically independent simplices of dimension (n-1). For example, a triangle, a 2-simplex, is bounded by three 1-simplices. These 1-simplices are geometrically independent if no two edges are parallel and no edge is of length 0 [Giblin 1977].

Figure 6: A 2-simplex composed of three 1-simplices.

A face of a simplex is any simplex that contributes to the composition of the simplex. For instance, a node of a bounding edge of a triangle is a face; another face of a triangle is any of its bounding edges.

A simplex S of dimension n has $\binom{n+1}{p+1}$ faces of dimension p ($0 \leq m \leq n$) [Schubert 1968]. For example, a 2-simplex has $\binom{2+1}{1+1} = 3$ 1-simplices as faces. Note that the n-simplex is a face of itself.

4.2 Simplicial Complex

A simplicial complex is a (finite) collection of simplices and their faces. If the intersection between two simplices of this collection is not empty, then the intersection is a simplex which is a face of both simplices. The dimension of a complex c is taken to be the largest dimension of the simplices of c.

The configurations in Figure 7, for example, are complexes, while Figure 8 shows three compositions which are not simplicial complexes.

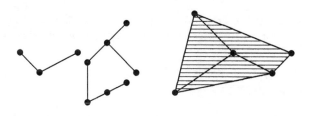

Figure 7: A 1- and a 2-complex.

4.3 Boundary

An important operation upon a n-simplex is *boundary*, denoted by ∂, which determines all (n-1)-faces of a simplex. The boundary of a n-complex is the (n-1)-chain of all (n-1)-simplices

The converse operation to boundary is *interior*, denoted by $\circ$. Interior determines the set of all (n-1)-simplices which are not part of the boundary of a n-complex. Figure 9 shows a 2-complex with five bounding 1-faces and two interior 1-faces.

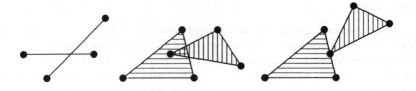

Figure 8: Three compositions which are not simplicial complexes.

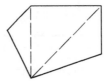

Figure 9: Boundary and interior of a 2-complex.

The property that two successive applications of boundary give the zero homomorphism is in agreement with the geometric notion that the boundary of a simplex is a closed surface.

4.4 Completeness Axioms

The simplicial model locates all spatial objects in the same world which is closed in analogy to the closed world assumption for non-spatial mini-worlds. The closed world assumption is extended by the two completeness principles for spatial data [Frank 1986]:

- Completeness of incidence: the intersection of two n-simplices is either empty or a face of both simplices.

- Completeness of inclusion: Every n-simplex is a face of a (n+1)-simplex. Hence, in a 2-dimensional space every node is either start- or end-point of an edge, and every edge is the boundary of a triangle.

5 An Algebraic Approach

The algebraic interpretation of the boundary operation is particularly useful for the subsequent formal investigations. For this goal the orientation of a simplex is introduced, fixing the vertices to lie in a sequence. The orientation of a 0-simplex is unique; the two orientations of a 1-simplex can be interpreted as the direction *from* vertex A to vertex B and reverse *from* B to A (Figure 10); the orientations of a 2-simplex are *clockwise* or *counterclockwise*.

Now suppose that the representation of the ordered n-simplex s_n be

$$s_n = \langle x_0, \cdots, x_n \rangle \tag{1}$$

then the boundary of s_n is determined by

$$\partial s_n = \sum_{i=0}^{n} (-1)^i \langle x_0, \cdots, \widehat{x_i}, \cdots, x_n \rangle \tag{2}$$

Figure 10: The two orientations of a 1-simplex.

where $\widehat{x}_i$ denotes that the face x_i is to be omitted [Schubert 1968]. The bounding simplices form a chain which is an additive (i.e., free Abelian) group. Hence, the boundary of a simplicial complex c_n can be determined as the sum of the boundaries of all its simplices s_n.

$$\partial c_n = \sum \partial s_n \text{ if } s_n \in c_n \tag{3}$$

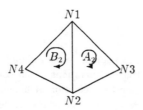

Figure 11: Calculating the boundary of the 2-complex C_2 from the boundaries of the two 2-simplices A_2 and B_2.

Figure 11 illustrates the following example: The two neighboring 2-simplices A_2 and B_2 have the following boundaries:

	simplex	∂
A_2	$\langle N1, N3, N2 \rangle$	$\langle N3, N2 \rangle - \langle N1, N2 \rangle + \langle N1, N3 \rangle$
B_2	$\langle N1, N2, N4 \rangle$	$\langle N2, N4 \rangle - \langle N1, N4 \rangle + \langle N1, N2 \rangle$

Table 2: Simplices and corresponding boundaries illustrated in Figure 11.

Then the complex C_2 formed by A_2 and B_2 has the boundary

$$
\begin{aligned}
\partial C_2 &= \partial A_2 + \partial B_2 \\
&= \langle N3, N2 \rangle - \langle N1, N2 \rangle + \langle N1, N3 \rangle + \langle N2, N4 \rangle - \langle N1, N4 \rangle + \langle N1, N2 \rangle \\
&= \langle N3, N2 \rangle + \langle N2, N4 \rangle + \langle N4, N1 \rangle + \langle N1, N3 \rangle
\end{aligned}
$$

5.1 Boundary Operator for Spatial Relationships

Unfortunately, the *boundary* operation as it is used in algebraic topology cannot be used immediately for the specification of spatial relationships. While the consideration of the faces of dimension $(n-1)$ is sufficient for the relationships among 1-complexes, it impedes the general treatment of relationships which are sometimes based upon common object parts of dimension $n-2$ or less. Figure 12 shows an example for a relationship which cannot be described by using *boundary* and *interior* in their purely mathematical sense. The intersection of the boundaries of the two-dimensional objects in one zero-dimensional object part is a crucial property of this neighborhood relationship; however, the intersection of the two boundaries does not identify any common parts, and applying the boundary operation upon these two objects does not help because boundary applied twice is always zero.

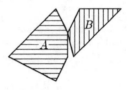

Figure 12: Two neighboring objects A and B sharing a common node.

5.2 Bounding and Interior Faces

To overcome these shortcomings, the two operations *boundingFaces* and *interiorFaces* are introduced. They are modified *boundary* and *interior* operations which consider all faces down to dimension 0. Their algebraic definition is based upon the definition of boundary (equation 2) and skeleton (equation 4). The *r-skeleton* of a complex c_q, denoted by $c_q^{(r)}$, is defined as the union of all simplices of dimension at most r.

$$c_q^{(r)} = \bigcup_{i=0}^{r} s_i \in c_q \qquad (4)$$

The *boundingFaces* of an n-dimensional complex c_n, denoted $\partial^f c_n$, is introduced as the (n-1) skeleton of the boundary of c_n.

$$\partial^f c_n = \bigcup_{r=0}^{n-1} c_n^{(r)} \in \partial c_n \qquad (5)$$

The *interiorFaces* of an n-dimensional complex c_n, denoted c_n^{of}, is the set of all faces of the n-skeleton of c_n which are not part of the *boundingFaces*.

$$c_n^{of} = c_n^{(n)} \setminus \partial^f c_n \qquad (6)$$

The dimension of the *boundingFaces* ∂^f of a complex c_n is defined to be the largest dimension of all faces in $\partial^f c_n$, i.e. n-1. In analogy, the dimension of the *interiorFaces* c_n^{of} is n. *BoundingFaces* and *interiorFaces* are sets upon which the traditional operations of set theory apply. In this context, only set intersection ($\cap$) will be needed.

Figure 13 shows the differences between *boundary* and *interior*, and *boundingFaces* and *interiorFaces*, respectively.

6 Formal Definition of Spatial Relationships

6.1 Formalism

Bounding and interior faces can be combined to form the four fundamental criteria of spatial relationships. These are: (1) common boundary parts as the intersection of *boundingFaces*, denoted by $\partial^f \cap \partial^f$, (2) common interior parts ($^{of} \cap ^{of}$), (3) boundary as part of the interior ($\partial^f \cap ^{of}$), and (4) interior as part of the boundary ($^{of} \cap \partial^f$). Subsequently, $\partial^f \cap \partial^f$ and $^{of} \cap ^{of}$ will be referred to as *corresponding*

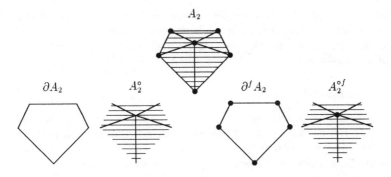

Figure 13: Boundary (∂), interior ($\circ$), bounding faces (∂^f), and interior faces ($^{\circ f}$) of a complex A_2.

intersections, and $\partial^f \cap {}^{\circ f}$ and $^{\circ f} \cap \partial^f$ as *opposite* intersections. With the binary values "empty" ($\emptyset$) and "non-empty" ($\neq \emptyset$) a total of 16 different specifications is given which provide the basis for the formal definition of the spatial relationships.

Lemma 1 *The 16 specifications as the Cartesian product of bounding and interior faces of two spatial objects with empty/non-empty values cover any possible constellation among them.*

Proof: Any two objects are completely described by bounding and interior faces. For the relationship between the two objects only the comparison with opposite object parts is significant, i.e. there are 2^2 comparisons. The Boolean values *empty* and *NOT empty* describe the full range of possible values for the intersections, i.e. each of the four constellations has two possible values resulting in 4^2 different specifications. □

The equivalence relation for two specifications is based upon the equivalence of the four components of a specification.

Lemma 2 *Two different pairs of objects o1, o2 and o3, o4 have the same relationship R if for each object pair the four intersections of the object parts have the same values, respectively.*

Proof: The equivalence relations *relationEqual* between two types of relationships is the conjunction of the equivalence relation *setEqual* for each of the 4 intersections of object parts. *SetEqual* be defined as follows:

```
OP setEqual: set_1 x set_2 -> boolean;
setEqual := (isEmpty (set_1) and isEmpty (set_2)) OR
            (NOT isEmpty (set_1) and NOT isEmpty (set_2));
```

SetEqual is an equivalence relation because it is reflexive, symmetric, and transitive.

Now *relationEqual* is defined for the four intersections of opposite object parts *o0_bound, o0_int, o1_bound, o1_int* in terms of *setEqual*:

```
OP relationEqual: o0_bound x o0_int x o1_bound x o1_int -> boolean;
relationEqual := setEqual (o0_bound, o1_bound) AND
                 setEqual (o0_bound, o1_int) AND
                 setEqual (o0_int, o1_bound) AND
                 setEqual (o0_int, o1_int);
```

Since *setEqual* is an equivalence relation it is implied that *relationEqual* as the conjunction of the four intersections is an equivalence relation as well. □

A geometric interpretation of the abstract definition will be given below. It is not a matter of the definition of terms for the relationships—a systematic terminology $r_0 \ldots r_{15}$ would provide the same service. Nevertheless, it is felt that meaningful names improve the understanding of the abstract definitions of the relationships.

6.2 n-Dimensional Relationships

This is to cover the relationships among volumes in 3-D, polygons in the 2-D plain, intervals along a line, and points in 0-D. Not all 16 potential relationships exist under this restriction. In a zero-dimensional space, for instance, the set of relationships between two 0-complexes is trivial since all 0-complexes are *equal*. Subsequently, a definition of the eight relationships *disjoint, meet, overlap, inside, contains, covers, coveredBy,* and *equal* is given in terms of *boundingFaces* and *interiorFaces*.

Definition 1 *If all four intersections among all object parts are empty, then the two objects are disjoint.*

Disjoint is linear, such that two objects are either disjoint or they are not. The specification for *not disjoint* follows immediately from the definition above, i.e., both objects must not share any common face. An interpretation of *disjoint* for 2- and 3-complexes in the corresponding spaces is given in Figure 14.

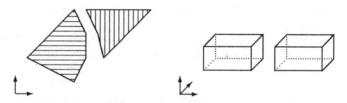

Figure 14: Two *disjoint* complexes in a 2- and 3-dimensional space, respectively.

Definition 2 *If the intersection among the bounding faces is not empty, whereas all other 3 intersections are empty, then the two objects* meet.

The nature of *meet* is such that it only matters that the two objects share at least one common bounding face.

Figure 15 shows two examples of pairs of 2- and 3-complexes which *meet*.

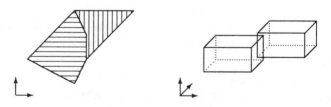

Figure 15: Two 2- and 3-complexes that *meet*.

Several different types of *meet* relationships exist which can be distinguished according to the dimension p of the common bounding faces. The detailed *meet* relations are called *p-meet*. Recall that the dimension of the bounding faces is defined as the largest dimension of all faces. The dimension of the intersection of two bounding faces is then the largest dimension of the faces being part of the intersection. Hence, there are n different types of boundary intersections between two n-dimensional objects.

Two n-dimensional objects can meet in n different ways. For example, the bounding faces of two 2-complexes can be of dimension 1 if the common part are one or several edges. Then the relationship is called 1-*meet*. The second *meet* relationship in 2-D, *0-meet*, requires that the dimension of the common bounding faces is 0 (i.e., the common bounding parts are only nodes). Figure 16 shows the difference between 1-*meet* and 2-*meet* for two pairs of 2-complexes.

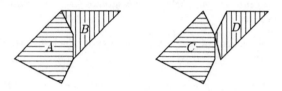

Figure 16: The 2 types of *meet* relationships among areal objects: 1-*meet* (A, B) and 0-*meet* (C, D).

Definition 3 *Two objects are* equal *if both intersections of bounding and interior faces are not empty while the two boundary-interior intersections are empty.*

Though this definition for equality may appear weak, it is sufficient for n-dimensional objects in an n-dimensional space.

For the sake of completeness, the stronger definition of equality is mentioned, too: Two objects are equal if they have the same bounding and interior faces. It is obvious that the former definition is a subset of this one. Due to the restriction that the objects and the underlying space have the same dimensions, any other constellations but *equal* are excluded under the requirement that the two opposite intersections are empty, while the corresponding intersections are not.

Definition 4 *An object A is* inside *of another object B if (1) A and B share interior, but not bounding faces, (2) if A has bounding faces which are interior faces of B, and (3) none of B's bounding faces coincides with any of A's interior faces.*

Inside has a converse relation *contains* which has the opposite definition of the boundary-interior intersections.

Definition 5 *An object A* contains *another object B if A and B share interior but no bounding faces; if B has bounding faces which are interior faces of A, and none of A's bounding faces coincides with any of B's interior faces.*

Figure 17: A 2-D object *inside* another 2-D object.

An integration relationship for *inside/contains* is *concur* which states that one of the two opposite intersections must be empty, while the other must not be.

Definition 6 *An object A* covers *another object B if both objects share common bounding and interior faces; if B has interior faces which are bounding faces of A; and if none of A's interior faces are part of B's boundary.*

Like *inside*, *covers* has a converse relationship, called *covered_by*, with corresponding specification which are the same except for the reverse opposite intersections.

Definition 7 *An object A is* covered_by *another object B if both objects share common bounding and interior faces; if A has interior faces which are bounding faces of B; and if none of B's interior faces are part of A's boundary.*

In analogy to *meet*, several versions of *cover/covered_by* exist which distinguish by the dimension of the boundary intersection.

Definition 8 *Two objects* overlap *if they have common interior faces and the bounding faces have common parts with the opposite interior faces.*

This definition does not include any statement about the relation between the two boundaries. Indeed *overlap* holds true no matter what the intersection of the two boundaries is. Figure 18 shows examples for overlapping lines and polygons with different boundary intersections.

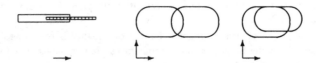

Figure 18: Overlapping complexes in 1- and 2-dimensional space.

7 Conclusion

A formalism for the definition of binary topological relationships between spatial objects was introduced. The formalism is based upon a sophisticated mathematical model for spatial data, the simplex theory. Crucial operations for the definitions of topological relationships are *boundingFaces* and *interiorFaces* which are modifications of the traditional operators *boundary* and *interior*. The comparison of bounding and interior faces with the binary values *empty* and *non-empty* gave rise to 16 different specifications.

The specifications for the relationships between two n-dimensional objects in the corresponding n dimensional space were investigated more thoroughly. A surprising regularity was obtained showing that the nature of topological relations is not erratic but rather systematic.

Further investigations are needed (1) to define the relationships of objects in higher-dimensional spaces, such as lines in 2-D or areas in 3-D, and (2) to verify that the specifications hold among objects of different dimensions as well. The Research Initiative 2 "Languages of Spatial Relations" of the recently established National Center for Geographic Information and Analysis will exploit the formalism proposed in this paper for more complex relationships.

Acknowledgement

Andrew Frank's expertise was a valuable contribution to this paper. Robert Franzosa helped clarify our understanding of combinatorial topology.

References

[Abler 1987] R. Abler. The National Science Foundation National Center for Geographic Information and Analysis. International Journal of Geographical Information Systems, 1(4), 1987.

[Carlson 1987] E. Carlson. Three Dimensional Conceptual Modeling of Subsurface Structures. In: ASPRS-ACSM Annual Convention, Baltimore, MD, 1987.

[Corbett 1979] J.P. Corbett. Topological Principles of Cartography. Technical Report 48, Bureau of the Census, Department of Commerce, 1979.

[Egenhofer 1987a] M. Egenhofer. Appropriate Conceptual Database Schema Designs For Two-Dimensional Spatial Structures. In: ASPRS-ACSM Annual Convention, Baltimore, MD, 1987.

[Egenhofer 1987b] M. Egenhofer. Relations Between Intervals In A One-Dimensional Space. 1987. Internal Documentation, University of Maine, Orono, Department of Surveying Engineering, Orono, ME.

[Egenhofer 1988] M. Egenhofer and A. Frank. Towards a Spatial Query Language: User Interface Considerations. In: D. DeWitt and F. Bancilhon, editors, 14th International Conference on Very Large Data Bases, Los Angeles, CA, August 1988.

[Egenhofer 1989] M. Egenhofer et al. Computational Topology: Data Structures and Algorithms. Technical Report, Department of Surveying Engineering, University of Maine, Orono, ME, January 1989. submitted for publication.

[Frank 1986] A. Frank and W. Kuhn. Cell Graph: A Provable Correct Method for the Storage of Geometry. In: D. Marble, editor, Second International Symposium on Spatial Data Handling, Seattle, WA, 1986.

[Franklin 1984] W.R. Franklin. Cartographic Errors Symptomatic of Underlying Algebra Problems. In: International Symposium on Spatial Data Handling, Zurich, Switzerland, August 1984.

[Giblin 1977] P.J. Giblin. Graphs, Surfaces, and Homology. Halsted Press, John Wiley and Sons, New York, NY, 1977.

[Güting 1988] R. Güting. Geo-Relational Algebra: A Model and Query Language for Geometric Database Systems. In: J.W. Schmidt et al., editors, Advances in Database Technology—EDBT '88, International Conference on Extending Database Technology, Venice, Italy, Springer Verlag, New York, NY, 1988.

[Herring 1987] J. Herring. TIGRIS: Topologically Integrated Geographic Information Systems. In: N.R. Chrisman, editor, Eighth International Symposium on Computer-Assisted Cartography, Baltimore, MD, March 1987.

[Jackson 1989] J. Jackson. Algorithms for Triangular Irregular Networks Based on Simplicial Complex Theory. In: ASPRS-ACSM Annual Convention, Baltimore, MD, March 1989.

[Peuquet 1986] D. Peuquet. The Use of Spatial Relationships to Aid Spatial Database Retrieval. In: D. Marble, editor, Second International Symposium on Spatial Data Handling, Seattle, WA, 1986.

[Pullar 1988] D. Pullar and M. Egenhofer. Towards Formal Definitions of Topological Relations Among Spatial Objects. In: D. Marble, editor, Third International Symposium on Spatial Data Handling, Sydney, Australia, August 1988.

[Robinson 1987] V.B. Robinson and R.N. Wong. Acquiring Approximate Representations of Some Spatial Relations. In: N.R. Chrisman, editor, Eighth International Symposium on Computer-Assisted Cartography, Baltimore, MD, March 1987.

[Schubert 1968] H. Schubert. Topology. Allyn and Bacon, Inc., Boston, MA, 1968.

[Talmy 1983] L. Talmy. How Language Structures Space. In: H. Pick and L. Acredolo, editors, Spatial Orientation: Theory, Research, and Application, Plenum Press, New York, NY, 1983.

NEW APPLICATIONS

Applying Neural Computing to Expert System Design: Coping with Complex Sensory Data and Attribute Selection

H.Tirri
Department of Computer Science
University of Helsinki
Teollisuuskatu 23
SF-00510 Finland[†]

ABSTRACT

Recently the relation of subsymbolic ("neural computing") and symbolic computing has been a topic of intense discussion. Our purpose is to focus this discussion to the particular application area of expert system design. We address some of the drawbacks of current expert systems and study the possibility of using neural computing methodologies to improve their competence. The topic can be discussed at various levels of integration: the higher the integration level, the more symbolic functionalities (such as an inference engine) are implemented directly at the level of the neural computational model.

In this paper we address the lowest levels of integration: neural networks that can be used to implement feature recognizers which allow symbolic inference engines to make direct use of complex sensory input via so called detector predicates. We also introduce the notion of self organization as a means to determine those attributes (properties) of data that reflect meaningful statistical relationships in the expert system input space, thus addressing the difficult problem of conceptual clustering ("abstraction") of information. The concepts introduced are illustrated by two examples: an automatic inspection system for circuit packs and an expert system for respiratory and anesthesia monitoring. The adopted approach differs considerably from the earlier research on the use of neural networks as expert systems, where the only method to obtain knowledge is learning from training data. In our approach the synergy of rules and detector predicates combines the advantages of both worlds: it maintains the clarity of the rule-based knowledge representations at the higher reasoning levels without sacrificing the power of noise-tolerant pattern association ("inference by memory") offered by neural computing methods.

[†]   This research is supported by TEKES through FINSOFT grant. This work was done while the author was visiting AT&T Bell Laboratories.

1. INTRODUCTION

Many of the current expert systems cannot be considered as theoretically well-founded artifacts. As most of them are designed based on a particular knowledge representation framework, their problem-solving performance may be severely restricted by the limitations posed by the selected representation technique. It can be argued that many of the fundamental problems in expert system design are due to this imperfect "knowledge compilation" as part of the domain knowledge cannot be expressed in the format dictated by the framework. Current expert systems, either domain-crafted or the ones produced with a shell programming tool, share the same general drawbacks: inflexibility in their problem solving capabilities, obscure explanation of the justifications of the results and difficulties in their modification. There are several attempts to improve this situation by making a distinction between "deep knowledge" and "shallow knowledge", the former usually meaning the use of semantics of domain objects to perform exhaustive search in the domain space if the explicit representation of the knowledge ("shallow part") fails [Davi 84]. Similarly causal knowledge is usually incorporated to provide rule justifications [WaSh 82]. In the case of rule-based systems many of the tools currently available try to address the problem of modifiability by providing semi-automatic facilities for consistency and completeness checking.

Our contribution to this research is to apply neural computing principles [AnRo 88], [RuMc 86] to improve the competence of expert systems in various domains. Although we adopt a purely engineering approach (as opposed to the competence modeling approach of [KeJo 86]) and do not try to mimic cognitive behavior of human experts, we still find an interesting starting point in studying those areas where human expertise clearly is superior to the capabilities of modern expert systems.

In spite of the underlying strong optimism in his book, Waterman [Wate 86] identifies several areas where programs have had little success of showing similar performance as human experts. Many of these problems are studied intensively in the artificial intelligence community, such as the problem of incorporating commonsense knowledge to expert systems (the CYC-project at MCC), but here we will address only two of them: *direct use of complex sensory input* and *conceptual clustering by learning*. Undoubtedly advances in capabilities in either of these areas would improve the applicability of expert systems significantly.

Recent years have seen an impressive growth in neural computing[1] research and many monographs have been published on the topic. As we do not have the possibility to review the various theoretical models and their properties appearing in the literature, we suggest for an uninitiated reader to study for example the two-volume set by the PDP-group [RuMc 86] and the monograph by Kohonen [Koho 88]. It should also be noted that our approach differs

---

[1] Depending on the research tradition adopted this research field is also called "Parallel Distributed Processing" or "Connectionism".

considerably from the earlier studies of using neural networks as expert systems (see e.g. [BePe 87], [BLMW 88], [DuSh 88] and [Gall 88]) where the only method to acquire knowledge is learning from training data. In our approach the highest levels of reasoning are always described within the rule-based paradigm. This reflects our view that for symbolic applications pure learning methods are computationally intractable unless a prior structure can be imposed on the knowledge domain by other means, i.e. programming.

2. EXPERT SYSTEMS WITH COMPLEX SENSORY INPUT

For pragmatic reasons in the following we will restrict our representation of symbolic knowledge to be in the form of rules [Wate 86]. This reflects our view of the importance of rules as a means to give rigorous formal expressions of knowledge about the problem domain.

Rule-based expert systems manipulate symbols that represent ideas and concepts. However, in many application areas complex sensory data (visual, auditory etc.) has to be transformed into symbols understood by the inference mechanism. This translation process inevitably loses information and depending on the application that information may be crucial to a successful operation of the overall system. For a moment let us study some typical rules from existing expert systems:

SPE [WeKu 84]

> **IF** THE TRACING PATTERN IS ASYMMETRIC GAMMA AND THE GAMMA QUANTITY IS NORMAL(CORRELATED TO AGE)
> **THEN** THE CONCENTRATION OF GAMMAGLOBULIN IS WITHIN THE NORMAL RANGE

TATR [CaWK 84]

> **IF** THE AIRFIELD DOES NOT HAVE EXPOSED AIRCRAFT AND THE NUMBER OF AIRCRAFT IN THE OPEN AT THE AIRFIELD IS GREATER THAN 0.25 TIMES THE TOTAL NUMBER OF AIRCRAFT AT THAT AIRFIELD
> **THEN**
> LET EXCELLENT BE THE RATING FOR AIRCRAFT AT THAT AIRFIELD

REACTOR [Nels 82]

> **IF** THE HEAT TRANSFER FROM THE PRIMARY COOLANT SYSTEM TO THE SECONDARY COOLANT SYSTEM IS INADEQUATE AND THE FEEDWATER FLOW IS LOW
> **THEN** THE ACCIDENT IS LOSS OF FEEDWATER.

> *Figure 1. Some typical rules from existing expert systems that illustrate the translation from sensory data to symbolic form.*

SPE is a typical example of an *interpretive expert system*[1] whose sole purpose is to infer situation descriptions from sensory data, in this case analyze waveforms from a scanning densitometer to distinguish between different causes of inflammatory conditions in medical patients. The rule from **TATR** is an example of rules in *planning expert systems* that create plans of actions to perform a given goal. **REACTOR** falls into the category of *monitoring systems* that compare actual system (in this case nuclear reactor) behavior to expected behavior. For all of the example rules from these different types of systems there exists a need for translation from sensory data to a symbolic representation, and the correctness of this translation is essential to the viability of the rule ("TRACING PATTERN IS ASYMMETRIC GAMMA" ..., "AIRFIELD DOES NOT HAVE EXPOSED AIRCRAFT"..., ..."COOLANT SYSTEM IS INADEQUATE").

Although all the above notions "PATTERN IS ASYMMETRIC GAMMA", "HAS EXPOSED AIRCRAFT" and "HEAT TRANSFER ... IS INADEQUATE" have a definite meaning, problems arise when one attempts to give a formal definition, e.g. in logic, to describe the condition. The situation is further complicated by the fact that the sensory data is usually noisy, sparse or incomplete (in worst case all of them). In the case of one-dimensional data it is sometimes possible to approximate these conditions by giving symbolic boundary expressions such as toleration intervals (e.g. $0.6 <$ HEAT TRANSFER < 0.9), but this approach does not generalize to higher dimensions where one has to recognize more complicated relations such as similarities of waveforms. Observe that in the literature there exist many studies on fuzzy logic [Zade 83] for approximate reasoning strategies which aim at a good estimate with uncertain data and imperfect rules. We adopt a different viewpoint and claim that *in many cases instead of describing the certainty factor of the truth value of a rule R it is sufficient to implement a reliable detector for this predicate P in the condition part of the rule*. This is based on the observation that very seldom (if ever) the rules themselves are fuzzy, but in many cases the detectors for the predicates are hard to describe algorithmically. This is usually modeled as the result from the corresponding inference step being uncertain with a given factor.

3. NEURAL NETWORKS AS DETECTORS FOR PREDICATES

Formally, a neural network *NN* is a dynamical system which has a topology of a directed graph and carries out information processing by means of its state response to (continuous) input [Hech 87a]. For the development of sensory data detectors one suitable class of neural networks are networks that directly approximate the target function $g:R^n \supset S \rightarrow R^m \supset S'$ after self-adjustment in response to a finite descriptive set of example mapping pairs $\{(i_1,o_1),(i_2,o_2),...,(i_k,o_k)\}$ (where $o_j = f(i_j) + \eta$, η being a stationary noise process). For example the layered networks presented in [Hech 87b] and [Werb 74] belong to this class.

---

[1] This classification of expert systems is from [Wate 86].

For these networks the nodes are simple computational elements: a node sums k weighted inputs and passes the result through a nonlinearity f as shown in Fig. 2. The topology of these networks is a DAG with usually less than three layers.

Much of the recent interest in these networks is due to the observation that they can be used as pattern classifiers (see e.g. [DuHa 73] in the d-dimensional feature space defined by the network inputs [Werb 74],[RuMc 86],[Lipp 87]. The decision boundary in the feature space is defined by the state of the network (connection topology, weight matrix $\mathbf{W}$, function f and threshold value vector θ). Although in principle the position of this decision boundary in the feature space could be "programmed" directly by setting arc weight values[1], the values of the weights are seldom known a priori. Hence the correct positioning of the boundary is approximated by a training process, where a set of examples of input instances $\{\mathbf{I}_1,...,\mathbf{I}_k\}$ and a correct classifications $\{\mathbf{O}_1,...,\mathbf{O}_k\}$ are presented to the network, and an algorithm called learning rule [RuMc 86] is used to calculate weight changes depending on network's performance with the current weights. As the network input includes also the correct classifications, this type of method is called *supervised learning* in the pattern recognition literature [DuHa 73]. Finally, the complexity of the shape of the boundary (linear, convex etc.) that can be realized is dependent on the number of layers (see [Lipp 87]), however for our purposes it is enough to know that any realizable shape can be produced by a three-layer network of the above elements - at least in principle.

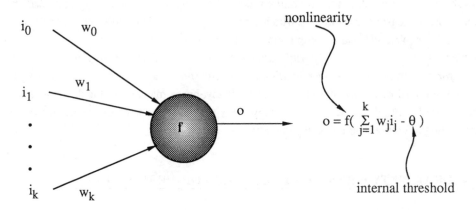

Figure 2. The computational element in a layered neural network.

For the above layered networks many learning algorithms have been suggested [Lipp 87]. Since our current purpose is to use neural networks as detectors in rule-based systems (rather than developing learning theory *per se*) we feel free to restrict ourselves to backpropagation

---

[1] Usually the only modifiable components of the network state are the weight matrix $\mathbf{M}$ and the threshold vector θ.

[Werb 74],[RuMc 86] and its variants [Werb 88]. Later on, in the context of knowledge acquisition and attribute selection we will discuss another network model with its associated learning algorithm. As in our case the details of the learning algorithms are not important, it is sufficient to state that backpropagation is an iterative gradient algorithm designed to minimize the mean square error between the actual and desired output of the multilayer network.

If NN solves a two-class classification problem, such as the question if an input $\mathbf{I}$ is regular/nonregular, in our knowledge representation formalism the network corresponds to a single data predicate $P_{NN}(\mathbf{I})$. However, in many cases a single network is capable of solving m-class problems and hence represents a set of (usually mutually excluding) predicates $P_{NN}(\mathbf{I}) = \{P_1(\mathbf{I}),...,P_m(\mathbf{I})\}$.

4. KNOWLEDGE REPRESENTATION WITH RULES AND DETECTOR PREDICATES

Our knowledge base consists of three (sub)knowledge bases: a rule base RB, a fact base FB and a neural network base NNB. Following the common expert system terminology a rule is understood as a condition-action -statement

rule i:	IF C_i THEN A_i;

with the natural semantics which assumes that if the condition part C_i is evaluated to be true, the action part A_i will be performed. A condition C_i is an expression containing one or more predicates P_{ik}. For our purposes it is sufficent to make a distinction between *detector and non-detector predicates*. The former predicates (denoted by PD) are implemented by neural networks in NNB.

An action A_i is a set of operations $\{o_{ij}\}$, each operation being either

- *internal*, i.e. it modifies the fact base FB and/or internal variables,
- *external*, i.e. call to an external procedure (e.g. for an alarm signal) or
- *adaptive*, i.e. call to a neural network in NNB in training mode.

Internal operations allow storing deduced knowledge for further use and external operations provide the interface to the real word environment where the expert system is functioning. These two types of operations are usually found in all monitoring, planning or interpretive expert systems. The adaptive operations, which are related to the adaptiveness of the data detectors, will be discussed in more detail in the context of dynamic behavior of this expert system architecture.

The fact base FB consists of facts stating that a particular predicate P holds for certain objects s_i in the object domain S of the expert system. The predicates appearing in the fact base FB can also be detector predicates. In this case the detector predicate on input $\mathbf{I}$ has already been evaluated. Hence a fact base acts as the "memory" of the expert system. In addition to the static part that states the universal facts about the problem domain, it also contains dynamically changing knowledge about a particular execution that can be later on erased.

The neural network base *NNB* contains a set of neural networks {NN_i}, each of which corresponds to one or more detector predicates. Like rules in the rule base, neural networks are active components of the system. They perform a classification operation that implements a predicate test on their input data and keep the latest data stored in an associated buffer. We call this process *knowledge translation, as the statistical relationships within the input data are translated into symbolic facts.* In this sense *NNB* is analogous to the rule base *RB*; the latter contains the knowledge for inference at the symbolic level, the former the knowledge for reasoning at the subsymbolic, sensory data level.

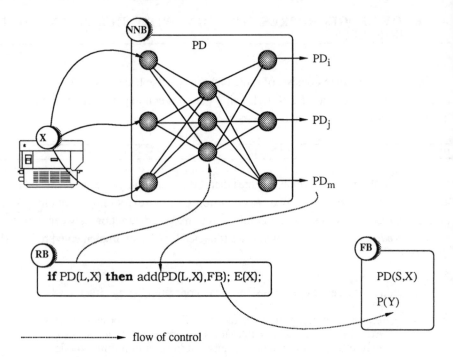

Figure 3. The behavior of a rule with a boolean detector predicate. If the value of the predicate cannot be decided based on the facts in FB the corresponding neural network (PD) is called with a pointer to the input device (X) and the name of the class to be tested (L). If the evaluation of the predicate is true, the fact is added to FB, in the other case all the subsequent evaluations of PD(L,X) in condition parts will be evaluated false without reconsulting the neural network.

The dynamic behavior of the expert system is illustrated in Fig. 3. The inference engine performs the normal backward/forward-chaining of rules. However, when it encounters a rule which has detector predicates $PD_1(L,X), PD_2(J,Y),\ldots$ in its condition part, and it cannot decide further, it performs a call for the corresponding neural network(s) with predicate arguments as parameters. *These parameters are not the actual input values to the neural network NN*, they define what classification result (L) is significant to the condition (as a multi-class classifier corresponds to a set of predicates $\{PD_i\}$) and the address of the input device (X). The actual input values *NN* receives from the sensory data equipment directly, *the arrival of the parameters acts only as a trigger to the classification process*. In the simplest form *NN* returns a boolean predicate value. If the predicate is true, the action part A of the rule in question has an operation o_i that stores the corresponding fact in the fact base. If it is evaluated false, the system automatically stores the negative fact. This is done in order to prevent the subsequent encounters with the predicate in some other condition parts from invoking the knowledge translation process again, i.e. the system "memorizes" the fact. Naturally this stored information is query-dependent and is removed after the query is completed. In the case of graded classifier output the value itself is stored in the fact base, i.e. a graded predicate always "succeeds".

Layered neural networks, such as the ones we are using, often require an extensive training period with a sample set adjusting the weights to reflect a good approximation of the decision boundary in the feature space. Obviously the larger and statistically more representative this training sample set is of the whole input space S, the better the performance (i.e. the accuracy of the approximation) is. Unfortunately in most cases it is not possible to gather enough data samples in advance to create a truly representative set. Therefore the system described must be prepared to continue adjusting the network weight matrix while already functioning by using the adaptive operations o_a in the action parts. If during the inference process there is substantial evidence of the fact $PD(L,X)$ in FB being incorrect, deduced either automatically or by human intervention an adaptive operation is performed. The adaptive operation is implemented as a call to the corresponding *NN* with the correct classification and the request to train to perform this classification. Observe that we required our *NN* modules to be able to store the latest input data whose classification was triggered, hence the symbolic reasoning module does not have to deal with the actual data at all. *This adaptation mechanism gives a way to gradually improve the accuracy of the detector predicate implementations with real input data.*

5. SELF ORGANIZATION AND ATTRIBUTE SELECTION

In practice one of the most difficult issues in the design of an expert system is the question of attribute selection for knowledge representation. As any real world process has infinitely many attributes, the problem is how to choose such a small attribute set for the knowledge base that it would be descriptive enough for the modeling purposes. This same problem is present especially when machine learning methods (either neural or symbolic, decision tree based ones such as ID3[Quin 79]) are used for knowledge acquisition.

Interestingly enough, one important organizing principle of sensory pathways in the brain is that the placement of neurons is orderly and often reflects some characteristic of the external stimulus being sensed [KaSc 85]. Inspired by this biological fact some of the neural network models and their associated learning algorithms promote *self organization* [Koho 88], [Gross 88]. As variants of these Kohonen networks can also be used directly as classifiers, they seem to be the most suitable candidates for our purposes.

In Kohonen networks the learning algorithm generates a mapping of a higher dimensional input space S onto (usually two-dimensional) discrete lattice M of output nodes. The map is generated by establishing a correspondence between the inputs in S and output nodes in M, such that the topological neighborhood relationships among the input instances are reflected as closely as possible in the arrangement of the corresponding nodes in the lattice. As a result of this process, a non-linearly reduced two-dimensional version of the input space is found. This data structure can be used to cluster input attributes.

The correspondence is obtained as follows. Each input instance is represented by a vector $s \in S$. For each training cycle an input instance $s \in S$ is chosen randomly according to a probability distribution $Pr(s)$. Each location $m \in M$ has an associated vector $w_m \in S$. These vectors w_m map lattice locations m to points in S. For each training cycle the mapping is modified according to the following abstract algorithm:

A1. Determine lattice location c for which

$$|| w_c - s || = min_{m \in M} || w_m - s ||$$

where s is the input chosen for the training cycle.

A2. For all nodes m in the neighborhood of c modify

$$w_m(new) = w_m(old) + \alpha \delta_{mc}(s - w_m(old)).$$

Here $0 \leq \delta_{mc} \leq 1$ is the adjustment function for the distance $|| w - s ||$ and α is a learning step size.

By decreasing the step size α and the width of δ_{mc} slowly during training, the algorithm gradually yields values for the vectors w_m which define a discretized neighborhood conserving mapping between lattice nodes m and points of the input space S [Koho 88].

We now turn to the problem of using this self organization process for attribute selection. Let us assume that our input space S is d-dimensional[1], i.e. each input instance is a vector $v = (v_1, v_2, ..., v_d)$. Let T be the training set, i.e. a set of such vectors. Further assume that the (output) nodes M are arranged as a grid (size k^2). In the training process an input instance enforces the sensitivity of the most responding node c (closest in d-space) and the nodes in its immediate neighborhood (defined by δ_{mc}), hence the resulting network has a tendency to form

---

[1] The dimension is typically large, $d > 100$.

clusters of nodes that are sensitive to similar inputs (see Fig. 4). After the completion of the training process, each cluster C_i is labeled with a meaningful attribute name A_i (semiautomatically) by finding an example set of vectors T_i from the training set such that the nodes in C_i are sensitive to these input instances. These example vector sets T_i help giving a meaningful interpretation for the clusters C_i. Observe that this process resembles multivariate methods such as factor analysis, but is nonlinear in nature.

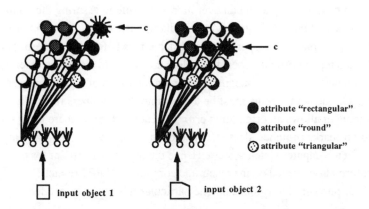

Figure 4. The self organization algorithm forms clusters among the output nodes. After a training period topologically close nodes are sensitive to similar inputs. In this example three clusters can be detected: one that is sensitive to round objects, second one to rectangular objects and the third one to triangular objects (objects are represented as a vector of gray-scale pixel values).

As the output of the cluster nodes c_i is graded, these attributes could directly be used in relational expressions to form detector predicates PD_i discussed above, e.g. sensor object s is a rock if detector predicate Is_rock(s) holds, where Is_rock(i) = $rock > .7$ (*rock* is an attribute defined by the clustering process). However, better results are obtained if this self organization process is used as a pre-processing step for a more sophisticated classifier. The clustering and labeling process gives the number and type of the classes after which a neural implementation of a nearest-neighbor method called LVQ [Koho 88] can be used to tune the classifier with the same training set T. This tuned classifier gives an alternate neural implementation to a set of detector predicates to those based on layered networks in Section 3, and is more viable in the cases where the structure of the expert system input space is not well-understood in advance.

6. EXPERT SYSTEM FOR AUTOMATIC INSPECTION

The ideas discussed have been applied to the design of an expert system for automatic inspection of circuit packs.[1] We will focus on showing the benefits of our overall approach in this particular application, readers interested in the details of the problem and a comparison of the different solution methods adopted should consult [MoRT 89a].

Computer vision is playing an ever increasing role in assuring the quality of manufacturing processes by making available low cost, reliable inspection. A computer vision system placed in-line after the placement operation can catch errors before the soldering process, thereby also reducing the repair cost. One special problem that arises in electronic assembly is the component orientation error. Although in sometimes even hundreds of components are placed on a single circuit pack, the components must be loaded into their hoppers manually and the symmetry of the component allows an orientation error to occur. Presently there is no standardization of the orientation marks (notches, dots etc.) and even if marks are used, they are often very hard to detect with a computer vision system. Hence the only starting point for the orientation detection is the information printed on the electronic component (DIP,SIP etc.).

For our purposes let us focus on one particular rule in the inspection expert system, namely

rule i: IF *orientation(chip_i) = orientation(chip_i) in design_db* THEN *check_pins(chip_i);*

that requires checking the component orientation before initiating the inspection of component pins. In principle one could use backward-chaining to solve the value of *orientation(chip_i)* and then compare it to the value accessed from the design database. One could imagine a set of rules that could be used to detect the orientation based on the features extracted from the image produced by the machine vision system. We challenge the reader to evaluate the viability of this solution as we describe some of the key requirements for this text orientation problem:

- There is no advance knowledge of font style or size.
- As opposed to Optical Character Recognition there is no opportunity to use contextual information (dictionaries) to resolve difficult-to-detect characters.
- The printing is often poor quality, e.g. characters are touching, misaligned and may contain nonchacter symbols.
- Many characters are invariant or almost invariant to a 180 degree rotation (or when rotated resemble some other character without rotation). Hence the system must be prepared to output also an "indeterminate" response.
- Detection must be carried out quickly (typically up to 50 characters/second).

Our solution to this problem was to implement a detector predicate *orientation()* as a feedforward network which was then called when executing the corresponding rule. In fact also

---

[1]   This research was performed as a joint venture with AT&T Bell Laboratories Systems Analysis Center, Holmdel.

an alternative implementation for the detector predicate based on the LVQ-method was tested and the performance of the two approaches were compared [MoRT 89b].

7. ON RESPIRATORY AND ANESTHESIA MONITORING

As a second example we will briefly compare the approach presented above to implementing an expert system with traditional rule-based techniques. Rather than inventing an artificial example of our own, we chose an example from the literature in the area of intelligent monitoring in medical environment. The original prototype system CAPS [RaCM 87], has been implemented by using various commercially available software tools for statistical analysis and expert system development.

One type of equipment malfunction during anesthesia is the accidental disconnection of the paralyzed patient from the life sustaining ventilator. If this occurs, no oxygen can be delivered to the patient and the carbon dioxide produced by the patient is not removed from the lungs. The result is a brain damage in less than five minutes. To prevent this from happening analyzers that produce carbon dioxide waveforms (capnograms) are used for monitoring purposes. A mass spectrometer produces a capnogram which is plotted against time and displayed on a CRT monitor together with some numerical information gathered. Unfortunately the capnogram and its relationship to physiological changes in the patient and to anesthesia equipment malfunction is not usually well understood by many anesthesiologists. Lack of experience with capnograms reduces the information gained and may cause misinterpretations. Therefore the work in [RaCM 87] aims at a real-time expert system for analyzing capnograms which could indicate whether the waveforms are normal or abnormal and suggest actions to fix the possible problem.

Before the design of CAPS rule base the authors used manually a statistical analysis package to analyze data stored in a capnogram database (each capnogram has also associated descriptive information about the case). Based on this analysis they chose 12 different capnogram types to be recognized with an associated feature set. In our approach this database would be used to train the self organizing network to find the initial clustering, i.e. the number of capnogram classes. In this case the input space would be d-dimensional, where d is the resolution of the waveform image stored in the database. This gives us a statistically rigorous method to determine different attributes that can be used to form detector predicates such as REBREATHING(CGRAM), NORMAL(CGRAM), CARDIOGENIC_OSCILLATION(CGRAM) etc. As discussed already in the previous sections, the LVQ-method could then be used to tune the classifier neural network that implements the set of detector predicates which describe the nature of the waveform.

In the original prototype system CAPS most of the 48 rules were used for deducing the classification from elementary features, i.e. they served pattern recognition purposes. Based on the experience with CAPS the authors predict that satisfactory operation in a delivered product would be achieved with 1000 rules! In our case the detector predicates perform the pattern recognition functions and free the rule base to describe only the necessary actions (less than 20 rules) and other higher level relationships based on this information. This considerable reduction in the number of rules has obvious performance benefits. As the real product system in the operating room should analyze several gases simultaneously (nitrogen, oxygen isoflurane etc.) our rules could also easily express complex relations between different classifications such as

$$\text{if HYPERVENTILATION(CGRAM) and NORMAL(NGRAM) then}$$
$$\text{check(ABNORMAL(OGRAM))}$$

and hence improve the expert systems ability to gain better evidence about the cause of a possible abnormality. Our claim is that the rule bases produced this way are easier to maintain and understand, since the low level reasoning for the pattern analysis is not mixed with the high level reasoning considering proper actions.

8. CONCLUSIONS

We have discussed the problem of integrating the subsymbolic and symbolic computing in the particular application area of expert system design. We have addressed only the lowest levels of integration: neural networks that can be used to implement feature recognizers which allow symbolic inference engines to make direct use of complex sensory input via detector predicates. We also introduced the notion of self organization as a means to determine those properties of data that reflect meaningful statistical relationships in the expert system input space. As our examples show, many isolated components of such systems already exist (LVQ-network simulators, design tools for rule bases etc.) but the integration itself requires considerable additional effort. The most obvious application domains for the concepts presented are fault-diagnostics and sensory data interpretation (satellite data, medical data). However, our work can be seen only as a first step towards the synergy of symbolic and subsymbolic computation as we undoubtedly have not reached the full potential of the applicability of neural computing for symbolic processing, an eminent source for future work.

REFERENCES

[AnRo 88] Anderson,J.A. and E.Rosenfeld (Eds.), *Neurocomputing. Foundations of research*. The MIT Press, 1988.

[BePe 87] Becker,L.E. and J.Peng, Using activation networks for analogical ordering of consideration: one method for integrating connectionistic and symbolic processing. IEEE International Conference on Neural Networks, San Diego, pp.367-371, 1987.

[BLMW 88] Bounds,D.G, P.J.Lloyd, B.Matthew and G.Waddell, A multi layer perceptron network for the diagnosis of low back pain. IEEE International Conference on Neural Networks, San Diego, pp.481-489, 1988.

[CaWK 84] Callero,M., D.A.Waterman and J.Kipps, TATR: a prototype expert system for tactical air targeting. Rand Report R-3096-ARPA, The Rand Corporation, Santa Monica, CA, 1984.

[Davi 84] Davis,R., Diagnostic reasoning based on structure and behaviour. Artificial Intelligence (24), 347-410, 1984.

[DuHa 73] Duda,R.O. and P.E.Hart, *Pattern classification and scene analysis*, John Wiley & Sons, 1973.

[DuSh 88] Dutta,S. and S.Shekhar, Bond rating: a non-conservative application of neural networks. IEEE International Conference on Neural Networks, San Diego, pp.443-450, 1988.

[Gall 88] Gallant,S.I., Connectionistic expert systems. Communications of the ACM (31), pp. 152-169, 1988.

[Gross 88] Grossberg,S.(Ed.), *Neural networks and natural intelligence*. The MIT Press, 1988.

[Hech 87a] Hecht-Nielsen,R., Neurocomputer applications. In R.Eckmiller and C.v.d.Malsburg (Eds.), *Neural computers*, Springer-Verlag, pp. 445-451, 1987.

[Hech 87b] Hecht-Nielsen,R., Counterpropagation networks. To appear in Applied Optics, 1987.

[KaSc 85] Kandel,E.R. and J.H.Schwartz, *Principles of neural science*, Elsevier, 1985.

[KeJo 86] Keravnou,E.T. and L.Johnson, *Competent expert systems - a case study in fault diagnosis*. McGraw-Hill, 1986.

[Koho 88] Kohonen,T., *Self-organization and associative memory*. 2nd Edition. Springer-Verlag, 1988.

[Lipp 87] Lippmann,R.P., An introduction to computing with neural nets. IEEE ASSP Magazine, pp. 4-22, 1987.

[MoRT 89a] Morris,R.J.T.,L.Rubin and H.Tirri, A computer vision system for font orientation detection: solution by optimal detection and learning vector quantization approaches. In preparation, preprint available from authors,1989.

[MoRT 89b] Morris,R.J.T.,L.Rubin and H.Tirri, A comparison of feedforward and self-organizing approaches to the font orientation problem. To appear in IJCNN'89,1989.

[Nels 82] Nelson,W.R., REACTOR: an expert system for diagnosis and treatment of nuclear reactor accidents. Proceedings of AAAI, 1982.

[Quin 79] Quinlan,R., Discovering rules from large collections of examples. A case study. In D.Mitchie (ed.), Expert systems in the microelectronic age. Edinburgh University Press, 1979.

[RaCM 87] Rader,C.D.,V.M.Crowe and B.G.Marcot, CAPS: a pattern recognition expert system prototype for respiratory and anesthesia monitoring. Proceedings of Western Conference on Expert Systems, Anaheim, CA, pp.162-168, 1987.

[RuMc 86] Rumelhart,D.E. and J.L.McClelland (Eds.), *Parallel distributed processing: explorations in the microstructures of cognition*. Vol 1,2. The MIT Press, 1986.

[WaSh 82] Wallis,J.W. and E.H.Shortliffe,Explanatory power for medical expert systems: studies in the representation of causal relationships for clinical consultations. Meth. Inform. Med (21), pp.127-136, 1982.

[Wate 86] Waterman,D.A., *A guide to expert systems*. Addison-Wesley, 1986.

[WeKu 84] Weiss,S.M. and C.A.Kulikowski, *A practical guide to designing expert systems*. Rowman&Allanheld (NJ,USA), 1984.

[Werb 74] Werbos,P., Beyond regression: new tools for prediction and analysis in the behavioral sciences. Ph.D. thesis, Harvard U. Committee on applied Mathematics, 1974.

[Werb 88] Werbos,P., Backpropagation: past and future. IEEE International Conference on Neural Networks, San Diego, pp.343-353, 1988.

[Zade 83] Zadeh,L.A., The role of fuzzy logic in the management of uncertainty in expert systems. Fuzzy Sets and Systems (11), pp. 199-227, 1983.

DATA SHARING

A Concurrency Control Algorithm for Memory-Resident Database Systems

Tobin J. Lehman
Computer Science Department
IBM Almaden Research Center

Michael J. Carey
Computer Sciences Department
University of Wisconsin-Madison

Abstract

Recent trends in memory sizes, combined with a demand for high-performance data management facilities, have led to the emergence of database support for managing memory-resident data as a topic of interest. In this paper we address the concurrency control problem for main memory database systems. Because such systems differ significantly from traditional database systems in terms of their cost characteristics, existing solutions to the problem are inappropriate; we present a new scheme based on two-phase locking that minimizes the overhead associated with concurrency control without overly limiting opportunities for concurrently executing transactions. We accomplish this by allowing the granularity of locking to vary dynamically in response to changes in the level of inter-transaction conflicts. Unlike hierarchical locking schemes, however, we avoid the expense of setting locks at multiple levels of a granularity hierarchy. We present a simple empirical analysis, based on instruction counts, to validate our claims.

1 Introduction

Memory-resident database management systems offer great potential for introducing high performance into the realm of relational database systems, and they also provide important new opportunities for the exploitation of set-oriented database operations and interfaces. For example, researchers have considered the use of relational databases for storing program data in program development environments [Powell 83, Linton 84, Horwitz 85] and for storing and analyzing performance data in an execution monitoring facility [Snodgrass 84]. Despite the advantages provided by such approaches, though, the relatively slow speed of general-purpose, disk-based relational database systems has tended to impede progress in these directions. Efficient processing techniques for memory-resident data can remove this impediment.

In previous work we have examined how the lack of disk accesses and the use of pointers can be exploited in data organization [Lehman 86b], index structures [Lehman 86a], query processing [Lehman 86c], and recovery [Lehman 87]. In this paper, we focus our attention on concurrency control.

This research was partially supported by an IBM Fellowship, an IBM Faculty Development Award, and National Science Foundation Grant Number DCR-8402818.

The many concurrency control algorithms in the literature fall into one of three categories: locking schemes, timestamp-based schemes, and optimistic (or certification-based) approaches [Bernstein 81]. Work on the performance of concurrency control algorithms has indicated that, in environments with finite physical resources and moderate to heavy workloads, locking schemes tend to provide the highest throughput [Carey 84, Agrawal 85]. The essential difference between locking and the other two approaches is that a locking protocol tries to block conflicting transactions, saving their state so that they may resume once the conflict has been removed. The other approaches typically abort many of the conflicting transactions, discarding work that must then be redone. Previous work on the cost aspect of concurrency control algorithms also suggests that locking is no more expensive than other approaches to concurrency control, at least in a centralized environment [Carey 83]. Since locking appears to be a good approach in terms of both throughput and relative cost, we are studying locking solutions to the concurrency control problem for high-performance, memory-resident database systems.

In a traditional disk-oriented database system, locking operations typically involve the manipulation of memory-resident data structures, while database references typically involve one or more disk accesses. The cost of acquiring a lock on a database entity is therefore only a small percentage of the total cost of retrieving it. In a memory-resident database system, however, this is no longer the case. The cost of acquiring a lock is likely to be on the same order as the cost of accessing a database entity; in fact, if *multiple* locks need to be acquired for a database reference, as might be the case in a hierarchical locking scheme, then the cost of acquiring a lock on a database entity could represent a significant (or even dominant) percentage of the total cost of retrieving the entity. Thus, it is necessary to examine ways of making the locking process for memory-resident database systems less expensive.

The remainder of this paper is organized as follows: Section 2 describes the salient features of the memory-resident database environment that are assumed throughout the remainder of the paper. Section 3 describes the locking algorithm that we propose for memory-resident database system use. Section 4 presents a simple analysis of our locking algorithm. Section 5 concludes the paper and discusses issues for future work.

2 The Memory-Resident Database Design

2.1 Main Memory Storage Organization

In this section we describe the storage structures used for organizing database objects in our main memory DBMS design [Lehman 86b]. We discuss the basic units of addressing and memory allocation, *segments* and *partitions*, and we describe how these units are used to organize relations, indices, and other system data structures. (For space considerations, some details have been omitted here. The interested reader should consult [Lehman 89].)

Direct addressability of database entities implies that close physical proximity of tuples is not as important for retrieval performance as in a disk-based system; indeed, the tuples of a relation *could* be scattered across all of memory. However, using random memory locations affects cache performance in some cases, and it would be more convenient for some components of the database system if tuples and index components were organized in a clustered, modular manner. For better cache performance and memory management reasons, each relation or index has its own separate memory space, which allows it to be created, reorganized, and destroyed without affecting other relations or indices.

Every database object (relation, index, or system data structure) is stored in its own logical segment. Segments are composed of fixed-size partitions, which are assumed to be the unit of memory allocation for the underlying memory mapping hardware. (We use the word 'partition' rather than 'page' to avoid any preconceived notions about the size or uses of this unit of memory allocation.) A partition is a unit of storage; database entities (*e.g.*, tuples) are stored in partitions and do not cross partition boundaries.[1] Partitions are also used as the unit of transfer to disk for checkpoint operations [Lehman 87].

Each relation partition holds control information, a tuple list that grows bottom up, and a string space heap that grows top down. The control information describes the state of the partition, including the amount of free space in the string space heap, a pointer to a list of free tuple entries, a count of existing tuples, a count of used string space bytes, and a latch control block that restricts access to a partition during update operations. The first partition in a segment is special, as it contains a data structure (the Relation Control Block) that manages the segment's lock data. Partitions for indices and other database objects are organized in a similar manner.

3 Locking in a Memory-Resident DBMS

3.1 Motivation

Common methods of accessing data in a memory-resident database system are by searching an index, by scanning a relation or index, or by traversing a link [Lehman 86a]. A traditional locking implementation employs a hash table to hold locks by entity name. If one were to use a traditional locking approach in a memory-resident DBMS, the cost of using an index to retrieve a database entity and locking it would be similar; both would involve a lookup in a memory-resident data structure. When using a scan or link to retrieve a tuple, the *relative* cost of tuple locking would be even greater— the retrieval cost would be a small fraction of the locking cost, a few instructions as compared to the expense of a hash table search/insert operation.

The cost of locking can be reduced by storing lock information in the database entity itself, as it eliminates the work of searching and dynamically allocating the lock control block. While such an approach would be costly if *every* database entity were to have its own lock control block, large entities such as relations do warrant their own statically allocated lock control blocks. Moreover, in the case of extremely high data traffic, it may be practical to allocate static lock data structures even at the tuple level.

The optimal lock granularity size for a database system is workload-dependent. Transactions that access large amounts of the database can lock their data most efficiently by using large granularity locks, while transactions that access small amounts of the database can maintain a higher degree of sharing by using small granularity locks.

---

[1] For simplicity, we assume that partitions, and therefore segments, completely contain database objects. Large entities, such as image or voice data, would be stored using a separate long field mechanism.

Hierarchical locking schemes have been proposed for use in disk-based database systems as a way to allow transactions to lock the appropriate amount of data efficiently [Gray 78]. In a study of locking granularity and performance, Ries and Stonebraker concluded that, when a mix of such transactions exists, a two-level lock hierarchy, using relation locks and tuple locks, seems to be best [Ries 79]. Such a hierarchy allows transactions accessing large amounts of data to set relation-level locks, while transactions accessing small amounts of data can operate by setting relation-level intention locks followed by tuple-level read and write locks. In a memory-resident database system, such an approach would further increase the (already high) cost of locking.

It appears that an ideal locking scheme for memory-resident data would be one which requires at most one lock per data item, and yet provides the functionality of a hierarchical locking scheme. Furthermore, the cost of the locking process should be as low as possible. If there is relatively little sharing for certain database objects, it would be beneficial if transactions could detect this and lock them all with one locking operation, particularly if this could take place dynamically. That is, we would like to be able to vary the locking granule size on a per-object basis to fit the current needs for sharing of that object. It is this "wish list" that guided the design of our scheme for locking in memory-resident databases.

3.2 Overview

The proposed locking algorithm uses two locking granule sizes: relation-level locks and tuple-level locks. Locking at the relation level is much cheaper than locking at the tuple level, so it is the preferred method when a fine granularity of sharing is not needed. When several transactions desire access to a relation that is locked with a relation-level lock, the relation lock is *de-escalated* into a collection of tuple locks; the higher cost for tuple-level locking is then paid, but the level of sharing is increased. To allow for the possibility of relation lock de-escalation, tuple-level write sets and read predicate lists for transactions are kept in a control block associated with each accessed relation so that they may be converted into tuple locks if the need arises. When fine granularity locks are no longer needed, tuple-level locks are escalated back into relation-level locks. Certain operations that require the use of an entire relation will be able to *force* lock escalation to the relation level and then disable lock de-escalation until they have completed.

Before describing the details of our approach, we review certain features of memory-resident database systems that will prove useful for concurrency control purposes. Memory-resident database systems do not have I/O-triggered process switches, so a process switch will occur only when a transaction's time slice has expired or when it is forced to wait for a lock. Except for long transactions, most transactions will need to use resources in the database system for only a relatively short time. If we were to assume that all transactions were short, and the database system was for uniprocessor use only, then exclusively locking the entire database might be a viable solution to the concurrency control problem [Salem 86]; however, we feel that both of these assumptions are far too strong. Even in a multiprocessor, though, transactions may be able to run without conflicting with one another on many relations, even using relation level locking. Other relations (*e.g.* catalogs) will be frequently accessed, so these must be locked at the tuple level or else too many transactions would be blocked.

With this background, we can now proceed with the presentation of our variable-granularity locking solution to the concurrency control problem for memory-resident database systems. We begin by discussing the two types of locking, relation and tuple locking, and we then describe how lock de-escalation and escalation work. We complete this section with a brief discussion of deadlock detection and resolution.

3.3 Relation Locks

A single lock at the relation level will lock both a relation and all of its associated indices. Thus, either all partitions of a relation can be accessed in a read-only fashion or else there is a single writer, so there is no need for lower-level locking to protect the consistency of the relation. As mentioned earlier, each relation keeps a small amount of static lock information in a relation control block (RCB). This control block is kept in a well-known location in the first partition of the relation's segment, so it is easily located given the address of any of the relation's tuples. (A tuple address has three parts: < Segment, Partition, Offset >.)

Relation Control Block (RCB)

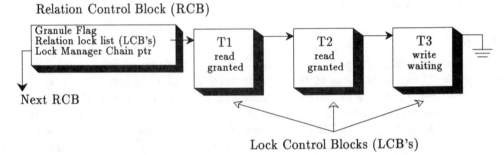

Figure 1: An Example of a Relation Lock Control Block Structure

Figure 1 shows the contents of a relation's RCB. A relation control block contains a lock granularity flag which shows the current locking size (either tuple-level or relation-level), a pointer to a list of lock control blocks (LCB's) that are kept by each transaction holding a lock on this relation, and an RCB chain pointer which links all of the active RCB's to a chain held by the lock manager.

Figure 2a shows the contents of a transaction's lock control block (LCB). Each transaction lock control block contains the owner's transaction id, a relation lock mode (shared or exclusive), the current lock status (held or waiting), a list of transactions waiting on predicate locks held by this transaction, a list of tuple pointers corresponding to its write set, and a list of predicates corresponding to its read set. A transaction *always* creates a lock control block for each relation it references, as it always maintains a write set and a list of predicates[2] specific to the relation, regardless of the relation's lock status value.

A relation's lock control blocks (LCB's) are managed in a manner similar to standard lock manager control blocks, as described in Gray's Notes [Gray 78]. The order of the

---

[2]Predicate locks are explained in section 3.4.1.

LCB's reflect the order in which transactions requested locks. When a transaction requests a lock that is not granted, it allocates an LCB, enters it at the end of the list, sets its lock status to waiting, and then suspends execution. When a held relational-level lock is released, the relation lock is granted to the transaction whose LCB is next in line in the LCB chain, and that transaction is allowed to continue. As shown in Figure 1, when transactions T1 and T2 finish, the relation lock will be given to T3 and T3 will be allowed to run.

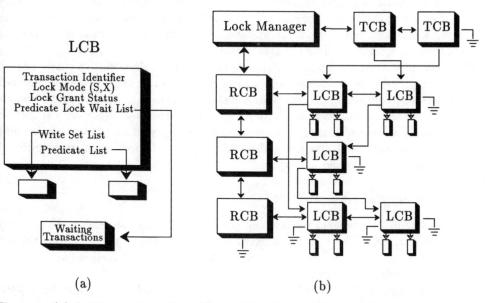

(a)   (b)

Figure 2: (a) A Transaction's Lock Control Block (LCB), and (b) Control Block Interaction

The locking status flag for a relation is kept in the relation's Relation Control Block (RBC). As a transaction runs it checks this locking status flag, which is protected by a spin latch (explained below), before each of its tuple references, and it sets the appropriate level of lock according to the lock status flag value. Since the locking status for a relation may change during the course of a transaction, it must be checked before each potential locking operation. This should not represent a significant cost, however, as it involves only a spin latch and test operation. Some types of transactions will force the use of a relation lock; such transactions would not need to test the lock status flag. Examples of such transactions are those used to create indices, perform relation scans, and checkpoint partitions.

Figure 2b shows the relationships between Transaction Control Blocks (TCB's), Relation Control Blocks (RCB's), Lock Control Blocks (LCB's), and the lock manager. The lock manager maintains a list of active RCB's so that it can easily find all of the relations that have locks, as well as the locks themselves. It also keeps a list of TCB's for deadlock detection purposes.

3.3.1 Latches

A latch, or short-term lock, is a low level primitive that provides a cheap serialization mechanism with shared and exclusive lock modes, but no deadlock detection [Gray 78]. In disk-based database systems, latches are used mainly by resource managers to gain temporary (exclusive) access to shared memory-resident

data structures or buffer pages. In a memory-resident database system, the entire database is a memory-resident shared data structure, so latches are needed to serialize updates to each of its parts. For example, a latch is needed to prevent readers from referencing a partition while it is being updated, as the update operation may cause its contents to be in a temporarily inconsistent state.

We use two varieties of latches: a spin latch with a single exclusive mode that is used to protect a very small critical section (or a critical section that is rarely referenced simultaneously by concurrent processes) and costs only a few instructions; and a regular latch with a share and exclusive mode that is used to protect a larger critical section and causes waiting transactions to be suspended while they wait for the latch to become available. The regular latch has the additional property of prohibiting preemption of the holding process (explained below).

3.3.2 Avoiding Convoys

Latches should not be held by inactive processes, as this can lead to the convoy problem [Blasgen 79]. The convoy problem is created when a preemptive scheduler preempts a process that is holding a critical resource in a critical section (*i.e.* a latch). All processes needing this critical resource block on the latch and wait for it to be released. When the holder of the latch is dispatched, it is likely to re-request the latch very shortly thereafter and, if scheduling is fair, the process must then wait until its turn to get the latch again. Once created, convoys tend to persist for a very long time, causing thrashing due to frequent context switches [Blasgen 79]. To prevent the convoy problem, a process holding a latch can also implicitly hold a "latch" on its processor, thus avoiding the possibility of being descheduled while holding an important shared resource in a critical section. In many systems, having a transaction disable a process switch would require an expensive kernel call, but this can be done inexpensively by having the database system share a data structure with the kernel. Setting a flag in this data structure will allow a transaction to run uninterrupted while it executes the operation requiring the latch. This is similar to the "open addressing" design of the Xerox open operating system [Lampson 79].

3.4 Tuple Locks

Tuple locks are managed differently than relation locks. Each tuple lock has dynamically allocated control block that holds its tuple address, its lock mode, its lock status, its transaction id, and (potentially) a queue of control blocks of waiting transactions. To reduce the lookup cost to a tuple lock's control block, simple bit operations are performed on the tuple address rather than a more expensive hash lookup. There are several additional costs involved in tuple-level locking. When tuple locks are used, latches (described below) are required for read and update operations on index structures and relation partitions. Each tuple read or write operation must set a latch on the tuple's partition, and if an indexed field is updated or the index is used in a search operation, an index latch must also be set. In addition, writers of tuples in a relation must check all outstanding read predicates for that relation, as predicates are used to prevent phantoms.

3.4.1 Predicate Locks

Simple tuple-level locking alone is not sufficient, as it doesn't solve the phantom tuple problem [Eswaran 76]. Phantom tuples are tuples that do not exist at the beginning of a transaction (and thus cannot be locked physically), but appear during the transaction, causing it to see an inconsistent view of the database. Solutions for preventing phantoms range from locking the entire relation to locking a range of values that cover the tuples being read. Locking a range of values can be done with a physical lock, as is done in R* via locks on index pages [Lindsay 85], or it can be done by locking predicates, as in the *Precision Locks* algorithm proposed by Jordan *et. al.* in [Jordan 81]. Precision Locks do not try to detect intersection of read and/or write predicates, as this problem is recursively unsolvable for general predicates [Eswaran 76]. Instead, writers of values simply compare each new value to be written against a list of all outstanding read predicates, and readers compare their read predicates against a list of all outstanding updated tuples. Since appropriate indices may not always be present to allow physical range locking, we propose a scheme similar to Precision Locks to handle the phantom problem.

Our method uses exclusive locks for write/write and write/read synchronization and requires readers to post predicates representing their read values to keep out writers of phantoms (read/write synchronization). In other words, our method uses tuple locks to prevent readers and writers from seeing or modifying the uncommitted data of other writers, and it uses read predicates (that writers must check) to allow readers to keep out writers of phantom tuples. This is similar to the Precision Locks mechanism in that it tests a writer's values against a list of read predicates, but it is different in that the Precision Locks algorithm must test a requesting reader's predicate against a list of outstanding updates for write/read synchronization, whereas our method uses simple exclusive locks for this purpose.

The Precision Locks algorithm performs well when there are only readers, as readers incur no locking costs other than posting their predicates. It does not perform well when there are many readers and many writers, as each newly written value must be checked against a list of read predicates, and each new read predicate must be checked against a list of newly written values. Note that writers must also post read predicates, as it is assumed that writers always read the values first. In our scheme, when there are only readers, locking will usually be set at the relation level, hence locking costs will be minimal. When there are readers and many writers, readers check only regular tuple locks, and writers check tuple locks and compare their new values against read predicates. Thus, readers incur a cost proportional to the number of database references they generate, as opposed to the number of active writers. In comparing the two methods, it appears that our predicate locking scheme benefits from the simplicity of relation locking under low to medium sharing, and incurs a smaller locking cost for readers under high sharing conditions; the cost for writers is about the same.

Read predicates can be created and compiled into executable code when transactions are compiled.[3] The predicates for a transaction are attached to its relation lock control block (as shown back in Figure 1), so each node in the predicate list holds a small portion of compiled code for testing potential write values against the predicate contained in the compiled code. If a writer blocks on a read predicate lock, it is entered in the transaction lock control block (LCB) of the transaction holding the predicate lock.

3.5 Lock De-escalation and Escalation

As mentioned earlier, our locking scheme is designed to allow the granularity of locking to vary on a per-relation basis in order to respond dynamically to the tradeoff between locking cost and the demand for shared data access. We now describe the details of this scheme.

3.5.1 Lock De-escalation

Typical high-performance transactions are assumed to be short, due to the lack of disk accesses, so most relations will not be referenced by more than one transaction at a time. There will, however, be some relations (e.g. system catalogs) that will be touched frequently and will probably need to be shared. Unless it is known in advance that a relation will need tuple-level locks, relations' RCB's are initialized with their locking granularity flag set to the relation level. Locks de-escalate in size when a relation-level lock held by one transaction significantly inhibits the progress of other transactions. The decision to de-escalate is determined by two factors: the number of transactions waiting on a lock and the amount of time they have been waiting. Each time a relation lock acquires another waiting transaction, the lock manager increments a de-escalation count for that relation. Also, the lock manager periodically increments the de-escalation count for all relations with one or more outstanding relation-level locks. When the de-escalation count for a relation lock reaches a specified threshold, the relation lock is de-escalated into tuple locks and predicate lists.

There are several ways that lock de-escalation itself could be accomplished for a relation. One approach would be to restart all transactions currently holding relation-level locks on the relation (thus quiescing the relation), changing its lock status, and then re-running the transactions at the new locking granularity. However, restarting transactions could potentially waste a large amount of work, especially since long transactions would be the most likely candidates to be aborted. Another way to de-escalate locks would be to wait until all active transactions finish their work on the relation, holding off new transactions until the relation becomes quiescent, and then to set the locking status to tuple-level and allow the blocked transactions to proceed. Unfortunately, it is not possible to predict when transactions holding the relation-level lock will finish, and concurrency may be significantly reduced in the meantime.

---

[3]When a predicate involves parameters rather than constants, the code will be generated with only placeholders and the actual values will be substituted at run time.

Instead of either waiting for or aborting active transactions in order to de-escalate
relation locks, the lock manager de-escalates relation-level locks into tuple-level locks "on
the fly" during normal transaction processing. This works as follows: transactions save
their tuple-level write sets and read predicates when running at relation-level lock status,
as mentioned earlier. These write/predicate sets are simply lists that are attached to the
transaction's relation-level lock control block (as indicated back in Figure 1). Inserting
a new entry into a transaction's read or write set is fast, as it (usually) requires only
a spin latch and a simple array indexing operation. When de-escalation of a relation's
lock(s) is required, the lock manager grabs the latch protecting the locking granule
flag, latches the processor so that it does not get interrupted while it de-escalates the
lock(s), and then de-escalates the relation's relation locks into tuple locks. The lock
manager's work of de-escalating locks does not affect other running transactions unless
they request a lock from the relation during lock de-escalation, in which case they'll
wait on the spin latch until it is released by the lock manager. Once the spin latch is
released, transactions will then see from the lock granularity flag that tuple locking is
in effect.

3.5.2 Lock Escalation

A relation is eligible for lock escalation when there are no write/write, write/read,
or read/write conflicts at the relation level. Since tuple-level locks are much more costly
to use than relation-level locks, tuple locks are escalated into relation locks as soon as
the relation is eligible. Once the locking granularity has returned to the relation-level,
transactions no longer need to incur the overheads of setting or checking locks or testing
read predicates.

There are times when a relation's lock status must be forced to the relation level so
that a relation-level operation can be performed without the need to acquire individual
tuple locks. An example of this type is the checkpoint operation which captures a
transaction consistent copy of a single partition [Lehman 87]. Although it would be
beneficial for the transaction that is waiting for a forced relation-level lock to prevent
other transactions from acquiring additional tuple-level locks, such a policy would cause
deadlocks. Therefore, to ensure that a transaction waiting for a relation-level lock is
given the lock as soon as possible without causing a deadlock with other transactions,
only those transactions already holding some tuple locks in a relation are allowed to
acquire more tuple locks (in that relation) when a forced relation-level lock is pending.

As mentioned previously, transactions create relation lock control blocks (LCB's)
for each relation they reference, regardless of the locking status of those relations. If
a transaction already has an active lock control block for a relation, then it is allowed
to ask for more tuple locks in that relation. If it doesn't have an active lock control
block, then it must wait in the LCB lock chain behind any transactions requesting
forced-escalation locks, just as normal requesters of relation locks would do in the case
of normal lock contention, as shown in Figure 1.

3.6 Deadlock Detection and Resolution

Methods for detecting and resolving deadlocks are well-known [Gray 78]. A waits-
for graph can be constructed by inspecting the lists of transactions that hold locks

and their transaction blocked lists; cycles of transactions waiting for other transactions can then be detected. Once deadlock has been found, the deadlock will be broken by restarting the transaction that has the smallest read and write sets in order to preserve transactions that are fairly far along in their execution [Agrawal 87].

4 Locking Cost Analysis

We will compare the relative locking costs of our locking method with that of two highly optimized disk based lock managers: the System R lock manager and the GAMMA database machine lock manager. Space considerations force us to present only an overview of the lock manager analysis here. A detailed lock manager cost analysis can be found in [Lehman 89].

4.1 Locking Cost Instruction Counts

Gray's "Notes on Database Operating Systems" claimed that the cost (at the time of writing in 1978) for setting and releasing a no-contention lock in System R was 350 IBM 370-level instructions. Gray predicted that he would be able to reduce the 350 instructions down to 120 by using more efficient techniques, such as using preallocated and preformatted lock control blocks and making use of in-line procedure calls. In actuality, Gray was able to reduce the lock cost to about 150 IBM 370-level instructions [Gray 89]. These 150 instructions include 5 instances of the complex *Compare and Swap* instruction which roughly corresponds to 20-25 normal instructions. The total in "real" instructions then, is approximately 250, using the more optimistic number of 20 instructions per complex compare and swap instruction. These instruction counts roughly correspond to a study of the GAMMA database machine, which claims to use about 230 VAX instructions for a lock/unlock pair in the no-lock-contention case [Ghandehari 89]. Although the above instruction counts are in CISC-level instructions, we will compare them in a 1:1 ratio with our RISC-level instruction counts to make our comparison more conservative.

We have a set of instruction counts taken from a preliminary implementation of our lock manager. The following numbers are for the no-lock-contention case. The instruction count for releasing the LCB structure is only approximate, as it is proportional to the number of tuple id's that have been posted, although the real cost is reflected in the graph in Figure 3.

MMDB Locking Costs	
Instruction Count	Operation
120	Acquire and Set 1 LCB (Relation lock), post 1 tuple id
100	Release LCB (Relation lock) and all tuple id's
60	Post an additional tuple id
190	Lock/Unlock 1 tuple

1.1 Comparing the Locking Costs

An examination of the static locking costs reveals that the instruction counts are comparable. The main difference between our MMDB locking approach and the traditional locking approach is not the static cost of the various locking levels, but the ability to chose the appropriate locking granularity *dynamically* depending on a relation's current level of data contention. Using MMDB locks, when the contention for a relation is low, the locking granularity will be set to the relation level. A traditional locking method, however, does not check the data contention level, so it would continue to lock at the tuple level.

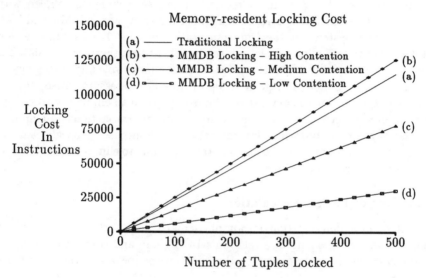

Figure 3: MMDB *vs* Traditional Locking Costs

The graph in Figure 3 compares the relative locking costs for different levels of lock contention as the number of tuple locks in a given relation varies. During low data contention, a transaction's database access cost with MMDB locking is less than the cost of traditional tuple-level locking, as the MMDB locks are setting relation-level locks and simply remembering which tuples were locked in case the relation-level locks need to be de-escalated. As data contention increases, more and more relations change their locking granularities to the tuple level until only tuple-level locks are used. Notice that the high contention case for the memory-resident locking method is slightly more expensive than traditional locking. In our current implementation, the combined cost of tuple posting with tuple locking is higher than traditional tuple locks. We are confident that we will be able to reduce the memory-resident locking cost with some additional effort so that it will be less expensive than traditional locking in every case.

2 Locking Cost *vs* Overall Transaction Cost

Although we have not yet implemented a memory-resident database management system, we can project the cost of a specific transaction with a detailed study of its function. A memory-resident DBMS implementation of the ET1 transaction, for example

[anon 85], would require about 2,000 instructions, <u>excluding</u> communication, operatin
system, and locking overhead. The 2,000 instructions figure represents the number o
instructions needed to manipulate the database system to perform the operations in th
ET1 transaction. The instruction count for an ET1 transaction in a disk-based databas
system is typically an *order of magnitude* higher than this for the same function.

Our projected cost for a memory-resident DBMS implementation of ET1 is signifi
cantly less expensive than disk-oriented DBMS implementations because the design o
our database system is significantly different existing disk-oriented DBMS's. In calcu
lating the transaction instruction counts for a memory-resident database system, w
are assuming the use of new memory-resident database techniques coupled with ne
general-purpose database techniques, such as those found in the GAMMA and EXODU
prototype database systems at the University of Wisconsin. For example, a memor
resident database system allows direct addressing of entities, therefore the database ca
be referenced as a simple set of data structures; no complex tuple addressing algorithm
record structures, or buffer management algorithms are necessary. Also, some usefu
database techniques include heavy use of in-line expansion to eliminate procedure cal
and software module crossings, *complete* compilation of transactions to eliminate an
run-time data-type or data-format interpretation, and the use of parallelism betwee
the database execution unit and the logging/recovery unit to eliminate logging overhea
from the main-line transaction cost.

4.3   The Cost of Lock De-escalation

The cost of lock de-escalation is not particularly high. It is mainly the cost o
traversing the saved tuple lists in a relation's LCB chain and turning the tuple entrie
into tuple locks, plus the cost of setting the latch on the locking granularity flag of th
relation.

The actual cost of acquiring the tuple locks is somewhat less than regular tupl
locking since all of the tuple locks are guaranteed to be granted (recall that all th
holders of the higher relation-level locks were compatible), thus the logic used to searc
for conflicts is therefore not needed. However, this savings could potentially be offset b
the waste of having transactions wait on the latch that guards the locking granularit
flag. Unfortunately we can't assign this "waste" a specific cost in instruction count
so we simply estimate that the cost of lock de-escalation would be a little more tha
the cost of regular tuple-level locking from the start. Notice that, although lock de
escalation is not overly expensive, it is not always a good idea. If a transaction holdin
one of the relation-level locks were referencing a significant percentage of the tuples i
the relation, then de-escalation would probably not be either cost effective or helpfu
from a sharing standpoint. Notice that this problem is easily prevented by including i
the de-escalation decision-making process the number of tuple locks to be obtained.

Part of the cost of the de-escalating locks mechanism is the cost of maintaining th
de-escalation counts in each relation containing relation-level locks. The de-escalatio
counter is incremented every time a transaction *waits* on a relation lock. Also, per
odically, a lock manager process will traverse the chain of RCB's and increment th
de-escalation counts and trigger a de-escalation operation if the count reaches the de
escalation threshold.

4.4 The Cost of Lock Escalation

The lock escalation operation is also inexpensive, as it only involves resetting the relation lock granule flag. The tuple locks acquired by a transaction are not immediately discarded; instead they remain with the transaction until its termination, being released as a normal part of the commit or abort procedure.

5 Conclusion

We have described the concurrency control problem for memory-resident data, arguing that standard solutions are inappropriate due to the high cost of concurrency control operations relative to data accesses. We presented a novel multi-granularity locking algorithm that attempts to reduce the overall cost of locking by using tuple locks only when doing so is necessary to reduce the level of data contention in the system; otherwise, less expensive, relation-level locks are used. Our approach involves the maintenance of write sets and sets of read predicates (for phantom prevention). Given this information, relation locks can always be dynamically de-escalated into tuple locks when a need for tuple-level sharing of data arises. We also described how the level of conflicts can be monitored on a per-relation basis, and how this information can be used for de-escalating and escalating the granularity of locking on a per-relation basis.

We have compared instruction counts of two highly optimized traditional-style lock managers with a preliminary implementation of our concurrency control scheme. The results indicate that the cost of our locking method for memory-resident data is significantly less than traditional locking in the case of low data contention, and about the same as traditional locking in the case of high data contention. Our cost estimates for a simple transaction, ET1, show that transactions implemented in a memory-resident DBMS may have significantly less pathlength than similar transactions implemented in a disk-based DBMS, and thus would incur a much higher *relative* locking cost if traditional methods were used.

We have shown that relation-level locking results in a smaller transaction instruction count, and thus a faster transaction response time, at the cost of reduced concurrency. Note that it is possible to extend our scheme to include completely serial execution through the use of a single database-level lock. While complete serialization may be desirable in some situations, as reported in [Li 88], it is not acceptable as the *only* choice of locking granularity. In particular, for applications that involve a mix of short and long transactions, and for multiprocessor-based architectures, fairness and throughput considerations (respectively) make it important to retain the ability to increase the level of sharing, even at the cost of increasing individual transaction path lengths.

6 Acknowledgements

We'd like to thank Jim Stamos for his numerous readings of this paper and his helpful suggestions on improving it. Also, our thanks to the referees for many helpful comments and suggestions.

7 References

[**Agrawal 85**] R. Agrawal, M. Carey, and M. Livny, "Models for Studying Concurrency Control Performance: Alternatives and Implications," *Proc. ACM SIGMOD Conf.*, May 1985.

[**Agrawal 87**] R. Agrawal, M. Carey, and L. McVoy, "The Performance of Alternative Strategies for Dealing with Deadlocks in Database Management Systems," *IEEE Trans. on Software Eng.*, December 1987

[**Anon 85**] Anon et al. "A measure of Transaction Processing Power", *Datamation*, Vol 31, No 7, April 1, 1985.

[**Bernstein 81**] P. Bernstein and N. and Goodman, "Concurrency Control in Distributed Database Systems," *ACM Computing Surveys 13, 2*, June 1981.

[**Blasgen 79**] M. Blasgen, J. Gray, M. Mitoma, and T. Price, "The Convoy Phenomenon," *Operating Systems Review 13, 2* April 1979.

[**Carey 83**] M. Carey, "An Abstract Model of Database Concurrency Control Algorithms," *Proc. ACM SIGMOD Conf.*, May 1983.

[**Carey 84**] M. Carey and M. Stonebraker, "The Performance of Concurrency Control Algorithms for Database Management Systems," *Proc. 10th VLDB Conf.*, August 1984.

[**Eswaran 76**] K. Eswaran, J. Gray, R. Lorie, and I. Traiger, "The Notions of Consistency and Predicate Locks in a Database System," *CACM 19, 11*, November 1976.

[**Ghandehari 89**] S. Ghandehari (implementor of the GAMMA database machine lock manager), Personal communication, February 1989.

[**Gray 78**] J. Gray, "Notes on Database Operating Systems," *Operating Systems, An Advanced Course*, vol. 60, Springer-Verlag, New York, 1978.

[**Gray 89**] J. Gray, Personal communication, February 1989.

[**Horwitz 85**] S. Horwitz and T. Teitelbaum, "Relations and Attributes: A Symbiotic Basis for Editing Environments," *Proc. ACM SIGPLAN Conf. on Lang. Issues in Prog. Env.*, June 1985.

[**Jordan 81**] J. Jordan, J. Bannerjee, and R. Batman, "Precision Locks", *Proc. ACM SIGMOD Conf.*, May 1981.

[**Lampson 79**] B. Lampson, "An Open Operating System for a Single-User Machine," *Proc. of 7th Symp. on Operating Systems Principles*, Pacific Grove, Calif., December 1979.

[**Lehman 86a**] T. Lehman and M. Carey, "Query Processing in Main Memory Database Management Systems," *Proc. ACM SIGMOD Conf.*, May 1986.

[**Lehman 86b**] T. Lehman, "Design and Performance Evaluation of a Main Memory Relational Database System," Ph.D. Dissertation, University of Wisconsin-Madison, August 1986.

[**Lehman 86c**] T. Lehman and M. Carey, "A Study of Index Structures for Main Memory Database Management Systems," *Proc. 12th Conf. Very Large Data Bases*, August 1986.

[**Lehman 87**] T. Lehman and M. Carey, "A Recovery Algorithm for a High-Performance Memory-Resident Database System," *Proc. ACM SIGMOD Conf.*, May 1987.

[**Lehman 89**] T. Lehman and M. Carey, *A Concurrency Control Algorithm for Memory-Resident Database System*, IBM Technical Report, April 1989.

[**Li 88**] K. Li and J.F. Naughton, "Multiprocessor Main Memory Transaction Processing," *Proc. Int. Symp. on Databases in Parallel and Distributed Systems*, December 1988.

[**Lindsay 85**] Bruce Lindsay, Personal Communication, November 1985.

[**Linton 84**] M. Linton, "Implementing Relational Views of Programs," *Proc. ACM SIGSOFT-SIGPLAN Symp. on Practical Software Development Environments*, April 1984.

[**Powell 83**] M.L. Powell and M.A. Linton, "Database Support for Programming Environments," *Proc. ACM SIGMOD Database Week*, 1983.

[**Ries 79**] D. Ries and M Stonebraker, "Locking Granularity Revisited", *ACM TODS 4, 2*, June 1979.

[**Salem 86**] K. Salem and H. Garcia-Molina, *Crash Recovery Mechanisms for Main Storage Database Systems*, Tech. Rep. No. CS-TR-0340-86, CS Dept., Princeton Univ., April 1986.

[**Snodgrass 84**] R. Snodgrass, "Monitoring in a Software Development Environment: A Relational Approach," *Proc. ACM SIGSOFT-SIGPLAN Symp. on Practical Soft. Dev. Env.*, April 1984.

Timestamp Ordering Concurrency Control Mechanisms for Transactions of Various Length

Xingguo ZHONG

Yahiko KAMBAYASHI

Department of Computer Science and Communication Engineering
Kyushu University
Hakozaki, Fukuoka, Japan

Timestamp ordering concurrency control mechanisms were considered to be quite suitable for distributed database systems, since transactions to be rolled back can be determined locally at each site. Experiments, however, have shown that timestamp ordering mechanisms do not seem to be efficient and has a starvation problem for long transactions. In this paper, to improve efficiency of timestamp ordering mechanisms we propose to use a termination timestamp which is defined by a predicted commitment time or a predicted last read/write request time of a transaction. Besides other advantages the mechanism simplifies operations required for abort selection. The abort selection method introduced by the authors tries to improve the efficiency by selecting a proper transaction to be rolled back when conflict occurs. Comparison of several timestamp ordering methods obtained by combining these techniques is also given.

1. Introduction

Concurrency control for database systems is very difficult since serializability is required. Although two-phase locking mechanisms are widely used in commercial systems, we need mechanisms which can be applied to areas where two-phase mechanisms are not suitable. The timestamp ordering concurrency control mechanisms were introduced by such motivation, which were expected to be used especially in the following two cases. (a) The ratio of read only transactions is high. (b) The system is distributed. The mechanisms are proved to be inefficient when there are long transactions. It was expected that the mechanism was suitable for distributed systems, since the transaction to be rolled back can be determined by local operations. In such systems, however, the transaction which requires many sites corresponds to a long transaction, and thus the mechanism is not efficient. As timestamp ordering mechanisms have many advantages, we will discuss methods to improve the mechanism.

In timestamp ordering mechanisms, transaction abort always occurs when a transaction requests an operation on a data item that has been operated by another transaction (called conflicting transaction) with larger timestamp than that of the requesting transaction. In conventional timestamp ordering mechanisms, when such a conflict occurs, the requesting transaction, which is the older transaction (i.e. with a smaller timestamp) is always aborted. This is very much different from two-phase locking mechanisms, where the transaction to be aborted can be selected from transactions contained in the deadlock cycle [ROS78], under the criteria of reducing re-execution cost and/or other costs. The problems of conventional timestamp ordering mechanisms are as follows.

(1) One advantage of timestamp ordering mechanism is that it does not have the deadlock problem which exists in two-phase locking, since the deadlock detection requires a large amount of costs in distributed database systems. Experiments, however, have shown that timestamp ordering does not appear to be efficient in distributed systems [LIN83, CAR84, CAR86].

(2) In conventional timestamp ordering, transactions with different lengths have very different possibilities of being aborted. Usually a long transaction has a high possibility of being aborted, which incurs high re-execution cost and may cause starvation of such long transactions.

(3) In order to realize efficient systems, we need to realize mechanisms that are able to abort a younger transaction when there is a conflict between two transactions. Such abort selection mechanisms also useful for other purposes.

(4) When we try to abort a younger transaction, however, the following problems must be handled.

(a) When a conflict occurs, the conflicting transaction with the larger timestamp may have been committed already and thus we cannot abort it.

(b) Even if the conflicting transaction has not yet been committed, to abort the conflicting transaction requires larger cost then aborting the requesting transaction if the conflicting transaction is being executed at some other site in distributed systems.

(c) A requesting transaction may cause conflicts with more than one transaction.

In [KAM87] we have introduced the concept of the oriental timestamp ordering mechanism, which tries to abort young transactions when there is a conflict. The name came from the fact that old persons are respected in oriental countries. The basic part to realize the mechanism is the abort selection one which can abort one transaction among conflicting transactions. In this paper we will introduce the termination timestamp ordering mechanism which utilizes a predicted commitment time or a predicted last read/write request time as timestamps. The mechanism has several advantages and it can realize abort selection easily if predicted time is correct. Since conventional timestamp ordering mechanisms utilize start time of each transaction as its timestamp, we call it *Start Timestamp Ordering*. The timestamp ordering defined above is called *Termination Timestamp Ordering*. In this paper, we do not distinguish the predicted commitment time and the predicted last read/write request time. Both of them are called the termination time for simplicity.

In many transaction oriented database systems a lot of similar transactions are executed. It may not be difficult to predict the length of computation for transactions in such frequently used types. Using statistics of database operations we can get data on average read/write time as well as communication time under various situations of the system. Precise termination time for each transaction is not required. An approximate value will be enough for our purpose. Problems caused by the prediction errors will be discussed in Section 5. In other sections of this paper, we suppose that the predicted termination time of each transaction is always correct in order to simplify the discussion.

The following four classes of timestamp ordering mechanisms will be discussed.

(1) Start Timestamp Ordering (STO)

(2) Start Timestamp Ordering with abort Selection (STOS)

(3) Termination Timestamp Ordering (TTO)

(4) Termination Timestamp Ordering with abort Selection (TTOS)

STO is the conventional timestamp ordering. STOS is the one trying to abort young transactions when possible. TTO is the same as STO except the definition of timestamp. TTOS is the combination of STOS and TTO. We will show that STOS is better than STO, if the additional cost required for aborting the conflicting transaction is not too high. TTO is also better than STO, since it takes the advantages that the requesting transaction may be young. TTOS has advantages of both STOS and TTO, and supposed to be the best choice among timestamp ordering mechanisms discussed in this paper.

We give basic concepts of concurrency control, timestamp ordering in Section 2. In Sections 3 and 4, we describe the two techniques to improve timestamp ordering concurrency control mechanisms. Section 5 discusses problems caused by prediction errors.

2. Basic Concepts

A database is a set of data items. Users operate on these data items by issuing transactions. A transaction is a unit of read and write operations on data items. An important concept on concurrency control is serializability [ESW76]. Several transactions are executed in the system concurrently. If the effect of executing these transactions is equivalent to that of executing these transactions serially in some order, the execution schedule of operations of these transactions is said to be serializable. Serializability is the most popular criterion to realize correct concurrency control algorithms. Because of the requirement of serializability, transactions being executed in the system may be aborted. A concurrency control mechanism must be designed to abort transactions as little as possible, because transaction abort affects the system efficiency and the response time of user transactions.

There are mainly two practical approaches in concurrency control, two-phase locking and timestamp ordering mechanisms. In this paper, we only discuss timestamp ordering mechanisms. In timestamp ordering mechanisms, each transaction has a timestamp which shows the starting time of the transaction. The transaction T_1, which has a smaller timestamp than that of T_2, must perform its read and write operations on a data item logically earlier than T_2, if T_1 and T_2 share the same data item. Such a mechanism is called a basic timestamp ordering mechanism. If we permit more than one version for each data, it is called multi-version timestamp ordering mechanism.

[Multi-version timestamp ordering mechanism]

a) Timestamp of each transaction is defined to be the starting time of the transaction. For each data item D, a set of read-stamps and a set of <write-stamp, version> pairs are stored by the system.

b) A read-stamp records the timestamp of the transaction that has read D.

c) A write-stamp records the timestamp of the transaction that has written D. The pair consists of the timestamp and the value produced by the write operation.

d) When transaction T_1 requests to read D, it selects the version with the largest write-stamp which is less than the timestamp of T_1.

e) When transaction T_1 requests to write D, it checks whether all read-stamps and write-stamps on D are smaller than that of T_1. If so, T_1 can write D. Otherwise, T_1 cannot write D and has to be aborted.

Multi-version timestamp ordering has the property that a read request does not cause any transaction abort. Transaction abort may only occur when a transaction issues a write request.

In this paper, we will use multi-version timestamp ordering mechanisms, since these are more efficient than basic timestamp ordering mechanisms.. The transaction processing model is supposed to be the same as [BER80]. two-phase commit protocol [GRA78] is also supposed.

A transaction reads and writes data items when it is executed. When a transaction starts its execution, a private space is given by the system for buffering the data items it can read and write. All read operations are performed by copying data items to its work space. Therefore a transaction will not read a data item more than once. Write operations of each transaction does not reflect the new values of data items to the database until the transaction is committed.

A transaction issues read and write requests to the concurrency control mechanism if read and write operations are required. The response of the concurrency control mechanism is one of the followings.

(1) The request is accepted (for read and write requests)

(2) The transaction is forced to wait (for read request)

(3) The transaction is judged to be aborted (for write request)

A transaction can be in one of two states. One is the active state which means the transaction is in execution. Another is the blocked state which means the transaction has to wait for uncommitted write of another transaction as shown in (2).

3. Abort Selection Method

In the timestamp ordering mechanisms always the older transaction is rolled back when there is a conflict between two younger (larger timestamp) and older (smaller timestamp)

509

transactions. By this way we can realize a simple mechanism to select the transaction to be rolled back, but in many cases the cost required for re-execution of the older transaction is higher than one of the younger transaction. Fig.1 shows an example of a conflict between transaction T_1 and T_2, where transaction T_1 is requesting to write data item D which conflicts with read operation already performed by T_2. Since T_2 is younger than T_1, we should abort T_2 instead of T_1, since re-execution for T_2 is usually smaller.

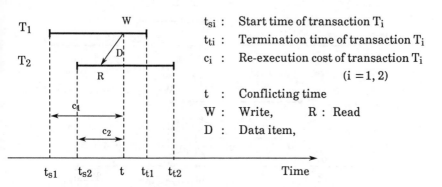

t_{si} :	Start time of transaction T_i
t_{ti} :	Termination time of transaction T_i
c_i :	Re-execution cost of transaction T_i
	$(i = 1, 2)$
t :	Conflicting time
W :	Write, R : Read
D :	Data item,

Fig. 1 An Example of Conflict on Data Item D

We will consider the case when there are transactions with very much different lengths. In the above example, when T_1 is very long, it is more desirable to abort T_2. There are the following three typical cases (See Fig. 2). Since we use multi-version concurrency control mechanisms, we need to consider the conflicts caused by a write operation on a data item which was already read by the conflicting transaction.

Case 1 : Both start and termination times of the long transaction T_1 are later than the times of the short transaction T_2. In this case, conflict occurs when T_2 issues a write request. Even if transaction T_1 should be aborted, since T_2 is short, aborting T_2 in conventional way does not cause a great problem.

Case 2 : Both the start and the termination times of transaction T_1 are earlier than those of T_2. In this case, conflict occurs when T_1 issues a write request on data item already read by T_2. In the conventional way, transaction T_1 is aborted with large re-execution cost. Since most of T_1 has been executed at the time of conflict, we should abort T_2 instead of T_1. Since T_2 is not yet committed, aborting T_2 is possible when conflict occurs.

Case 3 : The long transaction T_1 starts earlier but ends later than T_2. In this case, conflict may occur when the long transaction T_1 issues a write request on data item D that is read by T_2. In this case, since T_2 is committed, we have to abort T_1 with a high cost.

From the above discussion, we know that if the concurrency control mechanism performs abort selection under the principle of reducing total system cost, the system will become

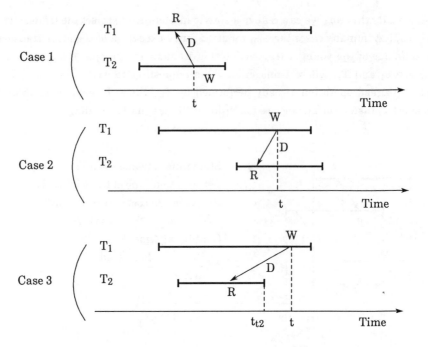

Fig. 2 Time Relationships for Conflict between a Short and a Long
Transactions

more efficient. The following three factors should be considered in determining strategy of abort selection.

(a) Cost of re-executing the transaction to be aborted

(b) Cost of aborting transaction

(c) Cost of aborting conflicting transactions (See Section 5)

Besides of the efficiency improvement, performing abort selection has the following advantages.

<1> Favor for long transactions

As mentioned above, the possibility for long transactions to conflict with short ones is much higher in conventional timestamp ordering. If a concurrency control mechanism could always perform abort selection whenever a conflict occurs, the old transaction would be prevented from abort. Once a long transaction is executed for a rather long period, it will be rather easy to be committed.

<2> Solution of starvation problem

Starvation problem is that a transaction (usually a long one) may be aborted too many times such that it will never be committed. In fact, even if it can be committed, aborting a transaction several times will affect the response time of the transaction. If a timestamp ordering mechanism could always perform the abort selection, the transactions with larger abort times could be given a high priority in the abort selection. Thus, all transactions will be committed within a certain period.

<3> Possibility of partial rollback

Partial rollback is a technique that when a conflict occurs, instead of aborting the transaction and re-executing it from the beginning, only some operations of the transaction are rolled back and redone [FUS81]. When the transaction with a smaller timestamp is aborted (as in conventional way), partial rollback cannot be realized, since the transaction aborted must be assigned a new larger timestamp in order to cancel the conflict. When the transaction with larger timestamp is selected to abort, the timestamp of this transaction does not need to be changed. The transaction can be re-executed starting from the point of the read operation which caused the conflict. Fig. 3 shows the case when T_1 conflicts to T_2 on data item D at time t and T_2 is re-executed from the operation of reading D. In this case the

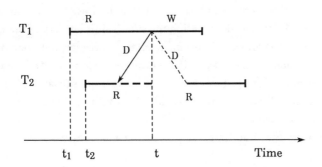

Fig. 3 Partial Rollback of Conflicting Transaction

timestamp for T_2 does not change, so there is a possibility of producing conflicts during the re-execution.

<4> Supporting other applications

In order to combine database systems with different concurrency control mechanisms, we need to control the order of serial schedule from outside[KAM84][KAM88]. The abort selection mechanism is a basic one to realize such control. Furthermore, priority control for real time systems can be realized.

One problem of performing abort selection is the case when the conflicting transaction has been committed when conflict occurs. In this case, we have to abort the requesting transaction. Fortunately, this situation can be avoided in many cases by termination timestamp ordering to be discussed in the next section.

In many cases, we do not need to perform the abort selection in termination timestamp ordering, since the requesting transaction is younger than the conflicting transaction. Fig. 4 shows this case that T_2 is younger than T_1. When transaction T_2 requests to write data item Y which conflicts to read operation of T_1, we can abort T_2 without abort selection. As described above, aborting the conflicting transaction usually needs additional cost in comparison with aborting the requesting transaction. By defining the timestamp to be termination time only, the objective of aborting young transaction is achieved in some degree.

(2) Favor for long transaction

Termination timestamp ordering also favors long transactions to commit, since a large timestamp is given for a long transaction.

(3) Version management

Version management is very important in realizing multi-version concurrency control mechanisms, which has been demonstrated by simulation of [CAR86]. For timestamp ordering mechanisms, the problem is how to get the smallest timestamp among ongoing transactions in the whole system. Evaluating the smallest timestamp of the whole system at each site requires message transmissions among sites. Moreover, the system usually has to hold some wasted versions of data, even if it performs such evaluation continuously. By termination timestamp ordering, however, all the ongoing transactions have timestamp larger than current time. We do not need to evaluate anything at all. Version management is then simplified and wasted versions of data are reduced.

We now summarize the four timestamp ordering mechanisms STO, STOS, TTO and TTOS.

STOS is better than STO, since it has advantages (1) efficiency improvement (2) favor for long transactions, (3) solution of starvation problem , (4) possibility of partial rollback and (5) supporting other applications.

TTO is better than STO for the advantages (1) possibility of performing abort selection, (2) efficiency improvement for the case that the requesting transaction is young, (3) favor for long transaction and (4) favor for version management.

TTOS is the best choice among the four mechanisms. It takes advantages of the both TTO and STOS. The comparison of TTO and STOS is rather difficult. It is very much dependent on system environment. For the system with high additional cost for aborting the conflicting transaction, TTO can play the roles of aborting young transaction in some degree. For systems that the termination time of transaction is very difficult to be predicted, we have to use STOS to improve system efficiency. Fig. 5 summarizes the relationship of the four timestamp ordering mechanisms from the view point of system efficiency.

4. Termination Timestamp Ordering

In principle, timestamp ordering guarantees the serializability of transactions by forcing all transactions to be executed in a total order. If each transaction could perform all its requests in an instant, there will be no conflicts among transactions. Since each transaction performs its requests during a rather long period of time, some point of time is selected as if the transaction is executed in that instant.

Conventional timestamp ordering selects starting time of each transaction to be the timestamp. This intuitively originated from the idea that transactions started earlier should perform their operations earlier than those started later. Evidently, if we define a predicted termination time to be the timestamp of each transaction, the idea becomes that transactions which will terminate earlier should perform their operations earlier than those terminate later.

One advantage of termination timestamp ordering is that the abort selection can always be performed since the conflicting transactions cannot be committed at the time of conflict.

Fig. 4 shows conflict situations of both timestamp definitions. When the timestamp of a

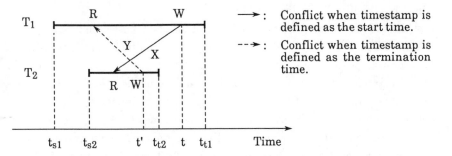

Fig. 4   Conflicts for Different Timestamp Definitions

transaction is defined to be the start time of the transaction, conflict on data item X at time t may occur and T_1 has to be aborted with high cost because T_2 is committed at t_{t2} before t ($t_{t2} < t$).

When we define the termination time to be the timestamp, the order of the two transactions T_1 and T_2 is exchanged. The request of T_1 on X will become legal, since the timestamp of T_1 is larger than that of T_2 ($t_{t1} > t_{t2}$). Instead of conflict on X, conflict on data item Y may occur as shown by the dotted line in the figure. In this case, the conflicting transaction T_1 is not committed yet, because the conflict time t' is always earlier than the termination time t_{t2} of T_2 and t_{t2} is earlier than the termination time t_{t1} of T_1.

Besides the advantage of the possibility of abort selection, termination timestamp ordering has the following advantages.

(1) Efficiency improvement

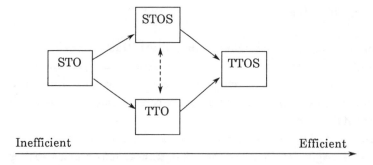

Fig. 5 Efficiency Comparisons of the Four Classes
of Timestamp Ordering Mechanisms

5. Problems Caused by Prediction Errors

We will discuss the problem caused by prediction errors for termination timestamp ordering in this section. A transaction may be terminated before or after the predicted termination time that is defined to be the timestamp of the transaction.

We first consider the case when the real termination time of a transaction is earlier than the predicted termination time. One strategy is to delay the commitment of the transaction in order to provide high possibility for abort selection. Committing a transaction earlier might cause abort of other transactions with smaller timestamp when they issue requests which conflict to this transaction. Case 1 of Fig. 6 gives an example of this situation. Timestamps of T_1 and T_2 are defined by their termination times t_{t1} and t_{t2} respectively. Suppose that T_2 terminated at time t'_{t2} which is earlier than the predicted termination time t_{t2}. When T_1 issues a request at time t which conflicts with T_2, T_1 has to be aborted if T_2 has been committed at t'_{t2}.

When the real termination time of a transaction is later than the predicted termination time, this transaction may issue a request on some data item which conflicts with some already committed transactions. In this situation, the abort selection cannot be performed. An example of this situation is shown in Case 2 of Fig. 6, in which transaction T_1 is predicted to terminate at time t_{t1}, but it does not terminate up to time t. When T_1 issues a write request at time t which conflicts with T_2, T_1 has to be aborted since T_2 is committed before conflict. A transaction may also read old data versions purged, if it does not terminated when the predicted termination time arrives. This is because that a transaction may execute at time t with its timestamp smaller than t (See version management of Section 4).

In principle, termination time of a transaction cannot be determined until the transaction terminates. Ideally, if the timestamp of each transaction is defined to be its real termination time except the situation it is aborted, the mechanism will be in optimum.

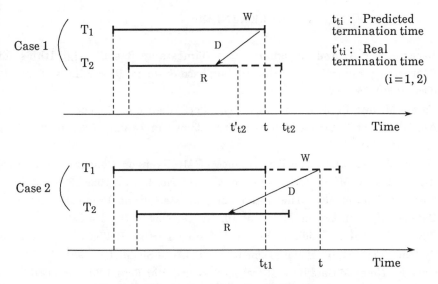

Fig. 6 Problems Caused by Prediction Errors

Termination timestamp ordering is acceptable, because it can usually define timestamps of transactions nearer to the ideal situation than that in start timestamp ordering.

Defining the predicted termination times too earlier will loss possibility of abort selection. Defining the predicted termination times too later will affect the response times of transactions. How to deal with the tradeoff of the two is very much dependent on requirement of applications.

We conclude that the predicted termination time of a transaction should be defined to be such a value that in most cases the transaction can terminate before that time. The value is not determined to be too large to affect the response time of the transaction.

Fortunately, update transactions are usually hoped to issue their write requests as early as possible, which makes the last read/write requesting time being more earlier than its commitment time. A transaction will not request any new data item after the last requesting time. Read only transactions do not cause transaction abort, hence, there is no problem caused by prediction errors.

6. Concluding Remarks

In this paper, we have introduced the termination timestamp ordering mechanism. The mechanism is supposed to be a simple and practical realization of the oriental timestamp ordering mechanism introduced by the authors. Performance evaluation by a simulator is being examined.

REFERENCES

[BER80] Bernstein, P.A. and Goodman, N. : Timestamp-Based Algorithms for Concurrency Control in Distributed Database Systems. Proceedings of VLDB, (Oct. 1980), 285-300.

[CAR84] Carey, M. and Stonebraker, M. : The Performance of Concurrency Control Algorithms for Database Management Systems. Proceedings of VLDB, (Aug. 1984), 107-118.

[CAR86] Carey, M. J. et al. : The Performance of Multiversion Concurrency Control Algorithms, ACM Trans. Computer Syst. Vol. 4, No. 4, (Nov. 1986), 338-378.

[ESW76] Eswaran, K.P. et al. : The Notions of Consistency and Predicate Lock in a Database System, Comm. ACM Vol. 10, No. 19, (Nov. 1976), 624-633.

[FUS81] Fussell,D., et al. : Deadlock Removal Using Partial Rollback in Database Systems, Proceedings of Management of Data (ACM SIGMOD), (1981), 65-73.

[GRA78] Gray,J. : Notes on Data Base Operating Systems, IBM Report RJ2188, (1978).

[KAM84] Kambayashi,Y. and Kondo, S. : Global Concurrency Control Mechanisms for a Local Network Consisting of Systems without Concurrency Control Mechanisms, Proceedings of AFIPS National Computer Conference, Vol.53, (July 1984), 31-39.

[KAM87] Kambayashi, Y. and Zhong, X., : Controllable Timestamp Ordering and Oriental Timestamp Ordering Concurrency Control Mechanisms, Proceedings of the IEEE Computer Society's International Computer Software & Applications Conference (COMPSAC), (1987), 554-560.

[KAM88] Kambayashi, Y., : Integration of Different Concurrency Control Mechanisms in Heterogeneous Distributed Databases, Proc. 2nd Int. Symp. on Interoperable Information Systems (ISIIS '88), ORM Publishing Co., (1988).

[LIN83] Lin,W. and Nolte,J. : Basic Timestamp, Multiple Version Timestamp and Tow-phase Locking, Proceedings of VLDB, (1983), 109-115.

[LIT88] Litwin, W. and Tirri, H., : Flexible Concurrency Conrotol Using Value Dates, IEEE Distributed Processing Technical Committee News Letter, Vol.10, No.2, (Nov. 1988), 42-49.

[ROS78] Rosenkrants,D.J., et al. : System Level Concurrency Control for Distributed Database Systems, ACM Trans. on Database Syst. Vol. 3, No. 2, (June 1978), 178-198.

SHARED VS SEPARATE INVERTED FILES

Elisabetta GRAZZINI

Dipartimento di Sistemi e Informatica - Università di Firenze
Via S. Marta 3, I-50139 Firenze, Italy

Fabio PIPPOLINI

Istituto per le Applicazioni della Matematica e dell'Informatica - C.N.R.
Viale Morgagni 67/a, I-50134 Firenze, Italy

Abstract

In this paper, two different structures for inverted files are analyzed and compared. The structures are called shared and separate inverted files. In the shared inverted file, the access keys can handle all the information usually handled by two separate inverted files. The results are given of some experiments which compare the shared structure with the separate one when the relational equi-join operation is executed. Moreover an evaluation is made of the memory space required by the shared and separate structures when a given application is taken into account.

1. Introduction

The most important relational operator is the θ-join; it operates on R and S relations so that all possible pairs of R and S tuples are selected which satisfy a given condition, called join condition. This condition is expressed by A θ B, where A and B are attributes of R and S, respectively, and θ is a comparison operator. The θ-join is also simply called join; as a particular case, when θ is the equality operator, the θ-join is called equi-join.

Since join requires a greater execution time than all other relational operators, various algorithms have been proposed for improving its efficiency. Initially, join algorithms can be divided into two groups: 1) algorithms which use auxiliary structures, such as indices, inverted files or pointers between tuples of different relations; 2) algorithms which do not use auxiliary structures.

The latter can be subdivided into two subgroups, according to the method used for comparing the tuples of the two relations together: 1) nested-loops algorithms [1]; 2) sort-merge algorithms [13]. Hash join algorithms are not taken into account because they may require a large quantity of main memory.

There are various auxiliary structures that can accelerate a join operation and many of them are well-described in [2]. Such structures are widely used on relational database systems (see, for example, [3] and [4]). Inverted files seem to be the kind of auxiliary structure most frequently used.

We refer to *separate inverted files* when there are inverted files on both the attributes of a join condition A θ B on the R and S relations. In this paper, we take into consideration also an inverted file structure, called *shared inverted file*, which allows us to put all the information that is usually contained in two or more inverted files into one inverted file.

This structure should be used when it is known that two attributes can belong to a join condition. When this structure is used with a join algorithm, no comparison among values is required because the join result is implicitly contained in the inverted file itself. The join is determined by means of a simple scan of the inverted file. The shared access keys can be the component records of whatever organisation of inverted files (B-trees, hash tables and so on).

The shared structure is therefore a method for keeping a join index, that is an index that makes it possible to calculate a join without accessing the tuples of the relations involved in the join itself. The notion of join index is also used by [5], [12] and, under other names, by [6], [7] and [8]. We point out that the shared structure is a sort of generalized access path structure as described in [6] and that the join index we refer to is completely different from the one described in [5] (for example, we avoid keeping two copies of the same join index as the author proposed in [5] in order to obtain the clustering of tuples for performance reasons).

The shared structure is analyzed and compared to the separate one in terms of both the amount of memory space required and a join execution time. The analysis of join execution time is made by taking equi-join into account. As far as space is concerned, it is proved that the shared structure reduces to varying degrees the amount of memory space required in the majority of actual applications. This is important even if memory space is not presently a real problem. In fact, we will show that, when a shared inverted file is used, the join execution time is linearly dependent on the amount of memory necessary to record it; therefore the smaller is the quantity of memory the more efficient is the join algorithm.

A join execution time, calculated by scanning a shared access key file, is the same whether or not the keys are sorted. When unsorted keys are used, the execution time is compared to that of both a nested-loops and sort-merge algorithms. Hash algorithms are not taken into account, becuase they can be executed only when a given large amount of main memory is available. The results show that the shared structure makes it possible to save a great deal of time in input/output operations involving the mass memory and in comparisons, moves and tests made in the main memory.

When the keys are sorted, the scan algorithm is compared to a merge algorithm; the results show: i) there is always a central unit time profit; ii) there is an input/output time profit whenever there is a space profit. At any rate, a sorted shared structure is advantageous even in situations that require greater mass memory space because there is always a profit in computing time in the main memory.

2. Inverted file structure

A relational database consists of a set of relations and each relation is defined by its schema R(A,B,C...), where R is the name of the relation and A, B, C... are the names of the attributes that R is defined on. For sake of simplicity, we assume that the attributes' names differ so that each attribute simply can be represented by its own name.

Attribute A of relation R is defined on its own domain **dom**(A), in the sense that only values taken from **dom**(A) can be associated with A in R's tuples. Several attributes can be defined on the same domain, i.e. it may be that **dom**(A) = **dom**(B) even if A $\neq$ B.

For each tuple r of relation R there is a *tuple identifier* (TID), a value that makes it possible to select r in the physical database. For example, if a relation R is recorded in the form of a sequential file, in which each record, of a fixed length, represents a tuple of R, r's TID can be the position of the record representing r in the sequential file.

For a given attribute A of relation R, $\mathcal{A}$ indicates all the values associated with A in R's tuples; $\mathbb{T}[A=v]$ is the list of the TIDs of relation R tuples having the same value v as attribute A.

A θ-join operation between R and S is represented by R $\triangleright\triangleleft_p$ S where p is the condition or join predicate of the A θ B form, in which A is an attribute of R, B is an attribute of S, and θ is a comparison operator. If θ is the equality operator, the join is called "equi-join", and if A and B are in a join condition, they must be defined on the same domain.

Two attributes are *potential join attributes* if they are defined on the same domain and can appear in the same join condition. As an example, let us take into account the following database schema: PARTS(P#,Pname,Pcity), SUPPLIERS(S#,Sname,Scity) and SHIPMENTS(SS#, PP#,Quantity); Pcity and Scity are potential join attributes and so are S# and SS# or P# and PP#, while Quantity and Weight are not, even though they are defined on the same domain (the set of Integers).

An attribute A in R's schema is *inverted* if there is a correspondence between **dom**(A)'s values and R's tuples, according to which, for each value v of actual **dom**(A), all R's tuples having v in correspondence of A are associated with itself. An inverted file for A represents this correspondence. Generally speaking, an inverted file is a file of *<access key,access list>* pairs.

An *access list* is a list of all the TIDs of R's tuples having the same value v associated with attribute A; this list is therefore $\mathbb{T}[A=v]$.

An *access key* is a triplet *<v,p,f>*, in which: 1) v is a value associated with A in at least one of R's tuples; 2) p is a pointer to access list $\mathbb{T}[A=v]$; 3) f is the number of TID's in $\mathbb{T}[A=v]$, that is, its length.

If two attributes, A and B, are inverted and are potential join attributes, we propose merging A's and B's inverted files into a single shared inverted file; its access keys appear as $<v,p_A,f_A,p_B,f_B>$, in which: 1) v is a value appearing at least once in $\mathcal{A}$ or in $\mathcal{B}$ or in both; 2) p_A is a pointer to the access list $\mathbb{T}[A=v]$; 3) f_A is the number of TID's in $\mathbb{T}[A=v]$; 4) p_B is a pointer to the access list $\mathbb{T}[B=v]$; 5) f_B is the number of TID's in $\mathbb{T}[B=v]$.

In other words, we propose maintaining an access key in correspondence to every value appearing in the union of $\mathcal{A}$ and $\mathcal{B}$; f_A and f_B represent the v frequency in attribute A and B, respectively; p_A and p_B are the pointers to two lists: the former consits of the TID's of tuples having v in correspondence with A, while tuples associated with the TID's in the other list have v in correspondence with B.

If v never appears in correspondence with A or B, a null value is codified in the corresponding <pointer, frequency> pair. It may be that s, s $\geq$ 3, attributes are inverted and are also potential join attributes: in such a case, it is possible to refer to a single shared inverted file; *s* is the inverted file's degree of sharing. An example of access keys, with *s* = 4, is illustrated in Figure 1.

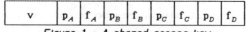

Figure 1 - A shared access key

It is worth noting that when there is a shared inverted file for A, B, C, etc., an operation regarding only one of the attributes involved (for example, an updating or search operation) can be carried out by means of traditional algorithms that only refer to the values and <pointer,frequency> pairs associated with the relevant attribute.

If f_A is 1 for a value v, the T[A=v] list can be recorded directly in p_A and therefore both space and time are saved for access to the list. As a matter of fact, if A is a primary key for the R relation, no access to lists is required during the search operations regarding the values associated with A.

From now on, we will assume that the attributes defined on the same domain are all either inverted or not inverted.

3. Performance evaluation

In evaluating a shared structure's perfomance, two elements are taken into consideration: 1) the equi-join operation's execution time; 2) the amount of space required for storing a shared index.

A comparison is made between an inverted file shared by two attributes, A and B, and traditional, separate structures having two inverted files, one for A and the other for B, and is based on the sets of parameters described in Tables 1 and 2.

Some parameters characterize the computer which the inverted files are stored and processed on (see Table 1), while others characterize the inverted file itself and therefore depend on the application chosen for evaluating the structure performance (see Table 2).

C_v	move time of a word in the main memory
C_o	comparison time for two bytes in the main memory
C_t	testing on 0 time
C_{to}	transfer time of a page between disks and main memory
P	page size
X	buffer size

Table 1 - System dependent parameters

b	length in bytes of each value in an access key
f	length in bytes of each frequency field in the access keys
p	length in bytes of each pointer field in the access keys
N_A	number of access keys in the inverted file for A
N_B	number of access keys in the inverted file for B
σ	number of values common to both A's and B's inverted files
P_A	number of pages in the inverted file for A
P_B	number of pages in the inverted file for B
P_S	number of pages in the shared inverted file for A and B

Table 2 - Application dependent parameters

As far as system dependent parameters are concerned, we assume that a page is the fixed amount of data transferred between any disk and main memory by a single I/O operation; moreover a certain part of main memory can be used as I/O buffer.

We remark that we will made a comparison with respect to the quantity of memory required for storing the inverted structures, even if this parameter is presently not so important as it was been in other moments in time (in other words memory space is not a real problem now). Nevertheless we will give some ideas about the quantity of memory used to record a shared inverted file as we will show that the time necessary to compute a join is linearly dependent on its size, as number of pages (see the scan algorithm in section 3.2.3).

3.1 Space evaluation

The space taken up by a shared inverted file for attributes A and B is compared with total amount of memory space used for representing the separate indices for the same attributes. The comparison proves that the shared structure is almost always the most advantageous one.

The number N of keys in the shared file for attributes A and B is given by:

$$N = N_A + N_B - \sigma$$

while the amount of space SI taken up by the shared file is given by:

$$SI = N * [b + 2(f + p)]$$

If we build an inverted file for both A and B, the total amount of space DI required for the two inverted files is given by:

$$DI = (N_A + N_B) * (b + f + p)$$

As a result, a shared inverted file for two attributes A and B is advantageous as far as taking up the total amount of memory space is concerned when $SI \leq DI$. In other words:

$$N * [b + 2(f + p)] \leq (N_A + N_B) * (b + f + p)$$

$$(N_A + N_B) * (f + p) \leq \sigma * [b + 2(f + p)]$$

Therefore, the memory space can be most advantageously taken up when

$$\sigma \geq \frac{(N_A + N_B) * (f + p)}{b + 2(f + p)}$$

If we let k be the ratio between the b length of value v and $f + p$, i.e the number of bytes used for representing the frequency and pointer fields in an access key, then we have

$$\sigma \geq \frac{N_A + N_B}{k + 2}$$

If $N_A \leq N_B$, then σ cannot be greater than N_A and so we can establish the following limits for σ:

$$\frac{N_A + N_B}{k + 2} \leq \sigma \leq N_A$$

If we set $N_B = a * N_A$, $(a \geq 1)$, we can then deduce from the limits established for σ that when k is less than $a - 1$ there is no advantage as far as taking up memory space is concerned in using a shared structure because the number of common values is never greater than N_A.

When $k > a - 1$, the shared structure is advantageous as far as taking up space in the memory goes when $\sigma \geq \frac{N_A + N_B}{k+2}$. If $k = a - 1$, then $\sigma = N_A$ and therefore the use of a shared inverted file is equivalent to using separate files only if all the values in attribute A are common to attribute B. We can summarize our conclusions as follows:

a) when k ($k > a - 1$), N_A and N_B are given, the advantage as far as space taken up in the memory is concerned increases as the number of values common to both A and B attributes increases;

b) as k increases, with N_A and N_B fixed, the lower bound of σ becomes smaller and therefore the number of possible situations in which the use of a shared structure is advantageous increases (in fact, it is sufficient a lesser number of values common to both attributes).

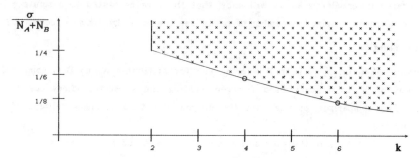

Figure 2 - Shared inverted file: space-saving applications ($a = 3$)

Since the f and p values are not very high (usually $f = 2$ and $p = 3$), it is easy for k to attain values high enough to make σ exceed its lower bound in most situations. For example, if $b = 30$, $f = 2$, and $p = 3$, then $k = 6$; in this case, it is sufficient that the number of common values be 12,5 per cent of the total number of values in $\mathcal{A}$ and in $\mathcal{B}$. If a is small enough (or $a = 1$, for example, when one of the relations represents a dependency), then it is enough for the two attributes to share only 1/4 of their values. If $b = 40$, and $k = 8$, it is sufficient that the number of common values be 10 per cent of all the values in both attributes.

In figure 2 each point in the shaded area represents a situation identified by the corresponding k and $\frac{\sigma}{N_A+N_B}$ values in which the use of a shared structure for an inverted file is advantageous in terms of space.

In this figure we set $a = 3$ and therefore a shared structure is never advantageous when k is less than 2. As a increases, the lowest advantageous value of k also increases, but, on the other hand, when k is greater than $a - 1$, the corresponding advantageous values of $\frac{\sigma}{N_A+N_B}$ decrease. For example, if $a = 4$, 5, 6,.... the lowest k values are 3, 4, 5,....... and the corresponding minimum values of $\frac{\sigma}{N_A+N_B}$ are 1/5, 1/6, 1/7........

3.2 Time evaluation

A shared inverted file's performance is evaluated by referring to the execution time of an equi-join on two attributes, A and B. A comparison is made between an inverted file shared by two attributes and two traditional, separate inverted files.

If the inverted files are not sorted, an equi-join's execution time on a shared structure is compared with the execution times of both a nested-loops and sort-merge algorithm on separate structures. If the inverted files are sorted, the comparison is made with a merge algorithm of the two separate indices.

In an equi-join algorithm, we are interested only in the creation of information for every value v appearing in both attribute A and B and this information makes it possible to access the tuples of R and S containing v itself. As far as our evaluation of an algorithm's cost is concerned, this means that the operations regarding access to the R and S tuples involved in the resulting equi-join relation will not be taken into consideration (in other words the join output cost is ignored). As a consequence we can ignore all effects (value distribution, clustering, hot spot data) which may influence locality of tuples in the database.

We feel that this approach is realistic because a query usually requires the execution of various relational operators and therefore it may be appropriate to make some other operations on the inverted files in order to reduce the number of R and S tuples to be accessed in order to obtain the relation that answers the query (see, for example, [9] and [12]).

The analysis of algorithms is presented in a detailed manner in the style used in some important recent papers about performance analysis of database algorithms (for example, see [10], [12], [13], [14] and [15]).Performance is expressed in terms of profit percentage $P(S/A)$ in the execution time $T(S)$ of algorithm S on a shared structure versus the execution time $T(A)$ of algorithm A on separate structures, that is:

$$P(S/A) = \frac{T(A) - T(S)}{T(A)}$$

In evaluating an algorithm's execution time, we use the approach described in [10], which consists in: 1) choosing a certain number of basic operations, called tasks, to be made on the data contained in the indices; 2) defining a cost function for each task. The cost function takes into consideration both the information described in the indices and the performance parameters of the computer involved in executing the tasks themselves.

An algorithm execution time is calculated by establishing what tasks have to be carried out and how many times each of them must be performed. The parameters we use are listed in Tables 1 and 2. We assume that there is a buffer available in the main memory which allows us to carry out input/output operations between the main memory and the direct access mass memory that the physical database is stored on.

As far as the input/output tasks are concerned, they perform the read and write operations. The operating costs of these I/O tasks are both equal to C_{io}. As far as using the central processing unit is concerned, we take into account comparison, move and "test on 0" operations. The following are the tasks carried out in the main memory.

Page sorting

This task sorts the access keys contained in a page of a separate inverted file according to the values described in the access keys themselves. A sort algorithm for k records requires a number of comparisons and moves proportional to $k*log\ k$ (see [11]); in this case, k is the number of access keys contained in a page, namely it is the floor of $\frac{P}{b+f+p}$.

In our case, each comparison is made between two values of two different access keys and therefore requires b comparisons among the bytes. Each move refers to a whole access key and therefore requires $\left\lceil \frac{b+f+p}{2} \right\rceil$ word moves.

This task cost can be expressed as:

$$\mathbb{C}(sort) = \left\lfloor \frac{P}{b+f+p} \right\rfloor * log\left(\left\lfloor \frac{P}{b+f+p} \right\rfloor\right) * \left(b * C_c + 2\sigma * \left\lceil \frac{b+f+p}{2} \right\rceil * C_v\right)$$

Merge

This task merges the access keys in a page of the inverted file for A to those of the inverted file for B. The pages have already been sorted internally. The merging deals with the values described in the access keys and aims at identifying the pointer and frequency fields described in the access keys referring to the pairs of values which satisfy the join predicate. The percentage of such values during the merge of two pages is assumed to be equal to $\frac{\sigma}{N_A+N_B}$; it is also assumed that $\frac{b}{3}$ bytes of two values must be compared to each other before deciding that the two values are different.

If $\left\lfloor \frac{P}{b+f+p} \right\rfloor$ is the number of access-keys in a page, $2\left\lfloor \frac{P}{b+f+p} \right\rfloor * b * \frac{\sigma}{N_A+N_B}$ byte comparisons must be made in order to identify the pairs of values which satisfy the join predicate, while $2\left\lfloor \frac{P}{b+f+p} \right\rfloor * \frac{b}{3} * \left(1 - \frac{\sigma}{N_A+N_B}\right)$ byte comparisons must be made in order to identify the pairs of values that do not satisfy the join predicate.

When a pair of values satisfies the join predicate, the pointers and frequency fields referring to them are moved to a convenient area; the number of word moves required is therefore $4\left\lfloor \frac{P}{b+f+p} \right\rfloor * \frac{\sigma}{N_A+N_B} * \left\lceil \frac{f+p}{2} \right\rceil$. The merge cost is

$$\mathbb{C}(merge) = 2\left\lfloor \frac{P}{b+f+p} \right\rfloor * \left(b * \frac{\sigma}{N_A+N_B} + \frac{b}{3} * \left(1 - \frac{\sigma}{N_A+N_B}\right)\right) C_c + 4 \frac{\sigma}{N_A+N_B}\left\lfloor \frac{P}{b+f+p} \right\rfloor * \left\lceil \frac{f+p}{2} \right\rceil C_v$$

Page scan

This task deals with a page in a shared file for two attributes, A and B, and is like the merge task because it makes it possible to identify the pairs of pointer and frequency fields referring to the values of A and B that satisfy the join predicate.

As a result, this task's aim is to identify the values in the access keys appearing in both A and B, and, in order to do this, it is sufficient to make a test on 0 for fields f_A and f_B of all the access keys in the page and move the pairs p_A, f_A and f_B, p_B of the access keys that satisfy the test. Its cost is:

$$\mathbb{C}(scan) = 2 \left\lfloor \frac{P}{b+2f+2p} \right\rfloor * f * C_t + 2 \sigma \left\lceil \frac{f+p}{2} \right\rceil * C_v$$

since $\left\lfloor \frac{P}{b+2f+2p} \right\rfloor$ is the number of access keys in a page of the shared inverted file.

3.2.1 A nested-loops algorithm on separate inverted files

In the nested-loops algorithm taken into consideration, the external inverted file is the largest, and the following steps are to be carried out:

1) X - 1 pages of the external inverted file are transferred onto X - 1 pages in the buffer; each page that is read is sorted internally;

2) a page of the internal inverted file is read in the buffer and sorted internally;

3) X - 1 merge tasks are performed on the values described in the internal inverted file's

page currently stored in the buffer and the values described in each $X-1$ page of the external inverted file;

4) steps 2 and 3 are repeated for each page of the internal inverted file;

5) some other $X-1$ pages of the internal inverted file are read and steps 2, 3 and 4 are repeated until all the pages in the external inverted file have been examined.

It can be noted that each page in the internal inverted file is read several times and it is also rewritten after being sorted internally; therefore additional internal sorting is no longer necessary (and so it also eliminates the cost of internal sorting which is comparable to the cost of a input/output operation). This algorithm's cost is:

$$NL = \left[P_B + P_A * \left(1 + \left\lceil \frac{P_B}{X-1} \right\rceil \right) \right] * C_{io} + \left(P_A + P_B \right) * \mathbb{C}(sort) + P_A * P_B * \mathbb{C}(merge)$$

3.2.2 A sort-merge algorithm on separate inverted files

A sort-merge algorithm for a join consists of an external sort step for each of the two files and a subsequent merge step; the sorting of the two files is done in accordance with the values that are to be compared in the join.

As far as external sorting is concerned, the following method can be used: the file is subdivided into numerous subfiles which are small enough to be contained in the buffer (we assume that each subfile is $X-1$ pages long because the buffer's page left over is used for the resulting file); each subfile is entirely read in the main memory and sorted by means of an internal sort algorithm.

The internal sorting is done by sorting each subfile's page separately and then by performing a $X-1$ way merge by means of a selection tree (see [11]) which makes it possible to choose the smallest value left to be examined by using only $X-1$ comparisons.

The sorted subfiles are recorded again in the mass memory. The cost of this step is

$$F * (2C_{io} + \mathbb{C}(sort)) + (X-1) * k * [(X-2) * c * C_c + r * C_v]$$

where F is the number of pages in the file to be sorted, k is the number of records per page, c is the length of the sorting field, and r is the length of the record. At this point, the sorted subfiles must be treated in such a way as to obtain a single entirely sorted file. This is done by means of a series of merge steps: in each step, $X-1$ sorted subfiles are merged into one sorted file until a single completely sorted file is obtained.

The procedure followed for the merge step is the same as the one used for sorting, except that when all the records in a page of a subfile that has to be merged have been examined, that page has to be substituted by the next page (if there is one) in the same subfile. Each merge step's cost is therefore the same as that of a sort step except for the additional cost of each page's internal sorting; that is

$$F * 2C_{io} + (X-1) * k * [(X-2) * c * C_c + r * C_v].$$

It is evident that the total number of steps required for sorting the file is $log_{X-1} \left(\frac{F}{X-1} \right)$ and so the total sort cost is

$$log_{X-1} F * F * 2C_{io} + F * \mathbb{C}(sort)) + log_{X-1} F * (X-1) * k * [(X-2) * c * C_c + r * C_v]$$

The following is the sort-merge algorithm for an equi-join calculated by using the two inverted files for the A and B attributes:

1) both inverted files for A and B are sorted by means of the preceeding external algorithm;

2) the first page of both inverted files is read;

3) the two pages are merged in order to find the pairs of access keys associated with the same value;

4) when the access keys in a page of one of the two inverted files have all been examined, the next page (if there is one) of the same inverted file is transferred to the memory and step 3) is repeated until one of the two inverted files is entirely examined.

As a result, a sort-merge algorithm's maximum cost is

$$
\begin{aligned}
SM = &\, 2P_A * log_{x-1} P_A * C_{to} + P_A * C(sort) + \\
&(X-1) * \left\lceil \frac{P}{b+f+p} \right\rceil * log_{x-1} P_A * \left[(X-2) * b * C_c + \left\lceil \frac{b+f+p}{2} \right\rceil * C_v \right] \\
&+ 2P_B * log_{x-1} P_B * C_{to} + P_B * C(sort) + \\
&+ (X-1) * \left\lceil \frac{P}{b+f+p} \right\rceil * log_{x-1} P_B * \left[(X-2) * b * C_c + \left\lceil \frac{b+f+p}{2} \right\rceil * C_v \right] \\
&+ (P_A + P_B) * C_{to} + P_B * C(merge)
\end{aligned}
$$

It is obvious that if the two inverted files have already been sorted, the join's cost is only

$$ SMO = (P_A + P_B) * C_{to} + P_B * C(merge) $$

3.2.3 A scan algorithm on a shared inverted file

The execution of an equi-join by means of a shared inverted file can be obtained by transferring file's pages one at time to the main memory and then performing the scan task on them; its cost is therefore

$$ SC = P_S * (C_{to} + C(scan)) $$

The scan algorithm's cost does not vary in the case of a sorted inverted file.

4. Analysis of the results

The algorithms we propose were evaluated and compared on the following three types of computers: personal computer, mini-computer and mainframe, so we were able to take into account the various kinds of computer facilities currently available.

The results turned out to be equivalent in terms of quality. The data regarding two experiments performed on personal computers are described in this section. The experiments differ only in the page size of main memory buffer.

The costs of operations in main memory refer to an INTEL 80286 processor with an 8 Mhz system clock, while the read/write costs refer to a SEGATE ST225 disk having 20 Mbytes with a transfer channel working at a speed of 512 Kbytes per second.

As far as tha database parameters are concerned, each experiment refers to the same number N_A in the inverted file for attribute A and to several numbers N_B of access keys in the inverted file for attribute B. For each combination N_A, N_B we also take into account several values for parameter σ expressing the number of values appearing in both join attributes. More exactly, we set always 4,000 access keys in the inverted file for **A** and we refer to a number of access keys in the inverted file for **B** varying from 4,000 to 28,000 counting by 4,000 at a time. For every pair of N_A and N_B values, the number of access keys belonging to both indices varies from 0 to 4,000 counting by 500 at a time. Table 3 illustrates all the parameter values used in the experiments.

C_v	1 μsec		P	4 Kbytes
C_c	1.5 μsec		b	30 bytes
C_t	0.75 μsec		f	2 bytes
C_{to}	47.8125 msec		p	3 bytes
			X	4, 16 pages

N_A	4,000						
N_B	4,000	8,000	12,000	16,000	20,000	24,000	28,000
σ	0 500	1,000	1,500	2,000	2,500	3,000 3,500 4,000	

Table 3 - Parameter values

Table 4 contains the exection costs of the scan algorithm on a shared inverted file; they are expressed in milliseconds. In the table, the first entry for each row σ and column N_B represents the algorithm total cost, while the second represents the I/O operations' cost and the third the cost of the operations in the main memory. These costs remain the same if the buffer size changes.

In the tables comparing the scan algorithm with nested-loops and sort-merge algorithms, the first entry represents the total profit percentage, the second represents the I/O operations' profit percentage, and the third the profit percentage of the operations in the main memory.

In the tables referring to the comparison between the scan and nested-loops algorithms and between the scan and sort-merge algorithms, it can be noted that the values shown are "regular" only if they are read in columns and this is because the merge task's cost, $\mathbb{C}(merge)$, and the scan task's cost, $\mathbb{C}(scan)$, both depend on parameter σ but in a different way.

Tables 5, 6 and 7 refer to a buffer size of 4 pages. Tables 5 and 6 refer to the scan algorithm's profit percentage versus nested-loops and sort-merge algorithms when the inverted files are not sorted, and table 7 illustrates the scan algorithm's profit percentage versus a merge algorithm on sorted inverted files.

Tables 8 and 9 refer to a buffer size of 16 pages and illustrates the comparison made between the scan algorithm and both nested-loops and sort-merge algorithms on unsorted inverted files. The costs of the scan algorithm and the merge algorithm on separate sorted inverted files are not illustrated because they do not depend on the buffer size.

In section 3.1, we saw that when ratio **k** is given, a shared structure is advantageous when the number of shared values belonging to both attributes is greater than a certain threshold which depends on the number of values in $\mathcal{A}$ and $\mathcal{B}$ and this advantage increases as the number of shared values increases.

It can be observed in the tables referring to the scan algorithm cost that when N_A and N_B are established, the cost decreases as the number σ of shared values increases. The I/O operations decreases because the shared inverted file size decreases. In tables referring to the comparison between the scan algorithm and traditional unsorted algorithms show that the profit percentage increases as σ increases when N_A and N_B are fixed.

It can also be noted that the operations in the main memory yield the highest degree of profit and this can be explained as follows:

i) The algorithms on separate inverted files require sorting at least for the pages (nested-loops method) and sometimes for the whole file (sort-merge method), while the scan algorithm is not involved in access key sorting.

ii) The algorithms on separate inverted files require page merging and this operation involves value comparing, while the scan algorithm only requires a test on 0 for any access key's frequency field.

In general it can be noted that execution time in join operations is saved by using the scan algorithm even when the shared inverted file is not advantageous as far as the amount of memory space taken up is concerned. This is true because there is always a decrease in the computing cost and this can compensate the increase in the disk reading cost.

When the inverted files are sorted, comparison is made exclusively between the scan and merge algorithms, and there is a saving in the total execution time of a join when the shared structure is advantageous as far as the amount of space taken up in the memory is concerned. However, even when there is no advantage in terms of total execution time, there is always a saving of operation execution time in the main memory.

N_B / σ	4000	8000	12000	16000	20000	24000	28000
0	3801.19 3777.19 24.00	5677.88 5641.88 36.00	7554.56 7506.56 48.00	9431.25 9371.25 60.00	11307.94 11235.94 72.00	13184.63 13100.63 84.00	15061.31 14965.31 96.00
500	3563.63 3538.13 25.50	5440.31 5402.81 37.50	7317.00 7267.50 49.50	9193.69 9132.19 61.50	11070.38 10996.88 73.50	12947.06 12861.56 85.50	14823.75 14726.25 97.50
1000	3326.06 3299.06 27.00	5202.75 5163.75 39.00	7079.44 7028.44 51.00	8956.13 8893.13 63.00	10832.81 10757.81 75.00	12709.50 12622.50 87.00	14586.19 14487.19 99.00
1500	3088.50 3060.00 28.50	4965.19 4924.69 40.50	6841.88 6789.38 52.50	8718.56 8654.06 64.50	10595.25 10518.75 76.50	12471.94 12383.44 88.50	14348.63 14248.13 100.50
2000	2850.94 2820.94 30.00	4727.63 4685.63 42.00	6604.31 6550.31 54.00	8481.00 8415.00 66.00	10357.69 10279.69 78.00	12234.38 12144.38 90.00	14111.06 14009.06 102.00
2500	2613.38 2581.88 31.50	4490.06 4446.56 43.50	6366.75 6311.25 55.50	8243.44 8175.94 67.50	10120.13 10040.63 79.50	12044.63 11953.13 91.50	13921.31 13817.81 103.50
3000	2375.81 2342.81 33.00	4252.50 4207.50 45.00	6129.19 6072.19 57.00	8053.69 7984.69 69.00	9930.38 9849.38 81.00	11807.06 11714.06 93.00	13683.75 13578.75 105.00
3500	2138.25 2103.75 34.50	4062.75 4016.25 46.50	5939.44 5880.94 58.50	7816.13 7745.63 70.50	9692.81 9610.31 82.50	11569.50 11475.00 94.50	13446.19 13339.69 106.50
4000	1948.50 1912.50 36.00	3825.19 3777.19 48.00	5701.88 5641.88 60.00	7578.56 7506.56 72.00	9455.25 9371.25 84.00	11331.94 11235.94 96.00	13208.63 13100.63 108.00

Table 4 - Scan algorithm: total, I/O and CPU costs

σ \ N_B	4000	8000	12000	16000	20000	24000	28000
0	87.41 83.88 99.64	89.79 87.02 99.70	90.86 88.48 99.73	91.27 89.00 99.74	91.53 89.32 99.75	91.80 89.68 99.75	91.91 89.82 99.75
500	88.44 84.90 99.66	90.36 87.57 99.71	91.25 88.85 99.73	91.57 89.28 99.74	91.77 89.55 99.75	92.00 89.87 99.75	92.08 89.98 99.76
1000	89.43 85.92 99.66	90.92 88.12 99.72	91.63 89.21 99.74	91.86 89.56 99.75	92.01 89.78 99.75	92.20 90.06 99.76	92.26 90.15 99.76
1500	90.38 86.94 99.67	91.46 88.67 99.72	92.00 89.58 99.74	92.15 89.84 99.75	92.25 90.00 99.76	92.40 90.25 99.76	92.43 90.31 99.76
2000	91.30 87.96 99.68	91.98 89.22 99.73	92.36 89.95 99.75	92.44 90.12 99.75	92.48 90.23 99.76	92.59 90.44 99.76	92.60 90.47 99.77
2500	92.18 88.98 99.68	92.49 89.77 99.73	92.72 90.32 99.75	92.71 90.40 99.76	92.70 90.46 99.76	92.75 90.59 99.77	92.74 90.60 99.77
3000	93.02 90.00 99.69	92.99 90.32 99.74	93.06 90.68 99.75	92.94 90.63 99.76	92.90 90.64 99.77	92.94 90.78 99.77	92.90 90.76 99.77
3500	93.84 91.02 99.69	93.40 90.76 99.74	93.35 90.98 99.76	93.21 90.91 99.76	93.12 90.87 99.77	93.13 90.96 99.77	93.07 90.93 99.77
4000	94.49 91.84 99.70	93.87 91.31 99.75	93.68 91.34 99.76	93.48 91.19 99.77	93.34 91.09 99.77	93.31 91.15 99.77	93.23 91.09 99.77

Table 5 - Profit percentages of the scan algorithm versus a nested-loops algorithm buffer size = 4 pages

σ \ N_B	4000	8000	12000	16000	20000	24000	28000
0	86.34 84.90 99.15	87.49 86.32 99.13	88.28 87.27 99.13	88.84 87.94 99.12	89.27 88.44 99.11	89.65 88.89 99.11	89.91 89.19 99.11
500	87.21 85.85 99.10	88.02 86.90 99.10	88.66 87.68 99.10	89.13 88.25 99.10	89.49 88.69 99.10	89.84 89.09 99.10	90.07 89.37 99.10
1000	88.07 86.81 99.06	88.55 87.48 99.07	89.03 88.08 99.08	89.41 88.56 99.08	89.72 88.93 99.08	90.03 89.29 99.09	90.23 89.54 99.09
1500	88.93 87.76 99.01	89.08 88.06 99.04	89.40 88.49 99.06	89.70 88.87 99.06	89.95 89.18 99.07	90.22 89.50 99.08	90.39 89.71 99.08
2000	89.78 88.72 98.97	89.61 88.64 99.01	89.77 88.89 99.04	89.98 89.17 99.05	90.18 89.43 99.05	90.40 89.70 99.06	90.56 89.88 99.07
2500	90.64 89.68 98.92	90.14 89.22 98.98	90.15 89.30 99.01	90.27 89.48 99.03	90.41 89.67 99.04	90.56 89.86 99.05	90.68 90.02 99.06
3000	91.50 90.63 98.88	90.66 89.80 98.96	90.52 89.70 98.99	90.49 89.73 99.01	90.59 89.87 99.03	90.74 90.06 99.04	90.84 90.19 99.05
3500	92.35 91.59 98.83	91.08 90.26 98.93	90.81 90.03 98.97	90.78 90.03 98.99	90.82 90.11 99.01	90.93 90.27 99.03	91.01 90.37 99.03
4000	93.04 92.35 98.79	91.61 90.84 98.90	91.19 90.43 98.95	91.06 90.34 98.98	91.04 90.36 99.00	91.12 90.47 99.01	91.17 90.54 99.02

Table 6- Profit percentages of the scan algorithm versus a sort-merge algorithm buffer size = 4 pages

N_B / σ	4000	8000	12000	16000	20000	24000	28000
0	-9.55 -12.86 80.46	-8.88 -13.46 85.14	-8.55 -13.77 86.72	-8.35 -13.95 87.52	-8.21 -14.08 88.00	-7.67 -13.69 88.38	-7.65 -13.82 88.60
500	-2.16 -5.71 81.95	-3.84 -8.65 85.92	-4.73 -10.14 87.26	-5.27 -11.05 87.93	-5.64 -11.65 88.34	-5.46 -11.62 88.66	-5.71 -12.00 88.84
1000	5.15 1.43 83.09	1.15 -3.85 86.58	-0.93 -6.52 87.73	-2.21 -8.14 88.30	-3.08 -9.22 88.64	-3.26 -9.54 88.92	-3.79 -10.18 89.07
1500	12.38 8.57 84.00	6.09 0.96 87.14	2.83 -2.90 88.15	0.83 -5.23 88.63	-0.53 -6.80 88.92	-1.08 -7.47 89.15	-1.87 -8.36 89.28
2000	19.54 15.71 84.74	10.99 5.77 87.61	6.56 0.72 88.51	3.84 -2.33 88.93	2.01 -4.37 89.17	1.10 -5.39 89.37	0.04 -6.55 89.47
2500	26.63 22.86 85.35	15.85 10.58 88.03	10.27 4.35 88.84	6.84 0.58 89.20	4.52 -1.94 89.40	2.87 -3.73 89.58	1.61 -5.09 89.65
3000	33.64 30.00 85.86	20.66 15.38 88.39	13.94 7.97 89.13	9.28 2.91 89.45	6.58 0.00 89.62	5.03 -1.66 89.77	3.50 -3.27 89.82
3500	40.58 37.14 86.30	24.54 19.23 88.71	16.92 10.87 89.39	12.24 5.81 89.68	9.07 2.43 89.82	7.17 0.41 89.95	5.39 -1.45 89.99
4000	46.13 42.86 86.68	29.27 24.04 88.99	20.55 14.49 89.63	15.19 8.72 89.88	11.55 4.85 90.00	9.30 2.49 90.11	7.27 0.36 90.14

Table 7- Profit percentages of the scan algorithm versus a merge algorithm buffer size = 4pages

N_B / σ	4000	8000	12000	16000	20000	24000	28000
0	74.87 54.86 99.64	77.70 57.71 99.70	78.90 59.01 99.73	80.28 62.45 99.74	80.56 62.46 99.75	80.81 62.52 99.75	80.95 62.51 99.75
500	77.40 57.71 99.66	79.33 59.50 99.71	80.09 60.31 99.73	81.17 63.41 99.74	81.31 63.26 99.75	81.45 63.20 99.75	81.51 63.11 99.76
1000	79.74 60.57 99.66	80.85 61.29 99.72	81.23 61.62 99.74	82.03 64.37 99.75	82.03 64.06 99.75	82.07 63.89 99.76	82.05 63.71 99.76
1500	81.90 63.43 99.67	82.27 63.08 99.72	82.30 62.92 99.74	82.86 65.33 99.75	82.72 64.86 99.76	82.67 64.57 99.76	82.58 64.31 99.76
2000	83.90 66.29 99.68	83.62 64.87 99.73	83.32 64.23 99.75	83.65 66.28 99.75	83.39 65.65 99.76	83.25 65.25 99.76	83.10 64.91 99.77
2500	85.76 69.14 99.68	84.88 66.67 99.73	84.30 65.54 99.75	84.41 67.24 99.76	84.04 66.45 99.76	83.75 65.80 99.77	83.54 65.39 99.77
3000	87.49 72.00 99.69	86.08 68.46 99.74	85.23 66.84 99.75	85.05 68.01 99.76	84.60 67.09 99.77	84.30 66.48 99.77	84.03 65.99 99.77
3500	89.11 74.86 99.69	87.06 69.89 99.74	86.01 67.89 99.76	85.76 68.97 99.76	85.21 67.89 99.77	84.84 67.17 99.77	84.51 66.59 99.77
4000	90.39 77.14 99.70	88.14 71.68 99.75	86.86 69.19 99.76	86.44 69.92 99.77	85.80 68.69 99.77	85.36 67.85 99.77	84.97 67.19 99.77

Table 8 - Profit percentages of the scan algorithm versus a nested-loops algorithm buffer size = 16 pages

Nb / σ	4000	8000	12000	16000	20000	24000	28000
0	78.53 / 68.87 / 99.57	78.85 / 71.34 / 99.50	79.30 / 73.05 / 99.44	79.72 / 74.27 / 99.40	80.08 / 75.19 / 99.37	80.49 / 76.04 / 99.35	80.76 / 76.61 / 99.33
500	79.89 / 70.84 / 99.54	79.75 / 72.55 / 99.48	79.97 / 73.90 / 99.43	80.24 / 74.92 / 99.39	80.51 / 75.72 / 99.36	80.85 / 76.48 / 99.34	81.07 / 76.99 / 99.32
1000	81.25 / 72.81 / 99.52	80.66 / 73.77 / 99.46	80.63 / 74.76 / 99.41	80.76 / 75.58 / 99.38	80.94 / 76.25 / 99.35	81.21 / 76.91 / 99.33	81.38 / 77.36 / 99.31
1500	82.61 / 74.78 / 99.49	81.56 / 74.98 / 99.44	81.29 / 75.62 / 99.40	81.28 / 76.24 / 99.37	81.37 / 76.77 / 99.34	81.57 / 77.35 / 99.32	81.69 / 77.73 / 99.30
2000	83.96 / 76.75 / 99.47	82.45 / 76.19 / 99.42	81.96 / 76.48 / 99.38	81.81 / 76.89 / 99.35	81.79 / 77.30 / 99.33	81.93 / 77.79 / 99.31	82.00 / 78.11 / 99.29
2500	85.31 / 78.72 / 99.44	83.35 / 77.41 / 99.40	82.62 / 77.34 / 99.37	82.33 / 77.55 / 99.34	82.22 / 77.83 / 99.32	82.22 / 78.14 / 99.30	82.25 / 78.41 / 99.28
3000	86.66 / 80.69 / 99.42	84.25 / 78.62 / 99.38	83.28 / 78.20 / 99.35	82.74 / 78.08 / 99.33	82.56 / 78.25 / 99.31	82.58 / 78.57 / 99.29	82.56 / 78.78 / 99.27
3500	88.01 / 82.66 / 99.39	84.96 / 79.60 / 99.37	83.81 / 78.88 / 99.34	83.26 / 78.73 / 99.31	82.99 / 78.78 / 99.29	82.94 / 79.01 / 99.28	82.87 / 79.15 / 99.27
4000	89.08 / 84.24 / 99.37	85.85 / 80.81 / 99.35	84.47 / 79.74 / 99.32	83.78 / 79.39 / 99.30	83.42 / 79.31 / 99.28	83.29 / 79.45 / 99.27	83.18 / 79.53 / 99.26

Table 9 - Profit percentages of the scan algorithm versus a merge algorithm buffer size = 16 pages

REFERENCES

[1] W. Kim: "A New Way to Compute the Product and Join of Relations". Proceedings of ACM/SIGMOD Int. Conf. on Management of Data, 179-187 (1980).

[2] T.J. Teorey, J.P. Frey: "Design of Database Structures". Prentice-Hall Inc., Englewood Cliffs, N.J., (1982).

[3] M.M. Astrahan et al.: "System R: A Relational Approach to Database Management". ACM Trans. on Database Systems 1(2), 97-137 (1976).

[4] M. Stonebraker et al.: "The Design and Implementation of INGRES". ACM Trans. on Database Systems 1(3), 189-222 (1976).

[5] P. Valduriez, H. Boral: "Evaluation of Recursive Queries Using Join Indexes". Proc. of Int. Conf. on Expert Database Systems, 197-208 (1986).

[6] T. Haerder: "Implementing a Generalized Access Path Structure for a Relational Database System". ACM Trans. on Database Systems 3(3), 285-298 (1978).

[7] M. Jarke, J. Schmidt: "Query Processing Strategies in the PASCAL/R Relational Database Management System". Proc. of ACM/SIGMOD Int. Conf. on Management of Data, (1982).

[8] D. Tsichritzis: "LSL: a Link and Selector Language". Proc. of ACM/SIGMOD Int. Conf. on Management of Data, 123-133 (1976).

[9] E. Grazzini, R. Pinzani, F. Pippolini: "A Physical Structure for Efficient Processing of Relational Queries". Foundations of Data Organization, Plenum Press, New York, N.J., 501-514 (1987).

[10] D. Bitton, H. Boral, D.J. DeWitt: "Parallel Algorithms for the Execution of Relational Database Operations". ACM Trans. on Database Systems 8(3), 324-353 (1983).

[11] D.E. Knuth: "The Art of Computer Programming: Sorting and Searching". Addison-Wesley, Reading, Ma. (1973).

[12] P. Valduriez: "Join Indices". ACM Trans. on Database Systems 12(2), 218-246 (1987).

[13] L.D. Shapiro: "Join Processing in Database Systems with Large Main Memories". ACM Trans. on Database Systems 11(3), 239-264 (1986).

[14] D.J. DeWitt et al.: "Implementation Techniques for Main Memory Database Systems". Proc. of ACM/SIGMOD Int. Conf. on Management of Data, 1-9 (1984).

[15] P. Valduriez and G. Gardarin: "Join and Semijoin Algorithms for a Multiprocessor Database Machine". ACM Trans. on Database Systems 9(1), 133-161 (1984).